SOCIAL STUDIES

MACMILLAN

Macmillan Social Studies

WORLD NEIGHBORS

SENIOR AUTHOR
John Jarolimek

J. Hubert Anderson
Loyal Durand, Jr.

Macmillan Publishing Company
New York

Collier Macmillan Publishers
London

Macmillan Publishing Company
866 Third Avenue, New York, New York 10022
Collier Macmillan Canada, Inc.

Printed in the United States of America
ISBN 0-02-147420-6
9 8 7 6 5 4 3

Acknowledgments

The publisher gratefully acknowledges
permission to reprint the following copyrighted
material:

Excerpt from *New Geographical Dictionary:*
By permission. From Webster's New
Geographical Dictionary © 1980 by Merriam-
Webster Inc., publisher of the Merriam-
Webster Dictionaries.

Excerpt from *A Journey From St. Petersburg to
Peking* by John Bell, edited by J. L. Stevenson.

Index from Encyclopedia International:
Adapted with permission of *Encyclopedia
International,* copyright © 1981, Grolier Inc.

Excerpt from *The Pyramids and Sphinx* by
Desmond Stewart is reprinted by permission of
Newsweek Books.

Graph adapted from *Cambridge Introduction to
the History of Mankind,* Book 2 edited by
Trevor Cairns. Published by Cambridge
University Press and used with their
permission.

CONTENTS

Learning About Maps and Globes 537

Reference Section 556

Enrichment 558

Reference Tables 602

Word List 611

Index 616

Maps

Diagrams, Charts, and Graphs

ATLAS

THE WORLD
POLITICAL

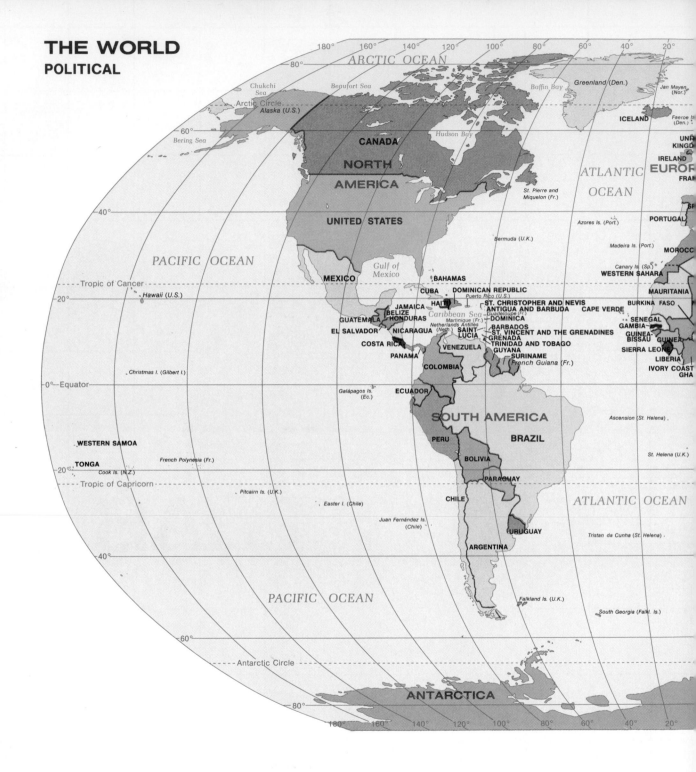

ARCTIC OCEAN

Chukchi Sea
Beaufort Sea
Greenland (Den.)
Jan Mayen (Nor.)
Arctic Circle
Alaska (U.S.)
Baffin Bay
ICELAND
Faeroe Is. (Den.)

60°
Bering Sea
Hudson Bay
CANADA
NORTH
AMERICA
ATLANTIC
EUROPE
UNITED KINGDOM
IRELAND
FRANCE

40°
UNITED STATES
St. Pierre and Miquelon (Fr.)
OCEAN
SPAIN
PORTUGAL

Bermuda (U.K.)
Madeira Is. (Port.)
MOROCCO

PACIFIC OCEAN
Gulf of Mexico
MEXICO
BAHAMAS
Azores Is. (Port.)
Canary Is. (Sp.)
WESTERN SAHARA

Tropic of Cancer
20°
Hawaii (U.S.)
CUBA
DOMINICAN REPUBLIC
Puerto Rico (U.S.)
MAURITANIA
BURKINA FASO
JAMAICA
HAITI
ST. CHRISTOPHER AND NEVIS
ANTIGUA AND BARBUDA
CAPE VERDE
BELIZE
Guadeloupe (Fr.)
SENEGAL
GUATEMALA
HONDURAS
Martinique (Fr.)
DOMINICA
GAMBIA
GUINEA-BISSAU
EL SALVADOR
NICARAGUA
Netherlands Antilles (Neth.)
SAINT LUCIA
BARBADOS
ST. VINCENT AND THE GRENADINES
GRENADA
GUINEA
SIERRA LEONE
COSTA RICA
VENEZUELA
TRINIDAD AND TOBAGO
LIBERIA
IVORY COAST
GHANA
PANAMA
GUYANA
SURINAME
COLOMBIA
French Guiana (Fr.)
Caribbean Sea

Christmas I. (Gilbert I.)
Galápagos Is. (Ec.)
ECUADOR

0° Equator
SOUTH AMERICA
Ascension (St. Helena)

WESTERN SAMOA
PERU
BRAZIL
TONGA
French Polynesia (Fr.)
BOLIVIA
St. Helena (U.K.)
20°
Cook Is. (N.Z.)
PARAGUAY
Tropic of Capricorn
Pitcairn Is. (U.K.)
CHILE
ATLANTIC OCEAN
Easter I. (Chile)
Juan Fernández Is. (Chile)
URUGUAY
Tristan da Cunha (St. Helena)

40°
ARGENTINA
Falkland Is. (U.K.)
South Georgia (Falkl. Is.)

PACIFIC OCEAN

60°
Antarctic Circle

ANTARCTICA
80°

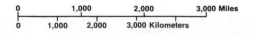

0   1,000   2,000   3,000 Miles
0   1,000 2,000 3,000 Kilometers

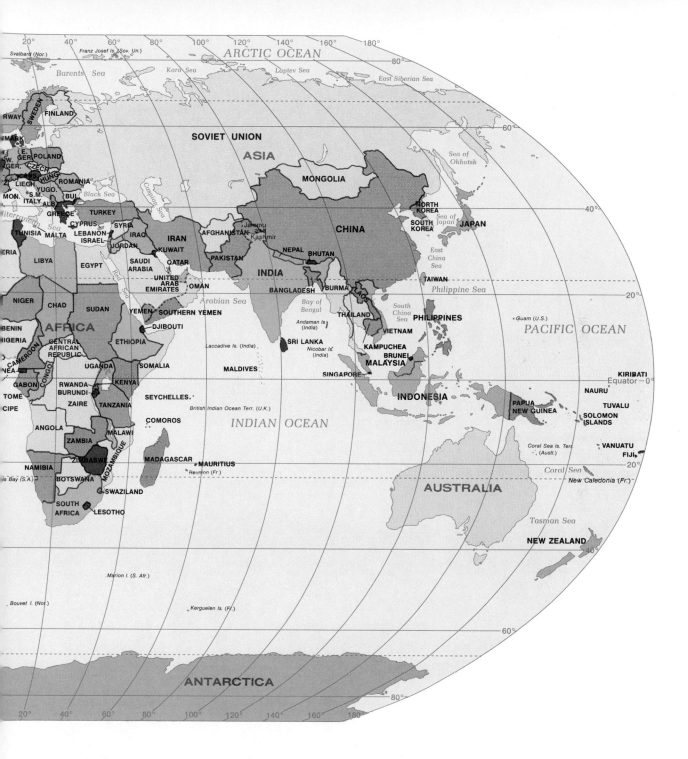

ALB. = ALBANIA
AND. = ANDORRA
AUS. = AUSTRIA
BEL. = BELGIUM
BUL. = BULGARIA
CZECH. = CZECHOSLOVAKIA
E.GER. = EAST GERMANY
HUNG. = HUNGARY

LIECH. = LIECHTENSTEIN
LUX. = LUXEMBOURG
MON. = MONACO
NETH. = NETHERLANDS
S.M. = SAN MARINO
SWITZ. = SWITZERLAND
W.GER. = WEST GERMANY
YUGO. = YUGOSLAVIA

A-3

World Climate

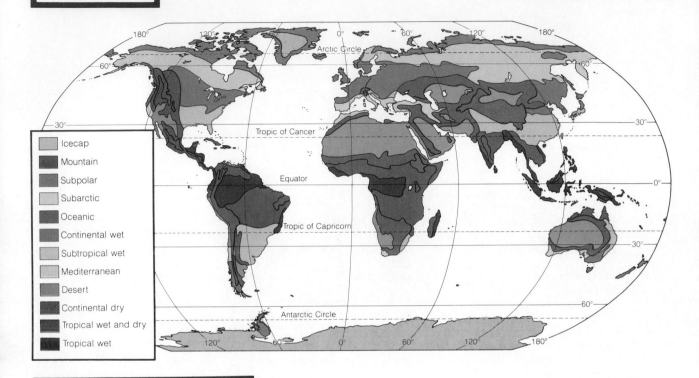

Icecap
Mountain
Subpolar
Subarctic
Oceanic
Continental wet
Subtropical wet
Mediterranean
Desert
Continental dry
Tropical wet and dry
Tropical wet

World Annual Precipitation

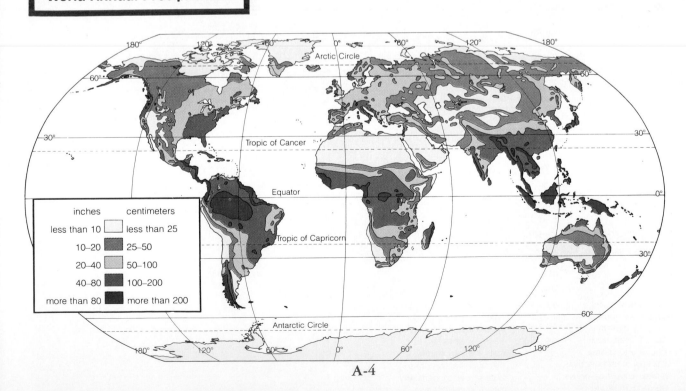

inches	centimeters
less than 10	less than 25
10–20	25–50
20–40	50–100
40–80	100–200
more than 80	more than 200

World Vegetation

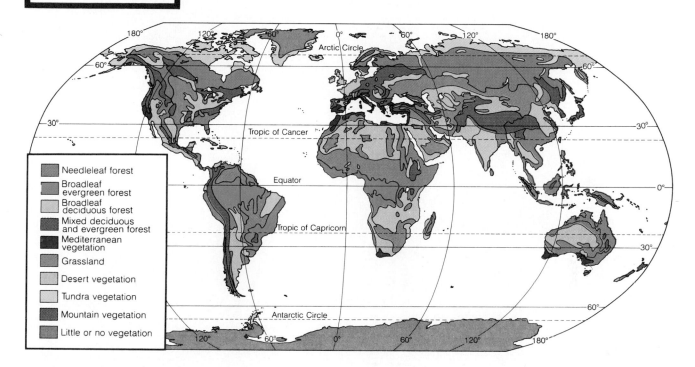

Needleleaf forest
Broadleaf evergreen forest
Broadleaf deciduous forest
Mixed deciduous and evergreen forest
Mediterranean vegetation
Grassland
Desert vegetation
Tundra vegetation
Mountain vegetation
Little or no vegetation

World Population

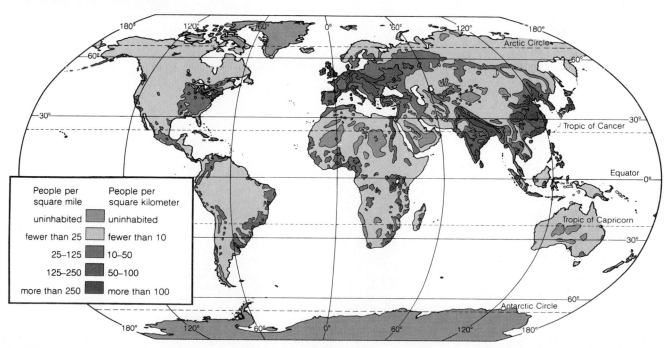

People per square mile	People per square kilometer
uninhabited	uninhabited
fewer than 25	fewer than 10
25–125	10–50
125–250	50–100
more than 250	more than 100

ASIA

ARCTIC OCEAN

Greenland Sea

ICELAND

Chukchi Sea

Lincoln Sea

Greenland (Denmark)

Bering Sea

Beaufort Sea

Baffin Bay

Alaska (U.S.)

Arctic Circle

Ellesmere Island

Fairbanks

Victoria Island

Baffin Island

Anchorage

Nuuk

Gulf of Alaska

Great Bear Lake

Juneau

Yukon R.

Frobisher Bay

Labrador Sea

Mackenzie R.

Yellowknife

Great Slave Lake

Hudson Bay

Lake Athabasca

CANADA

Newfoundland

N. Saskatchewan R.

Gulf of St. Lawrence

Edmonton

Lake Winnipeg

Vancouver Island

S. Saskatchewan R.

Québec

Vancouver

St. Lawrence R.

Winnipeg

Seattle

Montréal

ATLANTIC OCEAN

Portland

Missouri River

Ottawa

Lake Superior

Boston

Minneapolis

Lake Michigan

Lake Huron

Toronto

Lake Ontario

New York

Snake River

Detroit

Lake Erie

Philadelphia

Great Salt Lake

Salt Lake City

Platte River

Chicago

Washington

San Francisco

Mississippi R.

UNITED STATES

St. Louis

Colorado R.

Bermuda (U.K.)

Ohio River

Los Angeles

Atlanta

Phoenix

Dallas

Tropic of Canc.

Ciudad Juárez

PACIFIC OCEAN

Houston

New Orleans

Rio Grande

Miami

BAHAMAS

Monterrey

Gulf of Mexico

Nassau

Turks and Caicos Is. (U.K.)

ST. CHRISTOPHER AND NEVIS

Gulf of California

Havana

Virgin Is. (U.K.) (U.S.)

ANT AND BAR

MEXICO

Guadalajara

CUBA

DOMINICAN REPUBLIC

Puerto Rico (U.S.)

DOMINICA

Guadeloupe Martinique (Fr.)

SAINT LUCIA

HAITI

Mexico City

Port-au-Prince

Santo Domingo

Cayman Is. (U.K.)

Kingston

ST. VINCENT AND THE GRENADINES

BARBA

JAMAICA

GRENAD

NORTH AMERICA
POLITICAL

Belmopan

BELIZE

Caribbean Sea

Netherlands Antilles (Neth.)

Port-of-Spa

TRINIDAD A TOBA

—— National boundary

GUATEMALA

HONDURAS

⊛ National capital

Guatemala City

Tegucigalpa

• Other city

San Salvador

NICARAGUA

EL SALVADOR

Managua

0   500   1,000 Miles

San José

Panama City

0   500   1,000 Kilometers

COSTA RICA

PANAMA

SOUTH AMERICA

A-6

Equato

NORTH AMERICA

| 0 | 100 | 200 | | 400 | | 600 Miles |
| 0 | 161 | 322 | | 644 | | 966 Kilometers |

⊛ National Capitals   • Other Cities

Mountains   Hills

Plateaus   Plains

A-7

© Rand McNally & Co.

Map labels (geographic features):

BERING SEA · Nome · Point Barrow · BEAUFORT SEA · PARRY ISLANDS · ELLESMERE · Thule · GREENLAND · Ice Cap

ALASKA · Fairbanks · Mount McKinley 20,320 ft. · Anchorage · Yukon River · Mackenzie River · VICTORIA ISLAND · Baffin Bay · BAFFIN ISLAND · Nuuk · DAVIS STRAIT · Cape Farewell

Juneau · Ketchikan · Prince Rupert · ARCTIC CIRCLE · Great Bear Lake · River · Great Slave Lake · CANADA · Hudson Bay · Churchill

PACIFIC OCEAN · Vancouver · Victoria · Seattle · Portland · Columbia River · Fraser River · Peace River · Edmonton · Calgary · Regina · Winnipeg · Lake Winnipeg · Thunder Bay · Québec · St. Lawrence River · Gaspé · NEWFOUNDLAND · GULF OF ST. LAWRENCE · Halifax

Cape Mendocino · Missouri River · Duluth · Minneapolis · St. Paul · Great Lakes · Montréal · Ottawa · Toronto · Detroit · Milwaukee · Cleveland · Boston · New York

San Francisco · Great Salt Lake · UNITED STATES · Salt Lake City · Denver · Omaha · Chicago · Cincinnati · Ohio River · APPALACHIAN MOUNTAINS · Philadelphia · Washington · Norfolk · Cape Hatteras

Los Angeles · Colorado River · River · Arkansas River · Kansas City · St. Louis · Mississippi River · Memphis · Atlanta · Charleston · Savannah

Phoenix · Red River · Tulsa · Vicksburg · Dallas · Mobile · New Orleans · ATLANTIC OCEAN

TROPIC OF CANCER · El Paso · Ciudad Juárez · Rio Grande · Houston · Miami · BAHAMAS · TROPIC OF CANCER

Cape San Lucas · Laredo · Nuevo Laredo · Monterrey · GULF OF MEXICO · Havana ⊛ · CUBA · WEST INDIES · HAITI · DOM. REP.

Tampico · JAMAICA · CARIBBEAN SEA

Guadalajara · MEXICO · Veracruz · BELIZE

Acapulco de Juárez · Mexico City ⊛ · GUATEMALA · HONDURAS

Guatemala ⊛ · EL SALVADOR · NICARAGUA · CENTRAL AMERICA · COSTA RICA · Panamá · PANAMA

SOUTH AMERICA

CENTRAL AMERICA

Barranquilla   Caracas   TRINIDAD AND TOBAGO

Colón Panama Canal   Maracaibo   Port of Spain   10°

Medellín   LLANOS   Ciudad Bolívar   Georgetown   Paramaribo

Buenaventura   Bogotá   VENEZUELA   GUYANA   SURINAM   Cayenne   FRENCH GUIANA

COLOMBIA   GUIANA   HIGHLANDS

EQUATOR   Rio Caquetá   Rio Negro   Belém

ECUADOR   Quito

Guayaquil   Iquitos   Manaus   Fortaleza   Cape São Roque

Point Aguja   Amazon   Madeira River   Rio Tapajós

SELVAS   Recife

Trujillo   Rio   B R A Z I L   10°

Lima   Rio Tocantins   Rio São Francisco

Callao   PERU

Arequipa   Lake Titicaca   La Paz   BRAZILIAN   Brasília   Salvador

Mollendo   Cochabamba   Cuiabá   Goiânia

Arica   BOLIVIA   Sucre   HIGHLANDS   Rio

Atacama Desert   Potosí   Rio Paraguay   Belo Horizonte   20°

Antofagasta   CHACO   PARAGUAY   Rio Paraná   São Paulo   Rio de Janeiro

TROPIC OF CAPRICORN   Asunción   Curitiba   Santos   TROPIC OF CAPRICORN

Tucumán   Rio Paraná

Coquimbo   Rio Uruguay   Pôrto Alegre   30°

Córdoba   Santa Fe   Rio

Viña del Mar   Mount Aconcagua 22,834 ft. (6,960m)   Rosario   URUGUAY

Valparaíso   Mendoza

Santiago   Buenos Aires   Montevideo

Concepción   PAMPAS   Rio de la Plata

ARGENTINA

Bahía Blanca   40°

Puerto Montt

PATAGONIA

Comodoro Rivadavia

50°

Falkland Islands

Punta Arenas   STRAIT OF MAGELLAN   South Georgia

A-9

Tierra del Fuego   Ushuaia

PACIFIC OCEAN

ATLANTIC OCEAN

100°   90°   80°   70°   60°   50°   40°   30°

© Rand McNally & Co.

EUROPE
POLITICAL

— National boundary
✪ National capital
• Other city

AFRICA

A-10

0 ___ 150 ___ 300 Miles
0 ___ 150 ___ 300 Kilometers

ASIA
POLITICAL

— National boundary
---- Boundaries: indefinite, disputed or under treaty
⊛ National capital
• Other city

0 500 1,000 Kilometers
0 500 1,000 Miles

EUROPE

AFRICA

AUSTRALIA

A-12

ATLANTIC OCEAN

ARCTIC OCEAN

North Pole

SOVIET UNION

SIBERIA

PACIFIC OCEAN

INDIAN OCEAN

Arabian Sea

Bay of Bengal

South China Sea

Philippine Sea

Sea of Okhotsk

Bering Sea

Mediterranean Sea

Black Sea

Caspian Sea

Aral Sea

TURKEY
CYPRUS
LEBANON
SYRIA
ISRAEL
JORDAN
IRAQ
IRAN
SAUDI ARABIA
KUWAIT
BAHRAIN
QATAR
UNITED ARAB EMIRATES
OMAN
YEMEN
SOUTHERN YEMEN
AFGHANISTAN
PAKISTAN
INDIA
NEPAL
BHUTAN
BANGLADESH
BURMA
CHINA
MONGOLIA
TIBET
THAILAND
LAOS
VIETNAM
KAMPUCHEA
MALAYSIA
SINGAPORE
BRUNEI
INDONESIA
PHILIPPINES
TAIWAN
NORTH KOREA
SOUTH KOREA
JAPAN
SRI LANKA
MALDIVES
PAPUA NEW GUINEA

Ankara
Nicosia
Beirut
Damascus
Jerusalem
Amman
Baghdad
Tehran
Riyadh
Mecca
Medina
Kuwait
Doha
Abu Dhabi
Muscat
Aden
Sana
Kabul
Islamabad
Lahore
Karachi
Bombay
Ahmadabad
New Delhi
Delhi
Hyderabad
Madras
Calcutta
Kathmandu
Dacca
Rangoon
Mandalay
Bangkok
Kuala Lumpur
Singapore
Jakarta
Ujung Pandang (Makassar)
Lhasa
Chongqing (Chungking)
Canton
Wuhan
Shanghai
Tianjin (Tientsin)
Beijing (Peking)
Shenyang (Mukden)
Qiqihar (Tsitsihar)
Ulan Bator
Hanoi
Phnom Penh
Ho Chi Minh City (Saigon)
Manila
Quezon City
Taipei
Hong Kong
Macao (Port.)
Victoria
Pyongyang
Seoul
Luda (Dairen)
Vladivostok
Nagasaki
Osaka
Yokohama
Tokyo
Sapporo
Colombo
Male
Port Moresby
Jayapura

Moscow
Leningrad
Kishinev
Odessa
Kiev
Minsk
Vilnius
Tallinn
Murmansk
Arkhangelsk
Volgograd
Astrakan
Kharkov
Saratov
Tbilisi
Yerevan
Baku
Tashkent
Alma-Ata
Frunze
Karaganda
Omsk
Novosibirsk
Tomsk
Irkutsk
Yakutsk
Okhotsk
Anadyr

Arctic Circle

Tropic of Cancer

Equator

Tropic of Cancer

Red Sea
Gulf of Aden
Gulf of Oman
Persian Gulf
Gulf of Siam
Yellow Sea
East China Sea
Java Sea
Celebes Sea
Banda Sea
Flores Sea
Timor Sea
Lake Balkhash
Lake Baikal
North Sea
Baltic Sea
Barents Sea
Kara Sea

Socotra (S. Yemen)
Laccadive Is. (India)
Nicobar Is. (India)
Andaman Is. (India)
Sumatra
Borneo
Java
Bali I.
Celebes
Halmahera
Seram I.
Timor Island
New Guinea
New Britain
New Ireland
Luzon
Mindanao
Hainan
Taiwan
Okinawa I.
Ryukyu Is. (Japan)
Kyushu I.
Shikoku I.
Honshu I.
Hokkaido I.
Sakhalin Island
Kurii Islands
Kamchatka Pen.
Wrangel Is.
New Siberian Is.
Severnaya Zemlya
Novaya Zemlya
Franz Josef Is.
Guam (U.S.)
Mariana Islands (U.S.)
Caroline Islands

AUSTRALIA AND NEW ZEALAND
POLITICAL

— National boundary
— State boundary
⊛ National capital
★ State / Territory capital
• Other city

0   200   400 Miles
0   200   400 Kilometers

INDIAN OCEAN

ASIA

Timor Sea

Arafura Sea

Melville I.

★ Darwin

NORTHERN TERRITORY

Gulf of Carpentaria

• Larrimah

• Alice Springs

Broome

• Fitzroy R.

WESTERN AUSTRALIA

★ Carnarvon

★ Perth

• Albany

• Kalgoorlie

Great Australian Bight

SOUTH AUSTRALIA

Kangaroo I.

• Whyalla

• Port Augusta

★ Adelaide

L. Torrens

L. Eyre

Mt. Gambier •

Ballarat •

VICTORIA

★ Melbourne

King I.

Flinders I.

Bass Strait

TASMANIA

★ Hobart

QUEENSLAND

• Cloncurry

• Townsville

• Cairns

Great Barrier Reef

• Mackay

• Rockhampton

Fraser I.

★ Brisbane

Darling River

Murrumbidgee R.

Lachlan R.

NEW SOUTH WALES

• Charleville

• Dubbo

• Port Macquarie

• Canberra

AUSTRALIAN CAPITAL TERRITORY

★ Sydney

• Newcastle

Tasman Sea

Coral Sea

Solomon Sea

SOLOMON ISLANDS

Choiseul I.

Sta. Isabel I.

Guadalcanal I.

Malaita I.

San Cristobal I.

VANUATU

Espíritu Santo I.

Malekula I.

Efate I.

New Caledonia (Fr.)

Loyalty Is. (Fr.)

Fiji Sea

Tropic of Capricorn

Norfolk Island (Aust.)

PACIFIC OCEAN

NEW ZEALAND

Stewart I.

South Island

• Dunedin

• Christchurch

★ Wellington

North Island

• Auckland

A-13

Dictionary of Geographical Terms

archipelago (är′kə pel′ə gō′): a large group of islands

atoll (at′ôl): a ring-shaped coral island

basin (bā′sin): all the land drained by a river and its tributaries

bay (bā): an arm of a sea or lake, extending into the land, usually smaller than a gulf

butte (byo͞ot): a flat-topped hill with steep sides, smaller than a mesa

canal (kə nal′): a waterway built to connect two other bodies of water

canyon (kan′yən): a deep valley with steep sides

cape (kāp): a point of land extending from the coastline into the sea or a lake

channel (chan′əl): a wide stretch of water between two land areas

cliff (klif): a high, steep face of rock or earth

coast (kōst): land along a sea or ocean

continental shelf (con′tə nent′əl shelf′): the part of the earth's crust sloping gently seaward from the shoreline to the continental slope

cordillera (kôr dil′ər ə): a long mountain chain

dam (dam): a wall built across a river to hold back the water

delta (del′tə): land at the mouth of a river, made of sand and silt, usually shaped like a triangle

desert (dez′ərt): a very dry area where few plants can grow

dune (do͞on): a hill, mound, or ridge of sand formed by the wind

escarpment (es kärp′mənt): a steep slope or cliff

fiord (fyôrd): a deep, narrow inlet of the sea between high cliffs or banks carved by a glacier

foothills (foot′hilz′): a low line of hills lying between a mountain range and a plain

glacier (glā′shər): a large body of ice that moves very slowly over the land

gulf (gulf): an arm of a sea or lake extending into the land, usually larger than a bay

harbor (här′bər): a protected place on an ocean, sea, lake, or river where ships can shelter

hill (hil): a rounded and raised landform, not as high as a mountain

icecap (īs′kap′): a dome-shaped glacier covering a land area and moving out from the center in all directions

island (ī′lənd): a body of land entirely surrounded by water, smaller than a continent

isthmus (is′məs): a strip of land bordered by water that connects two larger bodies of land

lagoon (lə gōōn′): the water lying between an island shore and a reef or inside an atoll

lake (lāk): a body of water entirely surrounded by land

mesa (mā′sə): a flat-topped hill or mountain with steep sides, larger than a butte

moraine (mə rān′): a deposit of material carried by a glacier

mountain (mount′ən): a high rounded or pointed landform with steep sides, higher than a hill

mountain pass (mount′ən pas′): a narrow gap in the mountains

mouth (mouth): place where a river flows into the ocean or another body of water

oasis (ō ā′sis): a place in the desert that is fertile because it has a water supply

ocean (ō′shən): the body of salt water covering nearly three fourths of the earth's surface

peninsula (pə nin′sə lə): land extending from a larger body of land, nearly surrounded by water

plain (plān): an area of flat or almost flat land

plateau (pla tō′): flat land with steep sides, raised above the surrounding land

port (pôrt): a place where ships load and unload goods

reef (rēf): a ridge of coral rock that lies just above or just below sea level

reservoir (rez′ər vwär′): a body of water formed behind a dam

ridge (rij): a long and narrow chain of hills or mountains

river (riv′ər): a large stream of water that flows across the land and usually empties into a lake, ocean, or another river

sea (sē): a large body of water partly or entirely enclosed by land; the ocean

sound (sound): a long inlet or arm of the sea

strait (strāt): a narrow channel that joins two larger bodies of water

tributary (trib′yə ter′ē): a river or stream that flows into a larger river or stream

valley (val′ē): an area of low land between hills or mountains

wadi (wä′dē): a short, dry riverbed

waterfall (wô′tər fôl′): a flow of water falling from a high place

Map Symbols

Map symbols vary from map to map. Some maps use the same or similar symbols. Other maps use different symbols. You will see some of the commonly used symbols shown below on the maps in this book.

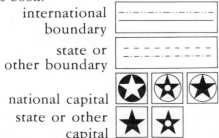

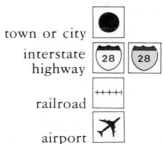

1 The Earth

Unit Preview

The earth on which we live is a place of great variety and contrast. It has landmasses that range from vast continents to tiny islands. Its bodies of water include great oceans, large seas, small lakes, and rivers.

Because of the earth's shape and its relation to the sun, the earth has many different climates. Each climate supports different forms of plant life. Jungles grow in the hot, moist regions near the equator. Barren deserts are found in hot, dry climates. Grasses, shrubs, and many kinds of trees grow in regions farther north and south of the equator. Near the poles, only small plants are able to survive in the cold temperatures.

The earth is always changing. Forces deep inside the earth produce earthquakes and build mountains. Many mountains are either volcanoes or great areas of folded rocks. Wind, water, and ice carve away the land. The rock material they carry builds up the land in other places.

Through the centuries, people have explored many parts of the earth. They have learned to make maps and globes that represent the earth. Maps show the location of landmasses, oceans, and rivers. They can also show countries, transportation routes, vegetation, and many other kinds of information.

People use soil, water, and other resources of the earth. Some resources are necessary to sustain life. Others, such as coal and oil, are important to the way we live. As some resources become scarce, people are learning ways to conserve them and develop new ones.

Things to Discover

If you look carefully at the picture, map, and time line, you can answer these questions.
1. What continents are shown on the map? What oceans are shown?
2. Parts of what continents are visible in the satellite photograph of the earth?
3. The outer layer of the earth is called the crust. The next layer is called the mantle. When was the boundary between these two layers discovered? By whom?
4. How many standard world time zones are there? When were they established?

Words to Learn

You will meet these words and terms in this unit. As you read you will learn what they mean and how to pronounce them. The Word List will help you.

alluvial plain	nonrenewable resource
aquifer	renewable resource
equinox	seismology
humus	silt
hydrosphere	solstice
lithosphere	strait
moraine	topography

10

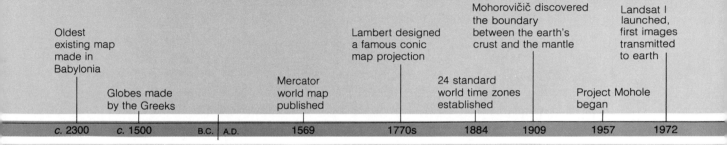

Oldest existing map made in Babylonia

Globes made by the Greeks

Mercator world map published

Lambert designed a famous conic map projection

24 standard world time zones established

Mohorovičič discovered the boundary between the earth's crust and the mantle

Project Mohole began

Landsat I launched, first images transmitted to earth

| c. 2300 | c. 1500 | B.C. | A.D. | 1569 | 1770s | 1884 | 1909 | 1957 | 1972 |

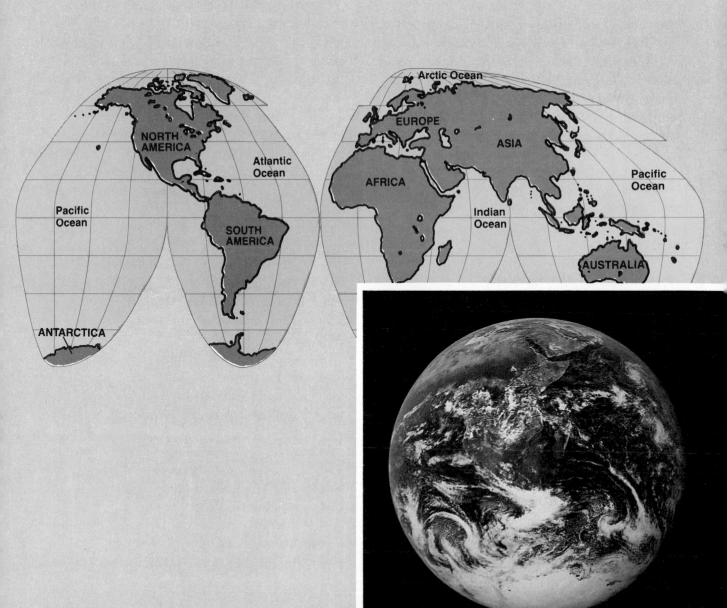

1
Land and Water

The photograph on page 11 is a view of the planet Earth taken from 18,900 miles (30,400 km) in space. As you study this picture, you can see areas of brown, blue, and white. The swirls of white are clouds. The areas of brown are land, and the vast blue regions are water. The total surface area of the earth is 196,951,000 square miles (510,103,000 sq. km). Only 30 percent of this area is land. About 70 percent is covered by water.

Land

The bodies of land on the earth's surface range in size from huge continents to tiny islands. Landmasses vary in shape as well as size.

The Shape of the Land

The largest landmasses on the earth are called continents. Continents cover millions of square miles or kilometers and are surrounded by water. Geographers generally agree that there are seven of these vast bodies of land. They are North America, South America, Europe, Asia, Australia, Africa, and Antarctica.

The map on pages 14–15 shows the earth's continents. The largest continent is Asia. It occupies about 17,120,000 square miles (44,339,000 sq. km) of the earth's surface. With Europe, it forms one large land area called Eurasia. The smallest continent is Australia, which covers about 2,968,000 square miles (7,687,000 sq. km). Australia is the only

continent in the world that is also a single country.

There are land areas smaller than continents that are also surrounded by water. Geographers call these areas islands. There are thousands of islands in oceans, rivers, and lakes throughout the world. They range in size from tiny dots of land called islets (ī′lits) to huge bodies of land. Greenland is the largest island in the world. It covers 840,000 square miles (2,175,600 sq. km). In some parts of the world, large numbers of islands form a group. One example is Hawaii, a group of 132 islands in the Pacific Ocean.

Peninsulas are another kind of landmass. A peninsula projects out from a larger landmass and is almost entirely surrounded by water. Florida, on the continent of North America, and Italy, on the European continent, are peninsulas. The largest peninsula in the world is Arabia.

An isthmus (is′məs) is a narrow strip of land bordered by water that links two larger landmasses. The Isthmus of Panama joins the continents of North America and South America.

Landforms

The surface of the earth has a variety of landforms. Mountains, hills, plateaus, plains, and valleys are landforms.

The highest of the earth's landforms are mountains. Mount Everest is the world's highest mountain. It soars 29,028 feet (8,848 m)

These islands are part of the Seychelles, a tropical country in the Indian Ocean.

above the level of the sea. Mount Everest is located in the Himalaya (him′ə lā′ə) Mountains of Asia.

Other mountains are far less impressive. The Appalachians (ap′ə lā′chē ənz) in the eastern United States, for example, are much lower and have gentle, rounded peaks. The highest mountain in this range, Mount Mitchell, is only 6,684 feet (2,037 m) above sea level.

Because mountains vary in height, geographers agree that a mountain must rise at least 2,000 feet (610 m) above its surroundings. Mountains cover about 20 percent of the earth's land surface.

Hills are another kind of landform. Sometimes it is hard to distinguish hills from low mountains. Geographers have no precise way to determine the difference between the two. In general, hills are smaller than mountains.

Plateaus are another kind of high land. They rise above the surrounding land, and steep cliffs form at least one of their sides. Unlike hills or mountains, however, plateaus have flat or gently rolling surfaces. Plateaus cover more than one-third of the earth's land surface.

Plains are large areas of flat or gently rolling land which are lower than the landforms next to them. Some plains are found along sea-

coasts. These plains slope gently up from the water toward plateaus or mountains. Other plains are found inland, and some of them cover vast areas. In the United States, for example, the Great Plains cover about one million square miles (2,590,000 sq. km).

Valleys are areas on the earth's surface that lie between hills and mountains. Some valleys have gentle slopes covered with plants and trees. Others have very steep walls and are called canyons. The Grand Canyon in Arizona is a dramatic canyon carved by the Colorado River.

One way to describe the surface of the earth is in terms of elevation. Elevation is the height to which a part of the earth's surface rises above sea level. The elevation of land at sea level is zero feet or meters. Another word for elevation is altitude.

Geographers use another term to describe the variations in height between landforms in an area. This term is relief. Mountainous regions are called areas of high relief because of the great difference in elevation between valleys and peaks. Plains are called areas of low relief because there is little difference in elevation between the highest and the lowest parts of the land.

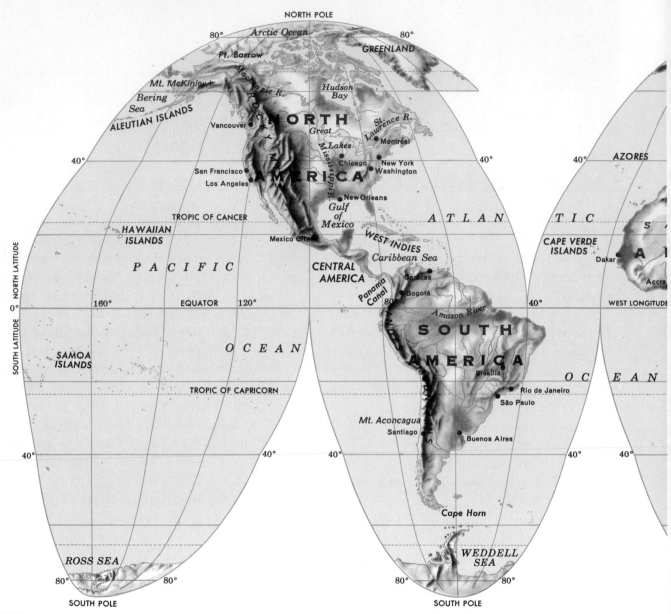

Water

About 70 percent of the earth's surface is covered by water. The water of the earth is called the *hydrosphere* (hī′drə sfēr′). The hydrosphere includes oceans, lakes, and rivers. Glaciers and icecaps, the water below the earth's surface, and the water vapor in the atmosphere also make up the hydrosphere.

Bodies of Water

The largest bodies of water are oceans. The earth is really covered by one huge ocean divided into four smaller oceans by the continents. These four oceans are the Pacific, the Atlantic, the Indian, and the Arctic. The largest ocean is the Pacific. Covering about 64 million square miles (161 million sq. km), it is vast

14

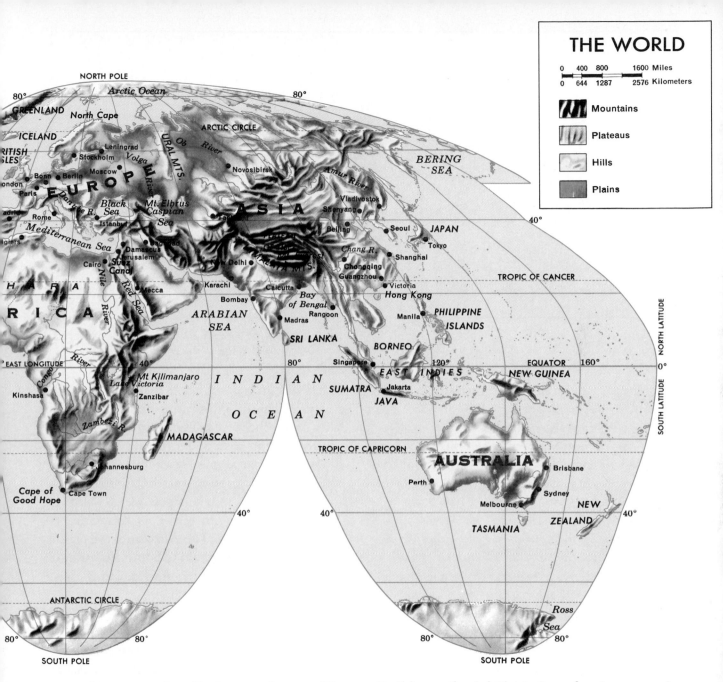

enough to contain all the continents. The smallest of the oceans is the Arctic. All of the oceans are saltwater.

The word *sea* is used to describe several different bodies of water. Sometimes the oceans themselves are referred to as seas. The word can also mean a section of the ocean partly cut off from the rest by land. The Caribbean (kar'ə bē'ən) Sea, for instance, is part of the Atlantic Ocean that is almost completely enclosed by the West Indies and Central and South America. Sometimes the word *sea* refers to large bodies of water that lie inland away from the oceans. Some of these seas, such as the Dead Sea, which lies between Jordan and Israel, are saltwater; others, such as the Sea

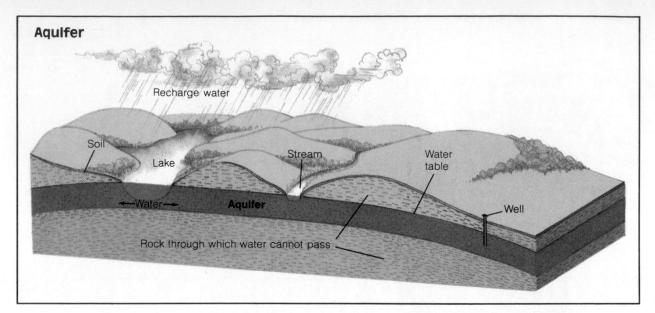

Aquifer

Recharge water

Soil

Lake

Stream

Water table

Water

Aquifer

Well

Rock through which water cannot pass

Aquifers are important sources of fresh water. What is the water table?

of Galilee, in Israel, are freshwater. Even though these landlocked bodies of water are called seas, they are really lakes.

Lakes are bodies of water completely surrounded by land. Lakes occur throughout the world and vary widely in size. Some lakes cover no more than 10 acres (4 ha). Some are so large it is impossible to see across them. Lake Superior, in surface area the largest freshwater lake in the world, is one of these.

Other bodies of water are extensions of oceans, seas, and lakes. One kind is called a gulf or bay. Gulfs and bays are formed when an ocean, sea, or lake fills an indentation in the shoreline. *Bay* and *gulf* are often used to describe the same bodies of water. However, a gulf is usually larger and deeper than a bay.

Another body of water is called a *strait* (strāt). A strait is a narrow channel that joins two larger bodies of water. The Strait of Gibraltar (ji brôl′tər) connects the Atlantic Ocean and the Mediterranean Sea. The Strait of Magellan, at the tip of South America, is the only strait between the Atlantic and Pacific oceans.

A river is a body of water that flows through a natural channel and empties into an ocean, a lake, or another river. The source of a river is usually high in mountains or hills. As a river flows down the slopes, it is joined by other streams called tributaries. A tributary is a stream that flows into a larger stream or river. A river together with all of its tributaries is called a river system. The Amazon is the major river of a vast river system in South America. It is fed by thousands of tributaries, and it empties into the Atlantic Ocean.

Ground Water

Ground water is water beneath the surface of the earth. As rainwater or water from lakes and streams seeps into the ground, some of it collects in the spaces, or pores, of rocks and between grains of gravel and sand. A rock layer that holds water and lets it pass through is called an *aquifer* (ak′wə fər). See the diagram on this page. The top surface of an aquifer is the water table. In the United States, 20 percent of fresh water comes from aquifers.

Glaciers

Glaciers are large bodies of ice found in the cold regions of the world. They form over land when the summer heat fails to melt all the snow which falls in the winter. Over many years, the snow builds up in thick layers and is gradually compressed into ice. When the ice becomes very heavy, gravity causes the glacier to move.

Thousands of years ago, glaciers covered large parts of the northern continents. Ice sheets stretched across North America, Asia, and Europe. Today, glaciers are found in polar regions and in high mountains. There are two kinds of glaciers—continental glaciers and valley glaciers. Continental glaciers cover large areas of land in the polar regions. Most of Antarctica and almost all of Greenland are covered by continental glaciers. Glaciers in mountainous regions are called valley glaciers. Valley glaciers are like rivers of ice moving between mountains.

The Changing Earth

The earth is very old, but it has not remained the same since it was formed. Its surface has changed slowly, but continuously, over the centuries. Forces have been at work that wear down the land. Other forces have worked to build it up. Glaciers have carved valleys on the earth's surface. Volcanoes have built mountains. Rivers, winds, and ocean waves have also helped to shape the surface of the earth. The forces that have changed the earth in the past are still at work today.

Glaciers such as this one in Canada carve out deep U-shaped valleys.

The Structure of the Earth

To understand some of the changes in the earth, it is necessary to know how the earth is constructed. The diagram on page 18 shows the structure of the earth. It shows that the earth is made up of several different layers. At the center is the core (kôr), which is divided into two sections. The center of the inner core is about 4,000 miles (6,450 km) below the surface of the earth. The distance from the center to the boundary between the inner core and the outer core is about 800 miles (1,300 km). The inner core is very hot, solid metal. Its estimated temperature is as high as 9,000° F. (5,000° C).

The outer core, which surrounds the inner core, is about 1,400 miles (2,250 km) thick. It is made of melted metal whose estimated temperature range is from 4,000° F. to 9,000° F. (2,000° to 5,000° C).

The mantle surrounds the outer core. The mantle is composed of solid rock and is about 1,800 miles (2,900 km) thick. Temperatures in the mantle are very high, too. They range from

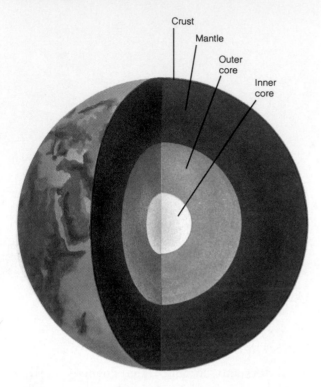

Crust

Mantle

Outer core

Inner core

The layers of the earth are shown in cross section. At the center is a core of very hot, solid metal.

4,000° F. (2,200° C) near the boundary with the outer core to 1,600° F. (870° C) near the boundary with the crust.

Above the mantle is the outer layer of the earth called the crust. The crust is sometimes called the *lithosphere* (lith'ə sfēr'). The crust, or lithosphere, is composed of solid rock that is lighter than the rock of the mantle. The lithosphere includes the continents and the rocks that lie under the ocean floors. The lithosphere varies in thickness from about 5 to 25 miles (8 to 40 km). Temperatures in the deepest parts of the crust may reach 1,600° F. (870° C).

A Yugoslavian geologist named Mohorovičič (mō hō rō'və chich) discovered the boundary between the earth's crust and mantle in 1909. In his honor, the boundary is called the Mohorovičič discontinuity (dis'kon tə nyōō'ə tē), or

Moho for short. In 1957, a group of scientists began Project Mohole to investigate the rocks of the Moho and the mantle. Several test holes were drilled using a drill as long as Mount Everest is high. Much important information was obtained before the project was abandoned in 1966.

While the lithosphere might seem to be a mass of solid rock, some scientists believe it is made up of several separate rigid plates. See the map on page 19. The plates float on a soft layer of rock. Scientists think that many changes in the earth's surface take place along the edges of the plates as they collide, pull apart, or slide past one another. The movement of the plates is caused by tectonic (tek tän'ik) activity. Tectonic activity may be caused by heat energy.

Tectonic Activity

Earthquakes, folding, faulting, and volcanic activity are all the result of tectonic activity. Folding, faulting, and volcanic activity often occur together and usually result in mountain building. Mountain building is always accompanied by earthquakes.

Earthquakes occur when there is a shift in the earth's crust along the edges of the plates. Earthquakes send shock waves called seismic (sīz'mik) waves through the earth. Seismic waves cause the earth to shake or vibrate. They often cause severe damage. The study of earthquakes is called *seismology* (sīz mol'ə jē). Scientists use an instrument called a seismograph to measure seismic waves. The strength of an earthquake is indicated on a scale called the Richter (rik'tər) scale.

Tectonic Plates

Plate movement is indicated by the direction of the arrows.

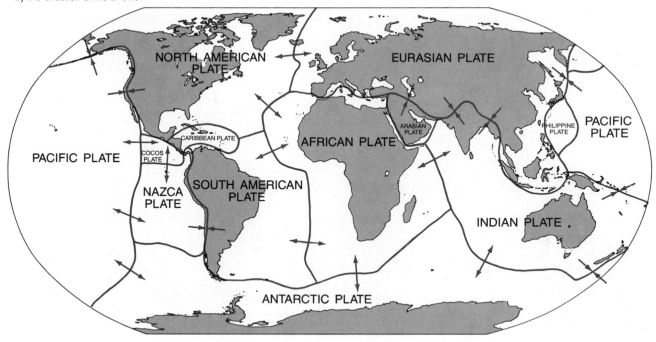

Earthquakes measuring below five on the Richter scale do not usually cause serious damage. An earthquake that measures eight or more on the Richter scale is usually very destructive. Sometimes buildings, homes, and lives are lost. Such severe earthquakes can also cause ocean waves to sweep onto the land, resulting in more destruction. The highest Richter number ever recorded was 8.9.

Folding and faulting are other changes in the earth's crust caused by tectonic activity. Pressure can cause layers of rock to bend in a series of waves or folds. Folding often results in the formation of mountains. See the diagram on page 20. The Appalachian Mountains, the Rockies, and the Alps were formed in part by folding.

Pressure in the earth's crust sometimes results in faulting rather than folding. Faulting

occurs when parts of the crust break into blocks. The blocks can move up, down, or sideways. The movement may be small or great. If it is great, mountains are formed. Mountain ranges created by faulting are usually very steep along one edge. Several mountain ranges in Nevada, Utah, and California were formed by the faulting of the earth's crust. Faulting helped to create the Sierra Nevada. See the diagram on page 20.

Few mountain ranges are created by either folding or faulting alone. The two actions almost always occur together in the formation of mountains.

Mountains can also be formed by volcanoes. Volcanoes are openings in the earth's surface that allow molten rock to escape. Molten rock inside the earth is called magma. Molten rock that escapes through cracks or craters is called

19

Mountain Building

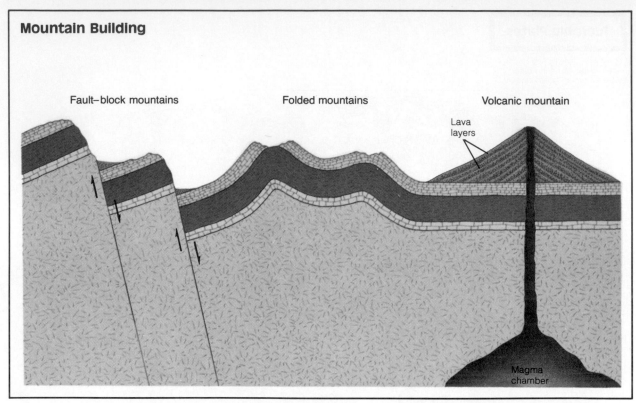

Fault–block mountains Folded mountains Volcanic mountain

Lava layers

Magma chamber

Mountains are formed by volcanic activity, by folding, and by faulting.

lava. During an eruption, gases, rock fragments, and ash may be expelled with lava. Volcanoes are found on land and on the sea floor. There are several different kinds.

One kind, called a shield volcano, is built up of lava that flows from the crater down the sides and hardens. When lava is thrown into the air, it hardens and falls to earth as ashes, cinders, and rock fragments. Volcanoes built up by this material are called cinder-cone volcanoes. Some volcanoes are built up by both lava flows and deposits of ashes and cinders.

The Hawaiian Islands are the tops of volcanoes whose bases are on the floor of the sea. Volcanoes are still active in Hawaii. Some are shield volcanoes. Their eruptions are not explosive. Lava flows down the sides of the craters and forms a low, wide cone-shaped mountain.

Parícutin (pə rē′kə tēn′), a volcano in Mexico, is a cinder-cone volcano. It began as a crack in the ground in 1943. Shortly after the crack appeared, violent eruptions began. Ashes and cinders were blown into the air. The explosions continued over a period of nine years, building up a fairly steep cone-shaped mountain that rises 1,345 feet (410 m) above the surrounding land.

Mount Fuji in Japan is an example of a volcanic mountain built up by lava, ashes, and cinders. It is an almost perfectly shaped cone.

Weathering

Tectonic activity often results in the building up of the earth's surface. Some forms of tectonic activity, such as volcanic eruptions, occur very quickly and are very dramatic. The folding of great mountain ranges, on the other

The 1980 eruptions of Mount St. Helens were the first in the continental United States outside Alaska in 59 years.

hand, takes place very slowly over long periods of time. The results cannot be seen in a single lifetime. Other forces change the surface of the earth less slowly than volcanoes, but more rapidly than tectonic folding. These forces result in the weathering, erosion, and deposition of rocks on the earth's surface.

Weathering refers to the breaking down of rocks into smaller pieces. It can occur in two ways. One way, called physical weathering, is caused by water, ice, plants, wind, and changing temperatures. Physical weathering occurs when water seeps into the cracks of rocks. As the water freezes, it expands and widens the cracks. Eventually the rocks break apart. Sometimes, the roots of trees and other plants grow down between cracks and cause rocks to split into smaller pieces.

Ocean waves are also agents of physical weathering. They pound against the land, breaking rocks into gravel and sand. Running water and wind also cause the breakup of rocks. Often water and wind carry small parti-cles of rocks that scrape other rocks. In some dry parts of the world, sand-bearing winds blowing steadily against rocks have a sand-blasting action. Many of the canyon lands in the western United States were weathered in this way.

Glaciers, too, break rocks up into smaller pieces. The rocks and boulders they carry along scrape and scour the rocks they move across.

Changes in temperature alone also cause physical weathering. During the day, the sun heats the earth's surface and causes rocks to expand. At night, the rocks cool and shrink. The continual expansion and shrinking eventually cause rocks to break into smaller pieces.

The other kind of weathering is called chemical weathering. Everything on earth, including rocks, air, and water, is made up of chemicals. Chemicals in rocks are broken down when they come in contact with chemicals in water. The dissolving action of water is one of the main causes of chemical weathering. Rain water, seawater, and the water in rivers and streams dissolve some of the substances in rocks and cause the rocks to crumble.

Weathering, both chemical and physical, breaks rocks into smaller and smaller pieces. The larger pieces are called boulders, smaller ones are called gravel and sand, and the very fine particles are *silt* (silt) and clay. Silt is finer than sand but coarser than clay. The small particles produced by weathering may eventually become soil. Soil is made up of bits of weathered rock and the decayed remains of plants and animals.

Erosion

Erosion also changes the earth. Erosion is the movement of weathered material and soil. Before rocks can be eroded, they must be made small enough to move. As weathered particles are eroded, more rock surfaces are exposed to weathering. Weathering and erosion work together to shape the land surface.

Some of the agents that cause weathering are also agents of erosion. Three important causes of erosion are water, wind, and glaciers.

Moving water is probably the main cause of erosion. Rain water running across the land washes soil away into streams. As rivers and streams flow down hills and mountains, they pick up more soil, rock particles, and silt and carry them along. Deep valleys and canyons are carved by running water. Waves and tides also erode the land. As they crash against the shore, they carry away rock, sand, and soil.

The wind is also an important force in erosion. In dry areas where there are few plants, the wind picks up sand, silt, and other fine particles and carries them away. Sometimes, hollows are created where earth materials have been blown away by strong winds.

In the past, huge glaciers that covered large areas of the earth's surface moved across the land, pushing mounds of boulders and soil in front of them. The glaciers also picked up rocks and soil and carried them along. Today large continental glaciers in Antarctica and Greenland and valley glaciers throughout the world act in the same way. As glaciers move, their tremendous weight scrapes away soil and rock.

Deposition

The same forces that cause erosion also cause deposition (dep′ə zish′ən). Eventually rains stop, rivers slow down, winds calm down, and glaciers melt. When these things happen, the materials carried by these agents are laid down, or deposited. Deposition changes the face of the earth by building it up.

As rivers slow down, they deposit the material they are carrying on their riverbeds. Near their mouths, rivers are usually moving very slowly. The only material they are able to carry is silt. As the rivers slow down even more, the silt is deposited, and large formations called deltas are built up. A large delta has been formed at the mouth of the Mississippi River near New Orleans, where the river enters the Gulf of Mexico.

Sometimes rivers overflow their banks and leave silt and other material behind as they recede. The material left forms an *alluvial plain* (ə lōō′vē əl plān′). Alluvial plains are also called flood plains. The fertile areas on both sides of the Mississippi River are alluvial plains. As floods recur, rich deposits of material are built up. Other important alluvial plains are in the valleys of the Indus, the Nile, and the Huang rivers.

Along the shores of lakes and oceans, water changes the shape of the land by depositing the material it carries. Sandbars and beaches are common formations.

Winds carrying particles of sand and dust deposit these materials when they slow down or stop. In deserts, along beaches, and in other sandy areas, deposition creates sand dunes. In some areas, sand dunes may reach heights of 500 to 600 feet (150 to 180 m). The dunes move slowly as sand from one side of the dune is moved to the other by the wind. Winds are also responsible for carrying volcanic ash and soil great distances. Great deposits of wind-borne soil are found in many parts of the world.

As glaciers melt, they deposit the rocks, soil, and other material they have pushed or carried along. Water from the melting glaciers often carries the material and spreads it out. A deposit of material carried by a glacier is called a *moraine* (mə rān'). Long Island, New York, is an example of a terminal moraine. This long, narrow deposit marks part of the edge of the glacier that once covered North America.

Do You Know?

1. Why are mountainous regions called areas of high relief? Why are plains called areas of low relief?
2. Name the four layers of the earth. Which layer is the hottest?
3. Name five causes of physical weathering. What is one of the main causes of chemical weathering?

2

Weather, Climate, and Vegetation

Weather and climate determine the kinds of lifeforms that can live in different regions of the earth.

Weather and Climate

Weather is the condition of the air in a place at any given time. Temperature, moisture, air pressure, and winds determine the weather of a region at a specific time.

Temperature is a measure of the amount of energy in the air. This energy is supplied by the sun. Warm air has more energy than cool air. Temperature is recorded in degrees Fahrenheit (F.) or in degrees Celsuis (C). The Celsius scale is part of the metric system and is based on decimals. On the Celsuis scale, water freezes at 0° C and boils at 100° C. On the Fahrenheit scale, the boiling point of water is 212° F., and its freezing point is 32° F.

The highest temperature ever recorded on the earth's surface was 136.4° F. (58° C) at Al' Aziziyah in Libya. The lowest temperature was -126.9° F. (-88.28° C) at Vostock in Antarctica.

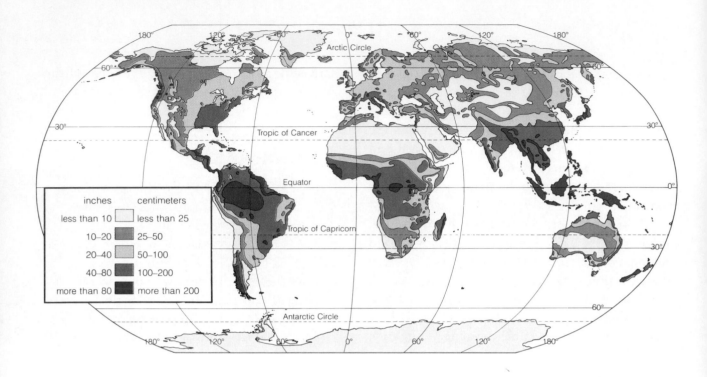

Temperature affects the humidity, or moisture in the air. Cool air holds less water vapor than warm air. When there is a great deal of moisture in the air, we say the humidity is high.

As air cools, its water vapor condenses, or turns into drops of water. Clouds are made of condensed water vapor. The water in clouds falls to earth as precipitation. Depending on the temperatures close to the ground, precipitation will be rain, sleet, hail, or snow.

Temperature also affects the pressure, or weight, of the air. Warm air is lighter than cool air and does not press down on the earth as much as cold air. The force of the air pressing on the earth is called air pressure. Areas covered by warm air are said to have low pressure. Cool air creates areas of high pressure.

Differences in air pressure areas cause wind. Air moves from areas of high pressure to areas of low pressure. As warm air rises, cool air flows in to take its place.

While weather is part of climate, the two things are not the same. Climate describes the kind of weather a place has year after year. To determine the climate of a region, meteorologists study daily weather conditions for many years. They record average rainfall and temperature ranges.

The Earth and the Sun

Many factors determine an area's climate. One of the most important factors is the relationship between the earth and the sun.

24

The sun is a great source of energy. In fact, nearly all of the energy on earth is provided by the sun. Most of the sun's energy is in the form of heat and light. Plants use the energy of sunlight directly. People and animals use the energy stored as food in plants. The sun also influences the weather. Heat from the sun affects temperatures and helps to produce clouds, precipitation, and wind.

Not all parts of the earth receive the same amount of energy from the sun. The amount of heat a place receives depends on the two movements of the earth in relation to the sun. These movements are rotation and revolution.

Rotation

Rotation is the turning of the earth on its axis. The axis is an imaginary line through the earth's center from one pole to the other. It takes the earth 24 hours to make one complete rotation. The rotation of the earth gives us day and night. On the side of the earth facing the sun, it is day. It is night on the side of the earth facing away from the sun. If the earth did not rotate, one side would always be in sunlight, and the other side would always be in darkness.

Revolution

As the earth rotates on its axis, it also moves around the sun. The movement of the earth around the sun is called revolution. The path of the earth around the sun is called its orbit. It takes the earth one full year to travel completely around the sun. See the diagram on page 26. Notice that the earth's axis is always tilted in relation to the orbit. The axis is tilted 23.5° from a right angle to the plane of the earth's orbit.

The tilt of the axis does not change as the earth revolves. As the earth revolves around the sun in its orbit, different regions on its surface receive different amounts of energy. The tilt of the earth and the changing relationship of the earth to the sun account for the changes that we call seasons.

The diagram on page 26 shows that more sunlight falls on places north of the equator when the northern end of the earth's axis tilts toward the sun. At the same time, the southern end of the axis is tilted away from the sun. When the earth is in this position, it is summer in the Northern Hemisphere and winter in the Southern Hemisphere. These conditions are reversed when the southern end of the earth's axis tilts toward the sun. At these times, the Southern Hemisphere has summer and the Northern Hemisphere has winter.

Equinoxes and Solstices

The length of daytime and nighttime in different parts of the world varies because of the tilt of the earth's axis and because of the earth's revolution. On the first day of summer, June 20 or 21 in the Northern Hemisphere, there are more hours of daylight than on any other day. This day is called the summer *solstice* (sol'stis). The solstice is either of two times during the year when the sun appears farthest from the equator. In Latin, *solstice* means "the sun stands still."

On June 20 or 21, the direct rays of the sun are over the Tropic of Cancer at noon. The

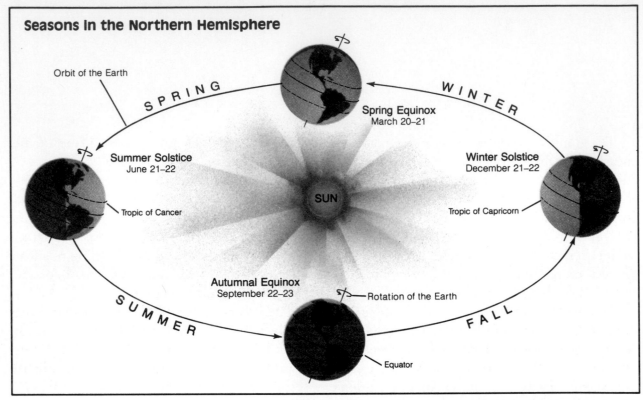

Seasons in the Northern Hemisphere

Orbit of the Earth

SPRING

WINTER

Spring Equinox
March 20–21

Summer Solstice
June 21–22

Winter Solstice
December 21–22

Tropic of Cancer

SUN

Tropic of Capricorn

Autumnal Equinox
September 22–23

Rotation of the Earth

SUMMER

FALL

Equator

The diagram shows how the earth's revolution causes the change of seasons. As the earth revolves around the sun, it rotates on its axis. What would happen if the earth did not rotate?

Tropic of Cancer is a line of latitude 23.5° north of the equator. The direct rays of the sun never shine north of the Tropic of Cancer. For six months after the summer solstice, the days grow shorter.

The first day of winter in the Northern Hemisphere is the winter solstice. It occurs on December 21 or 22. On this day, there are fewer hours of daylight than on any other day in the Northern Hemisphere. For the next six months, the days will grow longer. At the winter solstice, the direct rays of the sun at noon are directly over the Tropic of Capricorn. The Tropic of Capricorn is a line of latitude 23.5° south of the equator. The direct rays of the sun never shine south of the Tropic of

Capricorn. In the Southern Hemisphere, the summer solstice is on December 21 or 22 and the winter solstice is on June 20 or 21.

The *equinox* (ē′kwə noks′) is one of the two times of the year when the sun is directly over the equator at noon. During the equinoxes, day and night are of equal length in all parts of the earth. In Latin, *equinox* means "equal night." In the Northern Hemisphere, the spring equinox is March 20 or 21, the first day of spring. The autumnal equinox is September 22 or 23. It is the first day of fall, or autumn. In the Southern Hemisphere, the dates of the spring equinox and the autumnal equinox are the reverse of these dates in the Northern Hemisphere.

Other Factors Affecting Climate

Although climate is influenced greatly by the earth's relationship to the sun, many other things also affect climate. These include latitude, altitude, winds, ocean currents, and distance from the sea.

Latitude

Even though the sun provides heat to all parts of the earth, not all parts are heated equally. The reasons for this are the shape of the earth and the way the earth moves around the sun. Latitude helps explain some of the differences in temperature from place to place.

Latitude is the distance north or south of the equator. The regions lying between latitude 30° N. and latitude 30° S. are called the low latitudes. In the low latitudes, the rays of the sun strike the earth directly. The low latitudes receive most of the world's supply of solar energy. They are hot all year round.

Because of the spherical shape of the earth, the regions near both the North Pole and the South Pole receive only indirect rays of the sun. These regions, the part of the earth lying between 60° and 90° in both the Northern Hemisphere and the Southern Hemisphere, are known as the high latitudes. The high latitudes are very cold.

The regions of the world between the high latitudes and the low latitudes are called the middle latitudes. They lie between 30° and 60° in both the Northern Hemisphere and the Southern Hemisphere. In the middle latitudes, the rays of the sun are more direct near 30° latitude than near 60° latitude. The middle latitudes receive varying amounts of heat. In general, temperatures there are higher than those in the high latitudes and lower than those in the low latitudes.

Altitude

Altitude, or elevation, is another important factor in climate. Altitude has an effect on climate similar to that of latitude. The higher the land is above sea level, the colder it is. In fact, the temperature drops about 3° or 4° F. (2° or 3° C) with each 1,000 feet (300 m) of altitude. This is the reason that the temperature at the bottom of a mountain can be very warm while the temperature at the top is very cold. Mount Kilimanjaro, the highest mountain in Africa, lies near the equator in Tanzania. There are glaciers near the summit, while coffee, a tropical plant, grows on its lower slopes.

Winds

The air around the earth is always moving. The movement of air is called wind. Winds mix hot air from the equator with cold air from the poles. If the air of the earth did not move and mix, the low latitudes would get hotter and the high latitudes would get colder.

Differences in temperature between the high latitudes and the low latitudes cause differences in air pressure. Cool, heavy air has a high pressure. Warm, light air has a low pressure. The differences in air pressure cause the winds to move in certain patterns. They move from areas of high pressure to areas of low pressure. Winds that blow in patterns are called

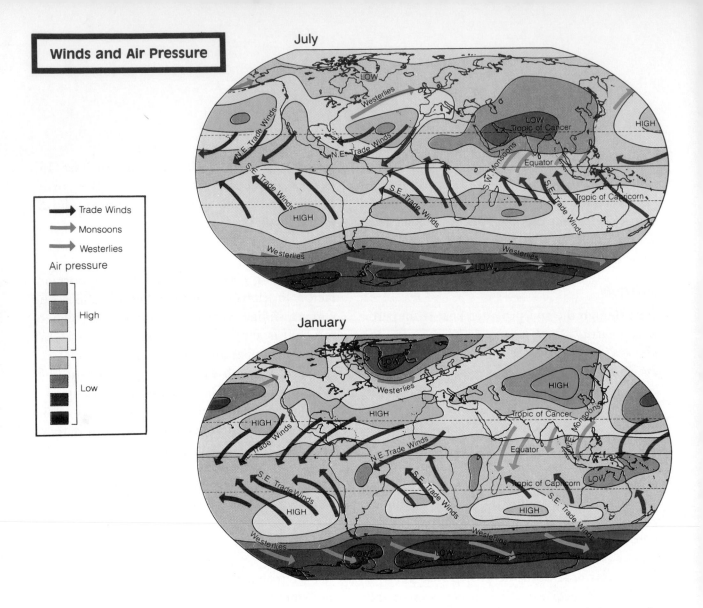

prevailing winds. Look at the map above. Notice the names of the prevailing winds and the directions from which they come. Winds are named for the direction from which they come. Winds coming from the west, for example, are called westerlies. There are both northeast and southeast trade winds.

Winds influence climate by moving moisture as well as heat. Water from the oceans or other bodies of water may evaporate and be carried by the wind. The moisture may later fall as rain or snow over the land. The shape of the land may determine where moisture falls. Winds rise on the windward side of mountains. The windward side is the side from which the prevailing wind blows. As the wind rises, the moisture condenses and falls as rain or snow. The other side of the mountains, called the leeward side, is usually dry as a result. Lands on the leeward sides of mountains are said to be in the rain shadow.

Winds blowing toward the land over ocean currents may help to warm or cool the land. If the current is warm, the wind will warm the land. If the current is cool, the wind blowing over it will cool the land.

Winds accompany tropical storms called hurricanes, typhoons, and cyclones. The winds have speeds greater than 75 miles (120 km) an hour. They may cover areas as wide as 300 miles (480 km). Such winds often cause great damage.

Differences in temperature and air pressure over land and water are the cause of the monsoons in Asia. Monsoons are seasonal winds. During the summer, the air over the continent heats more quickly than the air over the water. The warm air rises, and the heavier, cool air blows in from the sea, bringing rain. During the winter, the pattern is reversed. The land cools more quickly than the water, and cool, dry air from Asia moves out toward the ocean as the warm air over the ocean rises.

Ocean Currents

Like winds, ocean currents transfer heat. They transfer cold water and warm water from one part of the ocean to another. Currents are like rivers flowing through the oceans. Prevailing winds often help determine the direction of the ocean currents. Cold currents, which originate in polar regions, move toward the equator. Warm currents carry heat from the low latitudes toward the poles. The map below shows that most warm ocean currents flow along the eastern sides of continents. Most cold currents flow along the western sides.

Both prevailing winds and an ocean current moderate the climate along the northern Pacific coast of North America. This region is in the high latitudes and the northern part of the middle latitudes. It is not as cold as might be expected. The Japan Current brings warm

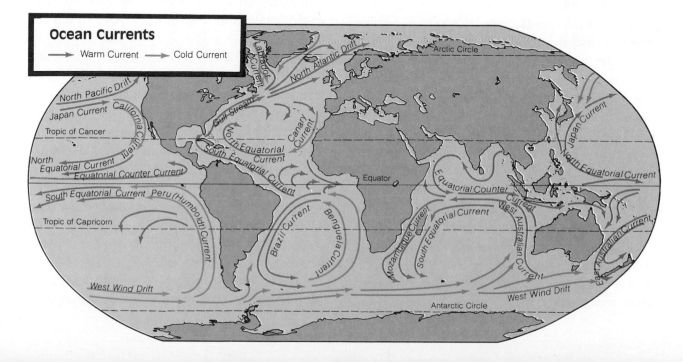

water from the South Pacific to this region. As a result, the ports along the coast are ice-free all year. Winds blowing across the current are warmed. They carry heat and moisture to the land. Great forests of evergreen trees grow along the rainy parts of the coast. In the mild climate, plants grow all winter.

Distance From the Sea

Regions near the sea or large lakes tend to have more moderate temperatures than regions far inland. As you have learned, land gains and loses heat more quickly than water does. In summer, the air over the water is cooler than the air over the land. Winds from the sea blow toward the land and cool the air. In winter, when the water is warmer than the land, the reverse takes place. The warm air over the water helps to keep the land warmer than it would be otherwise.

In general, lands near the ocean receive more rainfall than regions farther inland. However, the precipitation depends on the direction of the winds and the kinds of currents in the nearby waters. Some places along the Irish coast, for example, have as much as 100 inches (250 cm) of rain a year. Westerly winds passing over the warm waters of the North Atlantic Drift pick up moisture. The winds cool over the land and the moisture falls as rain.

The interiors of some continents are far from the sea. There is no nearby water to help moderate the climate. Regions far from the sea tend to have greater extremes, or wider ranges, of temperatures throughout the year. These land areas are always hotter in summer and colder in winter than regions near the sea. Continental interiors also tend to be drier than coastal regions. The moisture they do receive falls mainly in the summer, because the warm summer winds carry more moisture. The Great Plains in the interior of the United States is an example of a region that has little rainfall and a wide range between summer temperatures and winter temperatures.

Climate Zones

Climate can vary greatly within just a few miles because of landforms, winds, ocean currents, and elevation. Even though there are many variations in climate, scientists have classified climates into three main types or zones. The three major climate zones are tropical, temperate, and polar. A fourth kind of climate is called mountain climate. Throughout the world, regions of high altitude have mountain climates.

Within the major climate zones, there are several subgroups. The map on page 31 shows where the climate zones are located.

Tropical Climate Zones

The area directly north and south of the equator between the Tropic of Cancer and the Tropic of Capricorn is called the tropics. This area makes up the tropical climate zone. The sun's rays strike the earth most directly in this region. Within the tropical climate zone, there are wet and dry climates.

Lands with a tropical wet climate have high temperatures and plentiful rainfall throughout

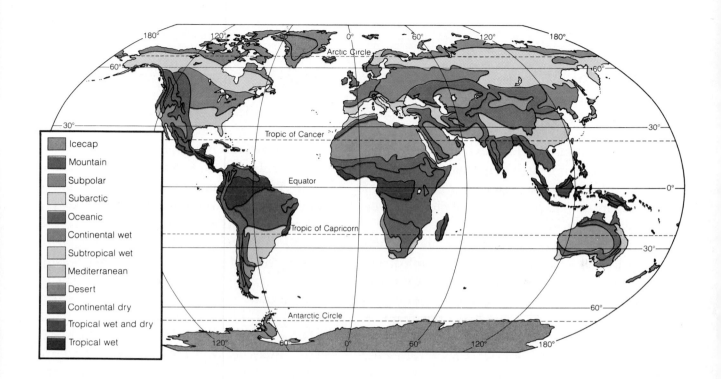

Icecap
Mountain
Subpolar
Subarctic
Oceanic
Continental wet
Subtropical wet
Mediterranean
Desert
Continental dry
Tropical wet and dry
Tropical wet

the year. The Amazon basin in South America, and Malaysia and Indonesia in Southeast Asia are in the tropical wet climate zone.

In the tropical wet-and-dry climate zone, temperatures are high all year. The amount of rainfall varies. Rain is most abundant during the summer. Much of Africa and India lie within this climate zone.

Some regions within the tropical climate zone are deserts. Temperatures vary greatly in these desert areas. Days are very hot, but nights are cool. The average amount of rainfall is very low. There are tropical deserts on every continent except Europe and Antarctica.

Temperate Climate Zones

The temperate climate zone lies north and south of the tropics. The sun's rays strike this region less directly than they do in the tropics. Temperatures in the temperate regions are therefore milder than those in tropical lands.

All parts of the temperate climate zone have summer and winter, but there are great variations in the seasonal climates of different regions. The main kinds of temperate climate are subtropical wet, Mediterranean, continental dry, continental wet, and oceanic.

In subtropical wet regions, summers are warm to hot. Winters are cool. There is moderate precipitation throughout the year. The southeastern United States and a great part of China have a subtropical wet climate.

The area around the Mediterranean Sea has hot, dry summers and mild, rainy winters. Such a climate is called a Mediterranean climate. Most of California, central Chile, and much of

Australia's southern coast have a Mediterranean climate.

Temperate regions that receive less rainfall than areas in the Mediterranean climate zone have continental dry climates. Much of Mexico and the western United States have a continental dry climate. Some regions in Africa south of the Sahara also have this kind of climate, even though they are in the tropics.

Continental wet lands have moderate precipitation all year. Summers are warm to cool and winters are cool. The midwestern and northeastern sections of the United States and much of eastern Europe have this kind of climate.

Regions with an oceanic climate are near large bodies of water. Summers are mild and warm, and winters are cool. There is moderate precipitation in all seasons. The northwestern United States along the Pacific coast, much of southern Chile, western Europe, Norway, and New Zealand have an oceanic climate.

Some regions within the temperate climate zone are deserts. These areas receive very little precipitation. Vast stretches of land in Asia are deserts. Australia, Africa, North America, and South America also have deserts.

Polar Climate Zones

Regions in the high latitudes lie within the polar climate zone. These areas of the world receive no direct rays from the sun. Within the polar climate zone, there are subarctic, subpolar, and icecap climates.

Most of the subarctic climate zone is directly south of the Arctic Circle. The areas in this zone have short, cool summers and long, cold winters. The amount of precipitation is small. North America, Europe, and Asia all have subarctic climate zones.

The region just north of the Arctic Circle is mainly a subpolar climate zone. A small peninsula in Antarctica has the same type of climate. In this climate zone, temperatures are always cold and summers are short and chilly. Because of the low temperatures, the ground in these areas is usually frozen solid. In the short summer, only the top one to five feet (30 to 50 cm) of the ground thaw. The part of the soil that never thaws is called permafrost.

Two areas in the world have an icecap climate. Antarctica and most of Greenland are covered by an icecap. In these lands, the temperatures never rise above freezing. Precipitation is always in the form of snow.

Mountain Climate

The climate of mountainous regions is usually different from the climate of nearby areas. Most mountain areas are cooler than the land around them. The windward side of a mountain receives abundant precipitation. The leeward side usually receives very little. Parts of most continents have mountain climates. Find these areas on the map on page 31.

Vegetation

Climate has a direct effect on the ecosystem of a particular area. An ecosystem includes the living and nonliving things in a region. Plants, animals, soil, water, sunlight, and air are parts

Lush rain forests are found in tropical wet lands. Sunshine and abundant rain result in the growth of hundreds of kinds of trees and other plants. This rain forest is in Ghana, West Africa.

of an ecosystem. There is a variety of plant and animal life within a given climate zone. The next sections describe the main kinds of vegetation found in different climate regions.

Rain Forests

The warm temperatures and abundant rainfall of tropical wet lands are ideal conditions for certain kinds of trees. The forests that grow in tropical wet lands are called rain forests. Most trees in tropical rain forests are broadleaf evergreen trees. These trees have broad, flat leaves. The trees are green all year long. There are hundreds of kinds of trees in tropical rain forests. Mahogany, balsa, teak, fig, rubber, bamboo, and palm are some of the trees that grow there. In many areas, sunlight cannot penetrate the thick treetops to reach the forest floor.

Regions in the temperate climate zone also have rain forests. There are rain forests along the Pacific coasts of Oregon and Washington. The trees in these temperate rain forests are mainly pine, spruce, and fir. Trees such as these are called needleleaf trees because they have narrow, needle-like leaves.

Needleleaf Forests

More than one-third of all forested lands are covered by needleleaf, or evergreen, forests. Hemlock, fir, spruce, and pine are needleleaf trees. Most needleleaf trees are evergreens. Needleleaf trees can grow in cool and cold regions. The northernmost areas of the temperate climate zone have needleleaf forests. Canada, Sweden, northern Europe, and Asia are vast needleleaf forest lands.

Needleleaf trees can also grow in warm areas. Much of Florida has needleleaf forests.

Broadleaf Deciduous Forests

Oak, maple, birch, poplar, elm, and hickory are just a few of the many kinds of broadleaf deciduous (di sij′o͞o əs) trees. Deciduous trees shed their leaves once a year. Deciduous forests in North America, Europe, and Asia are in the temperate climate zone.

Mixed Forests

Broadleaf trees and needleleaf trees grow together in mixed forests. The broadleaf trees are usually deciduous. They lose their leaves either in cold seasons or dry seasons. The needleleaf trees are usually evergreens. They remain green when the deciduous trees are

33

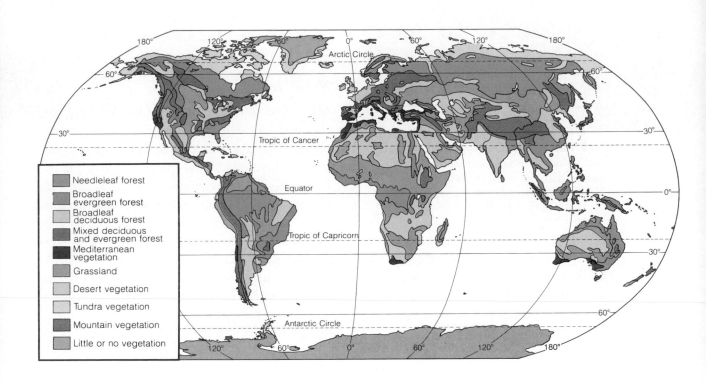

Needleleaf forest
Broadleaf evergreen forest
Broadleaf deciduous forest
Mixed deciduous and evergreen forest
Mediterranean vegetation
Grassland
Desert vegetation
Tundra vegetation
Mountain vegetation
Little or no vegetation

bare. Many parts of North America and Europe are covered by mixed forests.

Grasslands

There are three kinds of grasslands. They are savannas, prairies, and steppes. Both temperate and tropical climate zones have grasslands.

Savannas are tropical grasslands. Baobab (bā′ō bab′) and acacia (ə kā′shə) trees grow in the vast savannas of Africa. These trees are scattered throughout the stretches of tall grass.

Much of Argentina and the midwestern United States and the south-central region of Canada are prairie lands. Prairies have both tall grasses and short grasses.

Grasses are short and sparse on steppes because the amount of rainfall is small. Dry winds blow over steppe areas. The steppes in

34

the United States border the prairies to the west. The steppes in Africa and Asia border deserts.

Deserts

Deserts are very dry regions that are found in both the tropical and temperate climate zones. Most desert areas lie near the Tropic of Cancer and the Tropic of Capricorn. Some deserts in South America, Australia, and Africa are in coastal regions. Deserts in North America and central Asia are near mountainous regions. Deserts cover about one-seventh of the earth's surface.

Desert vegetation must be able to survive during long periods of little or no rain. Cactuses are well suited for such conditions. Some desert plants live only during the rainy season. They sprout, bloom, and produce seeds in a very short time.

Tundra

A tundra is a vast treeless plain in the subpolar climate zone. Only very hardy plants can survive in the cold, dry climate. The growing season lasts for only about three months when the top layer of the ground thaws. Mosses, lichens, dwarf shrubs, small grasses, and flowering plants grow in tundra regions. Vast sections of Alaska, Canada, Norway, and the Soviet Union are tundra lands.

Mountain Vegetation

At low elevations, the vegetation in mountainous regions is much like the vegetation of nearby areas. The vegetation changes at higher

Small but colorful plants appear in Canada's vast tundra during the short summer growing season.

elevations. Above a certain altitude, called the timber line, no trees can grow. Above the timber line, the growing season is too short and the soil is too rocky to support large plants like trees.

Vegetation differs on the leeward and windward sides of a mountain. Plants that grow on the leeward side require less moisture than those on the windward side.

Do You Know?

1. Where are the direct rays of the sun at noon during the solstices? During the equinoxes?
2. What are the low latitudes? What are the high latitudes? Which latitudes receive the direct rays of the sun?
3. What are monsoons? What causes them?

35

Before You Go On

Using New Words

equinox   alluvial plain
silt   seismology
strait   hydrosphere
moraine   lithosphere
aquifer   solstice

Number a paper from 1 through 10. After each number write the word or term from the above list that matches the definition.

1. A narrow channel that joins two larger bodies of water
2. A rock layer that holds water and lets it pass through
3. An area built up of silt and other material left behind after a flood
4. All the water of the earth
5. One of the two times of the year when the sun is directly over the equator at noon
6. The crust, or outer rock layer, of the earth
7. Either of two times during the year when the sun appears farthest from the equator
8. A deposit of material carried by a glacier
9. The study of earthquakes
10. Very fine particles of rock, smaller than sand

Finding the Facts

1. What is the total surface area of the earth? What percent is land? What percent is covered by water?
2. What are the earth's four oceans? Which is the largest? The smallest?
3. What are two kinds of glaciers?
4. What are some of the results of tectonic activity?
5. What instrument is used to measure the strength of an earthquake? What scale is used to indicate the strength of an earthquake?
6. Name two kinds of volcanoes.
7. What are three important agents of erosion?
8. What kind of geological formation is Long Island, New York?
9. What four factors determine the weather of a region?
10. How is temperature related to humidity?
11. What is the difference between the earth's rotation and its revolution?
12. Name four factors that affect climate.
13. What are prevailing winds? What are westerlies? Easterlies?
14. Name the three major climate zones. What is another important kind of climate?

3
Maps and Globes

Maps and globes are special tools that help us understand the earth. Maps and globes are only representations of the earth. Neither shows the world exactly as it is. If we know how to use them, maps and globes can tell us much about the earth, its places, and its people.

People long ago used maps and globes. The oldest known map was made about 2300 B.C. in Babylonia. The earliest maps must have been made long before then, however. People probably started to make maps as soon as they began to travel about the earth exploring it.

The earliest globes we know of were made by the Greeks about 1500 B.C. The Greeks knew that the earth is a sphere. Many of their measurements, including the circumference of the earth, or the distance around it, were quite accurate.

Modern maps and globes are more accurate than those made in the past. Today computers, photographs from space, and scientific instruments are used by map and globe makers.

Comparing Maps and Globes

Maps are drawings on flat surfaces of all or part of the world. A globe is a map of the entire earth drawn on a sphere. Because the earth itself is spherical, a globe is really a scale model of the earth.

Globes are useful because they show the earth's surface more accurately than maps do. A globe is made to scale, which means that it is a small copy of the real world. Distances, sizes, shapes, and directions are shown in their true relation to one another. North, for example, is always toward the North Pole. Most globes are mounted to show the tilt of the earth's axis.

The four features that can be shown accurately on a globe—distance, size, shape, and direction—cannot be shown accurately on a map. A map can give a true picture of only one or two of these features. Every map has some error, or distortion.

Maps, however, have some advantages that globes do not. Maps can be folded or rolled. They can be carried and stored easily. A map can show the world so that it can be seen all at once. On a globe, only half the world can be seen at a time. Maps are generally less expensive to make than globes.

The Grid System

If you look closely at a map or globe, you will see that there are two sets of lines drawn at some distance apart. The two sets of lines cross each other, or intersect. These intersecting lines make up a grid system. Grid systems help us find places on maps or globes and describe where they are.

Latitude and Longitude

The grid system divides the earth into parts both north and south, and east and west. The lines running north and south are called lines

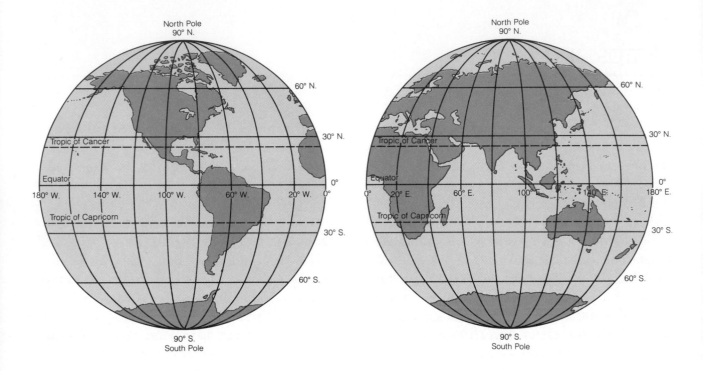

of longitude, or meridians. The lines that run east and west are called lines of latitude, or parallels.

Lines of latitude are measured in degrees north and south of the equator. The latitude of the equator is 0°. Lines of latitude are numbered from 0° to 90° both north and south of the equator. The North Pole is at 90° N. latitude. The South Pole is at 90° S. latitude. Lines of latitude are parallel to one another. That is why they are sometimes called parallels. Parallels never meet.

Lines of longitude run north and south. Each line of longitude is a half of a circle, and all lines of longitude, or meridians, meet at the North Pole and at the South Pole. By international agreement, the meridian that passes through Greenwich (gren'ich), England, is called the prime meridian. Its longitude is 0°, and all other meridians are numbered in degrees up to 180° east and west of the prime meridian.

The location of any place on earth can be described by giving its latitude and longitude. The latitude of a place gives us its distance and direction from the equator. The longitude of a place tells us its direction and distance from the prime meridian. The location of Bombay, for example, can be given as 19° N. and 73° E. This means that Bombay is 19° north of the equator and 73° east of the prime meridian.

On maps and globes, latitude and longitude are marked by labeled lines. Usually only a few of these lines are shown.

Sometimes we may want to give the location of a place more precisely than we can by using whole degrees. Degrees, which are represented by the symbol °, can be divided into smaller units called minutes. The symbol ′ is used for minutes. Perhaps you have seen this symbol in the index of an atlas. There are 60 minutes in one degree. If we want to give Bombay's location more precisely than we did above, we can give it as 18° 58′ N. and 72° 50′ E.

Hemispheres

A great circle is a line on the earth that divides the earth into two equal halves called hemispheres. The equator is the only line of latitude that is a great circle. Every line of longitude is half a great circle. Two lines of longitude together form a great circle if they are 180° apart.

The equator divides the world into a Northern Hemisphere and a Southern Hemisphere. All of Europe, Asia, and North America are in the Northern Hemisphere. Part of Africa and part of South America are in the Northern Hemisphere, and parts of each are in the Southern Hemisphere. All of Australia and Antarctica are in the Southern Hemisphere.

The boundary between the Eastern Hemisphere and the Western Hemisphere is not so precise as that between the Northern and Southern Hemispheres. To avoid cutting continents in two, the boundary is usually drawn along 20° west longitude and 160° east longitude. Africa, Australia, Europe, and most of Asia are in the Eastern Hemisphere. North America, South America, and a small part of Asia are in the Western Hemisphere. Antarctica is divided between the two hemispheres.

Time Zones

The way we measure time is related to the rotation and revolution of the earth. A year is the length of time it takes the earth to make one revolution around the sun. A day is the length of time it takes the earth to make a complete rotation.

How we divide the day to keep time is closely related to longitude. In one day, or 24 hours, the earth makes a complete rotation of 360° of longitude. In one hour, therefore, the earth rotates 15° of longitude. We can say that an hour is 15° of longitude wide.

Although the day is 24 hours long, we usually divide it into two 12-hour periods. The period from midnight to noon includes the A.M. hours. The period from noon to midnight includes the P.M. hours. Because of the earth's rotation, it is always noon somewhere on earth. Suppose it is noon where you are. Because the earth turns from west to east, noon has already passed at some place east of you. It has yet to occur at some place west of you. Every four minutes, noon moves one full degree of longitude west.

The sun time at any particular place is called local time. Local time was used for hundreds of years. As faster methods of communication and transportation developed, local time began to cause confusion. Before 1883, every locality in the United States set its own time by the sun. The railroads, in an attempt to make their schedules simpler, had established about 100 railroad times. In 1883, the railroads divided the United States into four standard time zones. The zones were centered on lines of

□ Irregular time

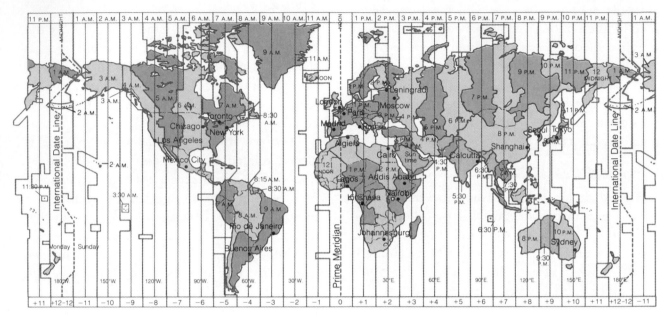

To find the time east of the prime meridian, hours are added. To the west, they are subtracted. What happens at the International Date Line?

longitude 15° apart. The Eastern Time Zone is centered on 75° W., the Central Time Zone on 90° W., the Mountain Time Zone on 105° W., and the Pacific Time Zone on 120° W.

In 1884, 24 standard time zones were established throughout the world. It was decided that places within each zone would follow the local time of the longitude passing through the center of that zone. The meridian passing through Greenwich Observatory in England was chosen as the center line of the starting zone. This meridian is the 0° meridian, or prime meridian. The prime meridian was used to determine noon for its zone. The meridian opposite the prime meridian, 180° longitude,

became the line for determining midnight. It is known as the International Date Line.

The model time zones set up in 1884 have been changed to make them more practical. The map above shows how the zones have been modified and changed. Many zones have been changed to follow state and national boundaries. The International Date Line has been redrawn to avoid as many land areas as possible. It does not follow the 180° meridian in all places.

In order to determine what time it is in different places around the world, you need to remember a few rules. Time in places east is always later than it is where you are.

Time in places west is always earlier than it is where you are. How much earlier or how much later depends on the number of time zones between two places. It also depends on whether the difference between any two zones is an hour, more than an hour, or less than an hour. In general, if you are going east, you must set your watch forward an hour for each time zone you cross. Going west, you must set it back an hour for each time zone you cross. If you cross the International Date Line, you must change days. If you cross it from east to west on a Sunday, the day becomes Monday. If you cross it from west to east on a Sunday, the day becomes Saturday.

Understanding Maps

People study maps to understand the earth. Maps can tell us much about the earth and the things on it, including its people. Some maps show the whole world, others show small parts of it in great detail. The information on all maps is presented by symbols. To get information from maps, we must be able to tell what the symbols stand for. We read maps by learning what their symbols mean and interpreting them.

Map Projections

A drawing on a flat piece of paper showing the global grid is called a projection. A map is drawn on a projection. There are many different projections, but none represents the earth's surface without some distortion. No single map can show shape, size, distance, and direction accurately. A map can show a true picture of one or two of these features, but it can never show a true picture of all of them. On maps covering only a small area, distortion is small. On maps of large areas, such as a continent or the world, distortion is very great.

Even though there are hundreds of map projections, only a few are commonly used. One of the most famous maps is a Mercator map. It is an example of a cylindrical projection. The diagram on page 539 shows how a cylindrical projection is made. Gerhardus Mercator, a Flemish geographer, invented this projection. In 1569 he published a world map using this projection. The Mercator projection is useful to travelers and navigators because a straight line drawn anywhere on the map shows a constant compass direction. The map stretches the lines of latitude and longitude, which results in keeping shapes true. Areas, however, are not shown in their true proportions. On a Mercator map, Greenland looks much larger than South America. It is really less than one-eighth as large as South America.

A famous conic map projection was designed by J. H. Lambert, a German mathematician, in the 1770s. The diagram on page 539 shows how a conic projection is made. Conic projections usually show only part of the world in the middle latitudes. Distance and directions are true along one or two parallels. Other distances, as well as shape, size, and direction, are fairly accurate, especially for small areas.

One of the most famous plane projections is the gnomonic (nō mon′ik) projection. The diagram on page 539 shows how this projection is made. A fixed point is the center of the map. Shape, size, and distance vary greatly. This projection is very useful to pilots, however. A straight line between the fixed point and any other place on the map is part of a great circle. The shortest distance between any two places in the world is always part of a great circle. Maps of polar regions are often drawn on gnomonic projections.

Map Scale

The scale of a map tells how much of the earth's surface is represented by a given measurement on the map. The scale can be expressed in words: *One inch equals 114 miles* or *one centimeter equals 145 kilometers*. Scale may also be expressed as a fraction. It might be written 1:62,500 or $\frac{1}{62,500}$. This means that one unit of measurement on the map represents 62,500 of the same units on the surface of the earth. This is a convenient way to express scale because the unit of measurement can be one inch or one centimeter. One inch would represent 62,500 inches, and one centimeter would represent 62,500 centimeters. A line called a bar scale can also be used to represent scale. See the map on page 62.

Maps are drawn to many different scales. Most maps can be described as small-scale maps or large-scale maps. Small-scale maps show large parts of the world. They do not show exact distances between places or great detail. Large-scale maps cover only small regions of the earth's surface. Large-scale maps can show many details. City maps are large-scale maps.

Map Symbols

The information on maps is shown by symbols. By using symbols, a great deal of information can be put on a map. Maps have a map key, or a map legend, that explains what the symbols mean. Symbols may be dots, stars, lines, dashes, triangles, letters, words, colors, or combinations of these things. Some symbols look like the things they represent. For example, a small tent may be the symbol for a campsite. Other symbols may have no resemblance to what they represent. A dot, for example, often represents a town or city.

Color is a special symbol on maps. On physical maps, color is commonly used to indicate landforms. On the map on pages 14-15, for example, mountains, plateaus, hills, and plains are shown in different colors. Color is also often used to show differences in rainfall, vegetation, elevation, and climate. Political information is also given by using color. Political boundaries are emphasized by showing countries in different colors. On most maps, constructed features are shown in black.

Kinds of Maps

Maps can be divided into two groups. General reference maps make up one group. The other group includes maps that are made for special purposes.

Most general reference maps show *topography* (tə pog′rə fē). Topography is the surface features of an area. Topography includes not only landforms, but many other natural and

The Landsat-1 satellite produced this view of the area around Washington, D.C. The light blue area is the city. The large dark blue area on the right is Chesapeake Bay.

Many of the maps in this book are maps of this kind.

Transportation maps are general reference maps familiar to almost everyone. Transportation maps show cities, roads, railroads, air routes, and shipping routes. One kind of transportation map, the road map, often shows rivers, lakes, parks, and campsites.

There are hundreds of different kinds of special-purpose maps. Weather maps, historical maps, land-use maps, language maps, and maps of the moon are just a few examples.

Developments in technology have made it possible to acquire more accurate information about the earth. Aerial (er′ē əl) photographs, computers, radar, and weather satellites are used to gather information. Landsat images of the earth are made by using information gathered by special satellites orbiting the earth. The first Landsat images were transmitted to earth from Landsat-1, which was launched into orbit in 1972. Landsat images show the earth in amazing detail. See the picture on this page.

constructed features such as rivers, lakes, roads, and bridges.

Physical maps, which are sometimes called graphic-relief maps, are one kind of general reference map. They show what kind of landforms and water features a region has. They sometimes indicate the elevation of the land. Political maps are another kind of general reference map. They show how the land has been divided into countries, states, and other political units. They show the location of cities and towns. Sometimes physical information and political information are combined on a single map called a physical-political map.

Do You Know?

1. What advantages do globes have over maps? What advantages do maps have over globes?
2. What do we call the two sets of lines that make up the grid system?
3. In what direction does the earth rotate? Is the time earlier or later east of where you are?

4

The Earth's Resources

Natural resources are all of the things on earth that people use. Materials of the earth are not resources just because they exist. They become resources when people use them for something. Resources change from time to time, from place to place, and from one culture to another.

Long ago, people did not know that coal would burn. Because people did not use coal, it was not a resource. When people began to burn coal to heat their homes, coal became a resource. Today, coal is used not only as a fuel, but as a source of many other materials.

Sometimes resources are abandoned for a time. Many years ago, people used windmills to generate energy. But when people began to use gas and oil energy, wind power was abandoned. Now that oil is becoming scarce, people are beginning to use wind power again.

Important Natural Resources

The most important resources are those that are essential to life. Four basic natural resources are sunlight, air, water, and soil. Two other important resources are plants and animals. Plants and animals supply us with food, clothing, and many other products. Minerals and fossil fuels are also important resources.

The Sun

The sun is vital to the existence of life on earth. The energy of the sun's rays warms the earth's atmosphere, land, and water. Plants need the sun's energy to make food. Animals and people eat plants or plant-eating animals for food. Without the sun's radiation, the exchange of food could not take place.

Energy from the sun, or solar energy, is the greatest source of energy in the world. Storing the sun's energy to use as heat, however, has always been a problem. New ways are being developed to collect and store solar energy. Today, solar energy is being used, but only in a limited way.

Air and Water

Air and water are earth's most valuable resources. Without them, life on earth could not exist.

Air, or the atmosphere that surrounds the earth, is made up of several gases. The most important is oxygen. People and animals breathe in air and use oxygen. They breathe out other gases, including carbon dioxide. Carbon dioxide is essential to green plants. Moving air, or wind, is used by sailboats and by windmills to generate power.

Water is also necessary to all forms of life. Land plants and animals need fresh water to survive. People cannot live without drinking water. Water is also important to people in their daily lives for cooking and cleaning, and in agriculture, industry, and transportation. Rushing water is used to generate hydroelectric power.

Although air and water are plentiful resources, people must be careful not to take them for granted. Factory wastes and car exhausts pollute the air. Water is polluted by sewage and industrial wastes. Fertilizers and insecticides used in farming can pollute the air and water. Pollution affects the quality of air and water and can be harmful to people and other living things. Scientists are now looking for ways to protect and purify the air and water.

Soil

Soil is an important natural resource that covers much of the earth's land surface. Plants need soil in order to grow. Without plants, people and animals would have nothing to eat. Soil supports all forms of life.

Soil is made up of minerals as well as decaying plant and animal matter called *humus* (hy$\overline{oo}$′məs). Particles of sand, silt, and clay make up most of the soil's mineral content. The humus is composed of decaying leaves, grasses, plant roots, and dead animals such as worms, insects, and small mammals. Soil rich in humus is black or dark brown. Humus has a spongy texture that helps the soil hold water. Humus is essential to the fertility of the soil.

Although soil covers much of the land, usable or fertile soil is very limited. Most of the food we eat comes from plants that grow in the upper layer, called topsoil. Topsoil, which is rich in humus, is only about ten inches (25 cm) deep. Conservation of this layer of the soil is important. It takes many years to replace a layer of topsoil.

Plants and Animals

Plants and animals are essential living resources. Plants provide food for people and animals. Animals are also a source of food for people and other animals. People eat the meat, milk, and eggs that come from animals. Fish from the world's oceans are also a source of food for people.

Many useful products are made from plants. Trees are used to build houses and make furniture. Wood is used to make paper and paper products. People also use plants for clothing, rope, and twine. Plants are also an important source of fuel. People burn wood to heat their homes and to cook their food.

People use animals for many things other than food. The fur, wool, and skins of animals are used to make clothing. Some animals are used for riding and pulling loads.

Minerals and Fossil Fuels

Minerals and fossil fuels are important resources found in the earth's land and oceans. Plants use the minerals in the soil to help them grow. Minerals used by people are taken out of the ground or from seawater. Minerals can be divided into two groups—metals and nonmetals. A third group of resources taken from the earth are called fossil fuels.

Most metals are solid and can conduct, or carry, an electric current. They can be made into many different things. Metals are especially useful in manufacturing and building. Iron, combined with other metals, is used to make steel for buildings, ships, cars, and all kinds of machinery. Copper can be drawn into wires

The first commercially successful oil well in the United States was drilled in western Pennsylvania in 1859.

used in the electrical industry. Aluminum is used in airplanes, wire, and foil.

Nonmetals include a great variety of useful minerals. The salt we use to flavor food is a common nonmetallic mineral. The lead in pencils is a mineral called graphite. Cement is a mixture of several minerals.

Fossil fuels are coal, natural gas, and petroleum. They are often classified as nonmetallic minerals. However, they are not really minerals. Fossil fuels were formed millions of years ago from the remains of plants and animals. When fossil fuels are burned, their stored energy is released.

Over 90 percent of all the energy used in the world today comes from fossil fuels. Petroleum, or crude oil, provides almost half of the world's energy. In addition to its use as a heating fuel, petroleum is used to make many valuable products. Gasoline, the most important of these, is used to power cars, trains, airplanes, and machines. Other petroleum products include plastics, dyes, and soaps. Coal now provides about one-third of the world's energy. It is used primarily to generate electricity. It is also used in the production of steel. Natural gas, another fossil fuel, is used for heating homes and cooking. Gas is also used for heat and power in many industries.

Distribution of Resources

Resources are distributed unevenly over the earth. An area of the world may be quite rich in some resources and poor or lacking in others. South Africa, for example, has some of the world's largest reserves of gold and uranium. However, it has very little gas and oil. Saudi Arabia, on the other hand, lacks most metallic minerals, but has large deposits of oil beneath the desert sands.

The variations in the distribution of resources are determined by natural conditions. The distribution of sunlight and water is affected by basic earth-sun relationships—rotation, revolution, and tilt of the earth's axis. Areas near the equator receive more energy from the sun. They also usually receive abundant rain.

The distribution of mineral resources and fossil fuels is related to changes that have taken place in the earth, rather than to latitude or climate. Metallic minerals are often found in rocks that were formed by tectonic activity. Fossil fuels, on the other hand, usually occur in sedimentary rocks, rocks formed by deposition. These different rocks do not usually exist in the same area. Unless a country is quite large, it is unlikely that it will have both metallic minerals and fossil fuels.

Because of the uneven distribution of resources, one nation does not usually have all of the natural resources it needs. For this reason, countries trade resources. They import those resources that they lack, and they export the ones they have in surplus. Trading resources makes up for uneven distribution and is essential to the world's survival.

Two Groups of Resources

A few resources are called permanent because they are so abundant. Water, air, and sunlight are often referred to as permanent resources. Most resources, however, are either renewable or nonrenewable. A *renewable* (ri noo′ə bəl) *resource* is one that can replace or rebuild itself. A resource that cannot be renewed or replaced is a *nonrenewable* (non′ri noo′ə bəl) *resource*. Once a nonrenewable resource is used, it is gone forever.

Renewable Resources

Most living resources, that is, plants and animals, are renewable. Soil is another important renewable resource. Water is plentiful, but can be used up or made unusable. However, water is renewed. Renewable resources can be replaced, but they should be used wisely.

Soil is sometimes washed away, or eroded. Erosion results when the soil is carried away by rivers or winds. Soil erosion can turn farming regions into deserts. Though soil is renewable, it takes many years for rocks to weather into the small particles that mix with humus to make soil.

Certain practices increase soil erosion and decrease the productivity of the land. Overusing of soil can rob it of important nutrients. Farmers today replace nutrients by adding fertilizers to the soil and by rotating crops. Overgrazing can also cause soil erosion. Ranchers can conserve grazing lands by limiting the number of animals and the time that their herds graze in one area.

Pumping too much water from wells may use up the water in the ground faster than it accumulates. If the top surface of the ground water, or the water table, drops below the bottom of a well, the well goes dry. The well has to be dug deeper in order to reach water.

The water of rivers in some irrigated parts of the world has been used in such quantities that the rivers cease to flow. In such regions, the river beds downstream also become dry stream beds.

All living things—animals and plants—are renewable resources because they can reproduce themselves. However, if all the plants or animals of any species are destroyed, the result is extinction, or disappearance forever.

Nonrenewable Resources

Unlike soil, water, plants, and animals, some resources cannot be replaced. This group of resources includes minerals and fossil fuels.

For thousands of years, the minerals in the earth were hardly used by people. During the

Although aluminum is a *nonrenewable resource,* it can be recycled. Crushed aluminum containers will be melted down and used again.

last 200 years, people have discovered many uses for minerals. Today, great amounts of minerals are necessary for industry. People are using minerals at a rapid pace. However, people have also found ways in which to conserve them and to find alternatives.

Most metals, for example, can be recycled, or made suitable for reuse. Aluminum can be used over and over by being melted down and reshaped. The development of the plastics industry is an example of how people create alternatives to nonrenewable resources. A wide variety of plastics has replaced metal and stone in thousands of products.

The supply of fossil fuels is also limited. Fossil fuels are burned in order to provide energy. There is no way to use fossil fuels without destroying them. The amount of fossil fuels used by people has nearly doubled every 20 years since 1900. This growth of energy use has put great strains on the supply of fossil fuels. Some scientists predict that petroleum will be scarce by the year 2000. Natural gas is also being used up quickly. Some experts predict that the earth's supply of natural gas will last only about 40 years. Coal, the most plentiful fossil fuel, may last for another 300 to 400 years.

One of the great concerns people have today is how to meet energy needs of the future when fossil fuels are gone. Some people are looking for ways to add to the world's reserves of fossil fuels. The oceans are being searched for new deposits of oil. People are also looking for less costly ways to extract oil from a rock called shale. Scientists know that other energy sources must be developed.

The most important factor in solving the problem of nonrenewable resources is human knowledge. People's skills, attitudes, and knowledge can lead to new discoveries. The ability of people to solve problems has created the complex world we live in, and the same ability can be used to meet the challenge of the future.

Do You Know?

1. What are four basic natural resources?
2. Why are water, air, and sunlight called permanent resources?
3. Why are living things said to be renewable resources?

To Help You Learn

Using New Words

moraine   nonrenewable resource
humus   lithosphere
topography   renewable resource

Number a paper from 1 through 6. After each number write the word or term from the above list that matches the definition.
1. A useful material that cannot be replaced
2. The surface features of an area
3. Decaying plant and animal matter that in part makes up soil
4. The crust, or outer rock layer, of the earth
5. A deposit of material carried by a glacier
6. A useful material that is capable of replacing or rebuilding itself

Finding the Facts

1. What percent of all fresh water in the United States comes from wells tapping aquifers?
2. What is weather? Temperature?
3. Name four kinds of needleleaf trees. Name four kinds of broadleaf trees.
4. Through what city does the prime meridian run? What is its longitude?
5. Name the four standard time zones in the United States established in 1883.
6. Why was the International Date Line redrawn? What happens if you cross the International Date Line from east to west on a Sunday?

7. What is a projection?
8. What does the scale of a map tell?
9. What is humus composed of?
10. How thick is topsoil?
11. Name three fossil fuels.
12. What percent of all the energy used in the world today comes from fossil fuels? What provides almost one-half of the world's energy? About one-third?
13. Where are metallic minerals often found? Where do fossil fuels usually occur?
14. Name three permanent resources.

Learning from Maps

1. Look at the map of tectonic plates on page 19. On what large plate does most of Europe and Asia rest? What small plate lies between this plate and the African Plate? What large plate is almost entirely covered by ocean? What are the plates under the United States?
2. Look at the map of world time zones on page 40. When it is 10 A.M. in Moscow, what time is it in Paris? In London? In New York? In Addis Ababa? In Shanghai? When it is 10 P.M. Sunday in Toronto, what time is it in Calcutta?

Using Study Skills

1. **Diagram:** Look at the diagram of mountains on page 20. What kind of mountain

resembles a cone? What kinds of mountains have steep edges along one side? Are fault-block mountains more closely related to folded mountains or volcanoes?

2. **Outline:** An outline is a list of the different parts, or headings, of a subject. It shows the plan of a book or of a part of a book. Outlines are useful for remembering information. Below is an outline of the climate zones section from this unit. Copy the outline, reread the text, and complete the outline.

    I. Climate zones
      A.
          1. Tropical wet climate
          2.
          3. Tropical deserts
      B. Temperate climate zones
          1.
          2.
          3. Continental dry climate
          4. Continental wet climate
          5.
          6. Deserts
      C.
          1.
          2.
          3. Icecap climate
      D. Mountain climate

3. **Library Resources:** The atlas and the geographical dictionary are two important reference books for social studies students. A world atlas contains many general-reference maps, including physical, political, and physical-political maps. These maps provide valuable information on world resources, climate, vegetation, population, and transportation. Find three maps in this book that could appear in a world atlas. Tell what kind of map each one is.

A historical atlas includes maps of early civilizations and maps that show political divisions of the past. Turn to the map of North America in 1750, on page 92. This is an example of the kind of map found in a historical atlas. Find three other maps in this book that could appear in a historical atlas.

A geographical dictionary provides basic information about regions, countries, states, departments, provinces, towns, and cities. A geographical dictionary also includes information about natural features, constructed features, and history. The information in a geographical dictionary is listed under entries arranged in alphabetical order.

Below is a sample entry from a geographical dictionary. Use it to answer the questions.

Fu·ji (foō′jē) *or* **Fu·ji·ya·ma** (foō′jē yämə) 1. Highest mountain in S cen. Honshu, Japan, about 70 miles (112 km) SW of Tokyo; 12,388 ft. (3,776 m); diameter of crater about 2,000 ft. (600 m); inactive volcano, last eruption 1707. 2. City, Honshu, Japan; pop. 180,639.

How is *Fuji* pronounced? What is another name for the mountain? Where is it located? How high is it? When did it last erupt?

Fuji is the name of a mountain, but it is also the name of a city. Where is the city located? How many people live there?

Thinking It Through

1. Explain the following statements: "Materials of the earth are not resources just because they exist. They become resources when people use them for something."
2. What problems would scientists have if they tried to drill to the earth's inner core?
3. Why is it important to conserve fossil fuels? What are some ways fossil fuels are being conserved?

Projects

One way to learn more about topics is to form committees to work together on projects. Each committee should select a leader to direct the committee's work on a particular project. Every committee should meet with its leader to plan its work, to decide what each member will do, and to schedule meetings to check on progress. After the committees have finished their work, they should share the information they have gathered by presenting reports, leading discussions, or creating displays. Students are free to join different committees throughout the year.

One group of students might like to belong to the Current Events Committee. This committee will use newspapers, magazines, radio and television broadcasts, and other sources to learn more about important events taking place today. The Current Events Committee might collect and display news items about active volcanoes, recent earthquakes, and storms.

Other students might like to join the Biography Committee. This committee will explore the lives of people of historical importance. Committee members might like to learn more about Andrija Mohorovičič, Gerhardus Mercator, and J.H. Lambert.

Another group of students can form the History Committee, which will research significant events from the past. Some members of the History Committee might find out more about ancient maps and globes: for example, the oldest known map, made in about 2300 B.C. in Babylonia, and the earliest known globe, made by the Greeks in about 1500 B.C.

A fourth group of students might like to join the Arts and Sciences Committee. This committee will look into current and past developments in science and art. Members of this committee might research the San Andreas Fault. They can prepare a report telling where the fault is, what tectonic plates are involved, and why there is risk of earthquakes along the fault.

2 People and the Earth

Unit Preview

From earliest times to the present, people on the Earth have had similar needs. To provide food, clothing, and shelter, early people used the materials they found around them. People today still have the same needs, but they meet them in different ways. Modern technology has permitted great choices in the way resources are used.

Early people were hunters and gatherers who moved from place to place in search of food. When people learned to farm and to herd animals, they began to settle in villages. Living in groups brought about changes that slowly led to the development of civilizations. Some of the changes were the development of laws and governments, written languages, technology, and art.

Four river valleys—the Nile, the Tigris and Euphrates, the Indus, and the Huang—provided the fertile farmland necessary to support large populations. The cultures that grew up in these valleys thousands of years ago were the earliest civilizations. These civilizations made many important contributions to the world. Later civilizations also contributed their cultural and technological achievements. The classical civilizations of Greece and Rome influenced much of the world through their developments in government and law.

In early times, people made their living by using resources directly. As technology advanced and societies became more complex, jobs became more specialized. Today people make their living in ways that use natural resources both directly and indirectly.

Things to Discover

If you look carefully at the picture, map, and time line, you can answer these questions.
1. The highlighted areas on the map show where some of the early civilizations were. On what continents are these areas?
2. The Step Pyramid in the picture was built in Egypt about 2750 B.C. How long after the establishment of the Kingdom of Egypt was this?
3. When did farming begin in the Middle East?

Words to Learn

You will meet these words and terms in this unit. As you read, you will learn what they mean and how to pronounce them. The Word List will help you.

arable	economic
archaeologist	gross national product
architecture	hieroglyphics
artifact	political
chronological	social
commerce	society
cultivate	standard of living
domesticate	

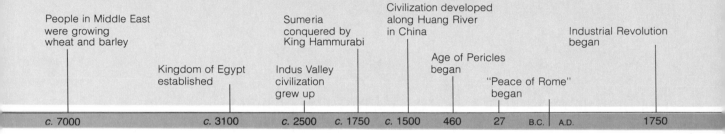

People in Middle East were growing wheat and barley

Kingdom of Egypt established

Sumeria conquered by King Hammurabi

Indus Valley civilization grew up

Civilization developed along Huang River in China

Age of Pericles began

"Peace of Rome" began

Industrial Revolution began

| *c.* 7000 | *c.* 3100 | *c.* 2500 | *c.* 1750 | *c.* 1500 | 460 | 27 | B.C. | A.D. | 1750 |

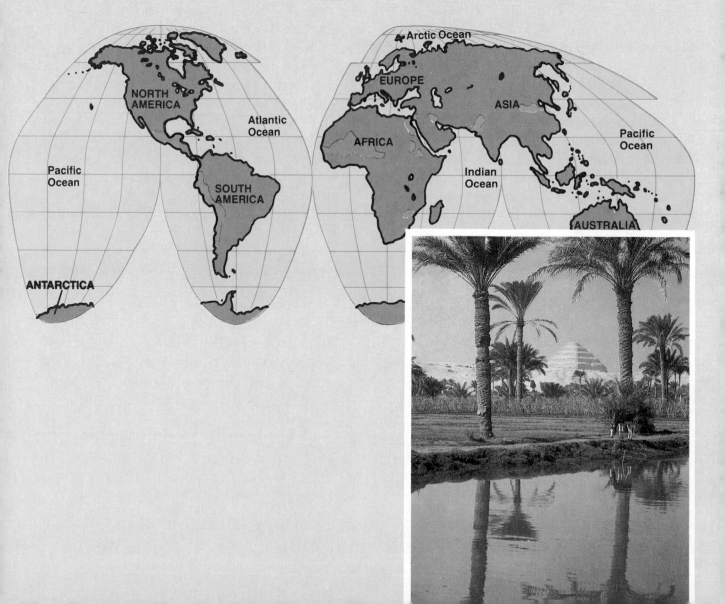

1

Basic Needs and Early Ways of Living

Food, clothing, and shelter are the physical needs of people who live on the earth. Early people learned to use the materials of their environment for the things they needed. Plants and animals provided food. People found ways to make clothing and build shelters from materials that were close at hand.

People also have other needs. Early people found that living in groups offered advantages. Hunting with others was safer than hunting alone. Building a shelter close to other shelters made people feel secure. As people formed groups, they developed ways to communicate with one another. They shared information and ideas.

Archaeologists search for *artifacts* to discover how early people lived. They mark out sections of earth to examine and carefully catalog their findings.

Basic Needs

From the time people first appeared on earth, they needed food, clothing, and shelter. The struggle to obtain these physical necessities occupied most of their attention.

Early people did not know how to write, so they did not leave written records. They did leave, in caves or communities where they had lived, certain tools and other articles they had used. Scientists call an object of this kind an *artifact* (är′təfakt′). An artifact is anything made or changed by humans. Tools, weapons, sculpture, pottery, and jewelry are examples of artifacts.

Scientists have found many artifacts in different parts of the world. Like detectives, scientists have studied these artifacts. They have pieced together much of the story of how early people lived.

An *archaeologist* (är′kē ol′ə jist) is a scientist who studies ancient ruins and examines artifacts. Archaeologists keep careful records of the sites they excavate. The discoveries of archaeologists tell us much about how early people met their basic needs for food, clothing, and shelter.

Food

Early people must have spent much of their time looking for food. They ate what they could find or catch. In grassy areas, they gathered wild seeds. In the forests, they picked berries and nuts and hunted birds and animals. Along rivers and beside the sea, they caught fish. Their methods of finding food can be called simple because they involved simple tools or no tools at all. Early people stayed in one place only as long as food was plentiful there. They moved to another place when food became scarce.

Hunting and Fishing

Early people learned to be skillful at fishing and hunting. At first, they probably waited beside a stream and grabbed a fish if they could. Early hunters may have come up behind a small animal and killed it with a club or a stone.

Later, people learned to kill fish with stone-tipped spears. They discovered how to make hooks from fish bones. They twisted vines or animal hairs together and made nets. With the spears, hooks, and nets, early people could catch more fish than they could with their bare hands.

Hunters also used spears to kill game. They developed the slingshot, which helped them heave stones faster and farther. They discovered how to make and use bows and arrows. With such weapons, early people could kill large animals. They could also keep a safe distance between themselves and their prey.

Even with tools, hunting and fishing took a great deal of time. People usually had to hunt each time they needed food. It was difficult for early people to preserve meat. It was also difficult for people to carry supplies of food while following herds of game.

The First Farmers

After thousands of years of hunting, fishing, and gathering, people discovered they could *cultivate* (kul′tə vāt′) plants. To cultivate is to improve the growth of plants by labor and care.

The first farmers probably tended fields of wild grains. They may have taken some wild plants and replanted them in new areas or nearer water. Later, people began to save part of their supply of seed in order to plant them. From each harvest, they gathered seeds for food and seeds for planting. As plants were tended and watered, they produced more and larger seeds.

Scientists are not sure where the first farmers lived. They do know that people in the Middle East were farming about 7000 B.C. There, near the Mediterranean Sea, early farmers grew wheat and barley. Rice was first grown in Asia. Indians in the Americas cultivated maize, or corn. These four grains—wheat, barley, rice, and corn—are still used as basic foods all over the world.

The First Herders

Gradually, early people also learned that they could tame animals. Hunters may have first tamed sheep and goats by making pets of young animals. In time, people learned to *domesticate* (də mes′tə kāt′) certain animals, or tame and keep them for human use.

At first, domesticated sheep and goats were kept only for meat. Later, they were kept for their milk and skins. As time went on, people also captured cattle and pigs and kept them as well.

By learning to farm and to herd animals, people did not have to hunt as often. They began to stay in one place for extended periods of time.

Storing Food

As they found new sources of food, people also learned to store and keep foods for future use. They knew that they would go hungry if supplies ran out before new crops were ready to be gathered.

Grain was the easiest food to store. Early seed gatherers learned to make pots and other containers. They used these containers to store seeds. The containers kept the grain dry and out of the reach of animals.

Meat, fish, fruit, and vegetables were harder to keep. Meat and fish were smoked or dried over a fire. Berries were also dried so that they could be kept through the winter.

Clothing

Early people needed clothing for warmth. They also needed clothing for protection. Clothing allowed early people to survive in harsh environments.

How Early People Dressed

Early people had to rely on the materials around them for clothing. They probably used animal skins for unfitted garments. These garments were made by drying the hides and softening them with oil or fat. Once people learned to make simple knives and bone needles, they could sew pieces of hide together.

These garments provided warmth and protection during the cold months.

During the warm months, early people probably wore garments of woven grasses or strips of bark. These garments provided protection from the rain and sun.

Improved Fabrics

Archaeologists cannot tell us exactly when or where better materials for clothing were first discovered. Experiments with plant fibers and sheep wool may have begun as long as 8,000 years ago. People in different parts of the world probably were finding new ways to clothe themselves at about the same time. Their materials and methods varied with the climate.

People who kept flocks of sheep and goats found out how to use wool. At first, they probably dressed themselves in sheepskins. Later, they found that they could cut tufts of wool from sheep and form the wool into strands. When people learned how to make simple looms, they could weave the strands of wool into cloth. Then they could sew the cloth with needle and thread.

The Egyptians began weaving linen cloth more than 4,000 years ago. Archaeologists have found pieces of the material in old tombs. It is finer, softer linen than is made today.

The people of India were probably the earliest to discover the usefulness of cotton. After experimenting with it, they learned how to spin cotton thread and to weave cotton cloth. As time went on, they learned to make fine cotton cloth and dye it beautiful colors.

The Chinese were the first people to produce silk. From the cocoons of a certain kind of caterpillar, they unwound the long, delicate strands. Then they twisted many of the strands together to make strong thread. From that thread, they wove the soft, shiny cloth that we know as silk.

Shelter

Early people sought protection from storms. They wanted shade on hot days and warmth in cold weather. They looked for places to make their homes where dangerous animals could not attack them. Shelters of various kinds provided protection and comfort. Caves in mountains and hillsides were probably the first shelters. Later, people found ways to use the materials in their environment to build shelters. They developed tools to help them build.

The First Builders

The first shelters that many early people made for themselves may have been caves dug with sharp stones in the side of a hill. In warmer lands, early people may have built huts from tree branches and thatched them with leaves or grass. People used the materials they could find around them to provide shelter.

Mud proved to be one of the most useful materials. People found that they could build a hut with mud walls or that they could plaster the sides of a grass hut with mud or clay. Mud or clay could be used to hold stones together in a wall. It could also be shaped and dried in the form of bricks.

Shelters of Many Kinds

Throughout history, people have built many different kinds of shelters. They have used a variety of materials. The kinds of shelters people built depended upon the climate in which they lived. The building materials they could find and use also affected the kinds of shelters people built.

People also considered the dangers they faced from animals and enemies when they built shelters. Some of the early people of Switzerland built their homes over the waters of lakes. To do this, they drove poles through the water deep into the mud below. Then they piled heaps of rocks in between the poles. On top of the poles and rocks they built wooden platforms to support houses made of twigs, mud, and grass. They used boats to go ashore.

In Ireland, stone was plentiful, so many Irish people built stone houses. If the builder could not find enough stones of the right size, the house might be made of sod. Sod is grass-covered earth. Builders cut chunks of sod and piled them up for walls, leaving openings for doors and windows. They covered the house with a roof of straw tied down with ropes of twisted grass.

The Cheyenne and other American Indians who roamed the Great Plains hunting buffalo made skin-covered tents called tepees. They chose this kind of dwelling because they were nomads who moved from place to place. Nomads need shelters that are easy to carry. The Indians covered the frames of their tepees with buffalo skins because buffalo were plentiful on the western plains.

Early Indians built cliff dwellings in what is now the southwestern United States. These are at Mesa Verde, Colorado.

Indians called Cliff Dwellers in what is now the southwestern United States built dwellings in cliffside caves. These cliff dwellings were built in stories, one above the other. These Indians built their homes high in the cliffs where they could see approaching enemies. They reached their homes by using ropes and ladders. These homes were more permanent than tepees.

Living in Groups

Securing food, clothing, and shelter took most of early people's time. People also had to protect themselves from foes and wild animals. They had to deal with an environment that was sometimes harsh. Early people discovered the advantages of living and working together in groups. People found that life was better when they had companionship. They also felt safer when they were with other people.

People began to work together, and in small ways they began to control their environment. Different groups developed different cultures, or ways of doing things. The way a group of people lives, thinks, and acts makes up its culture.

Greater changes came when people began to grow crops and domesticate animals. An increase in the food supply made it possible for people to live in larger groups. As people began to settle in villages, many *social* (sō′shəl) changes were introduced. *Social* means "having to do with human beings living together in groups."

Villages

As people began to farm, they began to live in small communities, or villages. A group of people who form a community and have common interests and culture is called a *society* (sə sī′ə tē).

In early agricultural societies, there was a supply of food. People no longer had to live as nomads. Where food was plentiful, the population increased. With more people to work, fields could be expanded and flocks increased.

As the population increased, the number of villages also increased. Early villages may have had 300 to 400 people. Not everyone was needed to raise food. People began to work at special tasks.

As people discovered their special abilities, a new system of working began to develop. It is called division of labor. Each family no longer tried to raise its own food and at the same time do all its weaving, building, and toolmaking. Division of labor meant that people could spend most of their time performing the tasks they did best.

Some people made pottery or worked at weaving. Other people made tools and weapons. Herders might have traded wool for finished cloth from the weaver. Farmers might have traded their grain for tools from the toolmakers. Extra food, tools, and cloth might have been traded with people from other villages. Division of labor meant that the *economic* (ek′ə nom′ik) system became more complex. *Economic* means "having to do with the production and use of goods and services."

Law and Government

As communities became larger, rules were needed to protect people's property and lives. Rules were also needed to regulate the buying and selling of land and goods. In complex societies, such rules are called laws.

In early times, groups of people chose leaders, or chiefs. They were often chosen for their bravery or their wisdom. Their duties included making decisions about hunting and planning for protection. The leaders also judged people who went against group customs.

In time, it was found that special people were needed to see that laws were obeyed. Laws became part of an orderly plan under which people could live in communities. The name for such a system of laws is government.

Establishment of a government required people to cooperate. They had to be willing to live under the laws of their community. People also found it desirable to join together in other enterprises. They found that by working together, they could improve their communities.

Early people had a simple form of government that was managed by their chiefs. When people began to settle in villages, new *political* (pə lit′ i kəl) systems arose. *Political* means "having to do with government." As villages grew, the need for laws grew. More officials were needed to carry out the laws.

Do You Know?

1. What four grains are used as basic foods all over the world?
2. Who were the first people to make silk?
3. Why were tepees suitable dwellings for the Plains Indians?
4. What were two advantages of living in groups?

Before You Go On

Using New Words

archaeologist   social
domesticate   society
artifact   economic
cultivate   political

Number a paper from 1 through 8. After each number write the word or term that matches the definition.

1. Having to do with human beings living together in groups
2. To improve the growth of plants by labor and care
3. To tame and keep animals for human use
4. A group of people who form a community and have common interests and culture
5. Having to do with government
6. Anything made or changed by humans
7. Having to do with the production and use of goods and services
8. A scientist who studies ancient ruins and examines artifacts

Finding the Facts

1. Name three examples of artifacts.
2. How were domesticated animals useful to early people?
3. What did early farmers grow in the areas near the Mediterranean Sea?
4. How did early people keep, or preserve, meat and fish?
5. How did early people prepare hides for clothing?
6. What tool did early people use to weave cloth?
7. What is division of labor? When did it become possible?
8. What are rules in complex societies called?
9. What were some of the main duties of early leaders?
10. What is the name for a system of laws?

2
Early Civilizations

Since people first lived on the earth, they have brought about many changes. The changes were small and slow at first. Later, they came about more rapidly. Two of the most important changes were the domestication of animals and the development of agriculture. These changes enabled people to live in larger groups and specialize in their work. The growth of villages brought about many social, economic, and political changes. These changes in turn led to civilization.

Culture and Civilization

The way of life of a people is called its culture. Culture includes a people's skills, languages, customs, and technology. Cultures can be either simple or complex. The societies that have simple cultures are called simple societies. Societies that have complex cultures are called complex societies. Complex societies are also called civilizations.

Simple Societies

Simple societies have no cities, only villages and small communities. The people may be herders or farmers.

Simple societies have languages but no systems of writing. Stories and legends are passed down orally. In this way, traditions are preserved for many centuries.

The social systems of simple societies are organized so that there are only a few leaders.

There may be a political leader, a religious leader, and a military leader. There is a unity among the people that is seen in its customs.

The economic system of simple societies is based on herding and farming. Trade is by barter, or exchange of goods and services.

Civilization

The most important part of a complex society, or civilization, is its cities. The word *civilization* comes from a Latin word meaning "citizen of the city." Agriculture also exists, as it does in simple societies.

Complex societies have large populations and control large areas of land. The social, political, and economic systems of a complex society are highly developed. All civilizations have systems of writing. Their written records include literature and history.

The Cradles of Civilization

The earliest civilizations developed along rivers after about 3000 B.C. The rivers are the Nile in North Africa, the Tigris (tī′gris) and Euphrates (yoo frā′ tēz) in the Middle East, and the Indus and the Huang (hwäng) in Asia. Find these rivers on the map on page 62. Because the civilizations that grew up along these rivers were the first civilizations, these river valleys are often called the cradles of civilization. The people who lived there made many important discoveries. The arts, sciences, and skills they

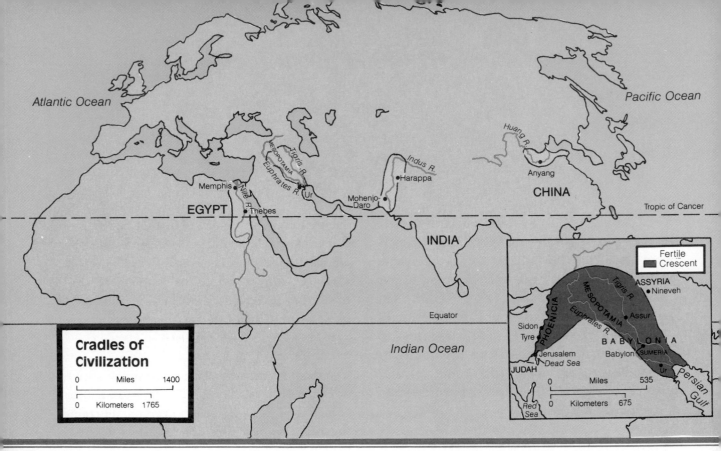

The green areas show the valleys where the earliest civilizations grew up. Why are they called Cradles of Civilization?

developed were passed down to later generations and spread throughout many parts of the world.

The rivers were important to the people who lived along them. The floods of the Nile, the Indus, the Tigris, and the Euphrates left rich alluvial deposits along the banks. Winds from central Asia deposited a great plain of fertile soil through which the Huang River flows. All the rivers provided water for irrigation. The climate of the river valleys was favorable for settlement. All four cradles of civilization lie between 20° N. and 40° N., in the subtropical or temperate zone. The mild climate, rich soil, and water available for irrigation resulted in abundant harvests. More than one crop a year could be raised in some places.

Because conditions in these lands were so favorable for agriculture, it was not necessary for everyone to work at producing food. Populations began to increase. Cities began to grow up. People in the cities worked at many different jobs. Well-organized forms of government developed. Each of the early civilizations had a system of writing that was used to communicate and to keep records.

Writing allows people to keep records of things that happen. The record of what has happened in the past is called history. History begins in the cradles of civilization.

The period before written records of events were made is called prehistoric time, or prehistory. We know about people in prehistoric times only through the study of artifacts.

The Nile Valley

Without the water of the Nile and its rich silt deposits, Egypt would have been part of the desert that surrounds it. As early as 5000 B.C., people were living along the Nile. They fished in the river, hunted along its banks, and used irrigation to farm the rich soil.

The river rose, flooded, and fell regularly. The Egyptians counted the days between the arrival of the floods and studied the stars. They determined that a year is 365 days long and divided their calendar into twelve months.

The early Egyptians developed a form of picture writing called *hieroglyphics* (hī′ər ə glif′iks). At first, pictures stood for objects. Later, the pictures came to stand for ideas and sounds. Eventually, Egyptian hieroglyphics came to be made up of 24 alphabet symbols that stood for consonant sounds.

The Egyptians used a reed plant that grew along the Nile to make a writing material. The plant is called papyrus (pə pī′rəs). The reeds were mashed into flat mats of pulp and dried. The writing material also came to be known as papyrus. Our word *paper* comes from this word. Ink was made from water and soot. Sharpened reeds served as pens.

The kingdom of Egypt was formed about 3100 B.C. It united Lower Egypt and Upper Egypt. Lower Egypt was the region of the Nile

Near the Great Pyramid at Giza stands the Great Sphinx. Except for its paws, it was built from one block of stone.

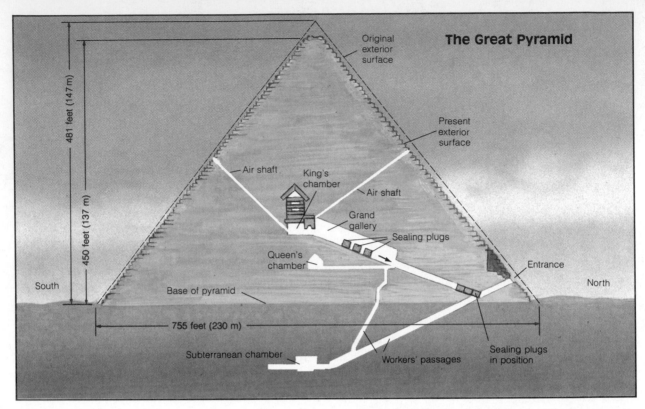

The Great Pyramid

Original exterior surface

Present exterior surface

481 feet (147 m)

450 feet (137 m)

Air shaft

King's chamber

Air shaft

Grand gallery

Sealing plugs

Queen's chamber

Entrance

South

North

Base of pyramid

755 feet (230 m)

Subterranean chamber

Workers' passages

Sealing plugs in position

This cross section shows the interior of the largest structure of ancient times. It was built about 2600 B.C.

delta. Upper Egypt was a narrow band of land on either side of the Nile south of the delta. The early kingdom of Egypt stretched nearly 700 miles (1,125 km) south of the Mediterranean Sea.

Egypt was ruled by very powerful kings. The people believed that the kings were descendants of gods. They also believed that the kings themselves were gods.

Beginning in the 1500s B.C., the Egyptians began to call their king pharaoh (fer′ō). The pharaoh was said to own all the land and people in Egypt. Actually, his power was shared with priests and nobles. The king handed down laws and punished wrongdoers. He collected taxes in goods and in labor.

Egyptian buildings included large temples and pyramids built of great blocks of stone.

During the first part of Egyptian history, more than 20 large pyramids were built. The pyramids were probably tombs for kings. Three famous pyramids were built at Giza (gē′zə), near the present-day city of Cairo (kī′rō). The largest, called the Great Pyramid, was built for a king named Cheops (kē′ops).

The Egyptians had a system of counting by tens. They measured distances by using long ropes with equally spaced knots. They surveyed the land to fix boundaries that were washed away each year when the Nile flooded.

During the final period of its early history, Egypt expanded to include the eastern end of the Mediterranean and lands far to the south along the Nile. By 1100 B.C., however, Egypt had begun to grow weak. Outsiders invaded the country and ruled it.

Mesopotamia and the Fertile Crescent

A curved, or crescent-shaped, belt of land stretches northwest from the head of the Persian Gulf, turns west to the Mediterranean, and continues south toward the Red Sea. See the map on page 62. This belt is called the Fertile Crescent. The Tigris and Euphrates rivers flow through a broad valley in the eastern part of the region. This area became known as Mesopotamia (mes'ə pə tā'mē ə). In ancient Greek, *Mesopotamia* means "between the rivers."

In Mesopotamia, as in Egypt, flooding was necessary to irrigate the fields. The Tigris and Euphrates, however, were not predictable rivers like the Nile. Flooding depended on the amount of snow in the mountains to the north. It was also affected by landslides along upper tributaries. The rivers might overflow without warning or change course unexpectedly. About 4000 B.C., the delta plain of Mesopotamia was swept by a great flood. The flood destroyed farms and villages and left a deposit of mud eight feet (2.4 m) thick.

The rich river lands were still the finest farming regions. Fish and game were abundant there. Between 4000 and 3000 B.C., people called Sumerians (sōō mer'ē əns) settled in southern Mesopotamia. They developed another of the world's earliest civilizations. From them the region took the name Sumeria.

A number of city-states grew up in Sumeria. Each had its own ruler, who was also a priest. The rulers were all-powerful, but unlike the Egyptian pharaohs, they were not considered gods.

The Sumerians developed canals for irrigation, learned to use the potter's wheel, and molded objects of gold and copper. The Sumerians also invented the arch. Our division of an hour into 60 minutes and a minute into 60 seconds is based on the Sumerian number system.

The writing developed by the Sumerians is called cuneiform (kyōō nē'ə fôrm'). Wedge-shaped marks that stood for syllables were made with sharp sticks in wet clay tablets. After the tablets were covered with writing, they were hardened by baking.

Archaeologists have found thousands of clay tablets covered with cuneiform writing. These records have helped scientists to put some of the events of Sumerian history in *chronological* (kron'ə loj'i kəl) order. Events in chronological order are arranged in the order in which they happened.

About 1750 B.C., Sumeria was conquered by a king named Hammurabi (hä'moo rä'bē). Hammurabi brought all of Mesopotamia under his rule. His capital city of Babylon (bab'ə lən) was so splendid that the entire region became known as Babylonia.

Hammurabi is remembered for his collection of laws. He ordered the laws of the kingdom examined and revised. He then had the laws carved on great stone blocks and set up in different parts of the kingdom. In this way, everyone would know what was lawful and what was not. The laws dealt with such matters as business, marriage, debts, and theft. Rights and duties, as well as punishments and penalties, were made clear.

The Sumerians invented cuneiform writing. Characters were scratched into wet clay. This tablet, found with its "envelope," concerns a court case.

About 1600 B.C., Babylonia was conquered by people called Hittites. The Hittites ruled for about 400 years. When their kingdom weakened, several small independent states grew up in the Fertile Crescent. One of these was Phoenicia (fənish'ə). The Phoenicians built two great cities at the eastern end of the Mediterranean and developed a great sea trade. The alphabet we use today came from the Phoenician alphabet.

Another important small kingdom was the kingdom of the Hebrews. The Hebrew religion, called Judaism (joō'dē iz'əm), had a belief in one god. Christianity and Islam are both based on Judaism.

By 700 B.C., another group of people, the Assyrians (əsir'ē ənz), had conquered all of Mesopotamia. Their empire also included lands to the east as well as Egypt. It was the largest empire the world had known up to that time. Many ancient writings were preserved in the library at Nineveh (nin'əvə), the capital. About 600 B.C., Nineveh was taken by the Chaldeans (kaldē'ənz) and Medes.

After the fall of Nineveh, the Chaldeans conquered all of the Fertile Crescent. Their king Nebuchadnezzar (neb'yəkəd nez'ər) rebuilt Babylon to make it a magnificent capital city. Its Hanging Gardens were one of the seven ancient wonders of the world. The gardens were planted on a building with many levels where earth had been laid. The Chaldeans were also well known for their studies in astronomy.

The Chaldean Empire began to fall apart after Nebuchadnezzar's death. It was eventually conquered by the Persians.

The Indus Valley

The site of the early civilization of the Indus Valley occupies nearly all the territory of present-day Pakistan. Civilization in this valley arose about 2500 B.C. Remains of more than 50 settlements have been found in the Indus Valley since 1870.

Little is known of the beginning of civilization in the Indus Valley. It is possible that it arose very suddenly. Most information comes from the two large cities of Harappa (hə rap' ə) and Mohenjo-Daro (mō hen'jō dä'rō).

The cities were laid out in a careful plan. Broad avenues were crisscrossed by narrower streets at right angles. The streets were paved with bricks and lined with shops and houses. Some houses were built around courtyards, and some had two stories. Brick-lined sewers ran under the streets and connected with bathrooms in the houses. Each Indus city had a fort in the center. Inside the forts were bathhouses, living quarters, and granaries.

Farming was the principal occupation in the lands surrounding the cities. Wheat, barley, melons, and dates were grown. The first cotton grown anywhere in the world was grown there. Like the early people of Egypt and Mesopotamia, the Indus Valley people had domesticated dogs, cats, and pigs.

Trade was also important. Boats traveled on the interior rivers and sailed as far as Mesopotamia. The Indus people traded with Egypt and India. Pearls, ivory, and cotton were traded for gold, copper, and gemstones. These were made into jewelry that was exchanged for more raw materials.

Many pieces of carved bone and ivory have been found near the Indus River. Archaeologists think they may have been used to make decorated furniture. Excavations have uncovered many small clay figures as well as figures of bronze and stone. Other discoveries include engraved seals. Some of the seals are covered with Indus writing, but scholars have not yet been able to translate them.

By about 1500 B.C., the Indus civilization had disappeared. Some natural disaster, such as a prolonged period of flooding, may have contributed to its decline. It is known that the Indus people were attacked by raiders from the north and west and that Harappa and Mohenjo-Daro were conquered.

The Huang Valley

As long ago as 4500 B.C., Chinese farmers were growing millet, a kind of cereal grain. By 3500 B.C., the Chinese were also raising silkworms and weaving silk cloth. People along the Chang River in southern China had learned to grow rice about 3000 B.C. The written history of China, however, does not begin until about 1500 B.C. About that time, a city called Anyang grew up north of the Huang River. The Huang River is the fourth great cradle of civilization. The civilization that developed there is the oldest continuous civilization in the world.

Anyang, like the cities of the Nile and the Fertile Crescent, was surrounded by rich farmlands. The kings controlled only a small region near that capital city. The city itself was divided into districts for different crafts. Weavers, potters, and blacksmiths had their shops in particular locations. Wheat and rice came from farms nearby.

Not much is known of the government, but warfare seems to have been constant. The kings of Anyang were buried in graves with weapons, tools, pottery, and ornaments. Offerings of flowers, fruit, vegetables, animals, and wine were made to spirits.

During this time, artists produced bronze works, especially beautiful vases. Other artists carved figures in marble, limestone, and jade. Jewelers also worked in jade, metal, and ivory.

Like the other early civilizations, the Chinese of the Huang Valley devised a system of writing. Their writing had more than 2,000 symbols. They also developed a calendar with a 30-day month.

One of the important sources of early Chinese history is the writing on pieces of animal bone. Some bones were used for keeping records. Fortunetellers also used bones for predicting the future. When 'the bones were

Bronze vessels of ancient China were often decorated with animal designs. This vessel has rams' heads for handles.

heated, they cracked. Then fortunetellers interpreted the cracks and wrote their messages on the bones.

Classical Civilizations

By about 1000 B.C., several new civilizations had begun to develop. Greece and Rome were two important civilizations that grew up around the Mediterranean. Their people were descendants of earlier settlers and invaders.

The civilizations of Greece and Rome developed independently. Through trading and wars, however, they came in touch with each other and influenced each other. Both Greece and Rome made contributions to science, education, art, literature, and government. Greece is the home of democracy. Many Greek ideas of freedom and equality were preserved by Rome. Rome developed an important legal system.

Greece and Rome are often referred to as classical civilizations. This means that they are thought of as models or ideals. The way many people live today is influenced by Greek and Roman culture.

Greece

As early as 3000 B.C., a civilization flourished on the shores and islands of the Aegean (i jē′ən) Sea. The Aegean Sea is the northeastern part of the Mediterranean Sea. For many centuries, the island of Crete was the center of Aegean civilization. Crete prospered from its overseas trade and metal industries. Then about 1400 B.C., the great palace at Knossos (nos′əs), the capital city, was destroyed by raiders. Invaders also destroyed other Aegean cities. By about 1100 B.C., the early Aegean civilization had almost disappeared.

The people we call Greeks were the descendants of the invaders and the earlier Aegeans. Slowly, the Greeks built their own civilization. By 750 B.C., the Greeks had become great manufacturers of pottery, textiles, weapons, and tools. Trade became profitable, and the population increased. The Greeks established more and more new settlements.

Greek settlements were established in valleys that were separated from one another by mountains. The isolation of these communities led to the formation of city-states. Each Greek city, together with its surrounding villages, was self-governing and independent. The Greeks had a strong sense of loyalty to their own city-state. City-states were often rivals for trade and power. Though Greece was not a

The Greeks made many contributions to *architecture*. The Parthenon, a temple overlooking Athens, was built during the Golden Age of Greece.

united nation, the Greeks thought of themselves as one people. They called themselves Hellenes (hel'ēnz), after Hellas, an area in Greece. The Greeks shared a common language, religion, and culture.

The city-state that made the greatest contribution to Greek civilization was Athens. Little of the land around Athens was *arable* (ar'ə bəl), or suitable for cultivation. To support themselves, the people of Athens turned to manufacturing and *commerce* (kom'ərs). Commerce is the buying and selling of goods or services.

Trade brought much wealth to Athens. For a long time, the wealth and power was in the hands of the aristocrats, or the nobles. After a long struggle, the people of Athens developed a new form of government. Citizens were given the right to make their own decisions and laws. Their form of government was called a democracy. The word *democracy* comes from the Greek words meaning "rule of the people." Other city-states followed the lead of Athens. By 500 B.C., there were democratic governments in most Greek city-states. Athens became the leader of the city-states.

Athens reached its greatest glory during the period from 460 to 429 B.C. This period is called the Golden Age. It is also sometimes called the Age of Pericles (per'ə klēz). Pericles ruled Athens during this time. He encouraged artists and builders to beautify the city. He also gave more rights and powers to the citizens.

Democracy in Athens was at its high point during this time. Athens had an assembly that met to discuss public matters and make laws. All citizens more than 18 years old had the right to speak and vote in the assembly. Citizens also served as jurors in court trials. Not all people were citizens, however. Women, slaves, and foreigners were not. Still, Greek democracy was a great achievement. The democratic way of life that developed in Greece became the ideal for many people.

During the Golden Age, the Greeks made outstanding contributions to the arts and sciences. Greek builders excelled in *architecture* (är'kə tek'chər), which is the art of designing and constructing buildings. One of the finest examples of Greek architecture is the Parthenon, a temple in Athens. Sculptors carved beautiful statues of bronze and marble.

Greek writers created many forms of literature, including drama and poetry. Herodotus (hə rod'ə təs) was the first Greek historian. He wrote the history of the world up to his own time. Hippocrates (hi pok'rə tēz) was a great Greek doctor. He wrote a pledge, or oath, that is still used by doctors today.

The Greek people loved beauty, truth, and individual freedom. They created a civilization so great that it will never be forgotten.

Like the Greeks, the Romans were skilled architects. The Roman Forum, with its classical buildings, was the city's *political* and *social* center.

Rome

Between 2000 and 1000 B.C., a number of tribes moved south through the Alps into the Italian Peninsula. One important group, the Latins, settled in the central part of the peninsula in the valley of the Tiber (tī′bər) River. The Latins established several villages on a hill near the Tiber. The city of Rome grew from these small villages.

About 600 B.C., the Latin tribes were conquered by the Etruscans, a group of people from the north. The Etruscans encouraged farming, manufacturing, and commerce. However, the Etruscan rulers were harsh. In 509 B.C., the Romans rebelled against the Etruscans and drove them out.

The Romans then set up a republic. A republic is a state in which the citizens elect officials to run the government. The nobles, or patricians (pə trish′ənz), were in control. The common people, or plebeians (pli bē′ənz), struggled to obtain a greater role in government. They elected their own officials, called tribunes, to protect their rights. About 450 B.C., the plebeians won the right to have laws put in writing. These laws were known as the Laws of the Twelve Tables. Roman citizens were required to know and obey these laws.

During the republic, the Roman state expanded. Rome joined with neighboring cities to form the Latin League. Rome soon controlled the central Italian Peninsula. By 270 B.C., Rome's strong, well-trained armies had conquered almost all of the Italian Peninsula. Loyal soldiers formed powerful legions, or military groups. Roman armies continued to conquer the lands surrounding Rome. By 100 B.C., Rome ruled almost all the lands around the Mediterranean.

As Rome grew, so did the differences among the Roman people. The upper classes became very wealthy. The common people remained poor. The struggle for power between the patricians and the plebeians resumed. Civil wars were fought in many parts of Rome.

By 50 B.C., a Roman general named Julius Caesar (sē′zər) had conquered lands to the north. He expanded Rome to include most of modern France and Belgium. Caesar's conquests made him popular with the Roman people. When Caesar returned home with his legions, he made himself head of the government. Later, he was elected dictator for life. During Caesar's rule, lands at the eastern end of the Mediterranean were conquered. He made plans to build new roads and temples.

His work was cut short. Julius Caesar was murdered in 44 B.C. by a group of Romans who thought he had too much power. The powerful days of the Roman Republic were over.

Before his death, Julius Caesar had made his grandnephew and adopted son, Octavian, his heir. In 27 B.C., Octavian took the name of Augustus and became the first emperor of Rome. The reign of Augustus marked the beginning of the Roman Empire.

The first two centuries of the empire were peaceful. This period, from 27 B.C. to 180 A.D., is known as the Pax Romana, or "Peace of Rome."

Rome made its greatest contributions to civilization during the Pax Romana. The most important achievement was the development of law. The Laws of the Twelve Tables written by the plebeians were expanded. Laws governing non-citizens were included. When new countries were taken into the empire, the Romans studied their laws. They adopted the best laws of the conquered countries. Roman law became the most useful and complete set of laws the world had ever known. Many modern nations have based their laws on those of ancient Rome.

The Roman language, Latin, was also a lasting gift. French, Italian, Spanish, Portuguese, and Romanian were all derived from Latin. These languages are called Romance languages. The English language has many words that come from Latin.

The Romans excelled in many areas. Fine examples of Roman architecture can still be seen today. The Romans built great roads and bridges, and magnificent temples and monuments. The Romans produced impressive works of art and literature. In government, language, and art, Roman civilization paved the way for many modern cultures.

Other Early Civilizations

Early civilizations are not limited to the places that have been mentioned here. Many other civilizations have developed and made important contributions to the world. About the time that Greece and Rome were emerging, a civilization was developing in India that still influences many ways of living. In China, as the early Huang Valley civilization ended, a new empire began to grow.

Later, important civilizations grew up in Africa, Central America, and South America. You will read about many of these later civilizations in the units that follow in this book.

Do You Know?

1. Along what rivers did the earliest civilizations develop?
2. For what purpose were the pyramids probably built?
3. Where did the Sumerians establish their civilization?
4. When did the early civilization of the Indus Valley arise?
5. What city-state was the center of classical Greece?

3

Living on the Earth

People have always had to work to obtain food, clothing, and shelter. These needs have not changed, but the ways in which they are met have changed.

As people developed tools and skills, they began to use the materials of the earth in different ways. Resources changed as people began to cultivate plants, harness the power of water and winds, and use fire.

As people began to learn how to control their environment, life became easier. People began to specialize in their work. This division of labor meant that people spent less time filling their basic needs. The materials of the earth began to be used for things that made life more comfortable.

As society became more complex, it offered people a wide choice of ways in which to make a living. Today there are many occupations from which to choose.

Technology

Technology is the way in which people use the materials of the earth. It includes tools and skills. It also includes ideas about how to make and use tools and how to use skills.

Technology is a part of culture. In early times, technology was very simple. Modern technology, in comparison, is extremely complex. Satellites, computers, lasers, robots, and radio telescopes are only a few examples of the advanced technology of today.

Early Technology

You have read about some of the technologies of early societies. Early people developed the skills required for hunting and fishing. They learned to make weapons and tools from stone. Later, when people began to farm and herd, they developed new technologies. They had tools for cultivating the soil and grinding grain. They learned to spin and weave. They also learned to make pottery.

Many other discoveries and inventions were important to the development of early societies. One of the most important was fire.

It probably took thousands of years for people to learn to use fire. Early people may have learned about fire from lightning or volcanoes. Fire was used for warmth, protection, and light. Later, fires were used to cook food, to shape metal, and to harden pottery.

One of the greatest inventions was the wheel. Before the wheel was invented, people probably dragged things from place to place on sleds. It is not known exactly how and when the wheel was invented. Many experiments were necessary. One step may have been placing logs or poles under a sled. As the sled was pulled forward, it would move more easily as the logs turned under it.

The stone tools and weapons used by early people were easily chipped or broken. People began to learn to use metals for tools and weapons. Metal lasted longer and could be shaped more easily. At first, copper was used.

Changes in technology do not occur everywhere at the same time. In some regions today, people plow with tractors. In other places, oxen are used.

Later, copper and tin were melted together to make a metal called bronze. Bronze was harder than copper. It could also be shaped easily and gave a sharper cutting edge. Iron came into widespread use much later.

Other important inventions included the sailboat, the potter's wheel, and the plow. With sailboats, sailors could take advantage of prevailing winds. The potter's wheel made it possible to produce a greater number of pots in a shorter time than before. The pots could also be more uniform in size and shape.

The plow was developed from an earlier invention, the hoe. Larger fields could be farmed with plows and oxen than by people using hoes. Another important development in farming was the use of irrigation. Ditches and canals were dug to bring water from lakes and rivers to the fields where crops were growing.

In early civilizations, most of the energy to do work came from people or animals. Heat from burning wood was another source of energy. Later, people learned to use the energy of falling water to drive waterwheels. Waterwheels were used to grind grain or raise water for irrigation. Windmills used wind power to raise water. Wind also powered sailboats.

Later Technology

Changes in technology came about very slowly. For centuries, the exchange of ideas and goods was a difficult and long process. Trade and communication were slow and expensive. Developments came about first where there were good water routes.

By 1600, improvements in transportation had helped speed up the transfer of technology among different parts of the world. Better ships had been designed and built. Such inventions as the astrolabe (as′trə lab′) and compass made long voyages possible. The astrolabe was an instrument for measuring the positions of the stars and planets. By using the astrolabe and the compass, sailors could determine the position of their ships. As the technology of transportation grew, so did trade.

Another important development was in the field of science. Between 1500 and 1700, scientists described many of the laws that govern the universe. Technology was able to apply the discoveries of science to daily life.

The interaction of science, technology, and trade brought about an important change in the way of living shortly after 1750. That change is called the Industrial Revolution. One of the important results of the Industrial Revolution was the shift of workers from agriculture to manufacturing. The Industrial Revolution came about when machines began to do the work that only people and animals had done before. The energy supplied by human and animal muscle was replaced first by the steam engine. Later, oil, gas, and electricity were used to power machines. You will read more about the Industrial Revolution and developments in technology since the Industrial Revolution in the units that follow.

Occupations

In early times, people did most things for themselves. They farmed or hunted for food. They made their own clothes and built their own homes. Advances in technology made it easier for people to meet their basic needs. Farmers could grow enough food to feed many families. Food surpluses allowed people to work at jobs other than farming. People began to specialize by doing certain kinds of work. They started to depend on other members of the community for goods and services.

In a complex society, people have many occupations, or ways of making a living. Some types of work are directly related to natural resources. Other occupations are related to natural resources in only an indirect way.

Using Natural Resources Directly
Some jobs make direct use of natural resources. Examples are jobs in farming, mining, lumbering, and fishing.

People who work in mines have jobs related to direct use of natural resources. Minerals such as sulfur are dug from the earth. What are some other jobs directly related to resources?

Farmers make up the largest group of workers who use natural resources directly. About one-half of the world's people today live on farms and raise crops. Farmers in Europe, Canada, and the United States produce about 44 percent of the world's crops. Yet only about 8 percent of the workers in these lands are farmers. Modern technology has allowed these farmers to increase their production.

Growing and harvesting crops are basic farming activities. Some farmers specialize by growing just one crop. They cultivate large fields of wheat, corn, cotton, or other crops. Other farmers tend orchards of fruit or nut trees.

Raising livestock is also part of farming, or agriculture. Cattle on dairy farms provide milk and cheese products. Sheep and cattle ranches produce meat products. Goats and hogs are other kinds of livestock. Geese, turkeys, chickens, and ducks are raised on poultry farms.

People who work in mines and quarries also use natural resources in a direct way. Quarry workers cut huge blocks of stone from the earth. Marble, granite, limestone, and other kinds of rock are taken from quarries. Miners dig copper, iron, and other ores or precious materials, such as gold or diamonds, from the earth. Many workers are involved in mining coal and drilling for oil.

Lumbering is another occupation that makes direct use of natural resources. Some people cut down trees. Others saw the logs into boards. The gum and sap of certain trees are collected to make turpentine and many other products.

Many people earn a living by catching and selling fish. Some fishers collect sponges. Others dredge for clams and mussels. Fishers set traps for lobsters and other shellfish. Large fish, such as tuna, are caught in huge nets. Some fishers freeze their catch on board their boats. Smoking and drying are other ways fishers preserve their catch.

Using Natural Resources Indirectly

People who earn their living by indirect use of natural resources work in many jobs. Occupations in manufacturing, commerce, transportation, government, and services are not directly related to the use of natural resources.

Workers in scientific laboratories use raw materials to develop products such as fertilizers, medicines, and paint.

People who earn their living by manufacturing work in factories. In factories, raw materials are made into finished goods or products. The raw material may be a bale of cotton. The finished product will be cloth. The cloth may be shipped to another factory where it again becomes a raw material. Here it is manufactured into shirts or dresses. Other examples of raw materials and finished products are wheat and flour, flour and bread, iron ore and steel, steel and machines. The finished products of one factory often become the raw materials of another factory.

Many of the raw materials are natural resources or come from natural resources. Cotton and wheat are farm products that are turned into cloth, bread, and cereals. Iron ore

Political Map of the World

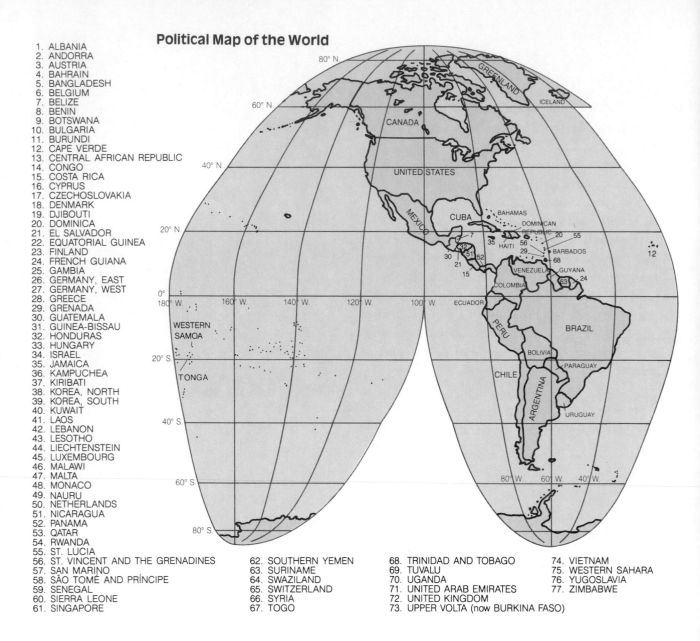

1. ALBANIA
2. ANDORRA
3. AUSTRIA
4. BAHRAIN
5. BANGLADESH
6. BELGIUM
7. BELIZE
8. BENIN
9. BOTSWANA
10. BULGARIA
11. BURUNDI
12. CAPE VERDE
13. CENTRAL AFRICAN REPUBLIC
14. CONGO
15. COSTA RICA
16. CYPRUS
17. CZECHOSLOVAKIA
18. DENMARK
19. DJIBOUTI
20. DOMINICA
21. EL SALVADOR
22. EQUATORIAL GUINEA
23. FINLAND
24. FRENCH GUIANA
25. GAMBIA
26. GERMANY, EAST
27. GERMANY, WEST
28. GREECE
29. GRENADA
30. GUATEMALA
31. GUINEA-BISSAU
32. HONDURAS
33. HUNGARY
34. ISRAEL
35. JAMAICA
36. KAMPUCHEA
37. KIRIBATI
38. KOREA, NORTH
39. KOREA, SOUTH
40. KUWAIT
41. LAOS
42. LEBANON
43. LESOTHO
44. LIECHTENSTEIN
45. LUXEMBOURG
46. MALAWI
47. MALTA
48. MONACO
49. NAURU
50. NETHERLANDS
51. NICARAGUA
52. PANAMA
53. QATAR
54. RWANDA
55. ST. LUCIA
56. ST. VINCENT AND THE GRENADINES
57. SAN MARINO
58. SÃO TOMÉ AND PRÍNCIPE
59. SENEGAL
60. SIERRA LEONE
61. SINGAPORE
62. SOUTHERN YEMEN
63. SURINAME
64. SWAZILAND
65. SWITZERLAND
66. SYRIA
67. TOGO
68. TRINIDAD AND TOBAGO
69. TUVALU
70. UGANDA
71. UNITED ARAB EMIRATES
72. UNITED KINGDOM
73. UPPER VOLTA (now BURKINA FASO)
74. VIETNAM
75. WESTERN SAHARA
76. YUGOSLAVIA
77. ZIMBABWE

is a natural resource from which iron and steel are made.

In addition to raw materials, factories depend on a number of other things. Some of these are money, machines, power, labor, and transportation.

Workers in commerce, or trade, are people who distribute and sell the goods made in factories. People who work in supermarkets and other stores sell products from factories. Other people in commerce have jobs in warehouses, where they unload and distribute goods.

Some people who work in commerce do not buy and sell goods. People who work in banks are a part of commerce, too.

76

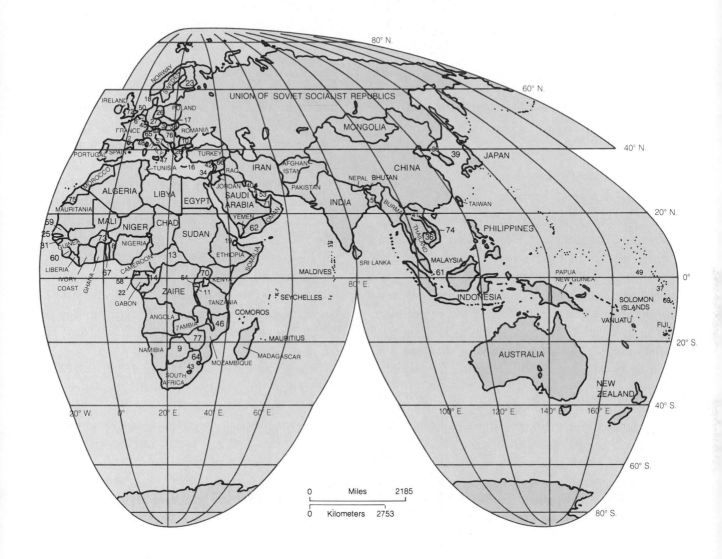

Transportation is an important part of manufacturing and commerce. Many people are involved in activities related to transportation. Some work on ships, barges, railroads, trucks, planes, and cars.

Millions of people all over the world make their living in government work. They work for countries, states, towns, and cities. Police officers, fire fighters, and letter carriers are all government workers. People in the armed services also work for the government. Many jobs in government involve keeping records, issuing licenses, and collecting taxes.

People in service occupations include doctors, lawyers, teachers, and architects. Restaurant workers, barbers, and flight attendants are also service workers. Service workers do not sell products. Instead, they sell services.

Standard of Living and Gross National Product

The changes that led from simple societies to complex societies did not happen at the same time in all parts of the world. Today, there are both simple and complex societies in the world. In countries with simple societies, many people spend much of their time in activities directly related to basic needs. In countries with complex societies, people spend less time filling basic needs. The division of labor in complex societies has led to the production of goods that are desirable but not strictly necessary for people to exist. The materials of the earth are used not only for necessities but also for things that make life more comfortable. The way in which people use their resources to provide for necessities and comforts can be expressed as the *standard* (stan'dərd) *of living*. The standard of living is the general level of goods and services available to a group or a country.

Standards of living vary from country to country. In countries with a high standard of living, people have comfortable places to live, enough to eat, and good medical care. They also are able to have a good education. Leisure time and nonessentials are usually part of life in countries with a high standard of living. In countries with a low standard of living, people generally do not have all of these things. Goods and services are limited.

Closely related to standard of living is *gross* (grōs) *national product*. Gross national product is often shortened to GNP. Gross national product is the total value of a country's goods and services produced in one year. To arrive at this figure, the value of all the goods produced in a country in one year is determined. The value of all the services performed is added to the value of the goods. The total is called the gross national product. Sometimes a country's GNP is divided by the country's population. The figure arrived at in this way is called the per capita (pər kap'ə tə), or per person, GNP.

In the units that follow, the GNP for each country studied will be given in the Regional Data Chart. You can use the figures to compare different countries. In general, countries with a high per capita GNP are countries with complex societies. Many of the people in countries with high per capita GNPs earn their living by using natural resources indirectly. In countries with low per capita GNPs, most people earn their living by using natural resources directly. They have simpler societies in which most of the land is used in traditional ways.

Do You Know?

1. What was the astrolabe? How was it useful?
2. What jobs involve direct use of natural resources?
3. Name three kinds of workers involved in service occupations.

To Help You Learn

Using New Words

hieroglyphics   chronological

standard of living   commerce

architecture   gross national

cultivate   product

arable   artifact

Number a paper from 1 through 9. After each number write the word or term that matches the definition.

1. Anything made or changed by humans
2. Arranged according to the order in which events happened
3. The buying and selling of goods and services
4. The total value of a country's goods and services produced in one year
5. To improve the growth of plants by labor and care
6. The art of designing and constructing buildings
7. Suitable for cultivation
8. A form of picture writing used by the early Egyptians
9. The general level of goods and services available to a group or a country

Finding the Facts

1. What are people's basic physical needs?
2. What tools did early people use to catch fish?

3. Who were probably the first people to use cotton cloth?
4. What does culture include?
5. What is prehistory?
6. How did the early Egyptians make paper?
7. What does the word *Mesopotamia* mean?
8. What is cuneiform writing?
9. How did Hammurabi make sure that the people of Babylonia knew the laws of the kingdom?
10. What was in the center of each early Indus city?
11. What is an important source for learning about early Chinese history?
12. What was the Golden Age, or the Age of Pericles?
13. What were the nobles of ancient Rome called? What were the common people called?
14. What is technology?
15. Why is metal a better material than stone for tools?
16. What sources of energy were used before the Industrial Revolution?

Learning from Maps

1. Look at the map on page 62. What do the color areas show? In what hemisphere are all of these areas? Compare this map with the maps on pages 289 and 381. In what

modern countries are the four Cradles of Civilization? What present-day city is near the site of Memphis?

2. Look at the map and inset map on page 62. Which distance is greater, Memphis to Ur or Ur to Nineveh? About how far is it from Ur to Nineveh? What two cities are shown on the eastern coast of the Mediterranean? In what ancient kingdom were they?

Using Study Skills

1. **Library Resources:** *The Readers' Guide to Periodical Literature* is an index of periodical, or magazine, articles listed by subject and author.

   Look at the sample entry from the *Readers' Guide* below.

SCULPTURE, Greek
   Heroic bronzes of fifth century B.C.
   regain old splendor. A. Pearce. il
   Smithsonian 12:124–31 N '81

The subject heading for this entry is Greek Sculpture. The name of the article is listed first. The author is listed next. The letters *il* indicate that the article is illustrated. *Smithsonian* is the magazine in which the article appears. The first number always stands for the volume of the magazine. The next two numbers are the numbers of the pages on which the article appears. *N '81* is an abbreviation for November, 1981.

Use the sample below to answer the questions that follow.

ART, Roman
   Image of Augustus. M. Henig il
   Hist Today 31:61 S '81

What is the name of the article? Who wrote it? Is it illustrated? On what page does it appear? What magazine does it appear in? When was it published? What is the general subject area of the article?

2. **Time Line:** Making a time line is one way to arrange events in chronological order, or the order in which they happened. Often a time line deals with a specific country, area, period, or subject.

   Look at the time line of ancient Rome below. Some of the dates and events are missing. Fill them in by looking back at the section about Rome in this unit. Then answer the following questions: How long did the Etruscans rule the Romans? How many years after Julius Caesar's death did Augustus begin his rule of the Roman Empire?

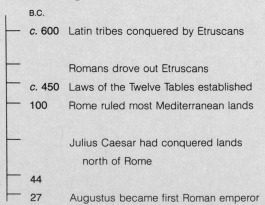

B.C.

c. 600   Latin tribes conquered by Etruscans

           Romans drove out Etruscans

c. 450   Laws of the Twelve Tables established

100   Rome ruled most Mediterranean lands

           Julius Caesar had conquered lands
             north of Rome

44

27   Augustus became first Roman emperor

3. **Diagram:** Look at the diagram on page 64. This diagram is a cross section. It is based on an imaginary cut through the Great Pyramid to show the interior and underground construction. How many chambers are shown inside the pyramid? What chamber is below ground level? What was the original height of the pyramid? On which side of the pyramid is the entrance? To which chamber do the air passages lead? After the workers released the sealing blocks, how did they get out of the pyramid?

Thinking It Through

1. How do complex societies differ from simple societies? Describe the kinds of social, political, and economic systems each kind of society has.
2. Name two examples of recent developments in technology and describe the effects of each.
3. How is the per capita GNP calculated? Use the information on the Regional Data Chart on page 126 to calculate the per capita GNP for the United States and Canada. Because the GNP is given in millions of dollars, it will be necessary to round off the population figures to the nearest million before you divide. What is the per capita GNP for the United States? For Canada?

4. Compare the lower courses of the Tigris and Euphrates rivers on the inset map on page 62 with the lower courses of these rivers on the map on page 289. What difference do you notice? What might account for the difference?

Projects

1. The Biography Committee might like to prepare reports on archaeologists Howard Carter, who discovered King Tutankhamen's tomb in Egypt, and Sir Arthur Evans, who excavated the ancient palace at Knossos in Crete.
2. The Arts and Sciences Committee might like to find out more about Egyptian, Greek, and Roman architecture. Committee members could prepare models of temples or other buildings and explain their architectural features.
3. The Current Events Committee might like to explore the occupations most in demand today. Committee members might consult the *Readers' Guide to Periodical Literature* and the weekly employment section in the classified ads of the local newspaper. They could make a display of job openings and photos of workers grouped in categories such as agriculture, fishing, mining, commerce, manufacturing, government, transportation, and service occupations.

3 The United States and Canada

Unit Preview

The neighboring countries of the United States and Canada occupy most of the continent of North America. These two nations share boundaries that stretch from the Atlantic to the Pacific, and from the Pacific to the Arctic. They also share landforms, such as the Great Plains and the Rocky Mountains, and water features, such as the Great Lakes.

Parts of both the United States and Canada were once English colonies. Early ties with Great Britain are reflected in the democratic governments and in the English language, which is spoken in most places. Other European cultures, especially the French in Canada and the Spanish in the United States, have also had strong influences. Today the population of the United States and Canada is a rich mixture of many backgrounds, including the Indians and Eskimos of North America.

Climates ranging from subtropical to polar are found in the parts of North America occupied by the United States and Canada. Here also are found rich farmlands, high mountains, great forests, many lakes and rivers, and rich deposits of minerals. The great variety and abundance of minerals and other natural resources have helped make Canada and the United States two of the most prosperous nations in the world.

Neighboring Canada to the northeast in the North Atlantic are the sparsely populated arctic islands of Greenland and Iceland.

Greenland, most of which is covered by a permanent icecap, is part of Denmark. Iceland is an independent country.

Things to Discover

If you look carefully at the picture, map, and time line, you can answer these questions.

1. The photograph shows Niagara Falls on the Niagara River. This river forms part of the boundary between the United States and Canada, the region highlighted in North America. What oceans border this region?
2. From what country did the United States buy the Louisiana Territory? When?
3. When did Canada become independent?

Words to Learn

You will meet these words and terms in this unit. As you read, you will learn what they mean and how to pronounce them. The Word List will help you.

agribusiness	foothills
bayou	Gulf Stream
bilingual	industrial crop
butte	maritime
cobalt	mesa
conterminous	negotiations
cryolite	ratification
ferroalloy	urbanization
fishing banks	

82

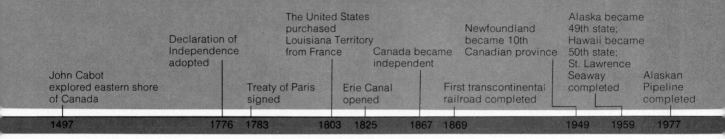

John Cabot
explored eastern shore
of Canada

Declaration of
Independence
adopted

Treaty of Paris
signed

The United States
purchased
Louisiana Territory
from France

Erie Canal
opened

Canada became
independent

First transcontinental
railroad completed

Newfoundland
became 10th
Canadian province

Alaska became
49th state;
Hawaii became
50th state;
St. Lawrence
Seaway
completed

Alaskan
Pipeline
completed

| 1497 | 1776 | 1783 | 1803 | 1825 | 1867 | 1869 | 1949 | 1959 | 1977 |

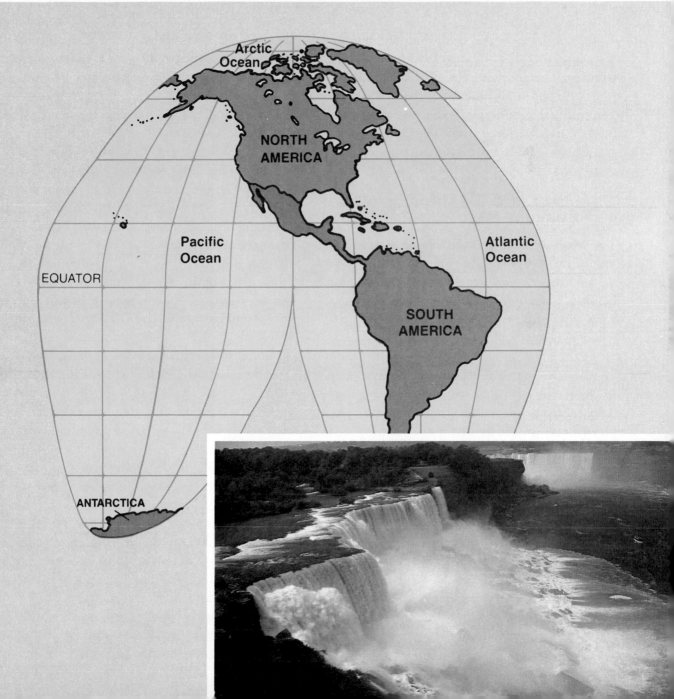

Arctic
Ocean

NORTH
AMERICA

Pacific
Ocean

Atlantic
Ocean

EQUATOR

SOUTH
AMERICA

ANTARCTICA

1

The Land and the People of the United States and Canada

Canada is the world's second-largest country. The United States is the world's fourth-largest country. Together the United States and Canada cover about 13 percent of the world's land. Yet neither country is densely populated. Fewer than 6 percent of the people in the world live in these two countries.

The Land of the United States and Canada

The United States and Canada are countries of great diversity. Lying between the frozen Arctic and the tropics are high mountains, wide beaches, vast plains and plateaus, barren deserts, and great river systems.

Landforms

The United States and Canada occupy the part of North America north of the Rio Grande. This area is bordered to the west by the Pacific Ocean and to the east by the Atlantic Ocean. The Arctic Ocean lies to the north of the continent. To the south, the United States is bordered by Mexico and the Gulf of Mexico. Great chains of mountains extend north and south in the western and eastern parts of the two countries. Lying between these mountain chains is a broad interior plain.

The continental United States and Canada can be divided into seven landform regions. These seven regions are the Pacific coast region, the intermountain region, the Rocky Mountains, the interior plains, the Canadian Shield, the Appalachian Mountains, and the coastal lowlands. Find these regions on the map on page 86.

Two parallel mountain chains stretch from Alaska into Mexico along the Pacific coast. The outer, or western, chain rises steeply from the Pacific. It includes the Coast Ranges of California and Oregon and the Olympic Mountains of Washington. The islands of the British Columbia and Alaska coast are partly submerged mountains belonging to this western chain. The higher inner chain of mountains lying to the east includes the Sierra Nevada, the Cascades, the Coast Mountains of British Columbia and Alaska, and the Alaska Range. Mount McKinley, the highest mountain in North America, is in the Alaska Range. It has an elevation of 20,320 feet (6,194 m) above sea level.

The two Pacific mountain chains are separated by a series of valleys and depressions. Among them are the Central Valley of California, the Willamette Valley of Oregon, the Puget (pyoo'jit) Sound lowland, and Cook Inlet in Alaska.

The intermountain region lies between the Pacific coast region to the west and the Rocky Mountains to the east. It is an area of high plateaus and basins. The Colorado Plateau and the Great Basin are in the southern part of this region. Death Valley, the lowest point in North America, is in the Great Basin. It lies

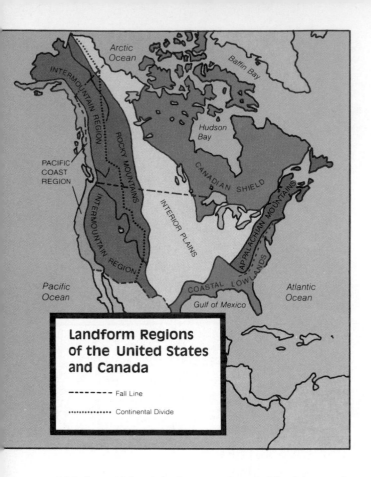

Landform Regions of the United States and Canada

- - - - - - - Fall Line

················ Continental Divide

North and east of the interior plains in Canada is the Canadian Shield. The Canadian Shield is also called the Laurentian (lô ren′shən) upland. It curves in the interior plains in a broad U-shaped outline around Hudson Bay. The Canadian Shield is an ancient landmass of very hard rock. It is an area of low relief, that is, there is little variation in the height of the land surface. There are, however, a few low mountain ranges, such as the Laurentian Mountains in southern Quebec.

South of the Canadian Shield, the Appalachian Mountains extend from Labrador into Alabama along the Atlantic coast. They lie parallel to the coastline and are separated from it by the Atlantic Coastal Plain. The Appalachians are lower and generally more rounded than the western mountains.

Coastal lowlands lie along the Atlantic Ocean and the Gulf of Mexico. They are made up of the Piedmont, the Atlantic Coastal Plain, and the Gulf Coastal Plain.

The Piedmont is a rolling plain that extends eastward from the Appalachians. Its eastern boundary is the fall line. The fall line marks the place where rivers drop to the lower plains in a series of falls and rapids.

The Atlantic Coastal Plain lies between the Piedmont and the Atlantic Ocean. It stretches from New England to Florida. In the north it is very narrow, but it broadens widely to the south. In Florida, the Atlantic Coastal Plain merges with the Gulf Coastal Plain. The Gulf Coastal Plain borders the Gulf of Mexico into southern Texas. Both coastal plains are areas of low elevation and low relief.

282 feet (86 m) below sea level. To the north of the Great Basin are the Columbia Plateau, the Interior Plateau of British Columbia, and the Yukon River Basin and Yukon Plateau in northwest Canada and Alaska.

The Rocky Mountains form the high backbone of North America. The different ranges stretch from the Sangre de Cristo Mountains in New Mexico to the Brooks Range of Alaska.

The interior plains extend eastward from the Rocky Mountains to the Appalachians. They form the large central lowland of the United States and Canada. The high plains in the western part of this region are called the Great Plains. An isolated mountain area, the Black Hills, rises in the central part of the Great Plains. The Ozark Plateau and the Ouachita (wäsh′i tô′) Mountains form another highland area in the southern part of the interior plains.

Water Features

The United States and Canada have irregular coastlines. Several large gulfs and bays indent the land. The largest of these are the Gulf of Mexico south of the United States and Hudson Bay in northern Canada. The continent is also cut into by the Gulf of Alaska, the Beaufort (bō'fərt) Sea, and the Gulf of St. Lawrence. Many irregularities in the coastline provide an abundance of good harbors, except along some parts of the Pacific coast.

The United States and Canada have a well-developed system of interior waterways. The crest of the Rocky Mountains forms the Continental Divide. The Continental Divide is sometimes called the Great Divide. It separates the waters that flow toward the Pacific Ocean from those that flow toward the Arctic Ocean, the Atlantic Ocean, and the Gulf of Mexico. The western drainage area is smaller and more rugged than the eastern drainage area. From north to south, the major westward draining river systems are the Yukon, Fraser, Columbia-Snake, Sacramento-San Joaquin, and Colorado.

The drainage system east of the Rockies is a broad area that is mostly plains. In the north, the main river systems are the MacKenzie and the Saskatchewan-Nelson. The St. Lawrence drains eastern Canada. The system formed by the Mississippi and Missouri rivers is the longest in North America. It drains the great interior plains of the United States. The Rio Grande flows south out of the Rockies to its mouth in the Gulf of Mexico. In Spanish, the word *río* means "river."

Most of the northern part of North America was covered by glaciers during the Ice Age. At the end of the Ice Age, the glaciers began to melt. The courses of many of the continent's rivers were set by water running from melting glaciers. Many lakes, including the Great Lakes, were also formed by glaciers.

The Great Lakes, in the central part of North America, are an important part of a great inland waterway system—the St. Lawrence Seaway. The boundary between the United States and Canada passes through the center of four of the lakes—Ontario, Erie, Huron, and Superior. The fifth lake, Lake Michigan, lies entirely within the United States. Lake Superior has the largest surface area of any freshwater lake in the world.

Scattered in a great arc across Canada to the northwest of the Great Lakes is a series of several other large glacial lakes. The three largest are Lake Winnipeg, Great Bear Lake, and Great Slave Lake.

A large lake not formed by glaciers is Great Salt Lake, a large, shallow body of salty water in Utah. Its waters are several times saltier than the ocean. It is the largest lake west of the Mississippi River and the largest lake of its kind in the Western Hemisphere.

Climate and Vegetation

Most of the United States and Canada lies in the middle latitudes, or temperate region. Within this region there is a great variety of climates and vegetation. Two important factors determining climate and vegetation are temperature and rainfall. The temperature regions of North America vary from north to south. The rainfall regions vary from east to west. Compare the maps showing rainfall, climate, and vegetation on pages 24, 31, and 34.

Southern Canada and the eastern part of the United States have long, warm summers with plenty of rain. The winters are cool or cold. Forests once covered this region but most of the land was cleared long ago for farms. In the southeast, Florida and parts of the Gulf Coast have a humid subtropical climate with very mild winters.

Much of the western part of the United States has a dry climate. The interior plain is prairie in the east and steppe in the west. Tall grasses grow in the areas of greater rainfall. Where rainfall is less, the short grasses take over. Deserts exist where the rainfall is less than ten inches (25 cm) a year. A large part of the intermountain region is desert.

North of Los Angeles, the Pacific coast has a Mediterranean climate. The summers are hot and dry, and the winters are mild and rainy. Farther north along the coast is a very rainy region with dense evergreen forests. It is sometimes referred to as a temperate rain forest.

Evergreen forests also cover much of the land in northern Canada and Alaska. The climate is cold and the growing season is short. To the north, the forest gives way to the tundra with its Arctic climate. Most of Greenland is covered by an ice cap.

The Hawaiian Islands have a tropical climate and a high annual rainfall. Because of the climate, more than one crop can be planted and harvested in one year.

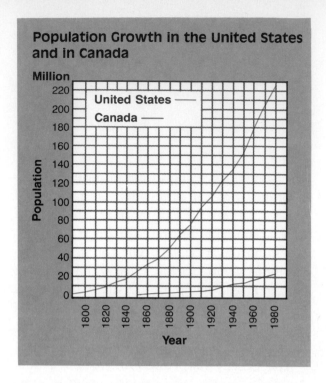

The People of the United States and Canada

When Europeans came to North America in the late 1400s, the only inhabitants were Indians and Eskimos. Hawaiians inhabited the Hawaiian Islands. Estimates are that fewer than one million people lived in the area that is now the continental United States and Canada. Today the combined population of the two countries is about 250 million.

The early settlement of North America north of the Rio Grande was made mainly by people from northern and western Europe. In the southern part of the United States, there was a strong Spanish influence. Africans, too, were among the first immigrants in several parts of North America. The cultures that developed were strongly influenced by the countries from which the settlers came.

Many of the social, political, and economic ideas of the United States and Canada come

88

Millions of immigrants entered the United States through an immigration station on Ellis Island in New York Harbor. Arrivals of 1910 are seen here.

from northwestern Europe. The common language is English. In both countries a rapid growth in cities and manufacturing began early in the nineteenth century.

The People of the United States

In both area and population, the United States ranks as the fourth-largest country in the world. More than 226 million people now live in the United States. This country has been called a "melting pot" because its people represent nearly every background and come from many countries of the world.

The majority of Americans, about 87 percent, are white. Between 11 and 12 percent are black. Fewer than 1 percent are American Indians.

English is the most widely spoken language in the United States, but many other languages are heard throughout the country. French, German, Italian, Chinese, Greek, Polish, and Yiddish are some of the languages spoken in different areas. About 5 percent of the population is of Spanish origin, and Spanish is widely spoken. Newspapers in many different languages are published in large cities.

Urbanization (ur'bəni zā'shən) has long been a trend in the United States. Urbanization is the change from rural to urban, or city, living. The first census of the United States, taken in 1790, reported only 5 percent of the population living in cities. Today, more than 70 percent is urban, and less than 30 percent lives in rural areas.

Population and Land Area

United States
226.5 million people
3.6 million square miles
9.4 million square kilometers

Canada
24.0 million people
3.9 million square miles
10.0 million square kilometers

= 25 million people

The people of the United States are a people on the move. In the early 1900s, most people moved only once or twice in their lifetime. Most moves were within the same county or state. By 1970, about 20 percent of the population changed their residence each year.

The People of Canada

The population of Canada is about 24 million. Canada is slightly larger in area than the United States, but the United States has about ten times as many people. Most Canadians live within 200 miles (320 km) of the country's southern border. About half the people live in the St. Lawrence-Great Lakes lowland. The proportion of rural inhabitants to urban inhabitants is roughly the same as it is for the United States. Only 6 out of every 100 rural inhabitants actually live on farms.

Canada was settled mainly by the French and the British, and most Canadians today are of British and French origin. People with British backgrounds account for about 45 percent of the population.

French Canadians make up about 30 percent of the population. Most French Canadians live in the province of Quebec, which differs from the other provinces because of the strong French influence. French customs and traditions are evident in many parts of Quebec.

A wave of immigration to Canada from countries other than France or England began in the late 1800s. It lasted until World War I. Another wave began after World War II. The immigrants settled mainly in the western provinces and in the growing industrial cities. The largest numbers came from Germany and the Soviet Union.

Canada's native population is made up of two groups, the Indians and the Eskimos. They account for less than 2 percent of the population. Most of the Indians live on reserves, or reservations, in Ontario and the western provinces. About 75 percent of the Eskimos live in the Northwest Territories. The other 25 percent live in Arctic Quebec and northern Labrador. Some Eskimos still support themselves by hunting and fishing, but many of them work for mining and transportation companies.

Canada has two official languages, French and English. Many Canadians are *bilingual* (bī·ling'gwəl). They speak and write both French and English. *Bilingual* means "using or capable of using two languages."

Do You Know?

1. What is the highest point in North America? The lowest point? Where are they located?
2. What is the Canadian Shield?
3. Where is the Piedmont?
4. What is the population of the United States? Of Canada? What percentage of the population in these two countries live in urban areas?

2
The Growth of the United States

Europeans came to the Western Hemisphere in the 1400s in their search for a way to the Far East by water. At that time, the Americas were inhabited only by Indians and Eskimos. The reports of a new continent rich in resources inspired many European explorers to cross the Atlantic. Vast regions of the Americas were claimed by the Spanish, French, and English. The colonies established to support these claims were the beginning of a new nation.

Claims and Colonies

Spaniards claimed land in what is now the southeastern and southwestern United States during the 1500s. Ponce de León's travels in the area that is now Florida established Spain's control in the Southeast. Francisco Coronado explored the Southwest and claimed all lands west of the Mississippi for Spain.

In 1683, the French explorer La Salle claimed all the land drained by the Mississippi

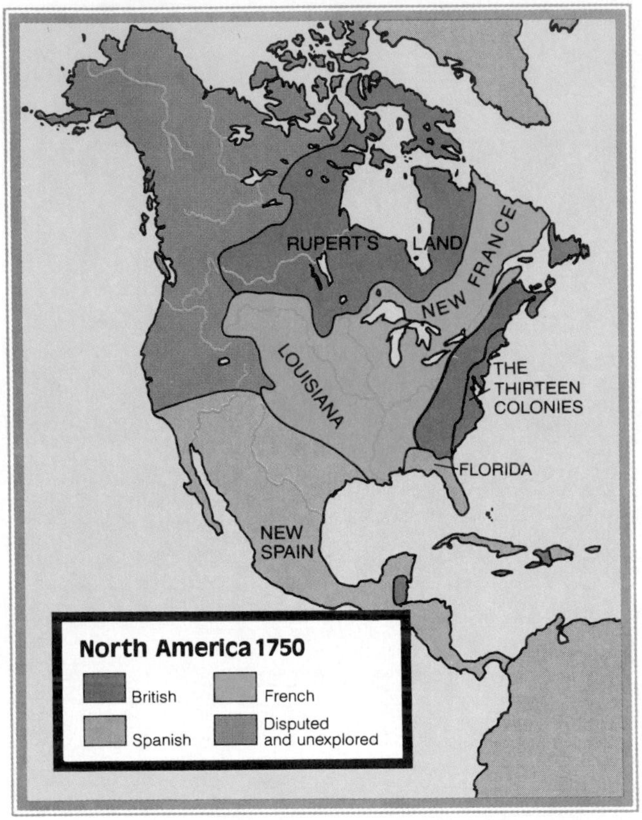
RUPERT'S LAND
NEW FRANCE
LOUISIANA
THE THIRTEEN COLONIES
FLORIDA
NEW SPAIN
North America 1750
British
French
Spanish
Disputed and unexplored

By 1750, large parts of North America were claimed by Great Britain, France, and Spain. Where were British colonies?

River system for France. The French traders set up trading posts along the river. Furs, fish, and lumber were shipped to the port of New Orleans and then on to Europe. By 1750 only 80,000 French settlers lived in the French territory. In that same year, there were almost two million British colonists in North America.

The first permanent British settlement in North America was established in 1607 at Jamestown. By the mid-1700s, British claims extended from what is now Maine southward to what is now Georgia. In the southern colonies, many large plantations were established. Rice, indigo, and tobacco were the chief crops of the southern colonies. Turpentine was also an important product.

In the middle colonies, grain and livestock were the main exports. New York and Philadelphia became trading and shipping centers. The ships that carried products to Europe were built in New England. Boston became one of the greatest seaports in North America. Shipbuilding, fishing, and farming were occupations of many colonists in New England. Water power from streams and rivers in the Northeast ran mills. Cloth, leather, and iron goods were produced by skilled workers.

The French and Indian War

The 13 British colonies along the Atlantic coast were bordered by lands claimed by the French to the north and west, and by those claimed by the Spanish to the south and west. By 1750, British colonists began to move into the area west of the Appalachian Mountains. The French were determined to hold this area because of the important fur trade. They built forts to discourage British settlement. Fort Duquesne (dōōkān′) was built at the point where the Monongahela and Allegheny rivers meet to form the Ohio River. War was formally declared between France and Great Britain in 1756. The conflict became known as the French and Indian War because Indians were allies of the French. The British also had Indian allies. In 1763, the war ended. The French surrendered all land east of the Mississippi to Great Britain. Spain, a French ally, gave up Florida to the British.

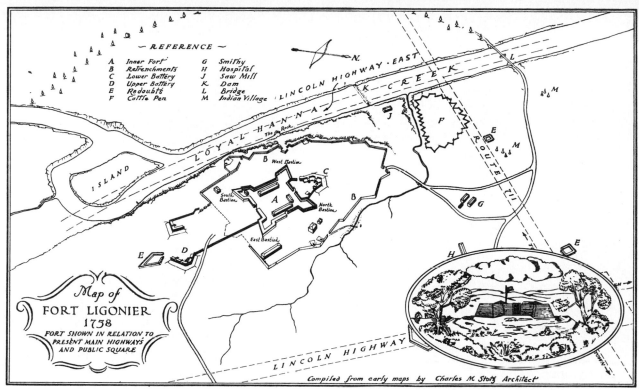

~ REFERENCE ~

A   Inner Fort
B   Retrenchments
C   Lower Battery
D   Upper Battery
E   Redoubts
F   Cattle Pen
G   Smithy
H   Hospital
J   Saw Mill
K   Dam
L   Bridge
M   Indian Village

Map of
FORT LIGONIER
1758
FORT SHOWN IN RELATION TO
PRESENT MAIN HIGHWAYS
AND PUBLIC SQUARE

Compiled from early maps by Charles M. Stotz Architect

The British built Fort Ligonier in southwestern Pennsylvania in 1758. From this base, they captured the French stronghold of Fort Duquesne, near the present site of Pittsburgh.

Independence

Great Britain became the leading power in North America, but the cost of victory was high. The British government levied new taxes and strict trading regulations in the colonies. The colonists protested against these laws made by a government that allowed them no voice in decisions. British troops were sent to the colonies, and in 1775, fighting broke out in Massachusetts.

By 1776, the colonists were convinced that a peaceful settlement was not possible. In that year, representatives of the 13 colonies broke with Great Britain by adopting the Declaration of Independence. The struggle for freedom from Great Britain had begun.

A New Government

The War for Independence, or the Revolutionary War, lasted until 1781, when the British General Cornwallis surrendered at Yorktown. The Americans had won the war, but the peace had to be settled. *Negotiations* (ni gō′shē ā′shənz), or discussions for the purpose of bringing about an agreement, continued until 1783. Four Americans—John Adams, Benjamin Franklin, John Jay, and Henry Laurens—represented the United States in Paris where the negotiations took place. By agreeing to the Treaty of Paris, Great Britain recognized the independence of a new nation, the United States of America. The British gave to the new nation all their land between the

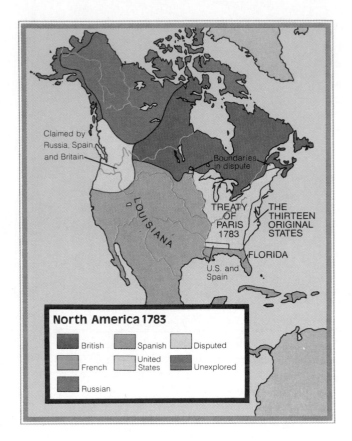

North America 1783

- British
- French
- Russian
- Spanish
- United States
- Disputed
- Unexplored

Claimed by Russia, Spain, and Britain

Boundaries in dispute

LOUISIANA

TREATY OF PARIS 1783

THE THIRTEEN ORIGINAL STATES

U.S. and Spain

FLORIDA

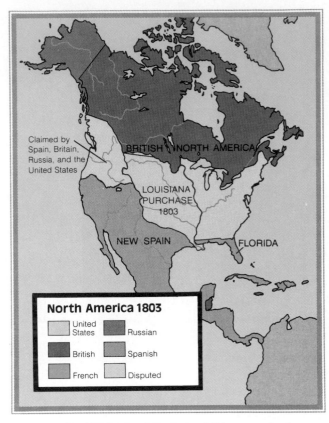

North America 1803

- United States
- British
- French
- Russian
- Spanish
- Disputed

Claimed by Spain, Britain, Russia, and the United States

BRITISH NORTH AMERICA

LOUISIANA PURCHASE 1803

NEW SPAIN

FLORIDA

In 1783, the Mississippi River marked the western boundary of the United States. The Louisiana Purchase doubled the size of the new nation in 1803.

Appalachians and the Mississippi River from the Great Lakes south to Florida.

A plan of government for the new nation was decided upon in 1787. The Constitution of the United States established three branches in the government: the executive (the President and Vice President), the legislative (the House of Representatives and Senate), and the judicial (the Federal court system). *Ratification* (rat′ə fi kā′shən), or official approval, of the Constitution had to be secured by the votes of nine states before it went into effect. By July of 1788, the necessary votes had been cast. After

ratification, the Constitution became the supreme law of the land. The new government was set up in 1789, with George Washington as the first President.

Territorial Expansion

In 1783, the United States extended from the Atlantic Ocean to the Mississippi River. The new nation continued to grow in the next century. In 1803, the country doubled in size when the French territory of Louisiana was purchased. The map on page 95 shows the

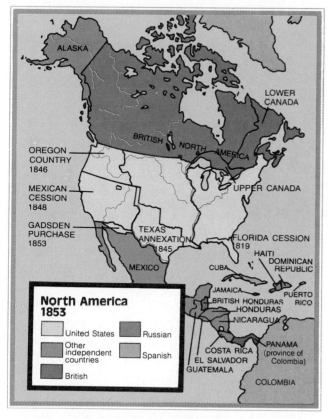

North America 1853

United States
Other independent countries
British
Russian
Spanish

ALASKA

LOWER CANADA

BRITISH NORTH AMERICA

OREGON COUNTRY 1846

MEXICAN CESSION 1848

GADSDEN PURCHASE 1853

UPPER CANADA

TEXAS ANNEXATION 1845

FLORIDA CESSION 1819

MEXICO

HAITI
DOMINICAN REPUBLIC

CUBA

JAMAICA

BRITISH HONDURAS
HONDURAS

PUERTO RICO

NICARAGUA

COSTA RICA
EL SALVADOR
GUATEMALA

PANAMA (province of Colombia)

COLOMBIA

By 1853, the United States stretched from the Atlantic to the Pacific. What parts of North America were still under European control in 1853?

areas acquired from Spain, Great Britain, and Mexico during the 1800s. By 1853, the United States stretched from the Atlantic Ocean to the Pacific Ocean.

Developments in Technology and Transportation

As the nation grew, it became increasingly important to provide connections between farms and cities and between inland and coastal regions. Transportation was essential for the exchange of goods.

Rivers and lakes had always been important means of transportation. To improve the nation's waterways, many canals were built during the 1800s. The Erie Canal, opened in 1825, made it possible for ships to travel an all-water route from the Great Lakes to the Atlantic Ocean. Products from the East were exchanged for the meat, grain, and lumber of the North Central States.

For the most part, the canals established east-west water connections. The Mississippi River was the great north-south connection. Floating goods downstream was the only way to use this great water highway. However, this one-way traffic was soon to be changed by the steamboat. In 1807, Robert Fulton demonstrated the power of his steamboat, the *Clermont,* by sailing it up the Hudson River. The river current no longer determined in what direction a boat could travel. By 1850, there were almost 800 steamboats on the Mississippi and its tributaries.

Improvements in overland transportation were also made. Work on the National Road began in 1811. When completed, the road led from Cumberland, Maryland, to Vandalia, Illinois. For many years, it was one of the principal routes to the West.

New inventions were also changing the way of life in the United States. In 1793, Eli Whitney's cotton gin allowed Southern plantation owners to clean cotton more rapidly than ever before. The demand for cotton increased as textile factories powered by steam engines grew up in the Northeast. The powerful new engines also ran saw mills and iron foundries.

Robert Fulton's steamboat, the *Clermont,* began a regular commercial run on the Hudson River in 1807. The boat was first called *The North River Steamboat.*

In 1846, Elias Howe's sewing machine made it possible to produce large quantities of clothing and shoes at low prices.

There were inventions that increased agricultural production, as well. In 1825, Jethro Wood manufactured the first iron plow. John Deere improved Wood's idea by making his plow of steel. Cyrus McCormick's mechanical seed drills, reapers, and threshing machines greatly increased the productivity of the nation's farms.

The new technology made transportation even more important. As the output of farms and factories increased, it was essential to have rapid ways to move the crops and products to markets. Farmers and manufacturers looked to the railroads as the solution.

Railroads had been in operation since the 1830s, but they were expensive to build and difficult to operate. The engineering problems were not fully solved until the 1850s. Between 1850 and 1860, the network of rails in the East grew from 9,000 miles (14,400 km) to more than 30,000 miles (48,000 km). In 1869, the first transcontinental connection was completed when the Union Pacific and Central Pacific lines met near Ogden, Utah.

Advances in transportation and technology continued to influence the way Americans used resources. The output of its factories and farms ranks the United States among the most productive nations in the world today.

Do You Know?

1. What explorer claimed the area that is now Florida for Spain?
2. What area did La Salle claim for France?
3. What lands were gained by Great Britain after the French and Indian War?
4. What inventions helped to increase the output of farms in the United States in the 1800s?

Before You Go On

Using New Words

negotiations   urbanization
bilingual   ratification

Number a paper from 1 through 4. After each number write the word from the above list that matches the definition.
1. Official approval
2. Using or capable of using two languages
3. The change from rural to urban living
4. Discussions for the purpose of bringing about an agreement

Finding the Facts

1. Name the mountains that form two parallel mountain chains in the Pacific Coast region.
2. What mountains form the boundaries of the interior plains?
3. What is the fall line?
4. Where is the Continental Divide?
5. Name the Great Lakes.
6. What are the official languages of Canada?
7. Where were the British colonies in North America in 1750?
8. What were some of the occupations of the New England colonists?
9. How did the constitution organize the government of the United States?
10. When was the Louisiana territory purchased? From what country did the United States buy it?
11. When was the Erie Canal completed? What all-water route did the canal make possible?
12. What inventions increased the output of textile and clothing factories?

3
Regions of the United States

The states of the United States can be divided into six regions. They are the Northeastern states, the Southeastern states, the North Central states, the South Central states, the Rocky Mountain states, and the Pacific states.

The Northeastern States

The Northeast is made up of two sections, the six New England states and the four Middle Atlantic states. Maine, New Hampshire, Vermont, Massachusetts, Rhode Island, and Connecticut are the New England states. New England is a hilly region with a rocky coastline. The Middle Atlantic states are New York, Pennsylvania, New Jersey and Delaware. The Appalachian Mountains extend through the Middle Atlantic States. The mountains separate the Atlantic Coastal Plain from the lowlands around the Great Lakes.

About 50 million people live in the Northeast. It is a region of many cities. The people of the Northeast are mainly urban. Some of them live just outside the city in the less densely populated suburbs. In many places the suburbs of a city meet or almost meet one another. Such a solidly built-up region is a metropolitan area.

Cities of the Northeast

In many parts of New England, life has long been centered in towns and cities. Factories run by water power were built in this area beginning in the early 1800s. Because workers were needed, people came to live near the factories, and towns and cities grew up.

Boston is the center of the largest metropolitan area in New England. Since its founding in 1630, Boston has grown from a small settlement into a great city. Many factories were built in and near Boston, and it became a trade center. Boston is also a great cultural center. It is a city where people can enjoy art museums, libraries, the theater, and concerts.

Let us now look at some of the cities of the Middle Atlantic states. Buffalo, in western New York, is a major industrial and transportation center. It is located on Lake Erie, at the western end of the Erie Canal. This canal connects the Great Lakes with the Hudson River.

Lake freighters carrying grain, lumber, and iron ore come to Buffalo from points farther west. At Buffalo some of this freight is transferred to canal barges or railroads and sent to cities east and south. On their return trips west, the lake freighters carry coal and goods made in the factories of the East. Some of the raw materials brought in are processed in Buffalo. This city ranks as the largest producer of flour in the nation.

Near Buffalo is one of the nation's scenic wonders, Niagara Falls. There the waters of the Niagara River drop over the edges of steep limestone cliffs in a great thundering spray. Behind the falls are steep tunnels that carry water to rotary engines. These rotary engines run generators to produce electricity. The electricity lights cities and supplies power for factories more than 200 miles (320 km) away.

Barges can travel east from Buffalo by canal to reach the Hudson River. This river cuts through the hills and plains of New York State and empties into New York Bay, on the Atlantic Ocean. Here in the largest, best-protected harbor on the Atlantic stands New York City. This city began as a small settlement built by the Dutch on Manhattan Island in 1624. In 1664, the Dutch city was taken over by the British.

The city grew slowly at first. After the Erie Canal was opened, thousands of boats were soon busy carrying freight and passengers between the Great Lakes region and the Atlantic. This all-water route saved both time and money. Farmers of the Middle West received good prices for the things they sold and paid lower prices for what they bought. The people of the East were able to buy western products for less and sell their own for more. Between 1825 and 1845, the city of New York more than doubled in population. Other cities along the canal and the Hudson River also grew in size. The state of New York quickly took a leading role in trade and in many industries.

Today New York City is the nation's largest city. Thousands of ships enter and leave this port each year. Incoming ships bring raw materials and manufactured goods from all parts of the world. Outgoing vessels carry industrial products from many parts of the United States. The Northeast produces 25 percent of the goods manufactured in the country.

Harvard University was founded in 1636 on the Charles River near Boston. Today Boston is the home of more than twenty colleges and universities.

New York City has famous skyscrapers. The World Trade Center is the second-tallest building in the world. The Empire State Building is the third-tallest building in the United States. Like Boston, New York is one of the nation's cultural centers. It has splendid museums, concert halls, opera houses, many theaters, great universities, and one of the finest public libraries in the world. It is the home of the United Nations and many large companies.

As in most big cities, transportation is a problem in New York City. The most rapid way to travel is by subway. New York City has more than 230 miles (370 km) of subway tracks. Every day trains and cars bring thousands of workers and shoppers from the suburbs to the city. Thousands of tourists visit the city every day. The heart of the business district is in Manhattan Island. It can be reached by tunnels and bridges.

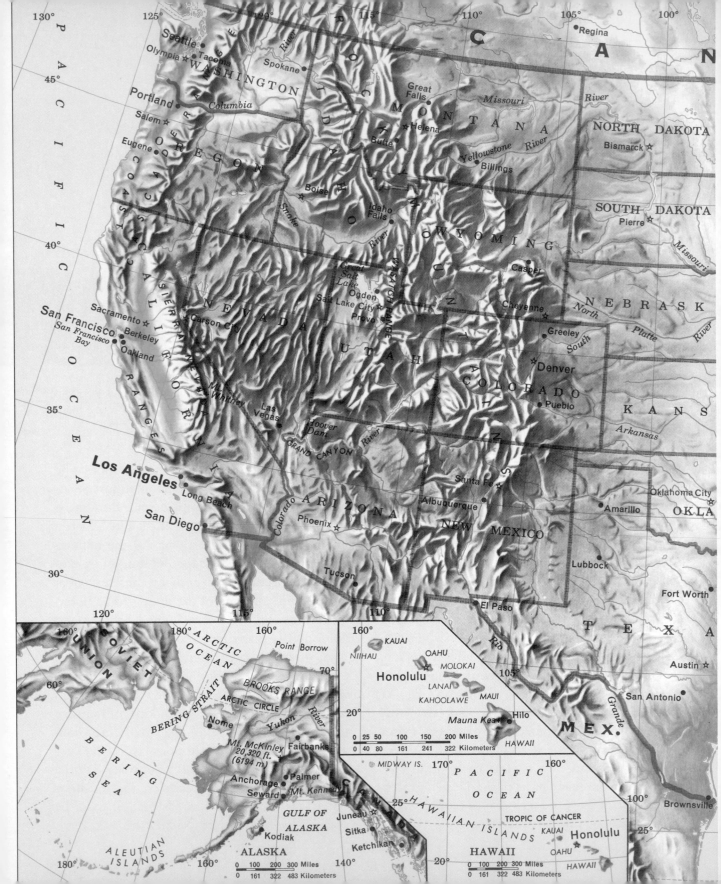

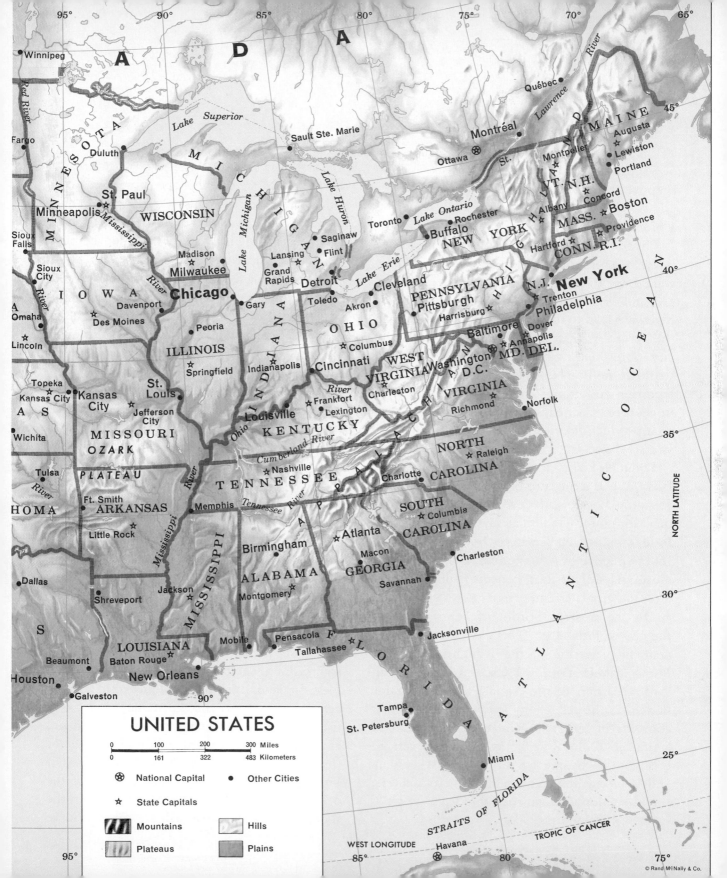

Southwest of New York City is the great seaport of Philadelphia. Today this city, founded by Quakers, is the fourth-largest in the United States.

Philadelphia is located on the Delaware River near the point where it flows into Delaware Bay. It is the center of a large industrial area in Pennsylvania and in New Jersey. Superhighways lead to the city and great bridges span the river. A network of railroads serves the city. Ships bearing cargoes from all parts of the world come to its docks. Products of the many factories and mines in nearby regions leave its harbor. Factories of this great industrial area produce textiles, clothing, and many iron and steel goods.

Philadelphia is a great modern city. Like Boston, it is a mixture of the old and the new. Standing beside tall new buildings are many that were built in colonial days. One of these is Independence Hall, where the Declaration of Independence was signed in 1776. With its museums, universities, concert halls, and theaters, the city is an important center of culture.

On the western border of Pennsylvania is the city of Pittsburgh. This city began as a fort near the junction of the Allegheny and the Monongahela rivers. These two rivers run through a part of the Appalachian Mountains known as the Allegheny Plateau, a region that abounds in minerals. The two rivers join to form the Ohio River. Raw materials can be brought in cheaply by way of the Allegheny and Monongahela rivers. Finished products can then be shipped down the Ohio River to cities in the South and the West.

Pittsburgh is a city of great blast furnaces and iron and steel mills. The bituminous coal fields of western Pennsylvania have helped make Pittsburgh a great industrial city. The soft coal is made into coke for use in the blast furnaces of the Pittsburgh region.

Pennsylvania has some iron mines, but most of the iron ore used in Pittsburgh's steel mills comes from the Lake Superior region of Minnesota, Wisconsin, and Michigan. It is shipped by boat through the Great Lakes, then by railroad to Pittsburgh.

Steel is the chief product of Pittsburgh. Iron is not the only metal used in steel production. Certain other metals, such as nickel, are sometimes used to give extra strength or toughness. Nickel is a *ferroalloy* (fer'ō al'oi). A ferroalloy is a metal mixed with iron to make a special kind of steel.

Factories in Pittsburgh and its suburbs manufacture other things, too. They include electrical goods, aluminum products, food, railway signals and safety devices, and plate glass.

Fishing and Farming

Most people of the Northeast make a living in cities. Many make a living from the sea and soil. Fishing is important all along the coast of New England. Boston and Gloucester, in Massachusetts, and Portland, in Maine, are leading fishing ports. Great quantities of cod, herring, and mackerel are caught on the *fishing banks* (fish'ing bangks') off the New England coast. Fishing banks are fairly shallow parts of the ocean where fish are usually plentiful. Near the shore lobsters and small fish are caught. Some

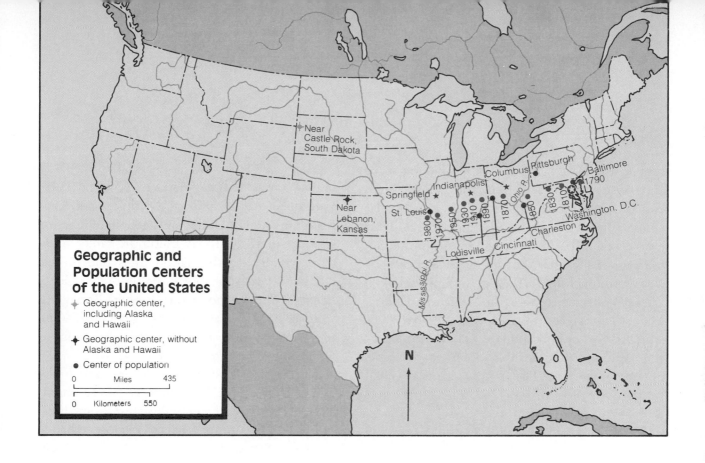

Geographic and Population Centers of the United States

- ✦ Geographic center, including Alaska and Hawaii
- ✚ Geographic center, without Alaska and Hawaii
- ● Center of population

| 0 | Miles | 435 |
| 0 | Kilometers | 550 |

of the catch is sold fresh, but most of it is processed for shipment inland.

New England is not an important farming area. The soil is thin. In northern New England the climate is too cool for many crops. There are truck farms, however, near many of the larger cities. The region is one of good dairy farms because ample rainfall allows pastures and hay to grow well. In rural areas potatoes are grown. Maine is noted for its fine potatoes. Apples and berries are grown in parts of New England and New York State.

The Middle Atlantic states have fertile plains and hills. Back from the wide, sandy beaches of the Atlantic stretches the low Atlantic Coastal Plain. New Jersey, New York, and Pennsylvania have many truck farms.

In the western part of the Appalachians is the hilly land of the Appalachian Plateau. In the valleys that extend far to the south, the land is fertile, and fine crops of many kinds are raised.

The Southeastern States

There are eleven states in the Southeast. One of these states, Maryland, lies north of the Potomac River. The other ten states—Virginia, West Virginia, Kentucky, Tennessee, North Carolina, South Carolina, Georgia, Florida, Alabama, and Mississippi—are all south of the Potomac and Ohio rivers. They lie between the Atlantic Ocean and the Mississippi River. Three of the states border the Gulf of Mexico. The District of Columbia, in which the nation's capital is located, is also in the Southeast.

The Appalachian Mountains extend through the eastern part of the Southeast from Maryland nearly to Atlanta, Georgia. One of the ranges, the Blue Ridge, is well known in story and song. Mount Mitchell, the highest peak east of the Mississippi River, is in the Appalachians. Its elevation is 6,684 feet (2,037 m) above sea level. The Great Smoky Mountain National Park is also in the Appalachians.

The rolling hills of the Piedmont lie between the Appalachians and the Atlantic Coastal Plain. The rivers of this region have their sources in the Appalachians. They flow across the Piedmont and tumble down to the plain along the fall line. The energy of the falls and rapids supplies power to many factories and cities in the area.

The plains and low hills of the Mississippi Valley lie to the west of the Appalachians. Find the Cumberland and the Tennessee rivers on the map on page 109. Notice that these rivers flow into the Ohio River and that the Ohio flows into the Mississippi.

The *Gulf Stream* (gulf′ strēm′) has its origin in the warm waters of the eastern part of the Gulf of Mexico, just southwest of Florida. The Gulf Stream is a warm ocean current that flows north along the Atlantic coast of North America. It then turns toward Europe. The Gulf Stream in part accounts for the mild climate of Great Britain and northwestern Europe. It is also a help to shipping. Ships traveling from South America to Atlantic coastal ports "ride" the Gulf Stream to save time.

Cities of the Southeast

Industry has grown rapidly in the Southeast in recent years. Manufacturing is scattered throughout the cities of the region.

The largest city in the Southeast is Baltimore. It was founded in the 1630s by Lord Baltimore. Although it is 200 miles (320 km) from the Atlantic, it has an excellent harbor on Chesapeake Bay. Today Baltimore ranks ninth in population in the nation. It is one of the country's largest seaports. Baltimore has long been an important factory center. Today its factories hum with activity. They turn out more than 2,000 different products, ranging from tin cans to great ships.

Large deposits of coal, iron ore, and limestone lie within a few miles of Birmingham, Alabama. Iron and steel mills were built there because these raw materials were close at hand. In the 1880s a city grew up around the new steel mills. It was named for Birmingham, England, which is also a steel city.

Norfolk and Mobile are important seaports of the Southeast. Louisville and Memphis are leading river ports. Several cities of West Virginia, including Charleston, have important chemical factories. Wheeling is a steel center. The discovery of oil in Mississippi did much to promote the growth of Jackson.

Piedmont cities such as Greensboro, North Carolina, and Greenville, South Carolina, are important producers of textiles. High Point is leader among North Carolina furniture manufacturing cities.

Atlanta has grown rapidly in recent years. About one-third of Georgia's population lives in the Atlanta metropolitan area. The city is the commercial center of the Southeast. Its factories produce aircraft, automobiles, chemicals, and transportation equipment. Many airlines, railroads, and trucking companies serve Atlanta. Its museums, theaters, and arts festivals contribute to the cultural life of the area.

Miami, Florida, is one of the most famous resort cities in the world. Many people visit Miami because of the pleasant climate and beautiful beaches.

Government is the main business of Washington, D.C., the nation's capital. It ranks fifteenth in size among the country's cities.

Fishing and Farming

Many people earn a living by fishing along the Atlantic and Gulf coasts. Dozens of different kinds of fish are caught in these waters. Some are used for food and some for making fertilizer. Chesapeake Bay and the coastal waters of North Carolina and South Carolina are famous for their oyster beds. Shrimp fisheries are found along the coast from western Florida to southern Texas. Near Tampa, sponges are gathered from the ocean floor.

The Southeast has long been the land of cotton and tobacco. Cotton is an *industrial crop* (in dus'trē əl krop'), as is tobacco. An industrial crop is a plant or plant product used in manufacturing, rather than for food. By growing industrial crops, farmers supply the materials that help many factory workers make a living. On many farms in the Southeast, corn is raised and fed to cattle and hogs. Florida has a climate that is excellent for citrus fruits. Sugarcane is also grown there. In winter, farmers grow vegetables for shipment to the Northeast. Other important crops of the Southeast are peanuts, soybeans, and peaches.

Cotton is picked by machine in most parts of the United States. Fibers are removed from the seeds at a cotton gin.

Lumbering and Mining

Forests cover large areas of the Southeast. Many people work in the hardwood forests of the Appalachians and in the pine forests of the coastal plain. Today nearly half of the nation's wood products come from this section of the Southeast.

Coal is mined in the Appalachian regions of West Virginia, Virginia, Kentucky, Tennessee, and Alabama. Western Kentucky also has large coal fields. Iron ore is found near Birmingham. Copper and zinc are mined in Tennessee. Florida leads all states in the mining of phosphate, a mineral used in the manufacture of fertilizer. In Georgia, marble and granite are quarried for building stone. Mississippi has important oil fields.

Living and Working in the United States and Canada

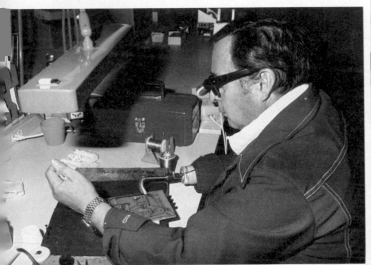

Abundant natural resources in both the United States and Canada are the basis for a wide variety of occupations. Skilled workers assemble electronics equipment. The *fishing banks* off Canada's Atlantic coast provide jobs for people in the *maritime* provinces. A mechanized conveyor belt speeds up the pineapple harvest in Hawaii. In the mountainous regions of Washington and Oregon, lumbering is an important industry.

Many indoor jobs are related to indirect use of natural resources. Steel workers in Chicago are protected from the heat and glare of a giant blast furnace by protective clothing and goggles. In a Houston oil refinery, an inspector relays information by radiophone. ■

The North Central States

The North Cental states are sometimes called the Middle West. Twelve states are included in this region. Six of them—Ohio, Indiana, Illinois, Michigan, Wisconsin, and Minnesota—border the Great Lakes. The Missouri River either crosses or forms a boundary of the other six states—Iowa, Missouri, North Dakota, South Dakota, Nebraska, and Kansas. About one-fourth of the people in the United States —about 59 million—live in the North Central states. Of these, more than 41 million live in the states east of the Mississippi River.

The Great Lakes are really inland freshwater seas. They are busy waterways. The average ship on the Great Lakes is larger than many ocean vessels. Duluth, Minnesota, and Superior, Wisconsin, together form one of the nation's largest ports, measured by the tonnage of freight moved.

Many rivers of this region, including the Illinois, the Ohio, the Mississippi, and the Missouri, are navigable. A navigable river is a river that is deep and wide enough to be used by boats. The Great Lakes are connected with these rivers by canals. Small boats and barges can sail from the Great Lakes to the Gulf of Mexico.

Cities of the North Central States

Many of the manufacturing cities of the North Central region are on waterways. The largest Great Lakes cities are Cleveland, Toledo, Detroit, Milwaukee, and Chicago. The twin cities of Minneapolis and St. Paul, in Minnesota, are on the Mississippi River, as is St. Louis. The two cities named Kansas City, one in Missouri and one in Kansas, form a large urban area on the Missouri River. Omaha, Nebraska, is also on the Missouri. Cincinnati is a large city on the Ohio River.

Several important cities are not on waterways. Akron is the world's largest rubber-producing center. Youngstown is the nation's fourth-largest steel center.

Chicago, the second-largest city in the United States, is the center of a large metropolitan area. It is one of the most important transportation centers in the country. It is the site of the nation's major grain exchange. Its mills supply great quantities of steel, as do those of Gary, Indiana, and Cleveland, Ohio.

St. Louis lies near the place where the Missouri River flows into the Mississippi River. It is the busiest inland port on the Mississippi and the nation's leading rail and trucking center. St. Louis began as a post built by French fur traders in 1764. During the 1800s, the city was a main port for Mississippi steamboats. It was also a gateway city for pioneers moving to the West. Today St. Louis is important in the production of transportation equipment and in the manufacturing of metals and chemicals. Large stockyards are located in East St. Louis. Among St. Louis's many cultural institutions is St. Louis University, the country's oldest university west of the Mississippi.

Detroit, Michigan, is the nation's leader in the manufacture of automobiles and trucks. Minneapolis, Minnesota, is important for its flour mills. Milwaukee, in Wisconsin, is known for manufacturing machinery, and Wichita, in

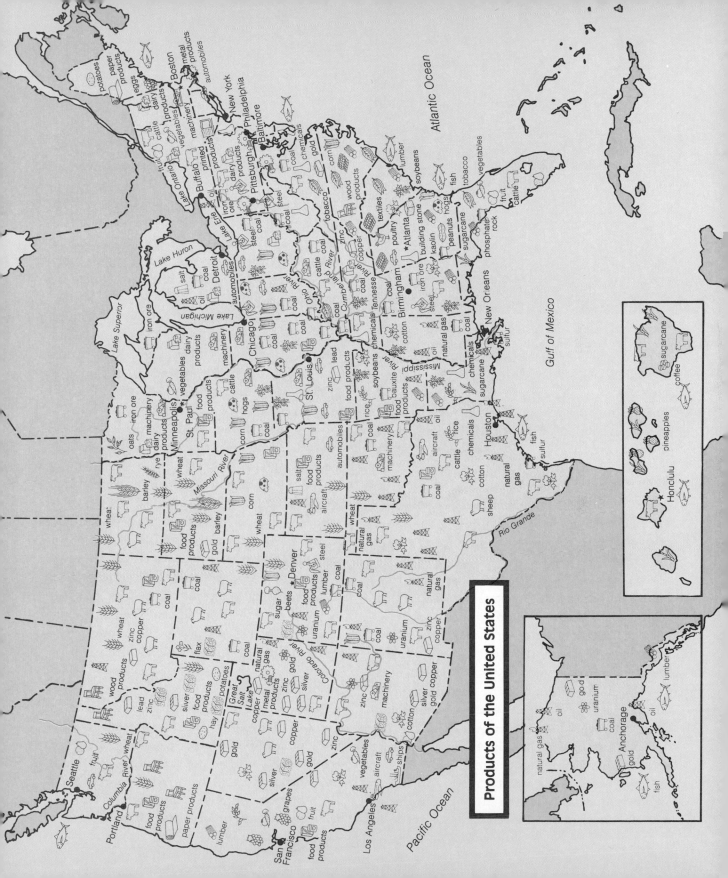

Products of the United States

Grain is harvested in the gently rolling plains near Milwaukee, Wisconsin. This region of fertile soil was once covered by a great ice sheet.

Kansas, for producing aircraft. Omaha, Nebraska, is one of the world's leading meat-packing centers.

Agriculture

By 1830, the plains of the North Central states were becoming a major farming region. Today this is the most important farming section in the United States.

Agribusiness (ag′rə biz′nəs) is an important industry in the North Central states. Agribusiness is the industry related to the production, sale, and distribution of farm products. About 40 percent of the workers in the United States are involved in some aspect of agribusiness. Fewer than 5 percent of these workers actually farm or raise livestock, however. The others have jobs related to the production of fertilizers and farm equipment, and to the processing and packaging of farm products.

Great dairy lands stretch across Michigan, Wisconsin, and Minnesota. Much of the cheese manufactured in the United States is made in Wisconsin. Minnesota leads in the manufacture of butter.

The farming area that stretches from Ohio westward across Nebraska is known as the corn belt. This is one of the world's most important farming areas. Much of the corn raised there is fed to cattle and hogs, which are marketed as meat.

In the western part of the North Central states are great wheat lands. Kansas and North Dakota are leading wheat states. Rye, barley, oats, and flax are also grown.

The North Central states are also important producers of soybeans. About 75 percent of the soybeans grown in the United States are raised here. Illinois, Iowa, and Indiana are the leading soybean-growing states.

The United States, which is the world's leading producer of soybeans, grows more soybeans than any other crop except corn and wheat. Soybeans are used as food for people, as feed for animals, and in industry. Soybeans are a cheap source of protein, and in many countries people eat them instead of meat and fish. A wide variety of products, including baby food, margarine, candles, soap, carbon paper, and fertilizers, is made from soybeans.

Mining

One of the greatest iron-producing regions in the world is near Lake Superior. There are both underground and open-pit mines. Railroads lead from the mines to docks at Duluth, Superior, and other nearby lake ports. There the iron ore is dumped into storage bins and later transferred to large boats for shipment.

The Houston Ship *Channel* makes the city a busy seaport. Skyscrapers of Houston are seen in the background.

Ohio, Indiana, and Illinois have important coal fields. There are lead and zinc mines in Missouri. Michigan and Kansas are important salt producers. South Dakota has the largest gold mine in the United States. Several of the North Central states produce oil. Kansas is the leading oil-producing state in the region.

The South Central States

The South Central states are Arkansas, Louisiana, Oklahoma, and Texas. About 24 million people live in this region. The Mississippi River is the eastern boundary, and the southern boundary is formed by the Gulf of Mexico and the Rio Grande. In the eastern part of the region, in Arkansas and Louisiana, the annual rainfall is heavy. The climate is much drier in Oklahoma and western Texas.

The Mississippi River flows into the Gulf of Mexico in the extreme southeastern part of this region. Each year the river empties about 133 cubic miles (554 cubic km) of water into the gulf. The situation is quite different in the extreme southwestern part of the South Central region. Here the middle course of the Rio Grande may be merely a dry river bed in late summer.

Cities of the South Central States

Much of the business activity in the cities of the South Central states has to do with oil. The nation's largest oil fields are in this region.

Houston, Texas, the largest city in the South Central region, is the headquarters of many oil companies. Once only a shallow river joined Houston with Galveston and the Gulf of Mexico. This river was widened and deepened so that a canal stretched across the coastal plain to the city, 25 miles (40 km) inland. Today ocean-going vessels can reach Houston, which ranks third among the nation's ports.

The Lyndon B. Johnson Space Center is just south of Houston. At the center, astronauts are trained, and space vehicles are tested.

Dallas is a center for the oil industry and a leading fashion center. Fort Worth manufactures airplanes and is a meat-packing center.

111

New Orleans, the great seaport on the Mississippi River, is one of the oldest and largest cities in the South Central states. It is built on the large delta formed from silt deposits. Founded by the French in 1718, the city grew slowly at first. It became a part of the United States in 1803.

New Orleans is one of the world's largest cotton markets. It also has important sugar refineries. Its great docks are crowded with ships from many foreign countries. Railroad tracks lead to the docks so that the products can be loaded directly on railroad cars for shipment inland. Barges also carry products up the Mississippi.

New Orleans is a meeting place of the old and the new. Tourists visit the city to see its old French buildings and eat the French food for which it is famous.

Mining

Little Rock, the capital of Arkansas, is the center for many farming and mining interests. Bauxite, the ore from which aluminum is made, is mined nearby.

The Gulf Coast of Louisiana and Texas has an important chemical industry. Sulfur deposits beneath this coast are mined for use in manufacturing many chemicals.

Oil, sulfur, and farm products have helped the region to grow rapidly. Texas is the nation's leading petroleum-producing state, and Louisiana ranks second. Today oil is being recovered from areas beneath the Gulf of Mexico. Oil wells are drilled from platforms built out in the gulf as far as 30 miles (48 km) from the shore.

Farming and Ranching

Many people of the region make a living in agribusiness. Cotton is the principal crop, and Texas is the leading cotton-growing state. Rice is grown in Louisiana, Texas, and Arkansas. Sugarcane is grown in Louisiana.

Wheat lands reach into western Oklahoma and northwestern Texas. These two states are among the top seven wheat-producing states in the United States.

The dry western part of Texas, the Gulf Coast, and the southern, narrow portion of the

Cattle raising is an important industry in the grasslands of the South Central states. These cattle are being unloaded at a ranch in Texas.

state that extends toward Mexico are important cattle lands. Large ranches in these regions produce thousands of beef cattle. Fort Worth, which is close to many of the great cattle ranches, is a major meat-packing center. Texas also has many sheep ranches and is an important supplier of wool.

Lumbering, Trapping, and Fishing

Arkansas and Louisiana, which lie in the rainy eastern part of the South Central region, are heavily forested. Many people there work in the lumber industry. The *bayou* (bī′ōō) country of the lower Mississippi River is a great trapping region. A bayou is a marshy creek or a sluggish, swampy backwater. Many people in the bayou country trap muskrats and sell the pelts to furriers. Much commercial fishing is carried on all along the Gulf Coast.

The Rocky Mountain States

The eight Rocky Mountain states cover a very large territory. On the north, Montana and Idaho share a border with Canada. To the south, New Mexico and Arizona border Mexico. The states in between are Wyoming, Nevada, Utah, and Colorado. About eleven million people live in the Rocky Mountain states.

From east to west the Rocky Mountain states stretch from the Great Plains westward across the Rocky Mountains, through the plateaus and basins of the intermountain region, to the Pacific Coast region.

The Rocky Mountain states take their name from the rugged, snow-capped mountains that extend through the region. This great mountain chain stretches from New Mexico through the states of Colorado, Utah, Wyoming, and Montana.

The Colorado Plateau covers western Colorado, much of eastern Utah, and parts of Arizona and New Mexico. Mountains rise above the level of the plateau. Deep canyons have been cut by the rivers. One of these is the spectacular Grand Canyon in Arizona. It is 18 miles (29 km) wide and one mile (1.6 km) deep. Layers of brilliantly colored rocks are exposed in the canyon walls. Grand Canyon National Park, an area larger than Rhode Island, was established in order to preserve the beauty of the canyon.

Erosion has shaped the features of the region. Wind and water have cut into the plateaus, removing much of the rock. As erosion continues, smaller parts of the plateaus are left standing. These parts, or formations, have special names. A *mesa* (mā′sə) is a flat-topped hill or mountain with steep sides. *Mesa* means "table" in Spanish. A mesa is smaller than a plateau, but larger than a *butte* (byōōt). A butte is a small flat-topped hill with steep sides, smaller than a mesa.

The Columbia Plateau covers part of southern Idaho. Between the Columbia Plateau and the Colorado Plateau lies the Basin and Range region. This is a vast area of mountains and lowlands. Faulting broke the earth's crust into huge blocks. Some of the blocks were raised to form ranges, others dropped to form basins. The Great Basin in Nevada and western Utah is part of the Basin and Range area.

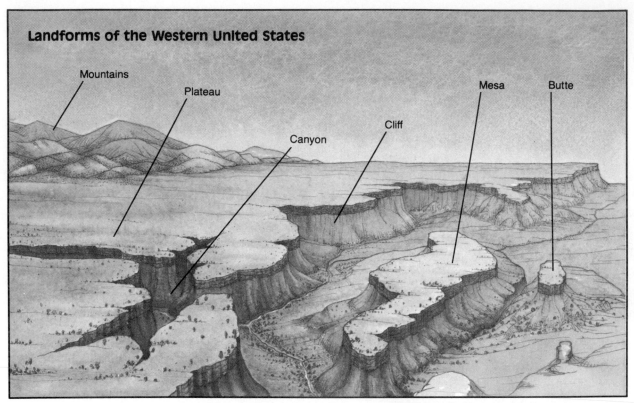

Landforms of the Western United States

Mountains

Plateau

Canyon

Cliff

Mesa

Butte

Erosion produces landforms like these in the arid intermountain regions of the western United States.

The Rocky Mountain states have a variety of landscapes and climates. Deserts border irrigated farms. Forests grow on the sides of snow-capped mountains.

Cities of the Rocky Mountain States

Phoenix (fē′niks), Denver, and Tucson (tōō′son) are the largest cities of the Rocky Mountain states. Other major cities include Albuquerque (al′bəkur′kē), Santa Fe (san′tə fā′), Salt Lake City, and Colorado Springs.

Phoenix, the region's biggest city, is a popular resort and retirement city. It has a pleasant, sunny climate. Cattle and fruit are raised in the surrounding area. Tucson is another resort city in Arizona. It has an important electronics industry. Much copper is mined in the surrounding area.

Denver, known as the mile-high city, lies on a plain at the base of the *foothills* (foot′ hilz′) of the Rockies. Foothills are a low line of hills lying between a mountain range and a plain.

The county courthouse in Tucson, Arizona, shows elements of several styles of *architecture*. A modern office building is seen on the right. Tucson was founded by the Spanish in 1775.

Denver was founded during the gold rush of 1859. It grew rapidly as a mining and transportation center. It is now the second-largest city in the Rocky Mountain states. A United States mint and many Federal government offices are in Denver.

Like Denver, Colorado Springs lies at the foot of the Rockies. It is the second-largest city in the state. The United States Air Force Academy is just north of Colorado Springs. Many tourists visit the city and nearby Pikes Peak.

Two important cities in New Mexico are Santa Fe and Albuquerque. Santa Fe, the capi-tal, was founded in 1610 as the capital of the Spanish colony of New Mexico. Santa Fe's adobe houses and narrow, winding streets attract many visitors. Pueblo Indians live in the areas surrounding Santa Fe. Albuquerque is the largest city in New Mexico. Like Santa Fe, it has a Spanish and Indian heritage. Today Albuquerque is an industrial, trade, and transportation center for a large area.

Salt Lake City in Utah is the center of a large irrigated area. It is the headquarters of the Mormons, a large religious group. Its beautiful temple is visited by many tourists each year.

National Parks

Many places of scenic beauty are found in the Rocky Mountain states. The government has established national parks to preserve these places for all people to enjoy.

Rocky Mountain National Park, in Colorado, has high snow-covered peaks, glaciers, lakes, and waterfalls. The park has more than 100 peaks that rise over 11,000 feet (3,350 m) above sea level.

Yellowstone National Park, most of which lies in Wyoming, is famous for its hot springs and geysers. Glacier National Park, in Montana, is noted for its glaciers, beautiful lakes, and towering mountains. This park was united to Waterton Lakes National Park in Alberta, Canada, in 1932, to become the Waterton-Glacier International Peace Park.

Zion National Park in Utah has many colorful canyons and mesas. Nearby is Bryce Canyon National Park, with its strangely shaped rock formations.

Long's Peak in Rocky Mountain National Park is one of Colorado's many peaks higher than 11,000 feet (3,350 m).

Carlsbad Caverns National Park in New Mexico includes the largest known cave in the world. One of its underground rooms is a half mile (.8 km) long, 400 feet (120 m) wide, and 348 feet (104 m) high. Mesa Verde National Park, in southwestern Colorado, has prehistoric Indian cliff dwellings. There are eight other national parks, including Grand Canyon National Park, in the Rocky Mountain states.

Mountains and Water

The most important problem nearly everywhere in the Rocky Mountain states is the water supply. The high mountains cause clouds to drop their moisture on the western slopes, which means that lands at low elevations receive little rain. Rain and snow falling on the mountains are the main sources of water. Most of the people of the Rocky Mountain states live close to the mountains or on rivers that lead from them. The sources of many large rivers are in the mountains. The mighty Missouri begins in Montana. It flows across the plains into the Mississippi River. The Snake River flows west from Yellowstone Park to join the Columbia. The Colorado, the Arkansas, and the Rio Grande all begin in the Rockies.

The fast-flowing rivers coming from the mountains are dammed, and their waters are used to irrigate the lowlands, where water is scarce. Great dams on the larger rivers provide power to generate electricity. Hoover Dam, on the Colorado River between Nevada and Arizona, and Hungry Horse Dam, on the Flathead River in Montana, are two of the largest.

Farming and Ranching

Some farming areas in the Rocky Mountain states receive just enough rain to grow wheat without irrigation. Most farms in the region must be irrigated. Water to grow crops is obtained from streams and rivers or from deep wells. Hundreds of cattle and sheep ranches are found in the dry plateaus west of the Rockies and on the plains of Montana and Wyoming.

Irrigation is widely used in the dry, flat farm country of Colorado. Great tracts that were once covered with sagebrush are now thriving farms. Alfalfa, sugar beets, corn, and wheat are important crops. Wheat farms dot northern Montana and eastern Colorado. Montana is one of the five greatest wheat-producing states. The Snake River plains of southern Idaho and the areas near Salt Lake City are irrigated. Idaho is noted for its fine potatoes.

Phoenix, in Arizona, is the center of an irrigated region. Oranges, lemons, grapefruit, and cotton are grown in southern Arizona. Some valleys have a climate hot enough to produce dates, which are a tropical fruit.

Mining and Lumbering

Mining is important in the Rocky Mountain states. Large copper mines are found in Arizona, New Mexico, Nevada, Utah, and Montana. One great open-pit copper mine near Salt Lake City is more than 2,000 feet (600 m) deep. The deep copper mines of Butte, Montana, are directly beneath the city. Silver, lead, zinc, and gold are produced in every Rocky Mountain state. In recent years important deposits of uranium have been discovered in Colorado, Utah, Arizona, and New Mexico.

Coal is mined in Colorado, New Mexico, Wyoming, Montana, and Utah. Iron ore is mined in Colorado and Utah. Steel is made at Pueblo, Colorado, and in a great plant near Salt Lake City. Coal and iron ore are shipped by rail from Utah to steel mills in California.

New Mexico, Colorado, Wyoming, and Montana are oil-producing states. Colorado has large deposits of oil shale, a rock that yields oil when heated. Scientists are developing efficient ways to recover the oil. Natural gas is pumped from gas fields in Montana. Many people work in the mines, smelting plants, and refineries of the Rocky Mountain states.

The region's forests provide other jobs. The largest forest in the Rocky Mountain states is in western Montana and Idaho. Many people are employed in cutting and moving trees, or logging. Others work in the mills where the trees are sawed into boards.

The Pacific States

The Pacific states are California, Oregon, Washington, Alaska, and Hawaii. All five states have coastlines on the Pacific Ocean. About 32 million people live in this area. More than 23 million live in California.

Alaska and Hawaii are the two newest states. With their admission to the Union in 1959, the United States became a nation of 50 states. Alaska occupies the northwestern part of North America. Hawaii is an island state in the Pacific Ocean. Alaska and Hawaii will be discussed separately at the end of this section.

Cities of the Pacific States

Los Angeles, San Diego, San Francisco, Portland, and Seattle are the largest cities on the Pacific coast of the continental United States.

Los Angeles and its suburbs spread over a wide area between the sea and the mountains. Los Angeles was once an inland city, but it is now connected with a harbor about 15 miles (24 km) away. Ships from many parts of the world move in and out of this harbor. The area around Los Angeles is rich in oil. Oil, movie, and airplane industries are important.

The plain on which Los Angeles is located is separated into several basins, or flat-floored valleys, by low mountain ranges. During the days of Spanish settlement the land was used for ranches. Later it was found to be fine for growing oranges. For many years oranges and other fruits and vegetables were the chief products of the Los Angeles area. The city grew rapidly. Houses and factories spread over the farmland. Today a very large part of the plain is covered by the city and its suburbs. Food for Los Angeles now must be shipped to the metropolitan area from long distances.

San Francisco is on a point of land between the ocean and San Francisco Bay. From the shore, the land rises in a group of hills. The first settlers built their houses near the water, but gradually the city spread over the hills. When gold was first discovered in California in 1848, San Francisco had only 800 inhabitants. Within a year the population was 30,000. Many people lived in tents and shacks. The city continued to grow, but in 1906 much of it was destroyed by an earthquake and the fire that followed. The people of San Francisco rebuilt their city from the ashes.

Today San Francisco is one of the banking centers of the nation. It has many factories where fruit and vegetables from the farming regions of the state are canned and where sugar is refined.

The harbor is a busy place. Shipbuilding is an important industry. Ships sailing through the Golden Gate to San Francisco Bay bring cargoes from all over the world.

A cold ocean current flowing near San Francisco causes fog to rise in the morning and evening. The current also keeps the cities around San Francisco Bay cool in the summer.

Part of the water supply for San Francisco and Los Angeles comes from the Sierra Nevada. Electricity generated by Hoover Dam is used by Los Angeles.

San Diego is only a few miles north of the Mexican border. The city is on a large bay that forms a good harbor. It is an important naval

The spectacular San Francisco-Oakland Bay Bridge spans San Francisco Bay. The tall buildings in the foreground are in San Francisco. The city is built at the northern tip of a peninsula.

base, and ships of the fleet are often in the harbor.

Sacramento, the capital of California, is on the Sacramento River in the Central Valley. The products of the surrounding farming and mining region are processed in Sacramento's factories.

The large cities of Seattle, Tacoma, and Portland are leading seaports north of California. Manufacturing in these cities is related to local products such as lumber, fish, and farm products. Seattle has large airplane factories. It is also the chief seaport and airport for travel to Alaska.

Spokane, on the east side of the Cascade Range, is near both the wheat fields of Washington and the forests of Idaho. Aluminum is a leading product of its many factories.

National Parks

The Pacific states include many places of scenic interest. There are 13 national parks in this region. The giant sequoia (si kwoi′ə) redwood trees of California can be seen in Sequoia National Park and Redwood National Park. These trees are the oldest living things on earth. Yosemite National Park, in the Sierra Nevada of California, has deep gorges and high waterfalls.

Snow-covered mountains and volcanic peaks rise high in the Cascades. Crater Lake, in Crater Lake National Park in Oregon, occupies the crater of an extinct volcano. The top of the volcano was blown off long ago by a great eruption. In 1980, another mountain in the Cascade Range, Mount St. Helens, erupted. It had been inactive for 123 years. The eruption removed a large quantity of rock. It spread a thick layer of ash over a large area.

Both Alaska and Hawaii have volcanoes that are still active. Hawaii Volcanoes National Park attracts many visitors.

Farming and Fishing

A series of fertile valleys stretch north and south between the coastal mountain chains. They are important agricultural regions.

Central Valley, in California, is one of these valleys. It is about 500 miles (800 km) long and about 100 miles (160 km) wide. This valley is one of the finest farming regions in the world. Fruit is the most important crop. The land is rich and nearly level. There is not much rain, but rivers bring water down from the mountains. Irrigation is used during the dry months

Machines harvest rice in California's Central Valley. Most crops in California are grown on irrigated land.

of the summer. Near Sacramento are great fields of rice. Fresno is a grape-growing center.

Imperial Valley, in southeastern California, has a tropical desert climate. Water from the Colorado River irrigates this valley. Vegetables find good markets in places that are too cold to grow crops during the winter. Some valleys near Imperial Valley grow dates.

The two large valleys west of the Cascade Range have mild winters, cool summers, and a high annual rainfall. This is an area of small farms. Many farmers of the Puget Sound lowland raise dairy cattle. In the Willamette Valley there are many kinds of farms. Some of these grow grain, some berries and other fruits, and some specialize in dairy cattle.

The valleys on the eastern side of the Cascades are irrigated because of the dry climate. These valleys are noted for their fine apples and other fruit. Washington leads the nation in apple production. The Columbia Plateau in eastern Washington is a great winter wheat region.

Fishing is a leading occupation in the Pacific states. Thousands of people work in the salmon fisheries off the coast of Alaska and Washington, in the Columbia River, and in Puget Sound. Halibut and other kinds of fish are caught as well. Fleets of fishing vessels are a common summer sight in nearly all waters. Many people work in the fish canneries and in the frozen-food plants. Fishing is also important along the California coast, where many tuna are caught. There are many fish canneries in San Diego and Los Angeles.

Lumbering and Mining

Lumbering is the chief industry of the mountainous sections of Washington, Oregon, and northern California. Oregon is the nation's leading lumber state. Giant trees are sawed into boards and other lumber at the mills. Many people work in factories making wood products. Wood pulp is made into newsprint and other kinds of paper.

Oil is Alaska's most important mining product. Today Alaska ranks third among the nation's leading petroleum-producing states.

California is the country's fourth-largest oil-producing state. The oil fields are in the southern part of the state.

Gold and other metals are mined in the Sierra Nevada of California and in Alaska. Each state has had gold rushes in the past. Today gold is obtained from river gravels by a sifting process called placer (plas′ər) mining.

Alaska

Alaska is part of the continental United States, but it is not part of the *conterminous* (kən tur′mə nəs) United States. *Conterminous* means "contained within the same boundaries." The conterminous United States includes the first 48 states and the District of Columbia, which completely fill an unbroken block of territory.

Alaska covers an area one-fifth as large as the other 49 states. It is a great peninsula that extends from the northwestern part of North America into the Pacific.

The Aleutian (ə l$\overline{oo}$′shən) Islands, which are a part of Alaska, reach across the Pacific toward Asia. Alaska is separated from Asia by the Bering Strait. At its narrowest, this strait is about 50 miles (80 km) wide.

The United States bought this great northern area from Russia in 1867 for $7.2 million. Before 1867, the Russians had controlled Alaska for more than 100 years. It was an important source of furs.

In 1896, gold was discovered in Alaska. Many people flocked to the region. Some of them stayed as settlers. During World War II, the Alaska Highway was completed. This road is the only major land route from Alaska to Canada and the "lower 48." It stretches 1,523 miles (2,451 km) from Dawson Creek, British Columbia, to Delta Junction, Alaska.

In 1957, a huge new oil field was discovered in northern Alaska. Between 1974 and 1977, the 800-mile-long (1,280 km) Alaska Pipeline was built to carry the oil from the north to the port of Valdez on the southern coast.

In 1959, Alaska became the 49th state of the United States. About 400,000 people live in Alaska. Most of them live on or near the Pacific coast. The Coast Ranges extend along this coast. The region has a climate of mild winters and cool summers.

Most of Alaska's large cities are found along the coast. Juneau, the capital, lies on a narrow strip of land between the coast and steep forest-covered mountains. Seward is an important port at the end of a railroad that runs to Fairbanks and Anchorage. Anchorage is the main transportation center of Alaska.

The interior of Alaska is a vast area drained by the great Yukon River. The Yukon is navigable during the summer. The city of Fairbanks is located on a tributary of the Yukon. It is the leading city of the interior.

The coastal forests continue into the interior. Northward they disappear. The far north is tundra.

Most of the people in Alaska work in the salmon fisheries, the lumber industry, the mines, and the new oil industry. Mining is Alaska's most important industry, and the leading mineral is oil. There are large coal fields, but only small amounts of coal are mined. A few people are farmers. The leading farming region is near Anchorage.

Hawaii

The beautiful Hawaiian Islands make up the newest state of the United States. Most of the islands lie in the tropics. In climate and vegetation, Hawaii differs greatly from the other 49 states.

The islands of Hawaii cover an area of 6,425 square miles (16,641 sq. km). This is about the area of Connecticut and Rhode Island combined. The population of the islands is about 965,000. Almost all of the people live on seven of the eight largest islands. These are Niihau (nē'hou), Kauai (kou'ī'), Oahu (ō ä'hoo), Molokai (mäl'ə kī'), Lanai (lə nī'), Maui (mou'ē), and Hawaii. Hawaii is the largest island. Eighty-five percent of the people live on Oahu.

All of the islands were formed by volcanoes built up from the ocean floor. The islands rise to different heights above sea level. Some have been eroded by waves. One of the volcanoes on Hawaii rises more than 13,000 feet (3,900 m) above sea level. The base of the volcano, on the ocean floor, is nearly 13,000 feet (3,900 m) below sea level. The volcano has a height of nearly 26,000 feet (7,900 m), but only the top half is above water.

Captain James Cook, an English explorer, visited Hawaii in 1778. He may have been the first European to stop there. Cook traded with the inhabitants, who were descendants of the Polynesians (pol'i nē'zhənz) who settled there more than 1,500 years ago.

Hawaii was a kingdom for many years. Whaling ships called at the islands. Missionaries from New England settled there, and ships on their way to Asia called there. Sometimes sailors and other passengers left the ships to settle in these beautiful islands. By the 1850s people from the United States and from England had started businesses in Hawaii. They built stores and plantations on the islands.

121

The planters brought in workers from other countries. People came from China, Japan, Korea, the Philippines, Puerto Rico, and Portugal to work in the sugarcane fields. Some of the workers brought their families. Others married Hawaiians.

In the 1890s, a group of foreign businessmen led some Hawaiians in a rebellion against their queen and set up a republic. The Hawaiian leaders who opposed the queen asked that Hawaii be made a part of the United States. The United States government learned that the matter had not been discussed with the Hawaiian people, and it refused the request.

A few years later, during the Spanish-American War, the Hawaiian people asked to join the United States. Because the Hawaiian people made the request and because the United States government did not want the islands to fall under the control of any other nation, it agreed. In 1898 the islands became a part of the United States. They were organized as the Territory of Hawaii in 1900. Hawaii was admitted to the Union as a state in 1959.

Hawaii specializes in the production of sugarcane and pineapples, for which there is a good market in the continental United States. Hawaii produces more than one million tons (900,000 metric tons) of sugar a year. It grows more than four-fifths of the world's pineapples. The sugar mills send much of the raw sugar to refineries in California. The island of Lanai is one large pineapple plantation. Boats take the fruit from Lanai to Honolulu to be canned.

Hawaii also has large cattle ranches. One of the largest cattle ranches in the United States is in Hawaii. Coffee is grown on the western side of the island of Hawaii.

Honolulu, the capital of Hawaii, is built on a good harbor on Oahu. Diamond Head, a small volcano, is the first landmark seen by arriving travelers. Suburbs of Honolulu lie across the mountains on the opposite shore of Oahu.

The entertainment of tourists is an important business in Hawaii. Honolulu is a favorite resort for tourists. The sandy beach of Waikiki (wī′kē kē′) lies along part of Honolulu's shore. Hotels and roadways line the beach. Surfboard riding is a famous sport.

Hilo (hē′lō) is the chief city of the island of Hawaii. Gardeners near Hilo grow many orchids. The orchids are sent by air to florists on the continental United States.

Pearl Harbor, the chief United States naval base in the Pacific, is six miles (9.6 km) west of Honolulu.

Do You Know?

1. What is the largest harbor on the Atlantic coast?
2. Why did Birmingham, Alabama, become a great producer of iron and steel?
3. What percent of workers in the United States are involved in some aspect of agribusiness?
4. Where is the Basin and Range region?

Before You Go On

Using New Words

ferroalloy   foothills

conterminous   bayou

butte   mesa

fishing banks   Gulf Stream

agribusiness   industrial crop

Number a paper from 1 through 10. After each number write the word or term from the above list that matches the definition.

1. Fairly shallow parts of the ocean where fish are usually plentiful
2. A low line of hills lying between a mountain range and a plain
3. A plant or plant product that is used in manufacturing
4. The industry related to the production, sale, and distribution of farm products
5. A flat-topped hill or mountain with steep sides that is larger than a butte
6. A marshy creek or sluggish backwater swamp
7. Contained within the same boundaries
8. A warm ocean current that flows north along the Atlantic coast of North America
9. A metal that is mixed with iron to make a special kind of steel
10. A flat-topped hill with steep sides that is smaller than a mesa

Finding the Facts

1. What two sections make up the Northeastern states?
2. What river separates the Southeastern states from the South Central states?
3. In what way do most of the people of the Southeast make a living?
4. Where does the Gulf Stream originate?
5. What are the North Central states sometimes called?
6. Name three cities of the North Central states that are on the Great Lakes.
7. What state is the nation's leading producer of oil?
8. Name two states that have active volcanoes.
9. Why was the Alaska Pipeline built?
10. What formed the Hawaiian Islands?

4
Canada

From east to west, Canada reaches from the island of Newfoundland in the Atlantic Ocean to Alaska and the Pacific Ocean. It reaches from the Arctic Ocean in the north to the United States in the south.

History and Government

The first European explorers to reach the eastern shores of Canada were the Vikings. However, they left no permanent settlements. It was more than 500 years before other Europeans came to explore Canada.

Early History

The first permanent European settlement in Canada was made by the French at Quebec (kwĭbek') in 1608. Other French settlements were made at Montreal and in the lands along the Atlantic. Quebec was built on a bluff overlooking the St. Lawrence River. It became the most important city in New France, as the eastern area of Canada was then called.

The English also had a claim to the area. In 1497, John Cabot, who sailed for the English, explored the eastern shores of what is now Canada. The English sent other explorers and later they made settlements near the Atlantic. As time went on, the power of the English grew. In 1713, the British captured the French settlements along the Atlantic coast. Then, in 1759, they captured Quebec. By 1763, they ruled New France.

Independence

Some colonists in Canada rebelled against the British in 1837 and 1838. Between 1840 and 1848, new laws were passed that gave the colonists more voice in the government. With their new freedoms, the colonists did not press for independence. Canada did not fight a war to gain its freedom from Great Britain. In 1867, the British government passed a law recognizing the new nation of Canada. Sir John Alexander Macdonald became the first prime minister. Canada has always maintained strong ties with Great Britain.

Government

Canada is made up of ten provinces and two territories. Provinces are like states of the United States.

The laws for the whole country are made by a parliament, which is much like Congress. Each province also has its own law-making body. The head of the Canadian government is the prime minister. The prime minister is also a member of parliament. Ottawa is the capital of Canada.

Canada is a member of the Commonwealth of Nations. This is a group of nations made up of lands that were once a part of the British Empire. Canada, like the other Commonwealth nations, belongs to the Commonwealth by its own choice. The Commonwealth nations are joined by ties of trade and defense. They meet to discuss matters of mutual concern.

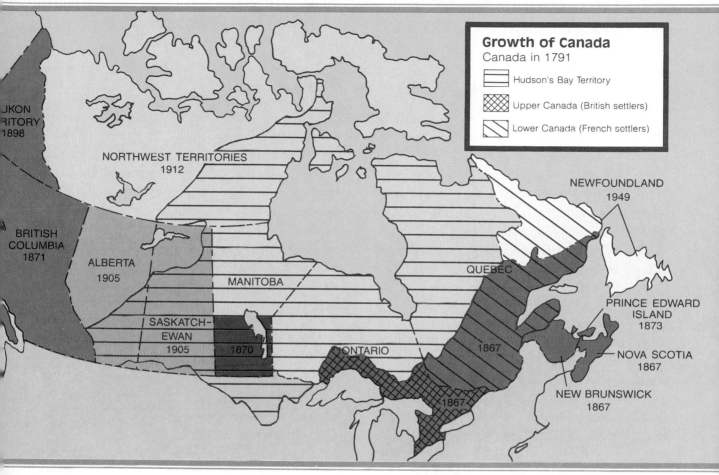

Growth of Canada
Canada in 1791

Hudson's Bay Territory

Upper Canada (British settlers)

Lower Canada (French settlers)

YUKON TERRITORY 1898

NORTHWEST TERRITORIES 1912

BRITISH COLUMBIA 1871

ALBERTA 1905

MANITOBA

SASKATCH-EWAN 1905

1870

ONTARIO

1867

QUEBEC

1867

NEWFOUNDLAND 1949

PRINCE EDWARD ISLAND 1873

NOVA SCOTIA 1867

NEW BRUNSWICK 1867

Alberta and Saskatchewan were created from parts of Hudson's Bay Territory. In 1912, other parts were added to Quebec, Ontario, and Manitoba.

Canada may be divided into five regions: the Atlantic provinces, Quebec and Ontario, the prairie provinces, British Columbia, and the northern territories.

The Atlantic Provinces

The Atlantic provinces are Newfoundland, Prince Edward Island, Nova Scotia (nō'və skō'shə), and New Brunswick. The Atlantic provinces are sometimes called the *maritime* (mar'ə tīm') provinces. *Maritime* means "bordering on or close to the sea." More than two million people live in the maritime provinces of Canada.

Newfoundland is Canada's newest province. When Canada became a nation, Newfoundland chose to remain a colony of Great Britain. It did not join Canada until 1949. Newfoundland includes the island of Newfoundland and part of the peninsula of Labrador. St. John's is the capital of Newfoundland.

Prince Edward Island, Canada's smallest province, is half the size of Connecticut. Charlottetown is its capital.

Nova Scotia is a peninsula. It is about as large as West Virginia. Halifax, a city of about 117,000 inhabitants, is its capital. Halifax is the largest city in the Atlantic provinces.

The province of New Brunswick lies northeast of Maine. Fredericton is the capital. New Brunswick is not quite as big as South Carolina.

Fishing and Lumbering

The people of Newfoundland make their living almost entirely by direct use of natural resources. They fish and they work in forests. The world-famous Grand Banks of Newfoundland are a continuation of the fishing banks off the New England coast. Fishing boats from Canada are joined on the fishing banks by vessels from New England, Nova Scotia, and even Europe. Cod is the chief fish along these rocky coasts. After the fish are caught, they are cleaned and dried. Dried fish can be easily shipped to markets.

Much of Newfoundland is covered by forests of spruce and fir. The soft wood of these trees is excellent for making wood pulp, from which paper is manufactured. Large pulp and paper mills are found in this province. Its rivers furnish water power.

Nova Scotia also has important fisheries. The interior of the Nova Scotia peninsula and the northern parts of New Brunswick are covered with great forests. Many people in these two provinces make a living by fishing and lumbering.

Regional Data Chart

Country	Capital	Area		Population	GNP (in millions of U.S. dollars)
		Square miles	Square kilometers		
Canada	Ottawa	3,851,809	9,976,185	24,000,000	$228,400
Iceland	Reykjavik	39,702	102,828	235,000	$2,400
United States	Washington, D.C.	3,615,122	9,363,166	226,505,000	$2,626,000

Nonindependent Area

Country	Capital	Square miles	Square kilometers	Population	GNP
Greenland (Denmark)	Nuuk	840,000	2,175,600	50,000	$390

Farming and Mining

Prince Edward Island, the coastal parts of Nova Scotia, and southern New Brunswick are good farming lands. The summers in these provinces are too cool for many kinds of crops to be raised, but hay, some kinds of fruit, and potatoes grow well. Most farmers specialize in dairying. They sell their milk to factories that make butter and cheese for export to Great Britain. New Brunswick raises many potatoes. The potato fields of this province join the important potato-growing lands in Maine.

Nova Scotia has fine apple orchards. Many of this region's agricultural products are shipped to markets in Great Britain.

Newfoundland has large iron mines near the sea. The island has no coal for smelting the iron ore, so the ore is shipped by water to England, to steel mills on the east coast of the United States, and to Nova Scotia. The steel mills of Nova Scotia have been built near its coal fields. Nova Scotia also ships its coal to Quebec and other Canadian cities by way of the Atlantic Ocean and the St. Lawrence River.

Halifax is an important seaport during the winter when the St. Lawrence River is frozen over and ships cannot reach Quebec and Montreal. In winter the seaport of Saint John, New Brunswick, is also busy. During the cold weather cargoes are brought to these ice-free ports and then shipped by rail.

Quebec and Ontario

The St. Lawrence lowland is the heart of Canada. It is the most heavily populated part of the nation.

The St. Lawrence Valley lies mainly in the province of Quebec. The plain north of lakes Erie and Ontario extends westward to Lake

Huge freighters like this one pass from the Great Lakes to the Atlantic Ocean through the St. Lawerence Seaway. This ship is beside a loading dock.

Huron in Ontario. The rivers of this area flow into the St. Lawrence River or into the Great Lakes, which drain into the St. Lawrence. Nearly all the inhabitants of the two provinces live in the St. Lawrence Valley or on the plain in Ontario. Seven of Canada's largest cities are in this region.

The Great Lakes are connected by rivers, but the rivers are not navigable. Canals with locks have been built so that ships can pass from lake to lake. The locks are necessary because the levels of the Great Lakes are not the same.

The canals make it possible for ships to go from Lake Superior through the other Great Lakes and out the St. Lawrence to the Atlantic. The governments of the United States and Canada cooperated to deepen and widen this water route, known as the St. Lawrence Seaway, so that it could be used by large ocean-going ships. The seaway was completed and opened to shipping in 1959.

French and British Influences

Many people of the St. Lawrence Valley, which was first settled by the French, speak French and continue to follow old French customs. The descendants of the French settlers are still French in their ways of living.

About 80 percent of the people in Quebec are of French descent. Many city dwellers in Quebec use English in their business dealings but speak French at home and in social gatherings. Many French-speaking people would like Quebec to have more independence from the Canadian government. Some would even like

Montreal, Canada's largest city, has strong French influences. What indicates that Canada is *bilingual* ?

Quebec to secede from, or be separated from, the rest of Canada. This question has been the cause of much hard feeling in the country.

Most of the settlers on the Ontario plain came from Great Britain. A large number of people loyal to Great Britain left the United States during and after the American Revolution and moved to this area. Later, people from the Atlantic provinces moved to the region.

Cities of Quebec

Quebec and Montreal are the two most important cities on the St. Lawrence River. Quebec, the capital of the province of Quebec, is a port. It can be reached by large ocean ships in the summer. During the winter, however, the river is closed by ice.

The city has two parts. One part is high up on a great cliff. It is called Upper Town. This part of the city has many old French buildings, including a fort. Upper Town is surrounded by a wall.

Below, near the water's edge, is Lower Town. Its narrow cobblestone streets, little houses crowded together, and its old churches are very much like those in France. Although Quebec is in North America, it is in many ways a French city.

Southwest of Quebec is Three Rivers, another old city on the St. Lawrence. Today it is important as a paper-manufacturing city, as are many other towns along the St. Lawrence. The paper mills use spruce and fir wood brought down the river from forests to the north. These mills manufacture paper for newspapers. Such paper is called newsprint.

Montreal is Canada's largest city, chief seaport, and leading banking and manufacturing center. A wide variety of products is manufactured in the city and its suburbs. Large new oil refineries receive and process oil from overseas and from the United States. The city has huge flour mills, great stockyards, and large meat-packing plants. The metropolitan area of Montreal covers much of the island on which the city is built. The city, which is 1,000 miles (1,600 km) from the open Atlantic, is the largest seaport in the country.

Cities of Ontario

Several large and many small cities are in the St. Lawrence lowland of Ontario. One of these is Ottawa, the capital of Canada. Ottawa also has important paper and lumber industries. Many electronics products are also made there.

Toronto, the chief city and capital of Ontario, lies on the north shore of Lake Ontario. The city is Canada's second largest. It is a great transportation center and manufacturing city. There are several reasons for Toronto's growth in importance. It has a fine harbor on Lake Ontario. It is served by many railroads. It lies in the center of a fine farming district. It receives cheap electric power from Niagara Falls. The city has grown as the St. Lawrence Seaway has come to be used more and more.

Hamilton is a steel city. Iron ore is brought to its mills by ships on the Great Lakes. Windsor, opposite Detroit, manufactures automobiles. London is the trading center of a rich farming region.

Mining, Lumbering, and Farming

The northern part of Quebec and Ontario is a region of lakes and forests that is part of the Canadian Shield, or Laurentian upland. The few towns of the area are lumber towns or mining towns.

The Canadian Shield is Canada's principal storehouse of minerals. Mines yield iron ore, nickel, gold, silver, and *cobalt* (kō'bôlt). Cobalt is a heavy and strong metal that does not rust or tarnish. Because cobalt can retain its hardness up to temperatures of 1,000° F. (538° C), it is used, mixed with other metals, in making jet engines and gas turbines. Cobalt is also used in making magnets, paints, varnishes, and medicine. More than 90 percent of the world's nickel comes from Ontario.

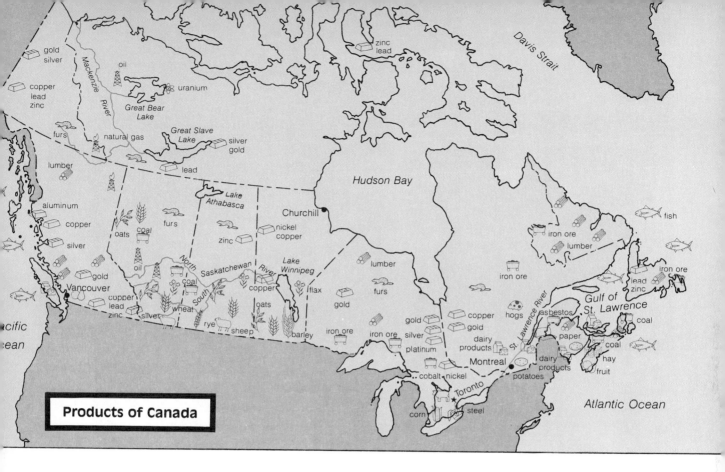

Products of Canada

Canada also has much platinum, a silvery-white precious metal. It is used chiefly for jewelry, but it is also used in the chemical industry.

Abundant water power has aided the industrial development of Quebec province. Large aluminum plants are located on the Saguenay (sag'ə nā') River. Canada imports the bauxite from which aluminum is made. The nation's great water-power resources make it possible to generate the electric power to produce aluminum at low cost.

The world's largest deposits of asbestos are in southern Quebec. Asbestos is a mineral used in making fireproof products.

Farms line the St. Lawrence River from its source in Lake Ontario to the Gulf of St. Lawrence—a distance of 750 miles (1,200 km). The lowlands of Quebec are quite cool in

summer. The farmers there sell milk to factories that make butter and cheese. Much of the farmland is pasture for the dairy cows. Potatoes are a principal crop. Sugar is made from the sap of the maple trees of the region.

The lowlands of Ontario extend farther south than do those of Quebec, and the climate is warmer. The farmers of Ontario raise dairy and beef cattle. They grow corn, wheat, and other grains. They also raise tobacco, which is processed in Canadian factories.

The Prairie Provinces

The provinces of Manitoba, Saskatchewan, and Alberta are called the prairie provinces. Winnipeg is the capital of Manitoba, Regina of Saskatchewan, and Edmonton of Alberta. The prairie provinces are Canada's great western

Combines harvest wheat on the plains of Saskatchewan. The prairie provinces produce most of Canada's grain.

farming lands. They are a part of the Great Plains that extend south into the United States. More than four million people live in these three provinces.

The prairie provinces were sparsely settled until 1885. In that year, the first Canadian transcontinental railroad was completed, and people began to move into western Canada in large numbers. Farmers from Europe, eastern Canada, and the United States settled there. By 1910, most of the farmland had been claimed. Today the prairies contain more crop land than any other section of Canada.

Cities of the Prairie Provinces

The cities of the prairie provinces serve as business centers for the farmers. Winnipeg is the largest city and leading commercial center. Regina, Saskatoon, Calgary, and Edmonton are the other chief cities. Mining industries provide jobs for many of the people who live in Alberta's cities.

The western edge of Alberta reaches to the Canadian Rockies. Many people in the town of Banff and on Lake Louise make their living by taking care of tourists.

Farming and Mining

The farmers of the prairie provinces grow wheat, rye, barley, oats, and flax, but wheat is by far the most important crop. Canada is one of the important wheat countries of the world.

Most of the wheat from western Canada is shipped east by rail to Lake Superior. There it is put on ships to be sent abroad. Wheat from the prairies is also sent by railroad to the seaport of Churchill, on Hudson Bay. There it is transferred to ocean vessels for shipment to Europe and elsewhere. Because ice forms in Hudson Bay in October or November, the time after harvest in which the Hudson Bay route can be used is very short.

Alberta has important coal and oil fields. Canada's greatest oil fields lie in this province.

British Columbia

British Columbia borders on the Pacific. This province is mountainous. It includes the western slope of the Rocky Mountains in the east and the Coast Mountains in the west. Long valleys lie between these mountain ranges. The Columbia River begins in British Columbia and flows through the United States to reach the Pacific. Another large river, the Fraser, flows through British Columbia and reaches the ocean near the port of Vancouver. Heavy rainfall and large rivers furnish British Columbia with abundant water power.

The coastline of British Columbia is indented by bays with numerous islands. The largest island is Vancouver.

Cities of British Columbia

Most of the people of British Columbia live in the southern part of the province. Vancouver is British Columbia's most important city and seaport. The western terminal of the Canadian Pacific Railway is Vancouver. This city has a large, ice-free harbor. It exports great shiploads of wheat and carries on an important shipping trade with the Far East. Vancouver is the lumbering center of British Columbia.

At the southeastern tip of Vancouver Island is the beautiful city of Victoria. It is the capital of British Columbia. The city is famous for its beautiful English gardens.

Farming, Fishing, Lumbering, and Mining

Most of the people of British Columbia live on ranches, in lumber camps, and in mining districts. Hay, potatoes, oats, and a little wheat are grown. Near Vancouver and Victoria are dairy farms. The Fraser Valley has fine fruit farms.

Along the coast are the great salmon and halibut fisheries of the Pacific. The chief fishing grounds are near Vancouver and the Queen Charlotte Islands. The Pacific coast of Canada produces almost as much fish as does its Atlantic coast. Many people in British Columbia work in the fishing industry.

The forests of British Columbia produce about one half of Canada's lumber. Much of the lumber is used to make newsprint.

British Columbia has deposits of gold, silver, copper, zinc, and lead. Soon after the gold rush to California, gold was discovered in British Columbia along the Fraser River.

In 1954, an aluminum plant was completed at Kitimat, about 400 miles (640 km) north of Vancouver. Docks were built on the coast to receive bauxite from South America. The Kitimat plant is one of the world's largest aluminum plants.

The Northern Territories

The northern part of Canada is divided into two territories. These territories do not yet have enough people to become provinces. Yukon Territory borders Alaska on the west. The Northwest Territories stretch across the rest of northern Canada.

The forests end in the southern part of northern Canada. The mosses of the Arctic tundra cover much of this section. Reindeer, caribou, and other animals live there.

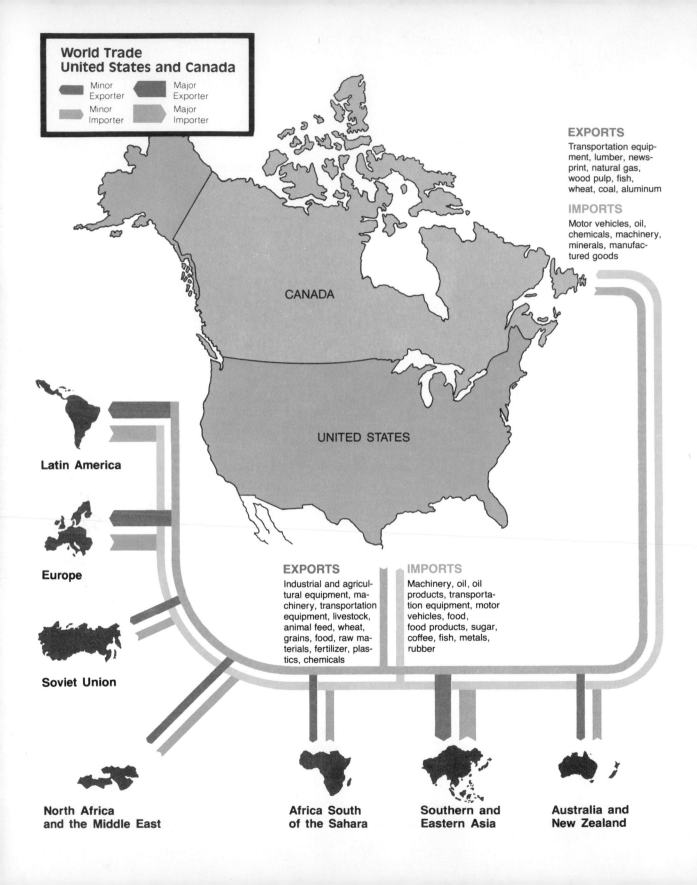

World Trade
United States and Canada

Minor Exporter
Major Exporter
Minor Importer
Major Importer

CANADA

UNITED STATES

Latin America

Europe

Soviet Union

North Africa
and the Middle East

Africa South
of the Sahara

Southern and
Eastern Asia

Australia and
New Zealand

EXPORTS
Transportation equipment, lumber, newsprint, natural gas, wood pulp, fish, wheat, coal, aluminum

IMPORTS
Motor vehicles, oil, chemicals, machinery, minerals, manufactured goods

EXPORTS
Industrial and agricultural equipment, machinery, transportation equipment, livestock, animal feed, wheat, grains, food, raw materials, fertilizer, plastics, chemicals

IMPORTS
Machinery, oil, oil products, transportation equipment, motor vehicles, food, food products, sugar, coffee, fish, metals, rubber

This small town lies on Greenland's east coast near the Arctic Circle. Colorful frame houses relieve the monotony of the frozen landscape.

The Yukon and Northwest Territories account for more than one-third of Canada's land area. Less than 1 percent of the population lives there. Most of Canada's Eskimos are included in this figure. No roads or railroads reach this distant region.

The territories are rich in zinc, natural gas, lead, gold, and silver. Canada has become a leading nation in the mining of uranium. On Great Bear Lake, at Port Radium, there is an important uranium ore deposit. One of the world's largest lead and zinc mines is on an Arctic island 875 miles (1,400 km) from the North Pole.

Greenland and Iceland

Greenland and Iceland are northeastern neighbors of the United States and Canada. Both countries are islands in the North Atlantic.

Greenland

Greenland is more than one-fourth as large as the United States. It is the largest island in the world. Most of Greenland is covered by a thick icecap. More than 50,000 people inhabit the island. Their homes are along the cold and rocky shore. Most of them earn a living by fishing. Greenland has some farms, and wheat, potatoes, and vegetables are grown there. Sheep are also raised. There are no forests.

Greenland is a province of Denmark. Nearly all the inhabitants are of both Eskimo and Danish descent.

Greenland is important for two reasons. One is that it lies on both the northern air route to western Europe and the air route across the North Pole to the Soviet Union. Meteorologists in Greenland can forecast the weather and warn navigators of storms. The second reason for Greenland's importance is its *cryolite* (krī′ə lĭt′). Cryolite is a mineral used in refining aluminum. Greenland has the only important cryolite deposits in the world.

Iceland

Iceland, 200 miles (320 km) east of Greenland, is an island with an area as large as that of Kentucky. From its name, you might expect that Iceland, like Greenland, is a land of ice and snow. Iceland does have mountain glaciers, but it also has farms and good pastures.

Iceland was settled by the Vikings, more than 1,000 years ago. As the population grew, its leaders formed a law-making council. Through this council the people developed a form of self-government that has been in operation since the year 930 A.D.

Iceland was once united with Norway. Between 1918 and 1944, Iceland was a self-governing country united with Denmark. In an election in 1944, the people voted for complete independence. Reykjavik (rāk′yə vēk′) is the republic's capital city and chief seaport.

About 235,000 people live in Iceland. Their language, Icelandic, is much like Danish. Out of every ten people in Iceland, one is a farmer, one fishes for a living, and eight work in industry. Fish processing is one of the important industries. Great quantities of fish are shipped to Europe. Hay and potatoes are the leading crops, and cattle and sheep are raised.

Iceland is sometimes called the "land of fire and ice" because hot springs, geysers, and volcanoes lie next to large glaciers. Geothermal power is used to warm houses in Reykjavik by piping heat from the hot springs and volca-

A geothermal power plant in Iceland taps the energy of hot springs. Steam turns turbines to generate electricity.

noes. Greenhouses are also heated in this way. Fruits and vegetables are grown in the greenhouses.

Iceland, like Greenland, lies on the northern air routes across the Atlantic. The airport at Reykjavik serves as a landing and refueling station.

Do You Know?

1. When did Canada become an independent nation?
2. In what province of Canada are most of the people of French descent?
3. What is the most important crop of the prairie provinces?
4. What country has the world's only important cryolite deposits?

136

To Help You Learn

Using New Words

maritime	cobalt
bayou	butte
cryolite	conterminous
industrial crop	negotiations
fishing banks	urbanization

Number a paper from 1 through 10. After each number write the word or term from the above list that matches the definition.

1. A plant or plant product that is used in manufacturing
2. Discussions for the purpose of bringing about an agreement
3. A heavy and strong metal that does not rust or tarnish
4. A mineral used in refining aluminum
5. Bordering on or close to the sea
6. Fairly shallow parts of the ocean where fish are usually plentiful
7. A flat-topped hill with steep sides that is smaller than a mesa
8. The change from rural to urban living
9. Contained within the same boundaries
10. A marshy creek or sluggish backwater swamp

Finding the Facts

1. How do the United States and Canada rank in size among the nations of the world?
2. What landforms are found in the inter-mountain region of North America?
3. What is the largest river system of North America?
4. Why did Spain have to give up its claim to Florida after the French and Indian War?
5. How many states had to ratify the Constitution before it became law?
6. Why did the Northeast become a region of many cities?
7. What is the chief product of Pittsburgh?
8. What are two important industrial crops of the Southeast?
9. What are the important industries of Akron, Youngstown, and Detroit?
10. What is an occupation of many people in the bayou region of Mississippi?
11. How was the Grand Canyon formed?
12. How does the cold ocean current affect the climate of San Francisco?
13. What states are not part of the conterminous United States? How many states are part of the continental United States?
14. How is Canada's government organized?
15. Where are many of the mineral resources in Canada found?
16. What are the two Canadian territories? Why are they not provinces?
17. Greenland is governed by what country?
18. How is geothermal power used in Iceland?

Learning from Maps

1. Look at the map on page 125. What four provinces existed in 1867? In what year did British Columbia become a province? What area was the last to become a province? In what year?

2. Look at the map on page 134. What regions are major trading partners of the United States and Canada? What products does the United States import as well as export? What products are major exports of Canada but not of the United States?

3. Look at the map on page 103. This map shows the geographic and population centers of the United States.

   The geographic center of a region is a balance point. Imagine that the United States is a sheet of paper. The point on which the sheet balances is the geographic center. What geographic centers are shown on the map? Where is the geographic center of the conterminous United States?

   The population center of a region is also a balance point, but it is a balance point for the distribution of people. Imagine that the people of the United States all weigh the same and that they are on a weightless platform. The point on which the platform balances is the population center. In what general direction has the center of population of the United States been moving since 1790? During what ten-year period did the center of population first move west of the Mississippi? Is the center of population of the United

States today east or west of the geographic center of the conterminous United States?

Using Study Skills

1. **Library Resources:**   A biographical dictionary is a reference book that contains short biographies of famous people. Biographical dictionaries may contain many thousands of entries about famous people from all times and all countries. These reference books may include only a few lines about each person, giving only the most important dates and events in the person's life. Locate a biographical dictionary in your school or public library. Use it to write a few facts about John Jay and Sir John Alexander Macdonald.

2. **Chart:**   A distance chart shows the distance between cities in miles or kilometers. Look at the chart on page 139. The cities are listed in alphabetical order. Suppose you want to know the distance between Chicago and Washington, D.C. Move one finger down the row of boxes under *Chicago*. Move another finger across the row of boxes left of *Washington, D.C.* The box where your fingers meet gives the distance between the two cities. Chicago is 709 miles (1,141 km) from Washington, D.C.

   Use the chart to answer the following questions: What is the distance between Houston and New York? Between Miami and Chicago? Between Washington, D.C. and Denver? Which is farther from Los

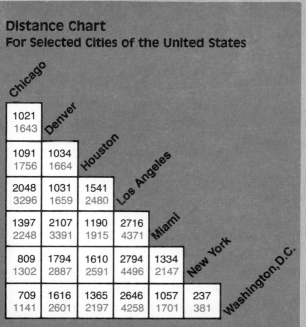

Distance Chart
For Selected Cities of the United States

Chicago	Denver	Houston	Los Angeles	Miami	New York	Washington, D.C.
1021 / 1643						
1091 / 1756	1034 / 1664					
2048 / 3296	1031 / 1659	1541 / 2480				
1397 / 2248	2107 / 3391	1190 / 1915	2716 / 4371			
809 / 1302	1794 / 2887	1610 / 2591	2794 / 4496	1334 / 2147		
709 / 1141	1616 / 2601	1365 / 2197	2646 / 4258	1057 / 1701	237 / 381	

Explanation
Black figures indicate miles. Red figures indicate kilometers. Figures given are for the shortest land routes between cities.

Angeles, Miami or Washington, D.C.? How much farther?

3. **Graph:** Look at the graph on page 88. What kind of graph is it? What does the graph show? For what years does the graph give information about the United States? About Canada?

The steepness of the lines on the graph indicates the rate of growth. The steepest lines indicate the fastest growth rates. Which country has had a faster growth rate?

In what ten-year period did the population first exceed 20 million in the United States? In Canada? In what ten-year period did the population of the United States first exceed 200 million?

Thinking It Through

1. The United States government has set aside many areas as national parks. What is the possible value of such a policy? What might have happened to these areas if they had not been protected?

2. Compare the history, government, and official languages of the United States and Canada. How do they differ? What do they have in common?

Projects

1. The Biography Committee might like to read more about the French explorers Samuel de Champlain and Sieur Duluth. Lake Champlain and the city of Duluth were named in honor of the explorers who first visited the areas where they are located. A biographical dictionary might be a good place to begin research about these two men.

2. The History Committee might like to do some research about North American forts. They could prepare a map showing where each of the following forts was located and the date when it was built: Fort Duquesne, Fort Dearborn, Fort Frontenac, Fort Necessity, Fort Niagara, Fort Ticonderoga, Fort Wellington, Fort William.

If there is a fort in your area, you might like to include it on your map.

4 Latin America

Unit Preview

Latin America includes Mexico, Central America, the West Indies, and South America. The region has both temperate and tropical climates. The mighty Amazon River, the towering Andes Mountains, and many lush islands are all found in Latin America.

The countries of Latin America share many traditions and customs. Much of their culture has been influenced by Europe. Spanish and Portuguese, which are based on Latin, are the two most widely spoken languages.

When European explorers first arrived in Latin America in the fifteenth century, they found Indians living there. The Mayas in Central America and the Yucatán, the Aztecs in Mexico, and the Incas in South America, all had highly developed civilizations.

European settlers soon followed the explorers. Spain, Portugal, France, the Netherlands, and Great Britain set up colonies in Latin America. Many Africans were brought in to work on the plantations. The people of Latin America today are the descendants of Europeans, Africans, and Indians.

Latin American colonies began to gain independence in the early 1800s. Today most countries in the region are independent.

In the past, most Latin Americans made their living by farming. Agriculture is still important, but industrialization is bringing change to many areas.

Things to Discover

If you look carefully at the picture, map, and time line, you can answer these questions.

1. The highlighted area on the map shows Latin America. On what continents are these lands?
2. Is more of Latin America in the Northern or in the Southern Hemisphere?
3. The Aztecs and Mayans had flourishing civilizations in America before Columbus arrived in the West Indies. The photograph shows the ruins of a Mayan city in Mexico. Spanish control of Mexico began when Cortés conquered the Aztec leader Montezuma. How long did Mexico remain under Spanish rule?
4. When was the Panama Canal completed?

Words to Learn

You will meet these words and terms in this unit. As you read, you will learn what they mean and how to pronounce them. The Word List will help you.

altiplano	fazenda
archipelago	junta
buffer state	nationalize
cash crop	selva
conquistador	sisal
cordillera	subsistence farming
coup	tourism
estancia	vanadium

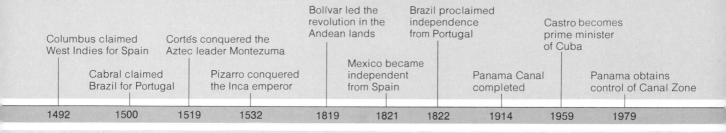

Columbus claimed West Indies for Spain	Cabral claimed Brazil for Portugal	Cortés conquered the Aztec leader Montezuma	Pizarro conquered the Inca emperor	Bolívar led the revolution in the Andean lands	Mexico became independent from Spain	Brazil proclaimed independence from Portugal	Panama Canal completed	Castro becomes prime minister of Cuba	Panama obtains control of Canal Zone
1492	1500	1519	1532	1819	1821	1822	1914	1959	1979

Arctic Ocean

NORTH AMERICA

Pacific Ocean

EQUATOR

Atlantic Ocean

SOUTH AMERICA

ANTARCTICA

1

The Land and the People of Latin America

The vast region called Latin America covers parts of both North America and South America. Latin America begins at the Rio Grande and extends south to Cape Horn at the tip of South America. Most of this region was colonized by Spain and Portugal. *Latin* refers to the Spanish and Portuguese languages, both of which are based on Latin. Spanish and Portuguese are widely spoken throughout Latin America today.

Latin America includes about 14 percent of the world's land. It is made up of Mexico and Central America in North America, the islands of the West Indies, and the continent of South America. Find these places on the maps on pages 149 and 163.

Latin America is not a densely populated region, but its population is growing quickly. The people come from a variety of backgrounds. The largest number of people are of European descent. Indians, blacks, and people of mixed backgrounds make up the rest of the population. Industrialization, improvements in transportation and communication, and new political systems are bringing about many changes in Latin America. Many areas, however, have remained isolated.

The Land of Latin America

Mexico and Central America occupy the southern part of North America. The Isthmus (is′məs) of Panama in the south of Central America links the continents of North America and South America. The West Indies is a long chain of islands stretching from Florida to the northern coast of South America. South America, the world's fourth-largest continent, is shaped somewhat like a triangle. Brazil, which is larger than the conterminous United States, is the largest Latin American country.

Landforms and Climate

Rugged chains of mountains extend from Mexico through Central America. They continue as the Andes down the west coast of South America. The Andes are the longest mountain chain in the world. A long mountain chain such as the Andes is a *cordillera* (kôr dil′ə rə). The principal mountain range of a continent is often called a cordillera. The Andes are higher than the mountains of North America, but they are not as high as the Himalayas. Many peaks in the Andes rise more than 20,000 feet (6,000 m) above sea level. Volcanoes are found in the Andes, as well as in the mountains of Mexico and Central America.

There are several large highland areas in Latin America. A high plateau extends through much of Mexico, and smaller plateaus lie among the mountains of Central America. In South America, the Guiana (gē ä′nə) Highlands extend across the north from Venezuela (ven′ə zwā′lə) into Brazil. The Brazilian Highlands in eastern South America are lower than the highlands of Patagonia in the far south.

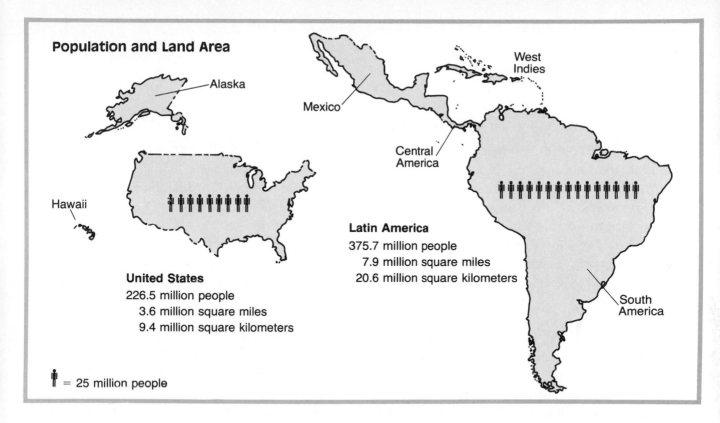

Population and Land Area

Alaska

Mexico

West Indies

Central America

Hawaii

Latin America
375.7 million people
7.9 million square miles
20.6 million square kilometers

South America

United States
226.5 million people
3.6 million square miles
9.4 million square kilometers

= 25 million people

The mountains and highlands have a great effect on the climate. Even though most of Latin America lies in the tropics, it is not hot everywhere. High altitudes in many parts of the region keep the temperatures cool.

The largest plain in South America stretches from the Atlantic to the Andes across Brazil. Here in the rain forest, temperatures are high throughout the year and rainfall is heavy. Savannas border the rain forest to the north and south. In Argentina, large grassy plains called the pampas have a temperate climate. Extensive plains in Venezuela, the llanos (län′ōs), have more rainfall than the pampas. Both *pampa* and *llano* mean "plain" in Spanish.

Coastal lowlands border most of Latin America. In general, the coastal plains are narrower along the western, or Pacific, coasts than they are in the east. The driest desert in the world, the Atacama, extends along the coast of Chile and Peru.

Some of the islands in the West Indies are tops of sunken mountain ranges. Others were formed by volcanoes or built up by coral. The climate is tropical and rainy.

Water Features

Latin America lies between the Atlantic Ocean on the east and the Pacific Ocean on the west. The cold Peru Current moving along the Pacific coast of South America cools the land. The Caribbean Sea is an arm of the Atlantic that is bounded by the West Indies on the north and east, and by Central America and South America on the west and south. The Caribbean Sea connects with the Gulf of Mexico to the northwest. Mexico lies west of the gulf.

Except for the Rio Grande, the rivers of Mexico, Central America, and the West Indies are short and not navigable. In South America, there are three great river systems. The Amazon, which drains an immense tropical lowland, is 4,000 miles (6,400 km) long. It is the second longest river in the world. North, in Venezuela, the Orinoco (ôr′ə nō′kō) River drains the flat grasslands of the llanos. The third great river system is the Río de la Plata in the southeast. The Río de la Plata is an estuary, or arm of the sea. Several rivers, including the Paraná (par′ə nä′), the Uruguay (yoor′ə gwā′), and the Paraguay (par′ə gwā′), are part of the Río de la Plata system.

Lake Titicaca (tē′tē kä′kə), on the border between Bolivia and Peru, and Lake Nicaragua (nik′ə räg′wə), in Central America, are the largest lakes in Latin America. Each lake has a surface area of slightly more than 3,000 square miles (8,000 sq. km). Lake Maracaibo (mar′ə kī′bō), in northern Venezuela, which is larger than either of these lakes, is really an extension of the Gulf of Venezuela.

The People of Latin America

The earliest inhabitants of Latin America were Indians. Christopher Columbus was the first European to reach the area. He landed in the West Indies in 1492 and claimed the islands for Spain. Soon after Columbus, other explorers from Europe began coming to the Western Hemisphere. During the 1500s, the Spanish ranged through Mexico, Central America, much of South America, and parts of what are now the United States. Settlers soon followed these explorers in large numbers. Many of the people of Latin America today are the descendants of the settlers and the Indians who lived in the region.

Indians in the Americas

Millions of Indians were living in the Western Hemisphere when the first European settlers came. The lands south of the Gulf of Mexico had far more people than northern North America. In Mexico and Central America, there were at least three or four million Indians. South America had not less than another four or five million.

Some Indian groups had highly developed civilizations. These included the Aztecs of central Mexico, the Mayas of Guatemala and the Yucatán Peninsula, and the Incas of the Andean plateaus.

The Aztecs, Mayas, and Incas built large cities. They constructed good roads and fine temples. Ruins of many of their buildings may still be seen today in Mexico, Guatemala, and Peru. Artworks of these early civilizations are displayed in museums.

The Aztecs, Mayas, and Incas had learned how to make a good living from the land. They cut terraces into the hillsides and used irrigation to increase the amount of land that could be farmed. The chief crops were maize, or corn, and potatoes. Neither corn nor potatoes were known in Europe until they were sent there from America.

Not all Indians were farmers. Skilled craftsmen produced fine textiles, ornaments of gold and silver, and pottery.

The rulers of the Aztecs and the Incas controlled large empires. The people paid taxes by working on government projects, by building roads and bridges, and by giving part of their goods and crops to the government.

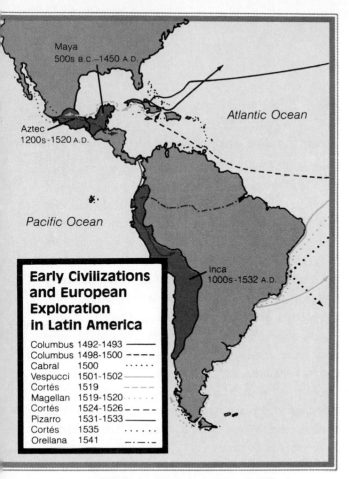

Early Civilizations and European Exploration in Latin America

Columbus	1492-1493	———
Columbus	1498-1500	— — —
Cabral	1500	· · · · · ·
Vespucci	1501-1502	———
Cortés	1519	———
Magellan	1519-1520	· — · — ·
Cortés	1524-1526	— — —
Pizarro	1531-1533	———
Cortés	1535	· · · · · ·
Orellana	1541	— · · — · ·

Three important Indian civilizations existed in the Americas before Columbus arrived there. What early explorers encountered each?

The Mayas had a system of city governments. Their rulers were also priests.

Religion was an important part of Indian life. There were ceremonies at times of planting and harvest.

The Aztecs and Mayas developed written languages. Scientists have not yet been able to decipher the ancient writing, which looks something like Egyptian hieroglyphics.

Other Indians, like the Chibchas of Colombia, lived in more simple societies. Some of them farmed, and others lived by hunting and fishing.

European Exploration

The first Spaniards came to the Western Hemisphere to find gold and silver rather than to make settlements. The island of Hispaniola became the Spanish base of exploration in the Americas. The city of Santo Domingo was founded there by the Spanish in 1496. It is the oldest city founded by Europeans in the Americas. Spanish explorers sailed to Santo Domingo and then set out on their expeditions of conquest. A Spanish conqueror in Latin America during the sixteenth century was called a *conquistador* (kon kēs′tə dôr′). The conquistadors set out to gain land for Spain, but they were also after gold and silver. They rode horses, which the Indians had never seen before, and had cannons and guns.

Hernando Cortés was a conquistador who sailed to Mexico in 1519. With a small army of about 600 Spaniards and 1,000 Indian allies, he conquered Montezuma, the great Aztec leader. Cortés imprisoned Montezuma and ruled the vast Aztec empire. He later brought much of what is now Mexico under his control.

From Mexico, the Spaniards pushed south to the land of the Mayas in what is now Guatemala. The Spanish soon controlled the entire region.

Another conquistador, Francisco Pizarro (fran sis′kō pi zär′ō), marched into the Inca empire of Peru. In 1532 he captured the Inca emperor. Pizarro demanded a huge ransom in gold and silver as the price for giving the emperor his freedom. After receiving the treasure, Pizarro had the emperor killed. Then he established Spanish rule over the Incas.

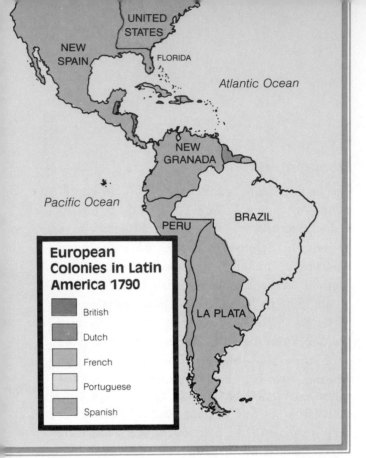

By 1790, European nations had claimed all of Latin America as colonies. Which country controlled the largest area?

Colonization and Independence

The period of exploration that began in 1500 was also a period of colonization. Between 1500 and 1800, huge numbers of Spaniards and Portuguese settled in Latin America. The rulers of Spain and Portugal gave large grants of land to members of the nobility who wished to settle in Latin America. These landowners developed large plantations where sugarcane, tobacco, and cacao were grown. The cacao tree produces beans from which chocolate and cocoa are made. Mining operations to extract gold and silver, emeralds, and diamonds were also important. Many people were needed to work on the plantations and in the mines. The landowners brought many people from Africa to work for them.

During the colonial period, most Latin American lands were controlled by Spain. Brazil, however, was claimed by Portugal. France controlled Hispaniola and other islands in the West Indies and an area on the northern coast of South America called French Guiana. The Netherlands claimed Dutch Guiana, an area west of the French coastal colony. The British had possessions in Central America and the West Indies.

Eighteen Latin American countries gained independence in the early 1800s. Since then, most of Latin America has become independent. The most recent lands to gain freedom are Suriname, in 1975, and Belize, in 1981.

Latin America Today

Today, more than 375 million people live in Latin America. They represent 8 percent of the

In the 1500s Spanish ships carried great treasures and riches from the conquered empires to Spain. The Caribbean Sea became a favorite hunting ground of pirates.

The Portuguese established their claim to land in the Americas in 1500. Pedro Cabral (pā′drō kə brāl′), a Portuguese sea captain, was on the way to the Far East when strong winds blew his ship off course. He landed on the eastern shore of what is now Brazil and claimed the land for Portugal. Look at the map on page 145 to find Cabral's route. It was not until 1532, however, that the first permanent Portuguese settlement in Brazil was made, near the present city of Santos, on the coast of southern Brazil.

This university in central Mexico is 250 years old. Its buildings are fine examples of Spanish colonial *architecture*.

guese and African backgrounds. The mestizos in Brazil have Portuguese and Indian ancestry.

In colonial times, large numbers of Africans were also taken to the West Indies as workers. Today most people in the West Indies are blacks or mulattoes. Many people of French descent also live there.

Spanish is the official language of most of Latin America, but Portuguese is the official language in Brazil. French, Dutch, and English are the languages in countries colonized by people who spoke them. In many countries, Indian languages are spoken.

Latin Americans make a living in a variety of ways. Agriculture is very important in most Latin American countries, and industry is expanding rapidly in some areas. Since World War II, the number of people living in cities has been growing significantly. Today about three-fifths of the people in Latin America live in urban areas.

world's population. The region's population is growing very fast.

Many people in Central America and western South America are descendants of Spanish or Indians, or are of mixed Spanish and Indian ancestry. People of mixed ancestry are called mestizos (mes tē′zōz).

In Argentina, Uruguay, and southern Brazil, the people are mainly of European ancestry. In early times, Africans were brought to Brazil to work on the sugar plantations. Many Brazilians today are mulattoes (mə lät′ōz), or people of mixed European and African ancestry. In Brazil, most mulattoes are of mixed Portu-

Do You Know?

1. In what two continents are the countries of Latin America?
2. What two countries colonized most of Latin America?
3. What is the name of the longest mountain chain in the world? Where is it found?
4. What early groups of Indians in the lands that are now part of Latin America had highly developed civilizations?

2

Mexico

Mexico lies between the United States on the north and Central America on the south. It is slightly less than one-fifth the size of the United States, and its population is more than 74 million. The majority of the people of Mexico live on a plateau in the central part of the country.

Geography

Mexico is mainly a highland country. A large interior plateau covers most of the northern and central parts. It lies between the Sierra Madre Occidental in the west and the Sierra Madre Oriental in the east. Find the plateau and these mountain ranges on the map of Mexico, Central America, and the West Indies on page 149. You can see that the plateau is wide in the north but that it becomes narrower to the south. The mountains meet just south of Mexico City. Southern Mexico is a mountainous region. There are basins and river valleys in the mountains.

A narrow coastal plain lies between the western Sierra Madre and the Pacific. A somewhat wider plain lies between the eastern Sierra Madre and the Gulf of Mexico. The coastal lowlands are hot. North of the Tropic of Cancer, they are dry. South of the Tropic of Cancer, they are humid, with swamps and dense forests.

Mexico has two important peninsulas. On the southeast, the peninsula of Yucatán juts out toward Cuba. On the west is the peninsula of Lower California, or Baja (bä′hä) California.

Mexico is generally a dry land. In northern Mexico, desert covers about one-fourth of the country. The southern three-fourths of Mexico has a rainy climate. Most of the area is in the part of the tropics that has a rainy season and a dry season. In the extreme south, it is rainy all year.

History and Government

The Spanish ruled Mexico for about 300 years after Cortés' conquest. The struggle for independence in Mexico began in 1810. It was influenced by the American and French revolutions. The Mexican revolution was led by a priest named Miguel Hidalgo y Costilla (mē gel′ ē däl′gō ē kōs tē′yä). Although Spanish troops executed Hidalgo the following year, the Mexican War of Independence continued. Finally, in 1821, independence was achieved. Mexico became a republic in 1824.

Mexico's most famous president was Benito Juárez (be nē′tō wär′ez). He is still one of the most honored leaders of Mexico. Juárez was an Indian who gained an education through his own efforts. He was president of Mexico at the time Abraham Lincoln was President of the United States. Juárez was interested in bringing about reforms in the government. He helped write a new constitution for Mexico. One of the reforms of the constitution was a

MEXICO, CENTRAL AMERICA, AND THE WEST INDIES

National Capitals ⊗
Other Cities •

Mountains
Plateaus
Hills
Plains

Miles
0   100   200   300   400
0 80 161 322   433   644
0 50 100
Kilometers

© Rand McNally & Co.

Mississippi

UNITED STATES

Houston

El Paso
Ciudad Juárez
Nuevo Laredo
Laredo
Rio Grande
Chihuahua
Monterrey
Torreón
Durango
Mazatlán
San Luis Potosí
Guadalajara

M E X I C O

SIERRA MADRE OCCIDENTAL
SIERRA MADRE ORIENTAL
SIERRA MADRE DEL SUR

Tampico
Veracruz
Mexico City
Puebla
Taxco
Oaxaca
Acapulco

GULF OF MEXICO
TROPIC OF CANCER

GULF OF CALIFORNIA
Lower California
PACIFIC OCEAN

Mérida
Yucatán Peninsula

BAHAMAS
Nassau
Miami

C U B A
GREATER ANTILLES
Havana
Camagüey
Santiago de Cuba

WEST INDIES
JAMAICA
Kingston

CARIBBEAN SEA

BELIZE
Belmopan
GUATEMALA
Guatemala City
HONDURAS
Tegucigalpa
EL SALVADOR
San Salvador
NICARAGUA
Managua
Lake Nicaragua
COSTA RICA
San José
Limón

CENTRAL AMERICA

PANAMA
Panama Canal
Panama City
Gulf of Panama

Barranquilla
Cartagena
Medellín

80°
90°
20°
10°

OCEAN

Inset map

60°
70°
20°
60°
10°

GREATER ANTILLES
HISPANIOLA
HAITI
Port-au-Prince
DOMINICAN REPUBLIC
Santo Domingo
PUERTO RICO
San Juan
Virgin Islands

LESSER ANTILLES
Leeward Islands
ANTIGUA
Guadeloupe
DOMINICA
Martinique
ST. LUCIA
BARBADOS
ST. VINCENT
Grenadines
GRENADA
Windward Islands

TRINIDAD AND TOBAGO
Port of Spain

Curaçao
Willemstad
Netherlands Antilles

CARIBBEAN SEA
WEST INDIES

Gulf of Venezuela

provision to break up the large estates in order to distribute the land among the people. At that time, a few wealthy landowners controlled much of the farmland in Mexico. Their large holdings were called haciendas (hä sē en'dəz). The haciendas had been kept in many of the same families since the time of the Spanish conquest. The farmers who worked on the haciendas received little or no pay.

Juárez died in 1872 before he could carry out his ideas. Four years later, Porfirio Díaz (dē'äs) led a revolt that overthrew the government. Díaz ruled as president for 30 years. He made no effort to carry out the reforms of the Juárez constitution. He jailed or killed many of his enemies. Yet under Díaz, Mexico made some progress. Mines were opened, oil wells were drilled, and railroads were built. Most Mexicans did not benefit from these improvements, however. Wages remained very low, and during this period the people lost many rights, such as the freedom of the press.

The Mexican people finally grew tired of the rule of Díaz. From 1910 to 1915, the country was torn by civil war. Díaz fled, and throughout Mexico bandit leaders controlled small armies. In time, order was restored. A new constitution was drawn up in 1917, making Mexico a democratic republic. The new constitution included more reforms than Juárez had dreamed possible. Many of the large estates were broken up. The rights of workers were defined, public education was provided for, and freedom of the press and free elections were guaranteed. A period of social and economic change had begun.

Living in Mexico

Traditionally, Mexico had been a farming country, and today many of the people are still farmers. Today, however, Mexico is becoming more industrialized. Reserves of minerals are being developed, and new jobs are being created. While industry has drawn many people to modern life in the large cities of Mexico, many other people still live in traditional ways in rural areas.

Agriculture

Arable land is not plentiful in Mexico. Much of the country is hard to farm because it is steep and rocky. Most farmers work small plots of land and produce only enough food for their own use. Producing only enough food to supply the necessities of life is called *subsistence farming* (səb sis'təns fär'ming). Subsistence farmers produce no significant surplus of crops that they can sell.

Land reform has helped put the land into the hands of the farmers. In 1917, under the new constitution, the government began to take over the haciendas and divide the land among the workers. The smaller units of land are called ejidos (ā hē'dōz). Several families or groups of families own and farm the ejidos. On some ejidos, the farmers share the work and the profits. On others, the farmers have their own pieces of land to work. Ejido farmers do not own the land. They have it only as long as they farm it. The government helps supply seeds, fertilizer, and farm machinery. It also finances irrigation projects. The majority of Mexicans live on ejidos.

The dry north of Mexico is a region of many cattle ranches. Irrigated lands in the northern and western parts of the country produce good crops of wheat and cotton.

The best farming lands in Mexico are in the southern part of the central plateau. Volcanic ash has produced fertile soil, and the climate is temperate. Most of the crops are grown during the rainy season. To the south and on the higher lands of the mountains, crops can be grown throughout the year because of the high rainfall.

Because of the range in altitude from tropical lowlands to cool highlands, Mexican farmers can raise many kinds of crops. Sugarcane and bananas do well on the hot coastal plains. Cotton and other warm-weather crops are grown on the central plateau. Cooler uplands grow wheat, and coffee is produced in the highlands. Corn and beans are grown on most farms.

In northern Yucatán, large crops of *sisal* (sī′səl) are grown. Sisal is a tropical plant that produces fibers used in making binding twine and bags. The leaves of the plant are cut, and the long fibers are removed.

Mining and Manufacturing

The mountains of Mexico are rich in minerals. Mexico is one of the world's leading silver-mining countries. It is the world's leading producer of fluorite (flôr′īt), a mineral used in making glass. Coal, copper, gold, iron ore, lead, sulfur, tin, and zinc are also mined. Some of Mexico's minerals are exported, but many are used locally to manufacture such products

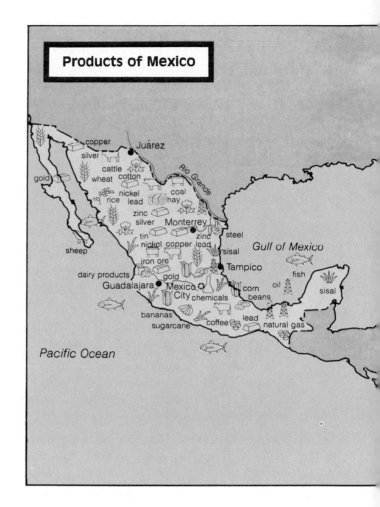

as medicines, chemicals, steel, fertilizers, farm machinery, and cement.

Petroleum is abundant in Mexico, and the oil industry is growing. In the early 1900s, foreign oil companies began to develop a large oil field along the Gulf of Mexico. In 1938, the government of Mexico decided to *nationalize* (nash′ən əlīz′) the oil industry. To nationalize means to change from private ownership to

The Plaza of the Three Cultures in Mexico City has Aztec ruins, a Spanish church of 1524, and modern buildings.

level. It is almost surrounded by mountains, some of which rise more than 10,000 feet (3,000 m) above the city.

Wide, tree-shaded avenues lead to the Plaza Mayor, or Great Plaza, at the center of the city. A beautiful cathedral, government buildings, old palaces, and many parks adorn the city. The steeples of numerous churches rise above the low buildings of the residential sections. On the edges of the city are the factories. Mexico City is a major industrial center.

Monterrey (mon'tə rā'), in the north, is the center of the Mexican iron and steel industries. Railroad cars and automobiles are made there. The city also has flour and cotton mills.

Puebla (pweb'lə), one of the oldest cities of Mexico, has a beautiful cathedral. Today, the city is a cotton-manufacturing center. Taxco (tas'cō) is famous for its silver and jewelry industries. Acapulco (ak'ə pool'kō) is a pleasant city on the Pacific Ocean that many tourists visit in winter. Veracruz, the chief port of Mexico, is on the gulf plain.

government ownership. The Mexican government now produces, refines, and sells the oil in Mexico. Crude oil is one of the nation's chief exports. In 1978, a new oil field was discovered in Mexico. Mexico's new reserves may be larger than those of Saudi Arabia.

Cities of Mexico

Mexico City, Mexico's capital and largest city, is also one of the largest cities in the world. More than nine million people live in Mexico City, which, like Washington, D.C., is in its own governmental district. The city lies on the central plateau, 7,400 feet (2,200 m) above sea

Do You Know?

1. What landform covers most of central and northern Mexico? What borders it on the west and east?
2. What country ruled Mexico for about 300 years? When was Mexican independence won?
3. Why is much of Mexico unsuitable for farming?
4. What is an ejido?

3

Central America and the West Indies

Central America is a strip of land 1,000 miles (1,600 km) long that stretches from Mexico to South America. Central America ranges in width from about 30 to 325 miles (48 to 520 km). The Panama Canal was cut through the isthmus at one of the narrowest places. The seven small countries of this region are Guatemala (gwä′təma′lə), Belize (beḻēz′), El Salvador, Honduras, Nicaragua, Costa Rica, and Panama.

The West Indies are a large group of islands, or *archipelago* (är′kəpel′əgō′). This chain of thousands of islands stretches for about 2,500 miles (4,000 km) in a curve that separates the Caribbean Sea from the Atlantic. There are three main groups of islands. They are the Greater Antilles, which include Cuba, Jamaica, Hispaniola, and Puerto Rico; the Lesser Antilles; and the Bahamas.

Geography of Central America

Mountain ranges stretch through Central America from Mexico to Panama. In a few places, notably in Guatemala and Nicaragua, small plateaus lie high above sea level between spurs of mountain ranges. The areas of high altitude have a cool climate.

A plain lies along the Caribbean coast of Central America. This plain, which is low, hot, and rainy, is covered by a dense, tropical forest. A narrower plain lies along the Pacific coast.

History of Central America

Indians lived in Central America for centuries before the Spanish came. The Indians who lived in an area now divided between Honduras, Guatemala, and Mexico were the Mayas.

The Mayas knew much about the positions of the sun, moon, and stars. They created a calendar, wrote numbers up to one million, and also had a form of picture writing. The Mayan civilization began to decline in the twelfth century for reasons that have never been fully understood. When the Mayas were conquered by the Spaniards in the sixteenth century, their way of life came to an end.

After 300 years of Spanish rule, Guatemala, El Salvador, Costa Rica, Honduras, and Nicaragua became independent in 1821. Mexico took control of these countries in the same year. Then they broke away from Mexico and joined together as the United Provinces of Central America. This union lasted from 1823 to 1825. By the middle 1800s, they were again independent countries.

Throughout the 1900s, many Central American countries have had trouble maintaining stable governments. Governments have often been replaced as a result of a *coup* (ko͞o), or a sudden, unexpected action that overthrows a government. In 1979, a coup in El Salvador brought a new government to power. The new government continued to be opposed by guerrillas, or bands of fighters, who disagreed with its policies and tried to overthrow it.

Living in Central America

Most of the people of Central America make their living on farms. Corn is the chief crop. Many are subsistence farmers, who raise only enough food to support themselves and their families.

Other farmers raise bananas or coffee as a *cash crop* (kash' krop'). A plant or plant product that is raised for income is called a cash crop. Bananas are grown on plantations on the tropical lowlands. Nearly all the bananas eaten in the United States come from Central America. Coffee is grown in the highlands. Central America produces 10 percent of the world's coffee. Cacao, sugar, cotton, and rice are other cash crops.

Some people make their living by cutting trees in the forests of the eastern plains. Mahogany is an especially important tropical wood because of its hardness and fine grain. Most Central American mahogany is exported to the United States, where it is used in furniture factories.

Guatemala and Belize

Guatemala is southeast of Mexico. It has the largest population of the Central American nations. More than half the people are descendants of the ancient Mayas. They live mainly in small villages in the highlands. They farm, herd, weave cloth, and make pottery.

Farming is the chief work in Guatemala. Farmers work on small farms or on large plantations. Corn, beans, rice, sugar, coffee, bananas, tobacco, and cotton are raised. Coffee and bananas are important exports.

Coffee plants are often started from seed in nurseries and later transplanted in fields. These small evergreen plants will become tall, dense shrubs or trees.

The name *Guatemala* means "land of trees." In the dense jungles of northern Guatemala, sapodilla trees are tapped for chicle. Chewing gum is made from chicle. Great forests of dyewood, mahogany, and cedar are valuable natural resources.

Guatemala City, the capital, is the largest city in Central America. It is the manufacturing and transportation center of Guatemala. The city is also a tourist center.

East of Guatemala is the newly independent country of Belize. Belize was a British colony until 1981.

Belize is a swampy land, and only one-tenth of it can be farmed. The country produces sugar, bananas, and citrus fruits. Dense forests are the country's most valuable resource. Cedar, chicle, and mahogany are chief exports.

154

El Salvador and Honduras

El Salvador is the smallest but most densely populated Central American country. It lies southeast of Guatemala on the Pacific coast. Its population is nearly five million.

Coffee is El Salvador's most valuable cash crop. Sugar, sisal, cotton, rice, and balsam are also exported. Balsam is made from the sap of a tree that grows along the coast. It is used in making perfume and medicine. Corn, beans, and wheat are grown as food.

Fine roads and railroads connect the capital, San Salvador, with other cities of the country. San Salvador is a busy modern city with parks and beautiful houses.

Northeast of El Salvador lies Honduras. The people of Honduras make their living from farms, mines, and forests. Bananas are the chief cash crop. They are grown along the hot and rainy Caribbean coast. Corn is the main food crop, but wheat, beans, and other temperate-climate crops are also grown. Cattle are raised in the highlands. Coffee is the second most important cash crop.

The rich silver mines first attracted Spaniards to the highlands of Honduras. They built a town near a mountain that the Indians called Tegucigalpa (tē gōō′sē gäl′pä), or "hill of silver." Tegucigalpa became the capital of Honduras in 1880.

Nicaragua, Costa Rica, and Panama

Nicaragua is southeast of El Salvador and Honduras. It has the largest land area of the Central American countries. Managua (mə nä′gwə) is the capital.

Nicaragua is mainly an agricultural country. Sugar, cotton, corn, and rice are grown on the plains around Lake Nicaragua. Coffee, cattle, and gold are the chief products of the central highlands.

Costa Rica lies south of Nicaragua. In Spanish, *Costa Rica* means "rich coast." As the name suggests, the land is fertile, and farming is the main activity. Coffee is a chief export. Bananas, meat, and sugar are also important exports. They contribute to Costa Rica's relatively high standard of living. The government has encouraged industry. San José (san′ hō zā′) is the capital.

Panama lies on the isthmus between Costa Rica and Colombia. The country is divided in two by the Panama Canal. The canal, which links the Atlantic and Pacific oceans, is one of the world's most important waterways. The United States completed the canal in 1914. For 65 years, the United States controlled both the Canal Zone and the operation of the canal. In 1979, a new treaty between Panama and the United States went into effect that gave Panamanians control of the Canal Zone. By the year 2000, Panama will control the operation of the canal as well.

Panama City, the capital, is near the Pacific end of the canal. The canal provides many jobs for people in Panama City and in cities near the Canal Zone.

Farming is the chief occupation outside the Canal Zone. Corn and rice are the leading food crops of small farms. Bananas and cacao are cash crops grown on large plantations. Stock raising and mining are growing in importance.

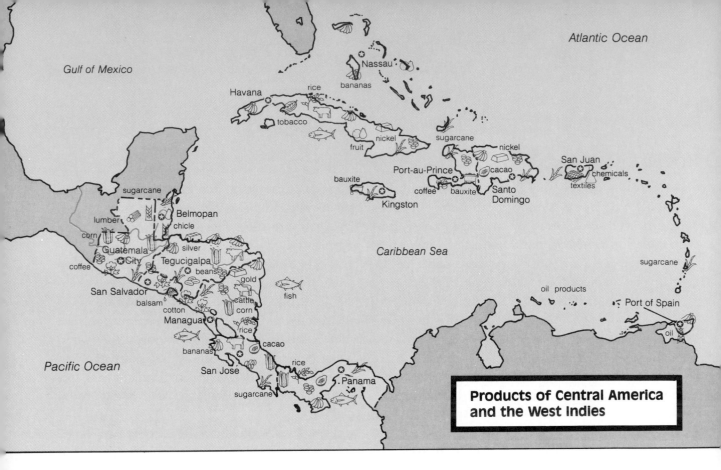

Products of Central America and the West Indies

Geography of the West Indies

The more than 7,000 islands of the West Indies were formed in several different ways. Some, including the large islands of the Greater Antilles, are the peaks of an underwater mountain chain. They are sometimes called the "Caribbean Andes." The small islands of the Lesser Antilles just off the coast of South America are also tops of sunken mountains.

Other islands in the Lesser Antilles were formed as volcanoes built up layers of lava. Several volcanoes have been active in historic times. One of the most destructive eruptions came from Mount Pelée (pə lā′) on the island of Martinique in 1902.

Coral islands are the third kind of islands in the West Indies. They are built up of limestone deposits from the skeletons of tiny sea animals. Most of the Bahamas are coral islands.

The West Indies lie in the tropics. Most of the islands are mountainous, but frost is unknown. The soil is rich, and abundant rains keep the islands green. In some places, there are thick forests.

Steady northeast trade winds help make the climate mild and bring much rain. The rainy season lasts from August to October. During this time, hurricanes sweep across the islands. A warm ocean current, the Antilles Current, flows northwest along the north coast of the Greater Antilles. It joins the Florida Current to form the Gulf Stream.

History of the West Indies

Columbus arrived in the West Indies and claimed them for Spain in 1492. The Spanish valued the West Indies because possession of those islands gave them control of the sea routes to Mexico, Central America, and northern South America. When they found that sugarcane grew well on those islands, they started sugar plantations. In the 1600s, Britain, France, the Netherlands, and Denmark took possession of some of the smaller islands.

Thousands of Africans were brought to work on the West Indian sugar plantations. Many inhabitants today are the descendants of Africans and Spaniards.

Since 1804, when Haiti won its freedom, most of the islands of the West Indies have become independent nations. Among the most recent to become independent are the Bahamas, in 1973; Grenada, in 1974; Dominica, in 1978; and St. Lucia and St. Vincent, in 1979.

The United States governs some of the Virgin Islands as a territory, and Puerto Rico is a commonwealth of the United States. France, Great Britain, and the Netherlands also control some West Indies islands.

The West Indies today are a favorite spot for vacationers. *Tourism* (toor′iz′ əm), the business of providing accommodations and services for tourists, is an important industry in many of the islands.

The Greater Antilles

The four main islands of the Greater Antilles are the largest islands in the West Indies. Hispaniola is divided into two independent nations, Haiti and the Dominican Republic. Cuba, Jamaica, and Puerto Rico are the other large islands.

Cuba

Cuba is the biggest country in the West Indies. It occupies one large island and some small nearby islands. Nearly ten million people live in Cuba. Havana is the capital.

Cuba became independent from Spain in 1898 as a result of the Spanish-American War. Cuba has often been ruled by dictators since its independence. In 1959, troops led by Fidel Castro (fē del′ käs′trō) were successful in a coup that removed President Batista from power. Castro then made himself prime minister. He began to nationalize industries and redistribute the land.

The constitution of Cuba was adopted in 1976. It established Cuba as a socialist state. However, Castro controls the government as a dictator, and the Communist Party is the only recognized political party in the country. To escape Castro's rule, thousands of Cubans left their country to live in the United States and other countries.

Cuba's climate is warm all year, and there is enough rain to raise good crops. Farming is the chief business. The principal crop is sugarcane. Sugar and tobacco are sold to Communist countries to earn money to buy manufactured goods and oil.

Jamaica and Hispaniola

Jamaica lies south of Cuba. Jamaica, an English-speaking nation, attracts many tourists. Kingston is the capital.

To the east of Jamaica is Hispaniola. This is the island where Columbus made his first settlement. The Spanish controlled the island until 1697, when France took over the western third that became Haiti. Today, two nations, Haiti and the Dominican Republic, share the island. Haiti's capital city is Port-au-Prince (pōrt′ō prints′). Santo Domingo, the oldest city in the Western Hemisphere, is the Dominican Republic's capital city. Rum and molasses are chief products of both countries, and the Dominican Republic also produces cement, cloth, and furniture. Many tourists visit the island each year.

Puerto Rico

Puerto Rico lies east of Hispaniola. With more than three million people, Puerto Rico is one of the most densely populated islands in the West Indies. San Juan is the capital.

Puerto Rico has been a part of the United States since the Spanish-American War and is organized as a commonwealth of the United States. Puerto Ricans elect their own governor and legislature. In 1952, they adopted their own constitution. Puerto Rico's leading political parties favor keeping ties with the United States. The Popular Democratic Party wants to continue the island's commonwealth status. The New Progressive Party wants Puerto Rico to become a state. A smaller group wants Puerto Rico to become independent.

More people in Puerto Rico make their living by manufacturing than by farming. Today the country has more than 2,000 factories. The workers in the factories make clothing, tools, chemicals, tires, paper, electronics equipment, and many other products. Puerto Rico is a rapidly changing land of big factories, new

San Juan, Puerto Rico, was founded by the Spanish in 1521 on a small island. This narrow, steep street in Old San Juan is lined with houses and shops.

tourist hotels and apartment buildings, and a rising standard of living.

The Lesser Antilles and the Bahamas

The Lesser Antilles includes the Virgin Islands, Barbados, Trinidad and Tobago, the Netherlands Antilles, and many small islands. The United States Virgin Islands lie east of Puerto Rico. The three inhabited islands are St. Croix (kroi), St. John, and St. Thomas. In 1917, the United States bought these islands from Denmark. Residents of the United States Virgin

Islands gained United States citizenship in 1927. Until 1970, the President of the United States appointed the governor. Today the Virgin Islanders elect their own governor. Many new industries have been started. Tourism provides jobs for many of the people.

The British Virgin Islands, a dependency of Great Britain, lie near the western end of the Lesser Antilles. A dependency is a Commonwealth area that does not have complete self-government. Agriculture and raising livestock are main ways of making a living.

Barbados is a very small island that was once a British colony. It became independent in 1966. Its chief products include sugar, molasses, rum, and cotton. Tourism is an important industry.

When the islands of Trinidad and Tobago won independence from Great Britain in 1962, they joined to form one nation called Trinidad and Tobago. Asphalt, oil, bananas, and cacao are main products.

Curaçao (koor'ə sou'), the main island of the Netherlands Antilles, is located off the northern coast of South America. The Netherlands Antilles also include a second group of islands east of Puerto Rico. An important industry is the refining of oil imported from Venezuela.

The Bahamas are a chain of about 3,000 coral islands and reefs that make up a single nation. They begin off the eastern coast of Florida and extend for 500 miles (800 km) to the northeastern tip of Cuba. Approximately 20 islands are inhabited, but more than three-quarters of the people live on two islands—New Providence and Grand Bahama.

Nassau, the capital of the Bahamas, has a colorful straw market. *Tourism* and sale of handicrafts provide most income.

Most of the people of the Bahamas have jobs related to tourism. Only a thin layer of soil covers the coral, so the land is not suitable for farming. Most food must be imported.

Do You Know?

1. What three island groups make up the West Indies?
2. When was the Panama Canal completed? What two oceans does it link?
3. What two nations share the island of Hispaniola?
4. What islands in the West Indies belong to the United States?

Before You Go On

Using New Words

conquistador
nationalize
archipelago
cordillera
subsistence farming

sisal
coup
cash crop
tourism

Number a paper from 1 through 9. After each number write the word or term from the above list that matches the definition.

1. Producing only enough food to supply the necessities of life
2. A tropical plant with fibers used to make twine and bags
3. A long mountain chain
4. A sudden, unexpected action that overthrows a government
5. A plant or plant product raised for income
6. A Spanish conqueror in Latin America during the sixteenth century
7. The business of providing accommodations and services for tourists
8. A large group of islands
9. To change from private to government ownership

Finding the Facts

1. What is the largest Latin American country?
2. What are South America's three great river systems?
3. Who was the first European to reach Latin America? When?
4. What is the oldest city founded by Europeans in the Americas? When was it founded?
5. Where did the Portuguese first establish claims in the Americas?
6. During the colonial period, how did Spanish and Portuguese landowners use the land of Latin America?
7. In what part of Mexico do most people live?
8. What are two important peninsulas of Mexico?
9. Name four important minerals mined in Mexico.
10. Name the seven countries of Central America.
11. What were three achievements of the Mayan civilization?
12. What important tropical wood used in furniture making is found in Central America?
13. Which Central American country has the largest population?
14. What is the most valuable cash crop of El Salvador?
15. What two currents join to form the Gulf Stream?
16. To what island group do the largest West Indian islands belong?

4
South America

More than 248 million people live in South America, the world's fourth-largest continent. The equator crosses the continent near its widest point, and more than three-quarters of the land is in the tropics. At its southernmost tip, the continent is 600 miles (960 km) from Antarctica.

The countries that make up South America can be grouped into three regions. They are the Andean lands, Brazil and the Guianas, and the Plata River lands.

The Andean Lands

The Andes cordillera runs through Venezuela, Colombia, Ecuador, Peru, Bolivia, and Chile. These are the countries called the Andean lands. The Andes are about 200 miles (320 km) wide in most places. Plains lie east and west of the Andes Mountains. The low coastal plains along the Pacific Ocean are less than 50 miles (80 km) wide at most points.

All the Andean lands except Venezuela and Bolivia border the Pacific. Venezuela borders the Caribbean Sea, and Bolivia is landlocked.

For several hundred years following the Spanish conquest, Spain ruled the Andean lands. Much gold and silver were taken to Spain. One-half of all the silver in use in the world in 1600 came from one Andean mine.

Lima, the capital of Peru today, was built by the Spanish in 1535. For many years, it was their center of government in South America.

In colonial times, Spaniards born in Spain held all the government offices and controlled all the trade. The Indians and the mestizos did the hard work on farms and in mines. Spaniards born in the colonies, or Creoles, paid high taxes but had little part in the government. As time passed, the Creoles and the mestizos became dissatisfied and began to think of becoming independent of the European powers that controlled them. The success of the American Revolution inspired them to action.

During the 1800s, many South American nations gained independence. Simón Bolívar led revolutions against the Spanish in Bolivia, Colombia, Ecuador, Peru, and Venezuela. He became known as *El Libertador,* "The Liberator." Bernardo O'Higgins was the liberator of Chile and that nation's first president. José de San Martín fought with Bolívar in the Andean lands and led the struggle against the Spanish in Argentina. Brazil gained its independence from Portugal without a struggle.

Venezuela

Venezuela, the northernmost Andean country, is about half the size of Mexico. The map of South America on page 163 shows that the Andes Mountains do not cover a very large area of the country. Much of the country is a plateau. In the central and eastern parts of Venezuela, are the extensive grassy plains of the llanos. The mighty Orinoco River flows

Most of Venezuela's oil comes from fields under and around Lake Maracaibo. Off-shore rigs frame a pump on shore.

northeastward through the llanos to the Atlantic Ocean. In the east and south are the forested Guiana Highlands.

When the early Caribbean explorers first saw the shallow bay now called Lake Maracaibo, they found Indian villages built over the water. Wooden columns driven into the lake bottom supported the structures. The villages reminded the explorers of Venice, an Italian city also built over the water. So they named the country Venezuela, which means "little Venice."

Oil Fields and Iron Deposits

Towering oil derricks now rise above the waters of Lake Maracaibo and the nearby plain. Oil has also been found in other parts of Venezuela. The country is the largest producer of oil in Latin America. It is also one of the world's leading producers of oil. See the reference table on page 557. Venezuela's crude oil is shipped to the Netherlands Antilles and the United States for refining.

Venezuela uses the money from the sale of oil to build its industries and to construct roads, parks, and schools. Venezuela now has the best highway system of any nation in Latin America.

The oil boom has caused great changes throughout Venezuela. There are many jobs in the oil industry, and fewer people now work on farms. As a result, Venezuela now has to import some of its food.

Eastern Venezuela has large deposits of iron ore. It is mined from great open pits on the mountainsides. The Orinoco River flows near the mines and provides cheap water transportation to the sea. A steel mill has been built on the nearby Caroni (kär′ə nē′) River, and a large hydroelectric plant is also there.

Cities of Venezuela

A fine highway connects the seaport of La Guaira (lä gwī′rä) with the capital city of Caracas (kə rä′kəs), which lies in a wide valley of the Andes. Caracas itself has been almost completely rebuilt with oil money. There are new apartment buildings and houses, and a fine school system has been established.

In 1961, an entirely new city with schools and hospitals was built near the iron mines on the Orinoco. This planned city is called Ciudad Guyana (sē′ o͞o däd′ gī an′ə).

Colombia

Colombia is southwest of Venezuela. Much of Colombia is mountainous, but narrow lowlands stretch along both the Caribbean Sea and the Pacific Ocean. These coastal lands are hot tropical jungles. Across eastern Colombia stretch the low flat llanos. The southeast is covered by the thick tropical forests of the Amazon Valley.

162

SOUTH AMERICA

| 0 | 100 | 200 | 400 | 600 | Miles |
| 0 | 161 | 322 | 644 | 966 | Kilometers |

⊛ National Capitals
☆ Other Capitals
• Other Cities

Mountains
Plateaus
Hills
Plains

CENTRAL
AMERICA

Barranquilla
Colón Panama Canal
Maracaibo
Lake Maracaibo
Caracas
TRINIDAD AND TOBAGO
Port of Spain
10°
Medellín
Magdalena River
Bogotá
VENEZUELA
Ciudad Bolívar
River
Orinoco
LLANOS
Georgetown
GUYANA
Paramaribo
SURINAME
FRENCH GUIANA
Cayenne
Buenaventura
COLOMBIA
Río
Caquetá
Río Negro
GUIANA HIGHLANDS

EQUATOR
Quito
ECUADOR
Guayaquil
Iquitos
Amazon
Manaus
Madeira River
River
Río Tapajós
Belém
Fortaleza
Cape São Roque
Point Aguja
SELVAS
BRAZIL
Recife
Trujillo
Río
Río Francisco
10°
Lima
Callao
PERU
Lake Titicaca
La Paz
Cochabamba
Potosí
Sucre
BOLIVIA
Cuiabá
BRAZILIAN
Brasília
Goiânia
São Francisco
Río
Salvador
Arequipa
Mollendo
Arica
Atacama Desert
HIGHLANDS
Belo Horizonte
20°
TROPIC OF CAPRICORN
Antofagasta
CHACO
PARAGUAY
Río Paraguay
Río Paraná
São Paulo
Santos
Rio de Janeiro
TROPIC OF CAPRICORN
Tucumán
Asunción
Curitiba
Coquimbo
Córdoba
Santa Fe
Río Paraná
Río Uruguay
Pôrto Alegre
30°
Viña del Mar
Mount Aconcagua 22,834 ft. (6,960m)
Mendoza
Rosario
URUGUAY
Valparaíso
Santiago
Buenos Aires
PAMPAS
Montevideo
Río de la Plata
Concepción
ARGENTINA
Bahía Blanca
40°
Puerto Montt
PATAGONIA
Comodoro Rivadavia
PACIFIC OCEAN
ATLANTIC OCEAN
50°
Falkland Islands
Punta Arenas
STRAIT OF MAGELLAN
Tierra del Fuego
Ushuaia
South Georgia

© Rand McNally & Co.

Most of the people of Colombia live on the plateaus and in the Andean valleys. Many people also live in the valley of the Magdalena (mag'də lā'nə) River, which flows from the Andes to the Caribbean Sea. This river is an important transportation route. The upper valley of the Cauca (kou'kä) River, a tributary of the Magdalena, is one of the most densely populated parts of the country. Colombia was named for Columbus, who explored part of the region on his third voyage to the Western Hemisphere. For almost three centuries, Spain ruled the lands that are now Colombia, Venezuela, Ecuador, and Panama.

In 1819, Bolívar led a revolution that overthrew the Spanish. He then set up the Republic of Great Colombia. By 1830, both Venezuela and Ecuador had established their own governments. Panama broke away in 1903, leaving Colombia as a separate nation.

Farming and Mining

Some of the world's finest coffee comes from Colombia, which is second only to Brazil in world coffee exports. Colombian coffee is grown on the mountain slopes. Some farms are as high as 7,000 feet (2,100 m) above sea level. In Colombia, the coffee is grown on small farms. In other coffee-growing areas of South America, coffee is chiefly grown on large plantations. Highland farmers who do not grow coffee are mainly subsistence farmers.

Colombia is a leading oil-producing country in South America. It also has gold, silver, and platinum deposits. Most of the world's emeralds come from Colombian mines.

Cities of Colombia

Bogotá (bō'gə tä'), the capital of Colombia, lies in the Andes. It has a population of more than four million. Bogotá was founded by the Spanish in the early days of the conquistadors. Some of their descendants live in houses built during colonial times.

Barranquilla (bär'räng kē'yä) and Cartagena (kär'tə gā'nə) are Caribbean seaports. Barranquilla lies at the mouth of the Magdalena River. Cartagena, an old Spanish city, is surrounded by a high wall. The wall was built to keep out pirates in the days when gold and silver were shipped from Cartagena to Spain. Today, bananas are exported from these Caribbean port cities.

Ecuador

Ecuador is the Spanish word for "equator." The equator passes through the northern part of this small country. Ecuador stretches from the Pacific Ocean across the Andes to the jungles of the upper Amazon Valley.

The equator runs just north of the capital city of Quito (kē'tō). This city is nearly two miles (3.2 km) above sea level. Because of its altitude, Quito is cool even though it lies close to the equator. In the beautiful plaza in the center of Quito, however, tropical trees grow.

Mountains near Quito rise as high as 10,000 feet (3,000 m) above the city. These mountains are always covered with snow. Most of the people of Ecuador live on the Andean uplands and plateaus near Quito, but some live in the tropical lowlands.

Regional Data Chart

Country	Capital	Area		Population	GNP (in millions of U.S. dollars)
		Square miles	Square kilometers		
Argentina	Buenos Aires	1,072,067	2,776,654	27,400,000	$61,000
Bahamas	Nassau	4,404	11,406	225,000	$640
Barbados	Bridgetown	166	431	250,000	$610
Belize	Belmopan	8,867	22,965	160,000	$130
Bolivia	La Paz, Sucre	424,162	1,098,581	5,750,000	$3,000
Brazil	Brasília	3,286,470	8,511,957	127,000,000	$207,300
Chile	Santiago	286,396	741,766	11,275,000	$18,400
Colombia	Bogotá	455,355	1,179,369	28,500,000	$26,400
Costa Rica	San José	19,652	50,898	2,300,000	$3,900
Cuba	Havana	44,218	114,524	9,900,000	$13,900
Dominica	Roseau	300	777	85,000	$30
Dominican Republic	Santo Domingo	18,704	48,442	5,580,000	$5,200
Ecuador	Quito	105,685	273,724	8,625,000	$8,500
El Salvador	San Salvador	8,260	21,393	4,750,000	$3,000
Grenada	St. George's	133	344	110,000	$70
Guatemala	Guatemala City	42,042	108,889	7,470,000	$6,900
Guyana	Georgetown	83,000	214,969	890,000	$480
Haiti	Port-au-Prince	10,714	27,750	5,100,000	$1,300
Honduras	Tegucigalpa	43,277	112,088	3,825,000	$1,900
Jamaica	Kingston	4,411	11,424	2,225,000	$2,700
Mexico	Mexico City	761,600	1,972,547	74,500,000	$107,600
Nicaragua	Managua	57,143	148,000	2,750,000	$1,700
Panama	Panama City	29,306	75,903	2,000,000	$2,500
Paraguay	Asunción	157,047	406,752	3,165,000	$3,200
Peru	Lima	496,222	1,285,216	18,300,000	$12,600
St. Kitts-Nevis	Basseterre	101	262	44,500	—
St. Lucia	Castries	238	616	125,000	$90
St. Vincent and the Grenadines	Kingstown	150	389	120,000	$50
Suriname	Paramaribo	63,251	163,820	400,000	$950
Trinidad and Tobago	Port-of-Spain	1,980	5,128	1,145,000	$3,900
Uruguay	Montevideo	68,548	177,539	2,925,000	$6,100
Venezuela	Caracas	352,143	912,050	14,300,000	$45,200

Nonindependent Area

Country	Capital	Area		Population	GNP (in millions of U.S. dollars)
		Square miles	Square kilometers		
British Virgin Islands (Great Britain)	Road Town	59	153	12,000	—
French Guiana (France)	Cayenne	35,135	91,000	65,000	$100
Netherlands Antilles (The Netherlands)	Willemstad	371	961	275,000	$920
Puerto Rico (United States)	San Juan	3,421	8,860	3,300,000	—
U.S. Virgin Islands (United States)	Charlotte Amalie	136	352	95,000	—

Farming and Lumbering

Most of the people who live in the Andes are subsistence farmers. Large banana and cacao plantations are in the tropical forests. Ecuador is the world's leading exporter of bananas.

The forests of Ecuador yield mahogany, other tropical hardwoods, and balsa wood. Balsa is a very light wood used for making boats and airplane models.

Mining

Gold, copper, silver, lead, salt, and sulfur are mined. Copper mining increased significantly in the 1970s. Oil has been found along the Pacific coast and near the Putumayo River. In the early 1970s, Ecuador began to export petroleum.

Peru

Peru is the third-largest country in South America. It has more than 18 million people.

Most of Peru's cities, farms, and factories are in a narrow, dry strip of land along the Pacific coast. Although this region is a desert, the many rivers that flow out of the Andes to the ocean furnish water for irrigation. There is a ribbon of green land along each river. It is in these fertile regions that most of the people live. Each valley is separated from neighboring valleys by barren land.

High plateaus and the Andes are east of the coast. Lake Titicaca, the highest navigable lake in the world, lies 12,507 feet (3,812 m) above sea level in the southern highlands. Part of the lake is in Bolivia.

East of the Andes are foothills and low plains covered by rain forests and jungles. This area is drained by rivers that flow into the Amazon. Ships can travel up the Amazon itself to the city of Iquitos (ikē′tōs), 2,300 miles (3,680 km) from the Atlantic Ocean. Tropical products are shipped down the Amazon from Iquitos to foreign markets.

From the 1200s to the 1500s, Peru was the heart of the great Inca empire. By 1533, the conquistador Pizarro and his forces had overrun the Inca capital of Cuzco, killed the Inca emperor, and conquered most of Peru.

For nearly 300 years, Peru was a Spanish colony. In 1820, José de San Martín led an army of Argentines and Chileans into Peru to liberate the country from Spanish rule. Although much of Peru was still ruled by Spain, San Martín declared independence the following year. Then in 1823, Simón Bolívar, with troops from both Venezuela and Colombia, marched into Peru. One of Bolívar's generals won a major victory over the Spanish in 1824. With this victory, Spain's hold on Peru was broken. However, Spain did not formally recognize Peru's independence until 1879.

Farming

Farming is the chief occupation in Peru. The Indian farmers of the Andean plateaus grow corn, potatoes, and grain in tiny, rocky fields. They grow quinoa (kinō′ə), a tall plant cultivated by their Inca ancestors. The round seeds of the quinoa plant are eaten as a vegetable.

Horses are used to work in the fields, and burros to transport goods on steep mountain

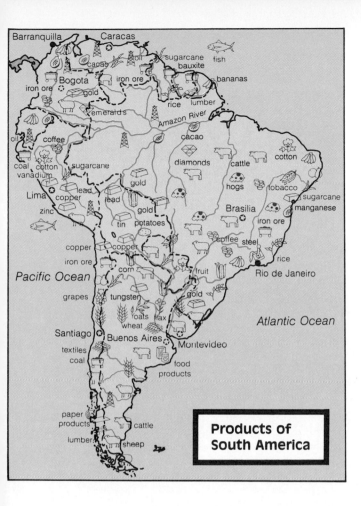

Products of South America

(Map labels) Barranquilla · Caracas · sugarcane · bauxite · fish · oil · cacao · Bogota · iron ore · bananas · iron ore · gold · rice · lumber · emeralds · Amazon River · oil · coffee · cacao · coal · cotton · sugarcane · diamonds · cattle · cotton · vanadium · gold · hogs · tobacco · Lima · lead · copper · lead · gold · Brasilia · sugarcane · zinc · tin · potatoes · manganese · gold · iron ore · copper · copper · coffee · steel · iron ore · rice · Pacific Ocean · corn · fruit · Rio de Janeiro · grapes · tungsten · gold · Atlantic Ocean · oats · flax · wheat · Santiago · Buenos Aires · Montevideo · textiles · coal · food products · paper products · cattle · lumber · sheep

to transport the ore from the mines to the coast. One Peruvian mine is the highest in the world. It is a *vanadium* (və nā′dē əm) mine, which is more than three miles (4.8 km) above sea level. Vanadium is a silver-white metallic mineral. It is one of the ferroalloys.

Petroleum deposits are found in the eastern part of the country. The oil is shipped out on the Amazon River. The government has nationalized many oil and mining companies.

Fishing

Peru is one of the world's chief fishing nations. Fish from the cold waters of the Pacific are processed in factories along the coast. Most of the catch is ground into fish meal that is used as feed for pigs and poultry.

Cities of Peru

Lima, the capital city of Peru, has about five million people. Lima is a city of contrasts. Spanish influence can be seen in its spacious plazas and boulevards and in the delicately carved balconies. However, Lima is also a modern city with many glass-and-concrete skyscrapers. The hillsides above Lima are crowded with Indians who have migrated to Lima in search of work.

The neighboring city of Callao (kə yä′ō′) is the port for Lima and is connected with it by highways. Callao is the only seaport in Peru where ocean liners can dock.

Southeast of Lima is the ancient city of Cuzco. Many tourists come to see the Spanish colonial churches and to visit the Inca ruins of Machu Picchu (mäch′yoo′ pēk′chyoo′).

trails. Thousands of sheep graze on the uplands and furnish meat and the wool for the warm clothing needed in that cool climate. Wool is also an important export.

Many of the large estates in the valleys of Peru were once owned by only a few families. They have now been made into cooperative farms. Sugarcane and cotton are grown in these valleys. The cotton is valued for its long fibers and brings a high price. Both raw sugar and cotton are exported from Peru.

Mining

Important deposits of minerals are found in the high mountains. The largest are copper and zinc mines. Roads and railroads have been built

167

Latin America is a region of contrasts. Great differences in ways of living exist between countries and within countries. Cultures change as industry grows and replaces traditional ways. In a Mexican automobile factory, an industrial worker pours molten metal into a mold. Operation and maintenance of the Panama Canal provides jobs for many people in the tiny nation of Panama.

In many rural areas, farming methods have changed little. On the small plots near this village in the Colombian Andes *subsistence farming* is practiced. Indian women sow seeds by hand. Coffee is an

important *cash crop*. On the Peruvian *altiplano* near the old Inca capital of Cuzco, an Indian boy tends baby llamas. Grown llamas are used for transportation, wool, and meat.

Throughout Latin America, traditional crafts are still practiced. In Peru, workers make adobe roof tiles by hand and set them in the sun to dry. A Mexican potter paints a design on a plate before firing it. ■

169

Bolivia

Bolivia lies southeast of Peru. It is the fifth-largest country in South America. That nation has two capitals. Sucre (sōō′krā), where the Supreme Court is located, is difficult to reach because of poor roads. The legislative and the executive branches of government meet in the larger city of La Paz. Bolivia is one of two countries without seacoasts in South America.

Most of the people live on the *altiplano* (äl′tiplän′ō′). The altiplano is the high plateau of the Andes. The altiplano straddles the borders of Bolivia and Peru. To the east, there is a tropical lowland that is drained by many rivers. Few people live in this part of Bolivia.

Bolivia declared its independence from Spain and Peru in 1825. The new republic was named after Simón Bolívar, who helped win its freedom and draft its constitution.

The Silver of Potosí

During the 1600s, the Spanish found a mountain of silver in Bolivia. At the base of the mountain, they constructed the city of Potosí (pōt′əsē′). Within a few years Potosí was the largest city in the Western Hemisphere.

Today, Potosí has far fewer people, but new ores have been discovered. The mountain now yields tin, copper, and lead.

Mining and Farming

Bolivia is supported by its mines. It is one of the world's chief tin-producing nations. However, Bolivia has no coal. The tin ore is exported by way of a port in Chile, because it cannot be refined in Bolivia.

Indians make up more than half the population of Bolivia. Some work in the mines, but most are subsistence farmers. The main food of many Indians is chuño (chōōn′yō). Chuño is made by first freezing, then drying, potatoes. It has been made the same way for centuries.

Chile

Chile is a long, narrow country south of Peru. The Indian word *chilli* means "place where the land ends." The country stretches 2,600 miles (4,160 km) from north to south. Its greatest width is only 225 miles (362 km). Earthquakes are common in this mountainous land.

The northern one-third of Chile is a part of the Atacama Desert. The Atacama extends along the coast of Chile south from the Peru-Chile border. The cold waters of the Peru Current help create the desert. Winds blowing from the west across the current lose their moisture before reaching the shore. In the Atacama, years pass without any rainfall.

The central part of Chile has a Mediterranean climate. The principal cities of the nation are located there. The southern third of Chile is heavily forested with pines and other evergreen trees. This region receives much rain. Mountains extend to the sea, and there are large lakes, bays, and fiords, as in Norway. The Strait of Magellan cuts through the southern end of Chile.

More than 30 rivers flow across Chile from the Andes to the Pacific Ocean. These rivers are not navigable because of their many waterfalls, but they do provide hydroelectric power.

The snow-capped Andes tower above modern high-rise buildings in Santiago, Chile. The city lies on a high plain.

Chile was under Spanish control from the early 1500s until independence was won in 1818. In 1823, Chile was the first nation in the Western Hemisphere to abolish slavery. Chile has been involved in several disputes with its neighbors. In 1973, Chile's president was over thrown in a coup. Military leaders then formed a government and banned political parties that opposed them. A small group, such as a group of military leaders, that rules a country after a coup is called a *junta* (hoon′tə). A junta rules without legal authority.

Farming and Lumbering

Many large estates from colonial times still exist in central Chile. Although some have been broken up, only a small percentage of the people own most of the land.

171

Many products are grown in the Mediterranean climate of central Chile. The land is irrigated during the dry summer with water from mountain streams that flow from the Andes. Orchards, vineyards, groves of orange trees, and wheat fields are important in this part of Chile. Much of the land is pasture for cattle and sheep.

Lumbering is important along the southern coast. Chile has a pulp and paper industry and it also exports lumber.

South of the Strait of Magellan is the large island of Tierra del Fuego (tyer′ə del fwä′gō). Part of the island belongs to Chile and part to Argentina. Tierra del Fuego is an important sheep-raising land. Wool is a major export.

Mining

The desert in northern Chile has deposits of nitrates, iron ore, and copper. Nitrates are used in making fertilizer. At one time Chile controlled most of the world's supply of nitrates. Although nitrates now are manufactured from the nitrogen in the air, natural nitrates are still exported by Chile.

The largest known single copper deposit in the world is found in northern Chile. Both copper and iron ore are exported to the United States.

Cities of Chile

Santiago (san′tē ä′gō), the capital of Chile, is the nation's largest city. It lies in a deep valley in the Andes. Low mountains separate Santiago from its seaport of Valparaíso (val′pə rī′zō). Valparaíso, Concepción (kən sep′sē ōn′) and Santiago are Chile's leading manufacturing cities. They produce textiles, steel, and paper products.

Brazil and the Guianas

Brazil occupies most of the northeast and east central part of South America. Along the Atlantic coast in the north lie the Guianas, an area less than 6 percent the size of Brazil. The term *Guianas* is a convenient way to refer to Guyana (gīan′ə), Suriname (soor′ə nam′), and French Guiana. Before 1966, when it became independent, Guyana was known as British Guyana. Suriname was known as Dutch Guiana before it became independent in 1975. French Guiana is not an independent country but an overseas part of France.

Five European powers, the Netherlands, Great Britain, France, Spain, and Portugal, explored and settled the region that is now Brazil and the Guianas. Today, people of Indian, European, African, Asian, and mixed ancestry live there.

Brazil

Brazil is the largest country in South America. It covers half the continent, an area almost as large as the United States. It is the home of 127 million people, more than half the people of South America. Brazil is the only South American nation where Portuguese is the official language.

Brazil lies almost entirely in the tropics. Much of the northern part of the country is a lowland covered by a vast tropical rain forest, or *selva* (sel′və). Brazil's selva is the largest rain forest in the world. The mighty Amazon, one of the greatest rivers in the world, drains this enormous region. In terms of volume of water and drainage area, the Amazon is the world's largest river. More than 15,000 miles (24,000 km) of the Amazon river system are navigable. Many of Brazil's Indians live in the densely forested Amazon region.

Much of eastern Brazil is a low plateau. The climate is warm, even hot in some places. There is sufficient rainfall to grow many different crops. The Guiana Highlands lie along Brazil's borders with Guyana, Suriname, and French Guiana.

A very narrow plain lies along the east coast of Brazil. The Brazilian Highlands rise sharply from the plain. They cover most of central and southern Brazil. The northern part of the highlands are in the Amazon drainage basin. The southeast part is drained by the Paraná (par′ənä′) River and its tributaries. Iguaçu (ē′gwəsoo′) Falls, a spectacular waterfall about two miles (3.2 km) wide, is on a tributary of the Paraná near the border of Argentina and Brazil.

Much of the western part of the Brazilian Highlands is a great tropical grassland, or mixed grass and thorn tree country.

Early Portuguese Settlements

Portugal's claim in northeastern South America was established in 1500 by Pedro Cabral. During the late 1500s and early 1600s, both the French and the Dutch made settlements in what is now Brazil, but the Portuguese drove them out.

The most important Portuguese settlements were along the coast between Recife (rəsē′fə) and Rio de Janeiro. The Portuguese, like the Spaniards, established large estates where sugarcane and cotton were grown.

Government

During the early 1800s, the French general Napoleon Bonaparte conquered large areas of Europe, including Portugal. The royal family of Portugal escaped and fled to Brazil. After Napoleon was defeated in 1814, the king returned to Portugal. The king's son remained in Brazil as head of the government. Brazil proclaimed its independence in 1822. Unlike the Spanish colonies, which set up republics with elected presidents, Brazil chose to keep the prince as its ruler. He became Pedro I, emperor of Brazil.

In 1831, Pedro II, the son of Pedro I, became emperor of Brazil. He carried out many social reforms during his long reign. In 1888, while Pedro II was in Europe, his daughter abolished slavery in Brazil. Her action was unpopular with the slave owners. The next year, Pedro II and his family were forced to leave the country. A republic was proclaimed, and a president was elected. Since that time, Brazil has undergone several revolutions.

In recent years, the government of Brazil has made great efforts to develop its vast resources. Farmlands are being cleared, new dams and power plants are being built, and new roads and railroads are being constructed.

Brazil's Tropical Coast

The people of Brazil's tropical coast make their living by working on farms and plantations and by fishing. Sugarcane, rice, cotton, cacao, and bananas are the most important crops of the coastal region. Cattle and sheep are raised in the south.

Few of the farmers own their own land, and many of the people of this region are very poor. Many unemployed farm laborers flock to such cities as Recife. However, there are few jobs for them there, and they add to the overcrowding of the cities. Since the 1960s, Brazil's government has started special programs to improve conditions in this region.

Brazilian Highlands

The most thickly populated region of Brazil is the rolling plateau inland from Rio de Janeiro. This part of the Brazilian Highlands, only one-tenth of Brazil's area, contains more than half its people.

The Brazilian Highlands produce a large percentage of the world's coffee. In Brazil, a coffee plantation is called a *fazenda* (fə zen'də). Some fazendas are very large and may cover several square miles. Each fazenda contains thousands of coffee trees.

The temperatures and the rainfall of the Brazilian Highlands are just right for growing coffee. The days are warm rather than hot, and there is no frost. The abundant rains of the rainy season help the trees grow. A dry, cool season follows the rainy period. The coffee berries ripen and are picked during the dry season. This season is fine, also, for drying the berries. Workers rake the beans on concrete floors where they are exposed to the warm sun.

Thousands of bags of coffee beans are shipped from each fazenda. Railroads take the bags from the plateau to the seaports of Santos and Rio de Janeiro. Brazil is the world's leading coffee-growing country. Coffee is the chief export of Brazil.

While the coffee trees are young and do not shade the ground completely, cotton is grown between the rows of trees. In the Western Hemisphere, Brazil is second only to the United States in the growing of cotton.

Minerals

Iron ore, manganese, and industrial diamonds are mined in the Brazilian Plateau. Industrial diamonds are used in cutting tools. The iron deposits are large. A great steel plant has been built between Rio de Janeiro and São Paulo. Most of Brazil's iron ore, however, is exported because Brazil does not have enough coal to smelt it.

Cities of Brazil

Rio de Janeiro has one of the world's most beautiful harbors. Mountains and hilly islands rise from the sea, and sandy beaches stretch along the shore. Hills have been leveled and swamps filled in to allow the city to expand. Modern apartments and hotels line the waterfront. Until 1960, Rio de Janeiro was the capital of Brazil.

The Brazilian government decided a new capital was needed. The government also wanted to promote settlement of the country's

Rio de Janeiro is built around Guanabara Bay. Sugar Loaf Mountain stands at the narrow entrance to the harbor.

underdeveloped interior. Brasília, the new capital city, is 600 miles (960 km) inland, in the highlands. The city was built according to a plan selected by an international jury. Brasília is a rare example of a completely planned city.

São Paulo is also in the Brazilian Highlands, near the great farming regions and above the port of Santos. São Paulo, which is Brazil's manufacturing center, is the largest city in South America. Many foreign businesses have headquarters there.

The chief city of the upper Amazon is Manaus (mänous′). It is an important river port. In the late 1800s, the rubber boom made Manaus prosperous. For many years, the city was in a decline, but the discovery of oil fields nearby and the renewed interest in the Amazon have revived it.

Belém (bəlēm′) is the chief port of the Amazon Basin. It lies on the Pará River near the mouth of the Amazon. Belém was another rubber boom town during the early 1900s. A coastal railway and an airport help Belém's trade. The city is now connected with Brasilia by a good highway.

The Guianas

Guyana, Suriname, and French Guiana all lie just north of the equator. They are tropical lands with an average annual temperature of about 80° F. (27° C). These countries receive a great deal of rain, more than 80 inches (200 cm) a year along the coast. Lowlands border the coast, and the Guiana Highlands rise in the south.

Guyana

Guyana is a small land, but much of it is still unexplored. Its capital is Georgetown. The country has many dense forests and some minerals. The soil in Guyana is rich, and there are many sugar plantations and rice farms. Other crops include fruits, cacao, coconuts, and coffee. Guyana is one of the world's main producers and exporters of bauxite, which is used in making aluminum.

Suriname

Suriname is the smallest country in South America. One person in three is of East Indian origin. Their ancestors were brought to this area from India to work on the plantations. There are also people of African, European, and Chinese descent. Most people live on the coastal plains. The official language in Suriname is Dutch. The capital, Paramaribo (par′ə mar′əbō′), is also the country's main port. Most of the country is mountainous and covered by a rain forest.

Suriname's timber is an important resource. Its main industry is the production of aluminum. Rice is an important cash crop.

French Guiana

French Guiana is smaller than Suriname. The capital of French Guiana is Cayenne (kīen′). As in Suriname, most of the people live along the coast. French is the official language. The interior of French Guiana has dense forests and has not been completely explored. The soil is rich, and there are valuable forests and mineral deposits. A new shrimp industry has been started. The resources in French Guiana have not been developed to any extent, however, and it depends on France for financial help.

The Plata River Lands

Paraguay (par′əgwā′), Uruguay (yoor′əgwā′), and Argentina are the Plata River lands. The rivers of the Río de la Plata system drain large parts of these countries.

The most important rivers are the Paraguay, the Paraná, and the Uruguay. These rivers are navigable for hundreds of miles, and they are important transportation routes. Both the Paraguay and the Uruguay rivers empty into the Río de la Plata. Buenos Aires (bwā′nəs er′ēz), the capital of Argentina, and Montevideo (mon′təvidā′ō), the capital of Uruguay, are important trade centers on opposite sides of the estuary.

The Paraguay, the Uruguay, and the Paraná rivers cover a vast area and drain more than one million square miles (2.6 million sq. km). A large part of this area is a fertile region known as the breadbasket of South America.

Paraguay

Paraguay is a tropical land with a population of more than three million. The people of the cities are mainly of Spanish descent. In rural areas, they are mainly mestizos.

The Paraguay River divides the country into two parts. The eastern region is an area of highlands that range from 1,000 to 2,000 feet (300 to 600 m) above sea level. The area west of the Paraguay River is the Chaco (chäk′ō′). It is a region of plains and lowlands covered with scattered forests.

History

Asunción (äsōōnsyōn′), now the capital, was founded as a port on the Paraguay River in 1537. It was important when the mines in the Andes were developed. Some of the silver from the great mine at Potosí was brought to Asunción to be shipped to Spain.

Paraguay became independent of Spain in 1811, without revolution or bloodshed. Its history as a nation, however, has been an unsettled one. Disputes over boundaries resulted in many wars. Military leaders became dictators and ruled with absolute power.

Today Paraguay has a small population and few skilled workers. The government has been trying to solve some of the country's economic problems by developing new industries. In 1973, Brazil and Paraguay agreed to cooperate in building a very large hydroelectric power plant on the Paraná River.

Farming and Forest Products

Paraguay is a nation of large estates and small farms. There are great differences in the standards of living of the large landowners and the very poor farmers. Sugarcane, cotton, and tobacco are leading crops. Cattle raising is important in the Chaco.

Some people work in tropical forests where two special trees, the quebracho (kābrä′chō) and the yerba maté (yer′bə mä′tä′), grow well. From the bark of the quebracho tree. a brown-ish juice, or extract, is pressed. Quebracho extract is used in the tanning of leather. The leaves of the yerba maté are made into a tea, which is a favorite drink in the Plata River lands and in southern Brazil. Yerba maté is one of Paraguay's chief exports. Lumber is also exported.

In some forest areas, castor beans are gathered from the castor oil plant. Large quantities of these beans are exported for the manufacture of castor oil. Castor oil is used as a medicine, in industrial processes, and as a lubricant for airplane engines.

Paraguay also has large orange groves, which are grown almost without cultivation. Oranges are exported to Argentina and Uruguay. Petitgrain (ped′ēgrän), an oil made from orange leaves, is a basis for flavoring and perfumes. Seventy percent of the world's supply of petitgrain, pressed from the leaves of wild orange trees, comes from Paraguay.

Uruguay

In South America, only French Guiana and Suriname are smaller than Uruguay. Uruguay is the only South American country where all the land is settled.

A narrow belt of sandy lowlands lies along Uruguay's Atlantic coast and along the Río de la Plata. In the east, highlands reach from the border between Brazil and Uruguay almost to the southern coast. The large area between the highlands and the Uruguay River to the west is pastureland. The country has a warm climate with rainfall throughout the year.

A Spaniard named Juan de Solís (hwän de sō lēs′) was the first European to explore the Río de la Plata in 1516. As soon as the Spaniards went ashore, they were killed by Indians. For many years, the Spaniards avoided the region. The first permanent Spanish settlement in what is now Uruguay was not made until 1625. The Spaniards called the region the Banda Oriental, meaning the "eastern bank."

Uruguay Today

Almost one out of every two people in Uruguay lives in Montevideo, the capital and the only large city in the nation. The city stands on the bank of the Río de la Plata, about 135 miles (216 km) southeast of Buenos Aires. Meat packing is the chief industry. Most people are descendants of Spanish and Italian immigrants who arrived during the past 100 years.

Among the countries of South America, the government of Uruguay is perhaps the most forward looking in the many kinds of benefits it provides for its people. Uruguay has a fine public school system, and workers have many benefits under Uruguayan laws. The government provides medical services.

Agriculture and Mining

Uruguay's wide, rolling, grassy plains make fine pastures, and the nation's chief industry is stock raising. Millions of cattle and sheep graze on the large estates of Uruguay. Gauchos, or cowhands, work on the estates. Uruguay has half as many sheep as Argentina and one-fourth as many cattle. Wheat and wool are leading exports.

Although Uruguay has no great forest lands, it does have some hardwood timber. There are large deposits of gold in the northern hills. Uruguay has abundant supplies of granite and marble in an amazing variety of colors. However, on the whole, Uruguay does not have important mineral resources.

Argentina

Argentina is nearly one-third as large as the United States. It has a population of more than 27 million. Most of the people are of European descent.

In the northwest, Argentina reaches into the plateaus of the Andes. South of these highlands, the Andes separate Argentina and Chile. Mount Aconcagua (ak′ən kog′wə), the highest peak in the Western Hemisphere, is located along Argentina's border with Chile. Mount Aconcagua rises almost 23,000 feet (7,000 m) above sea level.

Northern Argentina is in the tropics. The narrow southern part of the country is a dry, cold region called Patagonia. At the tip of Patagonia is Tierra del Fuego, the island that Argentina shares with Chile. On the southern shore of the Argentinian part of the island is Ushuaia (ōō swä′yə), the southernmost city in the world. Tierra del Fuego is about 650 miles (1,050 km) from Antarctica.

The heart of Argentina are flat, rich plains called the pampas. This area was a grassland when the first settlers arrived. Now much of it has been plowed up for farmland. It has a climate of mild winters and hot summers.

Ample rainfall creates good conditions for agriculture. Most of the people in Argentina live in the pampas.

Early Settlement and Independence

The Spanish, under the leadership of Sebastian Cabot, explored the coast of Argentina in the 1500s. On a voyage up the Paraguay River, Cabot met Indians who wore silver ornaments, so he called the land Argentina. Argentina means "silver" in Spanish. The fertile plains around the Río de la Plata were not settled by Europeans to any great extent until after 1800. Most Argentinians today are descended from Europeans who moved to the country after 1850. Many of these settlers came from Italy and Spain.

Argentina's great patriot, José de San Martín, led the country in its struggle for freedom from Spain. For a dozen or more years after independence in 1816, there was trouble over boundaries with Brazil. Finally, Uruguay was established as a *buffer state* (buf′ər stāt′) between Argentina and Brazil. A buffer state is a small country lying between two larger countries that are rivals or enemies.

The Pampas

Large crops of wheat, corn, oats, barley, flax, and alfalfa are produced on Argentina's pampas. Millions of cattle and sheep graze on excellent pastures. This region, with its rich soil, closely resembles the central plains of the United States.

A gaucho herds cattle on the Argentine pampas. Argentina is one of the world's leading producers of beef cattle.

World Trade
Latin America

Minor Exporter
Major Exporter
Minor Importer
Major Importer

MEXICO

CENTRAL AMERICA
AND THE WEST INDIES

SOUTH AMERICA

EXPORTS

Oil, oil products, sugar, molasses, coffee, cotton, aluminum, bananas, bauxite, gold, wood, chicle

IMPORTS

Machinery, transportation equipment, manufactured goods, chemicals, food products, livestock, paper, textiles, oil

EXPORTS

Oil, machinery, industrial equipment, coffee, chemicals, cotton

IMPORTS

Machinery, iron and steel, transportation equipment, motor vehicles, food products, chemicals

EXPORTS

Oil, oil products, coffee, copper, bauxite, tin, phosphate, silver, emeralds, soybeans, wheat, beef, machinery, electrical equipment, iron ore, transportation equipment, textiles, wool

IMPORTS

Minerals, chemicals, machinery, electrical equipment, motor vehicles, transportation equipment, manufactured goods

United States and Canada

Europe

Soviet Union

North Africa and the Middle East

Africa South of the Sahara

Southern and Eastern Asia

Australia and New Zealand

180

During the early settlement of Argentina, the Spanish granted large estates on the pampas. In Argentina, a large estate or cattle ranch is called an *estancia* (e stän′sē ə). Wealthy landowners, who maintain large herds of cattle and flocks of sheep, still own many estancias in the heart of the pampas region. Argentine gauchos work on the estancias.

The edges of the pampas to the north, west, and south lay beyond the region where estates were granted. These regions are farmlands owned chiefly by descendants of settlers who came to Argentina after 1850. Crops are more important than cattle and sheep on these farms. Corn is the chief crop in the north, and wheat is the main crop in the western and southern parts of the pampas. There is some dairy farming, as well.

This rich land produces much more food than the nation needs. Argentina has a great network of railroads that carry products of the farms and ranches to Buenos Aires for export.

The Tropical Northwest and Patagonia

In the tropical northwest, sugarcane grows well. There are irrigated vineyards at the base of the Andes. In Patagonia, in southern Argentina, the land is much too dry and too cold for crops. These conditions make it fine sheep country. Wool and mutton are exported. Important oil fields are found in Patagonia.

Cities of Argentina

Most people in Argentina's cities, from Buenos Aires to the smallest town, make their living by processing farm products. Other people have jobs in stores, selling goods to factory workers, farmers, and others.

Large meat-packing establishments are Argentina's chief manufacturing plants. Argentina also has many food-processing plants and leather and textile industries.

Buenos Aires, a city of more than three million inhabitants, is the capital and largest city of Argentina. Many of the city's people work for the government.

Broad boulevards, regular and straight streets, dozens of plazas, and fine government buildings beautify the city. The capitol is an especially beautiful building.

Buenos Aires is a cultural center, with art galleries, museums, an opera house, and many cathedrals and churches. Tall office and apartment buildings show the city's recent growth.

Rosario, Argentina's second-largest city, is a port on the Paraná River 180 miles (290 km) from Buenos Aires. It is an important grain-shipping center.

Do You Know?

1. In what climate zone does most of South America lie?
2. Name two leaders of independence movements in South America.
3. What present-day country was the heart of the Inca Empire?
4. What countries are known as the Plata River lands? Why?

To Help You Learn

Using New Words

conquistador   estancia

altiplano   junta

buffer state   fazenda

vanadium   selva

archipelago

Number a paper from 1 through 9. After each number write the word or term from the above list that matches the definition.

1. A small group, such as a group of military leaders, that rules a country after a coup
2. A large group of islands
3. A coffee plantation in Brazil
4. A small country lying between two large countries that are rivals or enemies
5. A vast tropical rain forest
6. A large estate or cattle ranch in Argentina
7. A Spanish conqueror in Latin America during the sixteenth century
8. A silver-white metallic mineral
9. The high plateau of the Andes

Finding the Facts

1. What four regions make up Latin America?
2. Where are Mexico's best farming lands?
3. Name the three kinds of islands in the West Indies.
4. In what climate zone are the West Indies?
5. Which of the Andean countries border the Pacific? Which country is landlocked?
6. Who became known as *El Libertador?* What countries did he help free?
7. What are the grassy plains of Venezuela called?
8. What is Latin America's largest producer of oil?
9. How does coffee growing in Colombia differ from coffee growing in other parts of South America?
10. What does *Ecuador* mean?
11. What is the highest navigable lake in the world?
12. Who conquered the Inca empire? When was the conquest completed?
13. What South American country has two capitals? Name them.
14. In what countries is the altiplano found?
15. Why does Bolivia export its tin ore?
16. What desert extends along the coast of Chile? What helps create this desert?
17. Why are Chile's rivers not navigable? How are the rivers useful?
18. Where is the single largest known copper deposit in the world?
19. What country was formerly British Guyana? Dutch Guiana?
20. What area in South America is not an independent country?

21. In what country is the world's largest rain forest? What river drains the region where the rain forest grows?
22. Why were Pedro II and his family forced to leave Brazil?
23. What city was Brazil's capital until 1960?
24. What are the most important rivers of the Río de la Plata system?
25. Who was Juan de Solíis?
26. What are the plains of Argentina called?
27. Between what countries was Uruguay established as a buffer state?
28. How do most people in Argentina's cities make a living?

Learning from Maps

1. Look at the map of South America on page 163. Through what countries do the Andes run? What countries are drained by the Amazon River and its tributaries? Through what countries does the equator pass?
2. Look at the map of early civilizations and early explorations in Latin America on page 145. When did Cortés reach the Pacific? Which explorer traveled farthest south? Which explorer first reached the eastern coast of South America? Which explorer traveled through the Inca empire? The Aztec empire?
3. Look at the map on page 146. What European country controlled the largest land area? What European languages might you expect to be spoken in Latin American countries today? What countries had colonies bordering on the Atlantic Ocean? On the Pacific Ocean?

Using Study Skills

1. **Library Resources:** An unabridged dictionary is the most complete edition of a given dictionary. One useful feature of an unabridged dictionary is the etymology (ət'ə mol'ə jē), or history, of words. The etymology is usually given in brackets at the beginning or end of an entry. The etymology of the word *yerba* might be given like this:

[fr AmerSp *yerba* herb, plant (fr L *herba* grass, herb)]

This entry shows that the word *yerba* comes from the American Spanish word *yerba,* which means herb or plant, and which in turn comes from the Latin word *herba,* which means grass or herb. You may need to consult the key in your dictionary to explain other abbreviations.

Find an unabridged dictionary in your school or public library. Use it to learn the etymology of some other interesting words used in this unit: cordillera, estuary, conquistador, hacienda, coup, junta.

2. **Graph:** You may need to refer to the text to help answer the questions about the graphs on this page. The graphs show the percentage of people in each region for whom each language shown is the official language. What kind of graphs are they? For what regions is information given? In what Central American country would you expect English to be the official language? Why? In what Latin American country would you expect Portuguese to be spoken? Why? What countries would you expect to have had colonies in the West Indies? Are there any Latin American countries with more than one official language? How do you know?

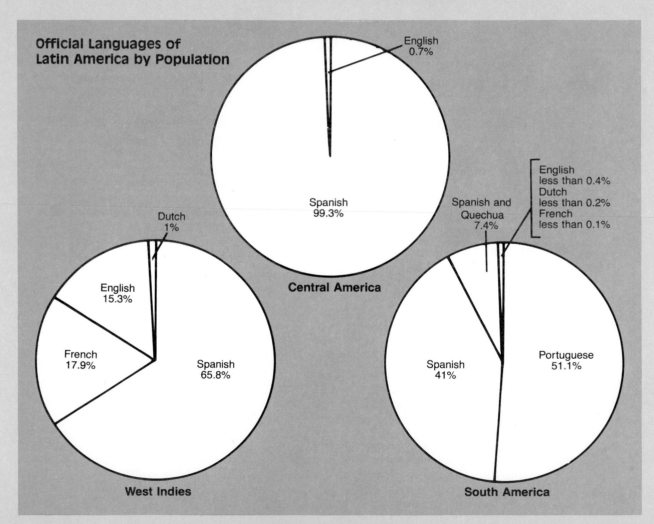

Official Languages of Latin America by Population

English 0.7%

Spanish 99.3%

Central America

Dutch 1%

English 15.3%

French 17.9%

Spanish 65.8%

West Indies

Spanish and Quechua 7.4%

English less than 0.4%
Dutch less than 0.2%
French less than 0.1%

Portuguese 51.1%

Spanish 41%

South America

Thinking It Through

1. Why were the land reform measures instituted by the Mexican government important to farmers?
2. What is the political status of Puerto Rico? Why might some Puerto Ricans favor maintaining this status?
3. The Brazilian government is encouraging people to settle in the interior of the country. It is also building highways through the jungle. What are some advantages and disadvantages of this plan?
4. Why is the Panama Canal an important waterway? Why do you think it was built where it was? What do you think might have been some of the problems in building the canal?

Projects

1. The History Committee might like to learn more about the Aztecs, the Mayas, and the Incas. What social, political, and economic systems did these groups develop? Where can ruins of their cities be seen? Share your findings with the class.
2. The Biography Committee might like to read more about such famous Mexican leaders as Benito Juárez and Porfirio Díaz. Committee members could use biographical dictionaries to write a short report on these men.
3. The Current Events Committee might like to read about political developments in Central America. Use *The Readers' Guide to Periodical Literature* to find interesting articles on Central American countries. Collect clippings from daily newspapers. Use the information to make a time line of important events that have occurred in Central America during the past six months.
4. The Arts and Sciences Committee might like to find out more about the operation of the Panama Canal. Students could prepare diagrams to show how the locks work.

5 Europe

Unit Preview

In this unit you will read about the more than 30 countries that make up the western part of the continent of Europe. The people of these countries speak many different languages and have many different customs and traditions. However, the nations of Europe share much the same history and cultural backgrounds.

Europe is a small continent, yet it has a large population. Fertile soil and a favorable climate allow farmers to produce abundant crops. Mineral resources provide raw materials for many industries. The Industrial Revolution began in Europe, and the European countries were among the first to become industrialized. Waterways that provide a convenient transportation network have long promoted trade among many European nations. European nations have also played a leading role in world trade.

The influence of many nations of Europe has extended beyond their borders. The classical civilizations of Greece and Rome have affected much of the Western world. During the fifteenth and sixteenth centuries, many European countries established colonies in different parts of the world. Millions of people outside Europe adopted European languages, customs, and technology. You have learned how Europe influenced the development of countries in North America and South America in Unit 3 and Unit 4.

Things to Discover

If you look carefully at the picture, map, and time line, you can answer these questions.

1. The highlighted area on the map is the continent of Europe, excluding the area occupied by the Soviet Union and Turkey. What oceans border Europe?
2. The photograph shows a castle along the Rhine River in Germany. For many years, German lands were divided into dozens of separately ruled states. In what year were the German states united?
3. At the end of World War I, Austria and Hungary became separate independent nations. For how many years had these two countries been united as the Austro-Hungarian Empire?

Words to Learn

You will meet these words and terms in this unit. As you read, you will learn what they mean and how to pronounce them. The Word List will help you.

alliance	heritage
Alpine	industrialization
channel	intensive farming
constitutional	loess
monarchy	nitrogen
dynasty	population density
emigration	self-determination
enclave	sirocco

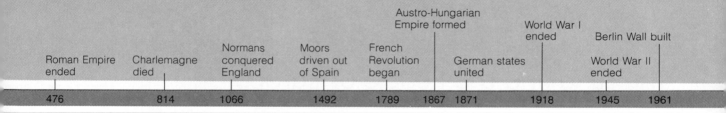

Roman Empire ended	Charlemagne died	Normans conquered England	Moors driven out of Spain	French Revolution began	Austro-Hungarian Empire formed	German states united	World War I ended	Berlin Wall built / World War II ended
476	814	1066	1492	1789	1867	1871	1918	1945 1961

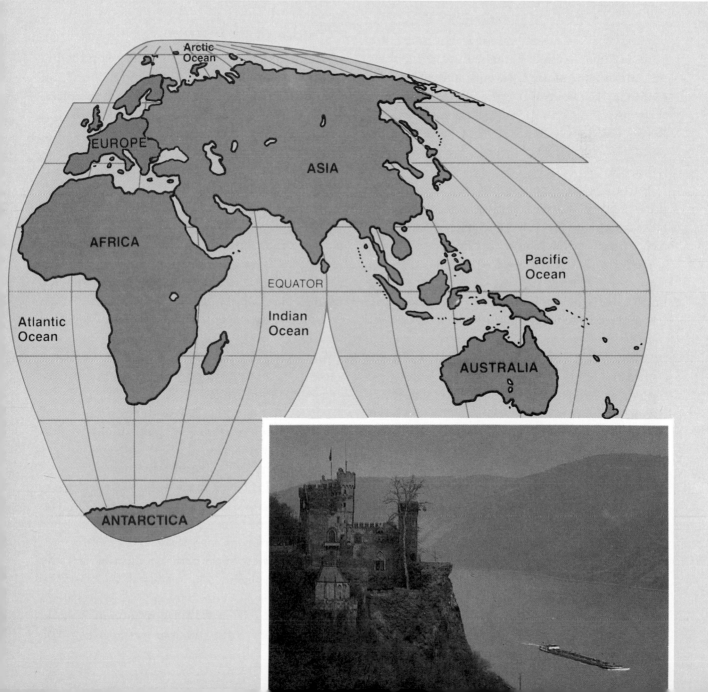

Arctic Ocean

EUROPE

ASIA

AFRICA

EQUATOR

Pacific Ocean

Atlantic Ocean

Indian Ocean

AUSTRALIA

ANTARCTICA

1
The Land and the People of Europe

Europe is a continent, but it is also part of a large landmass called Eurasia. Eurasia includes the continents of Europe and Asia. The land boundary between Europe and Asia is usually considered to be the Ural Mountains, the Ural River, and the Caucasus (kô′kə səs) Mountains. Only about one-fifth of the Eurasian landmass is Europe.

Europe is the second-smallest continent, yet it has a population larger than any other continent except Asia. More than half of Europe is part of the Soviet Union. In this unit, we will consider only the part of Europe that stretches from the Atlantic Ocean in the west to the border of the Soviet Union in the east. Throughout the unit, the term *Europe* will refer only to this region.

Although it is small, Europe is a land of great contrasts. There are more than 30 countries, ranging in size from France, which is somewhat smaller than Texas, to Vatican City and Monaco, each of which covers less than one square mile. Dozens of languages are spoken.

Europe has regions of low-lying plains, high plateaus, and towering mountains. Some countries are islands, others are landlocked nations. Many have at least one border on a sea or ocean.

After Columbus's voyages to the Western Hemisphere, Europeans set out to explore the world. They founded colonies and developed trade. European ideas and ways of life spread throughout the world.

The Land of Europe

Europe and Asia, unlike the other continents, are not surrounded, or nearly surrounded, by water. Europe is really a peninsula. It has often been called "a peninsula of peninsulas." To the north is the Arctic Ocean, to the west, the Atlantic Ocean, and to the south, the Mediterranean Sea. No part of the continent is more than a few hundred miles from the sea.

Landforms

Much of Europe is a plain. The largest plain stretches from the Atlantic along the North Sea and the Baltic Sea. Another great plain lies along the Danube River. Smaller plains are found in the Mediterranean countries. The plains are good farming regions. It is on the plains, too, that the great cities of Europe have grown up because the level lands offered easy transportation routes.

Plateaus and uplands rise to the southeast of the wide coastal plain. A plateau also covers much of Spain. The plateaus and uplands are cut by rivers and separated by plains.

Mountains cover most of Norway and western Sweden and part of northern Britain. The mountains of Norway and Sweden are higher and more rugged than those of Britain.

The highest mountains in Europe are the Alps. They lie in south central Europe. The Alps themselves are only part of a cordillera called the *Alpine* (al′pīn) mountain system. *Alpine* means "of or relating to the Alps." The

The Pyrenees mountains that extend along the border between Spain and France are part of the *Alpine* system.

word is often used to describe high mountain climate or scenery. Mountains of the Alpine system include the Pyrenees (pir′ə nēz′), the Apennines (ap′ə nīnz′), and the Carpathians. Find these mountains on the map on page 189.

Water Features

Many seas and bays cut into the land of Europe, making the coastline very long. In the north are the Gulf of Bothnia, the Baltic Sea, and the North Sea. The Bay of Biscay cuts into the coast of southwestern France and northern Spain. The Ligurian Sea, the Adriatic Sea, and the Aegean (ə jē′ən) Sea are northern extensions of the Mediterranean.

The river systems of Europe provide easy access to the sea. The Danube, flowing from southwest West Germany to the Black Sea, is Europe's longest river. The Rhine begins in the Alps and flows into the North Sea. Many rivers drain the broad European coastal plain and flow into the Baltic Sea, the North Sea, or the Atlantic. Canals link many of Europe's navigable rivers to form a transportation network.

Most of Europe's freshwater lakes are in Sweden and Finland. Several large lakes lie south of the Alps in Italy.

Climate

Europe lies in the middle latitudes between the Arctic Circle and 36° north latitude. Its climate is milder than the part of North America that lies in the same latitudes. The European winters are warmer and the summers are cooler. Except in the far north, winter temperatures seldom fall below freezing.

Europe's mild climate is a result of winds that blow from the west across the Atlantic. The winds pass over a warm current in the Atlantic known as the North Atlantic Drift. The North Atlantic Drift is an extension of the Gulf Stream. Find the Gulf Stream and the North Atlantic Drift on the map on page 29. During the winter, the winds warm the land. During the summer, they cool the land. A climate of warm summers and cool winters is called an oceanic climate.

Winds from the Atlantic also bring much rain to Europe. Inland regions receive from 20 to 40 inches (51 to 102 cm) of rain a year. Places near the shore and in the mountains receive even heavier rainfall.

Lands along the Mediterranean Sea have a different climate. Here the rainfall is seasonal, that is, most of the rain falls during one season of the year. The rainy season in the Mediterranean is from October to April. During the summer, little or no rain falls. A climate of hot, dry summers and cool, wet winters is known as a Mediterranean climate.

Population and Land Area

Alaska

Hawaii

United States
226.5 million people
3.6 million square miles
9.4 million square kilometers

Europe
491.4 million people
1.9 million square miles
4.8 million square kilometers

 = 25 million people

Natural Resources

Europe's most valuable natural resources are its fertile soil, its seas and rivers, and its mineral deposits. Europeans have made good use of their resources. Careful farming methods have led to the production of large crops. Fishing industries and shipbuilding have grown up along the coasts. An important sea trade has grown up among the countries of Europe and between Europe and overseas countries. The development of internal waterways has made transportation from one country to another easier.

Coal and iron are the most valuable of Europe's minerals. Coal and iron are necessary to produce steel. Machines, beams, and rails are all made from steel. Steel has made possible the many railways and highways that cross Europe and make it easier to transport goods. The important iron deposits are in Sweden, France, and Spain. There are large coal fields in Great Britain, Germany, Poland, France, and Belgium. Wells in the North Sea are now producing oil for Europe, but most oil is imported.

The mountainous parts of Europe have many waterfalls. The power of falling water or of swiftly flowing mountain streams is used to generate electricity. Power generated by falling water is called hydroelectricity. Hydroelectricity is used for light and heat and to power Europe's many factories.

The People of Europe

Europe's favorable climate, its geography, and its natural resources have made it possible for the land to support many people. Europe has a high *population density* (pop′yə lā′shən den′ sə tē). Population density is the average number of people living on a square unit of land in a country or other region. It can be given as

191

Highways, railroads, and waterways like these in the Moselle Valley of West Germany are part of Europe's efficient transportation network.

the number of people per square mile or as the number of people per square kilometer. Europe's population density is more than 260 per square mile (102 per sq. km). The population density of the United States is about 64 per square mile (25 per sq. km).

Because Europe is densely populated, it is important to produce as much food as possible. High productivity can be brought about in two ways. One way is to increase the amount of land under cultivation. The best farmlands in Europe are the flat or rolling plains. Yet farmers in Europe make good use of the hilly and mountainous regions. Orchards and vineyards are found in hilly regions. High areas in the Alps where it is too cold for trees to grow are used as pastures. In Europe, almost one-third of the land is cultivated.

Another way to increase agricultural productivity is to work the land with special care. Such methods of working the land are called

intensive farming (in ten'siv fär'ming). Often farmers plant two or more crops on the same field at the same time. Grapevines are grown on trellises built across a field of vegetables. Fruit trees and nut trees are planted along the edges of fields.

Even with intensive farming methods, Europe cannot produce enough food to feed its people. It must import food. It must also import fuel, because it does not produce enough for its needs. To help pay for its imports, Europe exports manufactured goods.

Trade has been important to Europe for hundreds of years. After 1500, many European nations established trade routes throughout the world. Later, they established colonies that supplied them with raw materials. Goods manufactured from the raw materials in Europe were then sold in the colonies. Today, the period of colonization is over, but European countries continue to trade throughout the world. In the past, there was much competition among countries for raw materials and for markets for manufactured goods. Today, many countries of Europe are cooperating in trade. They have formed an economic union called the European Economic Community, or Common Market. Member countries charge no taxes on imported goods, so goods can be exchanged freely. Today ten countries are members of the Common Market. They are the United Kingdom, France, Belgium, Denmark, West Germany, Ireland, Italy, Luxembourg, the Netherlands, and Greece.

In the following sections of this unit we will discuss the countries of Europe in four groups: western Europe, northern Europe, southern Europe, and eastern Europe. Although each country of Europe is unlike any other country, the countries in each group share certain geographic features and cultural patterns.

Do You Know?

1. What great landmass is Europe a part of?
2. What kind of climate does much of Europe have? What current is partly responsible for this climate?
3. In what ways does Europe increase its agricultural productivity?

2
Western Europe

The 12 countries of western Europe are the United Kingdom of Great Britain and Northern Ireland, Ireland, the Netherlands, Belgium, Luxembourg, France, Andorra, Monaco, West Germany, Austria, Switzerland, and Liechtenstein. Six of these countries have coasts on the Atlantic; two have coasts on the Mediterranean.

The United Kingdom and Ireland are island countries. They are separated from the rest of Europe by the English *Channel* (chan'əl). A channel is a wide stretch of water between two land areas. A channel links two larger bodies of water. The English Channel connects the Atlantic Ocean with the North Sea. The channel narrows to become the Strait of Dover. Channels and straits are both stretches of water that link large bodies of water, but a channel is wider than a strait. At its narrowest part, the Strait of Dover is 20 miles (32 km) wide. All of Europe except the United Kingdom and Ireland is often referred to as the Continent.

Most of western Europe has an oceanic climate. Rainfall is plentiful. Much of the region is a rolling plain that is the most productive agricultural land in Europe.

In the southeastern part of western Europe are the high and rugged Alps. They extend from France through Switzerland, Liechtenstein, and Austria. Many of the peaks are more than 12,000 feet (3,657 m) above sea level. The highest mountain in the Alps, Mont Blanc in France, rises 15,771 feet (4,807 m) above sea level. The Pyrenees, which are lower than the Alps, extend along the French-Spanish border.

The southern part of France borders the Mediterranean Sea. This region, known as the Riviera, has a Mediterranean climate.

The United Kingdom

The United Kingdom includes England, Wales, Scotland, and Northern Ireland. This island nation occupies the British Isles, which are made up of two large islands and several small ones. On the largest island are England, Scotland, and Wales. The Republic of Ireland occupies about three-fourths of the other large island. The rest of this island, known as Northern Ireland, is part of the United Kingdom. People often refer to the United Kingdom as Great Britain. All the citizens of the United Kingdom are British citizens.

The British Isles lie on the same latitude as Newfoundland in Canada. However, the British Isles are not nearly as cold as Newfoundland. Like most of western Europe, the United Kingdom benefits from the warm North Atlantic Drift.

The United Kingdom is about the size of West Germany, but almost 56 million people live there. Its population density and its location on islands have shaped the history and economy of the country.

Early Britain

The channel separating Britain from the European continent was not an obstacle to invaders in early times. The Celts of central and western Europe began crossing the channel about 700 B.C. The Gauls and Britons were two Celtic tribes who established permanent settlements throughout the island. These people were conquered by the Romans who invaded Britain in 43 A.D. The Romans ruled for 400 years, making Britain part of the Roman Empire. When the Empire began to decline in the early 400s, the Roman soldiers were called back to defend Rome. It was not long before other conquerors came to take their place.

The Angles, Saxons, and Jutes were Germanic tribes who came to Britain from the Continent. Their powerful kings ruled Britain for hundreds of years. King Alfred, who ruled from 871 to 899, was called Alfred the Great. He united the country and was strong enough to control the nobles who wanted to maintain their power through large armies and great land holdings. Alfred built a strong navy, created a system of local courts, and established schools. During the years immediately after Alfred's wise and just rule, no king was able to maintain a united kingdom.

Parts of a Roman wall still stand in Great Britain. Named for an emperor, Hadrian's Wall was built during the 120s A.D. across northern England.

In 1066, the Normans of France, led by William the Conqueror, crossed the English Channel and conquered the island. William became king, but he had to fight the nobles who resisted his authority. William established the feudal system. Under this system, the king granted lands to nobles who pledged their loyalty. The authority of the king was supreme. The nobles had only the powers granted by their ruler.

The nobles resisted the king's authority. In 1215, they succeeded in forcing King John to sign the Magna Carta, or Great Charter. This document limited the powers of the king, but it did not end the conflict. King John led an army against the nobles immediately after agreeing to the provisions of the Magna Carta.

A New Form of Government

The kings who came after John realized that they needed the support of the nobles. In 1295, King Edward I called a meeting of nobles, knights, churchmen, and representatives of towns. This meeting came to be called the "Model Parliament." King Edward not only asked the representatives for advice, he also gave them power. In 1297, he agreed that only Parliament could institute new taxes. The powers of Parliament increased during the next centuries. By 1689, Parliament alone had the authority to make laws. England had become a *constitutional monarchy* (kon′stə too′shən əl mon′ər kē). A constitutional monarchy is a form of government in which elected representatives have political power and the monarch has only symbolic authority.

In 1707, the Act of Union united England, Wales, and Scotland as one nation called Great Britain. Today England, Wales, Scotland, and Northern Ireland make up the United Kingdom of Great Britain and Northern Ireland. The United Kingdom is still a constitutional monarchy.

The Industrial Revolution

The late 1700s and early 1800s were years of important change in Britain. The Industrial Revolution is the term used to describe this period of *industrialization* (in dus′trē ə li zā′ shən). Industrialization is the process of changing to an economy that is based on manufacturing. Before the Industrial Revolution, Great Britain's economy was chiefly agricultural. Cloth, leather, and metal goods were made by hand in small shops or at home. People lived in villages and towns or on small farms.

During the Industrial Revolution, inventions and new sources of power transformed

Edinburgh Castle stands on a high rock above Scotland's capital and second-largest city.

the economy. Power supplied by humans and animals was replaced by machine power. Cloth that was woven on hand looms was produced faster and in greater quantities in factories with power looms. The small foundries that produced iron and steel were replaced by giant furnaces.

The first factories were small and were run by water power. They were built along the rivers of the plains of England and also along rivers and small streams that flowed out of the northern hills. Nearly all the sites suitable for developing water power were soon occupied.

In 1769, the steam engine was improved and made workable by a Scot named James Watt. The steam engine provided power for factories by burning coal, which heated water and turned it into steam. The steam engine was also the power source for railroads that transported raw materials and finished goods throughout the country. During the Industrial Revolution, hundreds of miles of railroad tracks were built.

Industrialization led to social and political as well as economic changes. As people moved closer to their places of work, cities grew up around factories. To find new markets for its finished goods and new supplies of raw materials for its factories, Great Britain looked beyond its borders to colonies. British colonies were established throughout the world.

The British Empire

Colonial trade helped Great Britain to prosper. Raw materials were imported from the colonies and were used to manufacture goods for sale at home and abroad. Britain's fleet of ships protected trade routes and found new places for colonies.

The British colonies along the Atlantic coast won their independence by 1783, but Great Britain still ruled Canada. British colonies were established in Latin America, Africa, and Southeast Asia. India, Australia, New Zealand, and many Pacific islands also became part of the vast Empire. It could once be said that "The sun never sets on the British Empire."

Great Britain Today

Great Britain is no longer an empire. Most of its colonies are now independent. Many former possessions are members of the Commonwealth of Nations. These nations are joined by trade and defense agreements.

Trade is important for the United Kingdom, which depends on other countries for most of its food supplies. Manufacturing is the most important industry. In 1974, offshore drilling operations in the North Sea began to produce oil for British industries.

Cities of the United Kingdom

Some of Great Britain's large manufacturing cities are near northern coal fields. They are Birmingham and Sheffield, famous for iron and steel; Manchester, a cotton-manufacturing center; and Bradford and Leeds, the woolen-goods centers. Farther north is the port city of Newcastle, a coal, iron, and steel center. Liverpool is the chief seaport for Britain's northern industrial area.

Glasgow and Edinburgh are the large industrial cities of Scotland. These port cities, too, are located near coal fields and near oil resources being developed in the North Sea.

London, the capital of the United Kingdom, is one of the world's largest cities. It is a great cultural center with world-famous museums, libraries, and theaters. It is also one of Britain's greatest industrial cities and has been an important seaport since the Middle Ages.

The oldest part of London is called "The City." Decisions made in the banks and businesses in "The City" affect businesses throughout the world. London's second-oldest section is Westminster. Both the royal palace and the houses of Parliament are in this district.

Northern Ireland

The United Kingdom includes the northern part of the island of Ireland. Belfast, the leading city of Northern Ireland, is a shipbuilding center. Belfast and Londonderry have large mills where flax is made into Irish linen.

Many people in Northern Ireland believe very strongly that their country should be independent of Great Britain. This has led to violence and acts of terrorism.

The Republic of Ireland

The Republic of Ireland is about one-fourth the size of the United Kingdom and has a population of nearly three and one-half million. Dublin is the capital city. Ireland occupies most of the island that is sometimes called the "Emerald Isle." It is called the Emerald Isle because it is so green. Mild temperatures and ample rainfall produce rich pastures on the plains.

Ireland is mountainous along the coast and flat in the interior. In the central part are many lakes and bogs. The island has few forests. Without oil, coal, or wood from forests, Ireland must use other sources of fuel. Many homes in Ireland are heated by burning peat. Peat is a spongy material composed of partially decayed grass and moss.

Ireland was part of the United Kingdom for 120 years. In 1921, it became independent. After winning independence, the Irish revived the old Irish language called Gaelic. Gaelic was taught in schools, and Gaelic place names were brought back into use.

One of the world's busiest seaports is Rotterdam. It is built on a branch of the Rhine that connects it with many other European cities.

The farms of Ireland are small. The Irish farmer's income is principally from raising beef cattle, sheep, and pigs. Potatoes and flax are also important farm products.

Ireland lacks coal for its factories, but hydroelectric power is available. The Irish government built a large dam on the Shannon River to supply electricity to farms and factories.

Shannon, a city in southwest Ireland, has a fine airport. Because of its western location, this airport is a servicing center for many planes crossing the Atlantic.

The Low Countries

The Netherlands, Belgium, and Luxembourg are often called the Low Countries. The word *Netherlands* means "lowlands." Much of the land in these countries is a low plain.

The Low Countries together are about the size of the Republic of Ireland, but they have about seven times as many people. The Netherlands has a population of more than 14 million, Belgium almost ten million, and Luxembourg 365,000. This is one of the most densely populated regions of Europe.

Geography

Belgium and the Netherlands lie on the great plain along the coast of the North Sea. There are low hills in southeastern Belgium that extend throughout Luxembourg. The Scheldt (shelt), Maas, and Rhine rivers flow through these lands, providing waterways to the sea.

History

The region of the Low Countries was ruled by Charles V of Spain in the mid-1500s. At that time, the Netherlands and Belgium were called Spanish Netherlands.

The Dutch revolted under the harsh rule of Philip II, Charles's son. The Netherlands won independence from Spain in 1581.

In their small area, the Dutch people developed a prosperous nation. Soon after they became independent of Spain, the Dutch became one of Britain's strong rivals for trade on the seas and in the founding of colonies. The Dutch founded New Amsterdam in North America, which later became the city of New York. The British, however, defeated the Dutch in a war in the 1660s and gained control of the Dutch colony. Nevertheless, the Netherlands still held a large overseas empire in the islands off the coast of Asia.

Belgium remained under Spanish rule for many years. Later, as a result of wars in Europe, it was passed back and forth between nations. In 1815, Belgium was joined to the Netherlands, but the Belgians did not like that arrangement. Fifteen years later, they revolted and became an independent nation under their own king.

Luxembourg became independent in 1867. Like the Netherlands and Belgium, Luxembourg is a constitutional monarchy, with a parliament elected by the people. It is ruled by a grand duke or duchess.

The Netherlands

The Dutch have built great dikes to keep the North Sea from flooding their land. About two-fifths of the country lies below sea level on land that has been reclaimed from the sea. In the past, windmills supplied the power to pump water to keep the reclaimed land dry, but now gasoline engines are used.

The dairy cattle of the Netherlands supply fresh milk for people in the cities. Cheese is an important Dutch product. Near the cities of Haarlem and Leiden (lī′dən) stretch field after field of tulips, lilies, and daffodils. Flower bulbs from these fields are shipped to gardeners all over the world, and freshly cut flowers are flown daily to many cities in Europe.

The mouth of the Rhine, the busiest river in Europe, is in the Netherlands. Two other rivers, the Maas and Scheldt, flow through the Netherlands. These rivers provide inland water routes and outlets to the sea.

Commerce is the leading activity of the Netherlands. Many products that are to be sent to Belgium, to Germany, and to Switzerland are unloaded at one of the Dutch ports. Then they are shipped inland on the rivers and canals. Products from inland countries also are exported from the Dutch ports. Dutch ships carry Dutch, German, Belgian, and Swiss products to many parts of the world.

Rotterdam and Amsterdam are the largest cities and seaports of the Netherlands. Rotterdam is built on one of the branches of the Rhine. Amsterdam, the capital of the nation, is reached from the sea by the large North Sea Canal. Many small canals thread the city, and houses are built right on their banks. Amsterdam has more than 350 bridges across its waterways.

The seaport cities of the Netherlands process many raw materials from overseas. Skilled craftsworkers cut and polish diamonds. Petroleum from overseas is refined. Pipelines carry the refined oil to West Germany.

Belgium

The flat plain of western Belgium is good farmland. The farmers raise dairy cattle and grow vegetables, flower seeds and bulbs, and flax. Flax is made into fine linen in the city of Ghent and nearby towns.

Manufacturing is an important occupation in Belgium. The country has coal, zinc, and iron ore deposits. However, most of the iron ore used in its steel mills is brought from Luxembourg and France.

The factory towns are built on the coal fields of the Meuse (mūz) River valley. Meuse is the French name for the Maas River. Steel is made there, and locomotives, heavy machines, and railroad cars are manufactured. Zinc ore is smelted and the zinc is used in many products.

Brussels, the capital of Belgium, is one of the large cities of Europe, with a population of one million people. Fine tapestries, carpets, and laces are made there.

High peaks in the French Alps remain snow-covered all summer. This valley is near Mont Blanc.

Luxembourg

The chief industry of Luxembourg, which is smaller than Rhode Island, is the manufacture of iron and steel. A large field of iron ore lies within its borders, and many people work in the mines. Coal is brought to the country from Germany, Belgium, and France. Iron and steel are manufactured in enormous quantities in this small country. Large amounts are exported to other European countries. The city of Luxembourg is the capital. Tourism is another important industry.

France

France is the largest country in Europe. It is about one-sixth the size of the United States. Its population is nearly one-fourth that of the United States.

France is located at the crossroads of many travel routes in western Europe. The location of the country has made it the center of much cultural activity, but it has also made it a target for invasion.

Geography

Although most of France is a large plain, the country has mountains too. The Alps form the border between France and Italy. The Pyrenees separate France and Spain.

The part of France near the English Channel has an oceanic climate. In contrast, southern France has a Mediterranean climate.

History

In ancient times, the country now called France was a part of Gaul. In 51 B.C., Julius Caesar, a Roman general, conquered Gaul and made it a part of the Roman Empire. When Rome lost its power and could no longer keep order, German tribes moved down from the north. One tribe, called the Franks, moved into the region that is now France. By the year 800 A.D., the land of the Franks was a part of Charlemagne's (shär′lə mänz′) empire. Charlemagne was a king of the Franks who had expanded his kingdom to include a large part of western Europe. After Charlemagne's empire broke up, Normans from Scandinavia swept across the North Sea and settled in

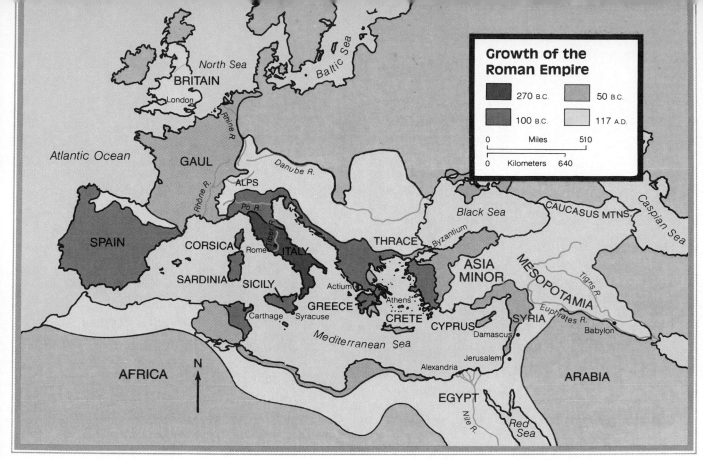

At its greatest size, the Roman Empire covered much of Europe, North Africa, and the Middle East.

northern France. The area became known as Normandy.

In the late 900s, a new *dynasty* (dī'nəs tē) came to power. A dynasty is a line of rulers from the same family. Hugh Capet was the first king in this dynasty. He strengthened the power of the monarch and increased the royal lands. By 1180, Paris was the capital of an area that was almost as big as France is today.

France was ruled by kings from a series of dynasties until 1789. In that year, the people rebelled against the king. France became a republic as a result of the French Revolution. That republic did not last long, however.

A French general named Napoleon seized control of the government and made himself emperor. Napoleon and his armies conquered much of Europe until several nations joined together and defeated him in 1815. After Napoleon's defeat, France restored the monarchy. In the 1840s, another revolution broke out, and a republic was again established. The president later declared himself Emperor Napoleon III. He involved France in a war with Prussia. Napoleon III's government collapsed, and in 1871 France was defeated. A third republic was set up after the war. France still has a republican form of government.

Farming

Although only ten of every 100 people in France make their living on farms, France is a

The Eiffel Tower is a famous Paris landmark. Built in 1889, it was for many years the world's highest structure.

leading food producer of western Europe. Abundant crops of wheat are grown on the western and northern plains. Sugar beets are raised in the north. There are dairy farms along the English Channel, in the central uplands, and in the French Alps. Corn is grown in the southwest. Thousands of sheep graze in the central uplands and in the Pyrenees Mountains. Grapes are grown in vineyards near the Mediterranean, in the area around Bordeaux (bôr dō′), and in regions south and east of Paris.

Manufacturing

France's industries manufacture automobiles, aircraft, plastics, and electronics products. There is also a large iron and steel industry. Iron ore is exported to Belgium and to West Germany. The French do not have enough high-grade coal for their steel industry, so they import coal from these two countries.

Cities of France

Paris, the capital of France, has more than two million people. All the main railroads and highways of France lead to Paris. The network of canals in western Europe leads into the Seine River, on which Paris is located.

Paris is one of the world's most beautiful cities. Art galleries, museums, old palaces, magnificent cathedrals, and theaters make Paris a cultural center that people from all over the world visit. Paris has long been recognized as a fashion center. The clothes created by its designers influence styles throughout the world.

Until recently, central Paris had no skyscrapers because the law restricted them. The one exception was the Eiffel Tower, which rises to a height of nearly 1,000 feet (300 m). The top of this tower is a fine place from which to view the city.

Le Havre and Cherbourg are the chief French seaports on the English Channel, and they are also shipbuilding centers. In the southwest, Bordeaux is the leading seaport, though it lies 60 miles (96 km) from the open ocean on the Garonne River. Marseille (mär sā′) is the largest seaport on the Mediterranean Sea. In Lyon (lē ōn′), on the Rhône River, fine French silks are woven. South of Lyon is Nice (nēs), the leading city of the French Riviera, a world-famous seaside resort.

Andorra and Monaco

Andorra and Monaco are tiny countries that border France. Both are independent yet share close ties with their larger neighbors.

Andorra

Andorra is a tiny country located in the Pyrenees Mountains between France and Spain. Andorra is about half the size of New York City and has a population of about 30,000.

Andorra is governed jointly by the French president and the bishop of Urgel, Spain. The two rulers have equal power. Andorra has two postal systems, one paid for by the French government and the other paid for by the Spanish bishop. The country also has both French and Spanish schools. The citizens use both French and Spanish money.

Although some crops are grown in Andorra, most of the land is mountainous and not good for farming. However, sheep and cattle are raised by the farmers there. Lumbering is an important industry, and furniture and timber are exported. Recently, tourism has become the main industry in Andorra. Tourists come to ski in winter and in the summer.

Monaco

Monaco (mon′ə kō) is a small hilly country on the Mediterranean coast. It is surrounded by France on its land borders. Monaco is ruled by a prince who governs with an elected council. Monaco's warm, sunny climate and beautiful beaches attract many visitors. Tourism is the chief industry.

West Germany

West Germany is about the size of the United Kingdom and has just slightly more people. Its capital, Bonn, is on the Rhine River.

Geography

The land of West Germany extends from the plains bordering the North Sea to the foothills of the Bavarian Alps in the south. The central part of the country is a region of highlands and plateaus.

The Rhine River flows from the Alps of Switzerland to the North Sea. It runs through West Germany and, for part of the way, forms the boundary between West Germany and France. The Rhine has carved a deep valley along part of its course.

The Ruhr River is a very small stream that flows into the Rhine. The valley of the Ruhr has the largest single coal field in western Europe.

Early History

Warlike tribes from northern Europe moved into the area that is now Germany as early as 1000 B.C. The Romans called these people *Germani*. These people resisted the attack of Roman soldiers. By the year 800 A.D., the people in what is now Germany had come under the rule of Charlemagne.

Soon after the death of Charlemagne in 814 A.D., his empire was divided among his three grandsons. One took the west, which became France. Another took the east, which became Germany. The third took the south, the northern half of the peninsula of Italy and an area across the Alps. About 100 years later, a new empire, called the Holy Roman Empire, came into being. That empire was made up of the lands and peoples of central Europe, including what is now known as Germany.

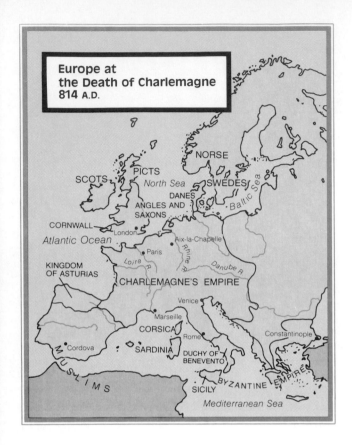

Charlemagne united much of western Europe in his empire. What lands were under Muslim control in 814? By 1360, many modern nations, such as England and France, had come into being.

Rival States

In the early eighteenth century, two powerful German states developed. One was Austria, in south-central Europe, and the other was Prussia, in northern Europe.

Prussia had a number of strong kings. One of these was Frederick the Great, who became king in 1740. With his well-drilled army, he waged war against his neighbors and seized much territory for Prussia. He also improved the welfare of his people by promoting education and science.

The rulers who followed Frederick were also interested in building up Prussia's strength. When William I came to the Prussian throne in

1861, his prime minister was Count Otto von Bismarck. Bismarck wanted to unify all the Germans under the leadership of Prussia. He built up a great army and waged three successful wars against Denmark, Austria, and France.

In 1871, at the end of the war with France, a united Germany was proclaimed. William I became the emperor. All the German states except Austria joined Prussia to form Germany. The new Germany became one of the most powerful nations in Europe.

A World at War

Germany's rise to power alarmed France, Great Britain, and Russia. By 1907, those three

Europe Before World War I
1914

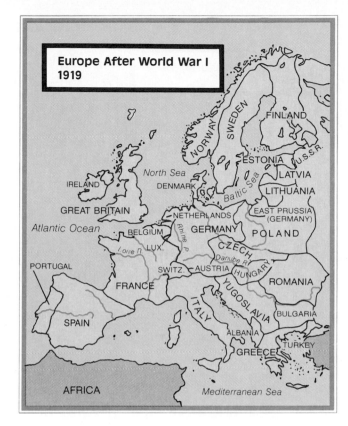

Europe After World War I
1919

Many changes occurred in European boundaries as a result of the peace settlement at the end of World War I. What nations in eastern and northern Europe became independent?

countries had signed agreements to support each other. Germany was united with Austria-Hungary and Italy by a similar arrangement called an *alliance* (ə lī′ əns). An alliance is an agreement between two or more nations to cooperate closely in such matters as defense or trade. Treaties and alliances among other European countries in the 1900s created a network of military and political connections.

In 1914, Archduke Ferdinand of Austria-Hungary was killed in Bosnia, a small Austrian territory that was claimed by Serbia. When Austria-Hungary declared war on Serbia, Russia, France, and Great Britain were committed to Serbia's defense. Germany and Italy

were pledged to support Austria-Hungary. The war that resulted came to be known as World War I. See the maps on this page.

Italy, Germany, and Austria-Hungary were called the Central Powers. Many other nations joined the fight against the Central Powers. Those nations were known as the Allies. The United States entered the war in 1917 on the side of the Allies. The United States sent many troops and military supplies. In 1918, the Allies defeated Germany.

After the war ended, Germany became a republic, but the republic was short-lived. A leader named Adolf Hitler came to power in 1933. Hitler built up a great army. He believed

Europe After World War II
1949

After World War II, Germany was divided into two countries. What happened to the Baltic countries?

A Divided Nation

The Allies divided occupied Germany into four zones. Within a few years, Germany was divided into two nations. See the map on this page. The zones occupied by the western allies became the new nation of West Germany. The Soviet zone became East Germany. Berlin was also divided. West Berlin became an *enclave* (en'klāv) in East Germany. An enclave is a country or an outlying portion of a country surrounded, or nearly surrounded, by the territory of another country.

After World War II, the Germans quickly regained their former leadership in manufacturing. In the early 1950s, people began to speak of West Germany's "economic miracle," as the country again made itself Europe's major industrial nation.

Between 1945 and 1976, more than 15 million people immigrated to West Germany, more than to any other country in the world during that period. Many of these people were from East Germany. In recent years, the growth rate of the economy has slowed somewhat. West Germany, though, remains a prosperous industrial country.

Farming

Much of Germany is too steep, too sandy, or too cool for growing crops. Only in central Germany do farmers engage in large-scale raising of crops. The farmers grow rye, oats, potatoes, and sugar beets. Farmers along the North Sea raise dairy cattle. The farmers of the south, who live in the hilly lands to the north of the Alps, also engage in dairy farming.

that Germany needed more land and prepared to take it by force. When he sent his armies into Poland in 1939, Great Britain and France came to Poland's aid. World War II had begun.

Hitler's armies were strong. They took over France with little trouble. Then Hitler attacked the Soviet Union, Germany's powerful neighbor to the east. Hitler's military machine was finally stopped by the Russians, who fiercely defended their homeland.

Meanwhile, the Allies on the western front had gained strength. In May 1945, the Allied armies of the United States, Britain, and France moved into Germany from the west. The Russians marched in from the east. The Allies met in Berlin and occupied all of Germany.

Cities of West Germany

On the Rhine River in West Germany are several large cities. Workers in these cities produce chemicals, cars, trucks, and machinery. Barges carry raw materials and goods from place to place. Railroad trains along the banks of the Rhine also move passengers and goods. A city of at least 100,000 persons is located every few miles along the Rhine, except in the Rhine gorge. Bonn, the capital, is located near the point where the Rhine leaves the gorge and flows into the plain again.

In the Ruhr Valley, so many mining and manufacturing cities have grown up that the area today seems to be one continuous city. Essen, the largest of the Ruhr cities, is an important iron, steel, and machinery center. The city of Duisburg (dōōs'boork'), located where the Ruhr flows into the Rhine, is Europe's largest and busiest river port. Dusseldorf, on the Rhine, is the banking and commercial center for the cities of the Ruhr Valley. Wolfsburg, near Hannover, has one of the largest automobile factories in the world.

Munich, in the south, near the Alps, is an important transportation and commercial city. Hamburg and Bremen, in the north, are great seaports. However, most manufacturers in the cities of the Rhine and Ruhr valleys market their products through Dutch ports at the mouth of the Rhine.

Austria

Austria is a nation a little larger than Ireland. It has a population of more than seven million.

Geography

Austria is a landlocked country, but the Danube River provides a waterway for transporting people and products. Austria has a small lowland region in the southeast, but most of it is an alpine region. A large portion of the land, especially in the south and west, is mountainous and forested.

History

Austria was part of the Roman Empire until the empire's collapse in 476 A.D. In the late 700s, it became part of the empire of Charlemagne. Otto I, king of Germany and emperor of the Holy Roman Empire, ruled Austria in 962.

The Hapsburg family came into control of the Holy Roman Empire in the late 1200s. Austria became the leading nation of the empire. For several hundred years, the Hapsburg dynasty controlled the empire. The crown of the Holy Roman Empire passed from one member of the Hapsburg family to another.

In 1867, Austria and Hungary were united into the Austro-Hungarian Empire. Each country had its own government, but the two countries had close financial and military ties to each other.

As a Central Power in World War I, Austria-Hungary shared Germany's defeat. During the peace negotiations in 1919, the empire came to an end. The Allies supported the principle of *self-determination* (self'di tur'mənā' shən). Self-determination is the right of a nation to choose its own form of government. Under that plan, Austria emerged as a separate independent country.

Germany took over Austria in World War II, but later in the war, the Allies occupied the country. In 1955, Austria became an independent country again.

Lumbering, Manufacturing, and Farming

Nearly half of Austria is covered with forests. The forests provide jobs for many people. Austria sells such forest products as lumber and wood pulp to nearby countries. To keep the forests from being used up, the government requires that young trees be planted in areas where older trees have been cut down.

Austria has steel and aluminum industries. Electrical equipment is an important export. Austrian manufacturers must import coal to power their factories. In the Alps, however, factories use hydroelectric power.

Only about 20 percent of Austria's land is used for farming. Sugar beets, potatoes, and dairy cattle are raised in the lowland region.

Cities of Austria

Vienna is located at the eastern end of the Alps, at the crossroads of central Europe. Because control of Vienna meant control of a wide area in the Danube Valley, this city has often been attacked by enemy armies.

The position of the city also made it a natural government center. It was the capital of the Holy Roman Empire and later of the Austro-Hungarian Empire. It is the capital of Austria today.

Vienna is much like Paris in many ways, for it has wide streets, many parks, great palaces, and art museums. In the city's small shops, pottery, leather goods, musical instruments, embroidered cloth, lace, and wood carvings are made and sold.

The winter Olympics of 1964 and 1976 were held in the alpine city of Innsbruck. Innsbruck is a rail center for western Austria. Salzburg, in the northwestern region of Austria, is famous for its music festivals.

Switzerland

Switzerland is about half as large as Austria. It has more than six million people. The capital city is Bern. French, German, Italian, and Romansch are spoken in different parts of the country.

Switzerland has three natural regions. To the north is a low range of mountains called the Jura (joor'ə) Mountains. The mighty Alps cover western and southern Switzerland. In the midland area, between the Juras and the Alps, are most of the nation's cities. This area is also the most important farming region of the nation.

Switzerland has been a republic for more than 600 years. Because of its location, Switzerland has often been overrun by foreign troops. However, Switzerland has stayed out of war. Even during World War I and II, when warring nations surrounded it, Switzerland remained neutral.

Farming

In the central area of Switzerland, farmers grow grain and fruit and have vineyards. Dairy farms are especially important in the central area and also in the valleys of the Alps. When the snow has melted in the spring, the farmers drive their cattle, sheep, and goats to mountain pastures. During the summer, they make cheese in dairies on these high pastures. Cheese and milk chocolate are important exports.

Manufacturing

Many Swiss people work in manufacturing. Most Swiss manufacturers produce products that require skilled workers and only small amounts of raw materials. Swiss workers make clocks, watches, instruments, toys, and textiles.

Swiss factories run on the hydroelectricity furnished by the waterfalls of the Alps. Swiss trains are run on electricity. The railroads move the manufactured goods and farm products of northern Europe to markets in Italy. Coal from the Ruhr is shipped southward, too. Returning trains bring Italian silks, fruits, and other southern products to the northern lands.

Tourism

Tourism is an important industry in Switzerland. Tourists visit Switzerland during the summer to enjoy the cool weather and the beauty of the lakes and snowy peaks. They come in winter for skiing. The money spent by tourists helps pay for the food and raw materials that Switzerland imports.

People visit Switzerland for business reasons, too. The country is a center of international banking. It is also the home of many international organizations. Geneva is the home of the International Red Cross, and Bern, the capital, is the home of the International Postal Union. Geneva is also a place where international conferences are held.

Liechtenstein

Liechtenstein is a tiny country in the Alps between Switzerland and Austria. It is about the size of Washington, D.C. The capital city is Vaduz. Most of Liechenstein is mountainous, but part lies in the Rhine Valley.

Liechtenstein has been independent since 1806. The country is ruled by a prince with limited power. Elected officials really govern the country. Liechtenstein has close ties with Switzerland. The two countries use the same money and have special trade arrangements. The Swiss government operates the post office and telephone system in Liechtenstein. Like Switzerland, Liechtenstein is a neutral country.

Liechtenstein is an active industrial country. The factories produce small machines and special tools. Liechtenstein has few people, so many workers come from other countries for jobs in these factories.

Do You Know?

1. What two island countries are part of western Europe? What is the name of the islands they occupy?
2. What was the Industrial Revolution?
3. What are the Low Countries? Why were they given this name?
4. What is the largest country in western Europe?

Before You Go On

Using New Words

enclave   population density
Alpine   intensive farming
dynasty   constitutional monarchy
alliance   self-determination
channel   industrialization

Number a paper from 1 through 10. After each number write the word or term from the above list that matches the definition.

1. A wide stretch of water between two land areas
2. The average number of people living on a square unit of land in a country or other region
3. Of or relating to the Alps
4. A country or an outlying portion of a country surrounded, or nearly surrounded, by the territory of another country
5. The right of a nation to choose its own form of government
6. An agreement between two or more nations to cooperate closely
7. A line of rulers from the same family
8. A form of government in which elected representatives have political power and the monarch has only symbolic authority
9. Working the land with special care to increase agricultural productivity
10. The process of changing to an economy that is based on manufacturing

Finding the Facts

1. What are Europe's highest mountains?
2. What is Europe's longest river? Into what body of water does it flow?
3. What is a Mediterranean climate?
4. Name Europe's most valuable minerals.
5. What is hydroelectricity?
6. Name the members of the European Common Market.
7. What stretch of water separates the United Kingdom and Ireland from the rest of Europe?
8. When did the Romans invade Britain? How long did they rule there?
9. What important event took place in 1066?
10. What did the Magna Carta do?
11. What are the parts of the United Kingdom?
12. What form of government do the Low Countries have?
13. What French general conquered much of Europe after the French Revolution?
14. Name three French seaports.
15. Where is the largest single coal field in western Europe?
16. What German state led the effort to unify Germany in the 1800s?
17. Why has Vienna often been attacked by enemy armies?
18. What languages are spoken in Switzerland?

3
Northern Europe

Norway, Sweden, Denmark, and Finland are the countries of northern Europe. Two Scandinavian countries, Norway and Sweden, occupy the Scandinavian Peninsula. The other Scandinavian country, Denmark, occupies the Jutland Peninsula. Finland, which is not part of Scandinavia, lies east of Sweden across the Gulf of Bothnia.

Geography

The countries of northern Europe share many geographic features. They are all lands with mountains, long, irregular coastlines, cool climates, and poor soils.

Natural Features

Northern Europe was shaped by ice sheets during the glacial period. As the ice sheets, or glaciers, moved across the land, they scraped material away and left rounded, polished hills. Today many lakes and bogs lie among the hills. Running water from the melting ice deposited layers of sand and gravel called moraines.

Most of the Scandinavian Peninsula is mountainous or hilly, as is Finland. On the west coast of Norway, the mountains rise steeply from the sea. In many places, glaciers carved out valleys and deepened them below sea level. Later, when the ice melted, sea water entered the valleys and extended far inland. Today

Deep, narrow bays called fiords indent the rugged coast of Norway. Some are large enough to admit ships.

these "drowned" valleys are deep, narrow bays called fiords.

Climate and Vegetation

Europe's northern lands lie in the high latitudes. The Arctic Circle passes through the northern part of Norway, Sweden, and Finland, yet most of northern Europe has a mild climate. It receives the warming effects of the North Atlantic Drift. The coastal areas do not have much snow, and the ports of Norway are ice-free all winter. The areas east of the mountains of Norway and the lands north of the Arctic Circle have cold, harsh winters.

The region north of the Arctic Circle is sometimes called the "Land of the Midnight Sun." The sun does not set there for two months, from the middle of May to the middle of July. Even at midnight, the sun still shines. In the middle of winter, from the middle of November to the end of January, the sun does not appear at all.

Rainfall is heavy along the western coast of Norway, and most of the region has ample rain. The moisture supports forests in much of Norway, Sweden, and Finland.

History of Scandinavia

In early times, Europeans talked about a northern island that they called Scandia. They did not know that Scandia was not an island but rather part of a great peninsula. From the early name Scandia comes the name Scandinavia. The Scandinavian Peninsula is the largest peninsula in Europe. It is separated from the Jutland Peninsula by straits that connect the North Sea and the Baltic Sea.

The lands of the Scandinavian Peninsula and the Jutland Peninsula were settled by the same Germanic people from the south. The people of Norway, Denmark, and Sweden today have many of the same customs and characteristics. Their languages, although not identical, are similar. Norway, Sweden, and Denmark have also shared much of the same history.

Early Scandinavia

More than 1,000 years ago, bands of warriors from Scandinavia called Vikings began to invade many parts of Europe. In their long, swift boats, they sailed to Great Britain, France, Ireland, Iceland, Greenland, and Russia. These seafaring people were both raiders and traders. They also made settlements in the lands they conquered. Vikings were the first Europeans to see North America.

About this time, Christian missionaries visited Scandinavia. Many Scandinavians became Christians. The raids and conquests stopped. The Scandinavians turned to farming and trading. Many became merchants. By 1000, the kingdoms of Norway, Sweden, and Denmark were well established.

Union and Independence

In 1397, Norway, Sweden, and Denmark were united under the Danish Queen Margrethe. At that time, they formed the largest kingdom in Europe.

In 1523, a strong Swedish leader, Gustavus, led his people in a successful uprising against the Danes and became king of Sweden. Under King Gustavus and his successors, Sweden became the most powerful country in Europe. Sweden's rule extended over much of northern Europe.

Sweden's glory was great but short-lived. In the early 1700s, Sweden's neighbors joined forces and defeated the Swedish army. Sweden was forced to give up much of its territory, including parts of Finland.

Norway and Denmark were ruled together for about 400 years. Then in 1815, Norway became a Swedish possession. The Norwegians wanted their freedom and demanded self-government. At times, civil war threatened. In 1905, in a national election, the Norwegians chose independence by an overwhelming vote of 186,000 to 184. The king of Sweden bowed to their decision and finally agreed to grant Norway its independence.

Scandinavia in the World Wars

When World War I broke out, Norway, Sweden, and Denmark made the decision to remain neutral. They agreed to work together for the best interest of all three countries.

Shortly after the beginning of World War II, German military forces attacked Norway and Denmark. These peace-loving countries were completely unprepared for war. Great Britain and France sent troops to help Norway, but the powerful German army soon took over the country.

Norway's king fled to England and set up a Norwegian government in London. Under the leadership of this government, the Norwegian

navy battled German submarines and carried supplies to help Britain.

The Norwegians and Danes refused to cooperate with the Germans and tried to undermine their power. They worked slowly and carelessly. They damaged machines, bridges, and railroads. Such actions are called sabotage.

Sweden was not attacked by Germany and did not take sides in the war. However, many thousands of refugees, fleeing from the conquering Germans, found safety in Sweden.

Scandinavia Today

Norway, Sweden, and Denmark are constitutional monarchies. Their monarchs, like the monarch of Great Britain, have little power. Each nation has a constitution, and the people elect their lawmakers and other officials.

The governments of the Scandinavian countries provide many benefits for their people. Norway and Sweden were leaders in setting up social welfare programs. Under the social welfare programs, the government provides such services as medical care, education, and pensions. Taxes, however, are fairly high in order to pay for these services.

The Scandinavian countries have limited resources. The climate is cool and the soil is sandy. Yet these countries are among the most prosperous in Europe.

Norway

Norway is a rugged, mountainous country that occupies the western part of the Scandinavian Peninsula. The long coast of Norway borders the Arctic Ocean, the Atlantic Ocean, and the North Sea.

Norway is about three-fourths as large as Sweden. It has the lowest population density of any country in Europe.

Farming

Most of Norway is extremely rugged country with little or poor soil. Only a very small percentage of Norway can be used for farming. The most important farming area is the lowland plain in the southeast. Farmers there grow crops of oats and potatoes and keep herds of cows and goats.

Raising enough food was once a big problem for the Norwegian people, but it is no longer. Farmers have learned to select plants and animals suited to the Norwegian climate. The farmers have improved production through the use of fertilizers and intensive farming methods. Ponds and marshes have been drained and forests have been cleared to make new farming land.

Fishing

No part of Norway is very far from the sea. Almost all Norwegians live along the coasts. Because arable and productive land is scarce, many Norwegians have turned to the sea for a living.

Norwegians fish for codfish near the Lofoten (lō′fō′tən) Islands north of the Arctic Circle. Herring are caught in the Atlantic Ocean between Norway and Scotland. The herring are sold to canneries and to factories that grind the fish into food for livestock. Norwegian waters are filled with small fish called sardines. Sardines are canned, often in oil, and are shipped throughout the world.

Water Power, Minerals, and Manufacturing

Norway has more waterfalls than any other country in Europe. The waterfalls are used to produce hydroelectricity. Electricity is a cheap source of energy in Norway. Factories have been designed and developed that use electricity, or "white coal," as it is sometimes called there. Copper, nickel, aluminum, and zinc ores from Norway's mines are refined in factories run by electricity. Nitrates, used in making fertilizer and in explosives, are produced from the *nitrogen* (nī′trə jən) which is in the air. Nitrogen is a colorless, odorless gas that makes up about four-fifths of the atmosphere. Much electric power is used to extract nitrogen from the air.

Even with its industries, Norway has electricity to spare. Some of it is sent to Denmark through wires set inside underwater cables.

Production of oil from the North Sea began in the 1970s. Since then, Norway has become an important oil-exporting country.

Shipping

Norway has one of the largest merchant fleets in the world. About half the ships are tankers used for hauling oil and other liquids from oil-exporting nations to oil-importing nations. Others transport agricultural products. Smaller ships sail along the Norwegian coast carrying supplies to the cities and other settlements.

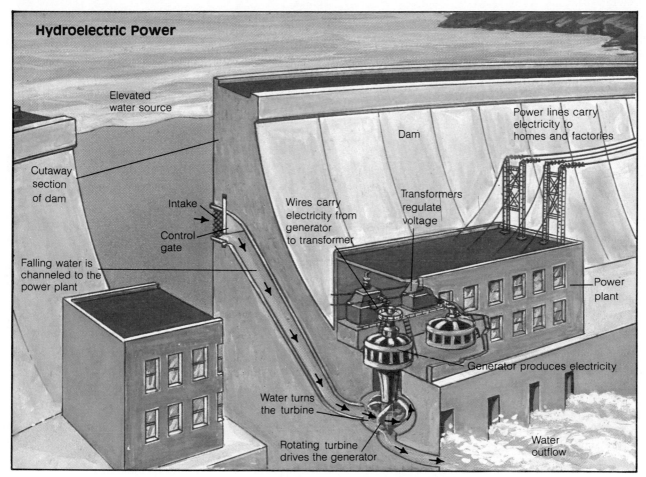

Hydroelectric Power

Elevated water source

Cutaway section of dam

Intake

Control gate

Falling water is channeled to the power plant

Wires carry electricity from generator to transformer

Dam

Transformers regulate voltage

Power lines carry electricity to homes and factories

Power plant

Generator produces electricity

Water turns the turbine

Rotating turbine drives the generator

Water outflow

Hydroelectricity is an important source of power in much of Europe. Falling water is the source of energy.

Cities of Norway

Oslo, the capital, is Norway's largest city and leading commercial, industrial, and cultural center. It is in the southeastern part of Norway at the head of a long arm of the North Sea. Oslo lies in the middle of Norway's richest agricultural lands. More than 10 percent of the people in Norway live in Oslo. Bergen, Norway's second-largest city, is the country's main shipping center. It is on the west coast, at about the same latitude as Oslo. The third-largest city in Norway is Trondheim (trän′hām). It was founded in 998 A.D. by King Olav I who brought Christianity to Norway. A famous cathedral that can be seen in Trondeim today was built in 1070.

Living and Working in Europe

Many European countries have the resources needed as raw materials in manufacturing. West Germany, in particular, has many factories. Welders in Munich work on an automobile production line. Many parts of Europe, however, are not heavily industrialized. In agricultural regions such as this one in Poland, animals are still used for farm work.

Europe's deposits of iron and coal provide jobs in the mining industry. Here, a coal miner uses sand to help control the blast from explosives. Lumbering is important in northern Europe. Lumberjacks in Sweden lash logs into giant bundles for river shipment. The seas and waterways of Europe abound with fish. Fishing provides employment for many people in Europe. A worker dries fish on racks on the coast of Portugal. ■

Sweden

Sweden extends about 1,000 miles (1,600 km) from north to south. It is the largest country of northern Europe, and it also has the largest population—more than eight million.

The mountains of Sweden lie to the west, near the border with Norway. In the south are rolling plains, where nearly 90 percent of the people live. Northern Sweden is almost covered with trees. Broad, rushing rivers flow from the mountains east across hills and plains to the Gulf of Bothnia. Sweden also has a great many lakes.

The effects of the North Atlantic Drift are not felt in northern Sweden. The mountains cut off the warm winds from the west. As a result, much of Sweden is covered with snow during the winter. In summer, Sweden is slightly warmer than Norway because the mountains block the cooling Atlantic winds.

Farming and Lumbering

Sweden has little land that is good for farming. The southern plain is the chief agricultural region. Most farms are small, but they are highly productive. Milk and meat are the most important farm products. Sweden produces almost all of the food it needs.

Forests cover much of northern Sweden. They provide work for many people. Trees are made into wood products, such as paper, boats, furniture, and matches.

Mining and Manufacturing

Sweden has large iron deposits. Much of Sweden's iron ore is exported. The ore from the north is sent by train to Narvik, in Norway, for export to Great Britain and West Germany. Narvik is ice-free all year. Swedish ports on the Gulf of Bothnia can be used only during the summer.

Although Sweden has much iron, it must import the ferroalloys needed to make steel. It pays for these imports by exporting manufactured goods. Among these are automobiles, aircraft, ships, precision instruments, and glass.

The factories in Sweden are run by hydroelectric power. Sweden has more water power than any European country except Norway. It has no coal or oil, however, and must import these fuels.

Cities of Sweden

A canal across southern Sweden connects the important cities of Stockholm and Göteborg (yoo′tə bôr′yə). The beautiful city of Stockholm, Sweden's capital, is on the Baltic coast. It is built on many rocky islands. Göteborg, at the western end of the Göta Canal, is a port on the North Sea. It is Sweden's second-largest city and most important seaport.

The Lapps of the North

In northern Sweden, and in nearby Norway and Finland, live people who are somewhat like the Eskimos of North America. These Arctic people, called Lapps, are not related to the Scandinavians. The Lapps make their living by farming, herding, and fishing. Some Lapps depend greatly upon reindeer. The meat, milk, and skins of the reindeer furnish the people with food and clothing.

Denmark

Denmark occupies a small peninsula and about 100 nearby islands. Denmark is the smallest country of northern Europe, but it has the highest population density.

Most of Denmark is a lowland dotted with many small lakes. Some of its smaller islands are rocky. Because of its many islands, Denmark has a very long coastline for such a small country.

About one-third of the people in Denmark live in Copenhagen, the capital. Copenhagen is the country's chief port and industrial center. Its location has given it an important role in trade between Baltic and Atlantic ports.

Farming

During the late 1800s, the government of Denmark divided the country's large farms into many small farms. These small farms were sold to the people, and Denmark became a nation of small farms.

Grass grows well in the Danish climate. The farmers, therefore, turned to dairy farming. Today about 75 percent of the land in Denmark is used for crops or pasture. Dairy cows feed on the thick grass of the pastures. The farmers specialize in three products: butter, bacon, and eggs.

Most farmers in Denmark belong to cooperatives. Cooperatives are businesses that are owned and operated by their members. The members share in the profits and other benefits. It is usually more profitable to buy and sell in large quantities. An individual farmer cannot always sell a product for as high a price as a

Hydrofoils carry passengers between Denmark and Sweden. A hydrofoil is a fast boat that skims over the water.

cooperative can. The cooperatives can also buy what the farmers need in large quantities at lower prices than individual farmers would have to pay.

Manufacturing

Dairy farming used to occupy most of the population. Now industry employs far more people. Workers produce machinery, furniture, and automobiles. Raw materials for Danish industries are imported from countries along the Baltic and the Atlantic. Manufactured products from Denmark are shipped to countries throughout the world.

Finland

Finland is not included among the Scandinavian nations because its people are of a different origin and speak a different kind of language. The Finnish language is unlike either the Scandinavian languages or Russian.

Finland is slightly larger than Norway and has slightly more people. Helsinki, on the southern coast, is the capital, largest city, and chief port.

Geography

Finland lies north of the Gulf of Finland and east of the Gulf of Bothnia. To the north, it

The art of glassmaking is an important industry in Finland. Here a worker removes a finished piece from a blowpipe. The glass is extemely hot.

borders Norway and to the east, the Soviet Union. The country has many lakes. One square mile out of ten is covered by water. The people call their country Suomi (swô′mē), which means "Land of Lakes."

History

Many centuries ago, people from Asia settled in what is now Finland. They took the country from the Lapps, who moved northward.

In the 1100s, after the Finns had made repeated raids on the Scandinavian coasts, Swedish armies invaded and conquered Finland. People from Sweden settled on the southern and western shores of Finland. The Finns were converted to Christianity and learned to speak Swedish. They also continued to speak Finnish. Finland remained under Swedish rule for more than 600 years. In the early 1800s, Russia, Finland's powerful neighbor to the east, seized the country and made it a part of Russia.

During the Russian Revolution in 1917, Finland rebelled against Russia and became an independent nation. Its freedom did not last long, however. Just before World War II, the Soviet Union attacked Finland and took away Finnish lands on the Gulf of Finland. After World War II broke out, Finland joined with Germany. The Soviets again attacked and defeated Finland. That time, they took valuable Finnish lands on the Arctic Ocean.

Today Finland is an independent nation with a president. Elected representatives make the country's laws.

Farming, Lumbering, and Manufacturing

The far south of Finland is an area of farms and forests. Meat, eggs, and dairy products are produced and shipped to Great Britain, Germany, and other countries of Europe. People on the coast often fish as well as farm.

Most of Finland is very much like the northern part of Sweden. Two-thirds of the country is covered with forests. Thousands of people work in lumbering industries. Lumber and wood products are Finland's chief exports.

In addition to making wood products, Finnish workers make locomotives, ships, and other products from iron and steel. Other important industries are chemicals, textiles, glass, and electronics. Copper from Finnish mines is used to make electric wires and cables.

Do You Know?

1. Name the Scandinavian countries.
2. What are cooperatives? In what Scandinavian country do most farmers belong to cooperatives?
3. What country has another name that means "Land of Lakes"?

4
Southern Europe

The lands of southern Europe either border or lie close to the Mediterranean Sea. They include Spain, Portugal, Italy, Yugoslavia, Albania, and Greece; the island countries of Malta and Cyprus; and the tiny countries of San Marino and the Vatican.

Most of the southern European countries occupy three peninsulas that extend into the Mediterranean Sea. From west to east, these peninsulas are the Iberian Peninsula, the Italian Peninsula, and the Balkan Peninsula. The peninsulas are largely mountainous. There are a few large plains with fertile soil. In much of the area, the land is steep and the soil is eroded. Most of the region has a Mediterranean climate. There are two periods for growing crops. One is in the fall when the rains begin, and the other is in the spring before the end of the rainy season.

Spain and Portugal

Spain and Portugal share the Iberian Peninsula. This peninsula is also referred to as Iberia. Portugal borders the Atlantic Ocean. Spain's northern coast is also on the Atlantic, but the country's longer coast is on the Mediterranean Sea. Most of Iberia is a high plateau called the Meseta (mə sā′tə). A few high mountains rise above the plateau. In the north, the Pyrenees form the border between Spain and France. The edges of the Meseta are steep and rugged as the land drops to the sea. There are only a

few areas of lowlands. Several broad river valleys cut back into the Meseta from the coast.

Most of Iberia has a Mediterranean climate. During the summer, there are often droughts. Northwestern Spain, however, has a climate much like that of western Europe. The oceanic climate does not reach the Meseta because the mountains block the rain-bearing winds.

History of Iberia

Iberia was once a part of the Roman Empire. As the power of Rome weakened, groups of Germanic peoples called Goths moved south and settled in the peninsula. They established a kingdom that lasted 300 years. Then early in the 700s, the Moors crossed the Mediterranean Sea from Africa and invaded the peninsula. The Moors, who were Muslims, conquered Iberia and controlled it for more than 500 years. Christians in the northwest of Spain united to drive out the Moors. In 1492, they finally succeeded.

In the late 1400s and early 1500s, Portugal and Spain became important nations. The Portuguese found a route to Asia around Africa. Later they founded colonies on both those continents and in South America as well. Spain founded colonies in North America, South America, and the Philippine Islands. Both Spain and Portugal grew rich from trade with the new lands. By the early 1600s, Spain and Portugal had begun to lose their power. In the

A finely detailed arch of the Alhambra frames a view of Granada. This palace-fortress is a splendid example of Moorish architecture in Spain.

early 1800s, Spain and Portugal lost most of their colonies through revolutions and wars.

For hundreds of years, Spain was a monarchy. In 1931, the Spanish king was overthrown and Spain became a republic. General Francisco Franco led a revolt against the new government, and a few years later, he became dictator of the country. When Franco died in 1975, Juan Carlos I became king. He established a democratic government.

Portugal also was a monarchy for hundreds of years. From 1926 to 1974, it was ruled by dictators. Only recently was a democratic form of government set up. Portugal now has an elected president and legislature.

Spain

Spain is the second-largest country in Europe and has a population of more than 37 million. Although half the population lives in cities, farming is the chief way of making a living.

Farming

Most of the land in Spain is used for subsistence farming. Much of the area is poor farming land, and yields are low. Most farmers cannot afford to buy machinery that could increase production. They continue to use farming methods practiced for thousands of years. In some places, however, farmers use irrigation and intensive farming methods to produce more food.

Wheat is raised on the Meseta. Vineyards and olive groves are cultivated throughout the south and southeast. Spain leads the world in olive production. Oranges, grown on the east coast, are exported. Potatoes are also an important crop.

Because it is dry, the Meseta is used for raising cattle, sheep, and goats. On some of the ranches, bulls are raised for the bull ring. Bullfighting is Spain's national sport.

Mining and Manufacturing

Many valuable minerals have been discovered in the mountains of Spain. Almost one-half of the world's supply of mercury is mined in Spain. Iron ore is also mined extensively in the north. Much iron ore is exported to Great Britain from Bilbao, on the north coast. Other important minerals of Spain are coal, lead, copper, manganese, silver, zinc, and sulfur.

Products of Europe

Norwegian Sea

fish

Narvik
iron ore

copper

aluminum

lumber

paper
products

textiles

lumber

steel

cobalt

chemicals

copper

zinc

copper

fish

dairy products

rye

oats

bauxite

potatoes

aircraft

iron ore

Helsinki

chemicals

nickel
copper

Oslo

copper

Stockholm

cattle

sheep

oats

cattle

dairy
products

flax

ships

coal

oil

North Sea

iron ore
coal

lead

machinery

dairy
products

glass

sugar beets

Dublin

hogs

Manchester

Baltic Sea

Copenhagen

Birmingham

textiles
metal
products

metal products

Atlantic Ocean

coal

steel

London

vegetables

Amsterdam

Hamburg

flowers

Rhine River

Berlin

oats

lumber

potatoes

coal

Vistula River

rye

sugar beets

Elbe River

ships

Warsaw

chemicals

oats

coal

copper

lead

zinc

coal

oil

ships

Brussels

Bonn

sugar
beets

iron ore

steel

rye

Prague

glass

coal

tobacco

potatoes

coal

Paris

Seine River

steel

iron ore

poultry

automobiles

oats

oats

Danube River

metal products

steel

iron ore

Loire River

hogs

chemicals

barley

Vienna

chemicals

bauxite

wheat

Bern

lumber

Budapest

corn

textiles

Rhone River

Milan

Po River

machinery

coal

oil

sugar beets

natural gas

corn

manganese

iron ore

tobacco

grapes

Turin

machinery

machinery

Belgrade

Bucharest

rye

fish

fruit

iron ore
coal
mercury

bauxite

Douro River

automobiles

mercury

building
stone

oats

Danube River

Lisbon

vegetables

grapes

Madrid

silver

Tagus River

mercury

fish

Rome

bauxite

fish

Sofia

cork

copper

textiles
metal products

oranges

goats

olives

Tirane

sulfur

potatoes

nuts

cotton

olives

lead

zinc

cork

tobacco

cork

Athens

sulfur

Mediterranean Sea

In recent years, Spain has become a modern industrial country. It produces machinery, textiles, automobiles, and ships.

Cities of Spain

Madrid and Barcelona are Spain's largest cities. Madrid, the capital, has fine public buildings and palaces, many of which date from the days of the Moors. Barcelona, on the Mediterranean, is an important manufacturing city and seaport. It is noted for its textiles, metal products, paper, and articles made of glass and leather.

Seville is the leading city of the south. Near Seville, reservoirs built by the Moors are still used to hold water for irrigation.

Gibraltar

At the southern tip of Spain is the British colony of Gibraltar. It has been a British possession since 1713. For years, the Spanish government tried to make Gibraltar part of Spain. In 1967, the people of Gibraltar voted overwhelmingly to remain part of the United Kingdom. Control of Gibraltar means control of the strait between the Atlantic and the Mediterranean. Most people on Gibraltar are involved with shipping and trade.

Portugal

Portugal is just a little larger than Austria. It has ten million people. Because Portugal is located on the ocean side of the Iberian Peninsula, it has both milder summers and milder winters than Spain.

Farming and Fishing

Most Portuguese are farmers who grow grains, vegetables, and fruit. They live in the fertile valleys of the rivers that flow westward into the Atlantic. Large vineyards supply grapes for Portugal's famous wines, one of the country's chief exports. Most of the olive crop is used to make olive oil. The best olive oil is used in cooking. Low grades of olive oil are used for making soap.

Cork-oak trees grow well on the Iberian Peninsula. The cork oak is a giant tree with a very thick bark. Once every 15 to 20 years, the bark is peeled off. From it, we get the light, woody material called cork. Cork ranks first among Portugal's export products.

Although a small country, Portugal has a large fishing fleet. Many of its people cross the Atlantic to fish on the Grand Bank of Newfoundland. Others fish for sardines, cod, and tuna in nearby waters.

Manufacturing

Portugal is less industrialized than Spain. However, the country has produced canned fish, textiles, chemicals, and fertilizers for many years. Now, Portuguese factories are beginning to produce metal products, ships, and petroleum as well.

Cities of Portugal

Lisbon, the capital and largest city of Portugal, lies at the mouth of the Tagus River. Lisbon is a beautiful seaport city with wide streets and many green parks and gardens. North of Lisbon is Portugal's second-largest city, Oporto.

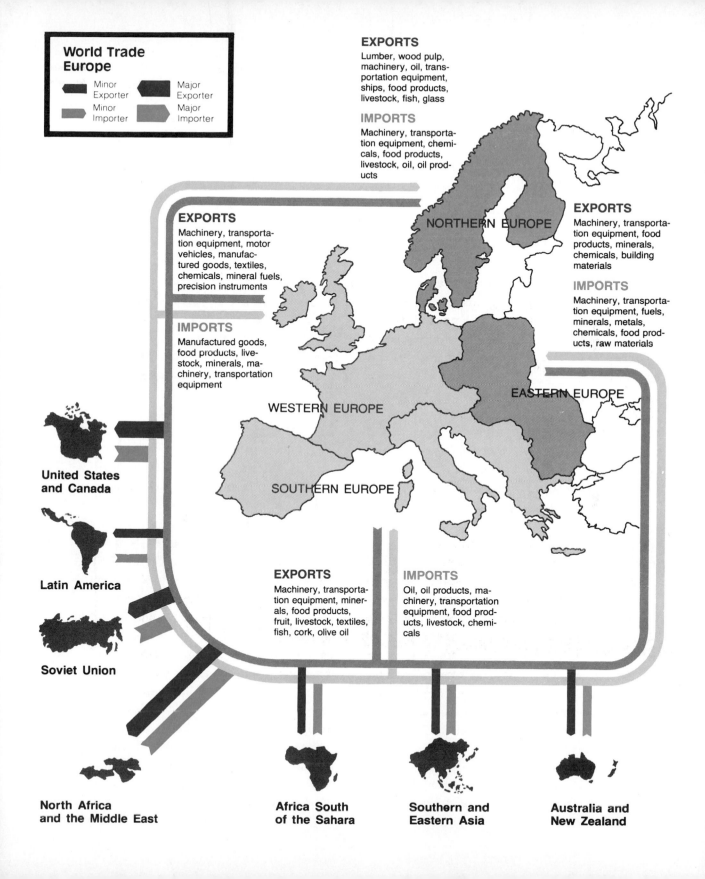

**World Trade
Europe**

Minor Exporter
Major Exporter
Minor Importer
Major Importer

EXPORTS

Lumber, wood pulp, machinery, oil, transportation equipment, ships, food products, livestock, fish, glass

IMPORTS

Machinery, transportation equipment, chemicals, food products, livestock, oil, oil products

EXPORTS

Machinery, transportation equipment, food products, minerals, chemicals, building materials

IMPORTS

Machinery, transportation equipment, fuels, minerals, metals, chemicals, food products, raw materials

NORTHERN EUROPE

EASTERN EUROPE

EXPORTS

Machinery, transportation equipment, motor vehicles, manufactured goods, textiles, chemicals, mineral fuels, precision instruments

IMPORTS

Manufactured goods, food products, livestock, minerals, machinery, transportation equipment

WESTERN EUROPE

SOUTHERN EUROPE

United States
and Canada

Latin America

Soviet Union

EXPORTS

Machinery, transportation equipment, minerals, food products, fruit, livestock, textiles, fish, cork, olive oil

IMPORTS

Oil, oil products, machinery, transportation equipment, food products, livestock, chemicals

North Africa
and the Middle East

Africa South
of the Sahara

Southern and
Eastern Asia

Australia and
New Zealand

Oporto is an important Atlantic port. Its most famous export is port wine, to which the city has given its name.

Italy

Italy occupies the long, narrow Italian Peninsula and the two large Mediterranean islands of Sicily and Sardinia. Only 100 miles (160 km) separates Sicily from the coast of Africa. Italy has more than 57 million people. Half of the people live in cities.

Geography

Italy has three natural regions. One region includes the Alps and the Piedmont in the north. A second region is the flat plain of the Po River Valley south of the Piedmont. The Po Valley has fertile soil and receives plentiful summer rains.

The third region includes the mountainous peninsula and the mountainous islands. The Apennine Mountains extend through the peninsula. Only a few narrow plains lie along the coast in this mountainous region. Melting snows high in these mountains supply water to streams during the spring. The Apennines are not as high as the Alps and do not receive much snow to furnish water. During the dry and sunny summers, water is scarce, especially in the southern part of the peninsula.

The peninsula, Sicily, and Sardinia have a Mediterranean climate. The Alps and the Po Valley have a climate more like that of central Europe. The southern part of Italy receives less rainfall than the northern part.

Italy and other parts of southern Europe are affected by a wind called a *sirocco* (si rok'ō). A sirocco is a hot wind that blows from northern Africa across the Mediterranean into southern Europe. Siroccos begin as hot, dry winds in Africa, but they become warm and humid as they pass over the Mediterranean. Siroccos often carry dust.

History

Rome, today the capital of Italy, was once the center of the Roman Empire. The city was founded more than 2,000 years ago. You have read about the civilization of Rome in Unit 2. At its height, the Roman Empire included all the lands around the Mediterranean Sea and parts of Britain. See the map on page 201.

In the 300s and 400s A.D., Germanic peoples from northern Europe crossed the Alps, spread through the peninsula, and eventually captured Rome. The great Roman Empire ended in 476 A.D.

In the thirteenth century, a number of Italian city-states became great trading centers. The most important were Venice, Florence, and Genoa. Italy became a center of learning and art during that period. Later, many different European powers controlled parts of Italy. It was not until 1861 that most of Italy became unified. In that year, Victor Emmanuel II of Sicily was proclaimed king.

Just after the end of World War I, Benito Mussolini came to power. Mussolini built up Italy's armies and ruled as a dictator. Italy entered World War II on the side of Germany and was defeated. After the war, Italy became a republic with a constitution and free elections. Today Italy has a president who is elected by the parliament.

Farming, Fishing, and Manufacturing

On the rich farmland of the Po Valley, farmers grow grains, vegetables, and fruit. Beef and dairy cattle graze in the meadows of this region. In the summer, they are taken to alpine pastures. Farmers in the Po Valley also raise silkworms. The raw silk is woven into cloth in nearby textile factories.

On the narrow coastal plains and in the valleys of the Apennines, the farmers raise drought-resistant crops, such as olives, almonds, chestnuts, and grapes. Where crops cannot be grown, many sheep and goats are grazed.

Sicily produces wheat and citrus fruit. Cattle are also raised there. Sardinia has valuable timber forests. The cork oak also grows on the island.

Along the coasts, farmers often fish to provide more food for their families. Their catches are small, as a rule, and are used by the families or sold to neighbors at local markets.

Italian industry is concentrated in the north of the country. Many of the factories process food. Others make fine silks and leather goods. The factories of Milan and Turin make machines, engines, electrical goods, chemicals, and automobiles. Turin also has iron and steel plants. Some of the power for the factories is furnished by hydroelectricity from the Alps. Some is furnished by coal from Germany.

Ancient buildings line the canals of Venice, which take the place of streets. Gondolas like this one, as well as motorboats, are used for transportation.

Cities of Italy

Rome, Italy's capital, is a very old city, with many ancient buildings and ruins. Rome is called the "Eternal City" because it has been important for more than 2,500 years. Today Rome is the center of a new and growing fashion industry.

The three chief manufacturing cities in the north are Milan, Turin, and Genoa. More than one and a half million people live in Milan. Turin has a population of more than one million. Genoa is Italy's largest and busiest seaport. The Apennines rise on three sides of the city. A low pass in the mountains provides an easy route between Genoa and the Po Valley.

Venice is an ancient city built on islands in a shallow lagoon connected with the Adriatic Sea. Its streets are canals, and people travel through the city by boats called gondolas.

Tourism is an important industry in both Venice and Florence. Florence is famous for its beautiful churches and art treasures.

Naples is a large seaport on the Bay of Naples, one of the most beautiful bays in the world. Close to Naples is Mount Vesuvius (vi soo'vē əs), a volcano that in times past has caused great damage by its eruptions. An eruption in 79 A.D. buried the nearby Roman cities of Pompeii and Herculaneum. Excavations in these cities have revealed many details about the people who lived there.

Vatican City

Vatican City is an enclave in Rome. This tiny independent state is the home of the Pope, the head of the Roman Catholic Church. The Pope is the ruler of Vatican City. Saint Peter's, the largest church in the world, is in this tiny state. Vatican City is a reminder that Rome was and is still a center of Christianity.

San Marino, Malta, and Cyprus

San Marino, Malta, and Cyprus are three small independent countries of southern Europe. San Marino is an enclave in Italy. Malta and Cyprus are Mediterranean island nations.

San Marino

San Marino is the smallest republic in Europe. The entire country covers only 24 square miles (62 sq. km) on the slopes of a mountain in east-central Italy. The walled city of San Marino, located near the top of the mountain, is the capital.

San Marino was founded in the fourth century A.D., during the days of the Roman Empire. Today, the people of San Marino speak Italian, but they have a separate history and do not think of themselves as Italians.

Sources of income in San Marino include farming and tourism. Cheese and woolen goods are important products. People all over the world buy the beautiful postage stamps of this tiny country.

Malta

Malta is a densely populated country of one main island and two smaller islands lying between Sicily and Africa. Between 1799 and 1964, Malta belonged to Great Britain. Today Malta is a republic, governed by a council of elected representatives. It has a president and a prime minister.

The islands do not have mountains or rivers. The soil is so rocky that few crops can be grown on the islands. Malta does have good harbors and a good location on major Mediterranean trade routes.

The Phoenicians founded a colony on Malta about 1000 B.C. In the early 1500s, the king of Spain inherited Malta. He gave the island to the Knights of St. John of Jerusalem, a religious order that had been active in the Crusades. In the mid-1500s, the Turks attacked Malta. The small group of Knights successfully defended their island.

During World War I and World War II, Malta was an important naval and military base. Today shipbuilding is the most important industry in Malta.

Cyprus

Cyprus, the third-largest island in the Mediterranean, lies south of Turkey and west of Syria. The location of Cyprus has made it important since the troubles in the Middle East began.

Cyprus was the site of early Phoenician and Greek colonies. It was ruled by many different countries until it was conquered by the Turks in the 1500s. The island was annexed by Great Britain during World War I. In 1960, Cyprus gained its independence. At the time of independence, about 80 percent of the population was Greek. Turks made up most of the other 20 percent. There has been constant conflict between the two groups. The Greeks want Cyprus to become part of Greece. The Turks do not want to become part of Greece. The constitution of Cyprus spells out a division of power between the Greek and the Turkish citizens. Both groups have their own elected representatives and their own schools.

Cyprus is mainly a farming country. It exports fruit, potatoes, and grapes. Other products include wine, clothes, and shoes. Tourism was once an important industry. Tourists came to enjoy the beautiful beaches, the rugged mountains, and the old castles. In recent years, the fighting between the Turks and Greeks has resulted in a decrease in tourism.

Yugoslavia

Yugoslavia is on the Balkan Peninsula. It lies east of Italy across the Adriatic Sea. The country is a little larger than Great Britain but has fewer than 23 million people.

Along the Adriatic coast of Yugoslavia are deep valleys and clear lakes. The few good harbors are protected by offshore islands. Rugged mountains, the Dinaric Alps, lie between the coast and the Danube Valley to the northeast.

Yugoslavia was controlled by other countries for many years. Before World War I, it was part of the Austro-Hungarian Empire. Germany occupied the country during World War II. After the war, the Soviet Union set up a Communist government in Yugoslavia. Yugoslavia is still a Communist nation, but it has broken ties with the Soviet Union. The economy is controlled by the government. However, there is more private ownership than in many Communist countries.

Farming is the principal occupation in Yugoslavia. Although it is a Communist nation, most of the farmland is privately owned, rather than owned by the state. On the plain in the north, many food crops are grown. In the mountains, the farmers raise sheep.

Belgrade is the capital and the industrial, political, and cultural center of Yugoslavia. Its factories produce machines and cloth. Electricity generated by hydroelectric plants is an important source of power for Yugoslavia's industries. Yugoslavia has some coal, oil, and natural gas. Bauxite, copper, and iron ore are other important minerals.

Albania

South of Yugoslavia lies the small Balkan country of Albania. Like Yugoslavia, Albania has a coast on the Adriatic. The country, which is about as large as Maryland, has a population of more than two and a half million. Albania's capital city is Tiranë (te rä′nə).

Albania is a mountainous land. Tiny villages are separated by towering peaks and high ridges. Along the Adriatic coast are several good harbors.

Albania became an independent nation after World War I. The Italians occupied the country during World War II. After the war, Albania came under Communist influence. It is still a Communist country, but it has broken its ties with the Soviet Union.

Most of the people of Albania earn a scanty living, chiefly by working their small hill farms. They raise crops in the valleys and graze sheep on the steep hillsides.

The development of Albania's coal, oil, and copper industries has been slow. Transportation is difficult in this country of poor roads and few railroads.

Greece

Greece lies at the southern end of the Balkan Peninsula. Greece is about half as large as Yugoslavia. Its population is nearly ten million.

Greece is a mountainous and hilly country. Its deeply indented shoreline provides many fine harbors. The southern part of peninsular Greece is the Peloponnesus (pel′ə pə nē′səs). It is connected to the northern part by the narrow Isthmus of Corinth. Hundreds of islands in the Aegean Sea make up the Greek archipelago.

The climate and scenery of the Greek islands attract many visitors. Here the whitewashed buildings of Mykonos rise gently above the harbor.

Most of Greece has a Mediterranean climate. Winters are rainy and mild, while summers are hot and dry. The high mountains have a cooler climate with summer rains and snow in the winter.

History

Greece has had a long history. More than 2,500 years ago, an advanced civilization developed there. You have read about ancient Greece in Unit 2. Ancient Greece did not have a national government. It was made up of many independent communities called city-states. The people of Greece were united by a common culture, language, and religion. Their

230

ideas about government, science, and human life have had a great effect on much of the world.

Greece was conquered in the fourth century B.C. It became part of the empire of Alexander the Great. About 200 years later, the Romans invaded Greece and made it part of the Roman Empire. Greek ways of living became part of Roman life. Greek influence spread throughout the lands ruled by Rome.

At the end of the fourth century A.D., the Roman Empire was divided into two parts. Greece became part of the East Roman, or Byzantine (biz′ən tēn′), Empire. This empire ended when the Turks seized Constantinople in 1453. The people of Greece remained under Turkish rule until 1829, when Greece became an independent monarchy. In 1967, a junta seized control of the government and set up a military dictatorship. In 1973, the monarchy was abolished, and the next year a civilian government took power. Today, Greece is a republic. Elected representatives choose the president.

Farming, Shipping, and Tourism

Only one-fourth of the land of Greece can be cultivated. Poor soil, steep slopes, and the dry climate make farming difficult. Much of the steep and rocky land is used as pasture to graze sheep and goats. Greek farmers raise olives, grapes, wheat, barley, and fruit. In Macedonia, along the northern shores of the Aegean, cotton and tobacco are grown.

Greece has always been a seafaring nation. Today, its merchant marine is the fourth largest in the world, and shipping accounts for much of Greece's income. Thousands of passenger ships, tankers, and freighters sail all over the world under the Greek flag.

Tourism also accounts for much income in Greece. Some people come to visit the historic cities and ancient ruins around Athens and in the Peloponnesus. Others come to enjoy the sunny climate and beautiful scenery of the islands.

Cities of Greece

Athens, the capital of Greece, has a population of three million. The ancient Acropolis, topped by the ruins of the Parthenon, rises above the city. Today, Athens is the industrial center of Greece. It has spread out across the plain to the port city of Piraeus (pī rē′əs), five miles (8 km) away. Piraeus is Greece's leading port.

Salonika (sə län′i kə) is the second most important port in Greece. It is located at the north end of the Aegean Sea. Salonika is also an important rail and manufacturing center.

Do You Know?

1. What three European peninsulas extend into the Mediterranean Sea?
2. What kind of climate do most countries of southern Europe have?
3. What is the smallest European republic?
4. What two countries of southern Europe have Communist governments?

231

Before You Go On

Using New Words

sirocco
enclave
nitrogen
alliance

Number a paper from 1 through 4. After each number write the word or term from the above list that matches the definition.

1. An agreement between two or more nations to cooperate closely
2. A hot wind that blows from Africa into southern Europe
3. A country or an outlying portion of a country surrounded, or nearly surrounded, by the territory of another country
4. A colorless, odorless gas that makes up about four-fifths of the atmosphere

Finding the Facts

1. What peninsulas do the Scandinavian countries occupy?
2. What is a fiord?
3. What is the "Land of the Midnight Sun"?
4. Who were the Vikings?
5. Who are the Lapps?
6. Why isn't Finland included among the Scandinavian nations?
7. What two countries occupy the Iberian Peninsula?
8. What is the Meseta?
9. What British colony is located at the southern tip of Spain?
10. What is Portugal's leading export?
11. Name three important city-states that became great trading centers in Italy in the thirteenth century.
12. What two nations of southern Europe are islands in the Mediterranean Sea?
13. What is the Peloponnesus?
14. What countries border the Adriatic Sea?

5
Eastern Europe

The countries of eastern Europe lie between western and southern Europe and the Soviet Union. They include East Germany, Poland, Czechoslovakia (chek′ə slə vä′kē ə), Hungary, Romania, and Bulgaria. All of these countries except East Germany and Bulgaria border the Soviet Union.

Like western Europe, eastern Europe is a land of mountains, hills, and plains. The Danube River flows through Hungary and forms part of the boundary between Romania and Bulgaria on the Balkan Peninsula. Because eastern Europe is farther from the sea than western Europe, its summers are hotter and its winters are cooler. The region has abundant rain, much of it in the summer.

Most of the people of eastern Europe are Slavs. They are descendants of people who came from regions to the east more than 1,000 years ago. Other people of eastern Europe come from a variety of other cultures. They speak different languages, use different alphabets, and have different religions. Each group has its own *heritage* (her′ə tij), or values and traditions passed down from earlier generations.

There is a reason for the great mixture of people in eastern Europe. For hundreds of years, this region has been invaded many times

Fertile farmlands cover the wide valleys of central Czechoslovakia. This region is known as Moravia. Cereal grains are the chief farm products.

by people from the east, the southeast, and the west. The southern part of the region was ruled by Turkey for many years. For centuries, the northern part has been a battleground between Slavs pushing west and Germans pushing east.

The peace conference that followed World War I changed the map of Europe. Poland, which had disappeared as a nation, was made a self-governing country again. Three new independent countries—Czechoslovakia, Austria, and Hungary—were created from Austria-Hungary. Both Romania and Bulgaria had become independent before the war. Romania, however, gained vast territories from Russia and the Austro-Hungarian Empire by the terms of the peace treaty.

Most of the eastern European countries became Communist during World War II. At that time, Soviet armies occupied many of these countries. Communist governments friendly with the Soviet Union were set up.

East Germany

The official name of East Germany is the German Democratic Republic. East Germany is less than half the size of West Germany.

Geography

East Germany is bordered by the Baltic Sea to the north and by West Germany to the west. The Oder River forms part of the boundary between East Germany and Poland to the east. A wide, sandy plain lies south of the Baltic. The Elbe River, flowing from southeast to northwest, crosses much of this plain. In the south, mountains rise along the borders with West Germany and Czechoslovakia.

History

From the late 1800s until 1945, Germany was one united country. Near the end of World War II, troops from the Soviet Union occupied the eastern part of Germany. After the war, this part of Germany was the zone controlled by the Soviet Union. German Communists worked with the Soviets to set up a Communist government.

In 1953, the government of East Germany tried to increase production by increasing the number of hours people had to work without increasing wages. This led to strikes and riots, which were put down by Soviet troops. In the 1960s, a new economic system allowed profits to be made. Trade, once limited to Communist countries, expanded to West Germany and other nations.

In 1973, East Germany became a member of the United Nations. The next year, the United States recognized East Germany, and the two countries established diplomatic relations.

Farming and Manufacturing

East Germany has the best farmlands in all of Germany. They are the lands near the Baltic Sea and in the south near Leipzig (līp′sig). Farmers in these areas produce barley, oats, potatoes, rye, wheat, and sugar beets. They also raise livestock, mainly hogs.

Farms are organized by the government and are under government control. Government farms are of two types. On one type of farm, the workers may share part of the profits. On the other, the workers are paid wages by the government.

The economy of East Germany did not recover from World War II as quickly as that of West Germany. In the 1960s, East Germany began to develop into a highly industrialized nation. Today East Germany manufactures machinery, ships, steel, chemicals, and furniture. It exports many of its products, mainly to the Soviet Union and other Communist nations, but to West Germany as well.

Cities of East Germany

Berlin is a divided city in East Germany. West Berlin is part of West Germany. East Berlin is the capital and largest city of East Germany. Until 1961, East Germans could cross the border into West Germany fairly easily. They visited family members and sometimes held jobs there. Many, however, left East Germany for good by passing from East Berlin to West Berlin. Between 1945 and 1961, more than three million who were unhappy under Communist rule fled to West Germany through Berlin. To halt this *emigration* (em′ə grā′shən), the East German government built a wall to separate East and West Berlin. Emigration is the act of leaving one place or country to live in another. Even with the wall, several thousand people leave East Germany each year.

East Germany's second- and third-largest cities, Leipzig and Dresden, are in the south. Leipzig is an important transportation and industrial center. It manufactures chemicals, cars, steel, and textiles. It was the center of Germany's book and music publishing industry. During the nineteenth and early twentieth centuries, many famous musicians and composers lived there. Dresden is a large inland port on the Elbe River. It is known for its fine optical instruments and glass. For centuries, Dresden was an outstanding center of the arts. The city was heavily bombed during World War II, and many of its famous landmarks were damaged or destroyed.

Poland

Poland is the largest country in eastern Europe. It has a population of nearly 36 million. Warsaw, a city of about one and a half million on the Vistula (vis′chə lə) River, is the capital.

Poland occupies part of the plain to the south of the Baltic Sea and extends southward into the Carpathian Mountains. Most of the land is level and is crossed by broad, slow-moving rivers.

About one-third of the people in Poland are farmers and live in small villages. The farms, however, are not very productive because modern farming methods are not used. Large crops of rye, oats, wheat, barley, potatoes, and sugar beets are grown. After World War II, the land was divided among the farmers. The farmers rebelled, however, when the government tried to organize government farms. About 80 percent of Poland's farmland is privately owned.

Since World War II, Poland has changed from an agricultural to an industrial country.

Slightly more than half the population lives in urban areas. The main industrial region is in the south, near the city of Cracow (krak′ou), where there are important coal fields. The coal fields supply coal for iron and steel mills, for manufacturing machinery, and for other industries. Polish workers also mine copper, lead, and zinc in the region. Many of the goods produced in Poland's factories are shipped to the Soviet Union.

The people of Poland have not benefited from the country's industrial production. They live with shortages of food and other goods. Housing in the cities is crowded and uncomfortable. These conditions have led to strikes and unrest in Poland. In the early 1980s, the Polish labor union, called Solidarity, led strikes for more rights and freedoms. The Polish government put down the strikes, causing great bitterness and anger among the Polish people.

Czechoslovakia

Czechoslovakia is a little larger than East Germany. Its population is more than 15 million.

Czechoslovakia is a long, narrow landlocked country. Along the northern border are high mountains. A band of hills stretches through the center of the country from east to west. On either side of the hills are rolling plains.

Wheat is grown on the *loess* (lō′əs) soil of Czechoslovakia. Loess is rich soil deposited by the wind. Areas of loess are the best farmland in Europe. Much of central and eastern Europe is covered with loess.

The Carpathian Mountains cover the eastern part of Czechoslovakia. This area of farms and forests is called Slovakia (slō väk′ē ə).

Bohemia, the western part of Czechoslovakia, is a hilly area, bordered on three sides by mountains. Here are found both factories and farms. Many minerals, including copper, coal, iron ore, and uranium, are mined in the mountains of Bohemia. Among the industries of the region are iron and steel, glass and china, and textiles and shoes.

Prague (präg), the capital of Czechoslovakia, is near the center of Bohemia. It is one of Europe's great cultural centers.

In the late 1960s, the president of Czechoslovakia tried to bring about some reforms. The Soviet leaders feared their control would be weakened. Czechoslovakia was invaded by Soviet troops, and Soviet control was reestablished.

Hungary

Hungary, like Czechoslovakia, is a landlocked country. It is the size of Portugal and has about the same number of people. Budapest is the capital and largest city. It was once two cities, Buda and Pest, lying on opposite sides of the Danube.

Most of Hungary is a flat, treeless plain. The loess soil makes it one of the richest farming areas in central Europe. The Danube River flows through the plain. The Carpathian Mountains protect the plain from north and northeast winds. The winters are mild and the summers are hot. Most rain falls in summer.

Budapest, the capital and largest city of Hungary, is built on both sides of the Danube River. Several bridges connect the two parts of the city.

Unlike their eastern neighbors, most of the people of Hungary are Magyars. They are descendants of Asians who settled on the plain in the tenth century. Hungarians speak a non-Slavic language called Magyar.

In 1956, the Hungarian people rebelled against their Communist government. The Soviet Union put down the uprising. Since then, the Communist government has worked to improve the economy of Hungary. In the 1970s, Hungarian leaders began to develop closer ties to Western nations. The government also granted greater freedom to the citizens of the country.

Hungary is sometimes compared to the corn belt of the United States because of its climate and crops. Large crops of wheat, potatoes, and corn are grown, and thousands of beef cattle, hogs, and sheep are raised.

Flour milling, sugar refining, and meat packing are important industries in Hungary. Chemicals, steel, and textiles are also produced. Near Budapest is a small oil field.

Romania

Romania is a little smaller than West Germany, but it has only one-third as many people. Its capital is Bucharest. Bucharest has nearly two million inhabitants.

Romania lies between Hungary on the west and the Black Sea on the east. A chain of mountains curves through the center of the country from north to south. Plains lie on both sides of the mountains. The western plains continue into Hungary. Those on the east extend to the Black Sea. The Danube drains both plains and empties into the Black Sea.

Regional Data Chart

Country	Capital	Area Square miles	Area Square kilometers	Population	GNP (in millions of U.S. dollars)
Albania	Tirana	11,100	28,748	2,800,000	$2,200
Andorra	Andorra la Vella	175	453	30,000	—
Austria	Vienna	32,375	83,851	7,515,000	$64,600
Belgium	Brussels	11,781	30,513	9,870,000	$107,300
Bulgaria	Sofia	42,823	110,912	8,875,000	$32,700
Cyprus	Nicosia	3,572	9,251	635,000	$1,900
Czechoslovakia	Prague	49,374	127,877	15,400,000	$80,500
Denmark	Copenhagen	16,615	43,033	5,130,000	$60,800
East Germany	East Berlin	40,646	195,273	16,730,000	$107,600
Finland	Helsinki	130,119	337,009	4,800,000	$39,400
France	Paris	212,973	551,600	53,950,000	$531,500
Greece	Athens	50,547	130,917	9,700,000	$36,700
Hungary	Budapest	35,919	93,030	10,725,000	$41,300
Ireland	Dublin	26,600	68,894	3,460,000	$13,800
Italy	Rome	116,304	301,225	57,150,000	$394,000
Liechtenstein	Vaduz	61	157	30,000	—
Luxembourg	Luxembourg	999	2,586	365,000	$4,500
Malta	Valletta	122	316	350,000	$890
Monaco	Monaco-Ville	0.7	1.9	30,000	—
Netherlands	Amsterdam	13,967	36,175	14,250,000	$143,200
Norway	Oslo	125,182	324,219	4,150,000	$43,500
Poland	Warsaw	120,359	311,730	35,900,000	$135,500
Portugal	Lisbon	35,340	91,531	10,000,000	$21,300
Romania	Bucharest	91,700	237,500	22,500,000	$41,800
San Marino	San Marino	24	62	20,500	—
Spain	Madrid	194,885	504.750	37,750,000	$162,300
Sweden	Stockholm	173,665	449,792	8,330,000	$98,600
Switzerland	Bern	15,941	41,288	6,375,000	$89,900
United Kingdom	London	94,250	244,108	55,900,000	$353,600
Vatican City State	—	0.2	0.4	1,000	—
West Germany	Bonn	95,999	248,637	63,305,000	$717,700
Yugoslavia	Belgrade	98,766	255,804	22,550,000	$53,800

Nonindependent Area

Country	Capital	Area Square miles	Area Square kilometers	Population	GNP (in millions of U.S. dollars)
Gibraltar (Great Britain)	—	2.3	5.8	30,000	$130

Romania was originally settled by the Romans. The Romanian language is one of the Latin languages.

Before World War II, Romania was a monarchy. After the war, Communists gained control of the government. Since the 1960s, Romania has tried to separate itself somewhat from the Soviet Union. Yet it remains a Communist nation.

The farmers in Romania grow corn and wheat. Corn is a staple food of the people. It also is used to feed livestock. High mountain pastures are used as grazing land for sheep.

Although Romania has many resources, it is one of the less industrialized countries of eastern Europe. In recent years, however, Romanian industries have begun to grow. Workers in the factories of Bucharest process farm products. Wheat, flour, meat, and corn are exported through ports on the Black Sea.

Romania has good supplies of oil, natural gas, and some minerals. Some oil is exported. In 1975, Romania and Yugoslavia completed a huge hydroelectric plant on the Danube. It increased Romania's electric power by 300 percent.

Bulgaria

Bulgaria is about the size of East Germany. Its population is about nine million. The country is south of Romania on the Black Sea.

Two mountain ranges extend east and west through Bulgaria—the Balkan Mountains in the north and the Rhodope Mountains in the south. North of the Balkan Mountains, the land drops steeply to the Danube Plain. A valley lies between the two mountain ranges and extends to the Black Sea. This valley has mild winters and hot, rainy summers. In contrast, the northern part of Bulgaria has very cold winters and dry summers.

Bulgarian farmers raise grain, tobacco, and fruit. On hills and mountains, sheep and goats graze. Wool from sheep and mohair from goats are exported. Mohair is used in the making of upholstery and clothing.

Parts of the central valley are great fields of roses. A fragrant oil, called attar of roses, is extracted from the rose petals and used in perfumes. It is exported to many countries.

Sofia, the capital of Bulgaria, has a population of more than one million. The city has factories that manufacture machinery, textiles, electrical equipment, chemicals, fertilizers, and metals.

Do You Know?

1. To what cultural group do most of the people of eastern Europe belong?
2. What divided city is in East Germany? To what two countries does the city belong?
3. Near what city is the main industrial region of Poland?
4. What important river flows through Hungary, Romania, and Bulgaria?

To Help You Learn

Using New Words

loess	channel
emigration	heritage
sirocco	self-determination

Number a paper from 1 through 6. After each number write the word or term from the above list that matches the definition.

1. A hot wind that blows from Africa into southern Europe
2. The act of leaving one place or country to live in another
3. Values and traditions passed down from earlier generations
4. A wide stretch of water between two land areas
5. Rich soil deposited by the wind
6. The right of a country to choose its own form of government

Finding the Facts

1. What mountains besides the Alps are part of the Alpine system?
2. Who was Alfred the Great? What did he do?
3. How did the British colonies help Great Britain to prosper?
4. What are two major industrial cities of Scotland?
5. What language was revived in Ireland after independence?
6. What rivers flow through the Low Countries on their way to the sea?
7. Who was Charlemagne?
8. Who governs Andorra?
9. Who was Otto von Bismarck?
10. Who were the Central Powers in World War I?
11. When was the Austro-Hungarian Empire established? When did it come to an end?
12. When and under what king did Sweden become the most powerful nation in Europe?
13. Why is control of Gibraltar important?
14. What valley in Italy is a rich farmland?
15. What is Vatican City?
16. What group of people founded a colony on Malta about 1000 B.C.?
17. What is the third-largest island in the Mediterranean Sea?
18. What two eastern European countries have broken their ties with the Soviet Union?
19. About how much of the farmland in Poland is privately owned?
20. What are the eastern and western parts of Czechoslovakia called?
21. Who originally settled in Romania?
22. What product exported by Bulgaria is used in making perfume?

Learning from Maps

1. Compare the map of the Roman Empire on page 201 with the map on page 189. What modern European countries in whole or part once belonged to the Roman Empire? What is the region once known as Gaul called today? When was Greece added to the Roman Empire?

2. Look at the maps of Europe before and after World War I on page 205. What happened to Austria-Hungary after World War I? What countries on the map of Europe after World War I include land that had been part of Austria-Hungary before the war? What country on the map of Europe after World War I is made up of lands that belonged to Russia, Germany, and Austria-Hungary before the war?

3. Compare the maps of Europe after World War I and after World War II on pages 205 and 206. What country was divided after World War II? What are the names of the two new countries? What countries became part of the Soviet Union between 1919 and 1949? What countries lost territory to the Soviet Union between 1919 and 1949?

4. Look at the map on page 223. What minerals are shown in Poland? In the North Sea? Where is cork grown? Cotton? Are grapes produced in the Rhone Valley?

Using Study Skills

1. **Diagram:** Look at the hydroelectric power diagram on page 215. What controls the amount of water channeled to the power plant? What changes the mechanical power of the falling water to electrical power? How is the electricity carried from the generators to transformers? What do transformers do?

2. **Time Line:** Find the dates for the following events and arrange them in chronological order: King John signed the Magna Carta, William I became king of Prussia, King Edward I called meeting of "Model Parliament," Frederick the Great became king of Prussia, William I crowned German emperor, Alfred the Great began rule as king of Britain.

   Then copy the time line below and complete it with the information you have found.

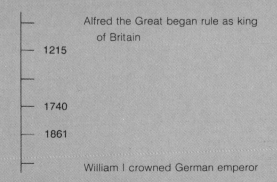

241

3. **Graph:** The population density of a country is determined by dividing the population of the country by its area in either square miles or square kilometers. Use the information on the Regional Data Chart on page 238 to find the population density in square miles for Belgium, Finland, Romania, Spain, and Switzerland. Round the numbers off to the nearest whole number. What is the population density of Belgium? Finland? Romania? Spain? Switzerland? Use the information you have to complete the graph below. What kind of graph have you made?

Thinking It Through

1. Why do lands north of the Arctic Circle have almost constant daylight from the middle of May to the middle of July?
2. Switzerland is the home of many international organizations. What reasons can you think of that explain Switzerland's growth as an international center?
3. It has been suggested that the Common Market countries might form a United States of Europe. What factors can you think of that would make this difficult? What advantages can you think of?

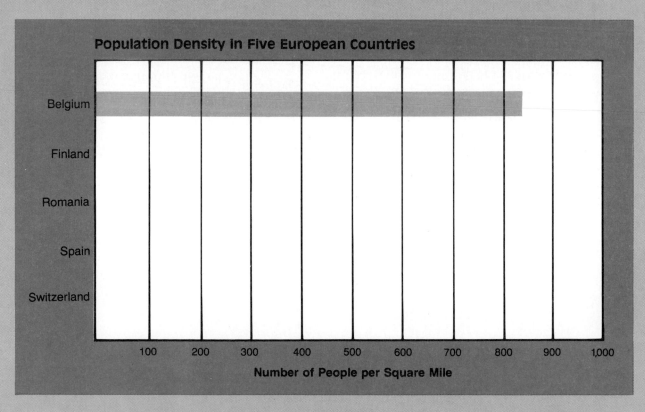

Population Density in Five European Countries

Belgium		
Finland		
Romania		
Spain		
Switzerland		

100 200 300 400 500 600 700 800 900 1,000

Number of People per Square Mile

Projects

1. The Arts and Sciences Committee might like to prepare displays of books by European authors and reproductions of paintings and sculpture by European artists. The local public library or your school library may have art reproductions that can be borrowed. Pictures from books or magazines could also be displayed. Committee members could provide brief biographies of the authors and artists included in the display.

   European authors might include Charles Dickens, Jakob and Wilhelm Grimm, Christina Rossetti, Robert Louis Stevenson, and Jules Verne. European artists might include Michaelangelo, Claude Monet, Pablo Picasso, Rembrandt van Rijn, Joseph M.W. Turner, Diego Velázquez, and Jan Vermeer.

2. Imagine that you are to spend a month in Europe. What countries and cities would you want to visit? How would you get from place to place? Use the map on page 189 to help arrange your route. Collect travel brochures and make a list of the things you want to see in each place. Then report to the class about your plans.

3. The History Committee could prepare a report on the Knights of Saint John of Jerusalem, who ruled Malta beginning in 1530. Committee members could find out about the work the knights did, the special symbol they had, and their defense of the island in 1565.

6 The Soviet Union

Unit Preview

The Soviet Union covers more land than any other country in the world. The nation stretches across both Europe and Asia, from the Baltic Sea to the Pacific Ocean.

The low Ural Mountains form part of the boundary between Europe and Asia. Plains on both sides of these mountains make up much of the interior of the Soviet Union. High, rugged mountains and several large lakes lie along the country's southern border. In the east is an upland region of plateaus and mountains. Climate and vegetation vary greatly throughout the country. They range from the arctic tundra of northern Siberia to the barren, arid deserts of Soviet Central Asia.

The Slavs and the Norse were early settlers in what is now Soviet Europe. During the thirteenth century, this region, then called Russia, was invaded and conquered by Tartars from central Asia. In 1480, Ivan the Great drove the Tartars from Russia. Russian expansion continued under later rulers called czars.

A revolution in 1917 overthrew the czars. Shortly afterward, a political group called Bolsheviks seized power. From the old Russian empire there gradually emerged the Communist nation known as the Union of Soviet Socialist Republics. The government of this country has a strong influence on the lives of its people.

Through a series of Five-Year Plans, the Soviet Union has grown into a modern industrial nation. In recent years, much effort has gone into the development of the rich but remote region of Siberia.

Things to Discover

If you look carefully at the picture, map, and time line, you can answer these questions.

1. The Soviet Union is highlighted on the map. On what two continents is it located?
2. The photograph shows Red Square in Moscow. Parades in this plaza celebrate the Russian Revolution each year. When did the Revolution take place?
3. When did the Tartars complete their conquest of Russia? How many years later were they driven out? Who led the Russian forces?

Words to Learn

You will meet these words and terms in this unit. As you read, you will learn what they mean and how to pronounce them. The Word List will help you.

abdicate	exile
accessible	proletariat
capital	propaganda
capitalist	quota
cede	regime
chernozem	satellite
ethnic group	taiga

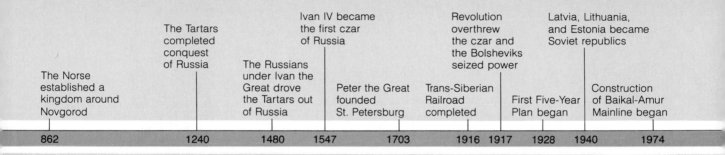

| The Norse established a kingdom around Novgorod | The Tartars completed conquest of Russia | The Russians under Ivan the Great drove the Tartars out of Russia | Ivan IV became the first czar of Russia | Peter the Great founded St. Petersburg | Trans-Siberian Railroad completed | Revolution overthrew the czar and the Bolsheviks seized power | First Five-Year Plan began | Latvia, Lithuania, and Estonia became Soviet republics | Construction of Baikal-Amur Mainline began |
| 862 | 1240 | 1480 | 1547 | 1703 | 1916 | 1917 | 1928 | 1940 | 1974 |

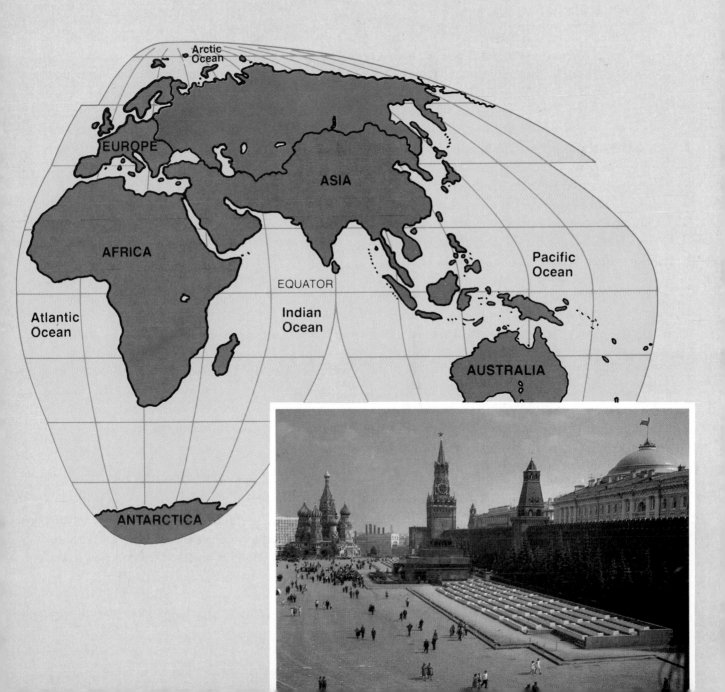

1

The Land and the People of the Soviet Union

The Soviet Union is the largest country in the world. It covers nearly one-seventh of the world's land area. It is larger than four of the continents. It shares borders with more countries than any other country in the world. It also has the longest coastline of any country.

Part of the Soviet Union is in Europe and part of it is in Asia. It stretches about 6,000 miles (9,650 km) from its borders with the countries of Western Europe in the west to the Pacific Ocean in the east. A narrow stretch of water, the Bering Strait, separates the Soviet Union from Alaska. From north to south, the Soviet Union's greatest extent is about 3,200 miles (5,150 km). The Arctic Ocean borders the country in the north, and several countries, including Iran, Afghanistan, and China, lie to the south.

The official name of the Soviet Union is the Union of Soviet Socialist Republics. Before 1917, this enormous land was called Russia, and it was ruled by czars (zärz). In 1917, the czars were overthrown by a revolution. The Communists took over and set up a number of areas called republics, which were united in the Union of Soviet Socialist Republics. Today there are 15 republics. Sometimes the Union of Soviet Socialist Republics is referred to as the U.S.S.R. or the Soviet Union. Many people also use the word *Russia* to mean the Soviet Union. Today the name *Russia* strictly refers to only the largest of the Soviet republics, the Russian Republic.

With a population of about 267 million, the Soviet Union ranks third among the nations of the world. Only China and India have more people. The number of people in the Soviet Union is only slightly larger than the number of people in the United States. The population density of the Soviet Union, however, is only about half that of the United States. The map on page 545 shows where most people live.

The Soviet Union is inhabited by people of many different cultures and languages. This is not surprising considering the great size of the country. For nearly a thousand years, Russia grew by adding territory on all sides. People from many different backgrounds came under its rule. After the Russian Revolution, the Communist government began to establish republics. The government tried to draw the boundaries on the basis of language or culture. As a result, the republics vary greatly in size. There is, however, a certain unity among the people who live in each.

The Land of the Soviet Union

The Soviet Union is a nation in two continents. Part of it is in Europe, and part of it is in Asia. The boundary between Europe and Asia is usually considered to be the Ural Mountains, the Ural River, the Caspian (kas'pē ən) Sea, the Caucasus (kô'kə səs) Mountains, the Black Sea, and the Mediterranean Sea. See the map on page 247.

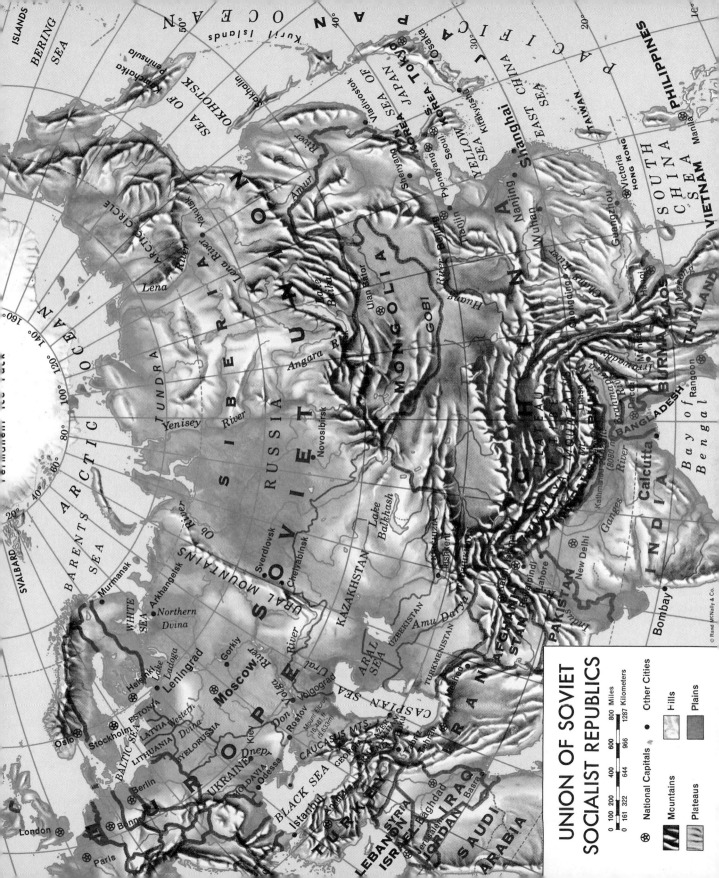

UNION OF SOVIET
SOCIALIST REPUBLICS

	National Capitals
•	Other Cities

Mountains

Hills

Plateaus

Plains

| 0 | 100 | 200 | | 400 | 600 | 800 Miles |
| 0 | 161 | 322 | 644 | 966 | 1287 Kilometers |

© Rand McNally & Co.

BERING SEA

ISLANDS

PACIFIC OCEAN

Kuril Islands

Kamchatka Peninsula

SEA OF OKHOTSK

Sakhalin

ARCTIC OCEAN

SVALBARD

BARENTS SEA

WHITE SEA

Murmansk

Arkhangelsk

Northern Dvina

Ob River

URAL MOUNTAINS

SIBERIA

TUNDRA

Lena

Lena River

Tunguska River

Yakutsk

ARCTIC CIRCLE

Yenisey River

Angara River

SOVIET

RUSSIA

Novosibirsk

Sverdlovsk

Chelyabinsk

KAZAKHSTAN

Lake Balkhash

ARAL SEA

UZBEKISTAN

Amu Darya

Tashkent

TURKMENISTAN

Meshed

MONGOLIA

Lake Baikal

Ulan Bator

GOBI

Amur River

Vladivostok

SEA OF JAPAN

JAPAN

TOKYO

Osaka

Kitakyushu

KOREA

NORTH KOREA

SOUTH KOREA

Seoul

Pyongyang

Shenyang

YELLOW SEA

Beijing

Tianjin

Huang River

CHINA

PLATEAU

Nanjing

Shanghai

Wuhan

Chang River

EAST CHINA SEA

TAIWAN

Guangzhou

Victoria

HONG KONG

SOUTH CHINA SEA

PHILIPPINES

Manila

VIETNAM

Hanoi

LAOS

THAILAND

BURMA

Rangoon

Bay of Bengal

BANGLADESH

Calcutta

INDIA

Ganges River

Deccan Plateau

New Delhi

Bombay

Brahmaputra River

Kathmandu

Lhasa

(8080 m)

PAKISTAN

Lahore

Rawalpindi

AFGHANISTAN

Mount Everest (8,848 m)

IRAN

Tehran

Tabriz

CASPIAN SEA

CAUCASUS MTS.

Mount Elbrus 18,481 ft. (5,633 m)

GEORGIA

Rostov

Don River

Volga River

Volgograd

Ural River

Gorkiy

Moscow

Leningrad

Ladoga Lake

Helsinki

Stockholm

BALTIC SEA

ESTONIA

LATVIA

Western Dvina

LITHUANIA

BYELORUSSIA

Kiev

UKRAINE

Dnepr

MOLDAVIA

Odessa

BLACK SEA

Istanbul

Ankara

TURKEY

SYRIA

LEBANON

ISRAEL

Jerusalem

JORDAN

IRAQ

Baghdad

Basra

SAUDI ARABIA

Berlin

EUROPE

London

Bonn

Paris

Oslo

NORWAY

The Caucasus Mountains stretch between the Black and Caspian seas in Soviet Asia. The snow-covered peak is Mount Kazbek.

The part of the Soviet Union west of this boundary is called Soviet Europe. Soviet Europe makes up one-fourth of the land area of the entire Soviet Union. The part of the Soviet Union east of the boundary is called Soviet Asia. The northern part of Soviet Asia lying between the Urals and the Pacific is a region called Siberia.

Landforms

Much of the Soviet Union is an area of low plains and plateaus. The northern part of the country was covered by ice during the Ice Ages. Moraines left by the ice are a major feature of the landscape.

Most of Soviet Europe is a gently rolling plain. The Carpathian Mountains of eastern Europe extend into the southwestern part of this region. At the southern edge of the plain, between the Black Sea and the Caspian Sea, are the Caucasus Mountains. Mount Elbrus (el'broos), the highest mountain in Europe, is in this range. It is 18,481 feet (5,633 m) high.

The European plain is separated from the great flat plain of western Siberia by the Ural Mountains. These mountains extend in an almost straight north-south line for 1,500 miles (2,400 km). They reach from the Arctic Ocean in the north to the Aral Sea in the south. Even though the Urals are called mountains, they are really little more than hills. The general elevation is 2,000 feet (610 m). This is lower than the general elevation of the Appalachian Mountains in the United States.

The plain of western Siberia stretches east from the Urals. It is one of the largest flat areas in the world. Much of it is marshy because of poor drainage.

A lowland extends south of the Ural Mountains and the plains on either side of it. This region is the southernmost part of the Soviet Union. Much of it is low plateaus and deserts. The lowest point in the Soviet Union is here, on the eastern edge of the Caspian Sea. This point is 92 feet (28 m) below sea level. Not far away is Communism Peak, the highest point in the Soviet Union. This mountain rises 24,590 feet (7,495 m) above sea level.

The mountain range in which Communism Peak is found is part of a series of ranges that continues to the northeast. Along the borders with China and Tibet, peaks in these ranges rise to elevations of more than 12,000 feet (3,650 m).

North of these mountain ranges and east of the Siberian plain is the central Siberian plateau. The region slopes gently toward the north.

The eastern part of Siberia is an upland region of mountains and plateaus. Many of the mountains reach heights of more than 10,000 feet (3,050 m). They form several peninsulas. The largest peninsula, Kamchatka (kam chat' kə), extends southward into the Pacific Ocean.

Water Features

Along the northern coast of the Soviet Union, the waters of the Arctic Ocean are divided into several seas. To the north of Soviet Europe is the Barents Sea. South of the Barents Sea, the water cuts into the land even more to form the White Sea.

The northern part of the Pacific Ocean between Alaska and the Soviet Union is called the Bering Sea. Two other parts of the Pacific border the east coast of the Soviet Union. The Sea of Okhotsk (ō kätsk') lies west of the Kamchatka Peninsula. Farther south, the Sea of Japan separates the extreme southeastern part of the Soviet Union from Japan.

Soviet Europe has boundaries on the Baltic Sea, the Black Sea, and the Caspian Sea, as well as on the White Sea and the Barents Sea. The Gulf of Finland extends east from the Baltic to separate the southern part of Finland from the Soviet Union. Not far inland from the head of the Gulf of Finland is Lake Ladoga. This lake is the largest lake in Europe.

The Black Sea and the Caspian Sea form part of the southern boundary of Soviet Europe. The Black Sea is connected with the Mediterranean by a waterway passing through Turkey. The Caspian Sea is the world's largest inland body of water. Although it is called a sea, it is really a lake. The Caspian Sea has no outlet. It loses more water by evaporation than it receives from rivers that flow into it. The Caspian is an unusual body of water in another way. Its surface is below sea level.

Two large bodies of water east of the Caspian Sea are also lakes with no outlets to the sea. One is the shallow Aral Sea. It is much like the Great Salt Lake in the western United States. The other, Lake Balkhash (bal kash'), lies at the foot of a high mountain range and is fed by streams from melting snow.

Lake Baikal (bīkôl') is a large lake in south central Siberia. It is the deepest freshwater lake in the world. It is more than one mile (1.61 km) deep, and it is nearly 400 miles (640 km) long. From January to May, the surface of the lake is frozen.

Some of the longest rivers in the world are in Siberia. They include the Ob (äb), the Yenisey (yen'əsā'), and the Lena. All of these rivers rise in the south and flow northward into the Arctic. The Amur (ämoor') River forms part of the boundary between the Soviet Union and China. It flows eastward into the Pacific.

The longest river in Soviet Europe is the Volga. It flows into the Caspian Sea. Several other rivers arise in the same region as the Volga, but they flow in different directions. The Don and the Dnieper (nē'pər) flow south into the Black Sea. There are two rivers called the Dvina (dəvē'nä). The Northern Dvina flows into the White Sea, and the Western Dvina flows into the Baltic Sea. These rivers of Soviet Europe, as well as many others, are navigable.

The rivers of Siberia, however, are of little use for transportation. Most of them flow north to the Arctic, which is frozen over most of the year. Because the rivers flow north, they flow from areas that are warmer to areas that are colder. In the spring, the ice in the southern parts of the rivers thaws before that in the north. The water flows north to places where the rivers are still blocked by ice. Floods result as the water backs up and is forced to spread out over the land. Much of the northern plain of Siberia becomes a swamp, or marsh. The rivers can be used only for a very short part of the year.

Climate

Almost every kind of climate except a tropical climate is found in the Soviet Union. Most of the country lies in latitudes that correspond to the latitudes of the northern United States and Canada. Much of the northern part of the Soviet Union lies within the Arctic Circle. Only in the extreme south is there a region with a semitropical climate.

Like much of North America, much of the Soviet Union has a continental climate. A continental climate is a climate of extremes. Most of the Soviet Union is far from large bodies of water that would help moderate the climate. The summers are hot for the latitude, and the winters are very cold.

In general, the farther north and the farther from the open ocean places are, the more extreme the temperatures will be. The highest temperatures in the Soviet Union are in the region east of the Caspian Sea. The coldest temperatures are in northeastern Siberia.

Northeastern Siberia is also noted for having the world's greatest temperature range, 118°F. (65°C). The average July temperature there is about 60°F. (15°C), and the average January temperature is about -58°F. (-50°C).

The long winters of the Soviet Union are famous. Snow covers more than half the country for at least six months of the year. Except in the south, the coastal waters, lakes, and rivers are frozen.

Another effect of the long periods of cold is permafrost. In nearly half of the country, the groundwater remains permanently frozen. Only the top few inches thaw in the summer.

In general, the Soviet Union is a dry country. Large parts of the country receive very little rain. The areas of low rainfall are in the far north and far south. Many areas of low rainfall in the north are also areas of low evaporation. As a result, there is enough moisture in such regions for forests to grow.

Vegetation

Climate has an effect on vegetation in all parts of the world. In the Soviet Union, the influence of climate on plant life is clearly seen. Its six major climate and vegetation regions stretch across the country from east to west in broad belts.

In the far north is the treeless tundra. The tundra stretches along the Arctic plain from the Barents Sea to the Bering Sea. In the short, cool summers, mosses, lichens, and low shrubs cover the region. The tundra of the Soviet Union resembles the tundra of Canada and the United States. The winters are extremely severe. All of the tundra has permafrost.

South of the tundra is a great needleleaf forest called the *taiga* (tī′gə). Most of the taiga is in subarctic regions. This forest extends across the Soviet Union from Finland to the Pacific. Except for the region that is tundra, nearly all of Siberia is taiga. The northern forests of Canada and Alaska are also taiga. The North American taiga is mostly spruce and fir. The Siberian taiga is mostly larch. Larches are a kind of pine and have needlelike leaves. Unlike most trees with needlelike leaves, larches shed their leaves in the fall.

South of the taiga region in Soviet Europe is another forested region. The trees in the southern part of this region are broadleaf deciduous trees. In the northern part, the trees are mixed evergreen and deciduous. Today much of the region is without trees because it has been cleared for farming.

A grassland region known as the steppe extends from the region north of the Black Sea almost to Lake Baikal. The steppe lies south of the mixed forest in Soviet Europe and south of the taiga in Soviet Asia.

Great loess deposits on the steppe have developed into a very rich black soil called *chernozem* (cher′nə zem′). In Russian, *chernozem* means "black earth." Chernozem is a fertile soil rich in humus. It is similar to the rich soil in the grain belt of the United States.

Rainfall on the steppe decreases from west to east. Trees and shrubs are found in the western parts. Grassy plains are found in the semiarid eastern parts.

Around the Caspian Sea, the Aral Sea, and Lake Balkhash is a desert. The desert extends to the base of the high mountains that lie along the Soviet Union's southern border. There is little natural vegetation in this desert region. Much of the area is covered with sand dunes.

The windward sides of some mountains along the southern borders of the Soviet Union receive heavy rainfall. Alpine grasses and forests grow in these moist regions. Other parts of the mountains are cold and barren.

The People of the Soviet Union

Much of the Soviet Union is too cold, too dry, or too mountainous to support many people. As a result, the population is spread out unevenly. About 75 percent of the people live in Soviet Europe. Here the population density is nearly ten times that of Soviet Asia.

The people of the Soviet Union come from many different backgrounds and speak many different languages. A group of people who share similar customs, languages, and other characteristics is called an *ethnic* (eth'nik) *group*. Other characteristics of ethnic groups are religion, history, and national origin.

In the Soviet Union, there are people of dozens of different ethnic backgrounds. People are grouped mainly by the language they speak. More than 150 different languages are spoken in the Soviet Union, but many of them are related to one another. School textbooks are translated into more than 50 languages for use in different parts of the country.

People who speak Slavic languages make up more than 75 percent of the total population. Russians make up the largest ethnic group among the Slavs. They account for more than half the total population of the country. Russian is the official language of the Soviet Union.

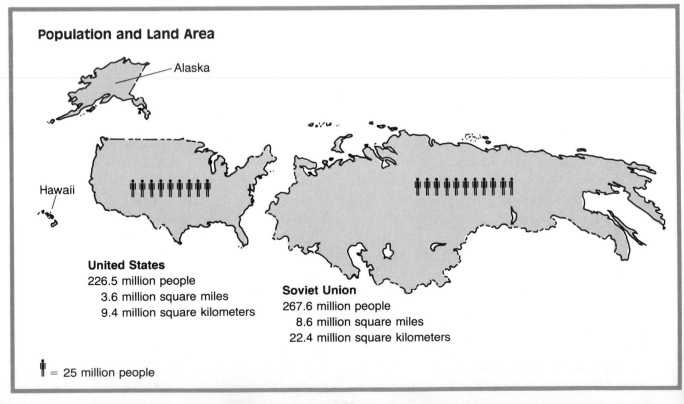

Population and Land Area

Alaska

Hawaii

United States
226.5 million people
3.6 million square miles
9.4 million square kilometers

Soviet Union
267.6 million people
8.6 million square miles
22.4 million square kilometers

⋔ = 25 million people

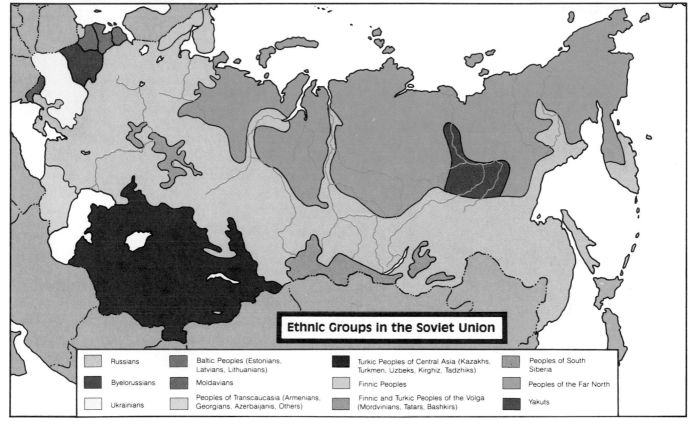

Ethnic Groups in the Soviet Union

Legend:
- Russians
- Byelorussians
- Ukrainians
- Baltic Peoples (Estonians, Latvians, Lithuanians)
- Moldavians
- Peoples of Transcaucasia (Armenians, Georgians, Azerbaijanis, Others)
- Turkic Peoples of Central Asia (Kazakhs, Turkmen, Uzbeks, Kirghiz, Tadzhiks)
- Finnic Peoples
- Finnic and Turkic Peoples of the Volga (Mordvinians, Tatars, Bashkirs)
- Peoples of South Siberia
- Peoples of the Far North
- Yakuts

Not all the people of the Soviet Union belong to the Russian *ethnic group.* This map shows the distribution of other important groups.

The word *Russian* is often used to refer to all the people of the Soviet Union. In a strict sense, the word is used to mean the Russian ethnic group or the Russian language. It is also used to refer to the Russian Republic.

Two other important Slavic groups are the Ukrainians and the Byelorussians (bel′ō rush′ ǝnz). Most people belonging to these groups also live in Soviet Europe.

Turkic peoples make up the second largest ethnic group in the Soviet Union. They speak languages related to Turkish. Most Turkic groups live in Soviet Asia, in the area between the Caspian Sea and China.

Other ethnic groups include people in the Baltic republics who are closely related to the Finns and Poles. Germanic peoples live in many places throughout the Soviet Union. There are several small groups in Siberia that are related to the Eskimos and Indians of North America.

The United States and the Soviet Union are not greatly different in size of population. Like the population of the United States, the population of the Soviet Union is made up of many different ethnic groups. There are several other ways in which the two countries are similar.

Both the United States and the Soviet Union are industrialized countries. In both nations, people have been on the move. The United States expanded by moving west. The Soviet

Russian Alphabet

Cyrillic letter		Roman letter equivalent	Sound in English
А	а	a	c*a*r
Б	б	b	*b*at
В	в	v	*v*ery
Г	г	g	*g*ame
Д	д	d	*d*ear
Е	е	ye	*ye*s
Ё	ё	yo	*ya*wn
Ж	ж	zh	sei*z*ure
З	з	z	*z*oo
И	и	i	m*ee*t
Й	й	y	t*oy*
К	к	k	*k*it
Л	л	l	*l*id
М	м	m	*m*an
Н	н	n	*n*ot
О	о	o	*aw*ful
П	п	p	*p*en
Р	р	r	th*r*ead (rolled)
С	с	s	*s*at
Т	т	t	*t*ag
У	у	u	f*oo*l
Ф	ф	f	*f*ine
Х	х	kh	blo*ck*
Ц	ц	ts	pi*ts*
Ч	ч	ch	*ch*in
Ш	ш	sh	*sh*oe
Щ	щ	shch	fi*sh ch*ips
Ъ	ъ	—	indicates a syllable break and a *y* sound before following vowel
Ы	ы	y	s*y*mpathy
Ь	ь	—	softens consonant preceding *y* sound
Э	э	e	n*e*t
Ю	ю	yu	*u*se
Я	я	ya	*ya*rn

The written Russian language uses 33 letters of the Cyrillic (si ril′ik) alphabet. This alphabet, based on Greek letters of the 800s A.D., is named after St. Cyril, a Greek missionary.

Union has expanded to the east. In both countries, there has been a move from the country to the city. Urban dwellers make up the largest part of both populations. In the Soviet Union, however, a much larger percentage of the population is involved in agriculture than in the United States.

In other ways, the United States and the Soviet Union are quite different. In the United States, freedom and responsibility are important ideas. In the Soviet Union, the government has much greater control over the lives of the people. Almost everything is owned by the government. Everyone works for the government. There are no private businesses. The government decides what work each person will do.

Do You Know?

1. On what two continents is the Soviet Union located?
2. What two ranges of mountains form part of the boundary between Europe and Asia?
3. What vegetation zone stretches across the northernmost part of the Soviet Union?
4. In what part of the Soviet Union do most of the people live?
5. To what ethnic group do most of the people in the Soviet Union belong?

2
The History of the Soviet Union

In early times, several groups settled in the lands that now make up the Soviet Union. The Slavs, the Norse, and the Tartars played important roles in Russia's early history. Strong rulers called czars established their power in the mid-1500s. The reign of the czars lasted for hundreds of years. Then in 1917, a revolution created the Communist nation known as the Soviet Union.

The Early History of Russia

The early Slavs lived in eastern Europe. During the late third century A.D., they began to occupy a region of plains that is now Byelorussia and eastern Poland. These Slavic people established many towns and villages and became involved in trading.

In the 800s, people from northern Europe called the Norse moved into the area. A Norse leader named Rurik led his warriors into the land of the Slavs. Some historians believe that the Norse invaded the area. Others believe that quarreling groups of Slavs asked the Norse for their help.

In 862, the Norse established a kingdom with Novgorod as its center. *Novgorod* means "new town." This kingdom lasted for more than 300 years. During this time, the Norse and the Slavs intermarried. They shared their traditions and technology. The term *Rus* was used to describe the Norse and Slavs. *Russia* means "land of the Rus."

Some of Rurik's followers traveled south and conquered the Slavs along the Dnieper River. They made Kiev the capital of the Norse possessions in Russia.

During the 900s, small city-states, some Norse and some Slav, arose throughout southern Russia. These city-states were ruled by dukes and princes. The rulers sent traders as far south as the city of Constantinople, now known as Istanbul.

From such contacts, the people of Russia became familiar with the Christian faith. In the 980s, Prince Vladimir (vlad′ə mir), the ruler of Kiev, converted to Christianity. Soon many people of Russia adopted Christianity as their religion.

The Tartar Conquest

Beginning in 1233, large and powerful troops of Mongols attacked Russia from the east. These were the Tartar armies. By 1240, the Tartars had destroyed Kiev and conquered Russia. For more than 200 years, the Tartars ruled the region. They forced the people to pay tribute, or taxes. The Tartars set up an empire with its capital near what is now Volgograd. The map on page 421 shows the extent of the Mongol empire in the 1200s.

Russian Independence

During the 1390s, armies from Central Asia attacked and severely weakened the Tartar empire. The grand duke of Moscow, Ivan III, decided to fight the Tartars while they were weak. Under his leadership, the Russians drove the Tartars back toward Asia in 1480. Ivan also extended his control over Novgorod. He is known as Ivan the Great because he laid the foundation of the Russian nation.

The Czars and Russian Expansion

Czars ruled Russia from 1547 until 1917. The title *czar* comes from the Latin name *Caesar*, meaning "emperor."

Ivan the Terrible

In 1547, Ivan IV became the grand duke of Moscow. He was crowned as Russia's first czar. He became known as Ivan the Terrible because he killed and plundered as he brought villages under his control. Special agents arrested and punished anyone who dared to criticize Ivan or his government.

Ivan made laws that forced Russia's peasants to work on the land of the nobles. The peasants, or serfs, had little freedom and lived in poverty.

Expansion to the East

Ivan extended the borders of Russia eastward. The Volga became a Russian river. This river gave Russia an outlet to the Caspian Sea. Under Ivan, Russia also gained possessions in Siberia.

At the outset of Ivan's reign, nomadic tribes of Mongols held the land east of the Ural Mountains. One of these tribes had its center at Sibir (sə bēr′). Ivan gave traders his permis-

sion to attack this tribe. In 1582, the traders defeated the Mongols, giving Russia control over western Siberia. This area was important for fur trapping.

For hundreds of years, Russia's frontier lay to the east. The Russians settled Siberia in much the same way as the people of the United States and Canada settled North America.

Russia's exploration and trading activities continued under other czars. They sent expeditions farther and farther east. In 1639, Russian explorers reached the shores of the Pacific Ocean.

Peter the Great

In 1682, a young man named Peter became czar. Historians call him Peter the Great.

Peter felt that Russia was a country behind the times. It was sparsely settled and had few contacts with Western Europe. It had little trade because it had no ports on the Baltic Sea or the Black Sea.

In his travels to Western Europe, Peter realized that his nation had been cut off from changes in the rest of the world. He decided to introduce the manners and customs of Western Europe into Russia. The people at Peter's court were more Asian than European in their manners and dress. Peter ordered that the long robes worn by men be replaced by European-style suits. He also ordered Russian nobles to shave off their long beards. Anyone who insisted on wearing a beard had to pay a heavy fine.

Peter founded schools to train engineers, sailors, and army officers. He brought in skilled workers from abroad.

**Expansion of Russia
1360–1917**

■ 1360	■ 1524–1689	···· Present-day boundary of the Soviet Union
■ 1360–1524	□ 1689–1917	⌁ Other present-day national boundaries

The map shows how Russia expanded in stages to cover much of Europe and Asia. Between what years did Russia reach to the Bering Sea? To the Caspian Sea?

Expansion in Europe

Peter knew that if Russia were to develop trade with Western Europe, it needed ports on the Black Sea and the Baltic Sea. He called such ports "windows to the West."

At that time, Sweden controlled the Baltic Sea. Between 1700 and 1721, Peter and his armies fought Sweden in the Great Northern War. When the Swedes were defeated, they were forced to *cede* (sēd), or give up rights to, a large area of land near the Baltic Sea.

Peter built a new city on the Neva River at the head of the Gulf of Finland. He called the city St. Petersburg. It became the chief trading port and capital of Russia. Through St. Petersburg, Russia had contact with Western ideas.

During Peter's reign, other nations realized that Russia was becoming a great power.

When Peter's daughter Elizabeth became empress of Russia, she also made war on Sweden. Her armies seized most of what is now Finland and added this land to Russia.

Catherine II was a German princess who married Peter III. She became empress of Russia after the death of her husband. During her reign, Russian armies defeated the Turks. As a result, the Turks ceded to Russia the north shore of the Black Sea. Catherine's armies also won most of what is now Byelorussia from Poland. Catherine II is often called "Catherine the Great" because of her military successes.

Expansion to the Southeast

During the early 1800s, Russia expanded to include territory that now makes up the republics in the region of the Caucasus Mountains. The czars then sent armies into Central Asia, to the region east of the Caspian Sea. Find these areas on the map on page 247. Expansion to the southeast was accomplished during the reigns of Alexander I, Nicholas I, Alexander II, and Alexander III.

The Soviet Union in the Twentieth Century

Under the czars, Russia expanded through exploration, settlement, and war. It became the world's largest nation. Cultural contact and trade with Western Europe were established. However, the czars did little to improve the lives of Russia's people. In the early twentieth century, Russia was still a land of wealthy, powerful nobles and poor peasants.

Crowds in Moscow protested against the czar in 1917. Many people had suffered from shortages of food and fuel during the harsh winter.

The Russian Revolution

When World War I broke out in 1914, Russia fought against Austria and Germany. Although Russian troops had some early successes, the Germans forced them into retreat by 1917. Many Russian soldiers were killed. People in Russia felt that the czar, Nicholas II, was mishandling the war effort.

The winter of 1917 was cold, and millions of Russians suffered. There were shortages of food, fuel, and housing. When hunger riots broke out in the capital, the czar did nothing to help the people. In March, an angry Russian parliament demanded that the czar *abdicate* (ab′də kāt′), or give up his power and position.

After the czar abdicated, the parliament set up a republic. This new republic lasted only until November. V.I. Lenin and his followers, who called themselves Bolsheviks, overthrew the government. On the night of November 7, 1917, the Bolsheviks seized the Winter Palace, where the government offices were. In the morning, when the parliament met, they found the Bolsheviks in control.

The Bolsheviks believed in Communism. They thought that the country's wealth should be shared among all people. In particular, they felt that the *proletariat* (prō′lə ter′ē ət), or the working class, should share in the wealth they produced. Under Lenin, the Bolsheviks seized the property of the nobles.

When Lenin died in 1924, Joseph Stalin's *regime* (rə zhēm′) began. A regime is a system of rule or government. During Stalin's regime, new plans for improving agriculture and industry were put into effect.

V.I. Lenin led the Bolshevik takeover of the government in October 1917. Here he addresses a crowd in Moscow.

The Five-Year Plans

In 1928, the Soviet government began a program of work to be accomplished within the next five years. During the first Five-Year Plan, Stalin combined small farms into larger farms called collectives.

The government already owned some of the nation's land. When farming began on the Siberian frontier, the government organized state farms from the land that it controlled. Stalin decided to keep this system of state farms. He expanded the system by taking control of the rest of the nation's agricultural land as well. By 1929, the government began to use force to gain control of privately owned farms. The farms around Soviet villages were "collected," or put together into larger farms.

The system of state and collective farming has remained in effect since Stalin's time. State farms and collective farms are similar. Under each system, farmers are paid wages. They may own limited amounts of livestock and may use small plots of land as their own private gardens.

On the collectives, crops are sold to the government and farmers share in the profits.

259

Each collective must fill its crop *quota* (kwō′tə), or a fixed amount or share of the total that is due to the government. After quotas are met, farmers may keep or sell the extra crops.

Stalin's first Five-Year Plan was also directed toward industrialization. Experts from other countries came to help with the program of building new power plants and factories and developing mines. Stalin put other Five-Year Plans into effect. The early plans were aimed at producing such items as machinery, steel, and construction materials. The system of Five-Year Plans continued under the leadership of later Soviet leaders.

Expansion of Soviet Influence

Since the revolution, the Soviet Union has expanded its borders and the area it influences. In 1920, the Soviets invaded the three independent countries of the Caucasus Mountains

There are 16 Communist countries in the world today. Which are *satellites* of the Soviet Union?

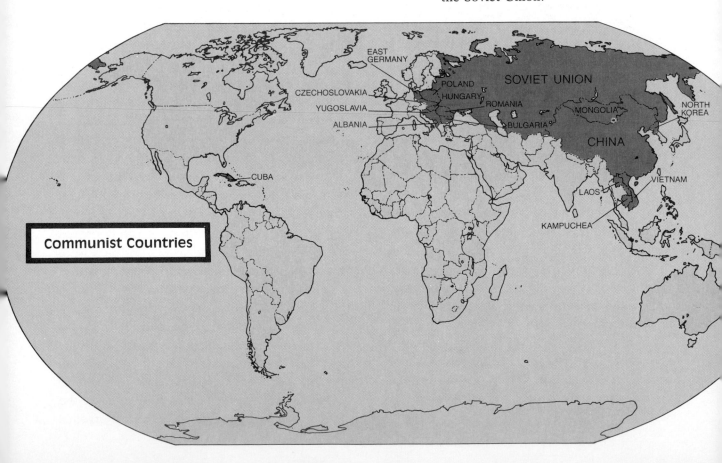

Communist Countries

that had once been under the control of the czars. These countries were made part of the Soviet Union.

In 1939, Finland was attacked by the Soviet Union. The Soviet Union won a great amount of Finnish territory in the war that followed. Latvia, Lithuania, and Estonia were invaded by the Soviet Union and made republics in 1940. In the same year, Soviet forces also overran Bessarabia, which was then part of Romania. Territory from Bessarabia became part of the new Moldavian Republic.

After World War II, the Soviet Union set up Communist governments in seven countries of eastern Europe. These were Albania, Bulgaria, Czechoslovakia, Hungary, Poland, Romania, and Yugoslavia. Each of these nations became a *satellite* (sat′ə līt′) of the Soviet Union. A satellite is a country under the control of another more powerful nation. The Soviet satellites do much of their trading with the Soviet Union. The economic and political decisions made in Moscow have a direct effect on the Soviet satellite nations.

Capitalism and Communism

The Soviet Union was the first country to establish a completely Communist state. Communism is an economic system. It is also a philosophy, or system of ideas. Communists have specific ideas about social, political, and economic systems. These ideas inspired the Bolsheviks who revolted in 1917. Today there are several nations with Communist governments. See the map on page 260.

Capitalism is another major economic system in the world today. Comparing capitalism and communism is one way to understand both systems.

Capitalism

Capitalism is an economic system. Free enterprise is one way that capitalism is put into effect. In the United States, Western Europe, and many other countries, people are allowed to own property. Individuals or groups of individuals own farms, ranches, stores, and manufacturing firms. When individuals are allowed to participate freely in business, they are part of a free-enterprise system.

In a free-enterprise system, an individual can own *capital* (kap′it əl). Capital is anything that can be used to produce wealth. Property, money, and natural resources are forms of capital. A *capitalist* (kap′it əl ist) is a person who owns capital. Capitalists in a free-enterprise system invest their wealth in whatever businesses they choose. The owners of the businesses decide what goods to produce and what prices to charge.

People who believe in capitalism feel that the opportunity to earn money and make a profit is a great motive for people to work.

Communism

In the nineteenth century, all of Europe was capitalistic. Some people believed that changes had to occur within the capitalist system. Philosophers such as Karl Marx believed that the industrial revolution had created poor working conditions for laborers. He saw that most of the working class lived in poverty. Marx believed that capitalists would become more and more wealthy. He thought the working class would remain poor. He wanted the working class to overthrow the capitalists so that wealth could be shared by all people. These ideas were the beginning of modern Communism.

Today the term *Communism* has a number of meanings. Some people still see it as a revolutionary movement. Others think of it as a philosophy, or way of life. To most people, Communism means a political and economic system. In a Communist state, all land and other natural resources and all industries are owned by the government. They are supposed to be used to benefit all the people in the country.

Communists believe that an ideal society does not have a middle class, a rich class, or a poor class. Communist governments make all decisions about what is produced, how much is charged, and how much workers are paid. The government owns or controls most land, natural resources, banks, industry, trade, transportation, and communication. Individuals own little, if anything.

One-third of the world's people live under Communist governments. These countries differ greatly, however, in how much control they think their governments should have.

Soviet Communism

Since its beginnings as a Communist state in 1917, the Soviet Union has become the leader of world Communism. Political and economic decisions made by the Communist Party affect the lives of all Soviet citizens. Their decisions also affect other Communist nations.

The Communist Party

The Communist Party is organized like a pyramid. At the base of the pyramid are hundreds of small units, or cells. Each school, farm, factory, and business has its own local Communist cell.

To be a Party member and join a cell, a person must be recommended by other Party members and approved by Party officials. The Soviet Communist Party has about 15 million members. This is only 5 percent of the Soviet population.

Above the cells in the pyramid are the district, region, and republic organizations. Each of these organizations is ruled by levels. The Secretary is at the top of the pyramid.

Elections for Party leaders are held at each level of the pyramid. However, only one person's name appears on the ballot for each position. The candidates are selected by those higher up in the Party. In this way, Party officials control all offices.

The Soviet Government

The Soviet government is separate from the Communist Party. However, it is directly controlled by the Communist Party. The government is influenced by the Party in all its decisions and actions. All government officials are members of the Communist Party.

The government of the Soviet Union is made up of soviets, or councils. There are soviets at different levels. At the highest level is the Supreme Soviet. The Supreme Soviet is the legislature of the Soviet Union. It passes laws proposed by the Communist Party.

The Supreme Soviet also elects the Presidium. The Presidium handles legislation when the Supreme Soviet is not in session. The chairman of the Presidium is the head of the Soviet government. He is called the premier. Joseph Stalin, Nikita Khrushchev, and Leonid Brezhnev were each premier and head of the Communist Party.

Life Under Soviet Communism

The government of the Soviet Union provides some important services for its citizens, including medical and child care. Education is also provided. However, the government must approve all courses and textbooks. Communist beliefs are stressed in Soviet schools.

All land and businesses are owned by the government. However, people are allowed to own their own homes, household goods, personal items, and savings. Government and Party leaders have many more privileges and luxuries than most people. In recent years, the Soviet government has given cash rewards for surpassing quotas and for special achievement. This has caused income inequality.

In the Soviet Union, people are denied the freedoms of a democratic society. Officials in the government make decisions about the publication and distribution of books. Newspapers, magazines, radio stations, and television stations are owned and run by the government. The government controls what information people receive about their own country and the rest of the world. The information given out by the government is often incomplete. It is sometimes changed. Government officials use the news media to publicize their point of view. Publicity used to make known the ideas of a group is called *propaganda* (prop′ə gan′də). Soviet propaganda is used by the government to promote Communist ideas throughout the world.

People who criticize the Soviet Union can be severely punished. They can be arrested and sent out of the country. In some ways the Soviet government is becoming less harsh. Since the Russian Revolution, the government's treatment of ethnic groups has changed. At first the government tried to make people do away with their traditions. Religious services were discouraged. Today ethnic groups are allowed to keep their languages and customs. There are also state-approved churches.

Do You Know?

1. Who was the first czar of Russia? What was he also known as?
2. What czar introduced many Western ideas and customs to Russia?
3. What important event took place in Russia in 1917?
4. Name three European countries that came under Soviet influence after World War II.
5. What is the political and economic system of the Soviet Union called?

Before You Go On

Using New Words

quota   proletariat

capital   ethnic group

taiga   capitalist

regime   chernozem

abdicate   propaganda

cede   satellite

Number a paper from 1 through 12. After each number write the word or term that matches the definition.

1. Anything that can be used to produce wealth
2. To give up rights to
3. A person who owns capital
4. A fixed amount or share of the total due
5. Publicity to make known the ideas of a group
6. The working class
7. Needleleaf forests of far northern regions
8. A country under the control of another more powerful nation
9. To give up power and position
10. People who share similar customs, languages, and other characteristics
11. A fertile soil rich in humus
12. A system of rule or government

Finding the Facts

1. What is the official name of the Soviet Union? What was the Soviet Union called before 1917?
2. What two countries have larger populations than the Soviet Union?
3. Where is Siberia?
4. What is the highest point in the Soviet Union? How high is it?
5. What is the world's largest inland body of water? Where is it?
6. What part of the Soviet Union has the world's greatest temperature range?
7. Why is Ivan III known as Ivan the Great? Why is Ivan IV known as Ivan the Terrible?
8. Why did Russia want ports on the Black and Baltic seas?
9. What kind of government was first set up after the revolution? What happened to it?
10. What are the two kinds of farms in the Soviet Union?
11. What percentage of the Soviet population belongs to the Communist Party?
12. Under Soviet Communism, what does the government own? What are the people allowed to own?

3
Soviet Europe

The early history of Russia began on the plains of Soviet Europe. The cities of Kiev and Moscow grew up there and became capitals of important kingdoms. The early rulers of Russia established their control in this region. From here, they pushed out in all directions to extend the boundaries of their empires.

Soviet Europe today is the center of the Soviet Union. It is not the geographic center of the country. It is, however, the region where the people and the political power are centered. Soviet Europe is the most densely populated and most heavily industrialized part of the Soviet Union. Most of the major cities are there. Most of the country's important agricultural lands are there.

There are seven republics in Soviet Europe. Three of them occupy more than 95 percent of the land.

Three Large Republics

The three largest republics in Soviet Europe are the Ukrainian Republic, the Byelorussian Republic, and the European part of the Russian Republic. The Russian Republic is the largest republic in the Soviet Union. About 75 percent of the country belongs to this enormous republic. Two-fifths of the Russian Republic is in Soviet Europe, and three-fifths of it is in Soviet Asia. The part of the Russian Republic in Europe is larger than any other European republic.

The people who live in the three largest republics of Soviet Europe make up the three largest ethnic groups of the Soviet Union. The Russian Republic, the Ukrainian Republic, and the Byelorussian Republic are each named for the largest ethnic group living within its boundaries. People of many other ethnic backgrounds also live in these republics.

Transportation

The geography of the Soviet Union has always made transportation a problem. For much of its history, the country remained cut off from the rest of the world. Mountains and deserts form barriers to the south. Although the country has a long coastline, much of it is locked by ice for most of the year.

The enormous size of the Soviet Union has made travel difficult within the country. Vast distances separate one part of the country from another. Most rivers are navigable fo only short periods of the year. At one time, however, waterways were very important to transportation.

The major waterways of the Soviet Union were developed west of the Ural Mountains. For hundreds of years, the Volga River has been used to transport people and goods. The Volga and many other rivers were widened and deepened so that large ships could use them. Canals were built to connect the rivers. The rivers and canals form an important transportation network. Major cities such as Moscow,

Leningrad, and Volgograd are linked to one another by waterways. It is possible to move goods by boat between the Caspian Sea, the Black Sea, the Baltic Sea, and the White Sea. Although it is far inland, Moscow is often called the "city of five ports."

Except in the south, the rivers and canals are navigable for only five to seven months a year because of ice. Ports on the Black Sea and the Caspian Sea are open all year long. Only a few ports on the Baltic remain open all winter. The entire Arctic coast except for the port of Murmansk (murmansk') is locked by ice for nine months a year. Murmansk is the largest city in the world north of the Arctic Circle. Its port is kept ice-free by a current that is part of the North Atlantic Drift. Atomic-powered ice-breakers keep some of the Arctic and Baltic ports open during the winter.

The waterways of Soviet Europe are limited in their usefulness. They are important, however, in the transportation of heavy goods, such as fuel, ore, and grain.

Railroads are the chief means of shipping goods over long distances in the Soviet Union. About half of the Soviet Union's freight and passenger traffic is carried by rail. The Soviet Union has more miles of railroad track than any other country in the world except the United States.

Most parts of Soviet Europe are connected by rail. Eleven main lines radiate from Moscow, the country's main transportation center. Moscow is also connected with parts of Soviet Asia by rail. The longest railroad in the world, the Trans-Siberian Railroad, connects Moscow

with Vladivostok (vlad'ə və stäk'), on the Pacific coast. This line is 5,600 miles (9,000 km) long. It took 25 years to complete. The fastest trains take seven days to make the run between Moscow and Vladivostok.

There are few paved roads in the Soviet Union. The heaviest concentration of roads is in Soviet Europe. In large areas of the Soviet Union, roads are difficult to build because of permafrost. In wet or snowy weather, roads may become impassable.

Because of the great distances in the Soviet Union, airplanes have become a major means of transportation. The government-owned airline provides flights between most large cities and to more than 80 countries. The airlines are important for both passengers and freight.

Agriculture

The Soviet Union has more farmland than any other country in the world. About 25 percent of the land in the Soviet Union is used for agriculture. Nearly 25 percent of the population works in agriculture. The major agricultural regions of the country are in Soviet Europe.

The most productive farmland is a triangular area that lies between Leningrad, Odessa (ō des'ə), and Lake Baikal. This region is sometimes called the "fertile triangle." The part of the fertile triangle lying east of the Urals is much like the Midwest of the United States. It can be divided into a northern and a southern part. The northern part corresponds to the mixed-forest vegetation zone. Here, where the land has been cleared, rye, potatoes, and feed crops are grown. Rye and potatoes are the most important crops. The Soviet Union is the world's largest producer of rye and potatoes. Dairy farming is also important in this region.

The southern part of the region is the steppe that stretches across the southern part of the Ukrainian and Russian republics. The rich chernozem soils here make this the most important farming region in the Soviet Union. Winter wheat, corn, sugar beets, barley, flax, and tobacco are grown. The Soviet Union leads the world in the production of wheat, sugar beets, barley, and flax.

Beef cattle, dairy cattle, and hogs are also raised in this region, particularly in the Ukraine. In recent years, the Soviet government has encouraged the production of beef cattle. Corn is an important feed grain for cattle. It requires more water to grow than wheat does. In order to grow more corn, the wheat fields were moved east to semiarid regions that had never been cultivated before. In years of high rainfall, wheat production was high. In dry years, however, the crops failed, and the Soviet Union had to import wheat from the United States.

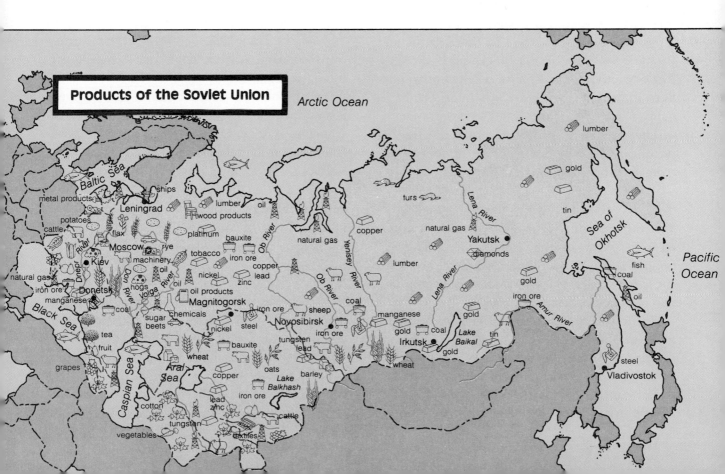

Products of the Soviet Union

The southern part of the Ukraine along the shores of the Black Sea has a Mediterranean climate. Citrus fruits, grapes, tobacco, and tea are grown in this sunny region. Tea is an important crop because many people in the Soviet Union drink tea.

Fishing and Lumbering

Fish such as cod, salmon, and herring are caught in the Barents Sea and the White Sea. A fish called the sturgeon (stur′jən) is caught in the lower part of the Volga River and in the Caspian and Black seas. The eggs of the sturgeon are a delicacy called caviar. There is a worldwide market for caviar.

Soviet fishing boats sail in the Atlantic and Pacific oceans and in the Black and Baltic seas. The Soviet Union is a major whaling nation. Its fleet of factory whaling ships hunt whales in many parts of the world.

The Soviet Union is the world's leading producer of lumber. Most of the lumber comes from the forests in Soviet Europe.

Mining

The Soviet Union is one of the richest countries in the world in kinds and amounts of minerals. The Soviet Union leads the world in the production of coal, iron ore, petroleum, and manganese. It also produces great amounts of natural gas, copper, gold, tin, lead, nickel, zinc, and bauxite.

Mineral deposits are found in all parts of the Soviet Union. Production of minerals has been going on longer in Soviet Europe than in Soviet Asia. The milder climate and better

Iron ore is loaded onto trucks at a mine near Belgorod in the Donets Basin of the Ukraine.

transportation systems have made it easier to mine, produce, and move the ores.

The Donets (də nets′) Basin of the Ukraine is an important area for the production of coal. Iron ore, natural gas, and manganese are also found in the Ukraine.

Rich reserves of oil and natural gas are being produced along the Volga River. To the northeast, in the Ural Mountains, there are important deposits of iron ore, copper, and bauxite. Petroleum is also found there.

Industrial Regions

Before 1928, the Soviet Union was mainly an agricultural country. Its chief exports were wheat, lumber, and furs. Today the Soviet Union is one of the leading industrialized countries of the world. It ranks second only to the United States in the production of manufactured goods.

In the middle 1920s, the government began a program to modernize the country through the development of its resources. Industrialization was carried out through a series of Five-Year Plans.

Part of the plan was to distribute industrial plants throughout the country. Each region would concentrate on the production of certain goods. Today factories are grouped in about ten industrial regions. The four most important industrial regions are in Soviet Europe. They account for about three-fourths of the country's industrial products.

In the large industrial region centered on Moscow, a great variety of goods is manufactured. Household appliances, chemicals, tools, textiles, automobiles, and farm machinery are some of the products. Moscow's location makes it easy to receive raw materials and distribute manufactured goods.

The Donets Basin in the Ukraine is another important industrial region. It is sometimes referred to as the Donbas. The Donbas has one of the largest iron and steel industries in the world.

A third industrial region is in the Ural Mountains. This region has large supplies of many kinds of metals. Fuel for industry must be shipped into the region. There are steel-making, metal, and engineering factories.

One of the newest industrial regions of Soviet Europe is the Middle-Volga District. Manufacturing industries use the oil and gas of the region to produce chemical products and plastics. Automobile and truck factories are also found here. A series of dams has been built along the Volga River in this region. Large amounts of hydroelectric power are generated to run the factories here. Power lines also carry electricity to other industrial regions. Pipelines carry oil and gas from the production fields to cities throughout Soviet Europe.

Moscow

Moscow is the largest and most important city in the Soviet Union. It is one of the largest cities in the world. Its eight million people give Moscow a population nearly twice that of the next-largest Soviet city.

Moscow is the capital of the Soviet Union. It is also the capital of the Russian Republic. About a million people work in Moscow's government offices. Headquarters for the Communist Party of the Soviet Union and the international headquarters of the world Communist movement are also in Moscow.

The Kremlin is the historic heart of Moscow. It consists of great cathedrals and palaces surrounded by walls. This fortress was built by the czars of Russia in the 1500s. Now it is the seat of the Soviet government.

East of the Kremlin is the vast open area known as Red Square. On special occasions, Red Square is used for great parades. Also on Red Square is St. Basil's Cathedral, now a museum. With its unusual ornamentation and eight onion-shaped domes, St. Basil's is one of Moscow's best-known landmarks.

Moscow is the Soviet Union's most important industrial city. More than a million people work in its factories. Steel, cars, textiles, and chemicals are major industrial products.

The Hermitage Museum in Leningrad is famous for its art treasures. The building was once the Winter Palace of the czars.

Moscow is also the transportation center of the Soviet Union. Major highways and railways connect Moscow with cities in all parts of the country. A major canal links the city to the Volga River. The city has three airports.

Moscow is a modern metropolis as well as an historic city. It has new buildings, hotels, and apartment houses. Its subway system, called the Metro, is one of the city's outstanding features. There are numerous libraries, museums, and theaters, including the famous Bolshoi Theater of opera and ballet. Moscow has a thriving publishing business and important educational and scientific institutions.

Moscow State University is the oldest and largest university in the Soviet Union. Its science building is Moscow's tallest skyscraper.

Other Cities of Soviet Europe

Leningrad is the second-largest city in the Soviet Union. It is located at the eastern end of the Gulf of Finland in the Russian Republic.

Peter the Great founded the city in 1703 as St. Petersburg. In 1712, Peter moved the capital from Moscow to St. Petersburg. The new capital became a leading cultural center.

In 1914, the city's name was changed to Petrograd, which means "Peter's city." The city was seized during the Russian Revolution, and the capital was moved back to Moscow in 1918. Petrograd was renamed Leningrad after Lenin died in 1924.

Peter planned his city to rival the other capitals of Europe. Leningrad is a beautiful city. It has broad avenues, wide squares, parks and gardens. Magnificent palaces, churches, and other buildings of the 1700s are still standing. The Winter Palace, once the winter home of the czars, stands in the center of the city. Next to it is the State Hermitage Museum, which houses a great art collection. Nearby is the St. Isaac Cathedral, whose golden dome rises high above the other buildings of the city.

Today Leningrad is a major port and a leading industrial city. It has an important shipbuilding industry and manufactures many other products. With its many museums, theaters, and educational institutions, Leningrad is still a leading cultural center.

Kiev is the third-largest city in the Soviet Union. More than two million people live in this city, which is the capital of the Ukrainian Republic. The city lies on the Dnieper River in a rich agricultural and industrial region. It is an important trading center.

Kiev is also one of the oldest cities of the Soviet Union. As early as the 600s A.D., Slavic people established a settlement where Kiev is. During the 800s, Kiev became the capital of the first Russian state. It was a leading city of Europe until Mongol invaders conquered it in 1240. Later, Kiev was ruled by Lithuania and Poland. It became part of the Russian Empire in 1654 and grew rapidly. In 1934, it became the capital of the Ukraine.

During World War II, Kiev suffered great damage, and much of the city had to be rebuilt. Today in Kiev, ancient and modern buildings stand side by side. Historic landmarks from the eleventh century include the Cathedral of St. Sophia. As the Ukrainian center of cultural life, Kiev has theaters, museums, a university, and a science academy.

Another major city in the Ukraine is Odessa, on the Black Sea. This city began about 800 B.C. as a Greek colony. At later times it was controlled by Tartars, Lithuanians, and Turks. It came under Russian rule in 1792.

Today Odessa is one of the Soviet's leading seaports. Its port is the home base of the Soviet fishing and whaling fleets. Odessa's refineries produce many petroleum products, and its factories make chemicals, machinery, and textiles. The city is an important point for transferring goods from railroads to ships.

Set on a terraced hillside above the harbor, Odessa has long been a popular seaside resort. It has a university and a number of museums, theaters, and specialized schools.

Four Small Republics

Four small republics are also part of Soviet Europe. Three of them that lie along the eastern coast of the Baltic Sea are known as the Baltic republics. The other republic, Moldavia, is near the Black Sea.

The Baltic Republics

The Baltic republics are Estonia, Latvia, and Lithuania. They occupy part of the coastal plain of northern Europe. Forests cover about one-third of the land. Many rivers flow through these republics and empty into the Baltic Sea. The region's chief river, the Western Dvina, flows from Byelorussia through central Latvia. There are small lakes and swamps throughout the region. Lithuania alone has more than 3,000 lakes. All of the Baltic republics have an oceanic climate. Their beaches are popular resort areas.

Estonia, Latvia, and Lithuania were ruled by various people, including Germans, Poles, Russians, and Swedes, throughout their history. By the end of the eighteenth century, all three countries had come under the rule of the Russian czars. The Baltic states declared their independence following Russia's defeat in World War I. Early in World War II, the Soviet Union took them over and made them Soviet republics.

Women in colorful *ethnic* costumes attend a song and dance festival in Lithuania.

Soviet rule has had a great effect on the social, economic, and political life in the Baltic republics. The people, however, have preserved their languages and customs. The colorful traditional costumes of these groups are an important part of their ethnic heritage and are worn during holiday festivals.

Today the Baltic republics are the most highly industrialized of all the Soviet republics. The region's factories produce machinery, metals, electronic equipment, and other important products. Wells in Estonia provide much of the Soviet Union's oil. Furniture, lumber, and paper are manufactured from the wood of local forests.

Agriculture and fishing account for about one-fourth of the value of goods produced in the Baltic region. The chief farm products include milk, butter, eggs, beef, and poultry. Farmers also grow apples, sugar beets, potatoes, barley, and rye.

The Moldavian Republic

Moldavia is bordered on three sides by the Ukraine. The Prut River, which flows southward into the Black Sea, forms the border between Moldavia and Romania. The Moldavian Republic is a hilly, partly forested region with fertile soil and a mild climate.

At one time, Romania controlled the region that is now the Moldavian Republic. At the end of World War II, the Soviet Union claimed the area and made it a Soviet republic.

Nearly four million people live in the Moldavian Republic. It has the highest population density of any republic in the Soviet Union. More than half the population is Moldavian. Ukrainians and Russians make up the rest of the population. Although Russian is spoken throughout the republic, the Moldavian language is still used by many people. Moldavian is similar to Romanian, but it is written in the Russian alphabet.

The fertile soil and mild climate of the Moldavian Republic make it an important agricultural region. The region produces much of the Soviet Union's tobacco and grapes. Other important crops include sugar beets, soybeans, and wheat. Farmers also raise dairy cattle and sheep.

Industries in the republic include tobacco and food processing. Shoes and textiles are manufactured in its factories.

Do You Know?

1. What is the largest republic in the Soviet Union? What percent of the country belongs to this republic?
2. What is the "fertile triangle"?
3. Name two of the major industrial regions of Soviet Europe.
4. Name the Baltic republics.

4

Soviet Asia

Soviet Asia is a vast area that makes up nearly three-fourths of the Soviet Union. It covers nearly two-fifths of the continent of Asia. Soviet Asia can be divided into three regions. They are Transcaucasia (trans′kô kāzh′ə), Soviet Central Asia, and Siberia.

Soviet Asia is a land of great variety. Although it is sparsely settled, many different ethnic groups live there. There are mountains, deserts, and vast stretches of tundra. The hottest and coldest places in the Soviet Union are found there.

Transcaucasia

Caucasia is the region between the Black Sea and the Caspian Sea. The great Caucasus Mountains divide this region into two parts. The northern part is in the Russian Republic. Three republics of Soviet Asia are in the part called Transcaucasia, which means "across the Caucasus." These republics are Georgia, Armenia, and Azerbaijan (az′ər bī jän′). Transcaucasia is bordered to the south by Turkey and Iran. Transcaucasia is not conterminous with the rest of Soviet Asia. See the map on page 247.

A high ridge of the Caucasus Mountains lies along Georgia's northern border. In the south, the land is crossed by another range of the Caucasus. A central plain lies between the two mountain ranges. Georgia's climate ranges from subtropical along the shores of the Black Sea to alpine in the high mountains.

Regional Data Chart

Country	Capital	Area		Population	GNP
		Square miles	Square kilometers		(in millions of U.S. dollars)
Soviet Union	Moscow	8,649,489	22,402,200	267,600,000	$1,082,000

Much of the Armenian Republic is high and mountainous. The temperatures vary greatly from season to season because the mountains block moderating winds from the sea.

Azerbaijan is the largest of the Transcaucasian republics. It lies along the Caspian Sea. Much of Azerbaijan is in the broad valley of the Kura River. The region is hot and dry in the summer and cold in the winter. The area near the Caspian Sea is marshy and humid. Azerbaijan's capital, Baku, is the fifth-largest city in the Soviet Union.

History

Three ethnic groups, the Georgians, the Armenians, and the Azerbaijanis, have lived in Caucasia for thousands of years. Each group has its own language, customs, and a deep pride in its culture. Many people of Transcaucasia are Muslims.

The region has been ruled and fought over for centuries by Romans, Turks, Mongols, Arabs, Persians, and Russians. During the late nineteenth and early twentieth centuries, the Armenians were harshly treated under Turkish rule. Nearly two million Armenians were killed, and thousands fled the area.

At the end of World War I, Georgia, Armenia, and Azerbaijan became an independent nation called the Transcaucasian Federal Republic. A month later, this republic broke up into three independent nations. In 1920, Russian armies invaded the area and took over most of it. The area under Soviet control became the Transcaucasian Federated Soviet Republic. In 1936, Georgia, Armenia, and Azerbaijan each became a separate republic of the Soviet Union.

Agriculture

Though much of the land is bleak and arid, the fertile plains and valleys of Transcaucasia make it an important agricultural region. In Georgia, farmers grow tea and citrus fruits near the Black Sea. Tobacco and grapes are raised in the inland valleys.

Armenia's best farmland is its irrigated valleys. Here cotton, tobacco, and orchards are cultivated. On terraced hillsides, wheat, barley, and sugar beets are grown.

Azerbaijan is one of the Soviet Union's great cotton-growing areas. Wheat and vegetables are grown in the Kura Valley. Farmers in the coastal regions grow tea, rice, fruits, and nuts.

274

In all three republics, cattle, sheep, and goats are grazed in the mountains. They are important for their production of meat, wool, and milk.

Mining and Manufacturing

Transcaucasia is rich in mineral resources. Georgia has rich deposits of coal and manganese. In Azerbaijan, oil is the chief source of wealth. The area near Baku on the north shore of the Caspian is a world-famous oil-producing region. Offshore oil wells have been drilled in the sea. Iron, copper, and lead are among the minerals mined in this region.

Georgia, Armenia, and Azerbaijan have all become highly industrialized. Hydroelectric plants supply the power for industry. Today Georgia has one of the biggest steel plants in the Soviet Union. Manufactured products of Transcaucasia include chemicals, machinery, and textiles.

Soviet Central Asia

Soviet Central Asia is the most southerly part of the Soviet Union. It is made up of five republics that lie south of the Urals and east of the Caspian Sea. The republics are Kazakh (kəzak'), Uzbek (ooz'bek'), Kirghiz (kir gēz'), Tadzhik (tä jik'), and Turkmen (tərk'mən). The largest of these republics is Kazakh. It is the second-largest republic in the Soviet Union.

Soviet Central Asia is the hottest and driest part of the Soviet Union. Deserts stretch from east to west across the central part of the region. The northern part of Soviet Central Asia is steppe. High mountains lie along its southern borders with Iran, Afghanistan, and China.

Westerly winds lose their moisture as rain or snow in these mountains. Rivers and streams flow out of the mountains across the desert. Some of the rivers flow into the Caspian Sea, the Aral Sea, or Lake Balkhash. Others evaporate in the dry desert air or disappear in the sands. This region is much like the Great Basin of the United States.

Most of the people living in Soviet Central Asia belong to Turkic ethnic groups. They speak closely related languages similar to Turkish. Many Turkic people are Muslims.

In recent years, large numbers of Russians have been resettled in this area. They were brought in to work on the farms and in the new factories.

For many years, the Turkic people of Soviet Central Asia were nomadic herders and small farmers. Market towns and villages grew up near oases. These settlements became important cities as overland trade routes developed between China, the Mediterranean, and India. The major overland route became known as the Silk Road. Great quantities of silk were exported from China by this route. Marco Polo was one of the first European travelers in this region. He crossed into China through one of the low passes in the mountains.

Different people, including Turks, Arabs, and Mongols, have ruled Soviet Central Asia throughout its history. The region did not come under the control of the Russian czars until the late 1800s.

Living and Working in the Soviet Union

The Soviet Union is a vast country with an abundance of natural resources and a great variety of climates. Much of it lies in cold northern latitudes. Atomic-powered ice breakers keep Soviet ports open in winter. In many parts of Siberia, hunting and trapping are important activities. Furs and skins are in world-wide demand. In the *taiga,* lumbering is also an important industry.

In the warm, dry steppes east of the Caspian Sea, cotton is grown under irrigation. Modern mills in the ancient city of Samarkand produce cotton cloth. An open-air market operates near ruins that date from the time of Mongol rule. In Leningrad, urban workers make their way by streetcar and on foot. ■

Shepherds on horseback tend their flocks in the Kirghiz Republic of Soviet Central Asia.

Transportation

The Trans-Siberian Railroad passes through only the very northern part of this region. An important branch line links the cities of Soviet Central Asia with the Trans-Siberian Railroad. It runs from Novosibirsk (nō′vō sə birsk′) through Tashkent to the Caspian Sea. Another line runs from Tashkent to Moscow. There are few good roads.

Agriculture

The steppe of northern Kazakh is part of the fertile triangle. Spring wheat is grown in the parts of this region that have sufficient moisture. Much new land in this region has begun to be cultivated as part of the Soviet land program. In the drier parts of the steppe and along the edges of the desert, sheep and goats are grazed.

Some of the richest irrigated croplands of the Soviet Union are in southern Soviet Central Asia. The farms are located along the rivers that flow out of the high mountains to the south. Irrigation has been practiced in this region for hundreds of years. Recently, new irrigation programs have been started.

The most important crop in the south is cotton. About two-thirds of the cotton grown in the Soviet Union is produced here. An important new kind of long-fibered cotton has been developed.

Other crops include fruit, rice, grapes, vegetables, and some grains. Cattle are raised on the rich pasturelands of the southeastern part of the region. Goats, sheep, and yaks are grazed in the drier areas. Wool is an important product of Soviet Central Asia.

Mining

Like most of the other parts of the Soviet Union, Soviet Central Asia has a rich supply of minerals. Large quantities of oil and natural gas are found in this region. Kazakh is the country's leading producer of copper. Other important minerals are iron ore, lead, and bauxite.

Industrial Regions

The major industrial region of Soviet Central Asia is located around the city of Tashkent. The cotton raised on the surrounding lands is made into cloth in factories here. Silk textiles are also produced, and both silk and cotton garments are manufactured. Other important products are leather goods and agricultural machinery.

The mineral wealth of Soviet Central Asia has led to the development of many new industries. Some of these are oil refining, smelting, and chemical production.

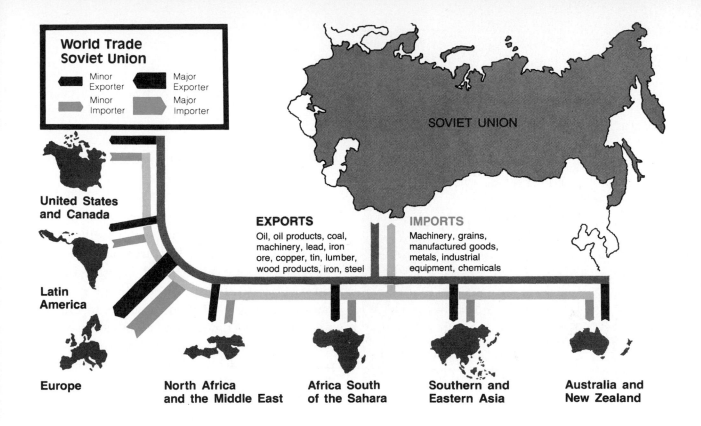

World Trade Soviet Union

Minor Exporter
Major Exporter
Minor Importer
Major Importer

SOVIET UNION

United States and Canada

Latin America

Europe

EXPORTS
Oil, oil products, coal, machinery, lead, iron ore, copper, tin, lumber, wood products, iron, steel

IMPORTS
Machinery, grains, manufactured goods, metals, industrial equipment, chemicals

North Africa and the Middle East

Africa South of the Sahara

Southern and Eastern Asia

Australia and New Zealand

Cities of Soviet Central Asia

Tashkent is the largest city in Soviet Asia. Its population of nearly two million makes it the fourth-largest city in the Soviet Union. Tashkent was one of the important cities on the early trade routes that crossed Central Asia. By the time the Russians conquered Tashkent in 1865, the city had declined from its former splendor. The Russians built a new city around the old one. Today, both parts of Tashkent survive. The old part still resembles an ancient caravan town.

In addition to being a major industrial and transportation center, Tashkent is an educational and cultural center. It has a university, an art museum, an opera house, and theaters.

Not far from Tashkent is the city of Samarkand. Samarkand is one of the oldest cities in the world. It was conquered by Alexander the Great in 329 B.C. In the eighth century, it came under Arab control. Muslim culture soon began to thrive there.

Like Tashkent, Samarkand was an important city on the Silk Road. The city was conquered in the fourteenth century by a Mongol leader, Tamerlane. Tamerlane established his capital at Samarkand. He promoted the arts and made Samarkand a center of culture and science. Remains of the city's splendid architecture from this period can still be seen.

Today Samarkand is part of the Tashkent industrial region. Its industries produce cotton and silk fabrics, clothing, and leather goods.

Siberia

Siberia is the name of the part of the Russian Republic that lies in Soviet Asia. Siberia makes up about half of the Soviet Union. Only one-eighth of the country's people live there. Ice

This part of the Trans-Siberian Railroad passes through southern Siberia. A worker clears loose rocks that might result in a rockslide.

and snow cover most of the region for much of the year. The name *Siberia* comes from a Tartar word meaning "sleeping land."

The taiga covers most of Siberia. In the north, a belt of tundra stretches along the Arctic Ocean. The steppe extends across the southernmost part of Siberia. Most of the people in Siberia live in the steppe region.

For centuries, Siberia was a place used by the government to *exile* (eg′zīl) people, or banish them. Criminals and political prisoners were forced from their homes. Many of these people were made to work in mines, in factories, and on the railroads. During the 1800s, more than 800,000 people were exiled to Siberia. Many freed serfs decided to settle in Siberia after 1861. They became small landowners there.

The Soviet government has tried to develop the rich resources of Siberia. As a source of useful minerals, timber, and water power, Siberia may be one of the richest areas in the world. There are, however, many problems in developing the region. Few areas are *accessible* (ak ses′ə bəl), or easily reached. Construction is difficult because of the cold. The permafrost causes railroad tracks and buildings to buckle and shift. Machines and equipment break down in the intense cold. High wages must be paid to attract workers to the harsh climate. Transporting food and equipment is costly.

Transportation

The development of Siberia began with the building of the Trans-Siberian Railroad. This railroad, which was completed in 1916, made possible the movement of goods and people across Siberia. Some of the villages and towns that grew up along the rail route have developed into industrial towns. Today, the Trans-Siberian Railroad has a double track. Trains going in one direction do not have to wait on sidetracks for trains going in the opposite direction to pass.

To further develop the mineral and forest resources of Siberia, the Soviet government began the construction of a new railroad in 1974. The new line is called the Baikal-Amur Mainline, or BAM for short. The BAM will run north of Lake Baikal parallel to the Trans-Siberian Railroad. This railroad is one of the largest construction projects ever undertaken. It will extend for about 2,000 miles (3,200 km) through seven mountain ranges. The cost was originally estimated at $15 billion. Completion of the BAM was planned for 1983. Because of difficulties in constructing the line, it may be 1985 before it is finished. The cost will probably greatly exceed the original estimate.

Agriculture

The fertile triangle of rich chernozem soil extends in a narrowing band across the steppe of Siberia. It is here that Siberia's productive farmlands are found. Spring wheat, barley, and oats are the major crops. Siberia has many dairy farms in the steppe. Cattle, sheep, and reindeer are also raised.

North of the steppe, agriculture is almost impossible. There is some attempt to grow vegetables and keep dairy cattle. There are places where farming can be carried on in areas of permafrost. Crops grow rapidly during the few summer weeks of almost continuous sunlight.

Mining

Siberia has a great abundance of mineral resources. Much of the Soviet Union's oil and natural gas come from vast fields near the Ob River and along the Arctic coast. Other important natural gas fields are found near Yakutsk (yə kōōtsk') in eastern Siberia.

Much of the country's coal is mined in the Kuznetsk (kooz netsk') Basin. Rich iron ore deposits are also found in this region.

Other important minerals mined in Siberia include gold, platinum, copper, tin, and diamonds. Many of Siberia's mines are located in cold, isolated parts of the region.

Crews prospect for oil in western Siberia. A derrick is being moved by boat to a new drilling site.

Lumbering, Fishing, and Trapping

Siberian forests produce about one-third of the Soviet Union's lumber. Most of the logging in Siberia is done in the winter. The logs are piled onto sleds, and tractors pull the sleds over snowy roads. Often the logs are taken to riverbanks where they are piled up until spring. When the ice melts in the rivers, the logs are floated downstream to lumber mills on the Arctic Ocean. The lumber is shipped to other parts of the Soviet Union.

Fishing crews catch cod, crabs, and salmon off Siberia's Pacific coast. Several Siberian cities have fish canneries.

Many fur-bearing animals are found in the northern forests of Siberia. Fox, ermine, and sable furs are sent by trappers to major Soviet cities. They are bought by fur dealers from all over the world.

Industrial Regions

Three important industrial regions have been developed in Siberia. The most important is the Kuznetsk Basin, or Kuzbas, as it is sometimes called. Nearby coal and iron mines make steel production an important industry. Steel products such as farm machinery, locomotives, and hardware are also manufactured here. The region around Vladivostok is another center for the production of steel and steel products. It is not as important as the Kuzbas, however.

An industrial region that is just beginning to develop is located near Irkutsk (ir kōotz′) on the Angara (än′gə ra′) River. This region has rich reserves of iron, manganese, tungsten, lead, and tin. There are also important timber reserves nearby. A dam and hydroelectric plant on the river will furnish power for developing industries. The new BAM will provide transportation for goods and materials.

Cities of Siberia

Novosibirsk, the largest city of Siberia, has more than one million people. The city lies on the Ob River in south central Siberia. Novosibirsk was founded in 1893 as a settlement for workers building the Trans-Siberian Railroad and grew rapidly as a transportation center.

Novosibirsk is an important Soviet manufacturing city in the Kuzbas. Among the great variety of goods made there are farm and mining machinery, wood and metal products, and textiles. The city also has engineering and chemical industries. An important scientific research center is located in one of Novosibirsk's suburbs.

Another industrial city of Siberia is Irkutsk. Irkutsk is a port on the Angara River. This city also grew as a transportation center after the railroad across Siberia was built. It is an important fur-trading center, and it is famous for its gold mines. Irkutsk is also the cultural and educational center of eastern Siberia. Today more than 500,000 people live in Irkutsk.

Vladivostok, like Irkutsk, has about 500,000 people. It is the most important Soviet port on the Pacific Ocean. The city lies at the eastern end of the Trans-Siberian Railroad, near the Soviet borders with Korea and China. Unlike the Pacific ports farther north, Vladivostok is open all year. Icebreakers are used in the winter months. The city is a base for fishing and whaling fleets. Industrial activities of Vladivostok include shipbuilding, fish canning, and metal refining.

Do You Know?

1. What three regions make up Soviet Asia?
2. To what ethnic group do most people of Soviet Central Asia belong?
3. What was the Silk Road? Name an important city that grew up along the Silk Road.
4. Why was the Trans-Siberian Railroad important in the development of Siberia?
5. What is the most important Soviet port on the Pacific? How is it kept open all year?

To Help You Learn

Using New Words

accessible
cede
abdicate
exile

Number a paper from 1 through 4. After each number write the word or term that matches the definition.
1. To give up rights to
2. Easily reached
3. To banish
4. To give up power and position

Finding the Facts

1. How does the Soviet Union rank in size among the nations of the world? In population?
2. What did Lenin and his followers call themselves?
3. What part of the Soviet Union is the most densely populated and heavily industrialized?
4. How much of the Russian Republic is in Soviet Europe?
5. Why are the waterways of Soviet Europe limited in their usefulness?
6. What railroad connects Moscow with Vladivostok? How long does it take the fastest trains to make the run between the two cities?
7. Why is it difficult to build roads in many parts of the Soviet Union?
8. About how much land in the Soviet Union is used for agriculture?
9. Why has the production of minerals been going on longer in Soviet Europe than in Soviet Asia?
10. Where is the Donets Basin? What major industries are located there?
11. What is the largest and most important city in the Soviet Union?
12. When was St. Petersburg the capital of Russia? What was the city called between 1914 and 1924? After 1924?
13. What leading Soviet seaport was once a Greek colony?
14. What country ruled Moldavia before World War II?
15. What is the chief source of wealth in Azerbaijan? Where is its famous oil-producing region?
16. Who was Tamerlane? What did he do?
17. What does the word *Siberia* mean?
18. Why did the Soviet government begin the Baikal-Amur Mainline? How long will this railroad be when completed?
19. Where in Siberia are oil and natural gas found?
20. How did Novosibirsk begin?

Learning from Maps

1. Look at the map on page 247. Find the mountains that form part of the boundary between Europe and Asia. What river rises in the southern part of these mountains? Into what sea does it flow? What high mountains lie between this sea and the Black Sea? How many countries border the Soviet Union to the south? Name them. Compare the map of the Soviet Union with the map of Europe on page 189. What European countries share boundaries with the Soviet Union?

2. Look at the map of Communist countries on page 260. Compare this map with the maps on pages 247 and 189 to name the countries bordering the Soviet Union that are not Communist countries.

3. Look at the map on page 253. What does this map show? What is the most widespread ethnic group in the Soviet Union? Compare this map with the map on page 247 to name the ethnic groups living west of the Caspian Sea and the Volga River, and south of a line from Moscow to Leningrad. What republics are inhabited by Baltic peoples? Where do Yakuts live?

4. Look at the map on page 257. During what period shown was the most land added to Russia? What regions shown were acquired by Russia between 1689 and 1917 but are not now part of the Soviet Union?

Using Study Skills

1. **Time Line:** Review the unit to find dates for the events listed below. Then make a time line by arranging the events in chronological order.

   Nicholas II abdicated
   Serfs were freed in Russia
   Russia gained control of western Siberia
   Lenin died and Stalin came to power
   Peter the Great became czar
   Odessa came under Russian rule
   Alexander the Great conquered Samarkand

2. **Outline:** A partial outline of material on Soviet Asia appears below. Study the outline and use it as a model to continue an outline for the material in the unit on Siberia.

   II. Soviet Central Asia
      A. Transportation
      B. Agriculture
         1. The steppe region
         2. The southern region
      C. Mining
      D. Industrial regions
      E. Cities of Soviet Central Asia
         1. Tashkent
         2. Samarkand

3. **Library Resources:** An almanac is a reference book that is compiled and published annually. It contains general information and statistics on many different subjects, including astronomy, business, education, the environment, people, religion, science, space, sports, weather, and countries. Almanacs are useful sources of information.

Find an almanac in your school or public library. Use it to answer these questions: What Soviet citizens have won the Nobel Prize for Literature? Where were the 1980 Summer Olympic Games held? What nation won the most medals at the summer games? How many medals did that nation win? Where were the Winter Olympics held in 1980? How did the Soviet Union rank in the awarding of medals in the winter games?

Thinking It Through

1. The czars greatly expanded Russia's territory and established trade and cultural contact with Western Europe, but they did little to improve the lives of the people. How might the history of Russia have been different if Nicholas II and earlier czars had done more for the Russian people? Why might today's Soviet leaders be concerned with providing more consumer goods for the people?

2. How did the industrialization of the Soviet Union differ from the industrialization of the United States? What helped the Soviet Union to industrialize rapidly? What factors made rapid industrialization difficult?

3. Voters in the United States often gather information about candidates running for office to help them decide whom to vote for. Would this practice be helpful to Communist Party members voting for party leaders? Support your answer.

Projects

1. V.I. Lenin, Joseph Stalin, Nikita Khrushchev, Leonid Breshnev, and Aleksei Kosygin have all been important in the political history of the Soviet Union. Members of the Biography Committee could prepare reports comparing these leaders and explaining their roles in the Soviet Union. Biographical dictionaries and encyclopedias would be good reference books to begin the reports.

2. Members of the History Committee might do library research on the Silk Road and the ancient cities of Tashkent and Samarkand. Committee members could present oral reports to the class. They could prepare large wall maps to show ancient trade routes to refer to during their reports. They might wish to illustrate their maps with drawings and pictures of caravans, ancient cities, and other sites along the route.

3. The Arts and Sciences Committee might wish to learn more about the Moscow Art Theater and the Bolshoi Theater Ballet. Some committee members could report on the plays of Anton Chekov and Leo Tolstoy presented in the Moscow Art Theater. Other students could use the *Readers' Guide* to find reviews or articles about Bolshoi performances in the United States, which began in 1959.

7 North Africa and the Middle East

Unit Preview

The countries of North Africa and the Middle East are among the hottest and driest on earth. The largest desert in the world, the Sahara, stretches across North Africa. Much of the Middle East is also desert. The Nile and the Tigris-Euphrates are the most important rivers in North Africa and the Middle East. The valleys of these rivers are two of the cradles of civilization you read about in Unit 2.

The Middle East is also historically important as the birthplace of three religions—Judaism, Christianity, and Islam. Religion continues to be an important part of the social and political life of the people today.

North Africa and the Middle East lie at a crossroads where three continents meet. In early times, camel caravans transported goods across the deserts. Merchants established markets along trade routes, and important cities grew up.

For thousands of years, farming and herding have been the chief occupations of the people in this region. Today many countries are becoming industrialized. Advances in technology have increased the amount of arable land. The discovery of oil has brought new wealth and new job opportunities.

Recent conflicts in North Africa and the Middle East have focused world attention on this region. Developments in this part of the world continue to influence other countries.

Things to Discover

If you look carefully at the picture, map, and time line, you can answer these questions.

1. The highlighted area on the map is North Africa and the Middle East. On what three continents is this region located?
2. The photograph shows an airport in Dhahran, Saudi Arabia. The architecture shows the influence of the Muslims, who are followers of Mohammed's teachings. When did Mohammed die?
3. When was the city of Carthage founded? By whom?
4. What was the capital of the Roman Empire in 330 A.D.? What group later captured this city? When?
5. The Suez Canal connects the Red and Mediterranean seas. When was it completed?

Words to Learn

You will meet these words and terms in this unit. As you read, you will learn what they mean and how to pronounce them. The Word List will help you.

aridity	Maghrib
caliph	pastoral
concession	pilgrimage
emirate	royalties
homeland	shadoof
kibbutz	sultan
Koran	wadi

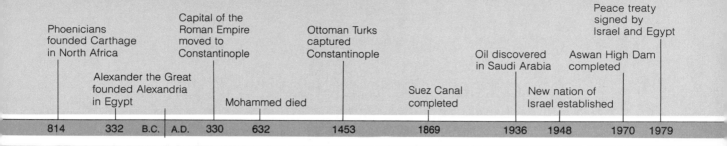

Phoenicians
founded Carthage
in North Africa

Alexander the Great
founded Alexandria
in Egypt

Capital of the
Roman Empire
moved to
Constantinople

Mohammed died

Ottoman Turks
captured
Constantinople

Suez Canal
completed

Oil discovered
in Saudi Arabia

New nation of
Israel established

Aswan High Dam
completed

Peace treaty
signed by
Israel and Egypt

| 814 | 332 | B.C. | A.D. | 330 | 632 | 1453 | 1869 | 1936 | 1948 | 1970 | 1979 |

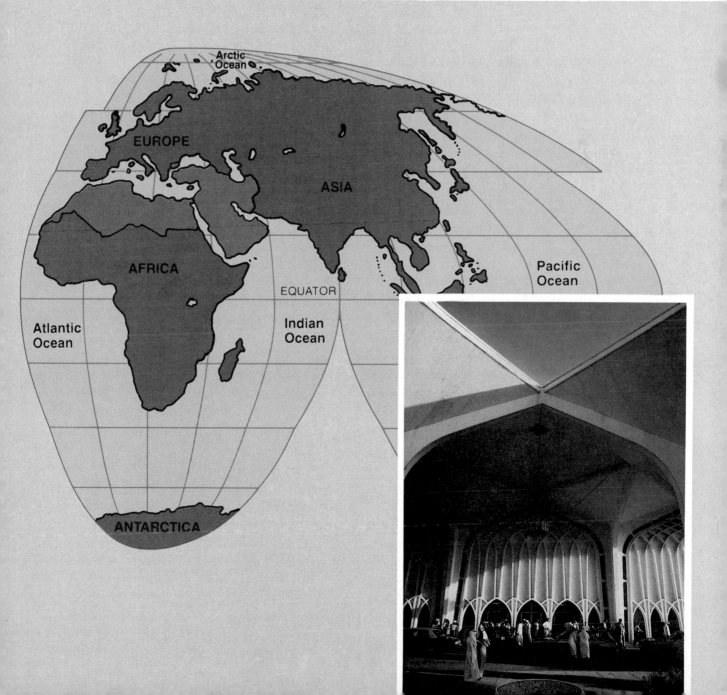

1

The Land and the People of North Africa and the Middle East

The region of North Africa and the Middle East borders the southern and eastern Mediterranean. It is located where the continents of Europe, Africa, and Asia come together. The countries of North Africa lie along Africa's northern coast. The Middle Eastern countries are at the eastern end of the Mediterranean in southwestern Asia. A small part of one Middle Eastern country is in Europe.

This vast region includes 20 countries. It stretches more than 4,350 miles (7,000 km) from the Atlantic Ocean to Afghanistan and the Arabian Sea. For the most part, it is made up of large deserts and broad plateaus. It is the hottest and driest area in the world. Lack of water is a problem throughout the region.

For centuries, North Africa and the Middle East was one of the most important areas in the world. Some of the earliest civilizations grew up here. Three of the world's great religions began here. Because of its location, this region has played an important part in the history of trade. It was a crossroads through which goods moved between the East and the West, and back and forth across the Sahara.

People and ideas, as well as goods, have moved through this region. The people of North Africa and the Middle East today are a mixture of many different ethnic groups. The religion, science, and art of the cultures in these lands have spread far and wide. They have influenced the lives of people in many other parts of the world.

The Land of North Africa and the Middle East

North Africa stretches for more than 3,000 miles (5,000 km) across the northern part of Africa from the Atlantic Ocean to the Red Sea. It includes about 19 percent of Africa.

The Middle East occupies the southwestern part of Asia. See the map on page 289. It is slightly larger than North Africa. The countries of the Middle East lie in the part of Asia south of the Soviet Union and west of Afghanistan and Pakistan.

Two large peninsulas make up a great part of the Middle East. The larger peninsula is called the Arabian Peninsula. It is separated from Africa by the Red Sea. The Arabian Sea lies to the south of this peninsula, and the Persian Gulf lies to the east.

The peninsula of Asia Minor extends west to the Aegean Sea. The Black Sea lies to the north, and the Mediterranean Sea lies to the south. This peninsula is sometimes called Anatolia (an'ə tō'lē ə).

The eastern part of the Middle East is bounded by the Caspian Sea on the north and the Arabian Sea on the south. A small peninsula southeast of the Mediterranean extends south into the Red Sea. It is called the Sinai (sī'nī').

Deserts

Deserts cover large areas of North Africa and the Middle East. The largest desert is the

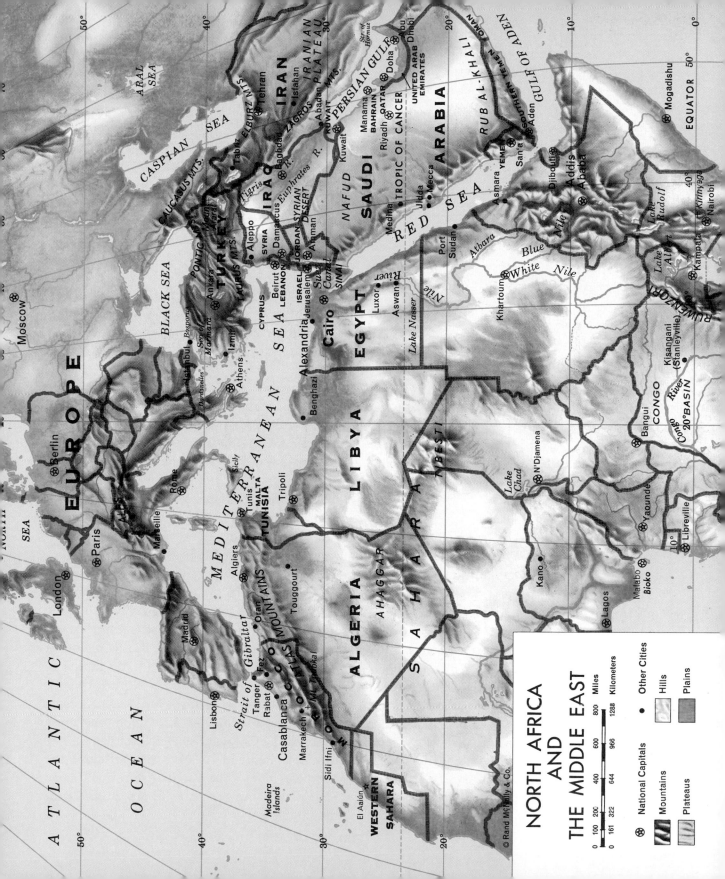

NORTH AFRICA
AND
THE MIDDLE EAST

© Rand McNally & Co.

Miles

0   100 200   400   600   800
0 161 322   644   966   1288
Kilometers

⊛ National Capitals   • Other Cities

☐ Mountains   ☐ Hills

☐ Plateaus   ☐ Plains

EUROPE

ATLANTIC

OCEAN

Moscow

Berlin

London

Paris

Marseille

Madrid

Lisbon

Madeira
Islands

Rome

Sicily

Tunis

MALTA

TUNISIA

Tripoli

Algiers

Tanger

Oran

Rabat

Fez

Casablanca

Marrakech

Mt. Toubkal

Sidi Ifni

El Aaiún

WESTERN
SAHARA

ATLAS MOUNTAINS

Strait of Gibraltar

Touggourt

ALGERIA

AHAGGAR

S A H A R A

LIBYA

NORTH
SEA

BLACK SEA

CAUCASUS MTS.

CASPIAN
SEA

ARAL
SEA

Istanbul

Bosporus

Sea of
Marmara

Izmir

Dardanelles

Athens

CYPRUS

PONTIC MTS.

TURKEY

Ankara

TAURUS MTS.

Mount
Ararat

Tabriz

ELBURZ MTS.

Tehran

Istahan

IRAN

IRANIAN
PLATEAU

ZAGROS MTS.

Abadan

Str. of
Hormuz

Abu
Dhabi

Aleppo

SYRIA

Beirut

LEBANON

Damascus

Amman

JORDAN

Jerusalem

ISRAEL

Benghazi

MEDITERRANEAN SEA

Alexandria

Cairo

EGYPT

SYRIAN
DESERT

SINAI

Suez
Canal

Tigris

Euphrates
R.

R.

Baghdad

IRAQ

Kuwait

KUWAIT

PERSIAN GULF

Manama

BAHRAIN

QATAR

Doha

UNITED ARAB
EMIRATES

OMAN

RUB AL-KHALI

SAUDI
ARABIA

NAFUD

Riyadh

Medina

Mecca

Jidda

TROPIC OF CANCER

RED SEA

Luxor

Aswan

Lake Nasser

Nile River

Nile R.

Port
Sudan

Khartoum

Atbara

White Nile

Blue Nile

Nile

SOUTHERN YEMEN

YEMEN

San'a

Aden

GULF OF ADEN

Djibouti

Asmara

Addis
Ababa

Lake
Rudolf

Lake
Albert

Mogadishu

EQUATOR

Kilimanjaro

Nairobi

Kampala

RUWENZORI

Kisangani
(Stanleyville)

CONGO

River

CONGO
RIVER

20° BASIN

Bangui

Libreville

Yaounde

Malabo

Bioko

N'Djamena

Lake
Chad

Kano

Lagos

TIBESTI

S A H A R A

50°   40°   30°   20°   10°   0°

50°

40°

30°

20°

10°

An oasis in the Libyan, or Western, Desert of Egypt stands out dramatically from the air. Drifting sand is seen at the bottom of the picture.

Sahara, which extends over much of North Africa. *Sahara* is an Arabic word meaning "desert." The Sahara is the largest desert in the world. It is about the size of the United States.

Although parts of the Sahara are made up of sand dunes, most of it is made up of low, flat, rocky plateaus. There are also wide areas covered with gravel.

The bare stretches of sand and rock extend for miles. Fertile watered areas called oases are scattered throughout the Sahara. The water in the oases comes from springs or wells. There are about 90 large oases in the Sahara.

In the Middle East, deserts extend from the eastern end of the Mediterranean throughout the Arabian Peninsula. The deserts of Arabia

have large areas covered by dunes. Deserts are also found in the area south of the Caspian Sea. Much of this area is like the Basin and Range region of the United States. Basins filled with sand and gravel lie between the steep, rocky ranges.

Plateaus and Mountains

Large parts of the Sahara are plateaus, most of the Arabian Peninsula is a plateau. The desert region south of the Caspian Sea is the Iranian Plateau.

Mountains and highlands rise above the desert plateaus. The highest mountains in North Africa lie parallel to the coasts of the Atlantic and Mediterranean in the northwest. These mountains are known as the Atlas Mountains. A range of lower mountains, called the Ahaggar (ä′hə gär′), are found in the south central Sahara. Highlands also lie along the Red Sea in southern Arabia and along the eastern end of the Mediterranean.

Four large mountain ranges extend in different directions from an area south of the east end of the Black Sea. This area is known as the Armenian (ärmē′nē ən) Knot. Mount Ararat (ar′ə rat′) is the highest peak in this region. It rises more than 16,000 feet (4,900 m) above sea level.

The Elburz (el boorz′) Mountains stretch east from the Armenian Knot along the south shore of the Caspian Sea. The Zagros (zag′rəs) Mountains extend to the southeast along the northeast side of the Persian Gulf. The Iranian Plateau lies between the Elburz and Zagros mountains.

Two mountain ranges run west of the Armenian Knot into Anatolia. The Pontic Mountains are in the north along the shore of the Black Sea. The Taurus (tôr′əs) Mountains extend along the shore of the Mediterranean Sea in the south. The interior of Anatolia is a high plateau rimmed by these mountains.

Water Features

The most important river systems in this region are the Nile and the Tigris-Euphrates. The Nile River flows north through the eastern part of the Sahara to empty into the Mediterranean Sea. The Nile is the longest river in the world. Its length is 4,187 miles (6,738 km).

The Tigris and Euphrates rivers rise in the Armenian Knot and flow south. They join to form the Shatt al Arab, which empties into the Persian Gulf.

Besides the Nile and the Tigris-Euphrates, there are few major rivers in North Africa and the Middle East. There are, however, many short, dry riverbeds in many parts of the desert. Such a dry, steep valley is called a *wadi* (wä′dē). Although wadis are usually without water, they may fill up for a short time after a heavy rain and even flood. Wadis often dry up very quickly as the water seeps down through the sand and gravel of the valley floor. Wadis may remain dry for many years. Although wadis are not dependable sources of surface water, there is usually underground water near wadis. Oases are often found near wadis.

The Jordan River is a small river at the eastern end of the Mediterranean. Its waters flow into the Dead Sea. The Dead Sea has no outlet. It is one of the saltiest lakes in the world. It is almost impossible for swimmers to sink in it. The surface of the Dead Sea is 1,299 feet (396 m) below sea level. Its shore is the lowest place on the surface of the earth.

There are hundreds of salt lakes with no outlets in many parts of North Africa and the Middle East. The Arab word for such a lake is shott (shät). Because of the irregular rainfall and the *aridity* (ərid′ətē), or dryness, the amount of water in these lakes varies greatly. Sometimes shotts dry up completely.

Climate and Vegetation

The Tropic of Cancer passes through the southern part of North Africa and through the middle of the Arabian Peninsula. Much of North Africa and the Middle East lies in the subtropics. Most of it is desert that receives less than ten inches (25 cm) of rain a year. This figure, however, is an average taken over many years. Months and years may pass without any rain. Sometimes violent rainstorms may bring several inches of rain in a few hours. Such storms often cause flooding in the desert.

Desert climates are not only arid, they are also hot. North Africa and the Middle East is the hottest part of the world. Average summer temperatures in the Sahara are 90° F. (32° C). Many places reach 110° F. (43° C). Winter temperatures average from 50° to 60° F. (10° to 16° C).

Most of the desert areas are far from the moderating effect of the ocean. The sands heat up and cool off quickly. Temperatures can vary as much as 45° F. (26° C) from day to night.

Few plants grow on the deserts. Some trees, shrubs, and grasses can exist in the dry conditions of the Sahara. The date palm is found in many oases. Many plants appear after rain showers, but they usually disappear within a few weeks.

Along the edges of the deserts are steppe regions. The rainfall in the steppes is slightly higher than in the deserts, and it supports a sparse growth of grasses. The interior of Anatolia and a region extending east from the Mediterranean to Pakistan are steppes.

Many areas along the coast of the Mediterranean have a Mediterranean climate of hot, dry summers and mild, rainy winters. Thorny bushes, low evergreen trees, and short grasses grow here. At one time, forests grew along some of the coastal areas of North Africa and the Middle East.

The heaviest rainfall in this region is in the high mountains. As much as 40 inches (100 cm) a year may fall in the Atlas Mountains and in the mountains of Anatolia. Winter temperatures in the mountains of the northern part of the Middle East may drop to 0° F. (-18° C), and snow is common.

The People of North Africa and the Middle East

More than 230 million people live in North Africa and the Middle East. This is about 5 percent of the total world population. The population is made up of many different ethnic groups. The largest are Arabs, Turks, Iranians, and Berbers.

The people are not evenly distributed throughout the region. Water largely determines where people live. Population densities are highest where rainfall is highest, or where streams or wells furnish water for farming.

For thousands of years, the most common occupations in North Africa and the Middle East were herding and farming. Most people today still earn their living by agriculture. Land reform programs have improved the lives of many farmers. Large irrigation projects and the use of modern equipment have increased crop production.

Handmade goods from the Middle East and North Africa have always been in demand in many parts of the world. The production of these goods is still important. Modern industry began in this region in the middle of the 1900s. Today most countries of the region have factories that employ many people.

Many parts of North Africa and the Middle East have become rich in recent years through the production of petroleum. The wealth, however, is not distributed evenly among all the countries. It is not evenly distributed within countries, either.

Some countries have begun to use oil money to improve the lives of their people. Governments are building hospitals, roads, and schools with oil income.

Judaism, Christianity, and Islam

Three great religions started in the Middle East. They are Judaism, Christianity, and Islam. All three religions are based on a belief in a single God.

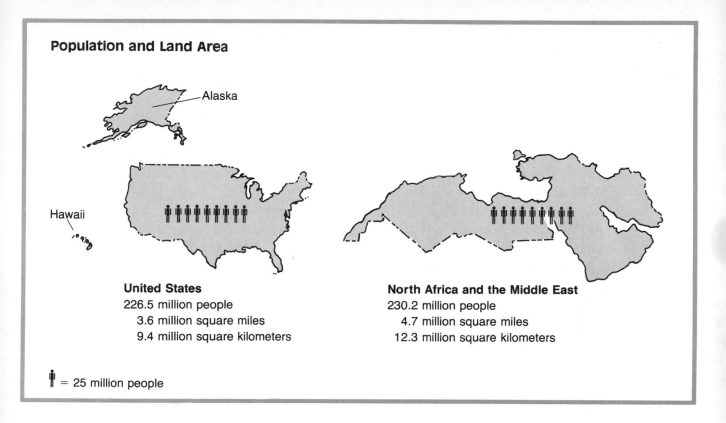

Population and Land Area

Alaska

Hawaii

United States
226.5 million people
3.6 million square miles
9.4 million square kilometers

North Africa and the Middle East
230.2 million people
4.7 million square miles
12.3 million square kilometers

= 25 million people

Judaism is one of the world's oldest religions. Jews trace their history to the 1700s B.C., when Abraham founded a community in the land of Canaan, near the Dead Sea. The Old Testament of the Bible tells the story of Abraham and his descendants. Both Jews and Christians consider the Old Testament to be a sacred book. In the Middle East today, only Israel has a large Jewish population.

Christianity began nearly 2,000 years ago in the area of the Middle East then called Palestine. Christianity is based on the teachings of Jesus Christ. His followers set down his teachings in the New Testament of the Bible. Lebanon is the only Middle Eastern country in which Christianity is a major religion today. Many Christians from all over the world, however, visit shrines of their faith in Israel.

The majority of people in the Middle East and North Africa are Muslims, or followers of Islam. The word *Islam* means "surrender to the will of God." The word *Muslim* means "a person who surrenders."

Islam began with the teachings of Mohammed, who was born in Mecca, in Arabia, about 570 A.D. Mohammed had a belief in but one God, called Allah. Mohammed's followers wrote down his teachings and gathered them together in a book called the *Koran* (kô ran'). To Muslims, the Koran is a holy book.

Mohammed's teachings were not accepted at first. The people of Mecca turned against him when he asked them to give up their idols and accept Islam. In 622, he fled to the Arabian city of Medina (me dē'na) for safety. The people of Medina accepted the new religion. They made Mohammed their religious leader. The year of Mohammed's flight to Medina became year one of the Muslim calendar. Mohammed later returned to Mecca in triumph.

Both Medina and Mecca are holy cities of Islam. All Muslims are supposed to make a *pilgrimage* (pil′grə mij) to Mecca at least once in their lifetime. A pilgrimage is a journey to a sacred place for religious reasons.

After Mohammed's death in 632, the Muslims were ruled by a *caliph* (kā′lif). *Caliph* was the title given to the successors of Mohammed who were the leaders of Islam. The caliphs and their followers spread the message of Islam to other countries. Arab armies conquered the Arabian Peninsula and moved into Persia. Other armies conquered Egypt and pushed westward across North Africa. Within one hundred years after Mohammed's death, Muslim Arabs had conquered much of Spain as well. Under the influence of the conquerors, many people became Muslims.

The Muslims, who were called Moors in Spain, remained there for hundreds of years. Their influence there came to an end in 1492, when Christian armies united to drive them out. The Moors retreated across the Mediterranean Sea to North Africa.

The Turks who took over many of the Arab lands after 1400 also became Muslims. Like the Arabs, the Turks were forceful in the spread of Islam. They overran western Asia, captured Constantinople, and moved into southeastern Europe. Many of the people they conquered became Muslims. Their empire was known as the Ottoman Empire.

European Colonialism

By the 1800s, the Ottoman Empire had begun to weaken. Parts of outlying districts broke away from Turkish rule. European nations began to take control of other parts of the empire.

Large parts of North Africa were taken over by France, Great Britain, and Italy before World War I. After the Turks were defeated in World War I, much of their remaining land was divided between France and Great Britain. Much of the Middle East became colonial territory. Not until after World War II did all the countries of North Africa and the Middle East win their independence.

Islam has remained the faith of the majority of the people in North Africa and the Middle East. Today the people of this region are spread throughout a large area and belong to many different nations. They are still closely united in their religious faith. Muslim unity is not only religious but also political. Leaders of Muslim countries meet to discuss problems and often take a common stand on issues.

Do You Know?

1. What two large peninsulas are in the Middle East?
2. What four large mountain ranges extend from the Armenian Knot?
3. What are the important rivers of North Africa and the Middle East?
4. What are the four largest ethnic groups in North Africa and the Middle East?
5. What three major religions began in the Middle East?

2
North Africa

The countries of North Africa are Egypt, Libya, Tunisia, Algeria, and Morocco. All of these countries border the Mediterranean Sea. All of them also extend south into the Sahara.

The North African countries west of Egypt are sometimes referred to as the *Maghrib* (məg′rəb). In Arabic, *Maghrib* means "the west" or "setting sun." Egypt lies at the eastern end of the Mediterranean near the countries of the Middle East. Because of its location and its cultural ties, Egypt is often considered part of the Middle East.

A very large part of North Africa lies in the Sahara. A narrow region along the coast has a Mediterranean climate. Here, westerly winds usually bring rain during the winter months. Some winters may pass without any rain. During the hot summer months, dry winds blow across the Sahara. They often create great sandstorms.

More than 93 million people live in the countries of North Africa. They represent many different ethnic groups and speak several different languages. Arabic and Berber are the most common languages. European languages are spoken in some regions. Almost the entire population is Muslim, and about half the people are farmers.

Egypt

Egypt lies in the northeast corner of Africa. Its northern coast is on the Mediterranean, and its eastern coast is on the Red Sea. A part of Egypt, the Sinai Peninsula, is in Asia. It is separated from the rest of Egypt by the Suez (soo ez′) Canal.

Almost all of Egypt is a desert. Its population, about 43 million, is the largest in North Africa. Egypt is able to support a large population because of the Nile River. The Nile provides almost all of the country's water.

The population density of Egypt is 114 per square mile (44 per sq. km). The population, however, is not spread out evenly over the country. Almost all of the people are crowded into the arable lands along the Nile. The parts where people live make up less than 4 percent of the entire country. In the Nile Valley, the population is more than 3,000 per square mile (1,160 per sq. km). This region is one of the most densely populated in the world.

Land and Climate

Most of Egypt is a low plateau covered by the Sahara. West of the Nile, the desert is called the Libyan Desert, or Western Desert. Several large oases dot the Western Desert. East of the Nile, the desert is known as the Eastern Desert, or Arabian Desert. The Eastern Desert rises to a range of mountains bordering the Red Sea. The Sinai Peninsula is a mountainous desert. The highest peak in Egypt is found there.

Egypt has a hot, dry climate. Rainfall is highest along the Mediterranean coast, where it averages only about eight inches (20 cm) a year. Precipitation decreases rapidly to the south. Cairo has only about two inches (5 cm) a year. The parts of Egypt to the south receive even less.

Summers in Egypt are hot. The temperature may rise to 100° F. (38° C). Winters are mild. The temperatures are generally about 20° to 25° F. (11° to 14° C) cooler. Temperatures are more extreme in southern Egypt.

The Nile River dominates Egypt. It flows for the last 960 miles (1,540 km) of its course from Egypt's southern border to the Mediterranean. A narrow green band of vegetation stretches along either side of the river as it winds its way north. About 100 miles (160 km) before it reaches the Mediterranean, the Nile branches out to form a broad delta. The delta of the Nile is known as Lower Egypt. South of Cairo, the Nile flows through a valley with low cliffs on either side. The valley of the Nile south of Cairo is known as Upper Egypt.

Because of Egypt's low rainfall, scarcely any water is added to the Nile as it flows through the country. The water that the Nile brings to Egypt comes from regions far to the south.

The Nile begins as a small stream in East Africa. The river flows out of Lake Victoria as the White Nile. The White Nile has an even flow of water all year.

The Blue Nile and the Atbara (at′bə rə) are eastern tributaries of the Nile that begin in the mountains of Ethiopia. Ethiopia has a rainy season and a dry season. During and after the rainy season, the Blue Nile and the Atbara are full of water. When these rivers are added to the White Nile, the lower parts of the Nile in Egypt rise and flood the land. During the dry season, the Blue Nile carries very little water, and the Atbara dries up altogether. At this time, nearly all the water in the Nile as it flows through Egypt comes from the White Nile.

History

An early Greek historian described Egypt as "the gift of the Nile." Each year, beginning in June, the Nile would spread out beyond its banks as it flowed across the desert. The yearly flooding took the place of rain in Egypt. After a few weeks, the water receded, leaving damp, rich soil in which crops could be planted.

People began to farm this region in very early times. It was here that one of the very first civilizations grew up. You have read something about this civilization in Unit 2.

The early Egyptians were great builders. Many of the pyramids, temples, and tombs they constructed are still standing and can be seen today. Carvings and paintings on these monuments give us a good picture of early Egyptian life. From hieroglyphics carved on buildings and written on papyrus rolls, much has been learned about Egyptian history.

Ancient Egypt began to weaken about 1000 B.C. For 1,500 years, Egypt was ruled by a series of outsiders. These included the Assyrians, the Persians, the Greeks, and the Romans. In the early days of Christianity, missionaries began to visit Egypt. Many Egyptians became Christians. In 642 A.D., the Arabs captured Alexandria, the capital of Egypt. Under the influence of the Arabs, most Egyptians were

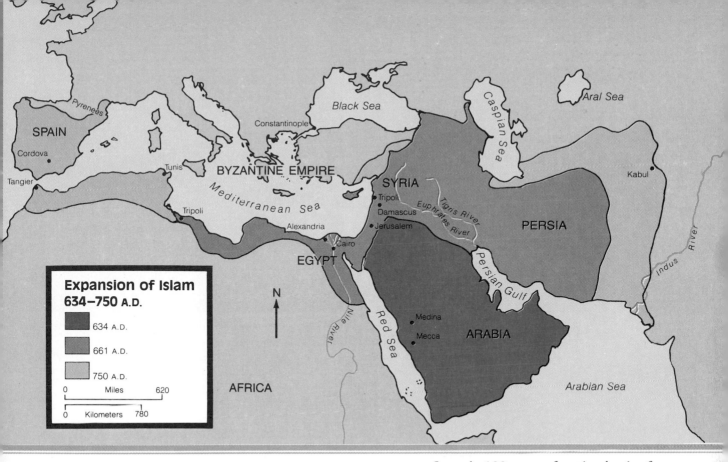

Scarcely 100 years after the death of Mohammed, Islam had spread throughout large parts of North Africa, the Middle East, and even into Europe.

converted from Christianity to Islam. They also began to speak Arabic.

For more than 800 years, Egypt was ruled by a series of dynasties. The Turks conquered Egypt in the early 1500s and made it part of the Ottoman Empire. Egypt remained a part of the Ottoman Empire until World War I broke out in 1914. When the Ottoman Empire sided with Germany in the war, Great Britain made Egypt a protectorate. A protectorate is a country that depends on another country for its defense. British troops had occupied Egypt since 1882, and the British had been the real power in Egypt for more than 30 years. During and after World War I, the Egyptians made demands for independence. Great Britain granted independence in 1922, and Egypt became a kingdom.

In 1952, the Egyptian army seized control of the government and forced the king to abdicate. The next year, the monarchy was abolished and a republic with a president as its head was established.

Egypt and many other Arab nations were opposed to the establishment of the Jewish nation of Israel. Since Israel's beginning in 1948, fighting has taken place off and on between the two countries. Egypt lost much of its territory in the Sinai. In 1979, a peace treaty between Egypt and Israel was signed. Agreements were made for the return to Egypt of lands in the Sinai.

The Aswan High Dam, completed in 1970, provides both electricity and irrigation water for Egypt. Farmers raise water to their fields by using a device known as an Archimedean screw.

The Suez Canal

The Suez Canal is a waterway that connects the Mediterranean and Red seas. The canal, designed by a French engineer, was completed in 1869. A company called the Suez Canal Company raised the money to build the canal. The company was given permission to operate the canal until 1968. The right to operate a business at a certain place is called a *concession* (kən sesh′ən).

In 1875, Great Britain bought a large interest in the company. The canal was an important link between Britain and its empire. In 1956, Egypt nationalized the canal. The next year, the canal was blocked by ships sunk during the Arab-Israeli war. The canal was not reopened until 1975.

The Suez Canal is a source of income for Egypt. Ships passing through the canal pay tolls for its use. The Suez Canal has no locks because there is not a great difference between the levels of the Red and Mediterranean seas.

The Aswan Dam

British engineers completed a dam across the Nile near Aswan in 1902. The height of the dam was later raised two times. The dam was built to hold back flood waters, to control irrigation, and to increase the amount of land that could be irrigated.

In 1960, Egypt began construction of a second dam a short distance upstream from the first Aswan Dam. The new dam, called the Aswan High Dam, was completed in 1970. The lake created behind the dam, Lake Nasser, is the world's largest artificial lake. Lake Nasser extends south from the dam more than 300 miles (480 km).

The Aswan High Dam has provided the same benefits as the earlier dam, but on a larger scale. With water stored by the dam, Egypt has been able to double its agricultural production. Two or three crops a year can be grown. A hydroelectric plant at the dam provides much of the country's electricity.

Although the Aswan High Dam has brought many benefits to Egypt, it has also brought problems. The silt formerly deposited in the fields by the floodwaters is now left behind at the bottom of Lake Nasser. Without the silt to enrich the soil, farmers must buy expensive fertilizers for their fields.

The dam has also caused erosional problems at the mouth of the Nile. The Nile no longer carries silt to deposit as it enters the Mediterranean. The processes of erosion are outstripping the processes of deposition. As a result, parts of the coast are being worn away. A third problem is that of poor drainage of the land near the dam.

Agriculture

About three-fifths of all Egyptians earn their living by agriculture. Farm products are the leading exports. Most of Egypt's farms are very small and privately owned. All crops in Egypt must be irrigated.

Cotton is Egypt's leading crop. It is an important cash crop for farmers in both Upper and Lower Egypt. The cotton raised in Lower Egypt has a long fiber that makes better cloth than short-fibered cotton. It brings a good price on the world market.

Other important crops are wheat, rice, sugarcane, millet, beans, and onions. Date palms grow on the desert oases. Goats and sheep are raised for meat, milk, and wool.

Many Egyptians still use age-old methods of farming and irrigating. Much work is done by hand or with the help of donkeys, oxen, or water buffalo.

Along the Nile, water is raised by using a water wheel. Another way of lifting water is to use a pole with a bucket at one end. In Egypt, this is called a *shadoof* (shä$\overline{oo}$f'). The pole is lowered over a crossbar to dip the bucket into the water. A stone is used to weight the other end of the pole, making it easier to lift the water. The water then flows through canals to the fields.

Mining and Manufacturing

Mining is not an important industry in Egypt. Petroleum and phosphate rock are found along the coast of the Red Sea and in the Sinai. Phosphate rock is used to make fertilizer. Iron deposits are being mined near Aswan.

Egypt's most important industry is the manufacturing of textiles. Egyptian cotton is made into cloth and clothing in factories in Cairo and Alexandria. Other important products include petroleum products, chemicals, fertilizer, and sugar.

Cities of Egypt

Cairo, the capital of Egypt, is the largest city in Africa. It has a population of more than six million. Cairo is located near the head of the Nile delta not far from where Egypt's early capital of Memphis stood.

Modern Cairo is an important manufacturing and distribution center. Its factories produce cloth, iron and steel, sugar, and many other products. Goods can be shipped into and out of Cairo by railroad and boat.

Much of Cairo is new, but in the old section are found splendid examples of early Muslim architecture. Much of the building stone was taken from the pyramids at Giza. Cairo is known for its many domed mosques with their slender towers called minarets.

Not far from Cairo are the famous pyramids of Giza and the Great Sphinx. Many treasures from Egypt's past are housed in the Egyptian Museum. Tourists who come to Egypt to visit the famous monuments of ancient Egypt along the Nile often begin and end their trip in Cairo.

Egypt's second-largest city and chief port is Alexandria. The city was founded in 332 B.C. by Alexander the Great when he conquered Egypt. It was the capital of Egypt for the next 300 years. It was famous for its great library. The lighthouse of Alexandria was one of the seven ancient wonders of the world. Today a new and modern harbor has been built on the Mediterranean. It handles most of Egypt's foreign trade.

Countries of the Maghrib

The countries of the Maghrib are Libya, Tunisia, Algeria, and Morocco. These countries cover more than 80 percent of North Africa. Their combined population is just slightly more than that of Egypt.

The Sahara covers most of the Maghrib. A coastal lowland with a Mediterranean climate extends from Libya to Morocco. It is much wider in the west than it is in the east. In Morocco, Algeria, and Tunisia, the high Atlas Mountains separate the coastal region from the desert interior. The mountain ranges act as barriers to keep rain from falling on the desert to the south.

A smaller group of lower mountains, the Ahaggar, are found in southern Algeria. From both the Atlas Mountains and the Ahaggar, dry wadis run out into the desert. Underground water can be found along the wadis for many miles. Oases are found along the wadis.

About 90 percent of the people of the Maghrib live in permanent communities along the Atlantic and Mediterranean coasts. The rest of the people live in oases or are nomads. There are several large oases south of the Atlas Mountains. Some of them are as densely populated as the Nile Valley.

The nomads move with their herds of sheep, goats, or camels to find good pasture. Herders who move from one pasture to another are called *pastoral* (pas'tər əl) nomads. *Pastoral* means "relating to shepherds or their way of life." The pastoral nomads of the Maghrib move to the high mountains in the summer. In the winter, they come down to the warmer valleys. The nomads often trade with the people of the oases. They exchange milk and meat for vegetables and dates.

History

The earliest known inhabitants of the Maghrib were the Berbers. They may have been there as long ago as 2000 B.C. The Berbers were subsistence farmers and pastoral nomads. They had no horses or camels.

The Phoenicians began to visit the North African coast as early as 1200 B.C. They founded the city of Carthage (kär'thij) in what

Colorful market streets like this one in Tunis are found in cities throughout North Africa and the Middle East.

is now Tunisia in 814 B.C. Carthage became the capital of an empire that extended along the coast from the present country of Morocco to Egypt. Carthaginian control of Sicily led to war with Rome. In 146 B.C., the Romans conquered Carthage. They ruled the coast of North Africa for the next 600 years. See the map on page 201. After the power of Rome declined, other groups gained control of North Africa.

The Arabs began to invade North Africa in the middle 600s A.D. By 732, they had conquered most of the region. The Arabs had a greater effect on the Berbers than any of the earlier invaders. The Arabs introduced the camel, the date palm, and the religion of Islam to the Berbers. The Berbers learned to speak Arabic and adopted many Arabic customs. The Muslim Berbers joined the Arabs in conquering Spain. The Muslim Arabs and Berbers became known as Moors.

During the 1500s, much of the North African coast came under control of the Ottoman Empire. Berbers who lived along the coast became pirates and slave traders. The region became known as the Barbary Coast. *Barbary* comes from the word *Berber*. To keep their ships safe from attacks, European countries and the United States paid tribute, or protection money, to the pirates. The United States fought a war against the pirates in the early 1800s. As a result, piracy had practically died out by 1805.

French control of Algeria began in the early 1800s. In the late 1800s, France made Tunisia a protectorate. In the early 1900s, Italy gained control of Libya. Parts of Morocco became French and Spanish possessions. Between 1951 and 1962, Libya, Morocco, Tunisia, and Algeria became independent.

Libya

Libya is more than one and a half times the size of Egypt. Its population is about three million. It has the lowest population density of any North African country.

Most of the people live on the coast in the areas around Tripoli (trip′ə lē′) and Benghazi (ben gäz′ē). Tripoli, an old Phoenician city, is Libya's capital, largest city, and principal port.

301

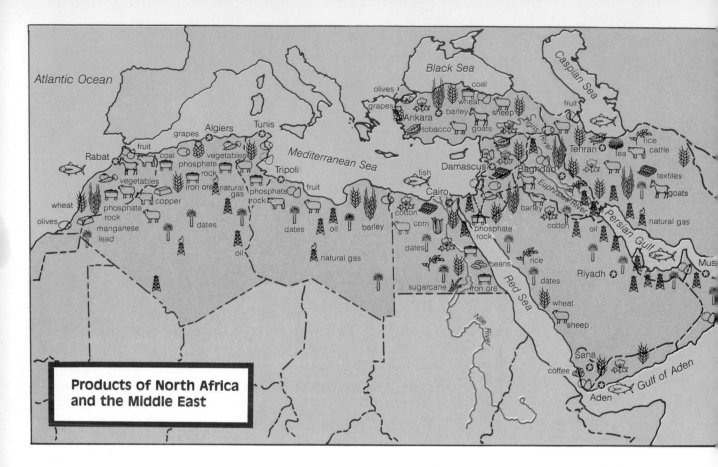

Products of North Africa and the Middle East

Although little of the land is suitable for agriculture, about 80 percent of the people make their living by farming or raising livestock. Cattle, sheep, and goats are herded. Important crops include dates, olives, wheat, and fruit.

In 1959, oil was discovered in the desert of Libya. Today Libya ranks as one of the ten top oil-producing countries in the world. Some of the oil money is being used by the government to improve farmland and build roads and schools.

Many roads and towns built in Libya when it was an Italian colony were destroyed in World War II. Italy lost Libya as a result of its defeat in the war. In 1951, Libya became an independent monarchy. The king was overthrown in 1969, and Libya is now ruled by a five-member group. The leader, Muammar El Qaddafi

(ghut dä′fē), has tried to increase Libya's power in African affairs.

Tunisia

Tunisia is the smallest country of North Africa. Its population is about six and a half million.

Since the days of Roman rule, Tunisia has been an important farming area. Much wheat is grown in a lowland between two ranges of the Atlas Mountains in the north. Cattle, sheep, and goats are raised on the plateau south of the mountains. Citrus fruits and olives grow on the fertile coastal plain south of Tunis.

Tunis is the country's capital, largest city, and chief port. It is located on the site of the ancient city of Carthage. Tunis is the industrial and transportation center of the country. Its factories produce textiles, carpets, olive oil, and cement.

Tunisia was under French control from 1881 to 1956, when it became independent. The French provided the country with a good network of roads and railroads. Although Arabic is the official language, French is spoken by many people.

Tunisia is a republic headed by a president. It has had only one president since independence. In 1975, the assembly voted to make him president for life.

Tunisia does not have important oil reserves. Its chief mineral resource is phosphate.

Algeria

Algeria is the largest country in North Africa. It has about 20 million people. The chief cities and richest farmlands are in the north.

Like Tunisia, Algeria provided food for the Roman Empire. Grains, including wheat and barley, have always been important. Algeria is also an important source of olives and grapes. Wine made from grapes is sent mainly to France. Herders raise sheep, goats, and cattle on the dry, grassy, high plateaus of the Atlas Mountains.

Oil and natural gas are the country's most important minerals. Iron ore, phosphates, and copper are also mined. Factories in the coastal cities process food and manufacture textiles.

Many of Algeria's cities grew up on the sites of early Roman towns. Algiers (al jirz'), the capital, is the largest city. Both Algiers and Oran are important ports. These cities are a mixture of the old and new. The older parts, called casbahs (käz'bäz), surround Arab palaces and forts.

The French began to colonize Algeria in 1830. To gain control of this vast region, they formed the famous French Foreign Legion. Algeria remained under French rule until 1962. Today it is a republic with a president as its head.

Morocco

The Atlas Mountains cover most of Morocco. Although Morocco is much smaller than Algeria, it has about the same population. Morocco is separated from Europe by the Strait of Gibraltar, which is only eight miles (13 km) wide at the narrowest part. Morocco is the only North African country with a coast on the Atlantic.

Most Moroccans are farmers or herders. The farmers grow wheat, barley, fruit, and vegetables in the lowlands. The herders raise cattle, goats, and sheep in the highlands. Timber and cork are important forest products. Some people make a living by fishing.

Morocco has important deposits of phosphates, coal, lead, and manganese. Factories process food and produce building materials, textiles, and cement. Morocco's handmade leather goods, jewelry, and textiles are famous.

Morocco has many colorful cities with both modern and old sections. Palaces, mosques, and marketplaces line the narrow streets of the crowded, old quarters. Casablanca, on the Atlantic, is Morocco's largest city and most important port. Rabat, the capital, is an important industrial and cultural center. Fez, a sacred city of the Muslims, has many fine mosques and one of the world's oldest universities.

Street merchants prepare mint for sale in Morocco. Many fresh fruits and vegetables can be bought on the streets.

France and Spain controlled much of what is now Morocco between the early 1900s and 1956. At first, they governed through local rulers. In 1956, France granted independence to French Morocco. Spanish Morocco became part of independent Morocco. The sultan became the king of Morocco. Today Morocco is a constitutional monarchy.

Spain had control of an area south of Morocco along the Atlantic from 1860 to 1976. From 1958 until 1976, this region was known as Spanish Sahara. When Spain gave up its control of Spanish Sahara in 1976, the region became known as Western Sahara. The northern part was claimed by Morocco, and the southern part was claimed by Mauritania. The people who lived in Western Sahara demanded independence. Although Mauritania has given up its claim and Morocco has claimed all of Western Sahara, the issue has not been resolved.

Do You Know?

1. Name the countries of North Africa.
2. What part of Egypt has the highest population density?
3. What waterway connects the Mediterranean and the Red seas?
4. Where do most of the people of the Maghrib live?

Before You Go On

Using New Words

Maghrib   pastoral
Koran   aridity
shadoof   concession
wadi   pilgrimage
caliph

Number a paper from 1 through 9. After each number write the word or term from the above list that matches the definition.

1. An irrigation device consisting of a pole on a pivot with a bucket
2. The title given to the successors of Mohammed who were the leaders of Islam
3. Relating to shepherds or their way of life
4. The right to operate a business at a certain place
5. The North African countries west of Egypt
6. A journey to a sacred place for religious reasons
7. A short, dry riverbed
8. Dryness
9. The holy book of the Muslims

Finding the Facts

1. What is the largest desert in the world? About how big is it?
2. What are the highest mountains of North Africa?
3. What is the lowest place on the surface of the earth?
4. Name two holy cities of Islam.
5. What is Lower Egypt? Upper Egypt?
6. What is the religion of most people in North Africa and the Middle East?
7. What is Egypt's leading crop? What is its chief industry?
8. Name the four countries of the Maghrib. Which is the largest? The smallest?
9. What is Libya's chief export?
10. Where is wheat grown in Tunisia?
11. What European country once ruled Algeria?
12. What country in North Africa has a coast on the Atlantic?

3
The Middle East

The term *Middle East* was first used by Europeans for the lands that lie between Europe and eastern and southeastern Asia. Eastern and southeastern Asia were called the Far East. Because the Middle East is close to Europe, it was also called the Near East. Today, both *Middle East* and *Near East* are used to refer to this region.

The Middle East is made up of 15 countries that cover nearly two and one-half million square miles (more than 6 million sq. km). It can be divided into four regions. They are the Fertile Crescent, Turkey, Iran, and the Arabian Peninsula. The Fertile Crescent extends from the eastern end of the Mediterranean in a broad curve toward the head of the Persian Gulf. Turkey occupies the Anatolian Peninsula to the north and west. Iran lies between the Caspian Sea and the Arabian Sea east of the Fertile Crescent. The Arabian Peninsula extends south from the Fertile Crescent to the Arabian Sea.

More than 136 million people live in the Middle East. Arabs, Turks, and Iranians are the largest groups. Most of these people are Muslims. The Jews are a small but important minority.

Like North Africa, much of the Middle East is hot and dry. Rainfall is heaviest along the shores of the Mediterranean and in the high mountains.

Much of the Near East is low plateaus covered by deserts and steppes. High plateaus and mountains are found in the northern and eastern regions.

The Middle East has more than half of the world's oil reserves. Most of the oil is found along the Persian Gulf and in the regions north and northwest of the gulf. Money from the sale of oil is rapidly changing the lives of many people in the Middle East.

The Countries of the Fertile Crescent

The Fertile Crescent extends along the eastern Mediterranean and follows the valleys of the Tigris and Euphrates to the Persian Gulf. As you learned in Unit 2, the plains of these rivers were once known as Mesopotamia. Some of the world's earliest civilizations grew up in this region. Today, the Fertile Crescent countries include Israel, Jordan, Lebanon, Syria, and Iraq. Israel, Lebanon, and Syria border the Mediterranean. Jordan has a short coastline on the Gulf of Aqaba (ăk′ə bə) at the head of the Red Sea. Iraq has a short coastline on the Persian Gulf.

Like the Nile, the Tigris and Euphrates furnish water to make farming possible. These rivers, however, are not as dependable as the Nile. Sometimes they bring very little water. Other times, heavy floods carry large amounts of sand and gravel instead of rich silt.

Much of the Fertile Crescent is desert and steppe. The Syrian Desert in the south covers a large area between the Tigris and Euphrates and the Mediterranean. Farther south lie the vast deserts of Arabia. Rainfall is low except in areas along the Mediterranean and in the mountainous northeast.

About one-fourth of the people of the Middle East live in the countries of the Fertile Crescent. Most of them are Muslims. The majority of people in Israel, however, are Jewish, and about half the people in Lebanon are Christians.

History

You have read about the early civilizations of Mesopotamia and the Fertile Crescent in Unit 2. One of the early civilizations in this region established Judaism. Many years later, Christianity developed here, too.

In ancient times, Mesopotamia was a crossroads between Asia and the Mediterranean. Ancient trade routes, traveled by camel caravans, followed the Fertile Crescent because food and water were available. Caravans avoided crossing the hot, dry Syrian Desert to the south and the rough mountains to the north and east. Today, important routes still follow the crescent.

Mesopotamia was an open plain with few natural barriers. Only in the north were there high mountains that were difficult to cross. After about 800 B.C., the early civilizations of the Fertile Crescent were destroyed by a series of invaders. The invaders included the Assyrians, the Greeks, and the Romans. By 700 A.D., the region was under the control of the Muslims.

The region of the Fertile Crescent was part of the Ottoman Empire from the 1300s until World War I. After Turkey's defeat in World War I, its lands in the Fertile Crescent were divided into several territories. These territories were governed by France and Great Britain. The Arabs who lived here had fought with the Allies against the Turks in the war. The Arabs demanded independence. Between 1932 and 1946, four territories became independent countries. They were Iraq, Lebanon, Syria, and Transjordan. Transjordan was later renamed Jordan.

Palestine

Palestine is the name of the region around the Dead Sea along the eastern shores of the Mediterranean. Palestine is sometimes called the Holy Land. Palestine is the *homeland* of the Jewish people. A homeland is the place where a people has its origins.

The Jewish people are descendants of the early Hebrews who practiced the religion called Judaism. The Hebrews lived in Palestine nearly 4,000 years ago. When the Romans took control of Palestine, they drove the Jews from Jerusalem. Many Jews fled from other parts of Palestine. From 135 A.D. until 1948, the Jews had no land of their own. For centuries, they lived in other parts of the world.

After World War I, Great Britain was asked to govern Palestine. Part of Palestine was to be developed as a national home for the Jewish people. Many Arabs lived in Palestine when the Jews began to move to the region. The numbers of Jewish refugees increased during

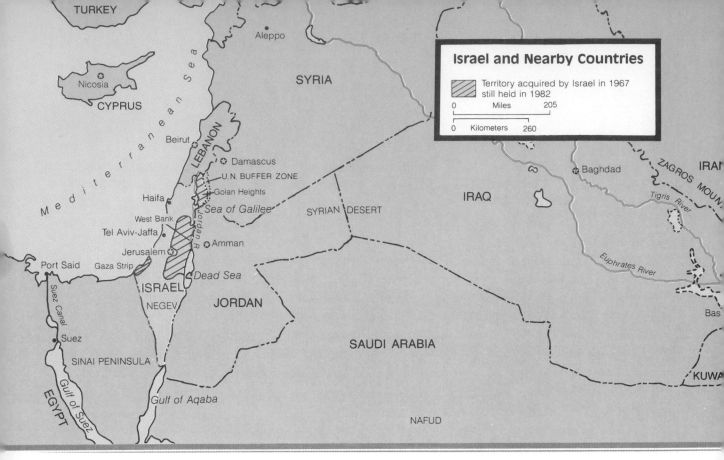

Israel and Nearby Countries

Territory acquired by Israel in 1967 still held in 1982

Israel returned the Sinai Peninsula to Egypt in 1982. Find the areas that Israel gained in 1967 and still controlled 15 years later.

and after World War II. In 1948, the United Nations voted to divide Palestine into two states. One part would be Jewish, and the other would be Arab. In 1948, the Jewish state of Israel was established.

The creation of Israel was strongly opposed by most Arab countries. Many Arabs fled or were driven from Israel. Almost immediately, the neighboring Arab states attacked Israel. Since 1948, there have been four wars between Israel and its Arab neighbors. Israel has resisted the invaders and taken over much of the land that was supposed to have been under Arab rule.

Much opposition toward Israel comes from the Palestine Liberation Organization, some-

times called the PLO. The PLO wants to establish a state for Palestinian Arabs.

A peace treaty was signed between Egypt and Israel in 1979. This treaty has not solved all the problems, but it has settled some.

Israel

Israel occupies most of ancient Palestine. About four million people live there.

About 10 percent of Israel's people make their living by farming. Israeli farmers created arable land by draining swamps and expanding irrigation. Most of the water of the Jordan River is used for irrigation. Today farmers produce about three-fourths of the country's food. The chief farm products are citrus fruits, eggs, milk, and poultry. Cotton, livestock, vegetables, and wheat are also raised. Many of Israel's farms are collective farms. In Israel, a collective farm is called a *kibbutz* (ki boots'). On a kibbutz, people share the land and divide the labor and profits. The land is rented from the government.

Israel is a highly industrialized nation. The majority of the people live in cities. Factories produce tools, textiles, clothing, and processed foods. Haifa (hī′fə), a city in the north, has a huge oil refinery and factories that assemble automobiles, electronics equipment, and appliances. Diamond-cutting is another important industry. Imported diamonds are cut and polished for the world market.

Tel Aviv and Jaffa, two cities on the Mediterranean, have been combined into one city. Tel Aviv-Jaffa is the largest city and chief industrial center in Israel. It is also a center for banking, publishing, and trade. Tel Aviv-Jaffa is one of the most modern cities in the Middle East. Shops and sidewalk cafes line the downtown streets. Part of the city's long coastline has been made into a beach resort.

Israel's second-largest city, Jerusalem, is the nation's capital. In 1948, the city was divided between Israel and Jordan. Israel controlled West Jerusalem, and Jordan held East Jerusalem. Israel captured East Jerusalem in 1967, and the city was united. The country's parliament is in the modern western part of the city. The Old City in eastern Jerusalem includes many places that are sacred to Christians, Jews, and Muslims. For this reason, Jerusalem is often called the Holy City.

Jerusalem landmarks include the Christian Church of St. Mary Magdalene and the Dome of the Rock, a Muslim shrine.

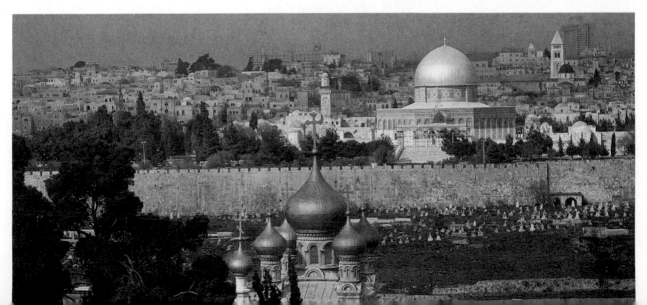

Living and Working in North Africa and the Middle East

Many people in North Africa and the Middle East live in traditional ways and do the same kind of work their parents and grandparents did. Kurdish shepherds in northern Iraq shear sheep in the spring. Many Kurds are nomads, moving with their flocks as pastures change. In the streets of Damascus, a woman transports a basket of eggplants on her head. Many changes have come to the area, however. With the aid of modern equipment, workers harvest dates on a kibbutz in Israel. Dates are an important crop throughout the region.

310

Development of mineral wealth has led to *industrialization* in some countries. The latest computer equipment is used by a worker in Saudi Arabia. Oil exploration requires complex technical equipment. A drilling crew surrounded by miles of desert works in the Rub al-Khali of Arabia. ■

Regional Data Chart

Country	Capital	Area		Population	GNP
		Square miles	Square kilometers		(in millions of U.S. dollars)
Algeria	Algiers	919,951	2,382,673	20,250,000	$28,900
Bahrain	Manama	240	622	400,000	$2,100
Egypt	Cairo	386,872	1,001,998	43,000,000	$18,600
Iran	Tehran	636,363	1,648,180	37,400,000	$81,700
Iraq	Baghdad	172,000	445,480	13,400,000	$30,400
Israel	Jerusalem	7,992	20,699	4,000,000	$15,700
Jordan	Amman	37,738	97,740	3,300,000	$2,600
Kuwait	Kuwait	7,780	20,150	1,440,000	$21,900
Lebanon	Beirut	4,015	10,400	3,230,000	$3,000
Libya	Tripoli	679,536	1,759,998	3,100,000	$23,400
Morocco	Rabat	171,953	445,358	20,500,000	$14,500
Oman	Muscat	82,000	212,380	920,000	$2,600
Qatar	Doha	4,247	11,000	230,000	$3,800
Saudi Arabia	Riyadh	831,313	2,153,090	8,650,000	$62,600
Southern Yemen	Aden	111,000	287,490	1,950,000	$890
Syria	Damascus	71,586	185,408	9,325,000	$8,900
Tunisia	Tunis	63,170	163,610	6,500,000	$7,000
Turkey	Ankara	301,380	780,574	45,500,000	$58,800
United Arab Emirates	Abu Dhabi	32,000	82,880	850,000	$13,000
Yemen	San'a	72,290	195,000	6,100,000	$2,400

Nonindependent Area

Western Sahara	El Aaiún	102,703	266,000	165,000	—

Jordan

The kingdom of Jordan borders Israel to the east. The Jordan River forms part of the boundary between the two countries. Although Jordan is much larger than Israel, it has only about three-fourths as many people. Most of the population is Arab. Amman is the country's capital and most important city.

Thousands of Palestinian refugees who fled Israel now live in an area west of the Jordan River and the Dead Sea. This area is called the West Bank. Once part of Jordan, the West Bank was taken over by Israel during the 1967 Arab-Israeli war.

About half of all Jordanians farm and live in villages in the Jordan Valley. The main crops are barley, lentils, wheat, and vegetables. Ol-ives, grapes, and other fruits are grown. Because of the lack of water, only about one-tenth of the land is arable. Most farmers use simple farming methods.

A little more than 5 percent of the people are nomadic herders. In many countries of North Africa and the Middle East, a nomadic herder with no permanent home is called a Bedouin (bed'ōo in). The Bedouins in Jordan herd camels, goats, and sheep.

Jordan has little industry. A plant near Amman refines oil from Arabia. Other factories produce cement and processed food.

Lebanon

Lebanon is a small, mountainous country on the Mediterranean coast between Israel and

Syria. The population is about three million. Beirut (bā ro͞ot′) is the capital and the only large city.

Lebanon occupies the land of ancient Phoenicia. The Phoenicians sailed throughout the Mediterranean in ships built of tall cedar trees from the Lebanon Mountains. Few of these famous "cedars of Lebanon" remain today.

Half the people in Lebanon are Christians, and most of the others are Muslims. In 1975, a bitter civil war broke out between the Christians and the Muslims. Thousands of people were killed, and much of Beirut was destroyed.

The PLO has carried on fighting with Israel from bases in southern Lebanon. Warfare has also continued between the Israelis and Palestinian refugees in Lebanon.

Before the civil war, Lebanon was an important banking center for the Middle East. It also had a thriving tourist industry.

Farmers make up about 40 percent of the population. They grow tropical fruits and tobacco along the coastal plain. On terraced fields on the mountainsides, farmers grow olives, grapes, peaches, apples, and potatoes.

Lebanon has oil refineries and factories that produce furniture, chemicals, and textiles. Many of Beirut's factories were destroyed in the civil war.

Syria

Syria lies along the Mediterranean between Turkey to the north and Lebanon, Jordan, and Israel to the south. Like Lebanon, Syria has mountains along the coast. Much of eastern Syria is desert and steppe. Most of the country's population of about nine million lives along the Mediterranean coast and at the eastern base of the mountains. Syria is almost 90 percent Muslim.

Farming is the chief occupation in Syria. Wheat, barley, tobacco, cotton, olives, and citrus fruits are the main crops. Sheep and goats are raised in the highlands.

The country has some small oil fields. Other resources include asphalt, iron ore, and natural gas. The chief industry is textile manufacturing. Since ancient times, Syrian fabrics have

Narrow streets wind through some parts of Damascus. Sections of the city are hundreds of years old.

Iraqis fish from a boat on the lower Tigris River. Fertile pastureland provides good grazing for sheep.

been prized. Chemicals, glass, processed foods, and tobacco are other manufactured products.

Syria's capital and largest city is Damascus, one of the oldest inhabited cities in the world. It occupies a huge oasis that provides food for the city. Damascus has been a trade center for thousands of years. Caravans crossing the Syrian Desert once stopped here. Today railroads and highways connect Damascus with many other cities.

Aleppo is another old and famous city of Syria that once depended on income from the caravan trade. Today a railroad connects the city with cities in Turkey and Iraq.

Iraq

Iraq is the largest country in the Fertile Crescent. It also has the largest population. About 13 million people live there. Muslim Arabs make up 80 percent of the people.

The Tigris and Euphrates rivers have created very fertile farmland in Iraq. Farmers grow barley, cotton, rice, and wheat in the irrigated lands along these rivers. To increase production, flood-control systems have been built. Water is stored during the rainy season and released during the dry season. Below the junction of the Tigris and Euphrates, in the Shatt al Arab, are large groves of date palms. Iraq grows more dates than any other country.

In the piedmont of the Zagros Mountains, wheat and barley are grown. On the steeper slopes, farmers cultivate grapes, olives, and fruit trees.

Outside the Tigris-Euphrates valley and the piedmont, most of Iraq is desert and steppe. In the steppes, nomadic herders move in search of pasture for their camels, goats, and sheep. One nomadic group called Kurds makes up about 15 percent of Iraq's population.

Only about 5 percent of Iraq's workers make their living in industry. Factories process food and produce cement, leather goods, soap, and textiles.

Iraq became a center for oil production in the 1930s. In 1972, the oil industry was nationalized. Recently, the Iraqi government has used money from oil to build schools, hospitals, roads, and irrigation systems.

Today Iraq is one of the largest producers of oil in the world. Pipelines from the oil fields cross the desert to ports on the Mediterranean Sea and the Persian Gulf. Tankers are loaded with oil for the journey to Europe and other parts of the world.

The ancient city of Baghdad is the capital of Iraq. It is one of the largest cities of the Middle East. The minarets and blue and gold domes of Baghdad's mosques rise above gray, flat-roofed houses in the city's old sections. Here also are narrow, winding streets and crowded bazaars. In the newer parts of Baghdad are factories, modern hotels, and office buildings.

Turkey

Turkey is the third-largest country of the Middle East. It has the largest population of any Middle Eastern country. About 45 million people live there.

Land and Climate

Most of Turkey occupies the peninsula of Anatolia in Asia. A small portion called Thrace is in Europe. Thrace and the western end of Anatolia are regions of plains and broad, gentle valleys. The Anatolian Plateau covers much of the interior of Turkey. High mountains surround the plateau to the north, the east, and the west. Narrow coastal plains separate the Pontic Mountains from the Black Sea and the Taurus Mountains from the Mediterranean.

The Pontic and the Taurus mountains meet in eastern Turkey. Here, in the Armenian Knot, are the headwaters of the Tigris and Euphrates rivers. Along the high ranges of the mountains in this region are Turkey's boundaries with the Soviet Union, Iran, Iraq, and Syria. See the map on page 289.

The climate of Turkey varies greatly from one region to another. The Aegean and Mediterranean coasts have a Mediterranean climate. The summers are hot, and rainfall averages from 20 to 30 inches (50 to 75 cm) a year. Summer temperatures are cooler along the coast of the Black Sea. Rainfall there is higher. In places it averages more than 60 inches (150 cm) a year.

The Anatolian Plateau is a dry steppe region. This plateau and the surrounding mountains have very cold winters. Summers are hot and dry on the plateau. The mountains are cooler and receive more moisture.

The Straits

Three bodies of water separate the European part of Turkey from the Asian part of Turkey. See the map on page 289. The Bosporus, the Sea of Marmara, and the Dardanelles (därd ə n elz′) form a water passage from the Black Sea to the Mediterranean. Together these waters are often called the Straits.

The Bosporus connects the Black Sea with the Sea of Marmara. It is 20 miles (32 km) long. Its greatest width is about two and one-half miles (4 km). Hundreds of years ago, the city of Constantinople grew up on the European side of the Bosporus. Eventually, the city expanded to the Asian side. The city's name was later changed to Istanbul (is'tän b‾oo‾l'). Today, a bridge spans the Bosporus.

The Sea of Marmara is connected to the Mediterranean at its western end by the Strait of the Dardanelles. The Dardanelles is 40 miles (65 km) long. Its greatest width is four miles (6.5 km).

Control of the Straits has been important since about 600 B.C., when the Greeks established colonies on the Black Sea. People have fought for control of the Straits for hundreds of years. Whoever controlled the Straits could control the movement of ships between the Black Sea and the Mediterranean. They could also control the overland movement of people and goods between Europe and Asia.

History

The earliest known people in Anatolia were the Hittites (hit'ïts'). By 1500 B.C. the Hittites had conquered much of the Fertile Crescent. Greeks, Persians, and Romans later ruled Anatolia. The capital of the Roman Empire was moved to Constantinople in 330 A.D.

Constantinople was the capital of the Eastern Roman Empire for more than a thousand years. The Eastern Roman Empire was also

A large ship passes through the *Straits* near Istanbul. The city is situated at the crossroads of Europe and Asia.

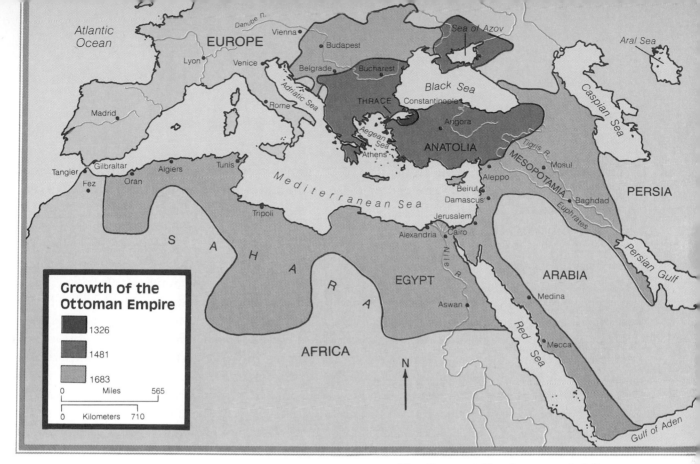

The Ottoman Empire expanded for more than three centuries. Constantinople was the capital of this vast empire, the world's largest during the 1600s.

called the Byzantine (biz′ən tēn′) Empire. Constantinople was named for the Emperor Constantine, the first Roman emperor to accept Christianity. His city became a center of Christianity in the East.

The Turks destroyed part of the Byzantine Empire in the 1000s. They originally came from a region in central Asia called Turkestan. This region is now part of the Soviet Union and China. Arabs, too, had been settling in Anatolia. The people of Anatolia began to speak Turkish and become Muslims.

About 300 years later, another large group of Turks arrived from the Caspian steppes. Their leader was Othman, and these Turks became known as the Ottoman Turks. In 1453,

the Ottoman Turks captured Constantinople. They changed its name to Istanbul and made it their capital. They closed the trading routes across Asia to the Far East.

The Ottoman Turks conquered large areas in southeastern Europe, the Middle East, and North Africa. At its greatest extent, the Ottoman Empire reached from the Danube River to the Red Sea. See the map on this page. When the Turks reached Vienna, in 1529, however, they were stopped by a large European army.

The Ottoman Empire eventually began to weaken. In 1783, Russia took control of Crimea. In the early 1800s, Greece became independent. The empire lost its North African possessions to Great Britain, France, and Italy.

The Ottoman Empire fought on the side of Germany in World War I. By the end of the war, the empire had lost all of its European and Asian lands except the small part that is now Turkey.

After World War I, a group of new leaders took charge of the empire's affairs. They set up the republic of Turkey in 1923. Mustafa Kemal became Turkey's first president. The capital was moved from Istanbul to Ankara, near the center of Turkey.

The new leaders made many political and cultural reforms. They decided to follow the Western custom of using surnames. Up to that time, Turkish people were given only one name. Kemal took the name *Atatürk*, which means "father of the Turks."

Atatürk introduced Western dress into Turkey. He also freed Turkish women from many old customs, such as wearing veils in public. Turkish women gained the right to vote and hold public office.

Atatürk, who valued education, started a campaign to increase the number of people who could read and write. Schools were started for all young people. Older people also were required to learn to read. The ancient Arabic script used to write Turkish was replaced by the Roman alphabet, which is used to write English and many other languages.

Farming and Herding

Turkey is an agricultural country. Six out of every ten people make their living by farming. Turkey is one of the world's ten leading wheat-producing countries. Wheat and barley are grown on the steppes of the Anatolian Plateau, where the government has introduced seeding and harvesting machinery.

Most of Turkey's farms are on the coastal plains of Thrace and western Anatolia. The rich alluvial valleys and delta plains are intensively farmed. Figs, grapes, citrus fruits, olives, cotton, and tobacco are grown. The region near Izmir is noted for its fine figs.

Turkey, like Egypt, is a major cotton producer. Cotton is Turkey's primary export. The government has been successfully encouraging increased cotton output since about 1960.

Many people make their living by herding. The hills and mountains of Turkey provide pastures for sheep, goats, and other animals. The hair of the Angora goat, called mohair, is used to make fine cloth. Much mohair is exported to the United States, where it is used to make clothing.

Mining and Manufacturing

Turkey has fairly abundant mineral resources, including large deposits of coal. It also mines copper, iron ore, and chromium ore. Turkey produces about half the petroleum it uses.

Almost 30 percent of the gross national product of Turkey comes from manufacturing. The main products are cement, processed foods, iron and steel, and textiles.

Cities of Turkey

Istanbul is one of the world's great cities. It is built on seven hills where the Bosporus joins the Sea of Marmara. Each of its hills is crowned by a mosque with a rounded dome and four

One of Istanbul's most famous mosques, with its domes and minarets, overlooks the Bosporus. Is it in Asia or Europe?

slender minarets. A harbor called the Golden Horn divides the European part of the city. This harbor was named for the great wealth from trade that was carried on there.

Today Istanbul is Turkey's largest city and a busy trade center. Its architecture and bazaars attract many tourists.

Ankara is Turkey's capital and second-largest city. Ankara is centrally located on the Anatolian Plateau. Izmir, on the Aegean coast, is a busy port and communications center.

Iran

Iran is bordered by Iraq to the west, Turkey and the Soviet Union to the north, and Afghanistan and Pakistan to the east. The southern coasts of Iran are on the Persian Gulf and the Gulf of Oman.

Iran's large central plateau is ringed by mountains. The mountains cut off winds that might otherwise bring rain. Most of the land is dry, except along the coasts. The tall peaks of the Elburz Mountains extend along Iran's northern border. Mount Damavand in the Elburz range is the highest point in the Middle East. In the low hills south of the Zagros Mountains are Iran's most important oil fields.

Iran is the second-largest country in the Middle East. More than 37 million people live there. The official language is Persian. Until 1935, the country was known as Persia.

History

In early times, the southwestern part of Iran was called Persis or Persia. By 500 B.C., the rulers of Persia had established a vast empire that extended from the Gulf of Oman to the Aral Sea, and from Greece and North Africa to India. See the map on page 320.

The Persian Empire was divided into provinces. The king, called "king of kings," had absolute power. He had a secret service that kept him informed about affairs throughout the empire. The members of the secret service were called the "eyes and ears of the king." A uniform system of laws was enforced in all the provinces.

Persian technology was complex. The Persians constructed irrigation systems to increase the amount of arable land. Water flowed through tunnels so it would not evaporate before it reached the fields. A vast system of roads extended throughout the empire. Horsemen delivered the mail quickly by using a relay system. Metal workers produced coins, weapons, ornaments, and housewares.

319

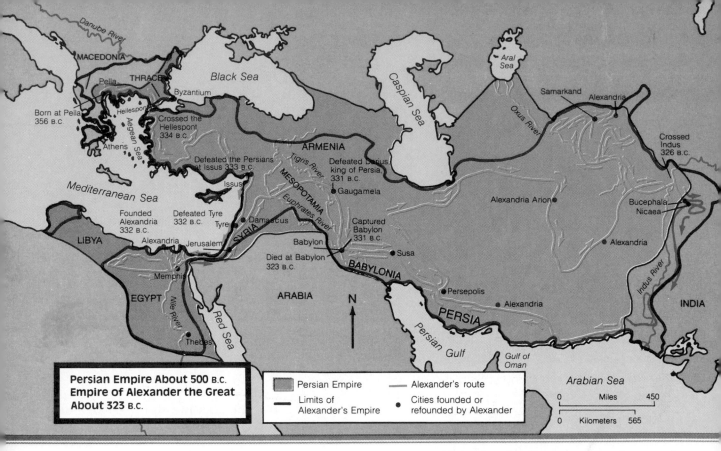

Alexander the Great conquered most of the Persian Empire. His empire lasted only a short time after his death.

Arab armies invaded Persia in the middle 600s A.D. Most Persians became Muslims. The Arabs ruled Persia for the next 200 years.

During the next centuries, first the Turks and then the Mongols conquered Persia. In the early 1500s, a Persian named Ismail united the Persians. Ismail began a dynasty that ruled Persia for the next 200 years. The ruler was called the *shah* (shä). *Shah* is a Persian word meaning "ruler."

In the 1800s, Great Britain and Russia competed for Persia's trade. Both countries eventually controlled much of Persia's trade. Many Persians worked for Russian and British companies. They became familiar with Western ideas through contact with these and other countries.

In the 1900s, many Persians wanted to reorganize the government. They wanted to limit the absolute power of the shah. In 1906, a new constitution established a parliament. Many people were not satisfied with the government, however. In 1926, a group of Persians overthrew the government. Reza Khan of the Pahlavi (pə lä′vē) dynasty became the new shah. In 1935, the shah officially changed the name of the country to Iran.

Mohammed Reza Pahlavi replaced his father as shah in 1941. He was responsible for many land reforms and social changes. Women voted for the first time in 1963.

In 1978, a revolution began in Iran. Students accused the shah of using a secret police force. Some people felt the social reforms of the shah were too extreme. Others were angry because the shah stressed the development of industry over agriculture. In 1979, the shah was forced to leave the country. The Ayatollah Khomeini (īyətō'lä hōmän'ē) took control of the government. Khomeini was a Muslim religious leader, the new government was based on Muslim laws.

Late in 1979, Iranian students captured the American embassy in Iran's capital of Tehran. Negotiations for the release of the Americans held hostage lasted until 1981. In January of that year they returned to the United States.

Farming, Herding, and Mining

More than half the people of Iran make their living by farming or herding. The main food crops are wheat, barley, and rice. Cotton, sugar beets, and tobacco are the chief crops that are exported.

Nomads raise cattle, goats, and sheep. The wool from the sheep is used to make the beautiful Persian carpets that Iran is famous for. Dyes for the wool are made from local plants.

Oil is Iran's most valuable resource. Among the oil-producing nations of the Middle East, Iran ranks third. Iran also has large deposits of natural gas. Iron, sulfur, turquoise, and coal are mined.

Cities of Iran

Tehran is the largest city in the Middle East. More than four million people live there. It became the capital of Iran in 1788. Many residents of the city work for the government.

There are several universities and museums in Tehran.

One of the most famous mosques in Iran is in the city of Isfahan. It is called the Royal Mosque and has a blue dome. Isfahan is a trading center. Its factories produce handicrafts, rugs, tiles, and textiles.

The city of Abadan has one of the largest oil refineries in the world. The refinery was damaged by forces from Iraq in the 1980 conflict between Iran and Iraq.

The Arabian Peninsula

The Arabian Peninsula is sometimes called Arabia. Arabia makes up nearly half of the Middle East. It has only about 15 percent of the population. Most of the people of the Arabian Peninsula live along the coasts.

Saudi (soud'ē) Arabia occupies most of the Arabian Peninsula. Seven smaller countries lie along the southern and eastern coasts. Kuwait (kəwāt'), Bahrain (bärān'), Qatar (kät'ər), and the United Arab Emirates border the Persian Gulf. Oman (ōmän') and Southern Yemen (yem'ən) have coasts on the Arabian Sea. Yemen is in the southwest corner of Arabia along the Red Sea.

Two gulfs of the Arabian Sea extend along the southern part of Arabia. In the east is the Gulf of Oman which is connected with the Persian Gulf by the Strait of Hormuz (hôrmōōz'). The Gulf of Aden (äd'ən) extends west. It is connected by a strait with the Red Sea.

Arabia is often divided into "desert Arabia" and "fortunate Arabia." "Fortunate Arabia" includes the mountainous regions along the southeast and southwest coasts. In these areas there is enough rain to allow farming. Most of Arabia is "desert Arabia." This sparsely populated region includes the large deserts of Nafud (nə food′) in the north and Rub al-Khali (roob′ al käl′ē) in the south. *Rub al-Khali* means "empty quarter."

Although the countries of Arabia are among the richest in the world, most of the people do not share in the riches. They still follow their traditional ways. Most are small farmers or Bedouin nomads. Some people have jobs in the oil fields.

History

The earliest inhabitants of the Arabian Peninsula may have come from Mesopotamia. Bedouin nomads have lived in the desert since early times. In 632 A.D., when Mohammed died, Muslim Arabs ruled most of the region. The Muslim armies conquered huge areas of the Middle East and North Africa. See the map on page 297. In the 700s, the empire was divided into individual states ruled by caliphs. Many different groups invaded the area during the next 700 years.

In the 1500s, the Ottoman Turks took control of parts of Arabia along the Red Sea. See the map on page 317. The Turks continued to control the area for hundreds of years. During the 1800s, Great Britain gained control of other parts of the peninsula. The British established protectorates in most of the coastal areas not ruled by the Turks. The inland areas were controlled by the Saud dynasty.

After World War I, the Turks left the peninsula, and a strong ruler of the Saud dynasty named Ibn Saud came to power. Ibn Saud defeated rival leaders and brought the desert sheikdoms under his control. A sheikdom is an area ruled by a sheik. Ibn Saud formed the country of Saudi Arabia in 1932. The name *Saudi Arabia* means "the land ruled by the Saud family." Ibn Saud became king of the new nation. In the 1960s and 1970s, Great Britain granted independence to its Arab protectorates.

Saudi Arabia

Saudi Arabia is the largest country on the Arabian Peninsula. Nearly nine million people live in this desert land with no rivers or lakes. Nomads roam the desert and herd camels, goats, and sheep. Near oases, farmers grow rice, wheat, dates, and other fruits. Farming and herding have been the traditional occupations of Saudi Arabians.

In 1936, oil was discovered in Saudi Arabia. Companies from other countries sent engineers to build refineries and pipelines. The Saudi Arabian government collected *royalties* (roi′əl tēz) from the foreign-owned oil companies. Royalties are shares of the income from a product paid to the owner in return for permission to use the property. The companies paid royalties for each barrel of oil that was produced in Saudi Arabia. The companies also secured concessions that allowed them to look for oil. In 1976, the oil industry in Saudi Arabia was nationalized. Today, Saudi Arabia ranks second among the oil-producing nations of the world.

The government has used oil income for many purposes. Irrigation projects have increased the amount of arable land. Hospitals and health programs provide medical care for many Saudi Arabians. The government has also built many schools.

Seaports on both the Red Sea and the Persian Gulf have been modernized. Airlines connect the country with other nations of the world. A railroad connects Damman, on the Persian Gulf, with the capital city of Riyadh (rē yäd′). Riyadh is a modern city of almost 700,000 people. It lies in a large inland oasis.

Mecca, on the Red Sea, is a religious center for the world's Muslims. The Great Mosque is in the center of the city. Near the center of the Great Mosque is a shrine called the Kaaba. Within the Kaaba, there is a large black stone. Muslims believe that an angel gave the stone to Abraham. Pilgrims to the shrine circle the stone seven times while they recite passages from the Koran. Making a pilgrimage to Mecca is one of the five duties of a devout Muslim.

Kuwait

Kuwait is a small country at the northern tip of the Persian Gulf. The nation is an *emirate* (ə mēr′āt). An emirate is a nation ruled by an emir. In some Arab countries, a ruling chief or prince is called an emir.

Oil was discovered in Kuwait in 1938. Today about 2 percent of the world's oil is produced in Kuwait. Pipelines carry oil to the coast for export. The people of Kuwait have benefited from the oil income. They pay no taxes, except on imported goods. There are jobs for every-

one, and the government provides education, medical care, and pensions.

Until recently, fresh water had to be brought to Kuwait on barges from Iraq. Now the government has constructed a large plant where salt is removed from seawater.

Bahrain

Bahrain is a tiny archipelago in the Persian Gulf off the coast of Saudi Arabia. It is the smallest country in the Middle East. Most of Bahrain's population lives on the largest island, which is also called Bahrain.

Oil is produced and refined on the island of Sitrah. The refinery there also processes much of Saudi Arabia's oil. Bahrain's oil reserves are limited, however. The government is preparing for the future when the oil will run out. An aluminum plant was built in the 1970s. A large shipyard repairs ships. Factories produce building materials and processed foods.

Some of Bahrain's people make their living by farming. They grow dates, other fruits, and vegetables. Fishing is also important for the nation's food supply.

Qatar

Qatar is another very small Arabian country. It occupies a peninsula that juts out from Saudi Arabia into the Persian Gulf. Most of Qatar's people live in Doha, the capital. The country is an emirate.

As almost everywhere on the Arabian Peninsula, oil is the major source of income. The government is also developing other industries. Qatar will not have to depend on oil in the future. The government runs a flour mill, a cement factory, and a fertilizer plant. The government also operates a large shrimp industry. Qatar's shrimp are sold all over the world.

United Arab Emirates

The United Arab Emirates is a federation of seven separate states at the southern end of the Persian Gulf. Each state is ruled by its own emir. The states were united in 1971. The population is almost one million, but workers who come in from other countries make up about half this number.

Most people in the United Arab Emirates live in cities. Abu Dhabi is the largest city and the country's capital. The cities have good schools, hospitals, and modern roads. In the villages, however, life is much simpler. Most people still live in thatched huts.

Oil is the chief product of the United Arab Emirates. The country also produces natural gas. In the four emirates that do not have oil, most people live on oases. They grow dates, vegetables, and citrus fruits. Some people in these emirates are pastoral nomads who herd goats, sheep, and camels.

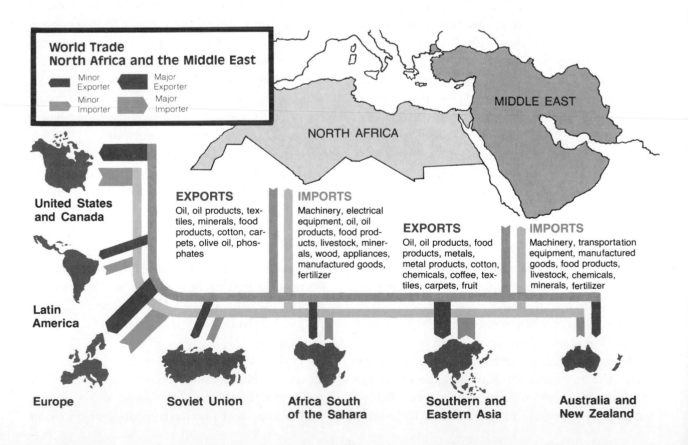

World Trade
North Africa and the Middle East

Minor Exporter
Major Exporter
Minor Importer
Major Importer

MIDDLE EAST

NORTH AFRICA

United States and Canada

Latin America

EXPORTS
Oil, oil products, textiles, minerals, food products, cotton, carpets, olive oil, phosphates

IMPORTS
Machinery, electrical equipment, oil, oil products, food products, livestock, minerals, wood, appliances, manufactured goods, fertilizer

EXPORTS
Oil, oil products, food products, metals, metal products, cotton, chemicals, coffee, textiles, carpets, fruit

IMPORTS
Machinery, transportation equipment, manufactured goods, food products, livestock, chemicals, minerals, fertilizer

Europe

Soviet Union

Africa South of the Sahara

Southern and Eastern Asia

Australia and New Zealand

Oman

Oman lies in the southeast part of the Arabian Peninsula along the Gulf of Oman and the Arabian Sea. It is one of the hottest countries in the world. Temperatures reach as high as 130° F. (54° C).

The ruler, or monarch, of Oman is called a *sultan* (sult'ən). *Sultan* means "ruler" in Arabic. Many Muslim countries were once ruled by sultans. Originally, the word was used as a title of respect, and anyone with political power could be called a sultan. After the eleventh century, the title was only given to the chief ruler of a state.

Oil was not discovered in Oman until 1964. The oil industry there is still developing. Oman farmers produce citrus fruits, coconuts, and dates. Some people make their living by fishing or herding.

Yemen and Southern Yemen

Yemen and Southern Yemen are countries in the southwestern part of the Arabian Peninsula. Yemen is sometimes referred to as Yemen (Sana), and Southern Yemen is referred to as Yemen (Aden). The name in parentheses is the capital of each country.

The interior plateau of Yemen is a fertile region that is part of "fortunate Arabia." It receives enough rain to support vegetation. Coffee, an important export, is grown here.

Gold and silver jewelry is made in the city of Sana. Craftworkers make leather goods and handwoven cloth. Sana has some unusual six- and seven-story "skyscrapers" made of mud bricks. The bricks are painted with whitewash.

Coffee, a leading *cash crop* of Yemen, is grown on terraced hillsides. The terraces help hold rainwater.

Less than 1 percent of the land in Southern Yemen is cultivated. Most of the country is in the Rub al-Khali. Southern Yemen has no oil, but it does have many refineries that process the oil from Saudi Arabia.

The capital city of Aden has been an important trading port since Roman times. Aden is built in the crater of an extinct volcano. On three sides of the city, the volcano forms a steep backdrop.

Do You Know?

1. What four regions make up the Middle East?
2. Why is Jerusalem often called the Holy City?
3. What three bodies of water are referred to as the Straits? Why have people fought over the Straits?
4. What was Iran called before 1935?

325

period of time. Find the line graph on this page. What does this graph show? Was there an overall increase or decrease in the amount of oil exported from Saudi Arabia between 1970 and 1980? During what two-year period did exports decrease? During what two-year period did exports increase the most?

A bar graph is often used to make comparisons. Find the bar graph on page 329. What does this graph compare? Which Middle Eastern country produced the most oil in 1980? The least? About how much more oil did Saudi Arabia produce than Iraq? About how much oil did Iran produce in comparison with Iraq?

Thinking It Through

1. How have the oil reserves of the Middle East affected the lives of the people in the region? How has economic development brought about social and political change?
2. Neither Islam nor the Ottoman Empire extended far inland from the Mediterranean coast of North Africa except along the Nile Valley. Why do you think this was so?

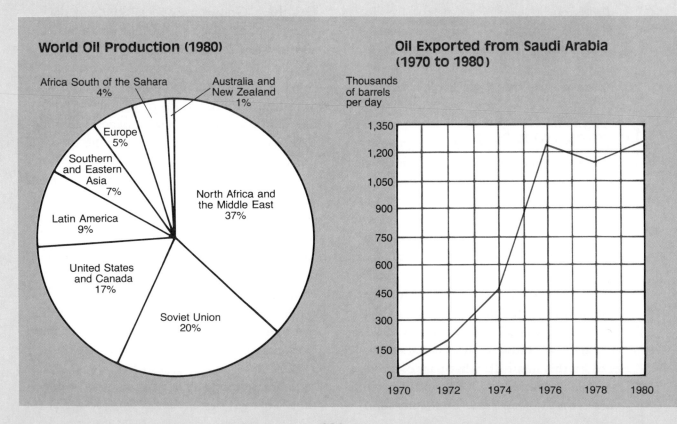

World Oil Production (1980)

Africa South of the Sahara 4%

Australia and New Zealand 1%

Europe 5%

Southern and Eastern Asia 7%

Latin America 9%

United States and Canada 17%

North Africa and the Middle East 37%

Soviet Union 20%

Oil Exported from Saudi Arabia (1970 to 1980)

Thousands of barrels per day

3. Why was control of the Straits important for hundreds of years? What other waterways allow ships to pass in and out of the Mediterranean? Do you think control of these waterways is as important today as it was in the past? Support your answer.

Projects

1. The Current Events Committee might like to find out about recent developments in the Middle East. Committee members could prepare a bulletin board display of current magazine and newspaper articles about Middle Eastern countries. Students might also include a map in the display.

2. Members of the Biography Committee might like to prepare reports on the following people: Mustafa Kemal, Golda Meir, Anwar el-Sadat, and Ibn Saud. How did these leaders influence events in their countries and in other countries?

3. The Arts and Sciences Committee might like to do some research on Islamic architecture. What are some distinctive features of mosques? What are some famous Islamic buildings and monuments? Where are they located? Remember that the Muslims in Spain and in parts of North Africa were known as Moors.

4. The Greek historian Herodotus, whom you read about in Unit 2, traveled throughout most of the known world as a young man in the fourth century B.C. The History Committee might like to find out about his travels in North Africa and the Middle East. Committee members could read interesting descriptions from Herodotus' *History* to the class.

5. Egyptians were not the only people to build pyramids. Early people in Mexico and Central America, including the Aztecs and Mayans, also built pyramids. The Arts and Sciences Committee could prepare a report on the pyramids of Egypt and those of Mexico and Central America.

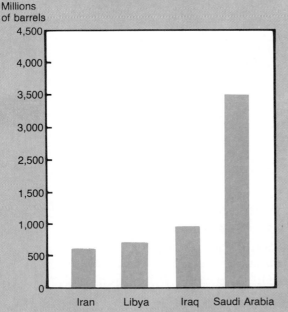

Leading Oil-Producing Countries in North Africa and the Middle East (1980)

Millions of barrels

8 Africa South of the Sahara

Unit Preview

The large part of Africa that extends south of the Sahara is part of a vast plateau lying mainly in the tropics. High mountains rise above the plateau in several places, and narrow lowlands stretch along most of the coast. Deserts, grasslands, and tropical rain forests are all found in this part of Africa.

Empires and kingdoms grew up along the southern edge of the Sahara very early. Other early kingdoms flourished farther south along the coasts of the Atlantic and Indian oceans. There were many African kingdoms when European explorers and traders reached the lands south of the Sahara in the late 1400s and early 1500s.

For centuries, the Europeans did not venture much beyond the coastal regions. Exploration of the interior did not begin until the late 1700s. By 1914, almost all of Africa had been taken over as colonies by European powers. Independence movements in Africa became stronger after World War II. Today almost all the countries of Africa are independent.

Most people living south of the Sahara are black Africans. There are also many people of European, Arab, and Asian background. Hundreds of African dialects are spoken, as well as several European languages. Although most African countries are becoming industrialized, agriculture remains the most important occupation of most Africans.

Things to Discover

If you look carefully at the picture, map, and time line, you can answer these questions.

1. The photograph shows zebras, hippopotamuses, and gnus at a watering hole near the lake in the highlighted area. What important line of latitude passes through this lake?
2. How long after the Kushites invaded Egypt did the Kingdom of Kush come to an end?
3. Ghana was the first West African country to become independent after Liberia. How long after Liberia became independent did Ghana become independent?

Words to Learn

You will meet these words and terms in this unit. As you read, you will learn what they mean and how to pronounce them. The Word List will help you.

Afrikaans	rift valley
anopheles	safari
chromium	shifting cultivation
developing country	sub-Saharan
escarpment	Swahili
famine	terra cotta
federation	tsetse fly
gorge	zebu
policy	

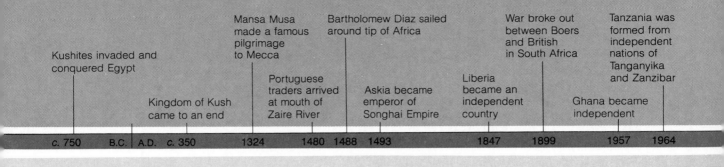

Kushites invaded and conquered Egypt

Mansa Musa made a famous pilgrimage to Mecca

Bartholomew Diaz sailed around tip of Africa

War broke out between Boers and British in South Africa

Tanzania was formed from independent nations of Tanganyika and Zanzibar

Kingdom of Kush came to an end

Portuguese traders arrived at mouth of Zaire River

Askia became emperor of Songhai Empire

Liberia became an independent country

Ghana became independent

| c. 750 | B.C. | A.D. | c. 350 | 1324 | 1480 | 1488 | 1493 | 1847 | 1899 | 1957 | 1964 |

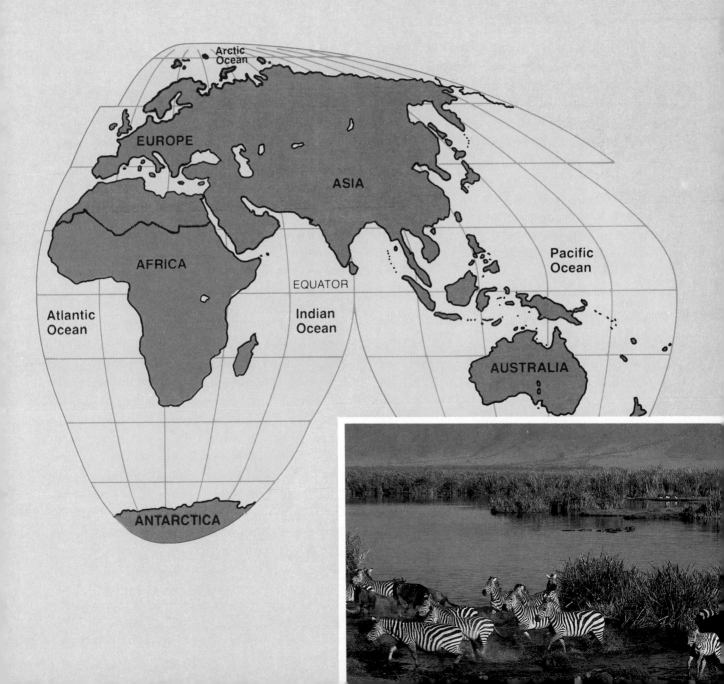

1

The Land and the People of Africa
South of the Sahara

Africa is the second-largest continent. It extends for about 5,000 miles (8,000 km) from the Mediterranean Sea in the north to the Cape of Good Hope in the south. From west to east, its greatest width is 4,500 miles (7,200 km). The vast Sahara separates North Africa from the rest of the continent. The region south of the Sahara makes up more than 80 percent of the continent. Nearly 388 million people, or 80 percent of Africa's total population, live there. The origins, cultures, and histories of the people who live south of the Sahara are generally unlike those of the people north of the Sahara.

The Land of Africa South of the Sahara

Africa is a roughly triangular-shaped continent with a bulge to the west in the northern part. The part of Africa south of the Sahara is known as *sub-Saharan* (sub'sə har'en) Africa. *Sub-Saharan* means "south of the Sahara." Most of sub-Saharan Africa is south of the Tropic of Cancer. The Atlantic Ocean lies to the west and the Indian Ocean to the east. The Gulf of Guinea (gin'ē) cuts deeply into the west coast near the equator. On the eastern coast, opposite the Gulf of Guinea, is the extension known as the Horn of Africa. North of the Horn, the Red Sea separates Africa from Saudi Arabia.

Sub-Saharan Africa is a region of deserts and highlands, of tropical forests and grasslands. Mighty rivers wind from the interior to the coasts, often descending in great waterfalls and rapids.

Landforms

Most of sub-Saharan Africa is a vast plateau that is generally lower in the north and west than it is in the south and east. Only along the bulge of western Africa does the land rise gently from the coast. Much of the plateau drops to the coast along an *escarpment* (es kärp'mənt). An escarpment is a steep slope or cliff. There are lowland areas along the coasts, but in most areas they are narrow. The coastline is straight, and there are few natural bays or harbors.

One of the remarkable things about the African plateau is the series of deep valleys that extend along its eastern edge in a north-south direction. Millions of years ago, the continent was broken by a series of faults, or cracks. Between the faults, parts of the plateau surface dropped down to form valleys. A long, steep-sided valley lying between two parallel faults in the earth's surface is called a *rift* (rift) *valley*. The Great Rift Valley is a series of valleys and depressions that extends 6,000 miles (9,600 km) from Mozambique (mō'zam bēk') to the Red Sea and on north as far as Syria. North of Lake Nyasa, the series of valleys forms an eastern and a western belt. The belts join again in Ethiopia. In 1969 American astronauts saw the Great Rift Valley from the moon.

Several areas of highlands and mountains rise above the surface of the plateau in sub-Saharan Africa. Eastern highlands extend from Ethiopia to Mozambique along both sides of the Great Rift Valley. Volcanic activity created most of the mountains there. Snow-capped Mount Kilimanjaro, the highest peak in Africa, is an extinct volcano, 19,340 feet (5,895 m) high. Not far from Kilimanjaro are the non-volcanic Ruwenzori (rōō wən zō′ rē) Mountains, sometimes known as the Mountains of the Moon. The highlands of the eastern half of the island of Madagascar, in the Indian Ocean, rise more than 9,000 feet (2,700 m).

Volcanic activity also produced the Tibesti Mountains in northern Chad; Cameroon Mountain, an extinct volcano rising 13,353 feet (4,070 m) along the Cameroon coast; and the mountainous Drakensberg region of south-west Africa.

Water Features

Sub-Saharan Africa has several important river systems that begin in highland areas. The longest river in the world, the Nile, flows north from east-central Africa to the Mediterranean. Most of the other major rivers, including the Niger (nī′ jər), the Zaire (zä ir′), the Senegal, the Gambia, and the Orange, empty into the Atlantic. The Zambezi (zam bē′ zē) and the Limpopo (lim pō′ pō′) flow eastward into the Indian Ocean. Waterfalls are common, especially along the escarpment. Victoria Falls, on the Zambezi River, is one of the most spectacular waterfalls in Africa. It is more than 350 feet (100 m) high.

Victoria Falls on the Zambezi River lies between Zambia and Zimbabwe. The explorer David Livingstone sighted the waterfall in 1855 and named it for England's Queen Victoria.

Most of Africa's large lakes have formed in the bottom of rift valleys in East Africa. Africa's largest lake, Lake Victoria, lies in a basin between two branches of the Great Rift Valley. Two large lakes in West Africa are Lake Volta and Lake Chad. Lake Volta was formed by a dam on the lower Volta River in Ghana. Lake Chad, on the border between Nigeria and Chad, was formerly a much larger lake. It has no outlet, and it varies greatly in size, depending on rainfall.

Climate and Vegetation

Africa has more tropical land than any other continent. More than 90 percent of sub-Saharan Africa lies north and south of the equator between the Tropic of Cancer and the Tropic of Capricorn. Only the extreme south of sub-Saharan Africa lies south of the Tropic of Capricorn in the temperate climate zone.

Except for the mountainous regions, all of Africa is warm or hot all year. There is not much difference between the summer and winter temperatures. There is often a great difference between daytime temperatures and nighttime temperatures, especially in the deserts. The variation can be as much as 60° F. (15° C). The highest temperatures of sub-Saharan Africa are not near the equator, but to the north in the Sahara and in the desert of Somalia along the Horn. The lowest temperatures are in the south and in the mountainous areas of the east. The mountains often have frost and snow.

Rainfall varies greatly throughout sub-Saharan Africa. Most of the land is covered

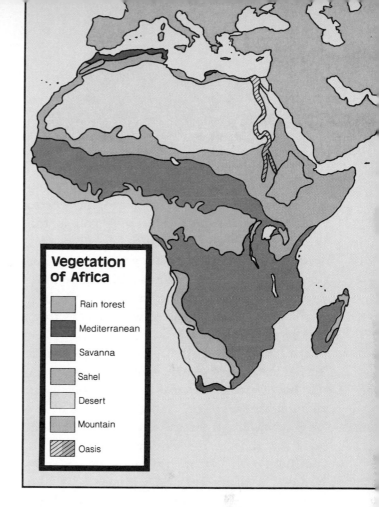

Vegetation of Africa

- Rain forest
- Mediterranean
- Savanna
- Sahel
- Desert
- Mountain
- Oasis

with grass. About one-fifth is desert, and less than one-fifth is forested.

The highest precipitation is in the equatorial belt of Africa, along the Guinea coast, and in the Zaire River valley. Throughout this region, more than 60 inches (152 cm) of rain falls each year. Parts of the highlands of Cameroon in West Africa receive as much as 300 inches (762 cm) of rain a year. In the equatorial belt, the rains fall throughout the year. In the rest of Africa, they are seasonal.

Some regions of Africa have almost no rain. The lowest rainfall occurs in the Sahara and Namib Desert. Along the coast of Namibia (nəmib'ēə), for example, rainfall averages less than one inch (2.5 cm) a year. In some parts of the deserts, years may pass without any rain.

The climate and vegetation zones of sub-Saharan Africa generally stretch across the continent in east-west bands. In the north, extending south from North Africa, is the Sahara. Almost no vegetation grows in this desert. The few plants found are those that can survive in high temperatures and require little water. The only parts of the desert that are fertile are the oases, where water comes from springs or wells.

Stretching across Africa south of the Sahara is a narrow belt of semiarid grassland known as the Sahel (sə hel′). *Sahel* is an Arabic word meaning "border" or "shore." The Sahel extends eastward from the coast of Mauritania (môr′ə tā′nē ə) to the Ethiopian highlands. It continues east of the highlands into Kenya. Winters in the Sahel are warm and dry. An average of 4 to 23 inches (10 to 58 cm) of rain falls during the hot summers, but there are often droughts, or dry periods. A few shrubs and low trees grow among the grassy patches.

The southern edge of the Sahel merges with the savanna, or savanna woodland. The savanna is a broad, grassy plain that receives between 20 and 60 inches (51 and 152 cm) of rain a year. The amount of rainfall increases from north to south in this zone, which extends across most of the widest part of Africa, from Senegal in the west to Ethiopia in the east.

The grassy plains of the savanna are broken here and there by trees. Two common trees are the baobab and acacia. The baobab has a thick trunk and short, stubby branches. It produces a fruit that can be eaten. The flat-topped acacia is shaped like an open umbrella. It is the source of gum arabic, which is used in making candy, medicines, and adhesives. Many of Africa's large wild animals live in the savanna.

South of the savanna is the rain forest. It extends east from the Guinea coast on both sides of the equator to the highlands of East Africa. In this forest, rain falls almost every day, and temperatures are high. Giant trees form a dense ceiling through which little sunlight reaches the ground. Most of the forest floor is open and clear. Monkeys, snakes, and birds live in the trees. Crocodiles and hippopotamuses swim in the rivers.

Some trees in the rain forest, such as mahogany, rubber, and oil palm, provide raw materials for the manufacture of such products as furniture, tires, and soap. The soil in the rain forest lacks humus. Many of the trees growing there are not suitable for lumber.

The climate and vegetation zones north of the rain forest are repeated in reverse order to the south. See the map on page 335. The savanna curves around the eastern end of the rain forest and spreads out south of it between the Atlantic and Indian oceans. South of the savanna lies an S-shaped region that is like the Sahel. It extends from the Atlantic coast of Angola almost to the Indian Ocean. Parts of this region in South Africa are large expanses of open grassland known as the veldt.

Deserts cover the southwest part of the southern part of Africa. The coastal region along the southern tip has a Mediterranean climate. North from there, along the east coast, a mixed forest grows in the humid subtropical climate.

The People of Sub-Saharan Africa

The people who live in sub-Saharan Africa make up about nine percent of the total world population. The majority of the people are black Africans. There are several million Africans of European descent and about one million of Asian ancestry. About 75 percent of the people live in rural areas.

Black Africans

The largest group of black Africans is the Bantu. The word *Bantu* also refers to a large number of related languages. *Swahili* (swä hē′lē) is a Bantu language used by many people in East Africa. Swahili includes many words borrowed from Arabic. Traders from the Arabian peninsula who came to the east coast of Africa learned Swahili and added their own words to it. There are more than 300 other Bantu languages.

The Khoisan (koi sän′) are another group of black Africans. The ancestors of the Khoisan were among the earliest inhabitants of Africa. Khoisan languages are spoken in southern Africa. Speakers of these languages make clicking sounds as they talk.

Neither the Bantu nor the Khoisan had a written language in early times. That did not mean, however, that they did not preserve their literature or their heritage. The names of ancestors and the deeds of great rulers were passed down from one generation to the next. The elders of a group told the children about their past. Accounts of past events, stories, and poems that are spoken rather than written are called oral tradition.

Traditional music remains very popular in Africa today. Here three musicians play drums in a procession to celebrate a wedding in Nigeria.

Some black Africans today have a way of life that is much like that of their ancestors. The Pygmies of Zaire, for example, are hunters and gatherers. The Masai (mä sī′) of Kenya, Uganda, and the Sudan are herders. The Yoruba of Nigeria have lived in cities for hundreds of years and farmed nearby areas.

Farming and raising livestock continue to be important occupations for Africans. Traditional ways of life are changing for most black Africans, however. The number of jobs in trade and manufacturing has increased with industrialization. Government service, education, construction, and transportation provide other job opportunities.

Africans of Asian and Arab Origin

People whose ancestors came from other parts of the world also live in sub-Saharan Africa.

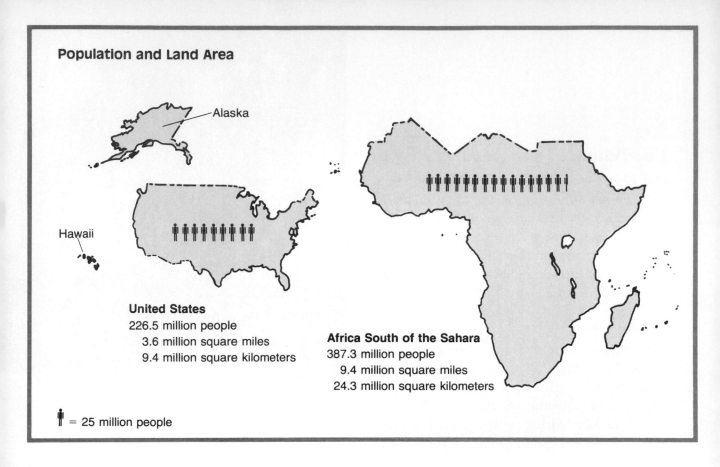

Population and Land Area

Alaska

Hawaii

United States
226.5 million people
  3.6 million square miles
  9.4 million square kilometers

Africa South of the Sahara
387.3 million people
  9.4 million square miles
24.3 million square kilometers

👤 = 25 million people

Soldiers and traders of ancient Egypt made their way south along the Nile River into the area now known as the Sudan. More than a thousand years ago, Berbers and Arabs from North Africa crossed the Sahara into West Africa. Other Arabs landed along the east coast. Today, many Muslims, or followers of Islam, in West Africa and East Africa speak and write Arabic.

Most Africans of Asian origin live in eastern and southeastern Africa and on the island of Madagascar. During the 1800s, many people from India, Malaysia, and what is now Pakistan came there to work on European-owned sugar plantations. Others came to help build the railroads in South Africa. Today, Africans of Asian origin live mainly in cities and towns.

Africans of European Origin

During the 1400s and 1500s, Portuguese traders set up forts and trading posts along the east and west coasts of Africa. Merchants and missionaries from other European countries also came to Africa during that time. European countries began to become involved in the slave trade. Plantations in North America and South America increased the demand for slaves.

During the late 1700s, Europeans began to explore the interior of Africa. During the 1800s, France, Great Britain, Belgium, Italy, Germany, Spain, and Portugal divided almost all of Africa into colonies. The map on page 343 shows the African lands claimed by European countries by 1914. European settlers farmed, raised livestock, and developed mines in their colonies. Until the colonies became independent, Europeans ran the government and controlled trade. Most Africans of European origin today are the descendants of early European settlers.

Because many languages are spoken in every African country, a European language is often used as the official language. English, French, and Portuguese are spoken by millions of Africans today.

Do You Know?

1. Name the land form that best describes Africa south of the Sahara.
2. In what climate zone is most of sub-Saharan Africa?
3. What is the name of the largest group of black Africans?

2

West Africa

The countries in the southern part of the western "bulge" of Africa are known as West Africa. Twelve West African countries border the Atlantic Ocean or the Gulf of Guinea. They are Mauritania, Senegal, the Gambia, Guinea-Bissau (gin′ē bis ou′), Guinea, Sierra Leone, Liberia, the Ivory Coast, Ghana (gä′nə), Togo, Benin, and Nigeria. Three of the countries, Mali, Burkina Faso (boor kē′nä fä′sō, formerly called Upper Volta), and Niger, are landlocked. Cape Verde is a group of islands.

The total population of West Africa is about 145 million. In general, the population density along the coast is higher than that of the interior. Nigeria has more people than any other African country. It has the highest population density of any West African country.

The people of West Africa speak many different languages. In Nigeria alone, more than 250 languages ard dialects are used. People in cities often have difficulty understanding one another. To make communication easier, most Africans speak at least two languages. They speak an African language or dialect and a European language. In West Africa, the European languages most often spoken are French and English. This is because most of the countries were once French or British colonies. See the map on page 343. French is the official language of Guinea, Mali, Niger, Senegal, and Togo. English is the official language of the Gambia, Liberia, Nigeria, and Sierra Leone. The people of Guinea-Bissau and Cape Verde speak Portuguese.

Geography

West Africa is mainly a plateau. Narrow bands of lowlands that border the coasts broaden in Senegal and Nigeria. Peaks rise as high as 5,000 feet (1,525 m) in the mountainous region of northern Niger known as the Äir (äir'). Many of West Africa's most important rivers rise in the slightly higher mountains along the Guinea-Liberia border. The Senegal and Gambia rivers flow west from there and empty into the Atlantic. The Niger, the third-longest river in Africa, begins by flowing northeastward, then turns sharply in a great bend to flow southeastward into the Gulf of Guinea. The Niger has built up an immense delta at its mouth.

All four of Africa's most important climate zones cross West Africa from east to west. From north to south, desert gives way to the Sahel, the Sahel to savanna, and the savanna to tropical rain forest.

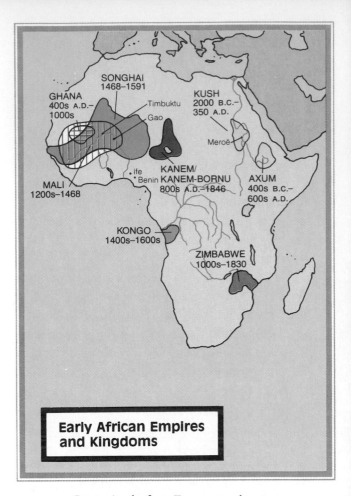

Early African Empires and Kingdoms

Centuries before Europeans began to colonize Africa, large kingdoms and empires existed south of the Sahara. The wealth of these early empires was based on trade.

History

West Africa has a long history. Hundreds of years ago, several powerful black African kingdoms existed there. See the map on this page. Beginning in the fifteenth century, European explorers began to come to Africa for gold, ivory, and slaves. Later, Europeans established colonies that lasted until the 1950s and 1960s, when the movement for independence began.

Early Empires and Kingdoms

About 400 A.D., the kingdom of Ghana began to develop in what is now eastern Mauritania and western Mali. This ancient kingdom has no connection with the modern country of Ghana. Ancient Ghana was a trading state. Gold, ivory, and slaves from the south were traded for salt and copper from the Sahara. The king claimed the right to all the gold nuggets that came from nearby mines. In that way, he could control the trade. He also taxed the goods that came into and went out of the kingdom. Ghana's greatest period of power began in the 700s and lasted about 300 years. In the eleventh century, a group of Muslim Berbers from the north captured Ghana's capital. The Berbers believed that they should convert people to Islam. The people of Ghana later won their capital back, but the empire never recovered. In the early 1200s, a leader of one of Ghana's provinces conquered the last king of Ghana.

The leader who conquered Ghana was called Sundiata (sōōn′dē ä′tə). The province he came from was called Mali. During Sundiata's rule, large territories came under Mali's power, and Mali became an empire. Mali took control of the Saharan trade and became very rich. The kingdom reached its peak of power and culture under Sundiata's grandson Mansa Musa (män′sə mōō′sə). In 1324, Mansa Musa made a famous pilgrimage to Mecca. His caravan included 500 slaves, each of whom carried 100 pounds (45 kg) of gold.

Timbuktu was the cultural center of Mali. Its famous library and other splendors drew travelers from all over the Muslim world.

Mansa Musa's successors were not able to control the Mali Empire. Sonni Ali (son′ē ä lē′), the king of one of Mali's provinces called Songhai (song′hī), captured Timbuktu in 1468. The Songhai Empire grew under Sonni Ali. A vast part of West Africa, stretching from the Atlantic to Lake Chad, was ruled from the capital of Gao (gou) on the Niger River. Songhai reached its greatest size and power under the emperor Askia, who began his rule in 1493. Askia set up a fair method of taxation, a centralized government, and a good system of communication throughout the kingdom. The empire came to an end in 1591, when a Moroccan army defeated the Songhai.

This ivory mask is an example of the famous sculpture of Benin. Benin flourished from the 1400s to the 1600s.

During the period when the great empires of Ghana, Mali, and Songhai rose and fell along the edge of the Sahara, other kingdoms and centers of culture grew up along the southern coast and in the forest lands of West Africa. The cities of Ife (ē′fā) and Benin, in what is now Nigeria, became important trading centers. Artists there produced sculpture that today is world famous. Some of the artists worked in bronze, ivory, and brass. Others worked in *terra cotta* (ter′ə kot′ə), a hard, brown-red earthenware. In Italian, *terra cotta* means "baked earth." Sculpture and pottery made of terra cotta are shaped from clay, then fired, or baked, to harden. Some of the oldest sculpture of black Africa includes terra cotta heads that are about 2,000 years old.

European Colonization

In the 1400s, Portuguese explorers sailed along the coast of West Africa while seeking a sea route around Africa to India. The Portuguese soon began trading European goods for African gold, ivory, and slaves. After 1600, Spanish, Dutch, French, and English traders joined the Portuguese in the slave trade. Millions of slaves were sent to the Americas.

The West African slave trade was at its height in the 1700s. In 1804, Denmark outlawed slave trade, and soon many other European nations followed Denmark's example. During the 1800s, the British navy used the region that is now Sierra Leone as a base for stopping the slave trade. Many Africans rescued from slave ships settled there.

Much of western and central Africa was looked on by Europeans as an unfavorable place to settle. The heat and humidity, along with such diseases as malaria, kept many Europeans from moving inland. Malaria is a disease of tropical Africa that is spread by the bite of the *anopheles* (ə nof'ə lēz') mosquito. People with malaria have chills and fever, and they often die. The anopheles mosquito thrives in the warm, moist climate of the African coast. For many years, almost all foreigners arriving in Africa came down with malaria. In the late 1800s, medicines were developed that lowered the death rate.

As the slave trade ended and malaria ceased to be a real danger, Europeans began to move into Africa and set up colonies. By 1914, all of Africa, except for Liberia and Ethiopia, was divided among European powers.

Colonial rule brought many changes to Africa. Some of the changes brought about by colonialism were helpful to the Africans. Cities and railroads were built. Schools and hospitals were founded. Other changes were harmful to the Africans. Africans who moved to the cities gave up their tribal way of life. The affairs of Africans were controlled by foreigners. Often the Europeans drew the boundaries of their colonies before they developed good maps of Africa. Tribes and clans were often separated. People who shared the same language, customs, and religions found themselves in different colonies. People of different tribes or clans, or groups unfriendly to one another often found themselves joined under one colonial power. The problems brought about by such situations continued after independence.

Independence

In 1822, a group of people from the United States bought a piece of land along the coast of West Africa. They called the land Liberia. There they helped freed slaves start a new life. In 1847, Liberia became an independent republic, the first in West Africa. Monrovia (mən rō'vē ə), its capital, was named after President Monroe of the United States.

With the exception of Liberia, no part of West Africa was independent before 1957. Some Africans had resisted colonization from the beginning. However, it was not until after World War II that the demands for independence became strong. Between 1957 and 1975, all the colonies in West Africa gained their independence.

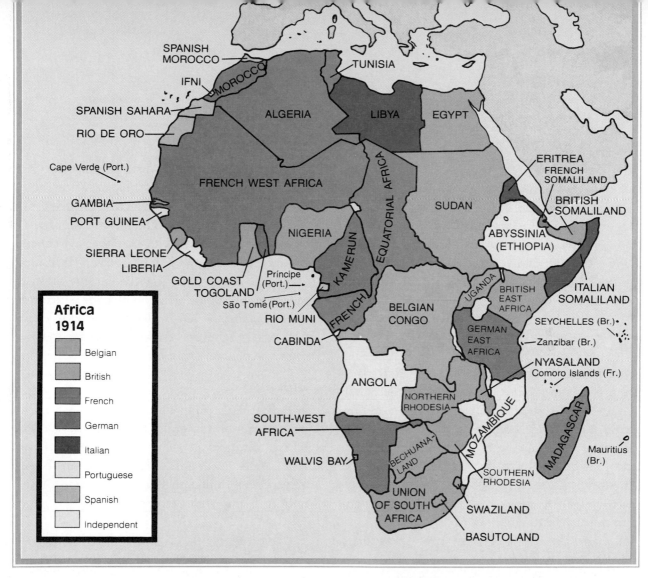

Africa
1914

Belgian

British

French

German

Italian

Portuguese

Spanish

Independent

SPANISH MOROCCO

IFNI

SPANISH SAHARA

RIO DE ORO

Cape Verde (Port.)

GAMBIA

PORT GUINEA

SIERRA LEONE

LIBERIA

GOLD COAST

TOGOLAND

Príncipe (Port.)

São Tomé (Port.)

RIO MUNI

CABINDA

MOROCCO

TUNISIA

ALGERIA

LIBYA

EGYPT

FRENCH WEST AFRICA

NIGERIA

KAMERUN

EQUATORIAL AFRICA

FRENCH

SUDAN

ERITREA

FRENCH SOMALILAND

BRITISH SOMALILAND

ABYSSINIA (ETHIOPIA)

ITALIAN SOMALILAND

UGANDA

BELGIAN CONGO

BRITISH EAST AFRICA

SEYCHELLES (Br.)

Zanzibar (Br.)

GERMAN EAST AFRICA

NYASALAND

Comoro Islands (Fr.)

ANGOLA

NORTHERN RHODESIA

MOZAMBIQUE

MADAGASCAR

Mauritius (Br.)

SOUTH-WEST AFRICA

WALVIS BAY

BECHUANA-LAND

SOUTHERN RHODESIA

UNION OF SOUTH AFRICA

SWAZILAND

BASUTOLAND

When World War I began, most of Africa was under European control. How many countries had African colonies?

The first West African colony to gain independence was the Gold Coast. In the 1950s, leaders there led strikes and demanded independence. In 1957, Great Britain granted independence, and the new nation decided to call itself Ghana.

When Nigeria became independent of Great Britain in 1960, the different groups in the country did not feel like one nation. The Muslims in the north, mostly Hausa (hou′sə), did not get along well with the Christian Yoruba in the southwest. In 1967, the Christian Ibo (ē′bō) tribe in the east tried to form a separate state. Their revolt developed into a civil war. After peace was restored in 1970, the country remained under military rule for nine years.

Guinea became independent of France in 1958. France granted independence to all of its other West African colonies in 1960. The new nations of Guinea, the Ivory Coast, Benin, Togo, Mauritania, Mali, Niger, Senegal, and Burkina Faso were created. Later in the 1960s, the Gambia and Sierra Leone gained independence from Britain. In the 1970s, Portugal granted independence to Cape Verde and Guinea-Bissau.

The Countries of the Sahel

Mauritania, Senegal, the Gambia, Mali, Burkina Faso, and Niger lie mainly in the Sahel. The Sahara covers much of northern Mauritania, Mali, and Niger. Few people live in the desert areas. Mauritania, Mali, and Niger, the three largest countries of West Africa, make up about 60 percent of West Africa. These three countries have only about 10 percent of the population, however.

Herding and Farming

Most of the people of the Sahel are nomads. They move with their herds from one pasture to another. Their movements are determined by the wet and dry seasons. Animals herded by the nomads of the Sahel include sheep, goats, camels, and a kind of cattle called *zebu* (zē′ byo͞o). The zebu is a domesticated animal related to the ox.

At the southern edge of the Sahel, people live in small farming villages. Peanuts, cotton, rice, and other grains are the main crops. Most agriculture consists of subsistence farming.

Water is an important part of life in the Sahel. A small amount can mean the difference between survival and disaster. In the late 1960s, a six-year drought began. Water holes dried up, and crops failed. The soil dried out and blew away. The drought caused a terrible *famine* (fa′min) in 1974. A famine is a great and widespread scarcity or lack of food. Thousands of people starved during the famine. Before the region could fully recover, drought began again in 1977. Today, several countries of the Sahel are working together to solve the problems of drought.

Mining

Although the Sahel countries of West Africa are not rich in minerals, some mining is done. There are deposits of iron in Mauritania, and rich uranium deposits are found in Niger. Phosphates mined in Senegal are one of that country's important exports.

Western dress and traditional African dress are seen side by side in the main square of Dakar, Senegal. Bright colors and bold patterns are typical of African clothing.

Cities of the Sahel

The largest city in the Sahel of West Africa is Dakar (də kär´), the capital of Senegal. Dakar is a modern city and busy port. Much of Dakar seems like a European city, but part of it is distinctly African. People shop in open markets where buyers and sellers bargain for goods. Bamako (bä mä kō´), the capital of Mali, is a trading and distribution center. It is connected by railroad with Dakar.

Cape Verde

Cape Verde is a small archipelago in the Atlantic, 385 miles (620 km) west of Senegal. These rugged volcanic islands have a climate like much of the Sahel. Average annual temperatures are between 68° and 77° F. (20° to 25° C). The low rainfall makes most of the land too dry to farm. Sandstorms often blow in from the Sahara. Cape Verde suffered from the drought that affected most of West Africa between 1968 and 1974.

Countries of the Savanna and the Rain Forest

Nine countries are located along the southwestern and southern coast of West Africa. They are Guinea-Bissau, Guinea, Sierra Leone, Liberia, the Ivory Coast, Ghana, Togo, Benin, and Nigeria. The northern borders of these countries are generally in the savanna, and the southern borders in the rain forest. The extreme northern part of Nigeria lies in the desert. The highest population density in Africa is along the coast of the Gulf of Guinea.

Farming and Herding

In the warm, moist climate of the coast, a disease-carrying insect has affected the use of the land. The *tsetse* (tset´sē) *fly* bites cattle and wild animals, causing a disease that often results in death. The tsetse fly also bites humans and transmits sleeping sickness. Because of the tsetse fly, cattle cannot be raised in most parts of the savanna and rain forest.

More than 60 percent of the people in the countries along the Gulf of Guinea are subsistence farmers. Their chief crops are millet, a root called manioc, and a special rice known as dry, or hill, rice. Food production in the region has not grown at the same rate as the population. Scientists are working to increase the production of food from the available land.

Most farmland in the area belongs to the community, not to individuals. Every member of a community has the right to farm a plot of land. The land, however, belongs to the tribe.

Farmers in the region have begun to raise more crops for export. Cotton, palm oil, and peanuts are cash crops. Ghana is the world's third-largest producer of cacao. The Ivory Coast is the largest producer of coffee.

Great changes have come to the farming villages of West Africa in recent times. Many people have left their home villages to work in mines and factories and to join highway and railroad construction crews. They earn money, and with it they buy many goods. When they return to their villages, they bring news of a different world. The presents they bring back make other villagers want to earn money to buy things. The stories they tell make the

An outdoor market operates in the heart of Abidjan, Ivory Coast. Abidjan is one of the busiest seaports in West Africa.

villagers eager to travel and to see the booming cities. The ancient pattern of village life has changed. Only a few very remote villages remain as they have been for centuries, untouched by modern ways of living.

Mining and Manufacturing

Nigeria is one of the most important oil-producing countries in the world. Oil amounts to 90 percent of the country's exports. Nigeria also produces coal, iron ore, limestone, and tin. Income from exports is used to expand Nigeria's universities and to build elementary schools. The income is also used to develop new industries. Nigeria has an oil refinery and a rubber-processing plant.

Liberia is another producer of iron ore, as are Guinea and Sierra Leone. Guinea also has more than one-third of the world's reserves of bauxite and manganese ore. Togo exports phosphates. Ghana, Sierra Leone, and Guinea mine and export diamonds. Ghana is a leading gold-mining country.

Since the early 1960s, the Ivory Coast has become a center of light industry. Factories there process agricultural products and lumber, and manufacture electrical equipment and textiles. The Ivory Coast is also a shipbuilding center.

Because of heavy rains and many rivers, the West African countries on the Gulf of Guinea may be able to develop industries run on hydroelectric power. A hydroelectric plant has been built by Ghana on the Volta River.

Cities of the Savanna and the Rain Forest

Many of the coastal cities of West Africa began as small market towns. They grew during colonial times, when many of them were administrative centers. Some of them became capitals of the new independent nations. The rapid growth of these cities today is due to migration from the inland villages and to high birth rates and low death rates.

Lagos, the capital and largest city in Nigeria, has a population of more than four million. From this port are shipped the products of Nigeria's farms and forests—animal hides and skins, cacao, palm oil, timber, and peanuts. Great tankers carry Nigerian oil to all parts of the world. Lagos is also the main manufacturing city in Nigeria. Workers there assemble motors and radios, and work in steel- and food-processing plants.

Ibadan (ē bäd'ən) is a centuries-old city of Nigeria not far inland from Lagos. It was founded by the Yoruba people and is one of the largest non-European cities in Africa. Its colorful markets attract people from all over the region, who come to buy and sell food, clothing, and handicrafts.

In the interior of Nigeria, in the north, is the ancient walled city of Kano (kän'ō'). Kano grew up at a crossroads where trade routes met. It was described by Arab geographers in the twelfth century. Today it is a religious center for Nigerian Muslims.

Abidjan (ab'i jän') is one of the busiest ports of West Africa. This city, the capital of the Ivory Coast, lies along a lagoon connected with the Gulf of Guinea by a canal. Abidjan's factories produce automobile parts and soap, and process cacao and coffee beans.

Accra (ə krä'), the capital of Ghana, is the country's largest city and main port. Like other cities in Africa, Accra displays many contrasts. Houses with mud walls and tin roofs are built in the shadows of tall modern buildings.

Do You Know?

1. Name two early kingdoms or empires of West Africa.
2. Why did Europeans at first look on West Africa as an unsuitable place to settle?
3. What was the first independent country in West Africa?
4. In what vegetation zone does the southern coast of West Africa lie?

3
Central Africa

Central Africa extends from the southern border of Libya in the north to the northern borders of Angola and Zambia in the south. It includes two landlocked countries, Chad and the Central African Republic; five countries that border the Atlantic, Cameroon, Equatorial Guinea, the Congo, Gabon, and Zaire; and the island country of São Tomé (sou' tə mä') and Príncipe (prēn'si pə). In size, the countries range from the second-smallest in Africa, São Tomé and Príncipe, to the second-largest, Zaire. Almost 48 million people live in this part of Africa.

Geography

Central Africa is a plateau with two large basins, or low-lying areas. One is in the north, centered on Lake Chad. The area surrounding the lake is a great swamp. Several rivers flow

Fishermen on the Zaire River wait patiently at dusk for their prey to appear.

into Lake Chad, but none flows out. The lake is very shallow. Evaporation of its water is causing the lake to shrink in size.

In the southern part of central Africa is the basin of the Zaire River. The Zaire and its tributaries drain a very large part of central Africa. The Zaire River rises in southeastern Zaire, flows first north, then turns in a broad loop toward the southwest. The Zaire River is 2,700 miles (4,370 km) long. It is the second-longest river in Africa. Much of the Zaire is navigable. Falls and rapids in several places make it necessary to transfer river traffic overland for short distances.

Along the coast of central Africa, there is a narrow strip of lowland. Mountains as high as 8,000 feet (2,400 m) rise near the coast in Cameroon. The Tibesti (təbes′tē) Mountains rise to heights of 11,000 feet (3,400 m) in the desert of northern Chad.

The equator crosses central Africa, and for this reason the region is sometimes called Equatorial Africa. The rain forest extends north and south of the equator to cover large parts of Cameroon, Equatorial Guinea, São Tomé and Príncipe, Gabon, the Congo, and Zaire. Much of southern Zaire lies south of the rain forest in the savanna. To the north of the rain forest, savannas cover most of the Central African Republic, northern Cameroon, northern Zaire, and southern Chad. A narrow part of central Chad lies in the Sahel, and the northern half of the country is desert.

History

Long ago, people from other parts of Africa moved into the rain forests of central Africa. They lived much as their ancestors had. They hunted with bows and arrows and trapped animals in snares. Using tools of iron, they cleared away vines and bushes, and cut down trees so that they could farm.

Early Kingdoms

In the 1400s, several kingdoms developed along the southern edge of the rain forest in central Africa. One of the largest was that of the Kongo. The king of the Kongo, called the Mani-Kongo, controlled the trade between the Kongo and kingdoms of the interior. Slave trade beginning in the 1500s weakened the Kongo, and by the middle of the 1600s, the kingdom had broken apart.

At Kanem, east of Lake Chad, a great empire began to grow up about 800 A.D. The

348

wealth of Kanem depended on trade. Salt, horses, and metals from the north were traded at Kanem for ivory and kola nuts from the south. The king of Kanem collected taxes from the traders. In the 1400s, the king moved his court from Kanem to Bornu, and the empire became known as Kanem-Bornu. After the fall of the Songhai Empire in 1591, Kanem-Bornu became one of the strongest and largest empires south of the Sahara. A king who ruled Kanem-Bornu about 1600 built up a cavalry. The riders were dressed like medieval knights. Both riders and horses wore chain mail and padded coverings.

In the 1700s and 1800s, Kanem-Bornu declined. One reason may have been that overland trade routes became less important as coastal trade grew. The last king of Kanem-Bornu was killed in 1846 in a religious war.

The cavalry of Kanem-Bornu was famous far beyond the borders of the kingdom.

European Colonization

In 1482, Portuguese traders and missionaries arrived at the mouth of the Zaire River. The Portuguese and the Africans were friendly at first, and some of the Africans were converted to Christianity.

In the early 1500s, the Portuguese began to export slaves from central Africa. Other European countries soon joined in the trade. They bought many of the slaves from the leaders of the kingdom of Kongo.

In the 1870s, an Englishman named Henry Stanley crossed the region that is now Zaire from east to west. See the map on page 361. Stanley made treaties with the Africans that helped King Leopold of Belgium claim the land for himself in 1885. In 1908, the Belgian government took control of the region. It became known as the Belgian Congo. The Belgians built river ports, railroads, schools, and hospitals, and opened mines in the southeast.

Most of what is now Chad, the Central African Republic, Gabon, and the Congo was part of French Equatorial Africa in colonial times. Cameroon was a German colony until after World War I, when the French and the British took control of it. What is now Equatorial Guinea was once controlled by Spain. São Tomé and Príncipe were Portuguese colonies.

Independence

In 1960, all but two of the eight central African countries became independent. Eight years later, negotiations with Spain led to independence for Equatorial Guinea. São Tomé and Príncipe became independent in 1975.

Independence did not solve all the problems of central Africa. There have been many civil wars, and several governments have been overthrown by coups.

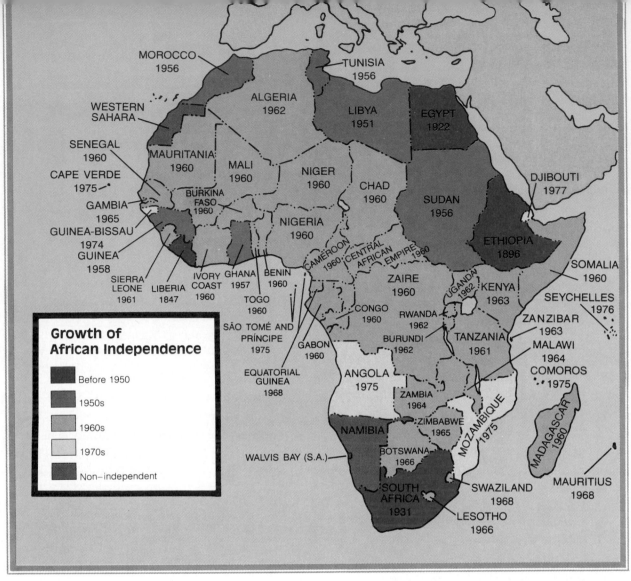

Growth of African Independence

MOROCCO 1956
TUNISIA 1956
WESTERN SAHARA
ALGERIA 1962
LIBYA 1951
EGYPT 1922
SENEGAL 1960
MAURITANIA 1960
MALI 1960
NIGER 1960
CHAD 1960
SUDAN 1956
DJIBOUTI 1977
CAPE VERDE 1975
BURKINA FASO 1960
GAMBIA 1965
NIGERIA 1960
ETHIOPIA 1896
GUINEA-BISSAU 1974
GUINEA 1958
CAMEROON 1960
CENTRAL AFRICAN EMPIRE 1960
SOMALIA 1960
SIERRA LEONE 1961
LIBERIA 1847
IVORY COAST 1960
GHANA 1957
BENIN 1960
ZAIRE 1960
UGANDA 1962
KENYA 1963
SEYCHELLES 1976
TOGO 1960
CONGO 1960
RWANDA 1962
ZANZIBAR 1963
SÃO TOMÉ AND PRÍNCIPE 1975
GABON 1960
BURUNDI 1962
TANZANIA 1961
MALAWI 1964
EQUATORIAL GUINEA 1968
ANGOLA 1975
COMOROS 1975
ZAMBIA 1964
MOZAMBIQUE 1975
NAMIBIA
ZIMBABWE 1965
MADAGASCAR 1960
WALVIS BAY (S.A.)
BOTSWANA 1966
SWAZILAND 1968
MAURITIUS 1968
SOUTH AFRICA 1931
LESOTHO 1966

Legend:
- Before 1950
- 1950s
- 1960s
- 1970s
- Non-independent

Most countries of Africa south of the Sahara gained independence after World War II ended in 1945. Which became independent first? Which most recently?

Chad

Chad, the northernmost country of central Africa, takes its name from the lake on its western border. It is a sparsely populated nation. Most of the people in Chad are farmers or nomadic herders.

Most of the northern half of Chad is covered by the dry sands of the Sahara. The people who live there are mainly Muslim nomads. They raise sheep, cattle, camels, and horses. The young men herd the animals from pasture to pasture. Other members of the family stay in permanent villages near oases.

In the savannas of the south, most of the people farm. They raise food for themselves and grow peanuts and cotton as cash crops. Cotton is the leading export. Fish are exported to neighboring countries.

Cameroon and the Central African Republic

Cameroon is a small country that borders the Gulf of Guinea. Except for São Tomé and Príncipe, it is the most densely populated country of central Africa. Most of its eight and a half million people are farmers. On the northern plateau, cattle and cotton are raised. Coffee, cacao, and other tropical crops are cultivated in the south.

Most of the people of Cameroon live in the southern third of the country. The two largest cities, Douala (dōō äl′ə) and Yaoundé (youn dā′), are there. Douala is an important port. A nearby aluminum plant processes bauxite from West Africa. Cameroon has good railroads built by the Germans during colonial times. A recently built highway connects different parts of the country.

Just east of Cameroon lies the Central African Republic. The Central African Republic is slightly larger than Cameroon. It has only about one-fourth as many people. Nearly all of the people live in rural areas, but only a small percent of the land is cultivated. The main way of making a living is subsistence agriculture. Some cotton and coffee are grown for export. Diamonds are the chief mineral export.

São Tomé and Príncipe and Equatorial Guinea

São Tomé and Príncipe are the two principal islands of a small country of the same name that lies about 125 miles (200 km) east of Gabon in the Gulf of Guinea. The tiny volcanic islands have an area about the size of New York City and a population of 90,000. Cacao and copra are grown on plantations that have been carved out of the jungle.

Equatorial Guinea is a country made up of a small territory on the coast and several islands in the Gulf of Guinea. The coastal part of Equatorial Guinea lies south of Cameroon and borders Gabon to the south and east. The population density is slightly lower than that of Cameroon.

Equatorial Guinea is the only area south of the Sahara that was colonized by Spain. Spanish, as well as several other languages, is spoken there. Coffee, cacao, and timber are the chief products of this hot, humid country.

The Congo and Gabon

Most of the area that is now the Congo and Gabon was once part of French Equatorial Africa. French is spoken throughout both countries. Gabon is on the coast south of Cameroon, and the Congo lies east and south of Gabon. The Congo has a short stretch of coast, about 100 miles (160 km), on the Atlantic. The Zaire River forms part of the border between the Congo and Zaire. The equator passes through both Gabon and the Congo.

Most people in the Congo live by subsistence farming. Cash crops are coffee, peanuts, sugarcane, and tobacco. Lumber is the chief export. Some crude oil is exported.

The Congo is an important transportation center. There is a railroad connecting the city of Pointe-Noire (pwant nə wär′), a very busy

351

port on the coast, with Brazzaville, 320 miles (515 km) inland on the Zaire River. Above Brazzaville, the Zaire-Ubangi river system provides transportation for 700 miles (1,100 km). Goods going to and coming from Chad and the Central African Republic move over the river system and the railroad.

Gabon is somewhat smaller than the Congo, but it has about one-third as many people. Most people are farmers who live in small villages along the coast or near rivers. The country has rich deposits of manganese, uranium, and oil. To help develop rich iron ore reserves in the northeast, the government began construction of a 350-mile (560 km) railroad in 1969. In addition to minerals, Gabon exports wood and wood products.

Gabon's capital is the coastal city of Libreville (lē′brə vil′), meaning "place of liberation." It was named by slaves freed from a slave ship captured by the French navy in 1849. Not far from Libreville is the inland town of Lambaréné (läm bə rā′nē), where the French doctor and missionary Albert Schweitzer built a famous hospital.

Zaire

Zaire is a very large country in central Africa that lies across the equator. It has only about 25 miles (40 km) of coastline along the Atlantic. The country has a population of about 30 million. Kinshasa is the capital and largest city. Many languages, mostly Bantu dialects, are spoken throughout the country. The official language is French, which is widely used.

Farming

In Zaire, as in many parts of Africa, a kind of agriculture called "slash and burn" is practiced. The ground is prepared by setting fire to it to clear away the bushes, shrubs, and grass. Seeds are planted, and the crops that grow are enriched by the ashes in the soil. After a few years, the soil wears out, and the farmers move to another place. The practice of moving farming to new land once the soil becomes infertile is called *shifting cultivation* (shif′ting kul′tə vā′shən). Shifting cultivation does not make the best use of the land.

Farmers grow corn, rice, and cassava for their own use. Cash crops include cotton, coffee, tea, and sugarcane.

Mining

Zaire has unusually rich natural resources. Copper is the most important mineral. Zaire is the world's largest producer of industrial diamonds. Cobalt, gold, manganese, and tin are also mined, and some oil is produced.

Do You Know?

1. What river system drains a large part of central Africa?
2. What country of central Africa is partly in the Sahara?
3. Where did the kingdom of Kanem grow up? When?
4. What country of central Africa is especially rich in mineral resources?

Before You Go On

Using New Words

famine	rift valley
Swahili	escarpment
zebu	terra cotta
anopheles	shifting cultivation
tsetse fly	sub-Saharan

Number a paper from 1 through 10. After each number write the word or term from the above list that matches the definition.

1. A long, steep-sided valley lying between two parallel faults
2. An insect that causes diseases in animals and humans
3. The practice of moving farming to new land once the soil becomes infertile
4. A great and widespread scarcity or lack of food
5. South of the Sahara
6. A Bantu language used by many people in East Africa
7. A hard, brown-red earthenware
8. A mosquito that transmits malaria
9. A steep slope or cliff
10. A domesticated animal related to the ox

Finding the Facts

1. How does Africa rank in size among the continents? What percent of Africa belongs to sub-Saharan Africa?
2. What is the Horn of Africa?
3. What is the highest mountain in Africa? How high is it?
4. What is the longest river in the world? Into what body of water does it empty?
5. What is the Sahel? What does the word *Sahel* mean?
6. What is oral tradition?
7. When did Europeans begin to explore the interior of Africa? When did they gain control over most of the continent?
8. Who was Mansa Musa?
9. By what date had all of West Africa become independent?
10. What country of West Africa is a major producer of oil?
11. What country has more than one-third of the world's reserves of bauxite and manganese?
12. What city is a religious center for the Muslims of Nigeria?
13. Who was Henry Stanley and what did he do?
14. What is the leading export of Chad?
15. Describe "slash and burn" agriculture.

4
East Africa

East Africa is the part of Africa that stretches along the east coast of the continent from the southern border of Egypt in the north to the northern border of Mozambique in the south. Somalia, on the Horn of Africa, borders both the Gulf of Aden and the Indian Ocean. Djibouti (jəbō͞ot′ē) also borders the Gulf of Aden. The Sudan and Ethiopia have coasts on the Red Sea. South of Somalia, Kenya and Tanzania (tan′zənē′ə) lie along the Indian Ocean. East Africa includes three landlocked countries, Uganda (yō͞ogan′də), Burundi (bərun′dē) and Rwanda (rō͞oän′də), and the island nation of the Seychelles (sāshelz′). More than 114 million people live in the ten countries of East Africa.

East Africa has deserts, highland forests, snow-covered peaks, and vast grasslands. The savannas of East Africa are the home of great herds of wild animals—antelope, deer, elephants, lions, leopards, and giraffes roam about freely in large game reserves. The game reserves of Kenya are famous throughout the world. An expedition to a game reserve to see the wildlife is often called a *safari* (səfär′ē). During colonial times, a safari referred to a hunting expedition in Africa.

The Sudan

The Sudan is the largest country in Africa. It extends more than 1,200 miles (1,900 km) from north to south, and in places stretches more than 1,000 miles (1,600 km) from east to west. The population is more than 18 million. Most people live in the southern part of the country or along the Nile and its tributaries.

Geography

The desert, the Sahel, and the savanna stretch across the Sudan in broad bands from east to west. See the map on page 335. Highlands extend along the southeast border, and in the southwest there is a small area covered by tropical forest. The northern part of the country is very dry, but parts of the south receive 20 to 40 inches (50 to 100 cm) of rain a year.

The two main branches of the Nile, the White Nile and the Blue Nile, rise in highlands to the south and east of the Sudan. Near Khartoum (kärtō͞om′), the two branches join and continue north toward Egypt. In the southern part of the Sudan, the White Nile breaks up into hundreds of channels and spreads out to form a marsh called the Sudd. The river moves very slowly through this wet lowland because it is clogged by plants.

History

As early as 2000 B.C., a kingdom called Kush developed along the Nile in what is now the Sudan. Kush was ruled by Egypt for many years, but about 750 B.C., the Kushites invaded Egypt, and the kings of Kush made themselves pharaohs of Egypt. About one hundred years later, the Kushites were driven back into their own land. They established their capital at Meroë (mer′ə wē′), not far from where Khartoum is today. The kingdom of Kush continued to flourish until about 350 A.D. The people learned to make tools and weapons from iron. They traded iron goods, as well as gold, ivory, and slaves, with Egypt, Arabia, and India. The Kushites invented a system of writing and developed styles of art and architecture. Ruins of their palaces and pyramids at Meroë can be seen today.

Many people in the area that is now the Sudan were converted to Christianity in the sixth century A.D. In the fourteenth century, much of the area was broken up into small states. Many of those states were Muslim. In the 1800s, the region was conquered by Egypt, and later it was ruled jointly by Egypt and Britain as part of the Anglo-Egyptian Sudan. The Sudan became independent in 1956.

Farming and Herding

Most of the Sudanese are herders whose cattle, sheep, goats, and camels feed on the grasslands in the southern part of the country. In recent years, the land suitable for herding has become smaller as water holes have dried up.

Acacia trees grow in some parts of southern Sudan. The trees can be tapped to yield gum arabic. The Sudan is the world's greatest producer of gum arabic.

The region between the White Nile and the Blue Nile is an important cotton-producing region. A dam built on the Blue Nile in 1900 furnishes water to irrigate this important agricultural region. Many of the farms are run as

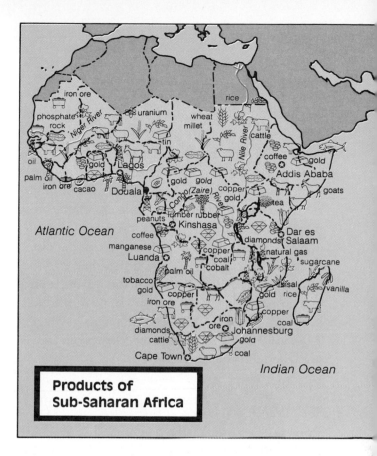

Products of Sub-Saharan Africa

cooperatives. The farmers provide the seeds and labor, and the government furnishes money and machines. Both the farmers and the government share in the profits. Cotton, peanuts, wheat, and sugarcane are grown.

Manufacturing

The irrigation system along the Nile in the Sudan is one of the most successful irrigation systems in Africa. However, crop and livestock production could be expanded even more in the Sudan. The country's economic growth has been slow because of the arid climate and lack of many resources. The Sudan is an example of a *developing* (di vel′ə ping) *country*. A developing country is one that is starting to develop industrially.

The government of the Sudan hopes to use the resources of the country to improve living conditions for its people. Today, there are a few factories that manufacture shoes, cement, soap, and textiles. The government is building more textile factories that will use the cotton raised in the country.

Transportation is important to the development of a country. The Sudan has a good network of roads throughout the north. It also has about 2,800 miles (4,510 km) of railroads and 3,000 miles (4,800 km) of navigable rivers. The government is now constructing canals and roads in the Sudd.

Ethiopia

Ethiopia lies east of the Sudan and has a coast on the Red Sea. It is about half as large as the Sudan, but it has more than one and a half times as many people.

Geography

Ethiopia is a highland country. The average elevation of the land is about one mile (1.6 km) above sea level. The mountainous parts of the country receive great amounts of rain. A desert extends along the coast of the Red Sea in the northeast, and semiarid grasslands cover much of the eastern part of the country.

The Blue Nile rises in the Ethiopian highlands and flows west through a *gorge* (gôrj), or deep, steep-sided valley, that is 700 miles (1,120 km) long and 7,000 feet (2,135 m) deep. The Great Rift Valley runs through Ethiopia from Lake Rudolf in the southwest to the Red Sea in the northeast. Lakes fill many of the depressions.

History

Beginning in the fourth century B.C., a powerful kingdom called Axum (äk'sōōm') grew up in East Africa. The present country of Ethiopia traces its roots to that kingdom. Axum grew rich and powerful through trade. Gold, ivory, and iron products from Kush and other parts of Africa were traded for goods from Egypt, Greece, Rome, and India. Products from Axum, including gum arabic and spices, were also traded.

In the early 300s A.D., the king of Axum was converted to Christianity, and Axum became one of the first Christian nations in the world. The same king defeated Meroe, which may have helped bring an end to the kingdom of Kush. Axum declined after the late 500s A.D., when the Persians conquered Arabia and made trading difficult. During the 600s A.D., the Muslim religion spread throughout much of Arabia and North Africa. For hundreds of years, the Muslims fought against Axum, but the mountains made conquest difficult. Axum lost its power, but its culture survived.

The modern country of Ethiopia was established by Emperor Menelik II in 1896. The emperor defeated an invasion by the Italians and added new territory to Ethiopia. In 1917, a railroad was completed between the capital, Addis Ababa (ad'əs ab'əbə), and the port of Djibouti on the Red Sea. The railroad helped to end Ethiopia's long isolation from the rest of the world. Today, Addis Ababa is the largest city in East Africa.

By the 1930s, Ethiopia was one of the few parts of Africa not under European control. In

1935, the Italians attacked Ethiopia and they defeated the armies of Emperor Haile Selassie (hī′lē sə las′ē). When the Italians in turn were defeated in World War II, they had to leave Ethiopia. Haile Selassie returned to power. The emperor tried to develop the country and bring about reforms. He was not able to solve all the country's problems, however. Much of Ethiopia's best land was owned by the church and the emperor's family. Many Ethiopians were short of food. A famine in 1973 made conditions worse. In 1974, Haile Selassie was overthrown by a coup. A military government took over and nationalized the rural land.

Farming and Herding

Most of the farming in Ethiopia is done on land between elevations of 6,000 and 8,000 feet (1,830 and 2,500 m). At this altitude, the temperatures are moderate and there is abundant rain. Coffee, the principal export crop, is grown here, along with wheat, corn, cotton, tobacco, grapes, olives, and sugarcane.

In the hot and arid lands below 6,000 feet (1,830 m), the people are mainly nomadic herders of sheep, goats, and camels. Livestock also grazes on the grasslands higher than 8,000 feet (2,500 m). Hardy grains such as wheat are grown there as well.

Mining and Manufacturing

The chief mineral mined in Ethiopia is gold. Factories in Addis Ababa include sugar refineries, cement plants, and iron manufacturing plants. Ethiopia also has some oil refineries and food-processing factories.

Djibouti and Somalia

Djibouti and Somalia share the Horn of Africa with Ethiopia. Djibouti is mostly a stony desert, but it has a few scattered plateaus and highlands. Most of Somalia is hot and dry, and there are deserts along parts of the coastal plain. The northern portion of the country is mountainous.

Djibouti

Djibouti was a French colony known as French Somaliland for many years. During the time that much of Africa was gaining independence, the colony voted twice to remain under French rule. When the country did become independent in 1977, it took the name of its chief port city on the Red Sea.

Most of Djibouti's income is from foreign trade. Most of the goods that move in and out of Ethiopia pass through the port of Djibouti, which is also the terminal of the Addis Ababa-Djibouti railroad.

Somalia

Somalia was formed of territory formerly under the control of Britain and Italy. Both Britain and Italy gave independence to their sections in 1960 so that the two parts could become one nation.

Most people of Somalia, called Somalis, are nomadic herders. Subsistence crops are grown along the rivers that flow into the Indian Ocean. Somalia exports some livestock and bananas. Fish, especially tuna, are also exported. The country has timber and uranium resources.

Living and Working in Sub-Saharan Africa

Farming and herding are the chief occupations in Africa. About 75 percent of all Africans live in rural areas, and agricultural products contribute more to Africa's GNP than any other single *economic* activity. Workers *cultivate* a field in Nigeria, where peanuts, corn, millet, and yams are important crops. Africa supplies the world with most of its diamonds.

Desert dwellers share their meal under the hot sun of the Sahara. Workers in a Nigerian textile factory fold lengths of finished cloth. The number of workers in industrial jobs is increasing. Many people in Africa work at traditional handicrafts. A man in Uganda begins to weave a basket. ■

359

Kenya, Tanzania, and Uganda

At one time, Kenya, Tanzania, and Uganda were part of the region known as British East Africa. English is spoken in all three countries, and it is an official language in Uganda and Tanzania. Swahili is an official language in both Kenya and Tanzania. Many other Bantu languages are spoken throughout the region. Most of the 49 million people in the three countries are farmers and herders.

Geography

Most of the land in Kenya, Tanzania, and Uganda is a high plateau. A low plain lies along the coast of Kenya and Tanzania. The Great Rift Valley extends through this region from the southern border of Tanzania to the northern borders of Kenya and Uganda. The Rift Valley is split into two sections. One section follows the western border of Tanzania and Uganda, where a series of lakes fills many of the depressions. Lake Nyasa, Lake Tanganyika (tan′gən yē′kə), Lake Kiva, Lake Edward, and Lake Albert are all lakes of this kind. The eastern part of the Great Rift Valley extends from Lake Rudolf to Lake Nyasa east of Lake Victoria. Highlands, steep cliffs, fault-block mountains, and volcanoes are found along the Great Rift Valley. Many of the mountains rise thousands of feet above the plateau. Many have elevations of more than 15,000 feet (4,575 m). Mount Kilimanjaro, in Tanzania, and Mount Kenya, in central Kenya, are two of the most famous volcanic peaks.

Kenya, Tanzania, and Uganda all border on Lake Victoria, the source of the Nile River. Water from Lake Victoria flows into Lake Albert and continues northward to become the White Nile.

Much of Kenya and Tanzania is hot, dry land that is Sahel or savanna. Even though Uganda is located on the equator, its climate is not hot because much of the land lies from 3,000 to 6,000 feet (900 to 1,825 m) above sea level. The mountainous parts of Kenya and Tanzania also enjoy a cool climate with plenty of rainfall.

History

The coastal regions of what are now Kenya and Tanzania were colonized and controlled by Arab traders as early as the 700s A.D. The Portuguese explored this area in the 1500s and had some influence on the trade until the 1600s. They established a trading post on the island of Zanzibar (zan′zə bär′), but they were driven out by Arabs in 1698.

In the middle of the 1800s, two Englishmen, John Speke and Richard Burton, explored parts of East Africa looking for the source of the Nile. A Scottish explorer and missionary, David Livingstone, joined the search in 1866. He was believed lost until Henry Stanley found him in 1871. Stanley had been sent to search for Livingstone by an American newspaper. Stanley later explored much of the region around Lake Victoria and traveled down the Zaire River to its mouth. The reports of Speke, Burton, Livingstone, Stanley, and other explorers and missionaries added much to the world's knowledge of Africa.

Parts of East Africa were divided between Germany and Great Britain in the late 1800s.

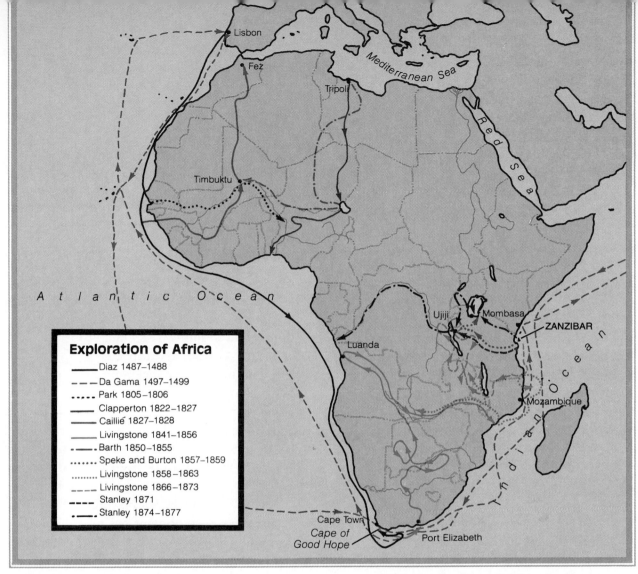

Exploration of Africa

——— Diaz 1487–1488
– – – Da Gama 1497–1499
••••• Park 1805–1806
——— Clapperton 1822–1827
——— Caillié 1827–1828
——— Livingstone 1841–1856
–•–•– Barth 1850–1855
•••••• Speke and Burton 1857–1859
•••••••• Livingstone 1858–1863
– – – – Livingstone 1866–1873
– – – – Stanley 1871
–•–•– Stanley 1874–1877

Early exploration of Africa by Europeans was confined to the coasts. Expeditions in the 1800s opened up the interior.

Britain controlled the region that is now Kenya, Uganda, and Zanzibar. The region now called Tanzania was part of German East Africa. After World War I, German East Africa came under the control of Great Britain and was called Tanganyika.

Kenya, Tanganyika, Uganda, and Zanzibar all became independent countries in the early 1960s. In 1964, Tanganyika and Zanzibar joined to form a single nation called Tanzania.

Kenya

A railroad from the port of Mombasa (mäm bäs′ə) to Lake Victoria was completed in 1901. This railroad helped open the rich agricultural lands of the highlands to European settlement. Large coffee and tea plantations were established there. Before independence, the British had begun a system of land reforms to help Africans buy land in this region. Through this program, land was peacefully

Masai lead their cattle to pasture in the grasslands of Kenya. The Masai are traditionally an independent people whose herds supply their basic foods.

transferred from the British to the Africans. Today in Kenya, some of the land is owned by the people, and some by the government. Most of the Kikuyu (ki koo′yoo), the largest tribe in Kenya, are farmers.

Only land in the southern part of Kenya is suitable for farming. In addition to coffee and tea, wheat, corn, cotton, and sisal are grown. Cattle and dairy products are also important. Recently the practice of shifting cultivation has ended in Kenya. The increase in population has made it necessary to use the land in a less wasteful way.

Along the border between Kenya and Tanzania live a group of nomadic herders called the Masai. The Masai are fond of their herds of sheep, cattle, and goats, and they take great pride in the animals' appearance. Wealth is measured in the size of herds. The Masai burn the vegetation to create open savannas where their herds can graze.

Nairobi, Kenya's modern capital, is an important transportation center. It has a large railroad yard, and many international flights land at its airport. People visiting the game reserves of East Africa often begin and end their safaris in Nairobi. Much of Kenya's income is from tourism.

Factories in Kenya produce cement, textiles, paper, and paper products. Food processing is an important industry. Oil from other countries is refined at a plant in Mombasa.

Tanzania

Lack of rain and the tsetse fly make much of Tanzania unfit for agriculture. The northern and central parts of the plateau are used for farming and herding. The chief crops are sisal, coffee, tea, cotton, and tobacco.

In Tanzania, the government owns the land. Farmers are being taught how to improve production through crop rotation and the use of machines and fertilizers. The government is also trying to improve the lives of the people by resettlement. People from isolated villages are being moved to larger villages where schools and hospitals can be built.

Tanzania's development has been helped by the building of a road, a railroad, and an oil pipeline from Dar es Salaam (där′ es′ sə läm′), the capital, to the interior of the neighboring country of Zambia. These transportation lines have increased trade in the port of Dar es Salaam. Dar es Salaam was founded in 1862 as a trading post by the sultan of Zanzibar. The name means "harbor of peace."

Tanzania has important diamond mines near Lake Victoria. Reserves of gold, silver, salt, and tin are also mined.

The Zanzibar Channel which is 22 miles (35 km) wide, separates the islands of Zanzibar from the rest of Tanzania. Cloves, coconuts, chili peppers, and citrus fruit are grown in the tropical climate of the islands.

Uganda

Uganda is more densely populated than either Kenya or Tanzania. Most of the people of Uganda live in the lowlands around Lake Victoria. Farmers there produce bananas, corn, and cotton. At higher elevations, coffee and tea are the chief cash crops and the chief exports. Copper is also an important export. It is smelted near Kampala (käm päl′ə), Uganda's capital, and sent to Kenya for shipment overseas.

Burundi and Rwanda

Burundi and Rwanda are two of the smallest but most densely populated countries in Africa. They have no large cities and few villages. Most of the people are subsistence farmers. Manioc, corn, bananas, and sweet potatoes are grown. Some coffee is grown for export. Tin is also exported.

Both Burundi and Rwanda were once part of German East Africa. After World War I, Belgium controlled both areas, which became independent countries in 1962. French is one of the official languages in both countries.

Burundi and Rwanda have a few surfaced roads, and neither country has railroads. Goods that are exported or imported must be moved many times from boats to railway cars through other countries.

The Seychelles

The Seychelles are an island country in the Indian Ocean 1,000 miles (1,600 km) east of Kenya. The archipelago is made up of 92 islands scattered over an area of 400,000 square miles (1,036 sq. km). The largest island is Mahe (mä hā′), where the capital of Victoria is located. Most of the people are descendants of French colonists and African slaves.

After Portuguese sailors discovered the Seychelles in the early 1500s, the islands were used as a hiding place for pirates for more than 200 years. In 1756, France claimed the islands and established plantations there. Slaves were brought from the east coast of Africa to work on the plantations. The islands passed to Great Britain in 1814. British rule ended in 1976, when the islands became independent.

Some of the islands of the Seychelles are coral and some are granite. The granite islands have mountains surrounded by wide, sandy beaches. The beaches and tropical climate attract many tourists. Tourism brings much income to the islands.

Farming and fishing are major occupations. The chief export crops are vanilla, coconut, cinnamon, and copra.

Do You Know?

1. What are the two main branches of the Nile River?
2. What two important kingdoms grew up in the northern part of East Africa about 2,000 years ago?
3. What three countries occupy the Horn of Africa?
4. Who are the Masai?

5
Southern Africa

Southern Africa includes the countries that lie south of Zaire and Tanzania at the tip of the continent. Three island nations are also considered part of Southern Africa. Almost 80 million people live in the 13 countries that make up this part of Africa.

The southernmost country, South Africa, borders both the Atlantic and the Indian oceans. North of South Africa, Namibia and Angola have coasts along the Atlantic. Mozambique (mō zam bēk′) lies along the Indian Ocean. The landlocked countries of southern Africa include Zambia (zam′bē ə), Malawi (mə lä′wē), Zimbabwe (zim bäb′wē), Botswana, Swaziland, and Lesotho (lə sō′tō′). The island country of Madagascar lies east of Mozambique across the Mozambique Channel. The Comoros and Mauritius (mô rish′əs) are two other island countries in the Indian Ocean. See the map on page 333.

Most of southern Africa is a plateau. Large parts are covered by flat or rolling grasslands. In this region of Africa, the escarpment is steep and even mountainous. Coastal lowlands border only the Indian Ocean. Much of southern Africa is rolling grassland, but deserts, forests, and swamps are also found there.

All the climate zones found in the rest of sub-Saharan Africa exist in southern Africa. In addition, two other kinds of climates exist south of the Tropic of Capricorn along the southern coast. They are the Mediterranean climate and the subtropical wet climate.

South Africa

The country of South Africa is about the size of Niger or Chad. It has a population of about 28 million, which is about one-third of the total population for all of southern Africa.

About 71 percent of the people are black Africans. Most of them are Bantu-speaking Zulus or Hottentots. South Africans of European origin make up 17 percent of the population. People of European descent are divided between those who speak English and those who speak *Afrikaans* (af′ri käns′), which is a dialect of Dutch. Afrikaans developed from the language spoken in South Africa by Dutch settlers in the 1600s. People of Asian origin make up about 3 percent of the population. Roughly 9 percent of the population is of mixed racial origin.

South Africa is the most industrialized country in Africa. It has many natural resources, particularly vast deposits of minerals. Its roads, railroads, airports, and harbors give it the best transportation system in Africa.

Geography

A plateau covers most of the interior of South Africa. Most of the plateau is a grassland referred to as the veldt. A coastal lowland stretches along the Indian Ocean, and mountains rise along the southern coast. The Namib Desert lies north of the mountains on the Atlantic Coast and extends into Namibia. In the interior, the Kalahari (kal′ə här′ē) Desert

Regional Data Chart

Country	Capital	Area		Population	GNP
		Square miles	Square kilometers		(in millions of U.S. dollars)
Angola	Luanda	481,350	1,246,700	7,250,000	$3,100
Benin	Porto-Novo	43,483	112,622	3,675,000	$860
Botswana	Gaborone	222,000	574,980	750,000	$560
Burundi	Bujumbura	10,747	27,834	4,650,000	$720
Cameroon	Yaoundé	183,569	475,442	8,650,000	$4,600
Cape Verde	Praia	1,557	4,033	330,000	$80
Central African Republic	Bangui	241,313	625,000	2,500,000	$560
Chad	N'Djamena	495,752	1,284,000	4,650,000	$490
Comoros	Moroni	838	2,171	330,000	$90
Congo	Brazzaville	132,046	342,000	1,580,000	$950
Djibouti	Djibouti	8,996	23,300	330,000	$140
Equatorial Guinea	Malabo	10,830	28,051	370,000	$70
Ethiopia	Addis Ababa	457,142	1,183,998	32,000,000	$4,000
Gabon	Libreville	102,317	265,001	550,000	$2,100
Gambia	Banjul	4,016	10,403	625,000	$150
Ghana	Accra	92,100	238,537	11,750,000	$4,500
Guinea	Conakry	94,925	245,857	5,115,000	$1,500
Guinea-Bissau	Bissau	13,948	36,125	580,000	$140
Ivory Coast	Abidjan	124,502	322,462	8,500,000	$8,600
Kenya	Nairobi	224,960	582,646	16,300,000	$5,800
Lesotho	Maseru	11,720	30,355	1,375,000	$440
Liberia	Monrovia	43,000	111,370	1,920,000	$890
Madagascar	Antananarivo	230,035	595,791	9,000,000	$2,500
Malawi	Lilongwe	45,747	118,484	6,125,000	$1,200
Mali	Bamako	464,873	1,204,021	7,100,000	$930
Mauritania	Nouakchott	419,229	1,085,803	1,675,000	$510
Mauritius	Port Louis	787	2,040	975,000	$970
Mozambique	Maputo	303,073	784,959	10,750,000	$2,600
Niger	Niamey	489,206	1,267,044	5,550,000	$1,400
Nigeria	Lagos	356,700	923,853	79,575,000	$55,000
Rwanda	Kigali	10,169	26,338	5,200,000	$970
São Tomé and Príncipe	São Tomé	372	964	90,000	$52
Senegal	Dakar	76,124	197,161	5,800,000	$2,400
Seychelles	Victoria	171	443	60,000	$90
Sierra Leone	Freetown	27,925	72,326	3,560,000	$840
Somalia	Mogadishu	246,155	637,541	3,750,000	$470
South Africa	Cape Town, Pretoria, Bloemfontein	471,962	1,222,382	28,280,000	$49,000
Sudan	Khartoum	967,491	2,505,802	18,750,000	$6,600
Swaziland	Mbabane	6,704	17,363	550,000	$350
Tanzania	Dar es Salaam	362,820	939,704	19,000,000	$4,700
Togo	Lomé	21,853	56,599	2,600,000	$860
Uganda	Kampala	91,134	236,036	14,000,000	$3,700
Upper Volta (Burkina Faso)	Ouagadougou	105,870	274,200	7,100,000	$1,000
Zaire	Kinshasa	905,063	2,344,113	29,450,000	$7,000
Zambia	Lusaka	290,724	752,975	6,000,000	$2,800
Zimbabwe	Harare	150,333	389,362	7,580,000	$3,400

Nonindependent Area

Country	Capital	Square miles	Square kilometers	Population	GNP
Namibia	Windhoek	318,261	824,296	1,000,000	$1,200
Mayotte (France)	Dzaoudzi	146	378	48,600	—

lies along the northern border and extends into Botswana. The Orange River rises near the east coast and flows 1,300 miles (2,090 km) west to empty into the Atlantic. The shorter Limpopo River flows into the Indian Ocean.

Almost all of South Africa lies south of the Tropic of Capricorn. Its climate is generally mild and sunny. Along the coastal lowland, the summers are hot and humid, and the winters are dry and mild. The area south of the mountains has a Mediterranean climate with winter rains. Rainfall decreases from east to west.

European Colonization

In 1488, the Portuguese explorer Bartholomew Diaz sailed around the southern tip of Africa. Because of the weather he encountered there, he named the point of land the Cape of Storms. When the king of Portugal learned that a sea route around Africa had been found, he renamed the cape the Cape of Good Hope. In the 1600s, a group of Dutch colonists established a supply base on the Cape for ships sailing between the Netherlands and the Dutch colonies in Asia. Soon other settlers from France and Germany began to arrive. The early Dutch, French, and German settlers of Cape Colony were known as Boers (bôrz), an Afrikaans word meaning "farmers." During the 1700s, some of the Boers migrated eastward and started farming along the Indian Ocean coast. Others went into the dry interior.

British Rule and Independence

In 1806, British soldiers took control of Cape Colony. Soon British colonists began to arrive and settle in both Cape Colony and the region along the coast to the northeast known as Natal. Asians, mainly Indians, came to work on British-owned farms in Natal. In 1843, Natal was taken over by Britain.

The Boers chose not to live under British rule. They moved north into the veldt, where they set up the free republics of Transvaal and the Orange Free State.

When diamonds and gold were discovered in the veldt, miners and adventure seekers from Britain and other countries came to South Africa seeking riches. Bad relations developed between the Boers and the newcomers. In 1899, war broke out between the Boers and the British. When the Boers surrendered in 1902, the Boer republics became British colonies.

During the years of trouble between the Boers and the British, both groups were also having trouble with the blacks. Between 1780 and the mid-1800s, a series of fierce battles took place between the Boers and the Zulus. The Zulus developed a well-organized fighting force. The superior fire power and cavalry of the Boers, however, enabled them to drive the Zulus back. The Boers were able to keep the best lands for themselves.

The Zulus also fought the British. By 1900, all of the black Africans had come under the control of colonial powers.

In 1910, Transvaal and the Orange Free State joined Cape Colony and Natal to form the Union of South Africa. The Union of South Africa was a self-governing colony within the British Empire. In 1931, Britain gave South

Africa full independence as a member of the Commonwealth of Nations. The Afrikaners, as the Boers had come to be called, took control of the government in 1948. In 1961, South Africa became a republic. It left the Commonwealth and cut its ties with Great Britain.

Cape Town, South Africa's legislative capital, oldest city, and chief port, was founded by the Dutch in 1652.

Apartheid

The government of the Republic of South Africa decided on a *policy* (pol'ə sē) toward non-whites. A policy is a general plan of action adopted by a government. The law limits the freedom of blacks and other non-white citizens. This policy of segregation, or separation, is called apartheid (ə pär'tīd). *Apartheid* is an Afrikaans word meaning "apartness." The policy of apartheid allows only whites to vote in national elections and to sit in the national assembly.

Apartheid also determines where people may live and the kinds of jobs they may hold. Whites, who usually live in cities, may move about fairly freely. The best-paying jobs are open only to whites. Blacks live in special areas outside the cities or on rural reserves. They must carry identity cards at all times.

Apartheid also includes the use of separate restaurants, restrooms, elevators, buses, parks, and beaches. Public buildings such as post offices and libraries have separate entrances and service areas for whites and non-whites.

Opposition to apartheid has grown in South Africa and throughout the world. Recently, the government of South Africa has set up homelands, or reserves, for blacks. Each homeland has an assembly elected by its people. In the 1970s, three homelands were declared independent. The government of South Africa claims that the blacks have self-government. The governments of many other nations disagree. They do not recognize the homelands as independent nations. Real control seems to be in the hands of the South African government.

Farming and Herding

South African farmers grow wheat and other cereal grains, wheat, citrus fruits, coffee, cotton, and tobacco. They produce more corn and sugarcane than any other country in Africa. Cattle and sheep are raised on farms throughout South Africa. Wool is South Africa's second-largest export.

Mining and Manufacturing

South Africa is Africa's richest country. Its wealth is partly due to its immense natural resources. They include gold, diamonds, iron ore, coal, and copper. South Africa is the world's largest producer of gold. The country produces more platinum, coal, and *chromium* (krō'mē əm) than any other country in Africa. Chromium is a silver-gray hard metallic mineral. It is used in making stainless steel.

367

Cities of South Africa

South Africa has three capitals. Cape Town, South Africa's oldest city, is the legislative capital. The administrative capital, Pretoria, is located in the northeast. Bloemfontein (bloom'fən tān), an old Boer city, is the judicial capital. Johannesburg (jō han'is burg') is the country's largest industrial center.

Swaziland, Lesotho, and Botswana

Swaziland, Lesotho, and Botswana were all British colonies at one time. In the early 1900s, they were known as the High Commission Territories.

Swaziland, one of the smallest countries in Africa, is nearly surrounded by South Africa. On the east, it shares a border with Mozambique. Lesotho, to the southwest, is an enclave completely surrounded by South Africa. It is slightly larger than Rwanda or Burundi. Population density is high in both Swaziland and Lesotho.

Botswana lies north of South Africa in the central part of southern Africa. It is about half as large as South Africa, but it has only about 750,000 people.

Geography

The western part of Swaziland is a high veldt. A series of plateaus descends to a low veldt in the east. Lesotho is a mountainous land. It is sometimes called the "Switzerland of Africa." Its mountains are part of the Drakensberg Range. Parts of the range rise more than 10,000 feet (300 m) above sea level. Most of

Botswana is a plateau with an average altitude of 3,000 feet (990 m). The Kalahari Desert covers much of the southern part of the country. In the northwest, there are swamps and salt lakes.

History

The Swazi are a Bantu-speaking tribe that settled in what is now Swaziland about 400 years ago. Bushmen were the original inhabitants in both Lesotho and Botswana. People of the Basatho group moved into the area that is now Lesotho in the 1600s.

During the 1800s, the entire area that is now Swaziland, Lesotho, and Botswana came under British protection. In 1966, independence was granted to Lesotho and Botswana. Swaziland gained independence in 1968.

Farming and Herding

Most of the people in Swaziland live by farming and herding. Lumbering is also an important industry. Wood products, citrus fruits, and sugar are among the country's exports.

In Lesotho, sheep and cattle are raised. Wool, mohair, skins, and hides are exported. The main occupation in Botswana is cattle raising. Botswana exports both canned meat and cattle.

Ties with South Africa

Many people from Swaziland, Lesotho, and Botswana have jobs in South Africa's mines and industries. Some companies offer contracts to workers for a six- or nine-month period. The workers receive part of their pay while they are working. The balance is paid when the job is completed. Families depend on the money sent to them from their relatives who work part of the year in South Africa.

Namibia

Namibia is sometimes called South West Africa. Namibia is about two-thirds the size of South Africa. About one million people live there. Most of them are black Africans, including some Bushmen and Hottentots. Whites make up 14 percent of the population. Namibia has 1,000 miles (1,600 km) of coast along the Atlantic Ocean. The Namib Desert lies along the coast. Most of the interior is a high plateau. The eastern part of the plateau is covered by the Kalahari Desert.

Namibia has a troubled history. In 1878, Britain claimed Walvis (wôl′vəs) Bay as a port for Cape Province in South Africa. Today, this city and the land around it are part of South Africa.

In the 1800s, Germany claimed the rest of the territory, which became known as German Southwest Africa. German colonists settled on the Atlantic coast and in the interior at Windhoek (vint′hook), Namibia's capital. The Germans established farms and mined diamonds.

During World War I, South African troops took control of the German colony. It then became known as South West Africa. In 1971, the International Court of Justice declared South Africa's control of South West Africa illegal. In 1974, the United Nations called for power to be transferred to the people of the territory, which became known as Namibia. South Africa has not given up its claims, and the situation is still not resolved. Many nations support Namibia's independence movement.

Namibia is a grazing country for sheep and cattle. The karakul (kar′ə kəl) sheep have dark curly fleece that is used for coats. The fleece is exported to many countries. Namibia also exports fish, maize, and peanuts. Rich mineral deposits, including diamonds, lead, copper, zinc, and uranium, are found in Namibia.

Angola

Angola is a country slightly larger than South Africa. Most of its seven million people belong to Bantu-speaking groups.

Angola stretches along the Atlantic coast north of Namibia. A narrow plain separates the coast from the high interior plateau. Most of the country is desert or savanna woodland.

In 1482, Portuguese explorers and sailors arrived in Angola and set up trading posts and missions along the coast. At the end of World War II, about 400,000 Portuguese were living in Angola. Africans seeking independence began a revolt in 1961. The struggle for independence was complicated by civil war. Three groups wanted to control the government. Angola gained independence in 1975, but the civil war continued. In 1976, a new government was established.

Most Angolans are farmers. They produce and export much coffee. They also export corn, sugar, cotton, palm oil, and tobacco. Iron ore, manganese, diamonds, and salt are mined.

Petroleum is the chief export of the country. Large oil fields are located in Cabinda, a part of Angola that is an enclave in Zaire.

Zimbabwe, Malawi, and Zambia

Zimbabwe, Malawi, and Zambia are three countries in the interior of southern Africa. Zimbabwe is about half the size of Namibia. Zambia is a little smaller than Namibia. Malawi is about a third the size of Zimbabwe. The combined population of all three countries is about 20 million, most of whom are black Africans.

All three countries lie on a plateau west of the Great Rift Valley. Much of the region is savanna. There are areas of fertile soil, adequate rainfall, and moderate temperatures.

History

Bushmen were probably the first people to live in what is now Zimbabwe, Malawi, and Zambia. In the eleventh century, a Bantu-speaking tribe called the Shona (shō′nə) moved into the area along the Zambezi River. See the map on page 333.

The Shona people conquered the hunters and gatherers who already lived in the region. They mined gold and traded with cities along the coast. Eventually, they established a kingdom called Zimbabwe. By the fifteenth century, the kingdom of Zimbabwe was wealthy and powerful.

Zimbabwe means "royal dwelling." The buildings of Zimbabwe were made of granite slabs. Walls were ten feet (3 m) thick. The

Ruins of the Zimbabwe kingdom can be seen in the modern country of Zimbabwe. The builders were expert masons.

stones fit so precisely that no mortar was needed to hold them together. Huge palaces and other buildings were built throughout the kingdom.

In the 1500s, Portuguese explorers tried to gain control of Zimbabwe, but they did not succeed. The kingdom survived until the 1800s. A tribe from the south conquered the region in 1830.

In 1890, the British South African Company led a caravan of white settlers into the area that is now Zimbabwe, Malawi, and Zambia. Soon more Europeans arrived, attracted by the fertile soil and mild climate. Great Britain established the colonies of Northern Rhodesia (rō dē′zhə), Nyasaland (nī as′ə land), and Southern Rhodesia.

After World War II, Great Britain united the three colonies in a *federation* (fed′ə rā′shən). A federation is a political union of two or more states or countries, in which each keeps the right to manage its internal affairs. From 1953 to 1963, Northern Rhodesia, Nyasaland, and Southern Rhodesia were members of the Central African Federation.

In 1964, Northern Rhodesia and Nyasaland gained their independence. Northern Rhodesia became the new country of Zambia, and Nyasaland became Malawi. The white minority in Southern Rhodesia did not want to lose their power to the black majority. The whites declared Southern Rhodesia independent of Britain in 1965. Black nationalists rebelled against the white rulers. The conflict ended when both blacks and whites received the right to vote. In 1980, the black majority formed a new government. The name of the country was then changed to Zimbabwe to preserve the memory of the early African kingdom of that name.

Agriculture and Industry

Zimbabwe, Malawi, and Zambia all produce tobacco, cotton, and sugar. Malawi exports coffee. Zimbabwe and Zambia raise cattle on grazing lands that are free of the tsetse fly.

The Kariba (kä rē′bä) Dam on the Zambezi River furnishes electric power to both Zimbabwe and Zambia. The energy is used in the mines of both countries. Zimbabwe and Zambia are one of the richest mining areas in the world. Zimbabwe is the world's second-largest producer of chromium. The country also exports large quantities of industrial diamonds. Zambia is a major world supplier of copper. It also has large reserves of cobalt. Both countries have deposits of iron, gold, vanadium, manganese and coal.

The factories of Zimbabwe, Malawi, and Zambia produce textiles, chemicals, fertilizers, and vehicles. Next to South Africa, Zimbabwe is the most industrialized African country.

Mozambique

Mozambique lies east of Zimbabwe and Malawi. It extends more than 1,500 miles (2,400 km) along the Indian Ocean and has a population of more than 10 million. Much of Mozambique, particularly in the south, is a coastal plain. The land rises gradually to the north and west to form a plateau. Two great rivers descend from the interior to the coast. The Zambezi flows through the middle of the country, and the Limpopo flows through the south.

In the early 1500s, Portuguese traders settled along the coast of Mozambique. For nearly 500 years, Mozambique was a Portuguese colony. The country became independent in 1975, after a ten-year war of rebellion.

Farming is the main occupation in Mozambique. Because of the tsetse fly, it is hard to raise cattle. Shipping trade with South Africa provides much of Mozambique's income.

Madagascar, the Comoros, and Mauritius

Madagascar, the Comoros, and Mauritius are independent island nations. They lie to the east of the continent of Africa. The people of the islands are Asian and African in origin.

Madagascar

Madagascar lies about 250 miles (400 km) east of the African coast. It is the fourth-largest island in the world. The population of Madagascar is about nine million. Much of the island is mountainous. There are few good natural harbors.

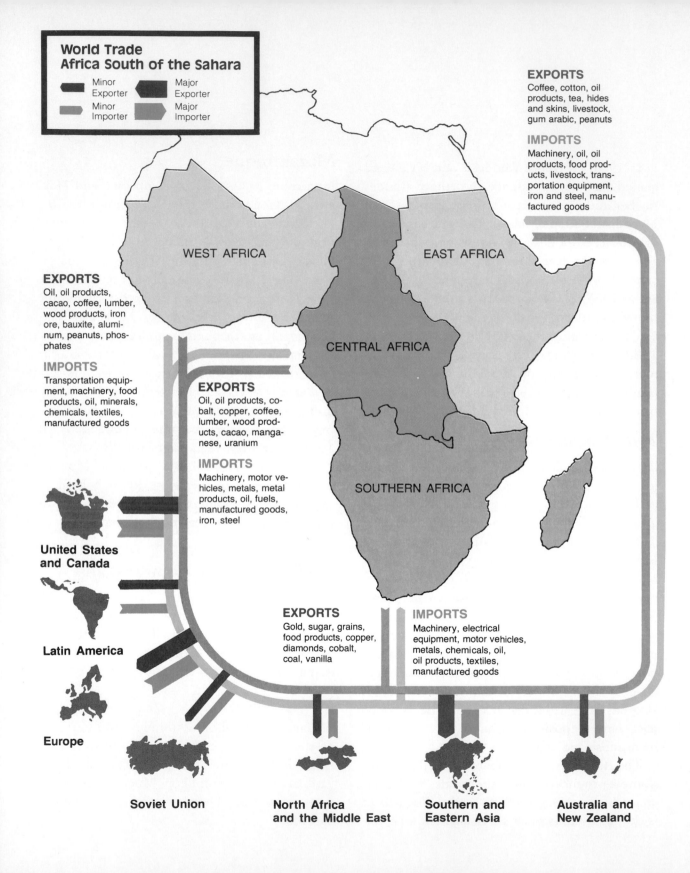

World Trade
Africa South of the Sahara

Minor Exporter
Major Exporter
Minor Importer
Major Importer

EXPORTS
Coffee, cotton, oil products, tea, hides and skins, livestock, gum arabic, peanuts

IMPORTS
Machinery, oil, oil products, food products, livestock, transportation equipment, iron and steel, manufactured goods

WEST AFRICA

EAST AFRICA

CENTRAL AFRICA

SOUTHERN AFRICA

EXPORTS
Oil, oil products, cacao, coffee, lumber, wood products, iron ore, bauxite, aluminum, peanuts, phosphates

IMPORTS
Transportation equipment, machinery, food products, oil, minerals, chemicals, textiles, manufactured goods

EXPORTS
Oil, oil products, cobalt, copper, coffee, lumber, wood products, cacao, manganese, uranium

IMPORTS
Machinery, motor vehicles, metals, metal products, oil, fuels, manufactured goods, iron, steel

EXPORTS
Gold, sugar, grains, food products, copper, diamonds, cobalt, coal, vanilla

IMPORTS
Machinery, electrical equipment, motor vehicles, metals, chemicals, oil, oil products, textiles, manufactured goods

United States and Canada

Latin America

Europe

Soviet Union

North Africa and the Middle East

Southern and Eastern Asia

Australia and New Zealand

More than 2,000 years ago, people from Indonesia settled in Madagascar. Later, black Africans and people from the Arabian Peninsula settled the coastal regions. Arab colonies were established there from the ninth to the fourteenth century. Europeans tried to establish settlements on the island during the next few centuries. The French established firm control in 1896 by ending a native monarchy. Madagascar voted to become the Malagasy Republic, a self-governing part of France, in 1958. It gained full independence in 1960, and changed its name to Madagascar in 1975.

The island produces most of the world's supply of vanilla. Farmers there also grow coffee, rice, and sugarcane.

The Comoros

The Comoros consist of four small volcanic islands in the Indian Ocean between Mozambique and Madagascar. About 330,000 people live there. The people are mainly of Asian and African origin. The islands were under French rule from 1886 until independence in 1975. The island of Mayotte (mä yôt') retains its ties with France.

The Comoros export vanilla, copra, and cloves. There is also a perfume industry in the islands.

Specimens of a fish called the coelacanth (sē'lə kanth') have been caught in the deep waters near the Comoros and Madagascar. Coelacanths are large blue to brown fish that are about five feet (1.5 m) long. Until a coelacanth was caught off the coast of East Africa in 1938, scientists thought these fish had been extinct for millions of years. Some people call coelacanths "living fossils."

Mauritius

Mauritius is a small, mountainous volcanic island about 500 miles (800 km) east of Madagascar. Nearly one million people live in this densely populated country. The majority of the inhabitants are descendants of Indians who came to work on the sugarcane plantations after slavery was abolished in 1834. The main sources of income are tourism and sugar.

The first Europeans to visit the island were the Portuguese in the early 1500s. Mauritius has been controlled by the Netherlands, France, and Great Britain at different times in its history. The British seized the island from the French in 1810. Mauritius and the Seychelles were administered as one colony until 1903. Mauritius became independent in 1968.

Do You Know?

1. What African country lies almost entirely south of the Tropic of Capricorn?
2. Who were the Boers?
3. What southern African country is named after an early kingdom of the region?
4. Name two of the island countries of southern Africa. In what direction are they from the African continent? In what ocean are they found?

To Help You Learn

Using New Words

gorge	developing country
safari	terra cotta
anopheles	Afrikaans
policy	federation
chromium	escarpment

Number a paper from 1 through 10. After each number write the word or term from the above list that matches the definition.

1. A silver-gray, hard metallic mineral
2. A hard, brown-red earthenware
3. A deep, steep-sided valley
4. A country that is starting to develop industrially
5. A political union of two or more states or countries, in which each keeps the right to manage its internal affairs
6. An expedition to a game reserve to see wildlife
7. A dialect of Dutch spoken in South Africa
8. A general plan of action adopted by a government
9. A mosquito that transmits malaria
10. A steep slope or cliff

Finding the Facts

1. Name the large bodies of water that border sub-Saharan Africa.
2. What two regions have the lowest rainfall in sub-Saharan Africa?
3. What empire became important in the region south of the Sahara after the fall of the Songhai Empire?
4. Name four minerals produced in Zaire.
5. What is the largest country in Africa?
6. What early East African kingdom became one of the world's first Christian nations?
7. What is the largest city in East Africa?
8. What lake is the source of the Nile? What countries border this lake?
9. What were Speke, Burton, and Livingstone all looking for in Africa?
10. Who owns the land in Tanzania?
11. What large island is part of Tanzania?
12. Name the landlocked countries of southern Africa.
13. What country is the most industrialized country in Africa?
14. What does the word *apartheid* mean?
15. Why is Lesotho called the "Switzerland of Africa"?
16. By what other name is Namibia known?
17. What is the chief export of Angola? What country controlled Angola before independence?
18. How does Madagascar rank in size among the islands of the world?
19. What kind of rock makes up Mauritius and the Comoros?

Learning from Maps

1. Look at the map of Africa on page 333. Near what city do the Blue Nile and White Nile join? On what river is Victoria Falls? Name the countries through which the Niger River flows. What lake lies on the border between Zambia and Zimbabwe? What city is near 0° latitude and 10° E. longitude?

2. Look at the map on page 340. Which of the early kingdoms of West Africa controlled the largest territory? Which kingdom shown was the first to develop? Which two kingdoms disappeared most recently?

3. Compare the maps on pages 361 and 333. Who explored the Niger River? The Zambezi River? The Zaire River? Who was the first explorer to reach the Cape of Good Hope? What explorer sailed around the tip of Africa?

4. Look at the maps on pages 343 and 350. What African nations were independent in 1914? What was the former name of the present-day country of Zaire? What country shown gained independence most recently? What European country formerly controlled it? How many African countries shown gained independence in the 1950s? How many of these countries are in sub-Saharan Africa?

5. Look at the map on page 355. Near what major city is manganese found? What agricultural product is grown near Cape Town? In what region of Africa is cacao grown? What does Madagascar produce?

Using Study Skills

1. **Library Resources:** The card catalog helps you find out what books a library has. There are three kinds of cards in the card catalog—author cards, title cards, and subject cards. The name of the author is given first on the author card. The title is first on the title card. On the subject card, the subject area is first. Each card also includes information about the copyright, the publishing company, and the number of pages. Cards are arranged in alphabetical order. Each card has a number, known as a call number, that helps you find the book on the library shelves. In some libraries, the card catalog is in book form.

Study the sample cards and answer the questions below.

Card A

963	Bennett, Susan
B	The Great Songhai Empire. San Francisco: World Press, 1982. 300 pp.

Card B

	AFRICAN HISTORY
963	Bennett, Susan
B	The Great Songhai Empire San Francisco: World Press, 1982. 300 pp.

Card C

The Great Songhai Empire

963   Bennett, Susan
B   San Francisco: World Press, 1982.
     300 pp.

Which of the cards is the author card? The subject card? The title card? Which card would you look for if you wanted to find information for a paper on African history? Which card would you look for if you wanted to find a book by Susan Bennett but could not recall the title of the book? What is the call number of this book? What company published the book? When? What does the number *300* stand for?

2. **Time Line:** Find the dates for the following events and place them in chronological order: Arabs drove Portuguese from East Africa; Boers surrendered; Sonni Ali captured Timbuktu; Songhai Empire ended; Kingdom of Zimbabwe conquered.

Copy the time line from page 331 and add the events listed above. Study the completed time line and answer the following questions: How many years did the Boer War last? How many years after Askia became emperor did the Songhai Empire come to an end? How many years before the Portuguese were driven out of East Africa did Portuguese traders arrive at the mouth of the Zaire River?

Thinking It Through

1. What reasons are there to believe that sub-Saharan Africa will become more prosperous in the future? What could prevent the achievement of greater prosperity? Why might some African nations make faster economic progress than others?

2. Why are European languages often used as the official languages in sub-Saharan African countries? What languages do you think will be used in Africa in the future? Support your answer.

3. Often European powers drew the boundaries of their African colonies before they developed good maps. How did this cause problems? How might Africa be different today if the boundaries had been drawn along tribal lines?

Projects

1. Members of the Current Events Committee might undertake a daily search for newspaper articles about the countries of sub-Saharan Africa. Have members of the committee share the most interesting items with the class. The committee might like to develop a bulletin-board display of the material they have collected.

2. Bartholomew Diaz, Dr. Albert Schweitzer, Emperor Haile Selassie, Jomo Kenyatta, the first president of Kenya after independence, and Shaka, the founder of the Zulu Empire, all have a place in the history of sub-Saharan Africa. The Biography Committee might like to collect information on

these men and prepare oral reports for the class.

3. The Arts and Sciences Committee might like to find out more about the establishment of African game preserves. They can find out what steps African governments have taken to help preserve wildlife. Committee members should share their findings with the class. Some committee members may like to illustrate their report with drawings or with illustrations from magazines.

4. The History Committee might like to do research on the Kingdom of Ghana, the Mali Empire, and the Songhai Empire. They could prepare a report explaining how these empires were alike and how they were different.

9 Southern and Eastern Asia

Unit Preview

Southern and eastern Asia includes more than half of Asia. It also includes the islands south and east of the continent. Within this vast area live more than half of the people in the world.

This part of Asia has a great variety of climates and vegetation. Deserts stretch across the interior of East Asia. Large areas of Southeast Asia are covered by tropical rain forests. Mountains of the region include the Himalayas, the highest in the world. Mountains and seasonal winds called monsoons greatly affect the climate.

In Unit 2, you read about the ancient civilizations that grew up along the Indus and Huang rivers in different parts of Asia. The cultures of India and China influenced the cultural development of other parts of Asia.

European exploration and settlement in South Asia and Southeast Asia began in the sixteenth century. Colonial rule lasted for more than 400 years in some areas. Japan and most of China did not share this colonial heritage. Until the nineteenth century, both countries remained almost totally isolated from the rest of the world.

Agriculture is the chief occupation of most people in southern and eastern Asia. Japan is an exception, however. It has become a major industrialized nation. Industrialization is becoming more important in other countries, especially India and China.

Things to Discover

If you look carefully at the picture, map, and time line, you can answer these questions.

1. The photograph shows terraced rice fields, or paddies, in Sri Lanka. Rice, a basic food throughout southern and eastern Asia, was grown in China during the Shang Dynasty. When did this dynasty begin?
2. The highlighted area shows the part of Asia you will be studying in this unit. How many large peninsulas can you find?
3. What oceans border the highlighted area on the map?
4. Marco Polo and Vasco da Gama were both Europeans who traveled to southern and eastern Asia during the Middle Ages. How long after Marco Polo arrived in China did Vasco da Gama reach India?

Words to Learn

You will meet these words and terms in this unit. As you read you will learn what they mean and how to pronounce them. The Word List will help you.

antimony	martial law
Brahman	Orient
civil servant	passive resistance
depose	samurai
evacuate	shogun
free port	subcontinent
mainland	

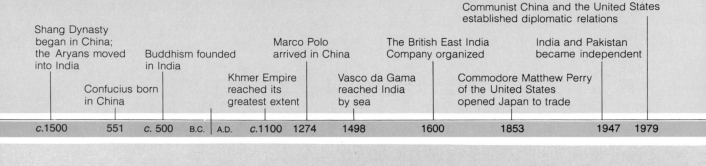

Shang Dynasty began in China; the Aryans moved into India

Confucius born in China

Buddhism founded in India

Khmer Empire reached its greatest extent

Marco Polo arrived in China

Vasco da Gama reached India by sea

The British East India Company organized

Commodore Matthew Perry of the United States opened Japan to trade

India and Pakistan became independent

Communist China and the United States established diplomatic relations

| c.1500 | 551 | c. 500 | B.C. | A.D. | c.1100 | 1274 | 1498 | 1600 | 1853 | 1947 | 1979 |

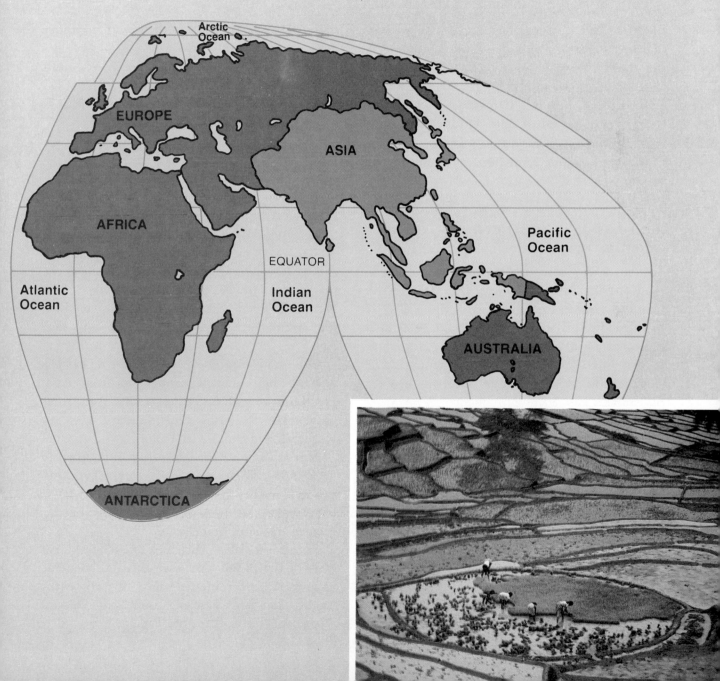

1

The Land and the People of Southern and Eastern Asia

Southern and eastern Asia is the part of Asia that lies south of the Soviet Union and east of the countries of the Middle East. This region also includes the groups of islands south and east of the continent. It makes up nearly 50 percent of the land of Asia, and includes more than 90 percent of Asia's population. Twenty-three independent countries are found in this region.

The Land of Southern and Eastern Asia

Southern and eastern Asia extends for more than 4,000 miles (6,400 km) from Iran in the west to the Pacific Ocean in the east. Its greatest distance from north to south is also more than 4,000 miles (6,400 km). The lands of this huge region lie between about 10° S. latitude and 55° N. latitude. See the map on page 381.

The Indian Ocean lies to the south of this region, and the Pacific Ocean lies to the east. The large peninsula of India extends south from the continent to divide the Indian Ocean into the Arabian Sea on the west and the Bay of Bengal (ben gôl') on the east. The Indian Peninsula and nearby areas are often referred to as South Asia.

Another large peninsula juts out from the continent between the Bay of Bengal and the Pacific. South and east of this peninsula are several large groups of mountainous, volcanic islands. The peninsula and the islands together make up Southeast Asia.

The part of the continent north of South Asia and Southeast Asia is part of East Asia. East Asia includes the chain of volcanic islands that lie off the coast in the Pacific.

Sometimes East Asia and Southeast Asia are referred to as the Far East. Europeans first called this vast region the Far East because it is in the part of the world farthest east from Europe. Another term for the Far East is the *Orient* (ôr'ē ənt), a word meaning "east."

Many high mountains are found in southern and eastern Asia. The highest mountains in the world, the Himalayas, lie north of the Indian Peninsula. They stretch east and west to form the boundary between South Asia and East Asia.

Mountain ranges extend from the eastern end of the Himalayas into Southeast Asia. From the western end of the Himalayas, other ranges fan out along the boundary between East Asia and the Soviet Union.

North of the Himalayas is a high plateau with surrounding mountains. Most of the important rivers of southern and eastern Asia have their source in the mountains of this plateau or in the Himalayas.

In the interior of East Asia are several large deserts, dry basins, and low plateaus. The wide valleys and rich alluvial plains of two of the world's longest rivers are found to the east where the rivers enter the Pacific.

SOUTHERN AND EASTERN ASIA

0 100 200 400 600 800 Miles
0 161 322 644 966 1288 Kilometers

⊛ National Capitals   • Other Cities
Mountains   Hills
Plateaus   Plains

SIBERIA

Yenisei River
Lena River
Lena River
SEA OF OKHOTSK
Kamchatka Peninsula
Kuril Islands
Sakhalin

SOVIET UNION

Ural R.
Novosibirsk
Angara R.
Lake Baikal
Amur River
HOKKAIDO

ARAL SEA
Lake Balkhash

MONGOLIA
Ulan Bator
MANCHURIA
Vladivostok
SEA OF JAPAN
HONSHU
Tokyo ⊛

Amu Darya
Tashkent
TIEN SHAN
SINKIANG
GOBI
INNER MONGOLIA
Shenyang
N. KOREA
Pyongyang ⊛
S. KOREA
Seoul ⊛
Osaka
Mt. Fuji
Kitakyushu
SHIKOKU
KYUSHU

AFGHANI-STAN
HINDU KUSH
KHYBER PASS
Kabul ⊛
Islamabad ⊛
Rawalpindi
Huang River
Beijing ⊛
Tianjing
YELLOW SEA
Shanghai
Nanjing

PAKISTAN
Lahore
Indus R.
HIMALAYA
KUNLUN MTS.
PLATEAU OF TIBET
Lhasa
QIN LING MTS.
Wuhan
Hangchou
EAST CHINA SEA

Karachi
Delhi
New Delhi
Agra
THAR DESERT
NEPAL
Kathmandu ⊛
Everest 29,028 ft (8,848 m)
MOUNTAINS
BHUTAN
Thimbu ⊛
Brahmaputra River
Chongqing
Chang River
Taipei
TROPIC OF CANCER

Jumna R.
Ganges River
Varānasi (Benares)
BANGLADESH
Dacca ⊛
Mandalay
Guangzhou
Macao
Victoria
HONG KONG

Narmada R.
INDIA
Calcutta
Irrawaddy
Red R.
Hanoi
HAINAN
LUZON

Bombay
DECCAN
Godavari R.
Krishna R.
WESTERN GHATS
EASTERN GHATS
BURMA
Saween
LAOS
Vientiane
VIETNAM
SOUTH CHINA SEA
Manila ⊛
PHILIPPINES
MINDANAO

Bay of Bengal
Rangoon
THAILAND
Menam R.
Mekong River

ARABIAN SEA
Madras
Bangkok ⊛
Phnom Penh ⊛
Ho Chi Minh City
S. CHINA SEA

Palk Strait
Colombo ⊛
SRI LANKA
Gulf of Thailand
KAMPUCHEA

MALDIVES
George Town
MALAYSIA
BRUNEI
SABAH
MOLUCCA ISLANDS
SULAWESI

Kuala Lumpur ⊛
SARAWAK
BORNEO

EQUATOR
STRAIT OF MALACCA
Singapore ⊛
SINGAPORE
SUMATRA

INDIAN OCEAN
INDONESIA
Timor
BALI
LESSER SUNDAS
Jakarta ⊛
JAVA

PACIFIC OCEAN

100° 120° 140° 160° 50° 40° 30° 20° 10° 0° 10°
70° 80° 90° 100° 110° 120° 130°

© Rand McNally & Co.

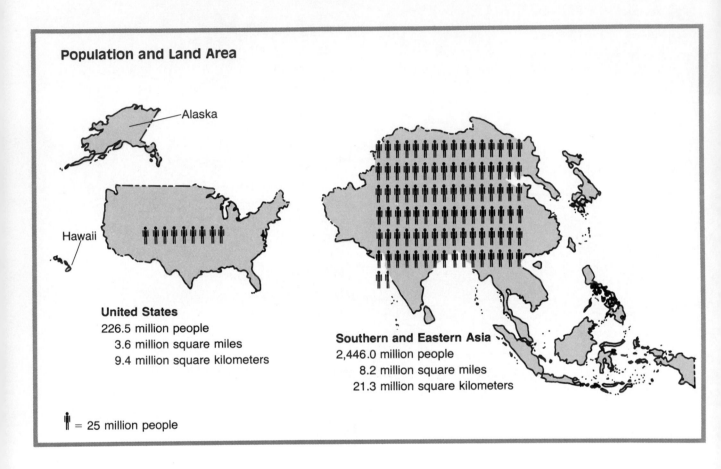

Population and Land Area

Alaska

Hawaii

United States
226.5 million people
  3.6 million square miles
  9.4 million square kilometers

Southern and Eastern Asia
2,446.0 million people
  8.2 million square miles
21.3 million square kilometers

👤 = 25 million people

Because of its great range in latitude and altitude, southern and eastern Asia has a great variety of climates. Here are found some of the driest, as well as the wettest, places on earth. The region also includes areas of very high and very low temperatures. Two of the most important factors in the climate of this region are monsoons and mountains.

Most of southern and eastern Asia is affected by monsoons. You have read about these seasonal winds in Unit 1. During the summer, monsoons blow from the sea toward the land, bringing the rainy season. During the winter, the direction of the monsoon winds is reversed. Cool, dry air blows from the land toward the sea. The winter monsoon brings the dry season.

The high mountains of southern and eastern Asia, especially the Himalayas, block the winds that blow across the region. The Himalayas keep the cold winter winds of Asia from reaching India. These mountains also block the warm, moist winds blowing toward the continent. They are the reason that much of central Asia is dry.

The People of Southern and Eastern Asia

There are nearly two and one-half billion people living in southern and eastern Asia. This is about 55 percent of all the people in the world. The land of this region makes up only 14 percent of the world's total. Few people live in the vast stretches of deserts and mountains. Some parts of this region, however, are very crowded. The population densities are among the highest in the world.

The majority of the people who live in southern and eastern Asia live in only two countries, China and India. The combined population of these countries makes up one-third of the total world population.

The cultures that developed in China and India have had a great influence on the other people of southern and eastern Asia. Religions that began in these countries are today practiced by millions of people throughout the region. Religion is one of the unifying forces among the diverse groups of people in this part of the world.

Many nations of southern and southeastern Asia share a colonial heritage. Beginning in the sixteenth century, Europeans established colonies throughout the region. Colonial rule in most places ended after World War II.

The people of China and Japan in East Asia chose to limit their contact with other nations until the nineteenth century. The traditional way of life in these countries began to change only in this century.

Japan has become one of the leading industrial countries in the world in a very short time. Industrialization is also growing in other parts of southern and eastern Asia. However, agriculture remains the occupation of most people. In many countries, a growing population requires more food than can be produced.

The nations of southern and eastern Asia have a variety of governments. There are democratic republics, Communist states, and monarchies. Stable governments do not exist in many Southeast Asian countries. Fighting between Communist and non-Communist groups continues to affect the lives of the people who live there.

Do You Know?

1. What are the highest mountains in the world? Where are they located?
2. What are monsoons? How do the summer monsoons differ from the winter monsoons?
3. In what two countries do most of the people of southern and eastern Asia live?
4. When did the traditional ways of life in China and Japan begin to change?

2
South Asia

South Asia lies south of the Himalaya and Hindu Kush (hin'doo koosh') mountains. It is separated from the rest of Asia by these high mountains on the north and west and by dense tropical forests on the east. The region made up of the Indian Peninsula and the lowlands south of the mountains is often referred to as the Indian *subcontinent* (sub'kon'tə nənt). A subcontinent is a large landmass that is somewhat isolated from the rest of a continent. See the map on page 381.

Eight countries make up South Asia. Five of them are part of the Indian subcontinent. They are India, Pakistan, Bangladesh (bäng'glə desh'), Nepal (nə pôl'), and Bhutan (byoo tan'). The mountainous country of Afghanistan lies to the northwest. South Asia also includes two island countries, Sri Lanka (srē' län'kə) and the Maldives (mal'dīvz').

Nearly one billion people inhabit this region of about two million square miles (5 million sq. km). Here more than 20 percent of the world's people live on about 3 percent of the world's land.

Geography

South Asia extends more than 2,000 miles (3,200 km) from Iran in the west to Burma in the east. The greatest north-south distance is also about 2,000 miles (3,200 km). South Asia stretches from the Soviet Union and China in the north to the Indian Ocean in the south. Sri Lanka is separated from southeast India by the narrow Palk Strait. The Maldives are in the Indian Ocean, about 500 miles (800 km) southwest of Sri Lanka.

Landforms

Great ranges of mountains extend along South Asia's borders with the Soviet Union and China. The towering Hindu Kush Mountains rise in northeast Afghanistan. From here, the Himalayas stretch in a great curve to the southeast for more than 1,500 miles (2,400 km). Along the border between Nepal and China is Mount Everest, the world's highest mountain. The crest of the Himalayas is made up of more than 40 peaks that are higher than 24,000 feet (7,300 m).

Lower mountains run southward from both ends of the Himalayas. Passes at each end of the Himalayas have been used for centuries as invasion and trade routes. One of the most famous is the Khyber (kī'bər) Pass on the border between Pakistan and Afghanistan.

South of the mountains are the great alluvial plains of India. They stretch from east to west across the subcontinent north of the Indian Peninsula. Most of the peninsula is a plateau. In the south, it is known as the Deccan (dek'ən) Plateau. A range of mountains called the Western Ghats (gôts) rises along the western edge of the plateau. A lower range of mountains, the Eastern Ghats, extends along its eastern edge. The Western Ghats drop

Mount Everest in the Himalayas is the world's highest peak. Because of great differences in altitude, almost every kind of climate is found in this range.

steeply to a narrow coastal plain. A broader coastal plain lies between the Eastern Ghats and the sea.

Water Features

The most important rivers of South Asia rise in the Himalayas. The Indus and its tributaries flow south from the western end of the Himalayas into the Arabian Sea. The Ganges (gan'jēz') and Brahmaputra (bräm'ə poo'trə) river systems drain the central and eastern parts of the Himalayas. The Ganges flows east along the south side of the mountains. The Brahmaputra flows east through canyons high in the mountains. It turns west around the eastern end of the Himalayas, then joins the Ganges in central Bangladesh. The joined rivers flow into the Bay of Bengal through a large delta.

The Indus and the Ganges have built up the vast alluvial plain south of the foothills of the Himalayas. As these rivers and their tributaries rush out of the mountains, they carry great quantities of sand, gravel, and mud. When they reach the plains and begin to flow more slowly, they deposit the materials they are carrying.

In the Indian Peninsula, the Narmada River forms the boundary between the plains to the north and the plateau to the south as it flows into the Arabian Sea. Other rivers, including the Godavari (gə däv'ə rē) and the Krishna, flow eastward across the plateau into the Bay of Bengal. These rivers may flood during the rainy season, but they are almost completely dry for a large part of the year.

Climate and Vegetation

Most of South Asia has a tropical monsoon climate. During the dry, warm winter, from October to March, the prevailing winds are from the northeast. From March to June, it is hot and dry. Winds are gentle, and although the air may be very humid, there is little rainfall. The wet monsoon season begins in June and lasts until September. During this season, prevailing winds from the southwest bring extremely heavy rains that continue for months. The temperature is a little lower during the rainy season because the rain clouds shade the earth.

There are great differences in the amounts of rainfall in different parts of South Asia. Rainfall is heaviest along the southwest coast of the Indian Peninsula and in the extreme northeast. The hills and mountains of the northeast receive an average of 450 inches (1,140 cm) a year. The Indus Valley, the western part of Afghanistan, and the interior of the Deccan Plateau receive very little rain.

The summer monsoon does not always bring the same amount of rain. If the monsoons are late or do not bring enough rain, the crops may fail. Sometimes the monsoon rains are heavier than usual, and serious floods result. Violent storms that often accompany the monsoons may increase the damage.

Frost is common in the Himalayas, the Hindu Kush, and the foothills. Summers there are cool and the winters are cold. Winter snows are heavy, and there are huge permanent glaciers among the high peaks. The word *Himalaya* means "house of snow."

Much of the original forest of South Asia was cut long ago to use as firewood and to clear the land for farming. Mixed evergreen and deciduous forests remain in mountainous regions. The northeast has great stretches of tropical forests and jungles.

In addition to cedars, pine, and birch, the forests include valuable timber trees such as teak and sandalwood. An unusual broadleaf evergreen tree called the banyan grows in India. Banyan seeds are dropped by birds in the branches of other kinds of trees. The seeds sprout and send out branches and roots. The roots establish themselves in the ground and eventually form trunks. As more branches and trunks develop, the tree becomes enormous. A single banyan tree with its hundreds of large trunks and thousands of small ones can look like an entire grove of trees.

History

Until recently, the name *India* referred to the entire Indian subcontinent. In discussing the history of this region, we shall refer to all of the subcontinent as India.

Aryans, Hinduism, and the Caste System

The early civilization that grew up in the Indus Valley had disappeared by 2500 B.C. About 1500 B.C., a group of people from central Asia moved through the mountain passes into India. These people called themselves Aryans. In their language, Sanskrit, *Aryan* referred to a person of noble family. When they arrived in India, the Aryans found the Dravidians (drə vid′i əns) living on the northern plain. Many Dravidians moved into southern India when the Aryans invaded. The Dravidians who stayed were conquered. The Aryans intermarried with the Dravidians and adopted some of their customs and ideas. During the next thousand years, the influence of the Aryans spread throughout much of India.

The Hindu (hin′doo) religion, or Hinduism, began in India during this time. Hinduism, unlike Judaism, Christianity, and Islam, is not based on the teachings of one person. Its beliefs developed over hundreds of years. It includes the idea that the universe is ruled by a single spirit made up of different gods and goddesses. An important belief of Hindus is that after death they will be reborn many times in new bodies. Hindus also believe that all living things have souls, and they have a respect for all forms of life.

The caste (kast) system is another part of Indian life. A caste is a social class. When the Aryans arrived in India, they wanted to keep a division between themselves and the people they had conquered. Gradually a complex social system developed, and all the people of India were organized into four large groups of castes. A member of the priest or scholar caste was called a *Brahman* (brä′mən). Rulers and warriors made up another group. A third group included landowners and traders. The fourth group was made up of servants and laborers.

People who did not belong to one of these groups were "outcastes" or "untouchables." The untouchables performed the most unpleasant tasks.

As time went on, the caste system became more complex and rigid. Thousands of new castes developed. People were born into the caste of their parents. They had to marry within their caste and do the kind of work that their caste allowed them to do. People could not move to a caste higher than the one into which they were born. According to Hindu beliefs, however, if people lived good lives and performed good deeds, they could be born again into a higher caste.

Buddhism

Another great religion arose in India about 500 B.C. It was founded by Siddhartha Gautama (sid′är′thə gô′tə mə). Gautama, who was a rich young prince, began to notice the suffering around him and wonder about the meaning of life. He left his wife and small son to become a monk. After many years of listening to others and meditating, Gautama believed that he had become enlightened, or found the meaning and purpose of life. Gautama's followers gave him the title the Buddha, which means "enlightened one" or "teacher of truth." The religion based on the Buddha's teaching is called Buddhism (bood′iz′əm).

Buddhism teaches that the pain and sorrow of life can be ended by living simply and learning to be unselfish. It also teaches that people should overcome anger by kindness, and evil by good. The Buddha believed that people should avoid extremes and follow moderation in all things.

During the time of the Buddha, India was divided into many city-states ruled by powerful rajahs. About 150 years after the Buddha's death, India was again invaded. In 326 B.C., the Greek general Alexander the Great reached the Indus Valley. The next year, Alexander crossed the Indus, but his soldiers convinced him to return to Persia. A new empire arose in India soon after Alexander left.

Asoka

Asoka was the grandson of the founder of the new dynasty. He greatly enlarged the empire he had inherited. See the map on page 388. Asoka, however, was shocked by the horrors of war. He suddenly turned to Buddhism and decided to devote his life to helping his people. He built roads and hospitals and began irrigation projects. He sent Buddhist missionaries to neighboring lands.

Asoka brought unity and peace to India. After his death in 232 B.C., his empire began to

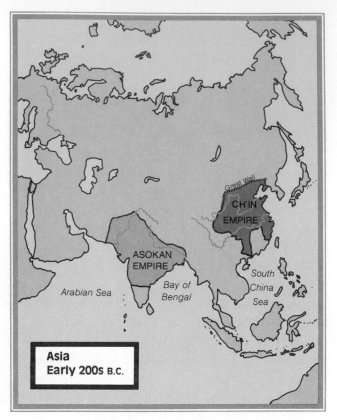

When much of India was united under Asoka, China expanded north and west under the Ch'in *Dynasty.*

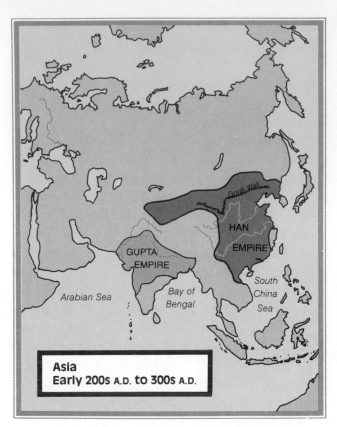

The Han ruled China from about 200 B.C. until 220 A.D. The Guptas did not come to power in India until 320 A.D.

crumble. Buddhism almost disappeared from India, and Hinduism again became the major religion.

India's Golden Age

About 320 A.D., a new line of rulers, the Guptas, came to power. Their rule, which lasted about 200 years, is known as the Golden Age of India. The Gupta emperors made their courts centers of learning and art. Doctors discovered how to treat wounds and perform surgery and mathematicians developed the decimal system. Sanskrit, the language of the early Hindus, was revived and used by scholars. Stories and fables, including those we know as *The Arabian Nights,* had their origin during this period.

Most of the Gupta emperors were Hindus. Both Buddhist and Hindu shrines and temples were built during the Gupta period, however.

The Golden Age ended with a new series of invasions from the northwest. The new invaders included first the Arabs and then the Muslim Turks. They brought Islam and Islamic architecture to India.

The Mogul Empire

In the early 1500s, a ruler named Baber (bä'bər) from central Asia won control of northern India. Baber began the period of Mogul rule. The word *Mogul* comes from the Persian word for Mongol. Under the Moguls, India became one of the most powerful and prosperous countries in the world.

One of the most famous Mogul emperors was Baber's grandson Akbar. At the age of 13, Akbar defeated a large Hindu army. Later he extended his rule over almost all of India. Akbar was concerned with his people's welfare, and he ruled the country with justice.

Akbar and later Moguls were great builders. Akbar designed many beautiful monuments. His grandson, Shah Jahan, built palaces and buildings throughout India. The most famous of these is the Taj Mahal, the tomb he built for his wife. The Taj Mahal is considered one of the most beautiful buildings in the world.

The Mogul Empire began to decline at the end of Shah Jahan's reign. Famines, wars, and religious struggles led to the end of the empire by 1750.

Europeans in India

Vasco da Gama, a Portuguese navigator who reached India in 1498, was the first person to find a sea route from Europe to India. Portugal soon established colonies in India and built up trade. After the middle 1500s, the British, French, and Dutch began competing for trade. They soon established bases in India. After the middle 1700s, the Dutch and French turned their attention to Southeast Asia. The British then controlled a large part of India.

The British in India

In 1600, the British East India Company was organized to handle Britain's trade with India. This company, acting for the British government, became the ruler of a region several times the size of Great Britain.

The Taj Mahal is reflected in a pool bordered by cypress trees. Minarets are a feature of Islamic *architecture*.

The British East India Company built cities, docks, and warehouses, and made trade agreements with the native rulers. The company had its own police force that acted as a private army. By the middle 1800s, it governed about half of India. The rest of India was governed by native rulers who had agreed to accept British control.

In 1858, Great Britain did away with the British East India Company. The British government itself, represented by a viceroy, took over control of affairs in British India. The rest of India was divided into about six hundred states ruled by Indian rulers called princes and maharajahs.

The British government built roads, railroads, schools, and universities. It also helped develop the country economically by improving agriculture and constructing factories. The British also improved medical care.

Under British rule, a number of young Indians were sent to Great Britain for an education.

There they learned about Western ideas of democracy. They returned to India with the desire for independence. The British tried to satisfy the Indians' demands for freedom by giving them positions in the government. A person who works for a government department other than the armed forces is called a *civil servant* (siv'əl sur'vənt).

The Independence Movement

The desire for independence began in the late 1800s and grew much stronger after World War I. India faced several problems in its struggle for self-government. One problem was the large number of native rulers, who wanted to keep their territories and live in wealth and comfort. The British supported the native rulers so that they themselves could carry on trade.

Another problem was the lack of a common language. This prevented people from exchanging ideas. Of the nearly 200 languages of India, only two are spoken by large numbers of people. Two other reasons for the lack of unity were the caste system and the differences between the Muslims and Hindus.

The outstanding leader of the freedom movement in India was Mohandas Gandhi (gän'dē). Gandhi, a lawyer educated in Great Britain, dedicated his life to helping the people of India. He was given the title *Mahatma*, which means "great soul."

Gandhi believed that India should be free, but he did not favor revolution by war or violent means. Gandhi urged the people of India to oppose the British government by quietly refusing to obey its laws and by refusing to cooperate with it. Such a method of resisting authority or protesting by nonviolent means is called *passive resistance* (pas'iv rə zis'təns). Gandhi planned to embarrass the British government in India. He urged people not to hold office, attend school, pay taxes, or buy British goods. Some of Gandhi's followers sat down on railroad tracks, forcing trains to stop. Under Gandhi's leadership, the Indian freedom movement gained strength.

Independence

When World War II broke out, Britain asked for India's help and promised independence after the war. Many Indian soldiers fought loyally in the British-Indian armies. After the war, Great Britain offered India independence as soon as a form of government could be agreed upon. This was difficult because of disagreements between the Muslims and Hindus. The final decision was to partition, or divide, the country into the mainly Muslim nation of Pakistan and the mainly Hindu nation of India. In 1947, Britain granted independence to both countries.

As a result of the partition, millions of Muslims in India fled to Pakistan, and millions of Hindus fled from Pakistan to India.

Pakistan was divided into two parts at the time of the partition. West Pakistan was separated from East Pakistan by nearly 1,000 miles (1,600 km). The political power was in West Pakistan, but most of the people lived in East Pakistan. The people in the two countries differed in languages and traditions. In 1971, a civil war resulted in the establishment of two separate and independent countries. West Pakistan became Pakistan, and East Pakistan became Bangladesh.

India

India is about one-third the size of the United States. It is the largest country in South Asia and the seventh-largest country in the world. With more than 680 million people, India ranks second only to China in population. About one out of every seven people in the world lives in India. The average population density is more than 550 per square mile (210 per sq. km).

The most densely populated parts of India are the Ganges plain and the Ganges-Brahmaputra delta. Most people in India live in villages and work on the land. One of the country's greatest problems is to increase food production to keep up with the growth in population.

The people of India speak many different languages and follow several different religions. Hindi is the official language, and many people speak English. Almost 85 percent of India's population is Hindu. The Muslim, Christian, and Sikh (sēk) religions are followed by most of the other 15 percent. A Sikh is a person who belongs to a religious group that has beliefs from both Hinduism and Islam. Sikhs believe in one God and do not follow the caste system.

The Hindu religion is one of the things most Indians have in common. Evidences of Hindu beliefs and ways of life are found throughout India. Cattle are considered sacred, and in some states there is a law against slaughtering healthy cattle. Cattle are used as work animals when they are young. When they grow old, they are allowed to wander freely over the countryside and through the village streets until they die.

The caste system is also an important part of Indian life. Although discrimination against untouchables was outlawed by the constitution of 1950, caste distinctions still exist. In the villages, particularly, caste is still important. In the cities, however, industrialization and education have helped to do away with some of the caste barriers.

Villages

About 80 percent of the people in India live in hundreds of thousands of small villages. The villages are nearly self-sufficient. Food comes from the surrounding land. Farmers live in the villages and go to the fields to work each day. The people in the village who do not farm provide other goods and services for the village. They are teachers, weavers, carpenters, and merchants. There is a market place where goods are sold. Most villages have mills that produce sugar and oil for the local market.

Living conditions in most Indian villages are very poor. Houses are usually made of mud, although some are made of brick or stone. Many villages lack electricity and plumbing. Water for drinking, bathing, and washing clothes is supplied by wells, ponds, and streams.

A young girl pumps water at a village well in northern India. The water is carried home in large metal jars.

Agriculture

About 70 percent of the people in India earn their living by farming. The average size of a farm is only a few acres. Work is done by hand or with the help of cattle and water buffalo. Nearly half of India is under cultivation, but the country does not produce enough food for its people.

Rice, wheat, and millet are the important food crops. India is the world's second-largest producer of rice. Rice can be grown only where there is enough water from rainfall or irrigation. Rice areas are the lower part of the Ganges and the eastern and western coasts of the Indian Peninsula. Sugarcane is also grown in the Ganges-Brahmaputra delta.

The western part of the Ganges plain is a drier region where wheat is grown. In the middle Ganges, wheat is grown in the winter and rice in the summer on the same land. Millet can grow in areas that are too dry for rice or wheat. Millet and similar grains are raised in the interior of the Deccan Plateau.

Cash crops in India include jute, cotton, tobacco, tea, and peanuts. On the Ganges plain near the delta, the major money crop is jute. Jute fiber is used to make burlap. Cotton and peanuts are raised mainly on the plateau. Tobacco is grown along the southern coasts of the peninsula and in the northeast. Tea is grown in the northeastern state of Assam. Coconuts, bananas, pepper, and rubber are produced for export.

Until recently, crop yields in India were very low. New varieties of wheat and rice that have short growing seasons, high yields, and resistance to pests and diseases are now being grown. New varieties and modern farming methods may help to solve some of India's food shortages.

Mining and Manufacturing

India has large deposits of iron ore and coal. These minerals, along with limestone and various ferroalloys, are found in the region around the city of Jamshedpur (jäm′shed pər), not far from Calcutta. This city is the country's chief steel center. Iron and steel manufacturing is one of India's major industries.

India's other important minerals include gypsum, magnesite, salt, and mica. India supplies a large part of the world's mica, which is used in electrical equipment. In general, India's mining industry has not been greatly developed.

India's two other major industries are cotton textiles and jute fabrics. Most of the cotton factories are found around Bombay, near the cotton-growing region of the Deccan. Calcutta is the center of the jute factories, which are supplied by jute from the surrounding delta lands. Factories that make wool, rayon, and silk are found in many parts of India.

India has long been known for its handicrafts. People working in small shops or at home produce textiles and rugs, and handmade brassware, jewelry, and carvings by hand.

Cities of India

About 20 percent of India's people live in cities, but the cities are growing at a much faster rate than rural India. India has nine cities with a population of more than one million each. The cities are scattered throughout India and connected with one another by the largest railway system in Asia.

Bombay, Calcutta, and Delhi are India's three largest cities. Bombay, the chief port of western India, has the finest harbor of the subcontinent. Calcutta, a busy port in eastern India, is connected with the Bay of Bengal by the Hooghly (hoo'glē) River. Calcutta's importance as a port declined after 1947, when East Pakistan, now Bangladesh, began to use other seaports. In recent years, silt deposits in the Hooghly have reduced its usefulness.

Much of the old city of Delhi (del'ē) was built by Shah Jahan. The British moved their capital from Calcutta to Delhi in 1912. The present capital, New Delhi, is a modern city just south of Delhi.

The *Orient* has long been known for its handmade rugs. This weaver in India works on a loom.

Delhi, New Delhi, and many other large cities are on the Ganges plain. About halfway between Delhi and Calcutta is the sacred Hindu city of Benares (bə när'əs). Three miles (nearly 5 km) of the river bank are lined with temples from which broad flights of steps lead to the river. Down these steps, millions of pilgrims descend to bathe in the river and drink its waters. Benares is also sacred to the Sikhs and Buddhists. It is believed that the Buddha preached his first sermon near here.

Pakistan

Pakistan lies northwest of India. It is about the second-largest country of South Asia. It is only about one-fourth the size of India, and it is much less densely populated. Most of its 85 million people are Muslims. During the 1960s, the Pakistanis built Islamabad to replace Karachi as the capital.

Pakistan became a republic in 1956. Military leaders took over the government in 1977, and since then the country has been under *martial* (mär'shəl) *law*. Martial law is military rule of a country during a war or other emergency.

Pakistan is mountainous in the north and along its borders with Iran and Afghanistan. In the southeast is the Thar Desert. The Indus River and its tributaries begin high in the mountains to the north and flow through this desert. The great plain occupied by the Indus and its tributaries is called the Punjab. The name *Punjab* comes from the Hindustani words meaning "five waters."

Agriculture

Most of the people of Pakistan are farmers in the Indus Valley. Rainfall is low because the summer monsoons have lost much of their moisture by the time they reach Pakistan. Water from the Indus and its tributaries is used for irrigation. The chief food crop grown is wheat, but some rice is grown in irrigated areas. The main export crop is cotton.

Water for irrigation has been increased and made more dependable by large dams on the headwaters of the Indus. The dams also provide the country with hydroelectric power.

One of the most serious problems that arose when India and Pakistan were created was the control of the province of Kashmir. When Kashmir joined India, the boundary between India and Pakistan cut across the headwaters of the Indus and its tributaries. India was able to control the water and make it unavailable to Pakistan. A war broke out over boundaries and water rights. A settlement gave Pakistan control of the western rivers. India was given control of the eastern rivers.

Mining and Manufacturing

Pakistan's mineral resources include iron ore, bauxite, salt, natural gas, and oil. Only about 10 percent of the country's workers are employed in manufacturing. The manufacturing of cotton textiles is the chief industry. Cement and fertilizer are other important products. Near Karachi, a plant makes steel from scrap metal. Pakistan is known for carpets, embroidered clothing, pottery, and metal items made in homes or small factories.

Bangladesh

Bangladesh is a small country at the head of the Bay of Bengal. It is completely surrounded by India on its landward side. Bangladesh's population of more than 90 million makes it one of the most densely populated countries in the world. Muslims account for about 85 percent of the population. Dacca is the capital and largest city. Between 1947 and 1971, Bangladesh was a part of Pakistan known as East Pakistan. Today, Bangladesh is a republic with an elected president.

Bangladesh occupies the low, wet plains of the Ganges, Brahmaputra, and Meghna (māg'nə) rivers. These rivers flow through a system of channels and canals across the world's largest delta into the Bay of Bengal. This region has rich, fertile soil. Heavy monsoon rains and high tides in the Bay of Bengal sometimes cause floods that destroy lives, crops, and property.

The majority of the people in Bangladesh are farmers. Rice and jute are the chief crops. Most of the delta land is used to grow rice. Three rice crops can be grown in a single year.

Jute is grown where the land is too deeply flooded to grow rice. When the jute is harvested, the stems are tied together and left under water for several weeks to loosen the fibers. The dried fibers are taken to factories to be made into burlap. Bangladesh is the world's largest producer of jute.

Wheat, corn, sugarcane, tobacco, and tea are grown in the drier areas where there is no flooding. Livestock is raised for skins and hides. Fish caught along the coast are an important source of food.

Bangladesh is a poor country that suffers from a shortage of food. It does not produce or import as much food as it needs.

Nepal and Bhutan

High in the Himalayas between India and the part of China known as Tibet (təbet′) lie the small independent countries of Nepal and Bhutan. Along their southern borders, both countries descend to the plains of India. In the past, Nepal and Bhutan were very difficult to reach. Their location helped them to remain independent. Both countries are constitutional monarchies ruled by a king.

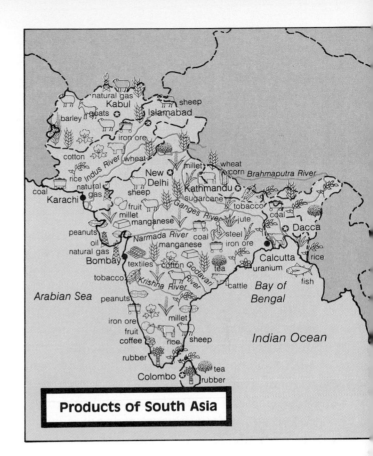

Products of South Asia

Nepal

Nepal is about the size of Bangladesh and has a population of more than 14 million. Hinduism is the official religion, but many Nepalese practice a religion that is a combination of Hinduism and Buddhism. Nepal is the birthplace of the Buddha.

Before Nepal was unified in the late 1700s, the region was made up of several small, independent kingdoms. The British controlled parts of Nepal in the early 1800s. In 1923, Britain recognized Nepal's independence. The monarchy was restored to power in 1951.

Most of Nepal is mountainous. The population is concentrated in the mountain valleys east and west of the capital of Kathmandu. These valleys have cool, rainy summers and cold, dry winters. Farmers here grow rice, corn, sugarcane, and wheat. Much of the farmland is terraced. Cattle, sheep, and yaks are raised in the mountain pastures.

On the plains south of the mountains, rice, wheat, and jute are grown. Part of this region has a tropical climate and is covered with jungles and swamps, where elephants, crocodiles, and tigers are found.

Most farming in Nepal is at the subsistence level, but some agricultural products are exported. The country also has income from tourism. Thousands of visitors, including many mountain climbers, arrive in Nepal each year. The Sherpas, a small Nepalese ethnic group, are known for their courage and skill as guides for the climbers.

Bhutan

Bhutan lies east of Nepal and is separated from it by the small Indian state of Sikkim (sik′əm). Bhutan is about one-third the size of Nepal, and it has a population of more than one million.

Bhutan was conquered by people from Tibet in the 800s. It became a separate state in the 1600s. During the days of British India, Great Britain controlled some of Bhutan's foreign affairs. Today, India handles most of Bhutan's foreign affairs.

Most of the people of Bhutan are descendants of Tibetans. A form of Buddhism is the official religion of Bhutan. Priests and monks of this religion are called lamas. They perform religious rites, treat diseases, and teach. They live in great fortress monasteries throughout the country.

The climate and landforms of Bhutan are much like those of Nepal. Most of the people farm and raise livestock in the mountain valleys. Barley, rice, and wheat are grown. The country produces and exports some coal.

Afghanistan

Afghanistan is a large landlocked country northwest of the Indian subcontinent. It borders Pakistan, Iran, the Soviet Union, and China. Afghanistan is about three-fourths the size of Pakistan. Its population of about 16 million gives it one of the lowest population densities in South Asia. Afghanistan is a Muslim country.

Much of Afghanistan lies high above sea level. The Hindu Kush Mountains in the northeast include many peaks more than 24,000 feet (7,300 m) above sea level that are always covered with snow. Set among the mountains are deep valleys with well watered streams fed by melting snow. In the southwest is a hot, dry desert. The country receives little rainfall.

History

Kabul (käb′əl), the capital of Afghanistan, lies in a valley near the passes through the Hindu Kush. The passes lead from central Asia to India. The Aryans who moved through these passes to invade India also conquered Afghanistan. Other early conquerors in the region included the Persians and Alexander the Great.

Arab armies, bringing Islam, reached Afghanistan in the seventh century A.D. Baber

A paved road now follows the famous Khyber Pass between Afghanistan and Pakistan. For centuries this route has been used for trade and invasion.

used Kabul as his base for the conquest of India in the early 1500s. Conflicts between rival Afghan tribes continued until the 1700s, when the country became unified. Twice during the 1800s, Russia and Great Britain struggled for control of Afghanistan. Britain wanted to protect its Indian Empire. Russia wanted an outlet on the Indian Ocean. In 1880, the British gained a certain degree of control over the area. British control ended in 1919, when Afghanistan became independent. A kingdom was established in 1926.

In 1973, a military coup overthrew the king, and a republic was set up. Five years later, the government was replaced by a Socialist government. In late 1979 and early 1980, Soviet troops invaded Afghanistan to put down a rebellion against the government. Resistance to the Soviet occupation has continued.

Farming and Herding

More than 90 percent of the people in Afghanistan live in rural areas and earn their living in agriculture. Wheat, barley, cotton, and sugar beets are grown on irrigated land in the mountain valleys. Nomadic herders graze sheep and cattle in the mountain meadows and in the valleys. Wool and skins of the native karakul sheep are exported.

Mining and Manufacturing

The lack of good transportation has made the development of natural resources difficult in Afghanistan. There are no railroads, no navigable rivers, and few good roads.

A few factories produce cotton and wool textiles, cement, and processed food. Rugs, leather goods, and jewelry are made by skilled workers in their homes.

Living and Working in Southern and Eastern Asia

Most people in southern and eastern Asia have jobs related to agriculture. In many places, work is done without the help of machinery. Tea is picked by hand on the mountain slopes of Sri Lanka. A nomadic herder on the plains of Mongolia carries a kind of lasso for catching horses. The portable tents, called yurts, are made of felt and canvas or hide.

Handicrafts are economically important in parts of Asia. An Indian brassworker marks a design on a plate.

Industrialization and mechanization have come to many Asian countries. A steel worker in India moves a red-hot steel bar. In Japan, rice is harvested by machine. Factory workers in China stack sheets of metal.

Sri Lanka and the Maldives

Sri Lanka and the Maldives are tropical island countries in the Indian Ocean. Both came under the control of the Portuguese during the 1500s. Later, both were ruled by the Dutch and then the British. Britain granted independence to Sri Lanka in 1948, and to the Maldives in 1965. Today both countries are republics with a president as head of the government.

Sri Lanka

Sri Lanka is about half the size of Nepal. The population of Sri Lanka is about 15 million. The population density—more than 590 per square mile (225 per sq. km)—is a little higher than that of India. The people are descendants of Indians, Europeans, Malaysians, and Arabs. The majority are Sinhalese, the descendants of people who came from northern India. Sri Lanka is the Sinhalese word for Ceylon, the name by which the island was known before 1972. Most Sinhalese are Buddhists.

A mountainous region in the south of Sri Lanka rises to 8,000 feet (2,400 m). A coastal plain with rich alluvial soil brought down from the mountains surrounds the mountains. Sri Lanka is a tropical country, but ocean breezes moderate the temperature. In the summer, monsoons bring heavy rains to the southwest side of the island, but the eastern side remains relatively dry.

The chief crops of the island are tea and rubber, which are grown on large plantations in the south. The rubber plantations are along the coastal plains and foothills. Tea is grown higher up on the mountain slopes. Rice and coconuts are grown as food crops, but Sri Lanka has to import much of the food it needs.

Valuable timber trees of Sri Lanka include ebony and satinwood. The island is famous for its spices and gemstones such as rubies and sapphires. Sri Lanka is a busy trading country. Its capital, Colombo, is an important port.

The Maldives

The Maldives are the smallest country in Asia. They are made up of about 2,000 very small coral islands populated by only 150,000 people. Most of the people are descendants of Sinhalese who came from Sri Lanka. Islam is the major religion.

The low-lying islands of the Maldives are covered with tropical vegetation, including coconut palms and fruit trees. The climate is hot and humid. Both the summer and winter monsoons bring rain. Fishing is the main industry of the islands, and dried fish are the chief export. Tuna are one of the main fish caught in the Maldives.

Do You Know?

1. What five countries are part of the Indian subcontinent?
2. What two religions began in India?
3. Who led the independence movement in India?
4. What was the former name of Bangladesh?

Before You Go On

Using New Words

subcontinent   martial law
passive resistance Brahman
Orient   civil servant

Number a paper from 1 through 6. After each number write the word or term from the above list that matches the definition.

1. Military rule of a country during a war or other emergency
2. A person who works for a government department other than the armed forces
3. A large landmass that is somewhat isolated from the rest of a continent
4. A member of the priest or scholar caste
5. A method of resisting authority or protesting against some law or act by nonviolent means
6. A word meaning "east" that refers to the Far East

Finding the Facts

1. What are the two most important factors affecting the climate of southern and eastern Asia?
2. What percentage of the world's people live in southern and eastern Asia?
3. What mountains border the Deccan Plateau?
4. What important rivers of South Asia have their source in the Himalayas?
5. What religion was founded by Siddhartha Gautama? When?
6. What dynasty ruled India during its Golden Age?
7. What was the result of the 1971 civil war fought in Pakistan?
8. What are three important cash crops in India?
9. What is the Punjab? What does the word *Punjab* mean?
10. What country is the world's leading producer of jute? What is jute used for?
11. What form of government do Nepal and Bhutan have?
12. When did Arab armies bring Islam to Afghanistan?
13. What are two island countries of South Asia?
14. What are the chief crops of Sri Lanka?

3
Southeast Asia

Southeast Asia separates South Asia from East Asia. It is bounded by India and Bangladesh on the west, and by China on the north. Nine countries make up this region.

Five Southeast Asian countries occupy the large peninsula that extends southeast between the Bay of Bengal and the South China Sea. This peninsula is known as Indochina. The countries of Indochina are Burma, Thailand (tī′land′), Laos (lä′ōs), Kampuchea (kam′ poochē′ə), and Vietnam (vēet′näm′). These countries are part of the *mainland of* Asia. The principal land of a continent is called the mainland. The mainland does not include small peninsulas and islands.

The rest of Southeast Asia is made up of the Malay (mā′la′) Peninsula and the Malay Archipelago. The Malay Archipelago is the largest group of islands in the world. It extends south and east of the mainland in a great arc between the Indian Ocean and the Pacific Ocean. The countries that occupy the Malay Peninsula and the Malay Archipelago are Malaysia, Singapore, Indonesia, and the Philippines.

Geography

The peninsulas and islands of Southeast Asia are made up of rugged mountains, wide valleys, and broad coastal plains. Great rivers flow through the valleys between the mountain ranges. Shallow seas separate the islands from the mainland and from one another.

Landforms

Several mountain ranges fan out from the eastern end of the Himalayas and stretch through Indochina. These mountains are not as high as the Himalayas, but they are steep. They become lower toward the south and east. The westernmost of these ranges lies along the border between India and Burma. It continues to the south through two groups of islands in the Bay of Bengal. The islands of Sumatra and Java are the tops of submerged mountains belonging to this range.

Another range of mountains extends along the border between Burma and Thailand. It continues south to form the Malay Peninsula. Along the border between Laos and Vietnam is a third mountain range.

Sumatra and Java are part of an island arc that continues northward through Sulawesi (soo′ləwā′sē) and the Philippines. All of these islands are the tops of submerged mountains. Active volcanoes exist among the mountains of the islands. The volcanoes can be very destructive, but they also produce great amounts of volcanic ash that enrich the soil.

Two large islands belonging to the Malay Archipelago are not part of the volcanic island arc. New Guinea, the second-largest island in the world, lies outside the arc to the east. Borneo, the world's third-largest island, is enclosed by the arc. Both Borneo and New Guinea are mountainous. Several peaks rise above 10,000 feet (3,000 m).

402

Water Features

The Bay of Bengal and the Indian Ocean lie to the east and south of Southeast Asia. To the east is the Pacific Ocean. The arrangement of the peninsulas and islands separates the Pacific into dozens of different seas. The most important of these are the South China Sea and the Philippine Sea. The Philippine Sea lies east of the Philippines, and the South China Sea lies between the Philippines and the mainland. To the south, the Arafura (ar'ə fōōr'ə) Sea separates Indonesia from Australia.

Hundreds of straits separate the islands and peninsulas. The Strait of Malacca (mə läk'ə) between the Malay Peninsula and Sumatra forms part of the most direct water route between southern and eastern Asia.

The most important rivers of Southeast Asia are in Indochina. Five large rivers flow south between the mountain ranges of the peninsula. From west to east, they are the Irrawaddy (ir'ə wäd'ē), the Salween (sal'wēn'), the Menam (mā näm'), the Mekong (mā'kong'), and the Red. The valleys through which these rivers flow broaden as they approach the sea. Here the rivers flow across wide alluvial plains. Where they enter the sea, the rivers have built up large deltas.

Climate and Vegetation

Almost all of Southeast Asia lies in the tropics and has a hot, humid climate throughout the year. Monsoons have a great effect on the climate. These winds, blowing from the ocean to the land, bring heavy rains to most of the region. Dry seasons occur when the winds blow from the land. Some parts of central Indochina are dry because they lie on the leeward sides of the mountains in the rain shadow.

In the areas of heavy rainfall in Southeast Asia, most of the original vegetation was tropical rain forest. Much of the rain forest has been cleared for farming, but large areas of lowland tropical forest still remain. In the drier regions are broadleaf deciduous forests and scrub woodland.

History

Traders, settlers, and missionaries from India came to Southeast Asia in the 200s B.C. The teachings of the Buddha and the Hindu religion were a great influence on the culture of the region.

People called the Khmer (kə mer') established an empire in what is now Kampuchea. By 1100 A.D., the empire included parts of present-day Thailand, Laos, and Vietnam.

The capital city of the Khmer Empire was Angkor Thom (ang'kər'tom'). The central temple of Angkor Thom was dedicated to the Buddha.

The temple of Angkor Wat (ang'kər'wät') was built close to the Khmer capital. Angkor Wat was dedicated to the Hindu god. The temple, which included pyramids and towers, was intended to be like the home of the Hindu gods. People used the high towers of the temple to observe the stars.

By the early 1400s, the Khmer Empire had become weak. Angkor Thom was captured by

Angkor Wat in Kampuchea was built as a Hindu temple. It was also used as an astronomical observatory and tomb.

invaders from Thailand in 1431. Other kingdoms and empires in Southeast Asia had lost their power and lands by the sixteenth century.

European exploration, settlement, and control of Southeast Asia began in 1511. In that year, the Portuguese arrived in the Malay Peninsula. Spanish explorers claimed the Philippines in 1565 and established a settlement there. After the Spanish-American War in 1898, Spain ceded the Philippines to the United States. The Dutch began to take over the islands of Indonesia in the 1600s.

British rule in India was extended to include Burma by the 1800s. In 1819, the British built a port on the island of Singapore. A large part of the Malay Peninsula came under British control in the 1800s. At about the same time, France took control of a region that included Vietnam, Kampuchea, and part of Laos. The French called the area Indochina.

In the late 1800s, Britain and France came into conflict over their interests in Southeast Asia. Both countries wanted to control Thailand, which lay between British Burma and French Indochina. To prevent war, the two countries agreed that Thailand would retain its independence and act as a buffer state between British and French colonies. Thailand is the only country in Southeast Asia that was never ruled by a European power.

Europeans valued the resources found in the tropical lowlands of Southeast Asia. They set up plantations where rubber trees, rice, and sugarcane were grown. Tin, nickel, and chromium deposits were mined.

During World War II, Japan gained control of all of Southeast Asia except for parts of Burma. When Japan surrendered to the Allies in 1945, the British, the French, and the Dutch regained their colonies in Southeast Asia. The

United States again controlled the Philippines. However, the desire for independence among the people in the colonies was strong. The return of the colonies to Western powers did not last long. One by one, the former colonies became nations.

After World War II, the Philippines and all the major British colonies were granted independence peacefully. The Indonesians fought against the Dutch to gain independent status. The French tried to retain their power in Indochina and kept their colonies longest.

In 1946, French forces fought Communist rebels in northern Vietnam. The fighting continued in Vietnam and in other parts of Indochina until 1954. In that year, a peace settlement put an end to the fighting. The settlement also established the borders of Laos, Vietnam, and Kampuchea. Vietnam was divided into two sections. South Vietnam became a republic. North Vietnam was ruled by a Communist government. French rule in Southeast Asia had come to an end.

In 1957, Communist forces called the Viet Cong began to attack areas in South Vietnam. The conflict developed into an extended period of fighting that involved the United States and several of its allies. It lasted until 1975, when South Vietnam surrendered to North Vietnam. In 1976, the Communists united Vietnam under a single government.

Conflict between Communist and non-Communist groups expanded into Kampuchea and Laos in 1975. In many parts of Southeast Asia today, fighting continues to disrupt the lives of the people.

Buddhist monks are a common sight in Burma. Flowers are often left as offerings in shrines.

Burma

Burma, the second-largest country of Southeast Asia, lies east of India on the Bay of Bengal. Almost 35 million people live in Burma, yet it is one of the least densely populated countries of Southeast Asia.

Burma is a land of mountains, forests, valleys, and plains. The great Irrawaddy River rises in the mountains of northern Burma and flows south through the center of the country. Burma's second-largest river, the Salween, rises in Tibet and flows through eastern Burma. Both the Irrawaddy and the Salween empty into the Bay of Bengal. Rangoon, Burma's capital, largest city, and main port, lies on a branch of the Irrawaddy near its mouth.

The Burmese call their country the "Golden Land" because the rice crops turn the land gold colored. Pagodas throughout the country are covered with gold, and Buddhist priests wear long yellow robes.

Burma was once a province of British India. Later, it became a separate colony. During World War II, Japan controlled the country. Burma became an independent republic in 1948.

Farming and Lumbering

Most Burmese live in bamboo houses in small villages. About 70 percent of the people make their living by farming or lumbering.

Burma's farms are on the Irrawaddy delta, in the river valleys, and on the coastal plains. More than half of the country's farmland is used for growing rice. Burma is one of the world's leading rice producers. Other crops include corn, cotton, peanuts, and sugarcane.

More than half of Burma is covered with forests. The most important forest product is teakwood, a hardwood used for making furniture and building ships. Elephants are trained to carry the teak logs between their tusks and trunks from the forests to river banks, where the logs are floated downstream.

Mining and Manufacturing

Rich petroleum fields lie in the Irrawaddy River Valley. Iron, tin, copper, and lead are mined in the mountains. The country also has deposits of precious stones.

Burma has few industries. The most important is rice milling. Small factories manufacture cotton yarn and cloth. Skilled workers make wood carvings, jewelry, cloth, and lacquered items.

Thailand

Thailand lies southeast of Burma and occupies part of Indochina and the Malay Peninsula. Thailand is somewhat smaller than Burma, but it has a larger population. Most of Thailand is on the Asian mainland. Northern Thailand is a mountainous region that lies between the Salween and Mekong rivers. Central Thailand is a wide valley formed by the country's chief river, the Menam. Southern Thailand is a long, narrow strip of land on the Malay Peninsula. Thailand has coasts on both the Andaman Sea to the west and the Gulf of Thailand to the south and east.

In the 1800s the country was known as Siam. In 1939, its name was changed to Thailand, which means "land of the free."

Thailand is mainly an agricultural country. More than three-fourths of the people are farmers. Rice is the major agricultural product and export.

More than 100,000 Thai earn a living by fishing. Thailand's rivers and coastal waters are filled with mackerel, shellfish, anchovies, and other fish. The fish are either eaten fresh or dried or smoked for export.

Thick forests provide Thailand with a successful lumbering industry. Thailand once produced more teakwood than Burma. However, many trees were cut down without being replaced, and the teak forests became smaller.

Farm produce goes to market by boat on canals near Bangkok, Thailand, once known as the "Venice of the East."

Tin is Thailand's most important mineral resource. It is mined in the southern part of the country, primarily for export. There are rich deposits of many other minerals, including tungsten, copper, iron, and precious stones.

Today Thailand is one of the most prosperous nations of Southeast Asia. Bangkok, the country's capital and largest city, is a fast-growing metropolis. Modern hotels, office buildings, and theaters have been built near the city's ancient temples and palaces.

Laos

Laos lies east of Thailand. It is bordered by four Southeast Asian countries and by China. It is the only landlocked country in Southeast Asia. Laos is a tropical area of forested mountains and rugged plateaus. There are fertile plains along the Mekong River, which forms Laos' boundary with Thailand. About four million people live in Laos. The capital and largest city is Vientiane (vyentyän′).

Most of what is now Laos was first united in 1353. The kindom of *Lan Xang,* which means "land of a million elephants," lasted until about 1700, when three separate kingdoms were formed. France occupied Laos in the late 1800s and ruled it as part of Indochina. In 1954, Laos became independent. Civil wars took place in the 1960s and the early 1970s. Laos became a Communist country in 1975.

Almost all of the people in Laos are subsistence farmers. Rice is the chief crop. Teak and other trees are cut for export. Tin is the only mineral that is produced and exported. The country has few industries.

Kampuchea

Kampuchea is also known as Cambodia. It is a small country with a high population density. The capital of Kampuchea is Phnom Penh (pənom′pen′). Kampuchea is at the southern end of Indochina. It has a short coast on the Gulf of Thailand. Most of Kampuchea is a large alluvial plain surrounded on three sides by mountains. The Mekong River flows from Laos through Kampuchea on its way to the South

China Sea. During flood time, the Mekong overflows into a large, shallow lake called the Tonle Sap (tän′lä sap′). Tonle Sap is found near the center of the country, just south of the ruins of Angkor Wat.

Kampuchea gained its independence from France in 1953. In the early 1970s, it became a major battleground in the Vietnam War. At the same time, Communists called the Khmer Rouge (kə mer′roozh′) fought a civil war with government forces. In 1975, the Khmer Rouge managed to *depose* (di pōz′), or remove from power, the ruler of Kampuchea. The Khmer Rouge took control of the country. In 1979, another group of Communists overthrew the Khmer Rouge government.

Most people in Kampuchea are farmers. Rice and corn are the main food crops. The country also produces rubber. However, many farms and rubber plantations were destroyed

Colonial control of Asia expanded from the 1500s to 1914. Asian countries furnished supplies of raw materials for Western nations.

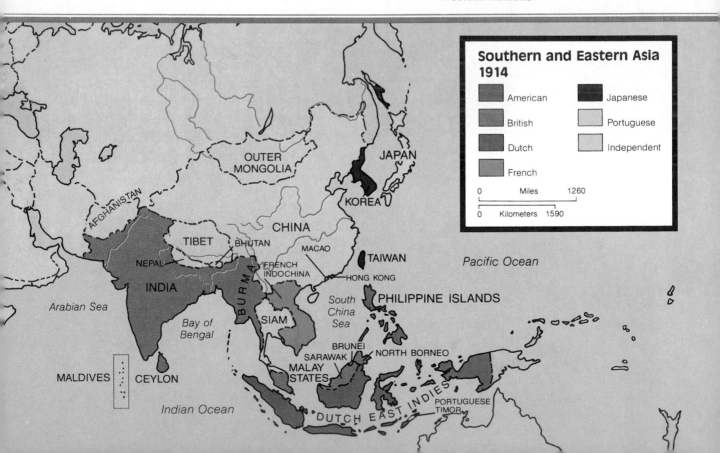

Southern and Eastern Asia 1914

American
British
Dutch
French
Japanese
Portuguese
Independent

0   Miles   1260
0   Kilometers   1590

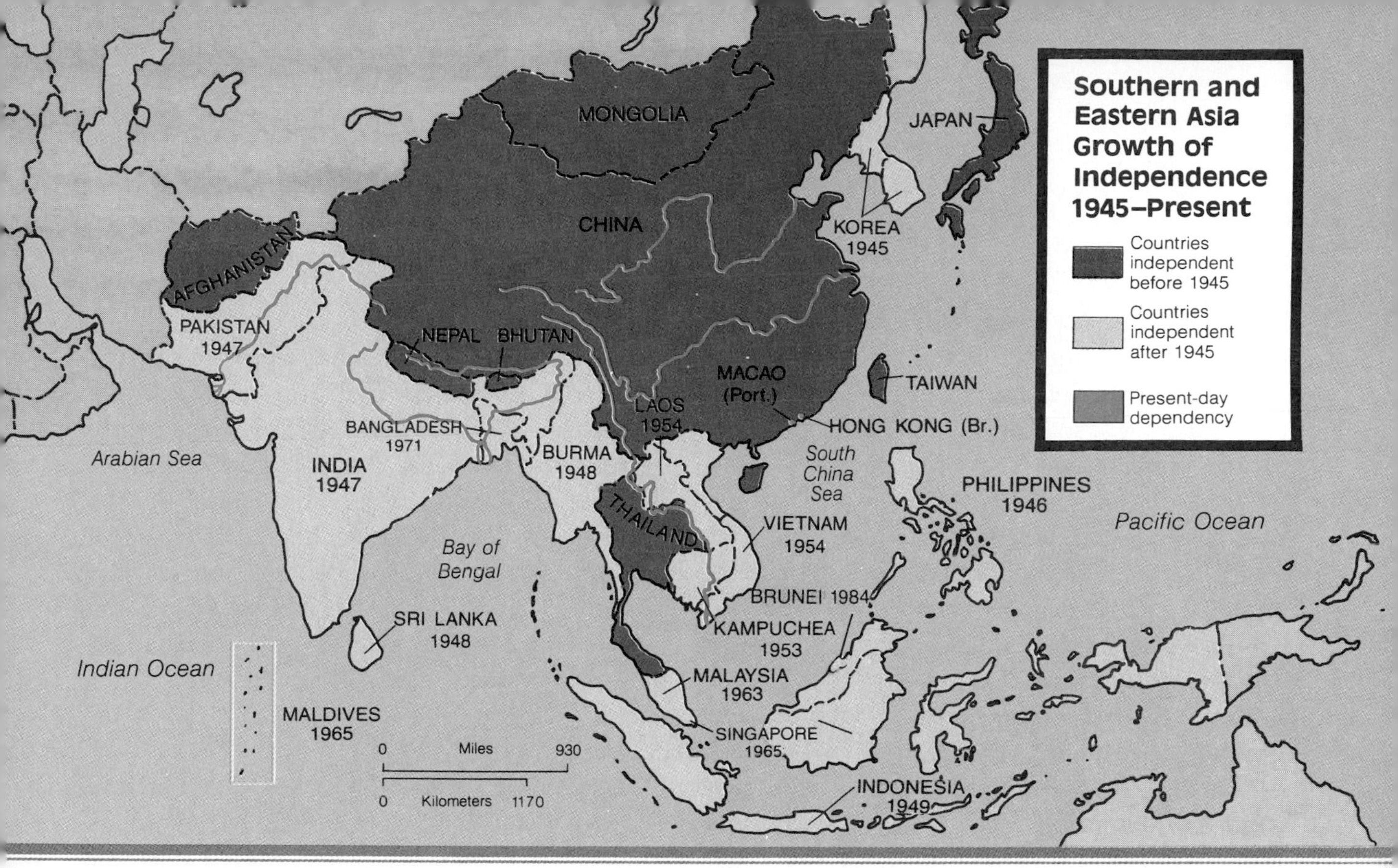
Southern and Eastern Asia Growth of Independence 1945–Present
Countries independent before 1945
Countries independent after 1945
Present-day dependency
MONGOLIA
CHINA
JAPAN
KOREA 1945
AFGHANISTAN
PAKISTAN 1947
NEPAL
BHUTAN
MACAO (Port.)
TAIWAN
HONG KONG (Br.)
LAOS 1954
BANGLADESH 1971
BURMA 1948
INDIA 1947
Arabian Sea
South China Sea
PHILIPPINES 1946
Pacific Ocean
THAILAND
VIETNAM 1954
Bay of Bengal
BRUNEI 1984
SRI LANKA 1948
KAMPUCHEA 1953
Indian Ocean
MALAYSIA 1963
MALDIVES 1965
SINGAPORE 1965
0 Miles 930
0 Kilometers 1170
INDONESIA 1949

Growing feelings of nationalism after World War II led to the end of colonialism in most parts of Asia.

during the recent wars. Agricultural production has remained low since the 1970s.

Fishing is an important activity in Kampuchea. The Mekong River and the Tonle Sap furnish Kampuchea with the greatest supply of freshwater fish in Southeast Asia.

Kampuchea also has forest and mineral resources. Pine and teak are cut for export, and iron ore is mined. A few industries manufacture wood, metal, and rubber products.

Vietnam

Vietnam extends south from China along the coast of the South China Sea in a narrow S-curve. Its coastline is nearly 1,000 miles (1,600 km) long. Hanoi is the capital, and Ho Chi Minh City, once called Saigon, is the largest city. Vietnam's population is about 53 million.

A chain of forested mountains runs along Vietnam's western borders with Laos and Kampuchea. The land slopes to a narrow plain along the coast. The Red River flows from China through the northern part of the country. It empties into the Gulf of Tonkin (tän′kin′) through a large delta. The Mekong River flows for a short distance through the south of Vietnam. It empties into the South China Sea through another large delta.

The French had gained control of the area that is now Vietnam by 1883. During World War II, the Japanese controlled the region, but French rule was restored in 1945. French forces were attacked by Communist groups in northern Vietnam in 1946. The fighting continued throughout Indochina until 1954. In that year, a settlement divided Vietnam into two parts by establishing the boundaries of North Vietnam and South Vietnam.

A major war between the two Vietnams began when Communist forces called the Viet Cong attacked South Vietnam. Between 1965 and 1973, the United States supported the South with supplies and troops. A cease-fire agreement was signed in 1973 by the United States, North Vietnam, and South Vietnam. Fighting continued, however, until 1975, when South Vietnam surrendered to the Communist forces of North Vietnam. The country was unified under a Communist government the following year.

The majority of the people in Vietnam are farmers. Rice is grown on the deltas of the Red and Mekong rivers. Rubber is produced in the south. Forests provide bamboo and timber. Fish are caught in rivers and along the coasts. Northern Vietnam has large deposits of coal and small quantities of several other minerals. Vietnam has a small iron and steel industry. The few factories manufacture textiles, paper, and cement.

During the war, Vietnam's transportation system was badly damaged, as were many farms, mines, and factories. The Vietnamese also suffered because of serious food shortages. During and after the war, thousands of people decided to *evacuate* (i vak′yoo āt′), or leave, the country. Many refugees left in small boats to find new places to live. They became known as "boat people."

Malaysia

Malaysia is made up of two regions separated by about 400 miles (640 km) of the South China Sea. West Malaysia occupies the southern part of the Malay Peninsula. East Malaysia is made up of Sarawak and Sabah on the northwest coast of Borneo. Malaysia is a mountainous tropical land, much of which is covered by rain forests. About 14 million people inhabit Malaysia. Malaysia is the world's leading producer of tin and rubber.

West Malaysia

West Malaysia shares a border with Thailand on the north. It is separated from Sumatra by the Strait of Malacca. The South China Sea borders it on the south and east. West Malaysia is the most heavily populated part of Malaysia. Most of the people are Malays, Chinese, and Indians. West Malaysia has about 80 percent of the population of the country, but only about 40 percent of the land. The capital of Malaysia, the modern city of Kuala Lumpur (kwäl′ə loom′poor′), is in West Malaysia.

Malays settled on the Malay Peninsula in ancient times. The area became a crossroads for trade between China and India about 2000 B.C. Between 800 and 1400 A.D., many small city-states grew up on the peninsula. The British, interested in protecting their route to China through the Strait of Malacca, established a trading post there in the late 1700s. Later, the British took over the settled native states. They developed the interior by establishing rubber plantations and opening tin mines.

West Malaysia was conquered by the Japanese early in World War II. Shortly after the war, most of the states that now make up West Malaysia were united as the Federation of Malaya and given independence. In 1963, the Federation of Malaya joined with Singapore, Sarawak, and Sabah to form Malaysia. Malaysia is a constitutional monarchy. Singapore withdrew from the federation in 1965.

West Malaysia is the more developed part of Malaysia. Most of the cultivated land, rubber plantations, tin mines, towns, and ports are found here.

Rubber is the most important industrial crop of Malaysia. Rubber is made from latex, a milky liquid that is collected from rubber trees. Tropical hardwood trees are cut for lumber and exported.

Rice is the chief food crop of Malaysia. About 80 percent of the country's rice is grown in West Malaysia. Other crops are palm oil, pepper, and pineapples.

The tin-bearing rocks of West Malaysia are part of a belt that runs south from China. Particles of tin are found in deposits of sand and gravel. The tin is recovered by large excavators that separate it from the sand and gravel by washing. Tin is West Malaysia's most important mineral. Bauxite is also produced.

Most of Malaysia's industries are found near Kuala Lumpur. About 10 percent of the population works in factories. Factories process tin, rubber, timber, and palm oil. New industries include oil refining, textiles, and chemicals. Another important industry is the processing and freezing of fish for export.

A Malaysian rubber plantation worker taps a tree for latex. Knives are used to make narrow downward-curving grooves. The latex collects in a cup below a spout at the bottom of the vertical cut.

East Malaysia

East Malaysia occupies about one-fourth of Borneo. Sabah is at the northern tip of the island, and Sarawak extends along the coast to the southwest. Between them on the coast is the tiny country of Brunei (broo′ nī). Brunei, Sarawak, and Sabah were once British colonies.

Most of the people of East Malaysia belong to several ethnic groups that have been there for a long time. Chinese account for about one-third of the population. Most of the population is concentrated along the coastal plain.

Farmers in East Malaysia produce rice and palm oil. Rubber is produced, and valuable hardwoods are found there, especially in Sabah. Oil is produced in Sarawak, and copper is mined in Sabah. Fish are caught, processed, and frozen for export in East Malaysia.

Native boats line the banks of a river flowing past modern skyscrapers in downtown Singapore. The main *economic* activities of this *free port* are moving goods and manufacturing.

Singapore

Near the tip of the Malay Peninsula lies the island country of Singapore, the smallest country in Southeast Asia. The country is made up of the island of Singapore and about 50 tiny nearby islands. The islands have a combined area of only 238 square miles (616 sq. km). Rain forests cover most of the main island, and there are swamps along its northern coast.

The country's capital, also called Singapore, is on Singapore Island. More than 90 percent of the people of Singapore live in the city. The majority of the people are Chinese.

The city of Singapore is one of the busiest ports in the world. It is a transfer point for ships traveling between Europe and Asia. At Singapore, goods are unloaded and reloaded for shipment to other Asian countries, Europe, and the United States. Singapore is a *free port* (frē pôrt). A free port is a port where goods may be moved in and out without payment of taxes, or duties.

The activities of the port provide many jobs and have helped Singapore become an important manufacturing center. Singapore's industries include petroleum refining, shipbuilding, and food processing. Singapore is one of the most prosperous countries in all of Asia.

Indonesia

Indonesia is the largest country in Southeast Asia. It is made up of five large islands and thousands of small islands. The islands stretch south and east of the Malay Peninsula for more than 3,000 miles (4,800 km). The three largest islands belonging wholly to Indonesia are Sumatra, Sulawesi, and Java. Indonesia also includes three-fourths of the island of Borneo and the western half of the island of New Guinea. The Indonesian part of New Guinea is called Irian Jaya (ir′ē än jī′yə).

Most of the 155 million people who live in Indonesia are Malays. The majority are Muslims. Indonesia is the fifth most populous country in the world. The most densely populated area is Java, where 60 percent of the people live. The country's capital and largest city, Jakarta (jə kärt′ə), is on Java. Irian Jaya is the least densely populated part of Indonesia.

Indonesia lies in the tropics, and tropical rain forests cover large parts of the islands. Most islands are mountainous, and the country has many active volcanoes. Java has more volcanoes than any other part of the world.

The ancestors of today's Indonesians came from the mainland of Southeast Asia between 2500 and 500 B.C. Indians, both Hindus and Buddhists, began settling in Indonesia in the

Dance is one of the most famous arts of Indonesia. A masked Balinese dancer performs as musicians play.

400s A.D. Hindu and Buddhist kingdoms were rivals for power for hundreds of years. In the 13th century, Muslim traders from Arabia and India introduced Islam to Indonesia.

The Portuguese, the first Europeans in Indonesia, arrived on the island around 1500. By the end of the 1500s, English and Dutch traders began to compete for influence in the area. The Dutch controlled the trade of most of the islands by the late 1700s. The region

became known as the Dutch East Indies. Indonesians began to demand independence early in the 1900s. The Dutch granted Indonesia independence in 1949.

Farming, Lumbering, and Fishing

The majority of Indonesians make their living by farming. The soil, enriched by ashes from the islands' volcanoes, is extremely fertile. The main crop, rice, is raised on terraces built on

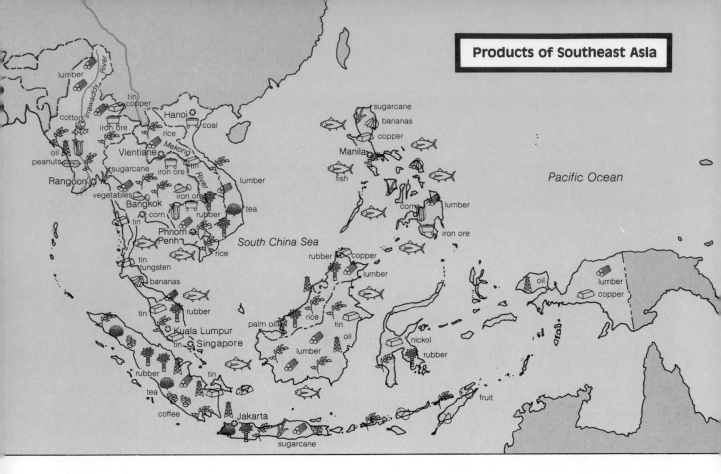

Map labels: lumber, tin, copper, cotton, iron ore, rice, Hanoi, coal, oil, peanuts, Vientiane, Mekong, sugarcane, iron ore, tin, Rangoon, vegetables, iron ore, lumber, Bangkok, corn, rubber, tea, tin, Phnom Penh, rice, South China Sea, tin, tungsten, bananas, rice, rubber, tin, rubber, palm oil, Kuala Lumpur, tin, Singapore, lumber, rubber, tin, tea, coffee, Jakarta, sugarcane, rubber, copper, lumber, tin, oil, nickel, rubber, fruit, corn, lumber, Manila, fish, iron ore, sugarcane, bananas, copper, Pacific Ocean, oil, lumber, copper

---

steep slopes. Coffee, tea, sugarcane, and rubber are produced on large plantations. These crops are raised for export.

Indonesia's forests have valuable hardwood trees, especially ebony and teak. Lumbering is important in Borneo and Java.

A wide variety of fish, including mackerel and tuna, is taken from the country's seas. Fish are also caught in inland rivers and raised in ponds.

Mining and Manufacturing

Indonesia is an important oil-producing country in Southeast Asia. Oil accounts for nearly 75 percent of the country's exports. Most of the oil comes from Sumatra, Borneo, and Java. Indonesia is also important for its tin.

Relatively few Indonesians work in manufacturing. Most of the factories are in Java.

They produce petroleum products, rubber goods, and textiles. Skilled workers of Indonesia use the batik method of waxing and dyeing cloth to make beautiful fabrics.

The Philippines

The Philippines is an island country that forms the northern end of the Malay Archipelago. The country lies north of Indonesia and is separated from the Asian mainland by the South China Sea. There are more than 7,000 islands in the Philippines. The two largest islands, Luzon (lōō zän′) and Mindanao (min də nä′ō), make up two-thirds of the country. See the map on pages 444–445. The country's capital and largest city, Manila, is on Luzon. Manila is a modern city. It has one of the finest harbors in Southeast Asia.

The Philippines islands are mountainous. Many are volcanic. Lowlands are found along the coasts, and there are wide interior plains on Luzon and Mindanao. The climate is hot and humid all year.

About 49 million people live in the Philippines. Most Filipinos are related to the Malays of Indonesia and Malaysia. Many are descendants of other groups of people who settled there. The Philippines is the only country in southern and eastern Asia where the majority of the people are Christians.

Ferdinand Magellan arrived in the Philippines in 1521. Magellan was Portuguese, but he was exploring a route to the East Indies for the king of Spain. The first Spanish settlement was established in 1565, and Spanish rule over the islands began. Under the Spanish, most Filipinos were converted to Christianity. In 1898 the United States gained control of the Philippines after defeating Spain in the Spanish-American War. The Philippines was given complete independence in 1946.

About half of all Filipinos are farmers. As in many parts of Asia, rice is commonly grown on terraced mountainsides. Corn, coconuts, bananas, and sugarcane are other leading crops. An important export crop is abacá, or Manila hemp. Its strong fibers are used to make rope and twine.

The forests of the islands include important timber trees, such as cedar, pine, and mahogany. The waters surrounding the Philippines have hundreds of kinds of fish.

Mining is important in the Philippines. Copper, found mainly on Luzon, is the most plenti-

Shoppers in the Philippines buy seafood just off the fishing boats. Fish are an important food in these islands.

ful mineral. There are large deposits of chrome and iron ore.

Manufacturing in the Philippines is growing rapidly. Factories process farm products and make chemicals, cement, and clothing.

Do You Know?

1. What is the name of the peninsula that extends between the Bay of Bengal and the South China Sea?
2. What is the largest group of islands in the world?
3. When did French control in Southeast Asia come to an end?
4. What country ruled the Philippines from 1898 to 1946?

Before You Go On

Using New Words

free port   mainland
evacuate   depose

Number a paper from 1 through 4. After each number write the word or term from the above list that matches the definition.

1. The principal land of a continent
2. A port where goods may be moved in and out without payment of taxes, or duties
3. To remove from power
4. To leave a country or place

Finding the Facts

1. Name the five countries of Indochina.
2. In what present-day country was the Khmer Empire established? Parts of what other present-day countries did it once include?
3. What are the two largest rivers in Burma?
4. What does the name *Thailand* mean?
5. What is the only landlocked country in Southeast Asia?
6. When did the Khmer Rouge take control of Kampuchea?
7. Who were "the boat people"?
8. What nation in Southeast Asia is the world's leading producer of tin and rubber?
9. Where is Singapore? Why is it an important port?
10. Why is Indonesia's soil rich and fertile?
11. What important resource accounts for most of Indonesia's exports?
12. When did Indonesia gain its independence? Which European nation gave up its control of Indonesia at that time?
13. What country in Southeast Asia exports abacá? What is abacá used for?

4

East Asia

East Asia is bounded by the Soviet Union to the north, South Asia to the southwest, and Southeast Asia to the south. The Pacific Ocean lies to the east. Six independent countries belong to this region. About one-fourth of all the people in the world live in East Asia.

China occupies most of the mainland of East Asia. China is a land of great mountain ranges, high plateaus, vast deserts, hills, and broad, fertile river valleys. North of China is Mongolia, a sparsely populated region of deserts and steppes. North Korea and South Korea occupy the peninsula that separates the Yellow Sea from the Sea of Japan. The islands of Japan stretch in an arc to the east of the Sea of Japan and the East China Sea. South of Japan

Regional Data Chart

Country	Capital	Area		Population	GNP (in millions of U.S. dollars)
		Square miles	Square kilometers		
Afghanistan	Kabul	251,000	650,090	16,250,000	$3,400
Bangladesh	Dacca	55,126	142,776	90,700,000	$8,300
Bhutan	Thimphu	18,100	46,879	1,325,000	$110
Brunei	Bandar Seri Begawan	2,226	5,765	225,000	$2,200
Burma	Rangoon	261,790	678,036	34,350,000	$5,100
China	Beijing	3,691,502	9,560,990	970,000,000	$517,000
India	New Delhi	1,229,737	3,185,019	683,810,000	$126,000
Indonesia	Jakarta	735,268	1,904,344	155,300,000	$52,200
Japan	Tokyo	143,574	371,857	117,650,000	$1,019,500
Kampuchea	Phnom Penh	70,000	181,300	9,000,000	$500
Laos	Vientiane	91,429	236,800	3,800,000	$300
Malaysia	Kuala Lumpur	128,328	332,370	14,000,000	$18,000
Maldives	Malé	115	298	150,000	$30
Mongolia	Ulan Bator	604,500	1,565,655	1,725,000	$1,300
Nepal	Kathmandu	54,362	140,798	14,325,000	$1,800
North Korea	Pyongyang	46,768	121,129	18,350,000	$19,700
Pakistan	Islamabad	310,724	804,775	85,000,000	$21,000
Philippines	Manila	115,707	299,681	49,000,000	$28,100
Republic of China	Taipei	13,592	35,203	18,000,000	$32,000
Singapore	Singapore	238	616	2,420,000	$9,100
South Korea	Seoul	38,022	98,477	38,800,000	$55,900
Sri Lanka	Colombo	25,332	65,610	15,000,000	$3,400
Thailand	Bangkok	198,455	514,000	48,175,000	$26,900
Vietnam	Hanoi	126,436	327,469	53,550,000	$8,900

Nonindependent Area

Country	Capital	Square miles	Square kilometers	Population	GNP
Hong Kong (Great Britain)	Victoria	398	1,031	5,156,000	$18,700
Macao (Portugal)	Macao	6	15.5	280,000	$540

and off the east coast of China is East Asia's other island country, the Republic of China.

In addition to these independent countries, East Asia includes the British colony of Hong Kong and the Portuguese territory of Macao (mə kou'). Both Hong Kong and Macao are on the southeast coast of China.

China

In both area and population, China is very large. It ranks third only to the Soviet Union and Canada in area. With more than 970 million people, it ranks first in population among all the countries of the world.

The western two-thirds of China is sparsely settled. Most of the people live in the eastern third of the country. Here are found most of the large cities and most of the good farm land.

Geography

China is made up of several regions. The extreme northeast of the country is known as Manchuria. The area just south of Mongolia is called Inner Mongolia. The western part of China is divided between Sinkiang (shin'jē äng') in the north and Tibet in the south. The part of China lying roughly east of a line drawn from Beijing (bā'jing') to Chongqing (choon'king') is called China Proper. See the map on page 381.

Landforms

Much of China is enclosed by high mountains that stretch along its borders. These mountain ranges include the Himalayas that separate China from South Asia. Other mountains extend to the northeast from the western end of the Himalayas to form much of China's northern boundary. Ranges stretching southeastward from the eastern end of the Himalayas separate China from Southeast Asia.

The Himalayas lie along the southern part of Tibet. Tibet is a high, dry plateau surrounded by high mountains. It is the largest region of high elevation in the world. The plateau averages 15,000 feet (4,600 m) above sea level. North of Tibet are the deserts and steppes of Sinkiang. This region, with its basins and salt lakes, resembles the Great Basin of the western United States.

Plateaus and mountains stretch eastward from Sinkiang into Inner Mongolia. The Gobi Desert covers much of this region. It extends to the western part of Manchuria. The central part of Manchuria is a plain surrounded by highlands to the west, north, and east.

China Proper is divided into two parts by an east-west mountain range called the Qin Ling (chin'ling'). North and east of the Qin Ling is the North China Plain. To the south is a hilly upland region.

Water Features

China has a long coastline on the Pacific. From north to south, the parts of the Pacific that border China are the Yellow Sea, the East China Sea, and the South China Sea.

The two great rivers of China are the Huang (hwäng) and the Chang (chäng). Both rivers rise in the eastern part of Tibet and flow through China Proper. The more southern river, the Chang, is the fifth-longest river in the world. In its lower part, it flows for 700 miles (1,120 km) across the North China Plain before entering the East China Sea. The world's sixth-longest river, the Huang, flows eastward through the deserts and steppes of Inner Mongolia. Here it picks up the yellow loess that gives it its characteristic color. *Huang* is the Chinese word for "yellow." The Huang also flows across the North China Plain. It empties into the Yellow Sea.

Both the Chang and the Huang have built up great alluvial plains near their mouths. This flat region made up of great deposits of mud, silt, and sand is known as the North China Plain. In times of heavy rain, the rivers often flood and cause great damage. Because of the destruction it causes, the Huang is often called "China's Sorrow."

China has about 100,000 miles (160,000 km) of navigable rivers and canals. The Chang is the single most important river for transportation. The Grand Canal, the world's longest constructed waterway, is more than 1,000 miles (1,600 km) long. It stretches from Beijing in the north to Hangchou (hän′jō′) in the south and connects the Huang and the Chang rivers.

Climate and Vegetation

Because it is so large, China has a great variety of climates. Most of China is affected by monsoons. In the summer, warm, moist winds blow across the Pacific toward China. The winter monsoons move cold, dry air from central Asia across China to the ocean.

The summer monsoons bring heavy rains to the hilly uplands of China Proper south of the Qin Ling Mountains. This region has a warm, humid subtropical climate. Some of the original forests still cover the land here, but much of it has been cleared for farming.

As the summer monsoon winds reach the interior, they become drier. Rain and snow fall in parts of Tibet. Little precipitation, however, falls in Sinkiang and Inner Mongolia. Much of this region is desert.

Manchuria and China Proper north of the Qin Ling Mountains receive more rain than Inner Mongolia and Sinkiang, but less than China Proper to the south. The summers are hot and dry. Cold winds blowing out of central Asia bring bitter winters to these regions.

History

You read about the early civilization of the Huang Valley in Unit 2. People have been living in China for at least 6,500 years.

Early Dynasties

The history of China began about 1500 B.C., with the rise of the Shang Dynasty. Shang rulers were not real kings or emperors. Powerful nobles controlled their own areas. However, the nobles recognized the Shang ruler as the head of the armies and as their religious leader.

In about 1125 B.C., the Chou (jō) people of western China overthrew the Shang and established a new dynasty. The Chou Dynasty, which lasted until 256 B.C., is often called

China's classical period. Chou rulers established a strong government and became active in the country's economic life. Canals were dug and irrigation systems were built. Cities prospered as people became skilled workers and merchants. Art and literature flourished. Beautiful bronze vases and carvings of jade and ivory have been found from this period.

Great thinkers and teachers lived during the Chou Dynasty. Kung Fu-tse, who became known as Confucius (kənfyōō′shəs), had a great influence on the Chinese people. Confucius was born in 551 B.C., just a few years after the Buddha. Confucius taught that people should always be kind and polite. He also believed that people should have respect for older people and ancestors, and for the ways of the past. This belief led to a practice called ancestor worship. Followers of Confucius combined his teachings and beliefs into a religion called Confucianism.

In 221 B.C., after the fall of the Chou, a new dynasty began. This was the Ch'in Dynasty, the dynasty from which China got its name. The country was united for the first time. The Ch'in ruler, China's first emperor, had absolute control. To protect China from northern invaders, he built a long wall known as the Great Wall of China. Later emperors extended the wall. Today it is more than 2,000 miles (3,200 km) long—the longest wall in the world.

In 202 B.C., the Han Dynasty took control and ruled for about 400 years. This was a great period of expansion for China. See the map on page 388. The Han Dynasty declined in the 200s A.D. A period of unrest and disunity

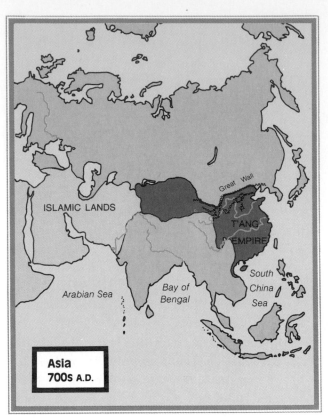

In the 700s A.D., Islam spread into southern Asia. In 751, Arab armies defeated the Chinese in Turkestan.

followed. China began to recover in the 600s A.D. under the T'ang Dynasty. The 300 years of T'ang rule was known as China's golden age. Some of China's greatest poets wrote during this time. The T'ang capital became a center for scholars from Asia and the Mediterranean. The invention of printing during this era made literature and scholarly writing available to many people.

The Mongols

In the 1200s, the Mongols invaded China from the north. They set up a new dynasty under the leadership of Kublai Khan (koo′blī kän′). For the first time, all of China came under foreign rule.

420

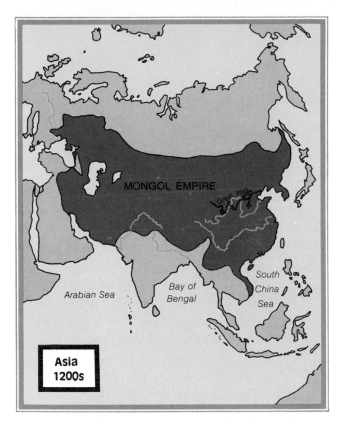

At its greatest extent, the Mongol Empire covered much of Asia and reached to the Danube in Europe.

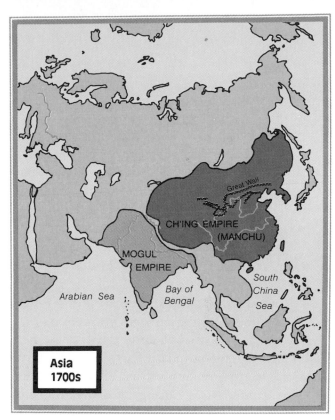

During the time of the Mogul and Ch'ing empires, European colonies began to grow in southern and eastern Asia.

During the late 1200s, the Western world learned of Chinese achievements through the reports of travelers and traders. In 1274, an Italian explorer named Marco Polo arrived in China and stayed nearly 20 years.

In time, Mongol rule weakened. The Chinese people rebelled against their foreign rulers and drove them out in 1368. The Chinese rulers of the fifteenth and sixteenth centuries did not welcome foreigners, and they limited trade with the West.

The Manchus

In 1644, China was invaded by the Manchu people of Manchuria, a land to the northeast. The Manchus established China's last dynasty, known as the Ch'ing Dynasty. They ruled a huge empire. See the map above. The last ruler abdicated in 1912.

Manchu rulers continued China's policy of isolation. China was prosperous during early Manchu rule. The new rulers expanded the empire to its greatest extent since the day of the Mongol emperors. In the nineteenth century, the Manchus signed treaties that gave trading rights to Great Britain, France, and the United States. Later, the United States persuaded China to accept an open door policy that allowed all nations to trade with China. Japan also took advantage of Manchu weakness at the end of the nineteenth century. In 1895, Japan won control of Korea and Taiwan.

The Republic

After a series of attacks against the Manchus, Chinese revolutionaries overthrew the Manchu empire. In 1911, the leaders of the revolution established a republic. Sun Yat-sen (soon' yät' sen') was elected president.

China did not become a united country when it became a republic. Military leaders from northern China, called warlords, organized their own armies. The warlords fought one another and the new government.

Sun Yat-sen tried to unite the Chinese people under the Nationalist Party, but he was not successful. After Sun's death in 1925, leadership passed to Chiang Kai-shek (chäng' kī'shek'). Chiang's armies fought the warlords and soon gained control over much of China. At the same time, another political party, the Communists, was growing. The Communists helped the Nationalists at first, but Chiang turned against them in 1927.

By 1931, the Communists had set up bases in southern and central China. Chiang's armies attacked the bases, forcing the Communists to move north. In 1934, the Communists began a walk that became known as "The Long March." By the end of 1935, they had walked 6,000 miles (9,600 km). Of the 100,000 who began the march, only a few thousand survived. Mao Tse-tung (mou' tsə toong'), the leader of the march, became the leader of the Communist Party in China.

While Chiang fought the Communists, Japan invaded China. In 1931, the Japanese occupied Manchuria. The Chinese could not turn back the Japanese attacks. By the end of 1938, Japanese armies controlled most of eastern China. The Nationalists withdrew to the province of Sichι an (se'chwän'), where they made Chongqing the wartime capital. China joined the Allies against Japan in World War II. Supplies were sent to Chongqing by the Allies, but the Nationalists were severely weakened by the costs of war.

Communist China

The war against Japan gave the Communists an opportunity for expansion. By the time the war ended in 1945, the Communists had control of northern China. In 1946, a full-scale war between the Communists and the Nationalists began. The Communists were victorious. In 1949, the Chinese mainland was united under the Communist rule. Under the leadership of Mao Tse-tung, the Communists set up the People's Republic of China. Chiang and the Nationalist armies were forced to withdraw to the island of Taiwan, which became known as the Republic of China.

The new Communist government took measures to improve China's economy. Large land-holdings were divided among the people. Later, private property was done away with. A series of five-year plans to promote industrialization were begun.

Contacts between China and other countries have increased in recent years. In 1971, the People's Republic of China was admitted to the United Nations. The following year, President Richard Nixon visited China. The United States established diplomatic relations with the People's Republic of China in 1979.

The main section of the Great Wall of China is about 2,000 miles (3,200 km) long. Built to keep out invaders, it did not prevent Mongols from conquering much of China in the 1200s.

Living in China

About three-fourths of the people in China today work in agriculture. The Chinese government has organized the rural areas into counties. Within the counties, the people are divided into communes. Each commune produces industrial and agricultural products to meet local needs.

Since the first five-year plans for industrialization, the population of China's cities has grown. Today, it is estimated that about 20 percent of China's population is urban. In the late 1960s, there was an attempt to move people out of the cities to live and work in the country. This plan to put city people in touch with country people was part of a movement called the Cultural Revolution.

Farming and Fishing

Only about 13 percent of the land in China is arable. Most of the arable land is in Manchuria and China Proper. The Chinese practice intensive farming. The farmland is carefully prepared, planted, and fertilized. Terraces and irrigation increase the amount of land that can be used.

Rice and wheat are the two main food crops of China. Rice is the most important crop south of the Qin Ling Mountains in the region called South China. North China, the area north of the Qin Ling Mountains, is the chief wheat-growing region.

South China has a long growing season. Rice is grown in paddies on the great river floodplains. In parts of the far south, two crops of rice are produced each year. In northern parts of South China, rice is grown in the summer, and wheat and vegetables are grown in the winter. China is the world's leading rice and vegetable producer.

Other crops of South China are cotton and tobacco. Tea is grown on the steep hillsides, and tropical crops are raised on Hainan (hī'nän') Island. They include bananas, coffee, and rubber.

The great wheat-growing region of North China is the valley of the Huang River. The rich loess soils here are highly productive. The

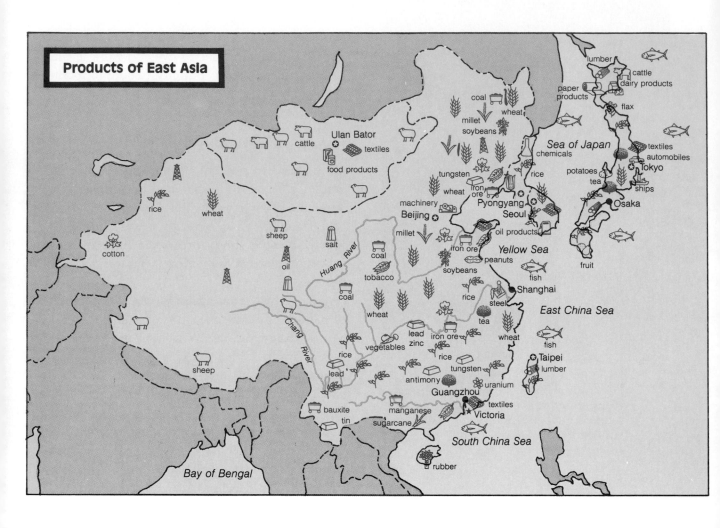

Products of East Asia

wheat grown is winter wheat, which is planted in the fall and harvested the following summer. To the north and in Manchuria, wheat is also grown. In the northern regions, however, the wheat is spring wheat. Spring wheat is planted in the spring of the year and harvested during the summer of the same year.

In addition to wheat, North China produces other grains such as millet and soybeans. Cotton, tobacco, and peanuts are also important crops. Northern China is too cold and dry for more than one crop a year.

China has a large fishing industry. Fish are an important part of the country's diet. The chief areas of sea fishing are off the coast in the East China and South China seas. Most farms have ponds that are stocked with fish, and fish are also raised in rice paddies.

Mining and Manufacturing

Coal and iron ore are found in many parts of China. These resources are used in the iron and steel industry. Coal is the major energy source in China, but oil is becoming more important. The largest oil field is at Da Qing (də king'), in Manchuria. During the 1970s, China began to export oil in large quantities.

China is first in world production of tungsten, a metal used in making tools and in the electronics industry. Tin and *antimony* (an'ti mō'nē) are also produced. Antimony is a bluish-white brittle metal. It is combined with lead to make an alloy. Antimony-lead alloys are used in batteries and cables. Zinc, salt, uranium, bauxite, lead, and manganese are other important mineral resources in China.

Industrial products make up more than 75 percent of China's exports. Steel, tools, machinery, and transportation equipment are the major industrial exports.

Cities of China

About 20 percent of China's people live in cities. China has about 15 cities of more than one million people. They include several of the largest cities in the world.

Shanghai (shang hī'), with nearly eleven million people, is China's largest city. It is on the banks of a small tributary of the Chang River. Shanghai's location has helped make it a leading port and industrial city. Ships carry products made in the city's factories to other parts of China and all over the world.

A common means of transportation in China is the bicycle. Riders pedal past the Great Hall of the People in the huge square outside Beijing's Forbidden City.

Beijing, also known as Peking (pē king′), is China's capital and second-largest city. Beijing is famous for its beautiful palaces, temples, and huge stone walls and gates. The palaces of former Chinese emperors are preserved in the old "Forbidden City." Surrounding the Forbidden City are lakes, parks, and the homes of China's government leaders. Beijing's many universities, libraries, and museums have made it the cultural center of China.

Southeast of Beijing is Tianjin (tan jin′). Tianjin is connected with the Huang River by the Grand Canal. It is the seaport for northern China and a major industrial center.

Guangzhou (gwäng′ jō′), also known as Canton, is the major city and chief port of southern China. It was the first Chinese port opened to foreign trade. The old city is surrounded by a wall with 12 gates. Many of the city's inhabitants live on houseboats.

The Republic of China

Nationalist China is called the Republic of China. It has been located on Taiwan and a number of smaller islands since 1949. Taiwan is about 90 miles (140 km) east of the Chinese mainland. The capital and largest city of Taiwan is Taipei (tī′ pā′).

Taiwan is separated from mainland China by the Formosa Strait. Thickly forested mountains cover the eastern two-thirds of Taiwan. Mountains drop sharply to the sea in the east. The land slopes more gently to a coastal plain in the west. This plain is the country's main agricultural area. About 80 percent of Taiwan's 18 million people live on this plain. The majority of the people are farmers.

Because of Taiwan's tropical climate, two or three crops a year may be harvested from the same field if fertilizer is used. High yields are important to the Taiwanese because only about one-fourth of the land can be farmed. The chief crops are rice, sugarcane, bananas, and sweet potatoes.

Taiwan's forests make lumbering an important industry. The lumber is used largely for construction and in the manufacture of paper. Many Taiwanese fish the waters around the island for mackerel, sardines, and tuna. Taiwan has deposits of coal and oil. Iron, copper, and sulfur are also mined.

Many manufacturing plants using modern machinery have been built in Taiwan. These include sugar refineries and cement, fertilizer, and textile plants.

Hong Kong and Macao

Two small areas on the southeast coast of China are still ruled by Europeans. Hong Kong is a British colony. It is made up of a peninsula, Hong Kong Island, and a number of other islands south of the peninsula. West of Hong Kong is the Portuguese territory of Macao.

Hong Kong

Hong Kong was part of China from ancient times until the 1800s. Hong Kong Island became a British colony in 1842 as part of the settlement in a war with China. Britain gained control of all present-day Hong Kong by the end

Colorful boats anchor off the China *mainland* in the *free port* of Hong Kong.

of the century. The head of government is a governor appointed by the British monarch.

Almost all of the people living in Hong Kong are Chinese. Most are immigrants who left China in the 1900s. Today there are about five million people living in Hong Kong. It is one of the most crowded places in the world.

Hong Kong is a center of international trade, finance, and tourism. Like Singapore, Hong Kong is a free port and serves ships from all over the world.

Hong Kong has also become an important industrial center. Its factories employ about half of its population. Hong Kong imports large quantities of raw materials for its manufacturing industries. Textiles, clothing, electronic equipment, and many other products are exported to the United States, West Germany, Great Britain, and Japan.

Victoria and Kowloon are Hong Kong's major cities. Victoria, on Hong Kong Island, is the capital. Kowloon, the largest city, is on the peninsula. The two cities lie on opposite sides of Victoria Harbor, one of the finest natural harbors in the world. Thousands of people cross the harbor each day on ferries or pass under it through a tunnel.

Macao

Macao is about 35 miles (53 km) southwest of Hong Kong on the China coast. Macao is made up of a peninsula and two small islands. The city of Macao occupies the peninsula. The total area of Macao is about six square miles (16 sq. km), and the population is about 300,000.

The Portuguese settled Macao in 1557. Although Portugal still formally controls Macao, the People's Republic of China has a major voice in the governing of the territory.

Macao attracts tourists from Hong Kong and has some industry. Like Singapore and Hong Kong, it is a free port. Almost all its food is imported from China.

Mongolia

Mongolia is a large landlocked country about one-sixth the size of China. It borders China to the south and the Soviet Union to the north. Mongolia is the homeland of the Mongols. In the past, the Mongols conquered large parts of Asia and extended their control into Europe. Mongol power reached its peak in the thirteenth century under the leadership of Kublai Khan. See the map on page 421.

Later, Mongolia was under Chinese rule for several centuries. Outer Mongolia, now Mongolia, declared its independence in 1912 after the fall of the Manchus. It became a re-public in 1924. Inner Mongolia remained under the control of China.

Today, Mongolia is a sparsely populated country. The population is less than two mil-lion. Mongolia's Communist government has strong ties with the Soviet Union.

The Gobi Desert covers much of Mongolia. Dry grasslands are found on the margins of the desert, and there are high mountain ranges in the west and north. Many Mongolians are pas-toral nomads who raise horses, cattle, sheep, and camels in the semiarid grasslands.

Most of Mongolia's factories are in Ulan Bator (yōō′län′bä′tôr), the capital and only important city. Textiles and processed foods are two of the important products.

North Korea and South Korea

North Korea and South Korea occupy the Korean Peninsula, which extends south from Manchuria. The peninsula is bounded by the Yellow Sea on the west, the East China Sea on the south, and the Sea of Japan on the east. Forested mountains cover much of the interi-or. There are plains along the coast.

For centuries, Korea was a single country, controlled by China. From 1895 until the end of World War II, Korea was controlled by Japan. After the war, Korea was divided along the 38th parallel. Soviet forces occupied the territory north of this line. United States forces occupied the territory south of it. Because the north and south could not agree on a single form of government, the division became per-manent. North Korea became a Communist country, and South Korea became a republic.

In 1950, North Korean troops invaded South Korea. The United States and other members of the United Nations sent troops to defend South Korea. China and the Soviet Union aided North Korea. Neither side could defeat the other. An agreement reached in 1953 left Korea divided.

North Korea

More than 18 million people live in North Korea. The people are divided equally be-tween the country's urban and rural areas. Pyongyang (pē′ong′yäng′) is the capital and largest city.

About half the people make their living by farming. All the farms are collective farms. Rice is the chief crop. Barley, corn, and wheat are also grown. Many people work in mines. North Korea has large deposits of graphite and magnesium.

Many people work in North Korea's government-owned factories. Manufacturing accounts for nearly 70 percent of the country's income. The chief factory products are chemi-cals, iron and steel, machinery, and textiles.

South Korea

South Korea is slightly smaller than North Korea, but its population—more than 38 million—is more than twice as large. The capi-tal and largest city is Seoul (sōl).

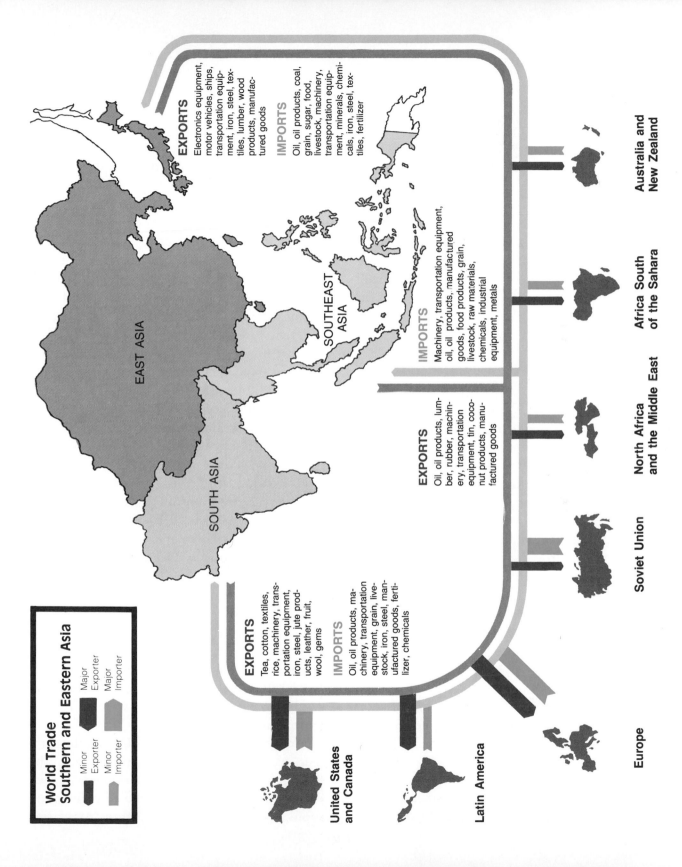

World Trade Southern and Eastern Asia

Major Exporter
Minor Exporter
Major Importer
Minor Importer

EAST ASIA

SOUTH ASIA

SOUTHEAST ASIA

EXPORTS
Electronics equipment, motor vehicles, ships, transportation equipment, iron, steel, textiles, lumber, wood products, manufactured goods

IMPORTS
Oil, oil products, coal, grain, sugar, food, livestock, machinery, transportation equipment, minerals, chemicals, iron, steel, textiles, fertilizer

EXPORTS
Oil, oil products, lumber, rubber, machinery, transportation equipment, tin, coconut products, manufactured goods

IMPORTS
Machinery, transportation equipment, oil, oil products, manufactured goods, food products, grain, livestock, raw materials, chemicals, industrial equipment, metals

EXPORTS
Tea, cotton, textiles, rice, machinery, transportation equipment, iron, steel, jute products, leather, fruit, wool, gems

IMPORTS
Oil, oil products, machinery, transportation equipment, grain, livestock, iron, steel, manufactured goods, fertilizer, chemicals

United States and Canada

Latin America

Europe

Soviet Union

North Africa and the Middle East

Africa South of the Sahara

Australia and New Zealand

As in North Korea, half of the people are farmers. The same crops are raised, but here the land is privately owned. The southern and western coasts are the main agricultural areas. Many farmers in these areas are also fishers.

Industry has developed rapidly since the war. In new factories in South Korea, imported raw materials are made into products for export. Manufactured products include clothing, petroleum products, electronics equipment, and chemicals.

Japan

Japan is an island nation that lies off the Asian mainland between the Sea of Japan and the East China Sea on the west, and the Pacific Ocean on the east. Japan is a small country that has a large population. In area, Japan is only 4 percent as large as the United States, yet its population is more than half that of the United States. With little land and few natural resources, Japan has become one of the most highly industrialized countries in the world. Its people have the highest standard of living in East Asia.

Geography

Japan is made up of a chain of four main islands and thousands of smaller islands. From north to south, the four large islands are Hokkaido (hä kīd′ō), Honshu (hän′shoo), Shikoku (shi kō′koo), and Kyushu (kē oo′shoo). Japan stretches in an arc from the northeast to the southwest for nearly 2,000 miles (3,200 km).

Mountains cover about 80 percent of Japan. Many of the mountains are volcanoes. Japan occupies an unstable part of the earth's crust. Earthquakes are common, and many volcanoes are still active. The highest peak in Japan, Fuji (foo′jē), is a volcano that last erupted in 1707. Fuji is 12,388 feet (3,776 m) high. Narrow lowlands lie along the coasts of the islands. Basins are found among the mountains.

Japan's rivers are all short, and most of them are fast flowing. They are not navigable, but they are important for irrigation and the production of hydroelectricity.

The coastline of Japan's four main islands is irregular, providing many small natural harbors. There are, however, few large good harbors.

Hokkaido, Japan's second-largest island, is separated from Honshu to the south by a narrow strait. Honshu is Japan's largest island. Between the southern end of Honshu and the islands of Shikoku and Kyushu is the nearly landlocked Inland Sea. No part of Japan is farther than 80 miles (128 km) from the sea.

The climate of the four main Japanese islands has a range similar to that from Maine to Florida in the United States. Because Japan is surrounded by the sea, however, its temperatures are a little milder. The southern and eastern coasts of Japan are warmed by the Japan Current.

Monsoons also affect Japan. During the summer, warm southeast winds bring rain to the eastern part of the islands. Hurricanes called typhoons often accompany the summer monsoons. Winter winds blowing from Asia bring cold weather and snow to western Japan. No part of Japan is dry. Rainfall varies throughout the islands from 40 to 150 inches (100 to 380 cm) a year.

History

An ancient Japanese legend tells about a god who dipped his sword into the ocean. When he shook the water off his blade, an island sprang up wherever a drop of water fell. A grandchild of this god became the first emperor of Japan.

All Japanese emperors were once thought to be descendants of the gods. The belief in a divine emperor became an important part of the religion known as Shinto. *Shinto* means the "way of the gods."

Chinese Influences

During the sixth and seventh centuries, Buddhists from China went to Japan. The Chinese told about their culture and technology as well as their religious beliefs. The Japanese adopted the Chinese style of writing. They learned about Chinese building, farming, arts, and crafts. Many Japanese became Buddhists, but Shinto beliefs were preserved.

Samurais and Shoguns

In the twelfth century, nobles who controlled vast estates in Japan became very powerful. They hired their own soldiers to protect their lands. These soldiers, who were very well trained and disciplined, were members of the warrior class called the *samurai* (sam′oo rī′). The most powerful samurai leader became

This old woodcut shows a *samurai* in full costume. This warrior class was abolished in 1871 by Mutsuhito.

known as the *shogun* (shō′gun′). The shogun was a military leader, but he was also a political ruler. The shogun respected the emperor, but the emperor's power was greatly reduced. Shoguns ruled Japan until the late 1800s.

Contacts with the West

The first Europeans to reach Japan were Portuguese sailors, who arrived in 1543. Portuguese and Spanish traders and Christian missionaries soon followed.

Europeans arrived in increasing numbers. The shoguns feared foreign control. In the late 1630s, Christian missionaries and all foreigners except the Dutch were forced to leave Japan. At the same time, the Japanese were forbidden to leave their country.

The United States was the first Western country to persuade Japan to reopen its ports to trade. In 1853, Commodore Matthew Perry took four American ships on a visit to Japan to ask for an "open door" in trade. He returned the following year for a reply. This time he had seven armed ships and many presents for the Japanese officials. The show of force and the gifts impressed the Japanese. They signed a treaty allowing American ships to trade at two ports. Within a few years, other Japanese ports were opened to trade with other nations.

A Time of Change

The power of the shogun was greatly reduced by the time of the open door policy. The emperor Mutsuhito (moo′tsoo hē′tō) was restored to a position of power by the samurai in 1868. The emperor used Meiji (mā′ji′) as his royal title. *Meiji* means "enlightened rule."

The period of Mutsuhito's rule became known as the Meiji restoration. During this time, schools were established and railroads and highways were built. A new land tax was instituted to raise money to build factories. In the next 50 years, Japan changed in many ways.

Expansion

In 1894, Japan attacked China, and, after a year of fighting, took control of Korea and Taiwan. Russia was also interested in Korea and northeastern China, where Japan had a foothold. The Japanese went to war against the Russians in 1904 and defeated them in 1905. In this way, Japan prevented Russian expansion in Asia.

In 1910, Japan made Korea a province. After World War I, Japan was given control of all the Pacific islands that had belonged to Germany. Japan invaded Manchuria in 1931. Control of Manchuria's mineral resources was important to growing Japanese industries.

In the 1940s, Japan continued its policy of expansion. Japan attacked the United States naval base at Pearl Harbor in 1941. This brought the United States into World War II. At the height of its power in 1942, Japan controlled most of Southeast Asia and many Pacific islands.

To bring an end to the war, the United States dropped atomic bombs on two Japanese cities, Hiroshima (hir′ə shē′mə) and Nagasaki (näg′ə säk′ē), in 1945. More than 132,000 people were killed. Japan surrendered and the United States army occupied the country.

Japan adopted a new constitution that went into effect in 1947. It made many reforms, and provided for a prime minister as head of state. The emperor lost all his political power.

Living in Japan

Most of the people of Japan live on the narrow coastal plains or in the small interior basins that make up less than 20 percent of the land. The rest of the land is mountainous and unsuitable for agriculture or cities.

About 30 percent of Japan's population is rural, but only 10 percent of the people farm. Most farmers own their own land. The most densely populated rural areas are in Kyushu and in the southwestern half of Honshu.

Workers in a Japanese factory assemble home computers. More than one-fourth of Japan's workers are employed in manufacturing.

Japan is mainly an industrial country. About one-third of the population works in industry. About 70 percent of the people in Japan live in cities. Japan's cities are growing at a very rapid rate. In order to spread the population more evenly throughout the country, the government has laid out several new cities and encouraged resettlement.

Agriculture

Only about 16 percent of Japan's land can be used for agriculture. Japan raises enough food, however, to feed its people and have a surplus. Intensive farming is practiced. Irrigation, fertilizers, machinery, high-yielding crop varieties, and terracing are important means of increasing crop production.

Farmland in Japan is scarce. Japan's farms are very small. The average size is less than two acres (9 hectares). About 90 percent of the farmland is used to grow food crops. The chief food crop is rice. In the southern part of Japan, two crops a year can be grown. Rice is the summer crop, and wheat, potatoes, soybeans, or barley is the winter crop. Where it is too dry or cool for rice, wheat, millet, barley, and oats are grown. In the latitudes south of Tokyo, fruit is grown.

Nonfood crops include tea, flax, hemp, and mulberry trees. The leaves of mulberry trees are used for feeding silkworms. The silkworms furnish the raw material for Japan's important silk industry.

Cattle raising in Japan has increased in recent years. Livestock production is important in the north, where the climate is suitable for feed crops. Hokkaido is the main area of dairy farming.

433

Transportation systems in Tokyo include seven subway lines. At some stations, attendants are on hand to move people into crowded cars.

Fishing

Japan's long coastline and many small harbors have been important in the development of its fishing industry. Today, Japan is one of the world's leading fishing nations. The shallow, warm coastal waters supply many fish. Japanese fishing boats sail as far as Alaska and South America. Japan's whaling fleet works in the Antarctic. Some of the large ships process the fish and whales on board. Canneries in Japan process and pack many kinds of seafood, including salmon, tuna, and crab. Japan is first in world tuna production and second in salmon.

Other important sea products are seaweed, sponges, and pearls. Seaweed is gathered near the shore and spread on racks to dry. Seaweed is used by the Japanese as a vegetable. Sponges are harvested in the tropical waters of southern Japan. The Japanese breed oysters for their cultured pearl industry. Cultured pearls are produced by inserting a piece of shell or other hard substance inside the oyster shell. To protect itself, the oyster covers the substance with layers of tiny mineral crystals. In time, the crystals form a pearl.

Lumbering

Japan has a higher proportion of forested land than any other densely populated country. More than half the country is covered with mixed broadleaf deciduous and evergreen forests. Japan produces more wood than any other country its size. The wood is used for fuel, railway ties, telephone poles, and for a variety of manufactured products including paper and rayon.

Japan's forests are very carefully managed. The number of trees cut each year is not allowed to exceed the number of new trees planted. In this way, Japan is conserving an important natural resource. Because of the rapid growth of industry, however, Japan does not have enough wood for its needs. It must import some wood from other countries.

Manufacturing

Japan is one of the world's great manufacturing nations. Japan has few mineral resources of its own and must import most of its raw materials. Manufactured products are exported from Japan to markets throughout the world. The large ships of the Japanese merchant marine bring in raw materials and then deliver finished goods to many countries.

Japan leads the world in the production of cars and in shipbuilding. The nation is also one of the largest producers of electronics equipment, precision tools, cameras and lenses, iron, steel, and transportation equipment.

Silk, cotton, and synthetic fabrics are important exports. Japan's paper-making factories supply the nation's printing and publishing industries. Chemical industries are becoming important in Japan.

Cities of Japan

Japan has ten cities with a population of more than one million each. More than half the population is concentrated in the large metropolitan areas along the Pacific coast of Honshu. Seven of Japan's ten largest cities are found in this small area, which is sometimes referred to as the Tokaido (tō kī'dō) megalopolis (meg' ə lop'ə lis). A megalopolis is a densely populated area made up of a number of adjoining cities.

Tokyo (tō'kē ō') is Japan's capital and largest city. With a population of more than eight million, Tokyo is one of the most crowded places in the world. The contrast between East and West in Tokyo is striking. Ancient Shinto shrines and Buddhist temples stand near modern skyscrapers. Tokyo's transportation system includes a monorail that carries passengers from central Tokyo to one of the city's large airports. Yokohama (yō'kə häm'ə), Japan's second most important port, is less than 20 miles (32 km) from Tokyo.

Southwest of Tokyo is the important manufacturing center of Osaka (ō sä'kə). Osaka's factories produce about 40 percent of the country's exports. Kobe (kō'bē), Japan's principal port, is just west of Osaka. North of Osaka and Kobe is the historic city of Kyoto (kyō'tō). Kyoto was Japan's capital for more than 1,000 years. Today it is an important cultural and religious center. The city's many palaces and museums house some of the world's finest collections of Japanese art.

Do You Know?

1. What are the two great rivers of China?
2. When did China become a Communist nation?
3. What parallel divides the Korean Peninsula into North Korea and South Korea?
4. Name three ways Japanese farmers increase crop production.

To Help You Learn

Using New Words

samurai   Brahman
depose   shogun
antimony

Number a paper from 1 through 5. After
each number write the word or term from
the list above that matches the definition.
1. A bluish-white brittle metal
2. Formerly, a military and political ruler in
   Japan
3. To remove from power
4. A member of the priest or scholar caste
5. Formerly, a member of the warrior class in
   Japan

Finding the Facts

1. What lines of latitude mark the north-
   south extent of southern and eastern
   Asia?
2. When did colonial rule end in most parts
   of Asia?
3. What high mountains are in northeast
   Afghanistan?
4. What is a caste? Who were "outcastes"?
5. Name the world's third-largest island.
   What island chain is it part of?
6. About how many people live in East
   Asia?
7. What is the largest region of high elevation in the world?

8. What is the world's longest constructed
   waterway? In what country is it located?
9. From what dynasty did China get its
   name? When did this dynasty begin?
10. What nation persuaded China to accept
    an open door policy?
11. When did the United States establish
    diplomatic relations with the People's Re-
    public of China?
12. What kinds of products make up more
    than 75 percent of China's exports?
13. What is Nationalist China? What areas
    does it occupy?
14. What British colony is on the southeast
    coast of China?
15. What country has formal control of
    Macao?
16. The Gobi Desert covers most of what
    country in East Asia?
17. What kind of government does North
    Korea have? South Korea?
18. What is an important influence on the
    climate of Japan's southern and eastern
    coasts?
19. About what percent of the population in
    Japan works in industry?
20. What are three important sea products in
    Japan besides fish?
21. What are five important industrial ex-
    ports of Japan?
22. What is a megalopolis?

Learning from Maps

1. Compare the maps on pages 395, 414, and 424. What cereal grain is grown in all three map regions? Compare the product maps with the map on page 381. Does this crop grow in areas of generally high elevation or low elevation? Compare the product maps with the maps on pages 24 and 31. Describe the climate and rainfall in regions where this crop grows.

2. Look at the maps on pages 388, 420, and 421. What empire shown covered the largest part of southern and eastern Asia? Did the Mogul Empire exist before, after, or at the same time as the Gupta Empire? What two Chinese empires controlled approximately the same territory? Which empire, the T'ang or the Ch'ing, extended farther south? Farther north? Had Islam spread to the Indian Peninsula by the 700s A.D.? About how many years are represented by this series of maps?

3. Look at the map on page 408. What part of the Asian mainland did Japan control in 1914? What other foreign countries controlled parts of southern and eastern Asia in 1914?

   Now look at the map on page 409. What foreign countries still control parts of southern and eastern Asia? What country shown became independent most recently? Compare the two maps to name the countries independent before 1945 that were also independent in 1914.

Using Study Skills

1. **Outline:** Taking notes is an important first step in preparing an outline. When you take notes, write down only the main points of a section or article.

   The incomplete notes below are based on the discussion of Communist China, on page 422. Read page 422. Then complete the notes.

   A. War against Japan gave Communists opportunity to expand
   B. Communists controlled northern China by 1945
   C.
   D. China united under Communist rule in 1949
   E. People's Republic of China established
   F.
   G. New Communist government began measures to improve economy
   H.
   I.
   J. Five-year plans started to promote industrialization
   K. China's contacts with other countries increased
   L.
   M. President Richard Nixon visited China
   N.

   Now use the completed notes to write an outline. Use *Communist China* as the title.

Country	Capital City	Major Products
Burma	Rangoon	Rice, teakwood, petroleum

2. **Chart:** Prepare a chart listing the nine countries of Southeast Asia, their capital cities, and their major products. Include at least two products for each country. The chart has been started for you above:

Thinking It Through

1. In order to be successful, Gandhi's policy of passive resistance required widespread support from the Indian people. Why was it difficult to achieve cooperation among great numbers of people in India?
2. How were the programs and projects begun during the Meiji restoration in Japan important in promoting the country's industrialization?
3. From 1947 to 1971, Pakistan consisted of two separate parts almost 1,000 miles (1,600 km) apart. What activities would be made difficult by such a separation?
4. Elephants are still used to haul teakwood in the jungles of Burma. With its many resources, Burma is a wealthy country. Why do you think elephants are still used when the country can afford to purchase heavy machinery to transport its products?

Projects

1. The Current Events Committee might like to find out about recent efforts to preserve the temples at Angkor Wat and Angkor Thom. Committee members could prepare reports about the discovery of the ruins at Angkor Thom by Henri Mouhot in 1860 and about the work of archaeologists since that time.
2. The Biography Committee might like to find out more about the leaders of independence movements in southern and eastern Asia. They could prepare short profiles of one of the following: Achmed Sukarno, Mohandas Gandhi, Mohammed Ali Jinnah, Sun Yat-sen, Chiang Kai-shek, or Mao Tse-tung. Committee members could share their findings with the class.
3. The Arts and Sciences Committee might like to do some research about mountain climbers who have scaled Mount Everest. They could also find out more about the

Sherpa people and their role in mountain-climbing expeditions.

4. The History Committee might like to prepare reports about Marco Polo and his travels and experiences in China. Polo's book, *Description of the World,* includes an account of his observations and impressions. Committee members could prepare a map showing the route taken by Polo, his father, and his uncle.

5. The Soviet Union and China were close allies when the People's Republic of China was established. Gradually the two nations grew apart and developed different ideas about Communism. Use the *Readers' Guide* to find articles that describe the different interpretations of Communism these two nations have.

6. Some students might like to find out about Chinese writing. By using paint and poster paper, they could prepare a display of some ideographs (id′ē ə grafs′), the written symbols used by the Chinese. The meaning of each symbol should be given.

10 Australia, New Zealand, and the Islands of the Pacific

Unit Preview

In its southern and southwestern part, the vast Pacific Ocean includes the continent of Australia, the islands of New Zealand, and thousands of small islands. These islands are grouped into Melanesia, Micronesia, and Polynesia. Most of them lie in the tropics on both sides of the equator. Northern Australia also lies in the tropics. New Zealand and southern Australia are in the temperate zone south of the Tropic of Capricorn.

Australia, New Zealand, and the islands of the Pacific are spread out over millions of square miles and separated by great stretches of water. Together they include only about one-twentieth of the world's land and less than 1 percent of its population.

When the first European explorers came to the Pacific in the sixteenth century, much of the region was inhabited by descendants of people who had migrated from Asia. Between the sixteenth century and the early twentieth century, many of the Pacific islands came under foreign control. They became important stations along shipping routes and provided raw materials to colonial powers.

Great Britain established colonies in both Australia and New Zealand. Today these countries are independent, but both have a strong British heritage. Both are also highly developed countries with predominantly urban populations. Their economy is based on agriculture.

Modern technology has brought changes in traditional ways of living to Melanesia, Micronesia, and Polynesia. Several former colonies have become independent since World War II.

Things to Discover

If you look carefully at the picture, map, and time line, you can answer these questions.

1. The photograph shows a village in the island nation of Western Samoa. When did this country become independent?
2. Western Samoa and many other islands discussed in this unit lie near the equator. What kind of climate and vegetation do you think they have?
3. Only one continent is also a single country. What is it? To whom did it belong before it became independent?

Words to Learn

You will meet these words and terms in this unit. As you read, you will learn what they mean and how to pronounce them. The Word List will help you.

artesian well	Oceania
atoll	outback
bight	reef
lagoon	sovereignty
marsupial	station
mutton	wallaby

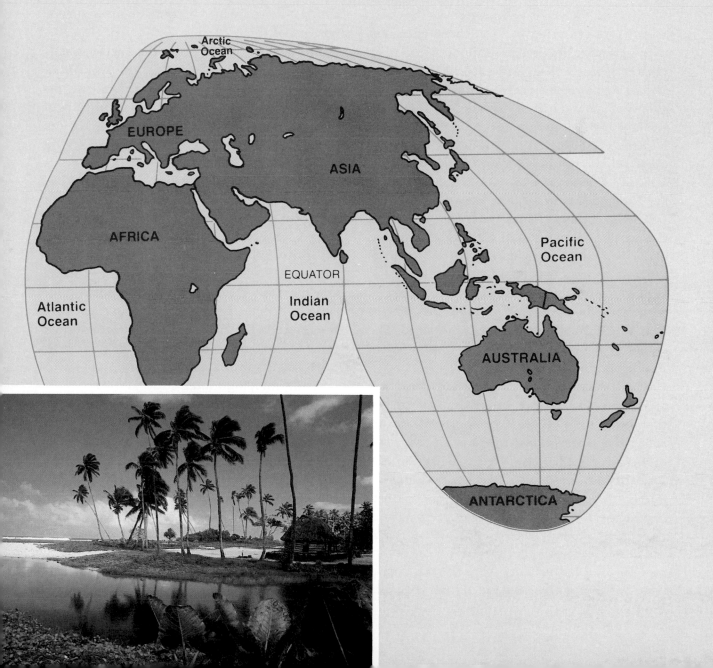

| 1521 | 1642 | 1770 | 1788 | 1840 | 1851 | 1901 | 1907 | 1962 | 1980 |

Magellan sailed across the Pacific

Tasman sighted New Zealand and reached Tasmania

Captain James Cook claimed Australia for Great Britain

Colony of New South Wales established in Australia by Great Britain

Great Britain gained control of New Zealand by treaty with the Maoris

Gold discovered in Australia

Australia became independent

New Zealand became a self-governing country within the British Empire

Western Samoa became first country in Oceania to gain independence in the twentieth century

Vanuatu became independent

Arctic Ocean

EUROPE

ASIA

AFRICA

Pacific Ocean

EQUATOR

Indian Ocean

Atlantic Ocean

AUSTRALIA

ANTARCTICA

1

The Land and the People of Australia, New Zealand, and the Islands of the Pacific

The Pacific Ocean is the largest and deepest body of water in the world. Its area, nearly 64 million square miles (166 million sq. km), is greater than all the earth's land surface. The Pacific covers about one-third of the earth and makes up almost half of its water surface. If the world's highest mountain could be dropped into the Pacific at its greatest depth, the top of the mountain would be more than 1.3 miles (2.1 km) below sea level. The average depth of the Pacific is about 14,000 feet (4,270 m).

The Pacific extends from the Arctic Circle in the north to Antarctica in the south, a distance of more than 10,000 miles (16,100 km). Its greatest width, just north of the equator between the Malay Peninsula and Colombia, is more than 11,000 miles (17,700 km). This is almost half the distance around the world. The equator divides the Pacific into the North Pacific and the South Pacific.

The northern part of the Pacific Ocean is a nearly empty expanse of water. Only a few islands are found there. The continent of Australia, the large islands of New Zealand, and thousands of small scattered islands lie in the southwestern part of the Pacific. Although no one knows exactly how many islands there are, geographers estimate the number to be between 20,000 and 30,000. Most of the Pacific islands lie between the Tropic of Cancer and the Tropic of Capricorn. The islands to the south of the equator extend farther east than those to the north. Australia, New Zealand, and the other islands account for less than 6 percent of the world's land.

The first people to settle the Pacific islands probably came from southeastern Asia thousands of years ago. These early inhabitants migrated throughout the islands by means of canoes. Most of the islands were settled by the time Europeans began to explore the region in the 1500s.

By the end of the 1700s, Europeans had visited many of the islands and established claims to some of them. Some of the earliest European settlements were made by the British in Australia and New Zealand. By the late 1800s, Great Britain, France, Germany, Spain, and the United States were all competing for control of the islands. These countries were interested in the Pacific islands because of their minerals and crops, and because of their location. The islands were important stopping places along shipping routes.

Australia and New Zealand became independent of Great Britain early in the 1900s. Several islands in this part of the Pacific have gained independence since World War II. Other islands and island groups are parts of trust territories governed by foreign nations.

It is estimated that about 24 million people live in the southwestern Pacific today. They include descendants of the original inhabitants, European colonists, and later immigrants from Asia. They make up less than 1 percent of the world's population.

The Land of Australia, New Zealand, and the Islands of the Pacific

The combined area of Australia, New Zealand, and the Pacific islands, almost three and one-half million square miles (9,000,000 sq. km), is only slightly smaller than the area of the United States. The continent of Australia and the islands of New Zealand account for about 90 percent of the area. The islands that make up the remaining 10 percent fall into three island groups—Melanesia (mel′ə nē′zhə), Micronesia (mī′krə nē′zhə), and Polynesia (päl′ə nē′zhə). See the map on pages 444–445. Together, these island groups are often referred to as *Oceania* (ō′shē an′ē ə).

Australia lies in the southwest of the region. It is bordered by the Indian Ocean on the west and south. The Timor (tē′môr′) Sea and the Arafura Sea separate Australia from Indonesia to the north. Two parts of the Pacific border eastern Australia. The Coral Sea lies off the northeast coast. The Tasman Sea to the southeast separates Australia from the two large islands of New Zealand. The island of Tasmania is south of the eastern part of Australia.

Melanesia includes the islands that lie north and east of Australia south of the equator. It extends southeast as far as New Caledonia (kal′ə dō′nyə) and the Fiji (fē′ jē′) Islands. The eastern half of the large island of New Guinea makes up the largest Melanesian country—Papua (pap′yə wə) New Guinea. The name *Melanesia,* meaning "black islands," refers to the skin color of the people who originally lived there.

Moorea, French Polynesia, is one of thousands of small volcanic islands surrounded by coral *reefs* in *Oceania*.

Micronesia means "small islands." Micronesia is made up of the islands lying north of the equator and west of 180° longitude.

Polynesia lies east of Melanesia and Micronesia. The name *Polynesia* means "many islands." The islands of Polynesia are spread out over a much larger area than the islands of either Melanesia or Micronesia. Polynesia extends from Micronesia and Melanesia on the west to Easter Island in the east. Historically, Polynesia included the Hawaiian Islands in the north and New Zealand in the south. Hawaii is now part of the United States. You read about the Hawaiian Islands in Unit 3. New Zealand will be treated separately here because culturally it is unlike Polynesia and more like Australia.

Kinds of Islands

There are three different kinds of islands in the southwestern Pacific. Continental islands are one kind. Continental islands are the tops of submerged mountains. A second kind are volcanic islands. These islands have been built up from the ocean floor by volcanic eruptions. Coral islands make up the third kind of island.

90° 120° 150°

• Vladivostok

NORTH KOREA
• Beijing Pyongyang ⊕ **JAPAN**

CHINA Seoul ⊕ **SOUTH KOREA** • Tokyo

30° Chongqing •

Nanjing ★ ★ Shanghai

INDIA **BANGLA-DESH**

Calcutta • **BURMA** ⊕ Guangzhou ★ Taipei ⊕ TROPIC OF CAN

Rangoon ⊕ Hanoi • Hong Kong (*Br.*) **TAIWAN**

Bay of Bengal **LAOS** *P H I L I P P I N E* MARIANA ISLANDS *(U.S. Trust)*

THAILAND *S O U T H* LUZON *S E A* GUAM *(U.S.)*

Bangkok ⊕ **VIETNAM** ⊕ Manila

KAMPUCHEA *C H I N A* CAROLINE ISLANDS *(U.S. Trust)*

Phnom Penh ⊕ **PHILIPPINES** PALAU *(U.S. Trust)*

Ho Chi Minh City • *S E A* MINDANAO *M I C R O N E S I A*

BRUNEI (*Br.*) EQUATOR

Kuala Lumpur ⊕ **MALAYSIA** NEW IRELAND

⊕ SINGAPORE *BORNEO* IRIAN JAYA **PAPUA NEW GUINEA** NEW BRITAIN

0° *SUMATRA* **SOLOMON ISLANDS**

INDONESIA Port Moresby ⊕

Jakarta ⊕ *N*

JAVA *BALI* *TIMOR* ARAFURA SEA *C O R A L S*

INDIAN OCEAN *TIMOR SEA* Darwin ★ GREAT BARRIER REEF

NORTHERN TERRITORY TROPIC OF CAPRIC

GREAT SANDY DESERT QUEENSLAND

NATIONS OF THE PACIFIC

WESTERN **A U S T R A L I A**

AUSTRALIA GIBSON DESERT SOUTH AUSTRALIA GREAT DIVIDING RANGE ★ Brisbane

GREAT VICTORIA DESERT *Lake* *Darling River*

	Plains	⊕ National Capitals
	Plateaus	★ Other Capitals
	Hills	• Other Cities
	Mountains	

30° NULLARBOR PLAIN *Eyre* **NEW SOUTH WALES** • Newcastle

Perth ★ *Great Australian Bight* *Murray River* ★ Sydney

| 0 | Miles | 750 |
| 0 | Kilometers | 950 |

Adelaide ★ Canberra ⊕

VICTORIA *TASMA*

Melbourne ★ *Bass Strait* *SEA*

TASMANIA ★ Hobart

90° 120° 150°

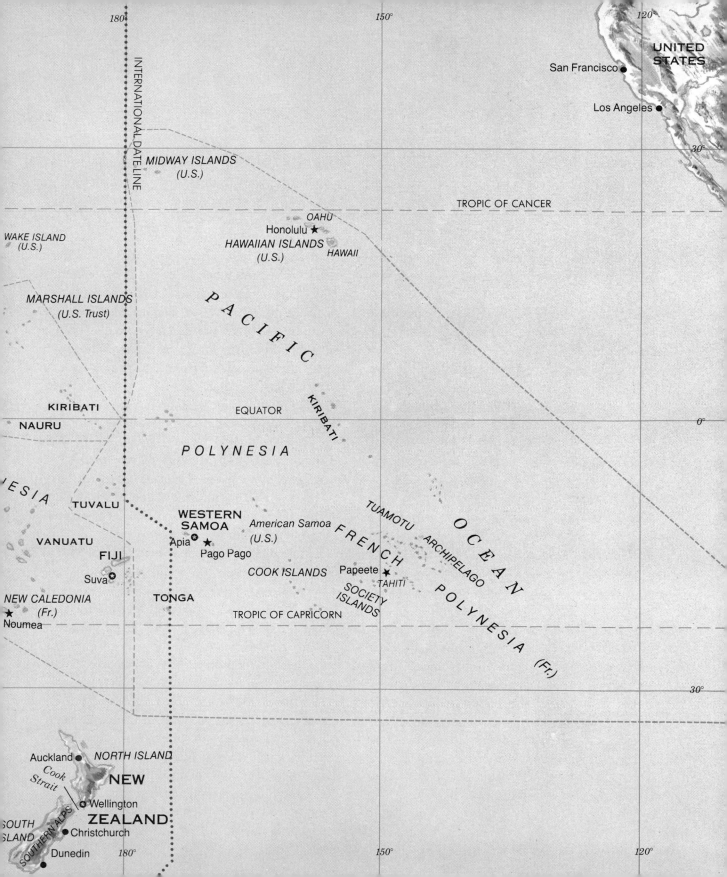

Most of the continental islands are found near Australia and the mainland of Asia. New Zealand, New Guinea, and many of the islands of Melanesia are continental islands. Thousands of years ago, during the most recent Ice Age, the continental islands were connected to one another. At that time, sea level was much lower than it is today. It was possible to travel between Asia, Australia, and New Zealand by land bridges that connected the islands and the continents.

Volcanic islands are found farther out in the Pacific. Polynesian islands such as Tahiti (tähē'tē) and some of the Cook Islands are volcanic islands. Volcanic islands often rise high above sea level as they build up layers of lava. For this reason, they are sometimes referred to as "high" islands. Volcanic islands have rich soil.

Coral islands are made up of the remains of tiny sea animals. There are billions of coral animals in the warm, clear waters of the Pacific. The skeletons they leave behind accumulate, and in time they form stretches of coral rock. A ridge of coral rock that lies just above or just below water level is called a *reef* (rēf).

Where conditions are favorable, reefs exist along the shores of islands. Reefs built around an island are called fringing reefs.

Many parts of Oceania lie along the unstable boundaries of the earth's tectonic plates. Many of the islands there are being slowly raised or lowered. If an island with a fringing reef is lowered, the area of the island becomes smaller and is separated from the reef by water. The reef continues to grow upward. The water lying between an island shore and a reef is called a *lagoon* (ləgoon'). See the diagram on page 447. The reef, which is now separated from the island, is called a barrier reef. The Great Barrier Reef off the northeast coast of Australia is a reef of this type. It is the largest coral reef in the world.

An island surrounded by a barrier reef may continue to sink. As the island sinks, the reef continues to grow upward. Eventually, only a ring-shaped coral island remains above sea level. Such an island is called an *atoll* (at'ôl). Most atolls have a circular or semicircular shape and surround or nearly surround a central lagoon. At some depth below the surface, the former island is submerged. See the diagram on page 447. Most atolls are small—less than two square miles (5 sq. km). Because they rise only about six to fifteen feet (1.8 to 4.6 m) above sea level, these coral islands are often called "low" islands.

If the ocean floor below an island with a fringing reef rises, the result is a raised reef. The reef, now high above sea level, forms a rim around the island, and a new fringing reef begins to grow. Raised coral islands usually have straight sides. Often there is a small lake or pond on the top of the island that is the remnant of an old lagoon.

Barrier reefs, atolls, and raised reefs are all kinds of coral islands found in Oceania. Many of the islands of Micronesia are low, coral islands. There are also many coral islands in the Coral Sea. The soil, made up of small bits of coral shell, is not fertile. Coconut palms, however, grow well on these islands.

Coral Reefs

Fringing Reef

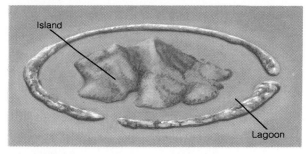

Barrier Reef

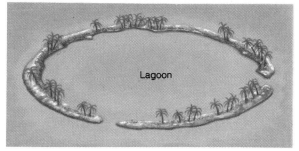

Atoll

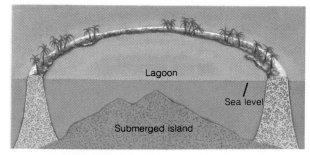

Cross Section of Atoll

Fringing *reefs*, barrier *reefs*, and *atolls* are found throughout *Oceania*. This diagram shows how *atolls* are formed. Why does the *atoll* remain above sea level when the central island sinks?

Climate

Ferdinand Magellan (mə jel'ən) was the first European to sail across the Pacific. He named the ocean *Pacific,* which means "peaceful," because it seemed so calm and quiet compared with the stormy Atlantic he had just left. Oceania, which lies almost entirely in the tropics, is generally a region of warm temperatures, gentle winds, and plentiful rain. At times, however, it is affected by violent, destructive storms.

The ocean, which covers large areas of Oceania, has a moderating effect on temperatures. Throughout most of the region, the weather is warm all year. It is rarely very hot, and it is never cold. The differences in temperatures between the hottest and coldest months are seldom more than a few degrees.

Trade winds blow from east to west across the Pacific, both north and south of the equator. See the map on page 28. Where the trade winds on either side of the equator come together, they rise and the moisture they are carrying falls as rain. Generally the rains are heavy, but they do not fall evenly on all the islands. Mountainous islands receive much more rain on their windward sides than on their leeward sides.

Windstorms bring much of the rain in Oceania. Sometimes the winds become very strong and develop into large storms known as typhoons. The typhoons move from east to west on both sides of the equator, usually in late summer and early fall. These storms are very destructive, especially the ones in the Northern Hemisphere. They cause extremely high

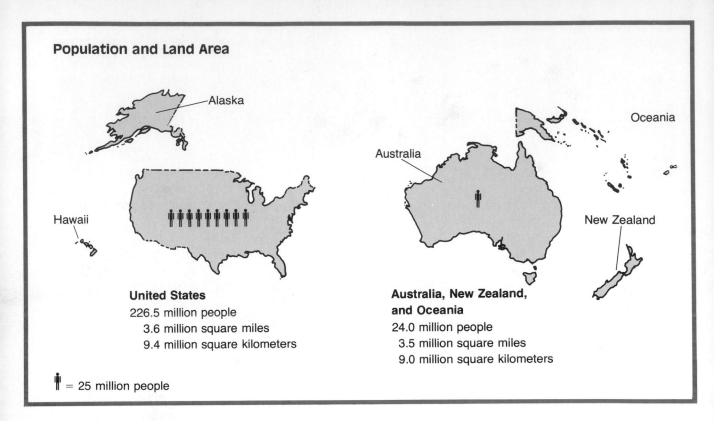

Population and Land Area

Alaska

Hawaii

Oceania

Australia

New Zealand

United States
226.5 million people
3.6 million square miles
9.4 million square kilometers

Australia, New Zealand, and Oceania
24.0 million people
3.5 million square miles
9.0 million square kilometers

= 25 million people

waves that wash across the low coral islands, destroying lives, crops, and buildings.

The northern part of Australia lies in the tropics and has a monsoon climate. The rest of the continent is in the temperate zone. Rainfall is heaviest along the coasts, and most of the interior is a dry desert. The southern coast has a Mediterranean climate. The extreme north of New Zealand also has a Mediterranean climate. The other parts of the islands, which lie in the temperate zone, have an oceanic climate of cool summers and mild winters.

The People of Australia, New Zealand, and the Islands of the Pacific

The southwestern Pacific is one of the least densely populated regions of the world. The original inhabitants of much of the area came from Asia. For thousands of years, the people

of the islands had little or no contact with outsiders.

The culture that later developed in Australia and New Zealand was largely influenced by the British. Great Britain ruled these two nations as colonies for many years. Thousands of British settlers came to live there.

Other islands of the Pacific were ruled by European nations and by the United States. The culture of the islanders was slowly changed. Traditional ways of living are still important to many islanders. Australia and New Zealand, however, have become highly developed nations.

Early Inhabitants

People from southeastern Asia migrated to the South Pacific thousands of years ago. At that time, the level of the oceans throughout the world was much lower than it is now. Land that is submerged today was then above water. It

448

was once possible to travel from the Malay Peninsula to Australia and New Guinea on an almost completely overland route. Dark-skinned people from southeast Asia made their way to Australia and New Guinea by using this land bridge. From New Guinea, people moved out to other islands in Melanesia.

Many islands in Micronesia were probably settled by people from Indonesia and the Philippines. These people used canoes with sails to travel between the islands.

The last area of the Pacific to be settled was Polynesia. A group of Polynesians called Maoris (mä′ôr ēz) were well settled in New Zealand by the 1500s. They were living there when the first Europeans arrived.

Exploration, Settlement, and Control

The first Europeans to explore the Pacific were Ferdinand Magellan and Sir Francis Drake. Magellan sailed across the Pacific in 1521. In 1580, the English explorer Sir Francis Drake followed a different route than Magellan. See the map on page 453.

A Dutch explorer, Abel Tasman, sighted New Zealand in 1642. Captain James Cook of the British navy sailed around New Zealand and along the eastern coast of Australia in 1770. Cook made a second Pacific voyage between 1772 and 1775. He died on a third Pacific voyage begun in 1776. On all his voyages, Cook made very detailed and accurate maps showing the location of many Pacific islands.

Cook claimed Australia for Great Britain in 1770. In 1840, a treaty with the Maoris established British control in New Zealand. Later Australia and New Zealand became independent nations and members of the British Commonwealth of Nations.

By the late 1800s, France, Germany, Spain, and the United States, as well as Great Britain, controlled islands in the Pacific. During World War II, the Pacific became a battleground between Japanese and Allied forces. Most of the islands were under Japanese control until Japan surrendered in 1945.

After World War II, the United Nations organized many of the Pacific islands into trust territories. The United States, Great Britain, Australia, and New Zealand were to administer these trust territories until the islands were ready for independence.

Do You Know?

1. What is the largest and deepest body of water in the world? About how much of the earth's surface does it cover?
2. What two countries account for 90 percent of the land area in the region covered in this unit?
3. What island groups are included in Oceania?
4. What three kinds of islands are found in the southwestern Pacific?
5. Where did the early inhabitants of Australia, New Zealand, and Oceania come from? How did they reach these lands?

2
Australia

Australia is both a country and a continent. It is the only continent in the world that includes just one country. It is the world's sixth-largest country. Australia is the only inhabited continent that lies entirely in the Southern Hemisphere. The name *Australia* comes from a Latin word meaning "southern." People in Great Britain often refer to Australia as the land "down under." If you look at a globe, you will see why. Globes are usually positioned with the North Pole at the top. Australia lies on the opposite side of the world from Great Britain. On a globe, it is "below" or "under" Great Britain. Actually, the world has no "up" or "down." There is only north, south, east, and west.

Geography

Australia is almost exactly the size of the conterminous United States. Like an island, Australia is completely surrounded by water, but it is classified as a continent because of its large size. It is the world's smallest, flattest, and driest continent.

Landforms

Most of Australia is low and flat. The western two-thirds of the country is a plateau. Ranges of low-lying mountains extend along the eastern coast of the country. Between the mountains and the plateau, a lowland stretches across the country from north to south.

Deserts cover most of the central part of the western plateau. In the north the desert is called the Great Sandy Desert, and in the south it is called the Great Victoria Desert. Between these two deserts lies the Gibson Desert. Together, these deserts make up the second-largest tropical desert in the world. Only the Sahara is larger. The Gibson Desert has a rocky surface, but the other deserts are areas of high, drifting dunes.

Low mountain ranges rise above the plateau along the west coast and in the center of Australia. South of the desert along the coast is the Nullarbor (nəl′ə bôr′) Plain. Its name comes from the Latin words for "no tree." The Nullarbor Plain stretches for 400 miles (640 km) along the Great Australian *Bight* (bīt). A wide bay or gulf formed by a curve in a coast is called a bight.

The highlands that extend along the east coast of Australia are called the Great Dividing Range. These highlands are a series of hills, plateaus, and low mountain ranges that separate the rivers that flow eastward into the Coral and Tasman seas from those that flow westward. The highest mountains in Australia are the Australian Alps at the southern end of the Great Dividing Range. Mount Kosciusko (käs′ē əs′kō′), the highest mountain in Australia, is in these mountains. It rises 7,316 feet (2,230 m) above sea level.

The western edge of the Great Dividing Range descends to the lowlands east of the plateau. This region has the lowest elevations in Australia. Part of it lies below sea level. The west-central part is a desert.

Water Features

Australia's major rivers are the Murray and the Darling. The Murray rises in the Australian Alps and flows westward. It empties into the Indian Ocean east of the Great Australian Bight. The Darling begins in the central part of the Great Dividing Range and flows southwest to join the Murray. Most of Australia's rivers are full only during the rainy season.

Most of Australia's lakes are also dry for long periods of time. The western plateau has hundreds of inland drainage basins called playas (plī′yəz). Playas fill with water only after a rain. Lake Eyre (ar), in the south-central part of the country, is Australia's largest saltwater lake of this kind.

There is an important source of underground water in Australia's central lowlands. Even where the climate is very dry in this region, a plentiful supply of water exists in rocks deep underground. These rock layers slope upward to the east, where they come to the surface in the Great Dividing Range. Here, where rainfall is heavy, water enters the rocks and seeps down the sloping rock layer to the west. Wells are drilled in the lowlands to tap this supply of water. The water does not have to be pumped up. It gushes or flows naturally to the surface. This happens because the water level in the east is higher than that in the west, so the underground water in the west is under pressure. A well in which water rises as a result of underground water pressure is called an *artesian* (ärtē′zhən) *well*. Much of the artesian water in the central lowlands is salty, but it can be used to water livestock.

Climate and Vegetation

Most of Australia is dry. Rainfall is highest along the eastern coast. The Great Dividing Range blocks the moisture-bearing winds from reaching the interior. Barren deserts receiving less than ten inches (25 cm) of rain a year cover about one-third of the country. Grasslands surround the deserts on the north, east, and south. Here the rainfall is about 10 to 20 inches (25 to 50 cm) a year.

The northern part of Australia lies in the tropics and has a monsoon climate. It is warm or hot all year. The rainy season lasts from November to April. Much of this region is a savanna. Rain forests are in the northeast.

The southern part of Australia lies in the temperate zone. It has warm summers and cool winters. Tasmania and the Australian Alps are the only areas that have freezing temperatures and snow in the winter. Like most temperate regions, southern Australia has four seasons. However, because it is in the Southern Hemisphere, the seasons are opposite those in the Northern Hemisphere. The hot, dry summer lasts from December to March.

The extreme southwestern part of the country and stretches along the Great Australian Bight have a Mediterranean climate. Westerly winds bring winter rains. Tasmania, which receives rain throughout the year, supports a temperate rain forest.

Native Animals and Plants

Australia has many native animals and plants that are quite unlike those found in other parts of the world. Australia was cut off from Asia at the end of the most recent Ice Age. Its animals and plants developed differently from those on the mainland.

The best known of Australia's animals is the kangaroo. The kangaroo is a *marsupial* (mär soo′pē əl). Marsupials are mammals that rear their young in pouches attached to the stomach of the mothers. Australia has more than 70 kinds of kangaroos. Some are very small, and others are more than seven feet (2 m) tall. Kangaroos are grazing animals that travel in herds. They can travel as fast as 30 miles (48 km) an hour by leaping and bouncing. The *wallaby* (wäl′ə bē) is a small or medium-sized kangaroo that can leap long distances, steering and balancing with its tail.

According to one story, kangaroos were given their name by Captain Cook. When he asked the inhabitants the name of this strange animal, they answered "kangaroo." In their language, this meant "I do not know."

The koala and the perching opossum are other marsupials found in Australia. The koala looks like a small teddy bear, but it is actually not a bear. The jerboa (jer bō′ə) is an unusual animal that resembles a rat. It stands on its hind legs and moves by jumping, like a kangaroo.

Two mammals that lay eggs are also found in Australia. They are the platypus (plat′ə pəs) and the echidna (i kid′nə). The platypus has a flat bill like a duck and is also called a duckbill. Spiny anteater is another name for the echidna.

It has a long tapering snout for poking into anthills. Australia also has wild dogs.

Australia's two most common trees are the eucalyptus (yoo′kə lip′təs) and the acacia (ə kā′shə). There are hundreds of different kinds of these trees. The eucalyptus is probably the best known because it has been transplanted to other parts of the world, including the United States. Koalas feed only on eucalyptus leaves. Australians call eucalyptus trees gum trees. They reach heights of 300 feet (91 m) and are among the tallest trees in the world.

Acacias are known in Australia as wattles. Australia is famous for its different wattle trees and shrubs. The bright yellow blossoms of one variety have been made the national flower.

History

The descendants of the southeastern Asians who first settled Australia came to be known as Aborigines. The word *aborigine* comes from two Latin words meaning "from the beginning." The Aborigines developed simple societies. They secured food by hunting, fishing, and gathering. The Aborigines were living in Australia when the first Europeans arrived.

European Exploration

The first European explorers who sailed near Australia were searching for an unknown continent. Many people in the 1500s believed that an undiscovered continent existed in the southern part of the world. They referred to this supposed continent as *Terra Australis Incognito,* or the Unknown South Land.

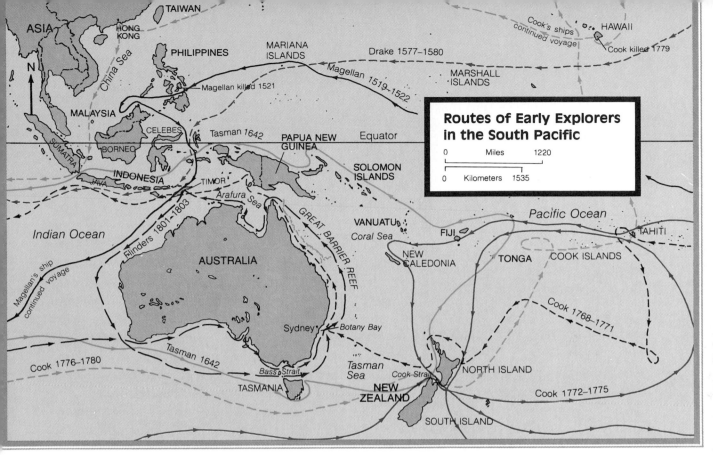

Routes of Early Explorers in the South Pacific

0 Miles 1220

0 Kilometers 1535

What explorer first crossed the Pacific? Did Cook or Tasman reach New Zealand first? Who sailed around Australia?

In 1606, a Dutch explorer named Willem Jansz landed on the northeastern coast of Australia. He was the first European to land in Australia even though he did not realize it. Jansz thought he had reached New Guinea.

Other Dutch explorers visited Australia in the 1600s. In 1642, Abel Tasman reached the small island south of Australia known today as Tasmania. He called the island Van Diemen's (van dē'mənz) Land. In 1644, Tasman sailed along Australia's western coast and named the area New Holland.

These early Dutch explorations were in the barren areas of the western, southwestern, and northwestern coasts of the continent. The Dutch did not settle in Australia because they thought the region was unsuitable for farming.

In 1770, Captain Cook became the first European to explore the more fertile eastern coast of Australia. He named the land he found New South Wales and claimed it for England. Sir Joseph Banks was with Captain Cook. Banks was a botanist, or scientist who studies plants. Banks discovered many new plants on the bay shore. Captain Cook named the area Botany Bay.

Early British Settlements

At first the British were not interested in faraway Australia. After the loss of their American colonies in 1783, however, they looked to Australia as a place to send prisoners.

In 1788, a shipload of convicts pulled into the cove of Botany Bay. They had been sent

Growth of Australia

Boundary of New South Wales in 1788

Western Australia 1829

Queensland 1859

South Australia 1836

New South Wales 1788

Added to South Australia after 1836

Colonial Period 1788–1901

Land taken from New South Wales for new colonies

Victoria 1851

Van Diemen's Land 1825 (renamed Tasmania in 1856)

Queensland

Western Australia

South Australia

New South Wales

Victoria
Melbourne

Independence 1901

National capital (temporary)

Tasmania

Northern Territory (North Australia 1927–1931)

(Central Australia 1927–1931)

Queensland

Western Australia

South Australia

New South Wales

Victoria

Canberra 1927

Melbourne 1901–1927

Changes Since Independence 1901–Present

National capital

Territory

Tasmania

Britain's six Australian colonies became states when Australia won independence in 1901. Northern Territory was part of South Australia until 1911.

from the overcrowded British prisons to found Australia's first colony. These first immigrants worked on community farms supervised by British troops. Within the next few years, free settlers from Great Britain began to arrive. They built a second settlement on Botany Bay and called it Sydney.

The early settlers did not venture far into the interior of Australia. No one knew the boundaries of the new land. Some people believed that New Holland was one island and that New South Wales was another. Between 1801 and 1803, Matthew Flinders sailed completely around the continent. His maps showed that no separation existed between New Holland and New South Wales. He suggested calling the landmass *Australia.*

British Colonies

The early settlements around Botany Bay were in the colony of New South Wales, the first British colony in Australia. In 1825, the British government estabished a colony on Van Diemen's Land. The island was officially re-named Tasmania in 1856.

The western part of the continent became the colony of Western Australia in 1829. Perth became its capital. The area between New South Wales and Western Australia became the colony of South Australia in 1836.

The area south of the Murray River in New South Wales was good grazing land for sheep. Many settlers moved into this area. In 1851, they asked the British government to create a new colony, separate from New South Wales. The new colony was named Victoria.

Gold was discovered in New South Wales and Victoria in 1851. Thousands of Europeans came to Australia to search for the precious metal. Although some prospectors became rich, many did not. Many of those who were unsuccessful decided to stay in Australia anyway. The population more than doubled in the years between 1850 and 1860.

In 1859, the colony of Queensland was established in the part of New South Wales north and west of Brisbane. The capital of the colony was Brisbane.

Independence

By 1890, the colonies of Australia were New South Wales, Tasmania, Western Australia, South Australia, Victoria, and Queensland. The colonies were self-governing, but Great Britain controlled their foreign policy and provided for their defense.

The desire for total independence became an important issue for many colonists. In 1897, a convention was called to draw up a constitution. The constitution was approved in 1899, and Great Britain granted independence in 1901. The six former colonies became states in the Commonwealth of Australia. In 1911, the part of north-central Australia between Queensland and Western Australia was established as a territory. The area is known as the Northern Territory.

The People of Australia

The majority of the people in Australia are European immigrants or their descendants. The greatest number of people of European

Aborigines were traditionally hunters. Now many work on farms and in cities.

descent trace their ancestry to Great Britain. After World War II, however, immigrants from other parts of Europe and from Asia came to Australia. The government instituted a new immigration policy after the war. Between 1945 and 1976, nearly five million immigrants came to Australia. Many came from Great Britain, Italy, Greece, Yugoslavia, the Netherlands, and West Germany. In the 1970s, people from Southeast Asia and New Zealand came in increasing numbers.

Less than 1 percent of Australia's population today is made up of Aborigines. Many Aborigines live in the Northern Territory. Although some Aborigines live in cities, the majority live in rural areas. Many have found work on ranches and farms. Those Aborigines who live in remote areas have preserved their culture and traditional ways of living.

Products of Australia and New Zealand

Living in Australia

Australia has a population of about 15 million. Although Australia has a population density of only five per square mile (2 per sq. km), this figure does not give the true picture of the distribution of the people. Few people live in the vast and isolated interior known as the *outback* (out'bak'). Desert areas of the outback are not populated at all. Australia's population is concentrated along the east, southeast, and extreme southwest coasts. About 85 percent of the population lives in the southeastern part of the country.

Australia is a prosperous country that has one of the highest standards of living in the world. People there live much as they do in Western Europe, Canada, and the United States.

Farming and Ranching

A little more than 60 percent of Australia is suitable for agriculture. Most of the agricultural land is used for grazing. Only a very small part is used to grow crops.

Australia is an important farming nation although only 7 percent of its workers are farmers. The farms are run efficiently by modern machinery. Australia produces nearly all the food it uses. Much of the country's wealth comes from the export of agricultural products. Meat, wheat, and wool are the main agricultural products. Sheep are raised for both wool and meat. In recent years, cattle raising has become more important. Cattle are being raised in the wetter regions, and sheep are being moved to drier lands. Australia is the world's leading producer and exporter of wool.

The Australian Merino (mərē′nō) sheep was bred in Australia to produce a very fine-textured wool. Australia is also one of the world's largest wheat producers. Many farm products from Australia are sent to Great Britain and to Japan.

The agricultural lands of Australia lie in seven regions, each of which has a different kind of climate. Find these regions on the map on page 456 as you read about them below.

One farming area is the coast of Queensland north of the city of Brisbane. In this rainy tropical region, products such as sugarcane, bananas, cotton, and pineapples are grown.

A second farming area is the coast of New South Wales. In the temperate climate of this region are important dairy farms. The farms lie in a narrow belt between the shore of the Tasman Sea and the highlands of the Great Dividing Range.

A third farming area is along the eastern and southern coasts of Victoria. The climate there is cool and temperate, like that of the British Isles. Dairy farming and raising beef cattle are the chief industries. Tasmania belongs in this farming region, too. It is noted for its fine apples.

Australia's leading farmlands are in the rich plain watered by the Murray, Murrumbidgee (mər′əmbij′ē), and Darling rivers. This plain, called the Murray-Darling Plain, is northwest of the Australian Alps. It lies away from the coast and is separated from it by mountains. From this region come most of the sheep, wool, and wheat of the continent. The Murray-Darling Plain is the largest area of artesian

wells in the world. Artesian wells supply water for livestock and irrigation. A water conservation project called the Snowy Mountains scheme has increased irrigation in the region.

On the Murray-Darling Plain, farmers make a living in three ways. In the east, near the Australian Alps, they grow large quantities of wheat and raise some sheep. This is the heart of the wheat belt, and wheat is the cash crop of these farmers. A little farther away from the mountains, farmers raise and sell both wheat and wool. On the drier side of the plain, farthest from the mountains, the farmers can raise only sheep.

Australia has two farming regions that have a Mediterranean climate. One of these areas is near Adelaide, in South Australia. The other is at the southwestern tip of the continent around Perth. These regions are important for sheep, wool, and wheat.

Australia's seventh farming region is northern Australia. The land there is more suitable for grazing animals than for raising crops. There are some very large cattle ranches in northern Australia and in parts of the interior. The cattle are marketed at a port in Queensland or at Darwin, in the Northern Territory.

Sheep Stations

In Australia a farm or ranch is called a *station* (stā′shən). Sheep stations are located throughout Australia. There are many sheep stations in Queensland, New South Wales, and Western Australia.

The headquarters of a sheep station is built around artesian wells, which furnish water for

This musterer uses a motorcycle at a sheep *station* in New South Wales. Part of the Great Dividing Range is seen.

the sheep and gardens. People who tend the sheep, called musterers, live in small cottages near the owner's house. There are large sheds where sheep are sheared and wool is stored. Other sheds are used for supplies such as gasoline. Gasoline is needed to run automobiles, trucks, and the pumps that distribute the water from the wells to the paddocks, or fenced fields where the sheep graze.

Sheep-shearing crews travel from station to station to shear the sheep. These crews often do no other work. An expert shearer can shear a sheep in only a few minutes' time.

Musterers drive from paddock to paddock each day to look after the sheep. They protect the sheep from wild dogs and keep the fences in repair. At one time they also helped keep rabbits under control. In the 1860s, some rabbits escaped from their pens. There were few natural enemies of the rabbit in Australia. The rabbits quickly increased in number and became a nuisance. They ate the grass close to the ground and destroyed pastures. Government programs to reduce the rabbit population have been quite successful in recent years.

Lumbering

Forests cover only a small part of Australia. Forests are found along the eastern coast, in the highlands, and in Tasmania.

In 1966, the Australian government began an important forestry program. Large plantations of softwoods, which included many acres of pine trees, were established. However, softwoods are still in short supply, and Australia produces only about 80 percent of the timber it needs.

Tasmania and Victoria have most of the nation's pulp and paper mills. Pulp and paper, plywood, boards, eucalyptus oil, tannin, and gums and resins are Australian forest products. Tannin is used to prepare, or tan, hides that will be used to make leather. Oil from the leaves of the eucalyptus is used as an antiseptic.

Mining

Australia is rich in mineral resources. Gold brought many people to Australia, and the mining of gold is still an important industry. Gold mines are found at Kalgoorlie (kal goor'lē) in Western Australia, and near Bendigo in Victoria.

One of the oldest of Australia's large mining centers is Broken Hill, on the edge of the desert in western New South Wales. Broken Hill's mines yield silver, lead, and zinc.

Australia also has great supplies of coal. The largest coalfields are on the east coast, near Sydney and Newcastle. Coal is sent by ship from Newcastle to Melbourne and to other port cities. Iron ore is mined in Western Australia and in Tasmania.

Australia is the world's leading producer and exporter of bauxite. Much of the bauxite comes from Western Australia and Queensland. Queensland is also Australia's leading producer of copper. Tin and tungsten are found in Tasmania.

Petroleum was discovered in Australia in the 1960s. Most of Australia's oil and natural gas comes from offshore wells in Victoria. There are also offshore wells in Western Australia.

Manufacturing

Until recent years, Australia was mainly an agricultural country. Today industry has been developed, and more people work in factories than on farms and in mines. Most of the country's income, however, is from farm products and minerals. Most of the goods that Australia manufactures are sold within the country. Victoria and New South Wales are the major manufacturing states.

Australia has an important iron and steel industry, centered on Newcastle and Sydney. Near the steel plants are factories that manufacture products made of steel. Australia has many assembly plants where automobiles and machinery are put together. Other leading manufactured products include processed food and household appliances.

Transportation

Because of Australia's great size and its distance from other industrialized parts of the world, transportation has always been a problem. The invention of the steamship and the building of the Suez and Panama canals were important early developments for Australia's commerce with the United States and Europe.

Transportation within the country has also posed problems. When Australia was first settled, it was made up of several regions that acted independently. When the country began to build railroads, there was no plan for a nationwide system. Each region built its own tracks, each using a different width between the tracks, called the gauge. This meant that goods going from one region to another had to be unloaded from one train and transferred to another. The government has now rebuilt some of the railroads using a single standard gauge. Today several railroads link the east coast to the interior. The Trans-Australian Railroad connects Sydney with Perth.

Automobiles are the most important passenger transportation. Paved roads connect the state capitals, but most of the outback roads are unpaved.

Airplanes have helped overcome problems of distance in Australia. They are particularly important in the outback for mail delivery and emergency medical services. The Australian government operates a major airline.

Australia's national emblem includes two native animals. The bird is an emu (ē′my̅o̅o̅). The window frames buildings in Canberra, the capital.

Cities of Australia

About 87 percent of all Australians live in cities. Australia is one of the most urbanized countries in the world.

Most of Australia's large cities are the capitals of their states. They are old cities located on rivers near good ports. See the map on pages 444–445. The capitals are centers of manufacturing and commerce. More than 60 percent of Australia's population lives in the six state capitals.

Canberra, the capital of Australia, is a city with more than 241,000 inhabitants. It is a beautiful inland city located in southeastern Australia. When Australia became a nation in 1901, neither Sydney nor Melbourne wanted the other to become the national capital. A federal district, like the District of Columbia in the United States, was set aside between them. The first government buildings were started at Canberra in 1913, but only since World War II have all the nation's government services been centered there. The majority of Canberra's people make their living in government work.

Perth, the capital of Western Australia, is situated on the Swan River, 10 miles (16 km) from the Indian Ocean. Perth is an important wheat-shipping center. Large ships stop at a small city on the coast that serves as Perth's ocean port.

Two state capitals, Sydney and Melbourne, together make up 40 percent of Australia's population. Sydney, the capital of New South Wales, is Australia's largest city and chief manufacturing center. More than three million people live there.

Melbourne, a city with about three million people, is a major manufacturing city. It is also the capital of Victoria. Both Melbourne and Sydney are wool- and wheat-handling cities.

Newcastle, an industrial city north of Sydney in New South Wales, is the largest Australian city that is not a state capital. Newcastle was built because of coal found nearby. Later, iron ore was brought to Newcastle from the mines at Iron Knob, not far from Adelaide. Newcastle then developed important iron and steel industries. Darwin, on the north coast, is the largest city in the Northern Territory.

Do You Know?

1. How does Australia rank in size among the continents?
2. Who are the Aborigines?
3. What country colonized Australia?
4. Is a larger percent of Australia's population rural or urban?

Before You Go On

Using New Words

reef   wallaby
lagoon   Oceania
station   outback
bight   marsupial
atoll   artesian well

Number a paper from 1 through 10. After each number write the word or term from the above list that matches the definition.

1. Any mammal that rears its young in a pouch attached to the stomach of the mother
2. A ring-shaped coral island
3. A well in which water rises as a result of underground water pressure
4. In Australia, a farm or ranch
5. A ridge of coral rock that lies just above or just below water level
6. The vast, isolated interior of Australia
7. A small or medium-sized kangaroo
8. The three island groups of the Pacific known as Melanesia, Micronesia, and Polynesia
9. The water lying between an island shore and a reef
10. A wide bay or gulf formed by a curve in a coast

Finding the Facts

1. In what part of the Pacific are most islands located? About how many people live in the southwestern Pacific?
2. What sea separates Australia from New Zealand?
3. What is the largest coral reef in the world? Where is it?
4. In what direction do trade winds and windstorms move across the Pacific?
5. Name three early European explorers of the Pacific.
6. How do Australia and the conterminous United States compare in size?
7. What is the name of the highlands along the eastern coast of Australia?
8. What is an important source of water in the central lowlands of Australia?
9. In what two major climate zones does Australia lie?
10. Name three marsupials of Australia.
11. Who was the first European to land in Australia? What nationality was he?
12. Where did the first European settlers in Australia come from? Who were they and why did they come there?
13. What event in 1851 resulted in a wave of immigration to Australia?
14. How many colonies were there in Australia just before independence in 1901? What did the former colonies become?
15. About how much of Australia is suitable for agriculture?
16. What are people who tend sheep called in Australia?

3

New Zealand

New Zealand is an island country in the South Pacific about 1,200 miles (1,930 km) southeast of Australia. It is made up of two large islands and several small islands. Its total area is somewhat larger than that of the Australian state of Victoria. New Zealand's population is a little more than three million. Its population density is about six times that of Australia.

Most New Zealanders, like most Australians, are of European origin. Many of them are descendants of the early settlers from Great Britain. Maoris make up about 9 percent of the population.

Geography

New Zealand's two large islands, known as North Island and South Island, are separated by Cook Strait. The relief is varied, but large areas are rugged and mountainous.

Landforms

North Island is smaller than South Island. A long, narrow peninsula of lowlands and hills occupies the northern end of the island. Mountains, hills, and plateaus cover the rest of the island. North Island's highest peak, Mount Ruapehu (rōō′ə pā′hōō′), is one of several active volcanoes. Mount Egmont, a snowcapped peak on the west coast, is one of the most perfectly shaped volcanic cones in the world.

The center of North Island is a volcanic plateau. This is a region of numerous hot springs and geysers, much like Yellowstone Park in the United States. Some of the geothermal steam is used to generate electricity.

South Island is more mountainous than North Island. The Southern Alps stretch along the western coast. Glaciers and snow fields are found in these mountains. Mount Cook, New Zealand's highest peak, rises in the central part of the range. The mountains descend steeply to the west, and many fiords cut deeply into the southwestern shore of the island. To the east, the Southern Alps descend more gradually to a low coastal plain.

Water Features

Lakes are found in both North Island and South Island. Many lakes lie in the high glacial valleys of the Southern Alps. The plateau of North Island is also a region of lakes. Here New Zealand's largest lake, Lake Taupo (tou′ pō), occupies the crater of an ancient volcano.

Short, rapidly flowing rivers rise in the mountains of both islands. These rivers, which tumble to the sea over hundreds of waterfalls, are an important source of hydroelectricity.

Climate

New Zealand lies south of the tropics in the middle latitudes. Most of the country has a climate much like that of Great Britain. Summers are mild and pleasant, and except in the high mountains, the winters are not very cold. Because no part of New Zealand is far from the sea, the ocean has a moderating effect on the climate of most parts of the islands. The northern peninsula of North Island, which reaches into lower latitudes, is warm and humid all year long.

Rainfall is heavy, especially on the western slopes of the Southern Alps. Moisture from the westerly winds fall here, leaving the eastern part of South Island in the rain shadow.

Native Animals and Plants

Like Australia, New Zealand has several unique kinds of animals and plants. The birds include several kinds that do not fly. One of these birds called the moa (mō'ə) stood about 12 feet (3.6 m) high and resembled an ostrich. The moa, now extinct, was hunted by the early Maori inhabitants of New Zealand. The kiwi (kē'wē), perhaps the best known of all New Zealand birds, still lives in the country's forests. It is the national emblem of New Zealand, and the name *kiwi* is used as a nickname for New Zealanders. Unlike all other birds, the kiwi has its nostrils at the end of its bill.

Many of New Zealand's native trees were cut down by the early settlers, and many of the native grasses were replaced by European grasses. The famous kauri (kour'ē) pines are now found in only a few places. The wood of the kauri pine is very fine, and its gum is used to make varnish.

History

The first people to settle in New Zealand were from islands in Polynesia. According to one legend, these early people left the home of their ancestors in a fleet of canoes. When they reached New Zealand, they called the islands "The Long White Cloud." Perhaps they chose this name because they saw steam rising from geysers.

Small groups of Polynesians may have come to New Zealand as early as 750 A.D. These early settlers survived by hunting moas. They lived on South Island along the coasts where the birds were plentiful.

Larger groups of Polynesians probably came to New Zealand between 1200 and 1400. They settled on North Island and became farmers. One of the crops they cultivated was the sweet potato. The Polynesians became known as Maoris. Maori means "the people."

When the first Europeans arrived in New Zealand, the Maoris lived mainly in the warm northern region of North Island. They were skilled in agriculture, building, and weaving.

Captain Tasman sighted the western coast of New Zealand in 1642. However, when members of Tasman's crew tried to land on South Island, they were attacked by Maoris. Tasman decided not to make further landing attempts. The land Tasman had found was called Nieuw Zeeland after a province in the Netherlands.

Captain Cook landed on North Island in 1769 and sailed around both North and South islands in 1769 and 1770. Cook made very accurate maps and recorded his impressions of Maori life and culture. In 1777, Cook published a journal about his voyages. He wrote that New Zealand would be a good place for colonies.

In the late 1700s and early 1800s, hunters, whalers, and traders came to New Zealand from Great Britain and other European countries, from Australia, and from the United States. These newcomers traded with the Maoris for kauri timber and flax. They hunted for seals and whales off the coasts of the islands.

In 1814, the first of many missionary groups arrived in New Zealand. By the 1830s, many settlers had come from Great Britain. They were attracted by New Zealand's good land and temperate climate.

New Zealand had no government or political organization until 1840. In that year, a British naval officer named William Hobson and a group of Maori chiefs signed the Treaty of Waitangi (wī′täng′ə). Under this treaty, the Maori chiefs gave Great Britain *sovereignty* (sov′rən tē), that is, political authority or control, over New Zealand. The British sovereign, or ruler, would also be the ruler of New Zealand.

The Maoris received British protection and a guarantee that their property rights would be respected. The Maoris agreed to sell their land only to the British government. After the treaty was signed, New Zealand became a dependency of New South Wales in Australia. In 1841, it was established as a separate British colony.

The arrival of large numbers of settlers led to tension between the Maoris, who did not wish to sell their land, and the settlers, who wanted farmlands. In 1845, tensions erupted into warfare. Fighting continued off and on until 1872, when Maori resistance ended.

In the early 1900s, New Zealand colonists began to feel that New Zealand should be an independent nation. Great Britain agreed to the colonists' request. In 1907, New Zealand became a dominion, or self-governing country within the British Empire.

Living in New Zealand

More than two-thirds of the people of New Zealand live on North Island. Like Australia, New Zealand has a high percentage of urban dwellers. About 80 percent of the population lives in cities. New Zealand is like Australia in other ways. Most of its income is from the sale of farm products, and more of its people work in factories than on farms. Its people also enjoy one of the highest standards of living in the world.

Farming and Ranching

New Zealand's climate is favorable for agriculture. It has warm temperatures and good rainfall. In addition, its many rivers furnish water for irrigation. Agriculture is the country's most important economic activity. It also supplies many raw materials used in manufacturing.

More than 50 percent of New Zealand is used for agriculture. Nearly 90 percent of this is grassland. Millions of sheep and cattle graze on these pastures. New Zealand has more than 20 times as many sheep and cows as people. The country is one of the world's leading exporters of lamb, dairy products, and wool.

Sheep are raised for both their meat and for wool. South Island and the hilly interior of

A series of mountain chains runs through the eastern part of New Zealand's North Island. The fertile slopes are important dairy-farming lands.

North Island are the great sheep lands. Sheep ranches extend into the Southern Alps from the hills of South Island. Both lamb and *mutton* (mut′ən) are produced. Mutton is the meat of a sheep that is more than one year old.

Cattle raising is almost as important as sheep raising in New Zealand. Cattle are either beef cattle or dairy cattle. Dairy farming is more important than beef production, however. New Zealand has developed some of the world's finest dairy farms. Most of these farms are on the small plains of North Island. The region south of Auckland (ô′klənd) and the plains around Mount Egmont are especially fine dairy areas. Butter, cheese, condensed milk and powdered milk are important dairy products.

The Canterbury Plains on the eastern side of South Island are New Zealand's important grain-growing region. Wheat, corn, oats, and barley are the chief crops. Some fruit is grown for export.

Mining and Manufacturing

Mineral resources are not abundant in New Zealand. Supplies of coal and iron ore are the basis for a steel industry. Some natural gas is produced, and there are small deposits of copper, silver, and gold.

Most of New Zealand's manufacturing industries process wool, dairy products, and meat for market. The production of farm machinery and other equipment needed by farmers is also important. Textiles, wood products, and chemicals are also produced.

Cities of New Zealand

New Zealand has no cities with a population of one million, but it has five with a population of more than 100,000 each. Many people in the

465

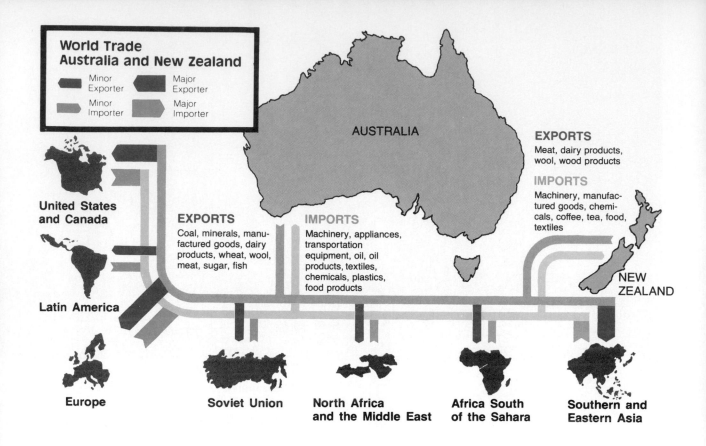

**World Trade
Australia and New Zealand**

Minor Exporter
Major Exporter
Minor Importer
Major Importer

AUSTRALIA

United States and Canada

EXPORTS
Coal, minerals, manufactured goods, dairy products, wheat, wool, meat, sugar, fish

IMPORTS
Machinery, appliances, transportation equipment, oil, oil products, textiles, chemicals, plastics, food products

EXPORTS
Meat, dairy products, wool, wood products

IMPORTS
Machinery, manufactured goods, chemicals, coffee, tea, food, textiles

NEW ZEALAND

Latin America

Europe

Soviet Union

North Africa and the Middle East

Africa South of the Sahara

Southern and Eastern Asia

cities make their living by handling the products of New Zealand's farms. Some work in factories where the products are processed. Others work in warehouses where the products are stored before being shipped. Loading, unloading, maintaining, and repairing ships are other important jobs.

Auckland, in the northern part of North Island, is the largest city and chief seaport of New Zealand. It is also the country's chief manufacturing center. Auckland, which is built on a narrow isthmus, has two harbors. One is on the Pacific, and the other is on the Tasman Sea. The Maoris thought the site of Auckland a fine one. When the first Europeans arrived, they found a large Maori settlement there.

Wellington, the capital of New Zealand, is the country's second-largest city. It is built on a harbor connected with Cook Strait. Wellington

is at the crossroads where traffic through the strait crosses the traffic from North Island to South Island.

Christchurch and Dunedin (dǝ'nēd'ǝn) are on South Island. Christchurch is on the Canterbury Plains just a few miles from the sea. Dunedin is a fine port on the southeastern coast. It has served as the headquarters of several expeditions to Antarctica. Admiral Byrd sailed from Dunedin to the South Pole.

Do You Know?

1. What are the two large islands of New Zealand called?
2. Who are the Maoris?
3. What is New Zealand's most important economic activity?

4
Oceania

The islands of Oceania have a total area of less than 300,000 square miles (777,000 sq. km), but they are spread out over about eight million square miles (20,720,000 sq. km) of the Pacific Ocean. You have read in the first section of this unit that the islands are divided into three groups—Melanesia, Micronesia, and Polynesia. You have also read about the three kinds of islands—continental, volcanic, and coral—found in Oceania.

The islands' location near the equator and the vast expanse of ocean that surrounds them are the chief influences on the climate of the region. Most of the islands lie in the tropics, where it is warm all year long. The ocean moderates the temperatures, which vary little from one month to another. Easterly trade winds bring much rain to the region, particularly to the eastern sides of the high islands. A warm ocean current moves from east to west on each side of the equator. Another current moves eastward between these two currents just north of the equator. Find the winds and ocean currents of Oceania on the maps on pages 28 and 29.

The International Date Line passes through the North Pacific and the islands of Oceania. See the map on page 40. This line determines the end of one day and the beginning of another. In general, the line follows the 180° line of longitude. Notice how the line zigzags so that the islands within certain groups are not on different sides of the line.

History

You have read about the early inhabitants of Oceania in the first section of this unit. The people who migrated from southeastern Asia settled first in Melanesia and Micronesia. Some islands had been inhabited for thousands of years when the first Europeans arrived there.

The navigators who explored Oceania from the 1500s through the 1700s prepared maps and reports that encouraged others to follow. Traders, whalers, and missionaries began to visit the Pacific islands in the 1800s.

Whaling ships were often at sea for several years. They used the islands as supply bases where they could get fresh water and food. Traders stopped at the islands to exchange goods with the islanders. Trading posts were established on many islands. Later, European settlers came to the islands to set up sugarcane, coffee, and pineapple plantations.

By 1900, almost all of the Pacific islands were controlled by several European nations and the United States. During World War II, the Japanese created an empire in the Pacific. Two important battles of the war in the Pacific were fought on Guadalcanal (gwäd′əl kə nal′) in the Solomon Islands and on Iwo Jima (ē′wō jē′mə).

After the war, colonial governments were reinstated on some of the islands. Other islands became trust territories governed by foreign nations. Nine island countries became independent nations between 1962 and 1980.

Living and Working in Australia, New Zealand, and Oceania

Both farming and fishing are important occupations in *Oceania*. Fish in the waters surrounding the islands are an important food source.

In parts of Melanesia and Polynesia, people wear clothing made of tapa cloth. Tapa cloth is made from the bark of the mulberry tree and is often decorated with patterns like the one this woman in Fiji is using.

Important *cash crops* of *Oceania* include copra, sugar, and bananas. Some islands grow special crops. In Tahiti,

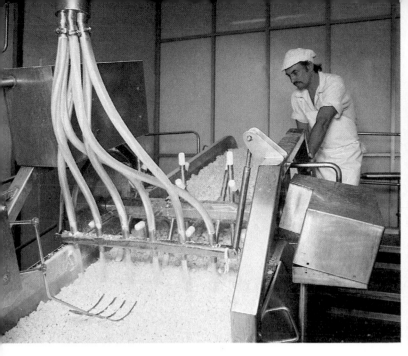

vanilla is raised for export. A worker
ties young plants to trees.

Both Australia and New Zealand are
industrialized countries, but most of
their income is from agriculture.
Agricultural products are also raw
materials for industry. In New Zealand,
a worker adds salt to cheese curds. At a
sheep *station* in Australia, sheep are
sorted and weighed. Australia is a
leading producer of wool, lamb, and
mutton. Wheat is Australia's most
valuable crop. It is loaded onto ships for
export. ■

Thatch houses like this one in New Guinea are found throughout *Oceania*. Buildings on stilts keep cool and dry.

Living in Oceania

Most of the people in Oceania are farmers. A basic food crop of the islands is taro. The taro plant has large leaves and a fleshy, starchy root. The roots are boiled and eaten like potatoes. The leaves can also be eaten. Breadfruit is another important food. The fruit of breadfruit trees can be cooked and eaten. It can also be dried and ground into flour.

Yams, bananas, coconuts, coffee, cacao, and sugarcane grow well in the tropical climate. They are food crops as well as cash crops. The most important cash crop is copra. Copra is ripe coconut meat that has been removed from the shell and dried. Coconut oil is extracted from copra and is used to make soap and margarine.

For many islanders in Oceania, life is much the same as it was for their ancestors. Villages are small and community ties are important. Fishing and farming provide food. Homes and clothing are made from local materials.

Change has come to some islands, and no island is completely isolated. Mining and other industries are being developed and cities are growing. Trading has increased contacts with other parts of the world.

Melanesia

The islands of Melanesia extend over the smallest part of Oceania, but they account for the largest land area. More than 80 percent of both the land and the people of Oceania are in Melanesia.

Almost all of the large islands of Melanesia are continental islands. Some of the islands are volcanic in origin, and there are still active volcanoes in the region. Papua New Guinea has more than three dozen active volcanoes. The islands of Melanesia have good soil. Thick, tropical rain forests cover much of the rugged, mountainous interiors of the larger islands. These places remained isolated until only fairly recently.

Parts of Melanesia formerly controlled by Australia, France, and Great Britain became independent nations between 1970 and 1980. They are Fiji, Papua New Guinea, the Solomon Islands, and Vanuatu (və n$\overline{oo}$′ə t$\overline{oo}$).

Papua New Guinea

Papua New Guinea is the largest country in Oceania and has more than half its people. It occupies the eastern half of the island of New Guinea, just north of Australia, and a number of outlying islands. The islands were visited by European explorers during the early 1500s. Australian rule began in 1905 and lasted until the country's independence in 1975.

The islands of Papua New Guinea have mountainous interiors. Large mineral deposits are found in the mountains. Copper, the country's most valuable resource, accounts for more than 60 percent of the value of its exports.

The highlands of Papua New Guinea are too cool for many tropical food crops. Yams and sweet potatoes are the main crops.

In the swampy areas along the island coasts, a different kind of agriculture is practiced. Sago (sā′gō) palms are raised for the soft, spongy material, called pith, found in their trunks. The sago pith is made into a white meal that is similar to tapioca. Sago is the main food for the people of these areas.

The Solomon Islands

East of Papua New Guinea are the Solomon Islands, a country that includes most of an archipelago of the same name. The first European to visit the islands was the Spaniard Alvaro de Mendaña, who arrived in 1568. He named the islands after King Solomon, who in legend had mines of gold. Few Europeans came to the Solomons until the 1700s. Great Britain controlled the islands from 1893 until independence was granted in 1978.

The islands are arranged in a double row. They have swampy coasts and mountainous, densely forested interiors. There are no gold mines, but there are some deposits of copper and nickel in the mountains. The forests provide timber, which is produced for export. The main activities are fishing and farming. Copra is produced for export. Taro, pigs, and chickens are raised for food.

A worker cuts sugarcane by hand on a Fiji plantation. Sugar is Fiji's most important export.

Fiji

The independent country of Fiji occupies the Fiji Islands, just west of the International Date Line and north of the Tropic of Capricorn. There are two large islands and more than 800 smaller ones, of which about 100 are inhabited. The main islands are volcanic in origin, but many of the others are coral.

Fiji has several fine harbors and is the crossroads of the South Pacific. It lies on major shipping routes between North America and both Australia and New Zealand. Fiji also has an international airport.

The British controlled Fiji from 1874 until 1970. During this time, thousands of people were brought from India to work on Fiji's sugar plantations. Today Indians outnumber native Fijians.

Sugarcane, coconuts, copra, and bananas are the most important products of Fiji. Industries that process these products have been developed. Fishing, mining, and lumbering provide jobs for many islanders. Fiji has also become a tourist center.

Vanuatu

Vanuatu consists of 80 small islands southeast of the Solomons. In the 1700s, Captain James Cook mapped the region and named the islands the New Hebrides. A joint British and French government was established in 1906. The New Hebrides became the independent nation of Vanuatu in 1980. The people of Vanuatu grow fruits and vegetables, raise chickens and hogs, and catch fish for a living.

New Caledonia

New Caledonia is an overseas territory of France lying east of Australia and south of Vanuatu. It includes the large island of New Caledonia and several small islands.

The island of New Caledonia is a volcanic island about 250 miles (400 km) long. Rugged mountains extend along the entire length of the island and descend to lowlands along the coasts.

The mountains are rich in mineral resources, and mining and smelting are the leading industries. New Caledonia is the third-largest producer of nickel in the world. There are also large deposits of chromium, iron, manganese, and cobalt.

Farmers in New Caledonia raise fruits, vegetables, and cattle for local use. There are also large plantations that raise copra, cacao, and coffee for export.

Micronesia

Micronesia is made up of about 2,000 small islands, many of which are atolls. Their total area is less than 1,000 square miles (less than 2,500 sq. km). Only about 100 islands are inhabited.

The main island groups are the Marianas, the Marshalls, and the Carolines. The United States controls most of the Micronesian islands as part of the Trust Territory of the Pacific Islands. The two independent island countries of Micronesia are Kiribati (kir′ə bas′) and Nauru (nä o͞o′ro͞o′).

Kiribati

Kiribati became an independent nation in 1979. Some of the islands that make up Kiribati were known as the Gilbert Islands when they were a British colony. Today the three island groups that make up the country are scattered over an area of about two million square miles (5 million sq. km). Two of the island groups are in Polynesia. Some of the islands are separated by more than 2,500 miles (4,600 km).

Most of the islanders are farmers, and copra is the chief export. Phosphate deposits mined on Ocean Island are an important export.

Nauru

The island of Nauru became independent in 1968. It is the third-smallest nation in the world. Its area is only eight square miles (21 sq. km), but about 8,000 people live there. The great population density of this small country, 1,000 per square mile (386 per sq. km), is matched by a very high per capita income. The source of Nauru's income is phosphate. Phosphates are chemical compounds extracted from phosphate rock used in making fertilizer.

Regional Data Chart

Country	Capital	Area		Population	GNP (in millions of U.S. dollars)
		Square miles	Square kilometers		
Australia	Canberra	2,967,909	7,686,843	14,900,000	$130,700
Fiji	Suva	7,055	18,272	625,000	$1
Kiribati	Bairiki	264	683	60,000	$40
Nauru	Yaren	8.2	21	8,000	$155
New Zealand	Wellington	103,736	268,676	3,150,000	$19,200
Papua New Guinea	Port Moresby	183,540	475,369	3,250,000	$1,900
Solomon Islands	Honiara	11,500	29,785	225,000	$90
Tonga	Nuku'alofa	290	751	100,000	$40
Tuvalu	Funafuti	10	26	7,000	$1
Vanuatu	Vila	5,700	14,763	110,000	$60
Western Samoa	Apia	1,133	2,934	160,000	$70

Nonindependent Area

Country	Capital	Square miles	Square kilometers	Population	GNP
American Samoa (United States)	Pago Pago	76	197	33,500	—
Easter Island (Chile)	Hanga Roa	64	166	1,600	—
French Polynesia (France)	Papeete	1,544	4,000	160,000	$970
Guam (United States)	Agaña	212	549	105,800	—
New Caledonia (France)	Nouméa	8,548	22,139	150,000	$870
Trust Territory of the Pacific Islands (United States)	—	717	1,860	143,000	—

Nauru is an unusual atoll that rises 200 feet (61 m) above the sea. Geologists believe that Nauru was raised and lowered several times. Each time the island was submerged, a layer of sea organisms was deposited on the coral rock. When the island rose, these deposits hardened into coral limestone. Over thousands of years, sea birds left deposits of guano (gwä'nō) on the limestone. Bird droppings are called guano. Under pressure, guano and limestone became phosphate of lime, or phosphate rock.

The people of Nauru know that their phosphate resources are limited. To provide for the future, they have invested their money. They own an airline, Air Nauru, which flies some of the most important routes in the Pacific. They built and own Nauru House, the tallest building in Melbourne, Australia. The government is also working to establish a shipping industry.

Trust Territory of the Pacific Islands and Guam

After World War II, the United Nations set up trust territories in the Pacific. One, called the Trust Territory of the Pacific Islands, includes about 2,100 islands in Micronesia. The Marshall, Caroline, and Mariana islands, except Guam, are part of this trust territory.

The United States was named as the trustee of the Trust Territory of the Pacific. The United States does not own the islands. It is responsible for administering island affairs.

The Mariana Islands are part of a volcanic mountain chain stretching from Guam almost to Japan. Volcanic eruptions still occur on some of the northern islands. When Magellan visited the Marianas in 1521, his crew gave them the name "Islands of Thieves." Some of the islanders took things from the ships while they were loading water and food supplies. Today the people of the Marianas produce copra and mine manganese and phosphate.

The island of Guam is the largest island in the Mariana group and in Micronesia. It is a territory of the United States and not part of the trust territory. The people of Guam became citizens of the United States in 1950. Much of the forested land in Guam has been cleared for airfields. The Pacific headquarters of the United States Air Force is on Guam.

The Marshall Islands were named for the British navigator who explored them in 1788. Two parallel island chains make up the Marshalls. The eastern chain is called the Sunrise Chain. The western islands are called the Sunset Chain. Because the Marshalls are coral islands, breadfruit trees and coconut palms are among the few kinds of plants that grow well there.

The Caroline Islands are an archipelago of more than 930 islands that stretch across the Pacific for more than 2,000 miles (3,200 km). One of the Carolines is the island of Yap. The islanders of Yap invented a very unusual kind of money made of huge wheel-shaped stones with holes in the center. Some of the stones weighed more than a ton, so the money did not change owners when it was used. Stone money is no longer used on Yap.

Polynesia

The thousands of islands of Polynesia are scattered widely throughout the largest part of Oceania. The total land area is about 20,000 square miles (52,000 sq. km). All of the islands of Polynesia lie east of the 180° line of longitude. Almost all of them are south of the equator.

The islands of Polynesia are inhabited by a group of people called Polynesians who speak a related group of languages and share many cultural traditions. The Polynesians, who were excellent sailors, originally came from Asia. It is believed that they later made voyages to and from the coast of South America.

Both volcanic and coral islands are found in Polynesia. High, rugged and mountainous volcanic islands make up Western Samoa (sə mō′ə) and many of the islands of French Polynesia. The fertile lowlands of the volcanic islands support most of the Polynesian population. Most of the islands, however, are low coral islands with poor soil and little drinking water. Part of the Tuamotu (too′ə mo′too) Archipelago and the Cook Islands are atolls.

Many of the Polynesian islands are under the control of the United States, France, Great Britain, or New Zealand. Three independent nations, Western Samoa, Tonga, and Tuvalu (too väl′oo), are part of Polynesia.

Western Samoa and American Samoa

The islands of Samoa lie in the southwestern part of Polynesia about half way between Hawaii and Sydney, Australia. The islands are divided into two parts. Western Samoa consists of two main volcanic islands. In 1962, Western Samoa became the first country in Oceania to become independent in the twentieth century. The several small volcanic islands and atolls of

Huts called fales are used for ceremonies in Samoa. Handwoven mats make colorful decorations.

American Samoa lie to the east of Western Samoa. These islands have been a territory of the United States since 1899. The capital, Pago Pago (päng′gō päng′gō), lies on the shipping route between the United States and Australia. Many ships stop there for supplies. Ships also stop at Apia (ə pē′ə), the capital and only port of Western Samoa.

Most people in Samoa live by farming and fishing. Some bananas, cacao, and copra are exported. Fish, especially tuna, are canned for export in factories on American Samoa.

In recent years, the population of Samoa has been increasing rapidly. Many American Samoans have migrated to Hawaii and the United States mainland. Today there are more Samoans in the United States than there are in American Samoa.

French Polynesia

French Polynesia is an overseas territory of France that is made up of several groups of islands lying east of Samoa and north of the Tropic of Capricorn. The Society Islands are the principal group. They are famous for the magnificent scenery of the mountainous volcanic peaks that rise thousands of feet out of the ocean. Most of the people in French Polynesia live in the Society Islands. More than half live in the single largest island, Tahiti. Tahiti is the political and commercial center of French Polynesia. Papeete (pə pēt′ē) is the capital and chief port of the islands.

Tahiti, which was claimed by the French in 1768, was one of the islands visited by Captain Cook on his voyage of 1769. The islands of French Polynesia were organized into a single colony in 1903.

Farming is important on some of the islands. Coconuts are the main crop. The coral reefs of the Tuamotu Archipelago east of the Society Islands have been a source of pearls and shells for buttons since the early days of European contact. Growing cultured pearls is an important part of the economy there today. Tourism is another important source of income.

475

The giant stone heads on Easter Island once stood on platforms. Many had been toppled when the first Europeans arrived.

Tonga and Tuvalu

Tonga is a group of about 180 coral and volcanic islands lying east of Fiji. Tuvalu is a group of nine coral atolls to the northwest of Fiji. Both groups of islands are independent countries.

Tonga, which gained independence from Great Britain in 1970, is a constitutional monarchy. The king of Tonga belongs to a dynasty that has ruled the islands for more than 125 years. All the land belongs to the king, but it is cultivated in small plots by the adult males of the islands. The people raise taro and yams as food crops. Bananas and copra are raised for export.

Tuvalu was also ruled by Great Britain before it became independent in 1978. It is one of the world's smallest nations and has one of the world's smallest populations. It has an area of 10 square miles (26 sq. km) and a population of a little more than 7,000. The soil is poor, but coconut palms grow well. Copra is the chief export.

Easter Island

Easter Island is a small island of volcanic origin lying about 2,400 miles (3,900 km) west of Chile. It belongs to Chile.

Easter Island was named by a Dutch admiral who arrived there on Easter Sunday in 1722. The inhabitants at the time of the arrival were later nearly wiped out by disease, war, and the slave trade. Today the people of Easter Island live by subsistence farming in restricted areas of the west coast. The rest of the island is used for sheep and cattle grazing.

Easter Island is famous as a "mystery" island because of its giant stone statues. There are more than 600 of these prehistoric carvings. Some of the largest statues are more than 30 feet (9 m) high and weigh more than 50 tons (45 metric tons). They were carved with stone tools out of rock from the island's volcanoes. How the statues were moved to their locations around the coasts of the island has never been fully explained.

Do You Know?

1. In what climate zone are most of the islands of Oceania?
2. What is the occupation of most people in Oceania?
3. Name three countries in Oceania that became independent in the twentieth century.
4. Which island group—Melanesia, Micronesia, or Polynesia—covers the largest part of Oceania?

To Help You Learn

Using New Words

reef	sovereignty
mutton	marsupial
lagoon	Oceania

Number a paper from 1 through 6. After each number write the word or term from the above list that matches the definition.

1. Political authority or control
2. The water lying between an island shore and a reef
3. A ridge of coral rock that lies just above or just below water level
4. The three island groups of the Pacific known as Melanesia, Micronesia, and Polynesia
5. Any mammal that rears its young in a pouch attached to the stomach of the mother
6. The meat of a sheep more than one year old

Finding the Facts

1. What do the terms *"high" island* and *"low" island* refer to?
2. Name the country that controlled most of the Pacific islands during World War II.
3. What are the states of Australia?
4. Where are Australia's leading farmlands?
5. What has a moderating effect on the climate of New Zealand?
6. Name three groups that came to New Zealand during the late 1700s and early 1800s.
7. What treaty gave Great Britain sovereignty over New Zealand? When was the treaty signed and by whom?
8. When did New Zealand become a dominion, or self-governing country?
9. What are the two most important kinds of livestock raised in New Zealand?
10. What is New Zealand's largest city? What is its capital?
11. What are the two chief influences on the climate of Oceania?
12. What important imaginary north-south line passes through Oceania? What line of longitude does it generally follow?
13. What is copra? What is taro?
14. What is the largest country in Oceania? What island does it occupy?
15. How are sago palms used?
16. Name three minerals found in New Caledonia.
17. Is Kiribati in Micronesia or Polynesia?
18. What is Nauru's chief source of income?
19. What is the Trust Territory of the Pacific?
20. What three independent nations are part of Polynesia?
21. What is the principal group of islands in French Polynesia?
22. What is Easter Island famous for? To what country does the island belong?

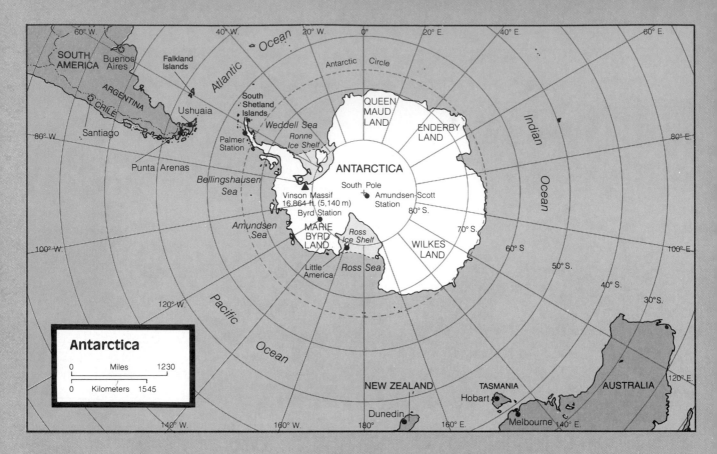

Antarctica

0	Miles	1230
0	Kilometers	1545

Learning from Maps

Look at the map on this page. This map is drawn on a plane projection centered on the South Pole. You may wish to review the special properties of plane projections on pages 41–42 and pages 538–539. Where is south on this map? If you traveled from the South Pole to any other point on the map in the most direct way possible, in what direction would you be traveling? If you traveled from the Ross Sea to the Weddell Sea along 70° south latitude, in what direction would you be traveling? What oceans border Antarctica? What lines of longitude bound the Ross Ice Shelf? What other continent is closest to Antarctica? About how far is it from Antarctica at their closest points? Admiral Byrd set out from Dunedin, New Zealand, for the South Pole in 1928. About how far did he have to go to reach the pole?

Using Study Skills

Library Resources: A cross-reference in an encyclopedia tells you where you can find additional information about a topic. The words *see also* indicate a cross-reference. In the sample below, the letter refers to the encyclopedia volume and the number refers to the page. Use the sample to answer the questions that follow.

Magellan, Ferdinand (navigator) **M:70**
 with picture, map
Maoris (people) **M:83**
 Sculpture **S:128** *with picture*
 Language **L:76**
 New Zealand **N:152**

Where would you look to find information about Maori sculpture? Which entries have maps? Which entries have cross-references? Under what other entry would you expect to find general information about Melanesia?

Cross-references are also used in the indexes in books other than encyclopedias. Use the index in this book to find out which of the following entries have cross-references: Maoris, James Cook, agriculture, Pacific Islands, climate, forests, artesian wells, North Island, Tonga, natural resources, ranching. Which of the following has a cross-reference and to what entry does it refer: Oceania, oil, petroleum, atoll, Polynesia, New Hebrides, Aborigines?

Thinking It Through

1. After World War II, Australia began a campaign to encourage immigration to that country. Australia also worked hard to develop more industries of its own. Why do you suppose Australia decided on these policies?

2. The United States administers the affairs of more than 2,000 islands in Micronesia. What are some of the advantages of this arrangement for the islanders? What are possible disadvantages?

Projects

1. The Biography Committee might like to find out more about Magellan, Drake, Cook, Tasman, and Flinders. What nationality were they? What countries were they sailing for? What difficulties did they encounter on their voyages? What impressions did they have of the Pacific?

2. The History Committee might like to report on the exploration of Antarctica. Students could read about the expeditions of James Cook, James Weddell, Charles Wilkes, James Clark Ross, Roald Amundsen, Robert Scott, and Richard Byrd. Some members of the committee might like to report on territorial claims in Antarctica.

3. The history of the Pacific has been called a history of improvements in transportation. The Arts and Sciences Committee might like to demonstrate this by making an illustrated time line for the classroom to show changes in transportation that affected travel in the Pacific. Interested students might read about Thor Heyerdahl's famous *Kon-Tiki* expedition—a 4,300-mile ocean journey by raft—and report to the class.

11 The United States in World Affairs

Unit Preview

The independence of the United States was formally recognized by Great Britain in 1783. Creating a strong plan of government was a major concern of the new nation. Leaders realized that the organization and authority provided by the Articles of Confederation were not effective. A new government structure was outlined in the Constitution.

In its early days, the United States adopted a policy of neutrality and avoided becoming involved in the affairs of other nations. This policy was challenged by the events that led to the War of 1812. The United States took a firm stand on the principle of "freedom of the seas."

President James Monroe emphasized the leadership role of the United States in the Western Hemisphere in 1823. He declared that the United States would not tolerate further colonization or interference in the Americas. The nation also took the lead in opening up trade with Japan and China.

Although the United States tried to remain neutral during the events that led to World War I, it was drawn into the conflict. The country also played an important role in World War II.

Relations between the United States and other countries became increasingly complex in the years following World War II. Hostilities between Communist and non-Communist countries were known as the Cold War. Efforts to promote peace and cooperation among the nations of the world became a major concern of the United States in its role as a world leader.

Things to Discover

If you look carefully at the picture, map, and time line, you can answer these questions.

1. The photograph shows the White House, the official residence of the President of the United States. It is an important symbol of national unity for the country. It was first occupied in 1800. How many years after the Constitution went into effect was this?
2. The United States occupies the third-largest continent and borders on three oceans. Name the continent and oceans.
3. What two important events that affected the United States took place in 1945?

Words to Learn

You will meet these words and terms in this unit. As you read, you will learn what they mean and how to pronounce them. The Word List will help you.

aggression	federalism
annex	isolationism
armistice	mandate
détente	manifest destiny
diplomacy	pact
doctrine	

United States
Constitution
went into effect

United States declared
war against Great Britain

Monroe Doctrine issued

Spanish-American War
began and ended

United States
entered
World War I

World War II ended;
United Nations established

President Nixon
visited China and
the Soviet Union

United States troops
withdrew from Vietnam

Peace treaty based on Camp David
Accords signed by Egypt and Israel

1788   1812   1823   1898   1917   1945   1972   1973   1979

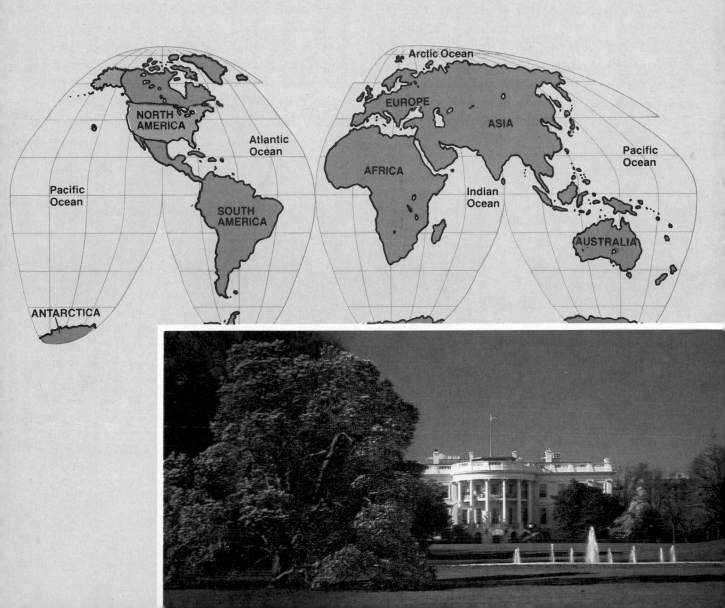

North America
South America
Atlantic Ocean
Pacific Ocean
Antarctica
Arctic Ocean
Europe
Asia
Africa
Indian Ocean
Pacific Ocean
Australia

1
Early Days of the Republic

You have read in Unit 3 how the 13 British colonies in North America became independent of Great Britain and established themselves as the United States of America. The movement toward independence began after the French and Indian War ended in 1763. Victory over the French had left Great Britain the leading power in North America. The British began to tighten control over the colonies. They began to enforce existing laws more strictly and to impose new taxes to help pay for the war. They also took away some of the rights of self-government that the colonists had been used to.

The American colonists resisted the British actions. Although they were British citizens, they had begun to think of themselves as Americans. More than 150 years had passed since the first English colonies had been established. The colonies had developed a new and

The Continental Congress adopted the Declaration of Independence in 1776. Thomas Jefferson, the tall red-headed man, was the author of the document.

different way of life. In 1776, they broke their ties with Great Britain by proclaiming their independence. The war that became known as the American Revolution, or the War for Independence, was formally declared.

Independence was won five years later when General Cornwallis surrendered to the Americans at Yorktown, Virginia. By the Treaty of Paris, signed in 1783, the British recognized the new nation as an independent country.

During the War for Independence, the 13 independent American states were governed by the Continental Congress. By 1781, all the states had ratified a plan of union called the Articles of Confederation.

Under the Articles of Confederation, the central government was made up of a congress of several delegates from each state. The new government was weak and ineffective. The consent of nine states was needed to decide important issues. Changes in the Articles required the unanimous vote of all the states. There was no executive branch to carry out laws, or courts to protect the rights of citizens. Congress had no power to collect taxes or regulate commerce. This lack of power made foreign relations especially difficult. The government could not make binding treaties, pay its debts, or maintain an army and navy.

In 1787, the nation's leaders met in Philadelphia to revise the Articles of Confederation. Instead of revising the old Articles, the delegates wrote a Constitution based on the idea of *federalism* (fed'ər ə liz' əm), or the division of powers between the national, or federal, government and the state governments. The Constitution was ratified by the required number of states and became the supreme law of the land in 1788.

The New Government

George Washington was inaugurated as President of the United States in 1789. The new Constitution provided a plan for the government. However, major decisions about how it would be put into effect had to be made. These decisions would serve as models for future leaders of the nation.

Important Concerns

The new government faced many problems. One of these problems was a huge war debt. During the War for Independence, France and other countries had supported the colonists by sending soldiers, equipment, and money. Repaying these debts was essential if the United States wanted to gain the respect of the other nations. The new government agreed to repay its debts by fixed yearly payments.

Another area of concern for the new government was relations with other countries. Government leaders had to develop a foreign policy, or set of principles and guidelines that would determine how the United States would deal with other nations.

In 1793, France went to war against Great Britain and Spain. Because France had helped the United States win independence, it thought America would support its cause. The United States had to decide how it would respond to the French request.

George Washington arrives in New York for his inauguration as President in 1789. Washington was met by cheering crowds all along his route.

Foreign Policy

The United States could not afford to become involved in a war with Great Britain or Spain. The American army was small, and the navy had been disbanded. British ships controlled the sea, and most of the nation's trade was with Great Britain. British troops were still stationed in the region between the Ohio and Mississippi rivers known as the Northwest Territory. This land had been ceded to the United States by Great Britain in 1783. Rumors about Indian uprisings supported by the British were cause for alarm.

Spain also posed a threat. The Spanish controlled the port of New Orleans at the mouth of the Mississippi. Many American goods passed through this port. Spain also controlled Florida. The border between the United States and this Spanish territory was in dispute.

President Washington issued a Proclamation of Neutrality in the spring of 1793. He stated that the United States would not take sides in the war.

President Washington believed in pursuing peace through *diplomacy* (di plō'mə sē). Diplomacy is a system for managing relations between nations and for carrying on negotiations between governments. Official representatives of a government who help carry out its foreign policy are called diplomats.

Washington sent diplomats to Great Britain and Spain to find a peaceful solution to the differences that existed. John Jay was sent to Great Britain, and Thomas Pinckney went to

Spain. Both diplomats negotiated treaties. Great Britain agreed to withdraw its troops from the Northwest Territory. Spain agreed to allow the United States free use of the Mississippi. The boundary of Florida was established.

Washington completed two terms as President in 1797. During his administration, the United States gained the respect of nations throughout the world. The new government repaid its debts, and it maintained peace.

In his Farewell Address, Washington warned the people of the United States against forming political alliances with foreign nations. He believed that *isolationism* (īsəlā'shəniz'əm), or a policy of avoiding involvements with foreign countries, was important for the development of the new nation. His advice became the basis of American foreign policy for many years.

The Louisiana Purchase

Shortly before Thomas Jefferson began his first term as President in 1801, Spain ceded Louisiana to France. At that time, Louisiana was an immense area that stretched westward from the Mississippi and included the port of New Orleans. See the map of North America in 1783 on page 94. At this time, France was at war with most of Europe. Jefferson feared that France might build up a powerful empire on the western border of the United States. He also feared that French control of the mouth of the Mississippi would limit American use of the river and the port of New Orleans.

Jefferson authorized the American minister in Paris to offer Napoleon ten million dollars for New Orleans and West Florida, the region along the coast east of the Mississippi. After many months of being urged to sell the port, the French minister suddenly asked how much the United States would pay for all of Louisiana. The United States agreed to pay about 15 million dollars for the territory of Louisiana. When this huge region became part of the United States in 1803, it was called the Louisiana Purchase. By acquiring the Louisiana Territory, the United States doubled in size.

Trouble at Sea

President Jefferson was committed to Washington's idea of isolationism. He wanted to avoid any "foreign entanglements." Events in other parts of the world, however, made America's isolation difficult to maintain.

An important principle of American foreign policy was "freedom of the seas." The United States believed that no nation had the right to interfere with the free passage of ships on the open sea. This principle was violated in the early 1800s, and Americans had to fight to protect their rights.

The Barbary Pirates

During the late 1700s, the merchant ships that sailed along the North African, or Barbary, coast were attacked by pirates. These raiders demanded tribute in return for safe passage. For nearly 20 years, the United States had paid large sums of money to protect American ships. President Jefferson refused to continue these payments.

In 1801, Jefferson sent a small fleet to fight the pirates. After four years of fighting, a treaty was signed with Tripoli. In 1815, Americans and Europeans joined forces to finally end the Barbary threat.

Great Britain and France at War

Conflict between France and Great Britain created an even greater threat to American ships than the Barbary pirates had. In 1803, the French and the British were again at war. Both nations depended on the supplies carried by American ships.

The French leader Napoleon Bonaparte had conquered most of western Europe by 1805. Napoleon was successful against the British on land, but he could not defeat them at sea. At that time, the British fleet was the largest and most powerful in the world. Napoleon decided to destroy British trade by forbidding other countries to trade with Great Britain. He also declared that any ships attempting to do so would be attacked.

The British were determined to prevent Napoleon's orders from taking effect. British traders feared that the United States would take over their trade with Europe. Competition between British and American merchants had been growing. The British had become alarmed by the expansion of American trade.

To counteract the French orders, the British forbade any ships to trade with France or with French-controlled areas. To prevent American ships from carrying any military supplies to France, the British began to stop and search American vessels. They also began to impress American sailors, or force them to serve in the British navy. In 1807, an American warship was fired on by a British ship. Several Americans were killed, and others were wounded.

Many Americans condemned these acts of *aggression* (ə gresh′ən), or hostile actions. They believed that the United States should go to war against Great Britain. Jefferson decided against war but urged Congress to pass the Embargo Act of 1807. An embargo is a restriction on imports or exports. The Embargo Act made it illegal for Americans to export goods to foreign countries. Jefferson hoped that the need for American goods would end the British and French restrictions and attacks.

The Embargo Act did not work. American farmers, manufacturers, shipowners, and traders were almost ruined. British aggression continued. James Madison, who became President in 1809, submitted a declaration of war to Congress in 1812. Congress approved the declaration, and the nation went to war against Great Britain.

The War of 1812

The War of 1812 was fought on land and on water. Early American attempts to attack British strongholds in Canada failed. In 1813, American troops raided and burned the Canadian city of York. American forces also defeated the British and their Indian allies north of Lake Ontario. The first naval victory also occurred in 1813. A small British fleet on Lake Erie was defeated by American ships, and Detroit came under American control.

The British burned the White House during the war of 1812. Badly damaged, the mansion was rebuilt by 1817.

In 1814, British resistance increased. Britain's war with France had ended, so Great Britain could turn its full attention to North America. The British attacked American cities along the Atlantic coast. British ships formed a blockade that prevented ships from entering or leaving American ports.

British troops captured Washington, D.C., and burned the Capitol and the White House. The British were forced to retreat, however, when they tried to take Baltimore. The Americans also turned back the British in an important battle near Lake Champlain.

By the end of 1814, the British and the Americans wanted to end the war. It seemed to both nations that fighting could go on indefinitely. In January 1815, the final battle of the war was fought at New Orleans. General Andrew Jackson defeated the British in a great American victory. Many Americans believed that this success meant that the United States had won the war. However, the battle took place after peace had been established. American and British representatives signed the peace treaty in December of 1814, but the news did not reach Jackson in time to prevent the battle.

The Treaty of Ghent that ended the war did not resolve the issues that had caused it. Each side had to return any land it had taken, so neither nation gained or lost territory. Impressment, blockades, and freedom of the seas were not even mentioned in the treaty. What the United States did gain by the war was security and confidence. Its victories and successful defense gave the nation new self-respect.

After the war, the United States returned to the foreign policy of President Washington. Americans did not become directly involved in European conflicts for nearly 100 more years.

Do You Know?

1. What document replaced the Articles of Confederation as a framework of government for the United States?
2. How did President Washington respond to the French request for support in its war against Great Britain and Spain in 1793?
3. Why did the United States go to war against Great Britain in 1812?
4. Who led the Americans against the British in the Battle of New Orleans?

2

A Growing Power

After the War of 1812, the people of the United States felt that a great future lay before them. They could load their products on ships and safely send them to all parts of the world. They could move westward into the lands of the Louisiana Purchase to clear farms and plant crops. There was plenty of room in which to spread out. Many of the nation's leaders, however, dreamed of adding even more territory to the country. They began to think of widening the boundaries of the United States.

The Monroe Doctrine

In 1808, Spain was defeated by the French forces under Napoleon Bonaparte. Spain's colonies in Latin America saw the defeat as an opportunity to seek independence. Although the United States was officially neutral, there was a great deal of sympathy for the Spanish Americans.

After Napoleon's defeat in 1815, Russia, Prussia, France, and Spain formed an alliance to suppress revolutions. The United States feared that the alliance might help Spain regain its former colonies in the Americas. By 1823, Mexico, Central America, and most of South America were independent. Great Britain still ruled Canada and several areas in the Caribbean, where the Netherlands, Spain, and France also controlled several small areas.

Russia, too, still had Alaska. In 1821, the czar claimed the Pacific coast of North America as far south as the 51st parallel. The Russians ordered American ships to stay more than 100 miles from the territory they claimed. Because this region was also claimed by both Great Britain and the United States, the United States was concerned. The establishment of Russian trading posts along the California coast was the cause for even greater concern.

The United States was faced with several problems of foreign policy in the 1820s. President James Monroe discussed them with his advisors. The result was a bold warning delivered as part of Monroe's annual message to Congress in 1823. The President told the nations of the world to keep hands off the Western Hemisphere. He warned them not to interfere in the United States and the newly independent Latin American countries. He also warned that there was to be no new colonization in the Western Hemisphere. President Monroe assured the European nations that their existing colonies were in no danger from the United States. He also said that the United States would not interfere in European affairs.

These warnings and reassurances became known as the Monroe *Doctrine* (dok′trin). A principle or set of principles is called a doctrine. The Monroe Doctrine restated President Washington's ideas of isolationism and Jefferson's desire to avoid foreign entanglements. It became the guiding principle of the foreign policy of the United States until the twentieth century.

James Monroe was President from 1817 to 1825. His Secretary of State was John Quincy Adams.

Continental Expansion

At the time of the Louisiana Purchase, it was not clear whether the United States had acquired the region known as West Florida. Boundary disputes continued until 1813. While Spain was involved in the revolutions of its Latin American colonies, the United States decided to *annex* (ə neks'), or to take possession of, West Florida. A few years later, Spain sold East Florida to the United States. A treaty fixed the boundary between the United States and the Spanish lands from the Gulf of Mexico to the Pacific. This treaty, signed in 1819, became known as the Transcontinental Treaty.

About this time, the United States made two important treaties with Britain. One, the Rush-Bagot Agreement, limited armed ships on the Great Lakes. It later led to the end of land fortifications along the boundary between Canada and the United States. The other treaty fixed the boundary between the United States and Canada from the Lake of the Woods west to the Rocky Mountains. This boundary followed the 49th parallel.

John Quincy Adams was the Secretary of State who was partly responsible for the Transcontinental Treaty and the Rush-Bagot Agreement. Adams once remarked that the world should become familiar with the idea that the United States might control the continent of North America. This idea that the United States was meant to expand and extend its boundaries to the Pacific, and perhaps to the north and south as well, became known as *manifest destiny* (man'ə fest' des'tə nē). During the 1840s, the United States did expand its boundaries enormously.

The Annexation of Texas

The region known as Texas became part of Mexico after Mexico won its independence from Spain in 1821. The Mexican government opened up Texas to settlers from the United States. In 1830, Mexico passed a law to stop further settlement. Mexico strengthened its army, and fighting soon broke out between the Texans and the Mexican army. In 1836, the Mexican president, General Santa Anna, attacked the fortified mission called the Alamo in San Antonio. The American defenders of the Alamo were killed. A few months later, Santa Anna was captured. He agreed to recognize the independence of Texas. Almost immediately, the Texans asked to join the United States. Annexation was put off until 1845. Texas became a state the same year. Mexico's government, which had refused to accept Santa Anna's treaty recognizing the independence of Texas, threatened to go to war with the United States.

The Mexican Cession

Late in 1845, President James Polk sent a diplomat to Mexico to discuss the question of the Texas-Mexican boundary and to offer to buy California. California, like Texas, had been inherited by Mexico at the time of independence. The Mexican government, angry over the annexation of Texas, refused to see the diplomat.

War broke out between Mexico and the United States in 1846 and continued for two years. During the first year, American troops gained control of California, New Mexico, and Texas. California was won with the help of local revolts. The people living there had earlier rebelled against the Mexican government because of the way it was ruling the region.

Mexico refused to make peace until 1848, after the capture of Mexico City by American forces. By the terms of the peace treaty, the United States gained California and most of what was then called New Mexico. This large area was called the Mexican Cession. A cession is territory that is ceded, or given up. See the map on page 95. The United States paid Mexico 15 million dollars and assumed some of Mexico's debts.

Oregon

In 1818, when part of the boundary between the United States and Canada was fixed at the 49th parallel, Britain and the United States agreed on joint occupation of Oregon for ten years. Until the mid-1830s, however, few people from the United States had moved into the territory. By 1846, the number of American settlers was more than 10,000. They were determined that Oregon should be governed by the United States. In 1846, it was agreed to divide Oregon between the United States and Great Britain along the 49th parallel. The United States would have the land south of this line.

The United States in 1853

By 1846, the idea of manifest destiny had, in part, come true. The United States stretched from the Atlantic to the Pacific. A boundary existed between the United States and Canada from one ocean to the other. The present-day boundary between the United States and Mexico was established when the United States bought a small area of land south of the Gila River. This land, known as the Gadsden Purchase, was acquired from Mexico in 1853. By this time, the conterminous United States had the same boundaries that it has today.

The Purchase of Alaska

In 1867, the United States acquired its last territory on the mainland of North America. This region was Alaska, which was purchased from Russia. The arrangements were made by the United States Secretary of State, William Seward. Seward, a believer in manifest destiny, wanted the United States to annex as much of North America as possible. When he learned that the czar wanted to sell Alaska, he arranged a purchase treaty within a few hours. The price paid for the vast region was a little more than seven million dollars.

Expansion Beyond the Continent

In 1867, the only territory outside North America controlled by the United States was the Midway Islands. By 1899, American possessions included many islands throughout the Pacific and the Caribbean. Much of this overseas empire was acquired as a result of the Spanish-American War.

The Spanish-American War

The Spanish had controlled Cuba since Columbus claimed it for Spain in 1492. A desire for independence had been growing among the Cubans throughout the 1800s, and they demanded their freedom in 1868. The war that followed lasted for ten years. When it ended, Spain was still in control, but the Spanish promised political reforms. Fighting began again in 1895. This time, Spain instituted harsh measures to control the Cubans.

Many Americans sympathized with Cuba's desire for independence. Some Americans had economic interests in Cuba. During the late 1800s, they had invested in Cuban sugarcane plantations. These investments were threatened by the unstable situation.

In 1898, a riot broke out in the Cuban capital of Havana. President McKinley sent the battleship *Maine* to Havana harbor. A huge explosion destroyed the ship and killed many

Theodore Roosevelt led the "Rough Riders" in the Spanish-American War.

American sailors. The cause of the explosion was unknown, but many Americans blamed the Spanish. Two months later, the United States declared war on Spain.

The first battle of the Spanish-American War did not take place in Cuba. As soon as war was declared, an American fleet set sail from Hong Kong for the Spanish-controlled Philippines. The Spanish ships in Manila Bay were completely destroyed in a single battle.

In the spring of 1898, American forces were sent to Cuba. They succeeded in ending Spanish resistance there by July. A short time later, American forces conquered Puerto Rico. After only four months, the war was over.

A Growing Empire

The peace treaty that ended the Spanish-American War established Cuban independence. The United States acquired the former Spanish possessions of Puerto Rico, Guam, and the Philippines.

491

In 1903, the United States gained the right to build a canal through Panama. Construction was completed in 1914.

The United States annexed the Hawaiian Islands in 1898 and acquired Wake Island in 1899. Britain, Germany, and the United States agreed to jointly govern the islands of Samoa in 1899.

Latin American Affairs

President Theodore Roosevelt came to office in 1901. Roosevelt believed that the United States should assume a larger role in foreign affairs. He took an active interest in promoting American commerce throughout the world. Roosevelt's policies in Latin America were based on the Monroe Doctrine, but they went a step further. Monroe had said that the United States would prevent European interference in Latin America. Roosevelt declared that the United States, as the leader of the Western Hemisphere, had a right to become involved in the affairs of Latin American lands.

In 1902, Roosevelt's policy was tested in Venezuela. The newly independent nation had not repaid its debts to several European countries. British and German ships blockaded the coast of Venezuela. Venezuela appealed to the United States for help. American intervention led to a peaceful settlement.

In 1903, Roosevelt negotiated a treaty to build a canal in the new nation of Panama. The canal, which would provide passage for ships going between the Atlantic and the Pacific, would be important for trade and also for defense.

American Influence in Asia

The Panama Canal and American possessions in the Pacific increased American trade with Asia. Much earlier, the United States had negotiated trade agreements with Japan. The Open Door Policy of 1854 had established

Commodore Matthew Perry, shown in a procession through Yokohama, opened Japan to American trade in 1854.

American trading rights and marked the beginning of American economic interests in Asia. Establishing trade with the Chinese was more difficult.

By the late nineteenth century, Great Britain, Germany, France, Japan, and Russia had taken over coastal areas in China and had restricted commerce in areas under their control. When the Chinese rebelled against these nations in 1900, the United States became involved in the fighting. After peace was restored, the United States proposed an Open Door policy for China. The terms of the policy guaranteed the right of all nations to trade with China. Great Britain, France, and Germany formally accepted the proposal.

Japanese and Russian rivalry over the Chinese province of Manchuria continued, and the two nations went to war in 1904. President Roosevelt invited both countries to the United States to work out a peaceful settlement. The Treaty of Portsmouth ended the war and reaffirmed the Open Door Policy. Roosevelt received the Nobel Peace Prize for his efforts in ending the war. The United States had assumed a role of leadership that was recognized throughout the world.

Do You Know?

1. What President issued a warning to the nations of the world about interfering in the Western Hemisphere?
2. What territory did the United States acquire as the result of the 1848 peace treaty with Mexico?
3. What secretary of state arranged for the purchase of Alaska? When? From whom?
4. What President negotiated a treaty to build a canal in Panama? When?

Before You Go On

Using New Words

doctrine   manifest destiny
federalism   aggression
diplomacy   isolationism
annex

Number a paper from 1 through 7. After each number write the word or term from the above list that matches the definition.

1. Hostile actions
2. The division of powers between the national government and the state governments
3. To take possession of
4. The idea that the United States was meant to expand and extend its boundaries to the Pacific
5. A system for managing relations between nations and for carrying on negotiations between governments
6. A policy of avoiding involvements with foreign countries
7. A principle or set of principles

Finding the Facts

1. What British actions following the French and Indian War led the colonists to break their ties with Great Britain?
2. What did Washington warn against in his Farewell Address?
3. What two concerns led Jefferson to acquire the Louisiana Territory?
4. How and by whom was America's "freedom of the seas" violated in the early 1800s? What did the United States do about it?
5. How did President Jefferson try to discourage French and British restrictions and attacks on American ships in 1807?
6. What treaty ended the War of 1812?
7. What warnings did President Monroe issue as part of the Monroe Doctrine?
8. What possessions did the United States acquire as a result of the Spanish-American War?
9. How did President Theodore Roosevelt expand the Monroe Doctrine?
10. What were the results of the Treaty of Portsmouth?

3
Global Involvement

The Spanish-American War marked a turning point for the United States. After 1898, the country acquired territories in the Pacific and the Caribbean. With its territories, the United States gained a new interest and a new role in world affairs.

The growing strength of the United States was tested in 1914 when World War I broke out in Europe. Many Americans wanted to stay out of the conflict, and the government at first decided to remain neutral. As the months went by, however, it became clear that as a major power the United States would become involved in the first global war.

World War I

World War I began in Europe when the Austrian Archduke Ferdinand was assassinated by a Serbian in the Balkan city of Sarajevo (sär′ə ye vô′). At the time this happened, 1914, Europe was divided into a system of rival alliances. One alliance was made up of Italy, Germany, and Austria-Hungary. Another alliance existed among France, Great Britain, and Russia. Smaller countries were allied to these great powers. Bulgaria and Turkey were on the side of Germany and Austria. Serbia was allied with Russia.

Austria-Hungary demanded compensation from Serbia for the assassination of the archduke. Serbia refused to meet the demands, and Austria-Hungary declared war on Serbia.

Germany backed Austria-Hungary. These countries and the nations siding with them became known as the Central Powers. Russia, France, and Great Britain backed Serbia. These countries and the others joining them were known as the Allied Powers, or the Allies. Italy joined the Allies in 1915.

America's Part in the War

The outbreak of war in Europe brought a declaration of neutrality from the President of the United States, Woodrow Wilson. Wilson said that the quarrels of Europe were not an American concern.

During the early part of the war, however, both Britain and Germany violated America's neutral rights at sea. Warfare at sea was endangering American ships. Wilson took the position that Jefferson had taken before the War of 1812. He demanded America's right to freedom of the seas.

The Central Powers and the Allies did not heed the demands of the United States. British warships halted American vessels headed for Germany. German submarines sank ships bound for Great Britain and France. In 1915, the British liner *Lusitania* was torpedoed and sunk off the coast of Ireland. The *Lusitania* was a passenger ship, but it was also transporting weapons. Because the Americans aboard the ship were drowned, many people in the United States thought the country should go to war. It was two years, however, before America entered the

When the *Lusitania* was sunk by the Germans in 1915, 128 Americans died. Americans were divided over war.

war. Germany announced that all ships in waters near the Allied countries would be sunk without warning. The United States responded with a declaration of war against Germany and the Central Powers on April 6, 1917.

Before the United States entered the war, it seemed the Allies might be defeated. About two million American troops were sent to France. Naval forces and equipment were also sent. America played an important part in the defeat of the Central Powers. On November 11, 1918, the Allies signed an *armistice* (är′mistis) with Germany. An agreement during a war or battle to stop fighting is called an armistice.

The Treaty of Versailles

President Wilson said that World War I was a "war to end all wars." Before the war ended, he told Congress that nations should join together in an organization that would help prevent wars. When the war was over, Wilson was eager to help establish such an organization.

The peace conference opened at the palace of Versailles (versī′) near Paris early in 1919. Delegates from 27 nations attended, including President Wilson from the United States. None of the defeated nations was represented. The meetings were dominated by the leaders of Great Britain, France, Italy, and the United States. These men, "the Big Four," met in secret to arrange the terms of the peace treaty. Under secret treaties made by the Allies before the United States entered the war, the Allies had planned to enlarge their boundaries and force Germany to make large payments. Although these secret treaties disagreed with his beliefs, Wilson stayed at the conference in order to introduce plans for a League of Nations into the peace treaty.

The treaty that ended World War I was known as the Treaty of Versailles. It was signed in June of 1919, and included plans for a League of Nations. The United States Senate refused to ratify the treaty because of the fear that the League would be an "entangling alliance." It was not until 1921 that the United States signed a peace treaty with Germany.

The League of Nations

The United States did not sign the Treaty of Versailles or become a member of the League of Nations. The League was an international organization for promoting peace and cooperation. It was dedicated to helping settle disputes between nations through the establishment of the Court of International Justice.

The Treaty of Versailles had made many changes on the world map. In Europe, several new independent states were created through the policy of self-determination. You have read about these countries in Unit 5. Germany's former colonies were given to different Allied countries under a *mandate* (man'dāt) system. Under the League of Nations, a mandate was a commission, or order, to administer some region. The governing countries had to account for their administration to the League of Nations. You have read about some of these mandates in Unit 7.

Foreign Policy After World War I

Although Wilson stressed the importance of building a lasting peace, the United States turned away from the responsibility of world leadership and retreated to a policy of isolationism. It was, however, an isolationism different from that of the nineteenth century. The United States had become too powerful not to be involved in many of the problems following the war.

Although the United States took no formal part in the League of Nations, it did cooperate with League agencies. Two Americans served as judges of the World Court. At a conference in Washington, D.C., in 1921 and 1922, the United States cooperated with Japan and European powers in arranging several treaties. These treaties had to do with cooperation in Asia and the Pacific. America took the lead in promoting a *pact* (pakt) to outlaw war. A pact is an agreement or treaty.

World War II

After World War I, new political leaders came to power in Italy, Germany, and Japan. These leaders were committed to extending their control beyond the borders of their countries. It became difficult for the United States to maintain its isolationism as these nations pursued policies of conquest.

Acts of Aggression

The new leaders of Italy and Germany were dictators. Benito Mussolini gained control of Italy in 1922. Adolf Hitler and the National Socialist, or Nazi, Party came to power in Germany in 1933. In 1936, Germany and Italy formed an alliance known as the Rome-Berlin Axis.

The same year, a civil war broke out in Spain. The rebels, led by Francisco Franco, wanted to overthrow the Spanish republic. Italian and German troops and support helped Franco become dictator of Spain in 1939.

The United States did not become involved in the Spanish conflict. In 1935, 1936, and 1937, Congress passed three neutrality acts. These were laws forbidding industries and banks to sell military supplies or lend money to warring nations. The acts also prevented Americans from traveling on ships of warring nations and prohibited American merchant ships from being armed.

While the United States pursued its policy of neutrality, the Axis powers began a policy of aggression. By 1939, Italy had invaded and annexed both Ethiopia and Albania. German troops conquered Austria and Czechoslavakia. When Hitler's forces invaded Poland, Great Britain and France supported Poland by declaring war on Germany.

Many Americans sympathized with the Poles and supported the British and the French. The embargo on military supplies was repealed so these nations could buy American weapons.

Hitler's conquests continued in 1940 with the invasion of Denmark, Norway, and the Netherlands. British and French troops were defeated by German forces in Belgium. Italy joined the conflict by declaring war on Great Britain and France. As German troops moved into France from the east, Italian forces gathered in the south. The French surrendered, and German troops occupied much of the country.

The German assault on Great Britain began a few weeks later. German aircraft bombed the cities and industries of southern England. British fighter planes destroyed much of the German fighting force, however, and no German invasion took place. In 1941, Congress passed the Lend-Lease Act, which allowed supplies and weapons to be sent to countries fighting against the Axis powers.

While the situation in Europe dominated American attention, Japan was carrying out invasions in the Far East. The Japanese had joined the Axis powers in 1940. By 1941, Japan controlled much of China and many Pacific islands. Japanese troops began to invade French Indochina. On December 7, 1941, in a surprise attack, Japanese planes bombed the American naval base at Pearl Harbor in Hawaii. The following day, Congress declared war on Japan. Germany and Italy, as allies of Japan, declared war on the United States.

The United States in World War II

The major battles of World War II were fought in Europe, North Africa, and the Pacific. German troops attacked the Soviet Union in 1941 and again in 1942. British and American tanks, trucks, and supplies were sent to help the Russians defend their country. By January 1943, the Germans were defeated in Russia. Four months later, British and American troops defeated German and Italian forces in North Africa.

On June 6, 1944, known as D-Day, British and American forces landed in Normandy, on the coast of France. As these forces pushed

French crowds cheer as Allied troops liberate Paris from the Germans in 1944. World War II ended in 1945.

eastward, the Russian troops moved toward the west. The German armies were caught between. The Allies began to liberate the countries occupied by Germany. In May of 1945, the Germans finally surrendered.

While some American troops were fighting in Africa and Europe, other American forces were involved in the Pacific conflict. During 1943 and 1944, Americans attacked the Japanese on islands throughout the Pacific. In 1945, the last of the Japanese-controlled islands were taken. American forces were ready to invade Japan, but the invasion never took place. President Truman urged Japan to surrender. He said the United States was ready to use a weapon powerful enough to destroy all of Japan. When Japanese officials refused to surrender, Truman ordered American planes to drop an atomic bomb on Hiroshima. This was the first time an atomic bomb was used in a war. Another bomb was dropped on Nagasaki. The destruction and loss of life that resulted shocked the world. Japan surrendered a few days later. World War II was over.

Do You Know?

1. What event led to the beginning of World War I?
2. What two groups of nations fought against each other in World War I?
3. What peace-keeping organization was established after World War I?
4. What incident led the United States to declare war on Japan in 1941?

4

The United States in a Complex World

The United States played an important role in bringing World War II to an end. As a major power, this country was involved in creating policies that affected the world after the war.

In February 1945, before the war ended, an important meeting took place at Yalta, in the Soviet Ukraine. British Prime Minister Winston Churchill, Soviet Premier Joseph Stalin, and President Franklin D. Roosevelt of the United States met to discuss plans for governing Germany after the war. It was decided to divide both Germany and the city of Berlin into four zones. Great Britain, the Soviet Union, France, and the United States would each control a part of Germany and a section of Berlin. The Yalta leaders declared that free elections should take place as soon as possible in the countries that Germany had conquered.

Plans for an organization to be known as the United Nations were also begun at Yalta. The United Nations was established as an international peace-keeping organization on October 24, 1945. The United States was the first country to ratify the United Nations Charter.

The Cold War

World War II was hardly over when the United States found itself in conflict with the Soviet Union. Disagreements between the two coun-

Allied leaders met at Yalta in 1945 to plan for peace. Seated left to right are Churchill, Roosevelt, and Stalin.

British and American planes provided food and supplies for more than two million Berliners during 1948–1949.

tries began in July 1945, when the Soviet Union insisted on keeping control of the territory it occupied in eastern Europe. A period of hostility that became known as the Cold War began. On one side were the United States and other countries of the free world. The Soviet Union and its satellites were on the other side.

The Truman Doctrine and the Marshall Plan

The Soviet dictator Joseph Stalin did not believe that peace was possible between capitalist and Communist countries. Soviet-occupied countries of Europe became satellites of the Soviet Union. See the map on page 260. Soviet control and suppression cut these countries off from the West. Winston Churchill said that an "Iron Curtain" had fallen across Europe.

Harry Truman, who became President of the United States in 1945, wanted to prevent the spread of Communism. He developed a policy of containment known as the Truman Doctrine. This policy was aimed at preventing the spread of Communism and helping free people maintain their freedom. Congress voted

money to help free countries strengthen their military forces.

Military aid was not enough, however, to stop Communism. Many countries had severe economic problems because of destruction caused by the war. In 1947, the United States approved a program to help European countries repair their transportation systems and get their farms and factories producing again. This program, called the Marshall Plan, or the European Recovery Program, was a great success. It was named for Secretary of State George C. Marshall, who first suggested the idea. As Western Europe became prosperous again, the appeal of Communism grew smaller.

While Truman was still in office, a crisis developed in the Cold War. The Soviet Union, which controlled eastern Germany, blocked all land transportation routes to Berlin in June of 1948. For ten months, British and American planes flew food and supplies to people stranded in the part of Berlin controlled by Great Britain, France, and the United States. The flights became known as the Berlin Airlift. The Soviets lifted the blockade in 1949.

501

The Korean War

The United Nations faced one of its first major problems in Korea. Korea had been divided at the end of World War II into Communist North Korea and independent South Korea. In 1950, North Korean armies invaded South Korea. The United Nations called on its members to aid South Korea. Several countries sent troops and equipment, but most were supplied by the United States. The United Nations' policy to fight a limited war ended in a stalemate, or deadlock. Negotiations continued for months. An armistice signed in 1953 left the country divided as it had been before the war.

The Vietnam War

Soon after the Korean armistice, another crisis threatened in Southeast Asia. The war that developed there became a serious problem for the United States.

In 1954, Vietnam was recognized as independent and divided into a northern and a southern part. An election to unite the country was never held. Vietnam continued as the Communist state of North Vietnam and the republic of South Vietnam.

Fighting soon broke out between the two countries. The United States was concerned about what would happen. President Eisenhower believed that if South Vietnam fell to the Communists, it would not be long before its neighbors also became Communist. Military advisors and millions of dollars for military aid were sent to South Vietnam in the late 1950s. In the 1960s, fighting grew into a full-scale war. The United States became more deeply involved and increased its aid. Thousands of American troops were sent to Vietnam. By the late 1960s, opposition to the war had become strong in the United States. Peace talks finally began in 1968.

American troops were withdrawn from Vietnam when a cease-fire agreement was reached in 1973. Fighting between North Vietnam and South Vietnam, however, continued. In 1975, South Vietnam surrendered to North Vietnam and the war ended. The next year, both countries were united under the control of the Communists.

The Vietnam War was the longest conflict in American history. Thousands of Americans were killed and wounded. America's involvement in Vietnam left the United States divided and angry.

The Bay of Pigs and the Missile Crisis

A problem closer to home faced the United States in the early 1960s. In 1959, the government of Cuba had been overthrown by Fidel Castro, who became the country's Communist dictator. The United States supported a plan to overthrow Castro's government by invading Cuba at a place called the Bay of Pigs. This invasion attempt failed completely.

In 1962, the United States learned that the Soviet Union was building missile sites in pro-Communist Cuba. President Kennedy demanded that the missile bases be dismantled and the missiles removed. He also set up a blockade to prevent the shipment of more weapons. The Soviet Union met the demands, and an armed conflict was avoided.

Efforts Toward Peace and Cooperation

American foreign policy after World War II was not totally dominated by the Cold War. The United States worked to promote peace and cooperation among different nations.

In 1953, Nikita Khrushchev became the new leader of the Soviet Union. Unlike Stalin, he seemed willing to pursue cooperation between Communist and non-Communist nations. In 1955, President Eisenhower met with Khrushchev and the leaders of Great Britain and France at Geneva. The President made a strong case for ending the weapons race. No agreement was reached, but the issue had at least been raised.

During the Eisenhower administration, the United States and Canada cooperated in building the St. Lawrence Seaway. The new waterway allowed large vessels to travel from the Great Lakes to the Atlantic Ocean. The seaway improved world trade for both nations.

Peace and Progress

John Kennedy became President in 1961. He established two programs that helped bring better living conditions to other nations. One of these was the Peace Corps. Peace Corps volunteers went to many countries throughout the world. They taught new methods of farming, helped to build homes and schools, and worked on a variety of projects.

Another program was the Alliance for Progress. Like the Marshall Plan, it was a program for helping countries help themselves. The Alliance used funds from member Latin Amer-

A Peace Corps teacher helps a student in Kenya. More than 15,000 Americans have served in this volunteer program.

ican nations and the United States for roads, schools, housing, and public works projects throughout Latin America.

Summit Conferences

President Nixon's inauguration in 1969 marked the beginning of a new approach to foreign policy. Nixon went to Romania and became the first President to visit a nation behind the Iron Curtain. He believed that the United States should try to improve relations with China and with the Soviet Union.

In 1972, President Nixon and Secretary of State Henry Kissinger visited China. A summit conference, or meeting with government leaders, was held in Beijing. It was a step toward establishing diplomatic relations between the United States and Communist China. Since 1949, the United States had only recognized the Chinese Nationalist government.

503

Nixon and Kissinger also visited the Soviet Union in 1972 for a summit conference. This Moscow meeting began a period of *détente* (dā tänt'). *Détente* is the easing of strained relations between countries.

Recent Foreign Policy

Bringing peace to the Middle East was an important goal of President Jimmy Carter. Disputes between Israel and Egypt had been going on since 1948 and had erupted into wars. In 1978, Israeli Prime Minister Menachem Begin (mə näk'əm bā'gin) and Egyptian President Anwar Sadat met with President Carter in Maryland. Agreements known as the Camp David Accords were the result. In 1979, Carter helped the two nations reach a compromise, and a peace treaty was signed.

President Carter tried to maintain good relations with Latin America. In 1978, he signed a treaty giving Panama control of the Panama Canal Zone. In 1979, Carter announced the establishment of diplomatic relations between the United States and Communist China. He was also concerned with human rights of people throughout the world. When Soviet troops invaded Afghanistan in late 1979 and early 1980, Carter banned grain shipments to the Soviet Union. He also asked the United States Olympic team to boycott the 1980 Olympic Games in Moscow.

In November 1979, Iranian students seized the American embassy in Tehran and took the Americans there as hostages. Negotiations for their release continued for more than a year. The day the hostages left Iran, Ronald Reagan

President Reagan appears with Prime Minister Margaret Thatcher of England after a meeting.

was inaugurated as the fortieth President of the United States.

Foreign affairs were an important concern of the new administration. The assassination of Egyptian President Sadat threatened to upset peace in the Middle East. In Poland, the Communist government imposed martial law. In Central America, revolutions disrupted governments in several countries. The arms race with the Soviet Union continued. A major task of the United States in the 1980s would be to help maintain peace in a complex world.

Do You Know?

1. What was the period of hostility between Communist and non-Communist countries after World War II called?
2. What were the goals of the Truman Doctrine?
3. What was the outcome of the Korean War? The Vietnam War?

To Help You Learn

Using New Words

pact   détente
mandate   armistice
annex   doctrine

Number a paper from 1 through 6. After each number write the word or term from the above list that matches the definition.

1. To take possession of
2. An agreement or treaty
3. The easing of strained relations between countries
4. A commission, or order, to administer some region
5. An agreement during a war or battle to stop fighting
6. A principle or set of principles

Finding the Facts

1. When did the movement toward independence in the American colonies begin?
2. What made up the central government of the United States under the Articles of Confederation?
3. What diplomat was sent by President Washington to settle differences with Great Britain? With Spain?
4. What acquisition resulted in doubling the size of the United States in 1803?
5. What is the principle of "freedom of the seas"?
6. Why did the United States Senate refuse to ratify the Treaty of Versailles?
7. What dictator came to power in Italy in 1922? In Germany in 1933?
8. What was the Rome-Berlin Axis?
9. How did the United States respond to the conflict in Spain in the 1930s?
10. After the invasion of what country did France and Great Britain declare war on Germany?
11. What did the Lend-Lease Act allow?
12. What happened on D-Day?
13. What American action brought about the surrender of Japan in World War II?
14. What world leaders met at Yalta in 1945? Why?
15. What international peace-keeping organization was established in 1945?
16. What were the goals of the Marshall Plan?
17. Name two programs established during the Kennedy administration to improve living conditions in other nations.
18. What steps did President Nixon take to improve relations with China and the Soviet Union?
19. What part did President Carter play in helping to bring about peace in the Middle East?
20. What were two events or situations that threatened world peace when President Reagan took office?

Learning from Maps

Look at the maps on pages 92, 94–95, and 100–101 to answer the questions below. According to the maps, what foreign countries had claims in North America in 1750? In 1853? What were the eastern and western boundaries of the United States in 1783? In 1853? Was Alaska part of the United States in 1853? In 1803, about how many times larger was the United States than it had been in 1783? What country had lost most of its North American claims by 1803? When did Texas become part of the United States? When did Oregon Country become part of the United States? What countries claimed this region in 1803? In 1783? Was Mexico an independent country at the time of the Gadsden Purchase?

Using Study Skills

1. **Library Resources:** A yearbook is a reference book published every year that has information about the preceding year. It is often published as part of an encyclopedia. A yearbook usually has articles about the significant events and developments that have taken place. It may include statistical information on industrial and agricultural production, GNP, imports and exports, and population. Yearbooks generally include a chronological list of the important events for the year. Other lists may include famous people who have died during the year, scientific achievements, major sports events, and technological developments.

The features of a yearbook are similar to those of an almanac. However, the lists in almanacs generally include information for more than one year. There are usually more general-reference articles in yearbooks than in almanacs.

Use the sample table of contents from a 1981 yearbook that follows to answer the questions below.

In what section would you look to find Ronald Reagan's margin of victory over Jimmy Carter in the presidential election? Where George Bush was born? How the United States boycott of the Olympics affected the Moscow games? The winner of the 1980 Nobel Peace Prize? When the shah of Iran died? The important developments in physics in 1980?

2. **Time Line:** Find the dates for the following events and list them in chronological order: Articles of Confederation ratified; Mexican Cession acquired; South Vietnam surrendered to North Vietnam;

President Eisenhower met with Soviet Premier Khrushchev; Alaska purchased by United States; Hawaiian Islands annexed by United States.

Copy the time line from page 481 and add the events you have listed. Use the completed time line to answer the following questions: How many years passed between the ratification of the Articles of Confederation and the ratification of the Constitution? Between the issuance of the Monroe Doctrine and the beginning of the Spanish-American War? Between President Eisenhower's meeting with Khrushchev and President Nixon's visit to the Soviet Union? Between United States withdrawal from Vietnam and the surrender of South Vietnam to North Vietnam?

3. **Outline:** Reread the sections about continental expansion on pages 489–491. Take notes on the developments that led to the territorial expansion of the United States from 1819 through 1867. Use your notes to write an outline. *Continental Expansion of the United States* could be the title of the outline. You may wish to use the dates 1819–1845 and 1846–1867 as subheadings. If necessary, review the discussions on outlining in Units 1, 6, and 9.

Thinking It Through

1. When Secretary of State John Quincy Adams spoke about the "manifest destiny" of the United States, he said that the entire continent of North America could one day become United States territory.

Why would this idea appeal to people in the United States? What arguments could they use to support this point of view? Why didn't Americans pursue the idea of trying to control all of North America?

2. Do you think a policy of isolationism was an advantage to the new nation of the United States? Why or why not? Do you think such a policy could be an advantage today?

Projects

1. Write to the Peace Corps to find out what skills are most needed and in what countries Peace Corps volunteers are currently serving. Request materials about this organization and arrange a display for your classroom. If possible, invite a Peace Corps volunteer to talk to your class about his or her experiences.

2. The History Committee might like to find out more about United States involvement in the Spanish-American War. Newspaper accounts in the New York *Journal* and New York *World* greatly influenced public opinion to support the war. Committee members could prepare reports on how the newspapers affected foreign policy decisions.

3. The Biography Committee could prepare a time line, listing the Presidents of the United States and the years each served. Significant developments in the foreign policy of each administration could be noted.

12 World Neighbors

Unit Preview

The part of the earth occupied by people is very small in comparison with the rest of the earth. Within the earth's populated regions, people are unevenly distributed. Population densities are related to the different ways land is used to obtain the necessities of life.

Factors that affect land use include natural resources, natural conditions, culture, and technology. Today about one-third of the earth's land is used for agriculture, and about half of the earth's people work in agriculture. Other land is used for lumbering, hunting, gathering, mining, cities, and industries.

Where land is used intensively, large numbers of people can be supported. After about 1650, the world's population began to grow rapidly as a result of technology leading to industrialization and better health practices. The extremely rapid increase in recent years has been called the population explosion.

Growing populations and the related problems of limited food supplies, dwindling resources, pollution, and the threat of war are problems shared by all the nations of the world. Long ago countries began trading with one another and discovered the advantages of exchanging goods and ideas. Today the nations of the world are linked to one another by a complex system of economic ties. Improvements in transportation and communication have made the world smaller. It has become increasingly important for countries of the world to share its resources and solve its problems so that they can live together peaceably as world neighbors.

Things to Discover

If you look carefully at the picture, map, and time line, you can answer these questions.

1. The photograph shows the United Nations headquarters. The UN was founded in 1945. Some of the UN's agencies are older than the UN itself. One is the Universal Postal Union. When was it established?
2. When were the first Olympics held? How many years later were the first modern games held?
3. What does NATO stand for? When was it established?

Words to Learn

You will meet these words and terms in this unit. As you read, you will learn what they mean and how to pronounce them. The Word List will help you.

balance of payments	geophysical
balance of power	interest
biosphere	investment
demography	literacy
deplete	malnutrition
finite	passport
free trade	profit

508

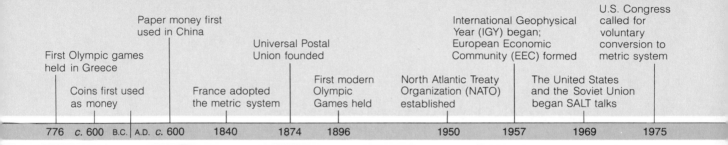

First Olympic games held in Greece

Coins first used as money

Paper money first used in China

France adopted the metric system

Universal Postal Union founded

First modern Olympic Games held

North Atlantic Treaty Organization (NATO) established

International Geophysical Year (IGY) began; European Economic Community (EEC) formed

The United States and the Soviet Union began SALT talks

U.S. Congress called for voluntary conversion to metric system

776 c. 600 B.C. A.D. c. 600   1840   1874   1896   1950   1957   1969   1975

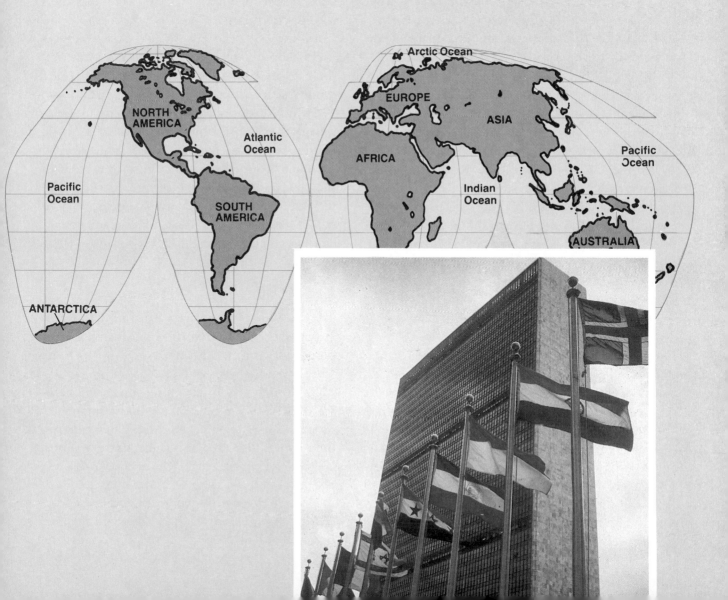

1

Land Use and Population Patterns

The planet Earth is the home not only of human beings but of many other living things. The part of the earth that supports plants and animals is called the *biosphere* (bī′əsfēr′). The biosphere is a thin zone at and near the earth's surface. The biosphere is small compared with the rest of the earth.

The part of the biosphere inhabited by people is also small. In general, people live only on the land portion of the earth. As you have learned in Unit 1, land makes up only about 30 percent of the earth's surface. If you look at the map on page 515, you will see that the world's population is not evenly distributed throughout the world. There are parts of the world where no people at all live.

People live only where they can obtain the necessities of life. Where people live depends on such things as natural resources, climate, and the physical character of the land. Where people live also depends on culture and technology. Since people first began cultivating crops, they have tended to live in places that are good for growing crops. These are places with level or gently rolling land, good soil, abundant rain, mild climates, and long growing seasons. Through technology, people are able to change their environment. They can use technology to alter the availability of necessary or useful resources. Whether societies do change their environment or not greatly depends on their culture and the complexity of their technology.

Simple societies still live in ways that have made few changes in the environment. Other societies have used complex technology to make great changes. People have modified natural conditions to increase the areas of the world that they can inhabit. Irrigation projects and scientific farming methods have increased the number of people that different regions of the world can support.

Natural resources also determine population patterns. As you have read in Unit 1, natural resources have changed from time to time and from culture to culture. Materials in the environment become resources when people use them to satisfy their needs. Where natural resources are plentiful or readily available, large cities have often grown up.

Land Use

The way land is used varies from place to place. It has also varied from time to time. The map on page 511 shows the main ways in which the world's land is used today.

Environment, or natural resources and natural conditions, is one of the most important factors in land use. Farming can be carried out only where there is good soil, sufficient water, and the proper climate. Mining activities must be located where there are minerals. Lumbering can be done only where there are trees.

Compare the map on page 511 with the map on page 515 to see what activities support the

510

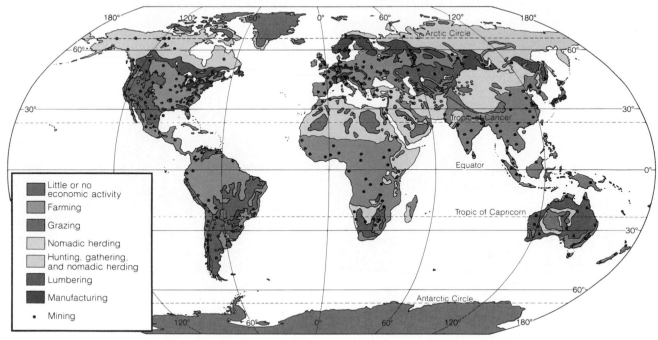

Legend:
- Little or no economic activity
- Farming
- Grazing
- Nomadic herding
- Hunting, gathering, and nomadic herding
- Lumbering
- Manufacturing
- • Mining

Land use is affected by such factors as mineral resources, water supply, climate, and culture. Land use changes as these factors change.

densest populations. Areas where small amounts of land support large numbers of people are areas of intensive land use. The opposite of intensive land use is extensive land use. In areas of extensive land use, large areas of land support few people.

Technology also affects land use. Before people learned to cultivate crops, land was used mainly for hunting and gathering. Until the technology for farming developed, the land could not be used to grow crops. Advanced technology allows greater choice in how land will be used. New exploration methods might reveal the presence of minerals on land used for farming. Modern methods of mining might mean that more money could be made by

mining the land than by farming it. Modern technology often leads to the increased use of land for commercial activities. Commercial activities are carried out where basic needs are provided for and surpluses can be sold for *profit* (prof'it). Money gained after expenses have been paid is called profit.

Culture also plays a role in land use. It was the custom among American Indians to own land in common as tribal lands. In the late 1800s, the United States government passed a law to break up tribal lands. The lands were divided into small units to be owned by individual Indians. The government hoped that individual ownership would encourage the Indians to become farmers. Although the land

Research to increase food production is part of the Green Revolution. Scientists here are experimenting with rice plants.

was suitable for farming, many Indians did not want to become farmers. They preferred to supply themselves with food in their traditional ways of hunting and fishing.

Habits and customs often determine what particular crops are grown in regions where many different kinds of crops can grow. Culture, however, includes not only habits and customs, but technology. Advances in technology have brought rapid changes in culture. For example, because of new irrigation projects in desert lands, some nomadic herders have become farmers. As cultures continue to change, land use will also change.

Agriculture

About one-third of the earth's land is used for agriculture. More land is used for agriculture than for any other purpose. About half the people in the world work in agriculture. The map on page 511 shows the areas of the world's land that are used for agriculture. A table listing some of the world's important agricultural products and the countries that lead in their production can be found in the Reference Tables on pages 556 and 557. Agriculture not only provides food but also raw materials for industry.

Agriculture includes both growing crops and raising livestock. Compare the map on page 511 with the maps on pages 24 and 31 to see how climate and rainfall determine whether crops will be grown or livestock raised in agricultural lands.

In industrialized countries like the United States and the countries of western Europe, agriculture is mainly commercial. Crops are raised to be sold. Scientific farming methods and modern machinery allow relatively few workers to produce great quantities of agricultural products.

In many parts of the world, for example in parts of South America and Africa, agriculture is at the subsistence level. People raise crops and animals chiefly for their own use. Shifting cultivation, which you read about in Unit 8, and nomadic herding, which you read about in Unit 7, are part of subsistence agriculture.

Lumbering, Hunting, and Gathering

Forest lands throughout the world are used for lumbering, hunting, and gathering. Today about 30 percent of the world's land is covered with forests. Logging is a commercial activity that provides materials for lumber, paper and paper products, and other wood products. Forests also provide latex for making rubber as well as valuable gums and resins.

In developing countries, wood is still the chief fuel for heating and cooking. Forests also provide simple societies who live there with wild game and food plants.

Mining

Minerals are distributed unevenly throughout the world. Their occurrence does not depend on climate or latitude, however. The distribution of minerals is related to rock types. Coal, petroleum, and natural gas are found in rocks that have been formed by deposition. Metals are usually found in association with rocks formed by tectonic activity.

Since the Industrial Revolution, demand for mineral resources has become greater. With

The demand for fossil fuels continues to grow. Oil and natural gas production in Nigeria has increased in recent years. Are these resources *finite*?

the greater demand have come improved methods for discovering and mining minerals.

All of the earth's crust is made up of minerals. Whether or not a mineral is mined depends on two things. It will not be mined unless it is useful. It will not be mined if the technology to extract it from the earth has not been developed. Some important minerals and the countries that produce them can be found in the Reference Tables on pages 557 and 558.

Although mining is an important activity, mining operations take up little of the world's land. Many minerals are found underground, and mining does not always affect activities at the earth's surface. In many oil-producing areas, crops are raised alongside oil wells. In areas where strip mining is carried out, however, it may be many years before the land can be used for other purposes.

Manufacturing and Cities

Use of land for manufacturing is often called industrial land use. Manufacturing usually takes place where raw materials are readily available. For example, Pittsburgh, which is an important steel-manufacturing center, is located near large coalfields. Iron ore from mines to the northwest is shipped by boat through the Great Lakes and then by rail to Pittsburgh.

Most manufacturing takes place in or near cities. The growth of manufacturing and cities is interrelated. As factories drew people to new jobs, cities grew. New factories were set up in cities where labor and transportation were available.

Today much manufacturing takes place in industrial parks. Industrial parks are areas outside cities that are devoted entirely to industry. When land is used for cities and manufacturing, location becomes more important than climate and soil fertility.

Other Uses of Land

Land use often changes through time. Farms and grazing lands give way to cities. Cities grow out from the center as suburbs are built up around the fringes. More and more land is needed just for people to live on. As countries become industrialized, more land is needed for streets, roads, highways, and airports.

Another fairly recent development in land use is the preservation of areas for enjoyment. Setting aside regions as wilderness areas and game preserves has grown in importance as more and more of the world's land has been taken over for economic purposes.

Brazil's new capital is the planned city of Brasília. The government has promoted *industrialization* of the country's sparsely populated interior.

Population Patterns

You already know something about population density and population patterns. In Unit 5, you learned that population density is the average number of people living on a square unit of land. You can find this number by dividing the number of people living in a given area by the amount of land in the area. In the first part of this unit, you learned that the uneven distribution of the world's population is related to land use. Look again at the map on page 515 and compare it to the graphs on page 535.

The study of populations is called *demography* (di mog′rə fē). People called demographers study records of births and deaths and other information. Much of the information demographers study is collected by governments in a kind of survey called a census. A census can provide information about such things as jobs, language, residence, income, ethnic background, education, and *literacy* (lit′ə rə sē). Literacy is the ability to read and write. Census information is used by demographers to dis-

514

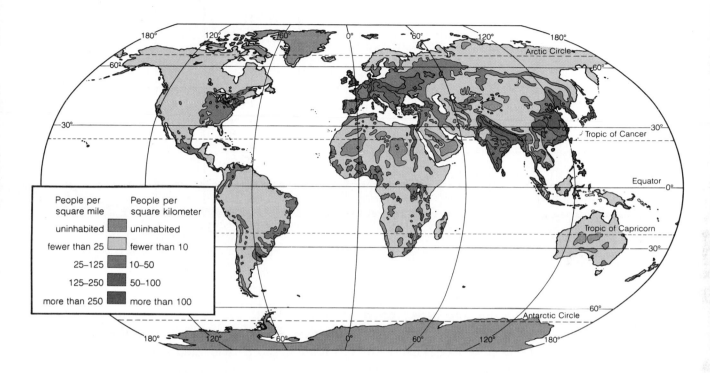

cover characteristics of populations and to describe population changes that have occurred. Predictions about future populations are made on the basis of the patterns and relationships discovered by demographers.

World Population and the Population Explosion

Today there are about four and one-half billion people in the world. This is the largest number of people that has ever lived on the earth at one time.

For many thousands of years, the population of the world grew slowly. Demographers usually consider the years before 1650 A.D. as the period of early population growth. The populations then were small compared with those today. The years since 1650 are considered the period of modern population growth. During this period, populations grew very rapidly. See the graph on page 516.

It is estimated that in 1650 the world population was about 500 million. Since then, the population has doubled three times. The first time was about 1850, the second time in the 1930s, and the third time in the 1970s. You can see that the number of years between doubling times has been decreasing. In the period of modern population growth, the first doubling time was about 200 years. Some demographers estimate that by about 2000, the population of the world will be about eight billion. If they are right, the world population will have doubled for the fourth time since 1650. The doubling time will have been shortened to about 30 years.

The rapid rate of population growth since 1650 is the result of improved health practices

World Population Growth

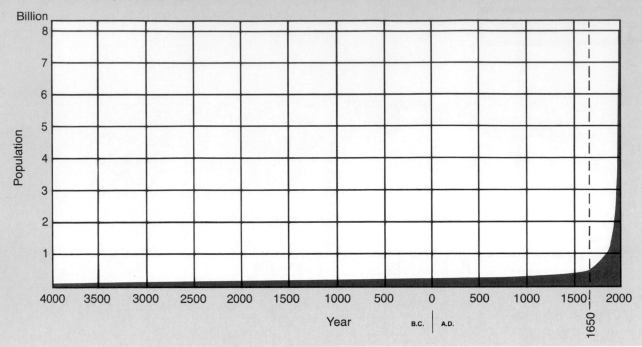

and industrialization. During the early period of population growth, birth rates were high, but the population grew slowly because death rates were also high. Many people died from diseases. Poor sanitary conditions led to other deaths. Beginning in the 1700s, medical advances and improved living conditions lowered the death rate. As a result, the population began to grow.

The Industrial Revolution also affected population growth. New machines and technology made it possible for food supplies to keep up with the increase in population. Industrialization made goods more easily available to more people. Improved health conditions and industrialization together resulted in a marked increase in population.

The tremendous growth of the population in recent years is often referred to as the population explosion. In parts of the world it has led to overpopulation. In these places, the number of people moving from rural areas to urban areas has been increasing at a rapid rate. Be-

tween 1950 and 1975, the number of world cities with a population of more than one million more than doubled. The standard of living is very low in such areas. Many people suffer from lack of enough food or the right kinds of food. This condition, called *malnutrition* (mal′no͞o trish′ən), lowers resistance to disease. As a result of malnutrition, disease, and famine, the death rate is high in overpopulated areas.

Growth Rate of Countries

To study population growth, two things must be considered. These are natural increase and migration. The rate of growth for a country must take these two factors into account.

The rate of natural increase is based on the birth rate and the death rate. The birth rate is the number of births each year for every 1,000 people. The death rate, also called the mortality rate, is the number of deaths each year for every 1,000 people. The rate of natural increase or decrease is the difference between

516

the birth rate and the death rate expressed as a percent of 1,000. If, for example, a country has a birth rate of 40 and a death rate of 10, the rate of natural increase is 3 percent. The difference between 40 and 10 is 30, and 30 is 3 percent of 1,000.

A country with a 3 percent rate of natural increase has a positive rate of natural increase. A country with a birth rate equal to its death rate has a zero rate of natural increase. A country with a birth rate lower than its death rate is said to have a negative rate of natural increase. Very few nations of the world have negative rates of natural increase.

Rates of natural increase do not tell the whole story about population growth for a country. Migration, or the movement of people from one country to another or from one part of a country to another, also influences population patterns.

People who migrate fom one country to another decrease the population of the place they leave and increase the population of the place they go to. The population growth rate for a country must take into account both natural increase and migration. In Australia, for example, natural increase and migration each account for about half of the annual growth rate. You read in Unit 10 about the large number of people who have migrated to Australia since World War II.

Urbanization

People within a country also often move from place to place. Sometimes this movement is called internal migration. The movement of

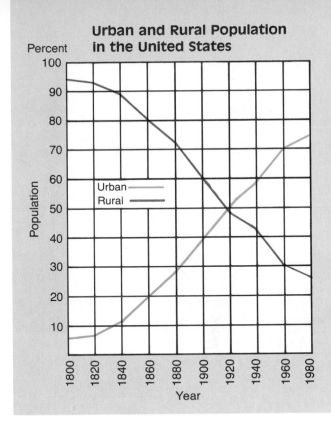

people from rural areas to urban areas has been taking place at a rapidly increasing rate. Between 1950 and 1975, the number of world cities with a population of more than one million more than doubled. The graph on this page shows how the United States has changed from a mainly rural to a mainly urban country since 1800.

Rapid urbanization causes problems in many parts of the world. Increases in city populations cause increases in demands for housing, electricity, water, schools, health services, public transportation and many other things. Often these needs cannot be met as rapidly as the population increases. In developing countries, many people who migrate to cities are not qualified for the jobs they want. Because they are illiterate or have little education, they may take low-paying jobs. Their standards of living are often very low.

517

Population Profiles

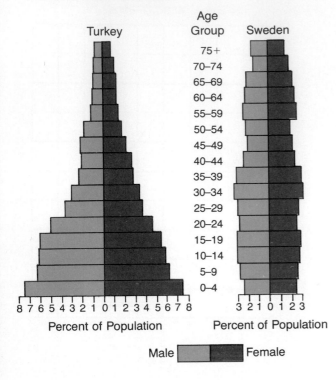

Turkey — Age Group — Sweden

Age Groups: 75+, 70–74, 65–69, 60–64, 55–59, 50–54, 45–49, 40–44, 35–39, 30–34, 25–29, 20–24, 15–19, 10–14, 5–9, 0–4

Turkey: 8 7 6 5 4 3 2 1 0 1 2 3 4 5 6 7 8
Percent of Population

Sweden: 3 2 1 0 1 2 3
Percent of Population

Male ☐ ☐ Female

Populations in Industrialized and Developing Countries

Density, distribution, and growth are only part of demography. Population studies provide information used to describe industrialized countries and developing countries.

Graphs called population profiles show a country's population by dividing it into males and females of different age groups. Look at the population profiles of Turkey and Sweden on this page. The right side of each profile shows the female population, and the left side, the male. The bars extending from the center line represent different age groups. Each bar represents the percent of males or females in each age group. Sweden's profile shows that nearly 3 percent of the population is made up of males between the ages of ten and fourteen.

If you compare the profiles for Sweden and Turkey, you will see that the shapes are quite different. Turkey's profile shows that the coun-

try has many young people and very few old people. The pyramid shape of the profile is typical for countries with high birth rates and low death rates. It indicates that the country is growing rapidly. Most developing countries have a high growth rate and have profiles similar to that of Turkey.

Sweden's profile does not show any great differences in the percentages for the different age groups. Its rectangular shape is typical of countries that have low birth rates and low death rates. Such countries are growing slowly. Low population growth is a characteristic of industrialized countries.

Industrialized countries can also be distinguished from developing countries by urban and rural population patterns, literacy rates,

Math class is held outdoors for these students in Nepal. The country is striving to raise its *literacy* rate.

518

and income. High urban populations are characteristic of industrialized countries. High rural populations are characteristic of developing countries. Literacy rates are high for industrialized countries but low for developing countries. As you read in Unit 2, gross national product, or GNP, is the value of a country's goods and services within one year. A country's GNP is divided by the number of people in the country to determine per capita GNP. Developing nations usually have lower per capita GNPs than industrialized nations.

The characteristics of industrialized nations and developing nations described above are generalizations. They are not true of all industrialized nations or of all developing nations. Many factors affect growth rates, GNP, literacy rates, and population patterns in the world's nations.

Do You Know?

1. How does intensive land use differ from extensive land use?
2. Name three factors that influence land use.
3. What is a census?
4. What is the population explosion?

2

World Markets

The world has many resources, but they are unevenly distributed. Some parts of the world have natural resources that can be used in industry. Other regions have the resources necessary for farming. The resources of nations also vary because the people of some countries are more highly trained than those of other lands. Nations find it desirable to exchange goods and raw materials, ideas, and information of many kinds.

The Growth of Trade

As you read in Unit 2, early people secured food, made clothing and tools, and built shelters for themselves. As settled communities grew, some people began to specialize by doing only certain kinds of work. With specialization, the exchange of goods and services within the community became important.

Trade between communities and between larger political units such as city-states and

In 1626, Peter Minuit bought Manhattan Island from the Indians using wampum and pelts for money.

Money and Banking

Early people exchanged, or traded, one product for another product. This system of exchange is known as barter. Later certain items such as hides, shells, metal tools, or articles of gold and silver became widely accepted in exchange for goods and services. These items were the first form of money. Money can be anything people accept in exchange for goods and services.

Coins may have been used as money as early as 600 B.C. Archaeologists have found coins stamped with the image of the ruler of Lydia, an ancient Turkish empire that existed at about that time. Each coin had a set value that came to be accepted by traders in different countries.

The use of coins led to the development of banking. The first bankers were probably money changers who bought the coins of other countries in exchange for local coins. The word *bank* comes from the Italian word *banco*, which means "bench." Early bankers exchanged money at benches along the streets. By the 1600s, banks became more than places for exchange. People began to use banks as places to store their coins for safekeeping.

When Marco Polo wrote about his visit to China in the 1200s, he described the paper money the Chinese used. Paper money had been used in China as early as 600 A.D. By the 1600s, banks in Venice began to issue paper bills called bank notes. The notes could be exchanged for coins deposited at the bank. These receipts, or notes, were easier to carry than coins. Using bank receipts made buying and selling easier. Until the 1800s, most paper

empires developed later. You have read about the trade between the kingdoms in Africa and the lands of the Mediterranean and the Middle East in earlier units. Commerce was also an important activity throughout the Persian and Roman empires.

During the Middle Ages, between 1000 and 1500 A.D., towns and cities grew up in Europe. Urban tradespeople, craftworkers, and merchants depended on an expanding network of trade for raw materials and finished goods.

In the 1400s, a great period of world exploration began. Several European countries established colonies in the Americas, Asia, and the Pacific. The Industrial Revolution, which began in the late 1700s, increased the value of colonial empires. Colonies provided raw materials for growing industries and became markets for manufactured goods.

As trading between nations grew, it became important to have an accepted standard of exchange. People needed to agree on a way to set the value of goods and services.

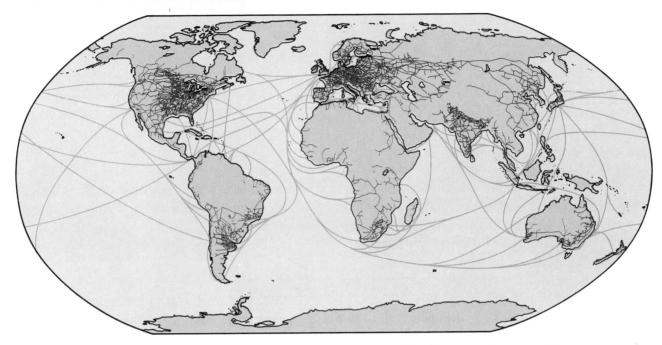

This transportation map shows the major railroads and shipping routes of the world. What other important transportation routes are not shown on the map?

bills were issued by banks or private companies. After that, governments began to issue paper money.

Today banks do not keep all of the money people deposit. Banks keep enough money to cover the amount they can expect people to withdraw. A banker may use money to make an *investment* (in vest′mənt). An investment is an outlay of money for income. People hope to make a profit when they invest. Banks lend money to individuals and to businesses, and charge *interest* (in′trist) on these loans. Interest is money paid for the use or borrowing of money, usually a percentage of the amount borrowed.

Banks encourage trade by lending money to individuals and businesses. Some banks also provide services for exchanging the money of different countries.

Transportation and Communication

World trade depends on rapid and efficient transportation and communication. A revolution in transportation began with the invention of the first engine-powered vehicles in the early 1800s. The improvement of the steam engine by the Scottish inventor James Watt in 1774 led to the development of railroads and steamships. Today supersonic jets travel faster than the speed of sound. International freight is transported mainly by ship, still the cheapest way to move goods. The nations of the world are connected by canals, railroads, and highways. Planes and ships follow routes that crisscross the earth. See the map on page 521.

Until the 1800s, the speed of communication depended on transportation. News could not travel faster than the messenger who brought it. Inventions in the nineteenth century changed the ways people could communicate. These inventions included the telegraph, the telephone, the camera, the typewriter, and the linotype machine, which set type for books, newspapers, and magazines.

Toward the end of the nineteenth century, developments in electronics began to revolutionize communication. The study of electronics made radio and television possible. Elec-

tronics also led to the development of computers that process information at high speeds. Electronic and computer equipment in communication satellites make worldwide television and radio broadcasts possible.

Developments in improved transportation and communication have increased the exchange of goods and information. Trade today is a worldwide activity that affects people in every nation.

Economic Ties

World trade makes it possible for people to buy products that otherwise would not be available to them. Because of trade, countries can specialize in producing certain products. It is difficult for most countries to be self-sufficient, or produce everything they need. Countries sell goods to other countries to pay for the products they buy. A country imports raw materials and goods it lacks and pays for them by exporting raw materials and goods it produces. The policies of governments have an important effect on the trade between nations.

Government Policies

Governments influence trade between countries by encouraging or discouraging *free trade*. Free trade permits people of a country to buy and sell without restrictions. People who favor free trade believe that it encourages competition and keeps prices low.

One way to encourage free trade is by establishing free ports. Singapore and Hong Kong are free ports where traders may bring in

Rapid communication is important to modern world trade. Computers process information at high speeds.

Many merchant ships are equipped to carry goods in containers that can be transferred to tracks or railway cars.

goods from foreign countries without paying taxes called import duties. There are few free ports in the world today.

Despite the advantages of free trade, most countries have some policies for protecting their industries from outside competition. One method countries use for such protection is to impose tariffs, or taxes on imports. Tariffs raise the price of imported goods. This encourages people to buy goods produced in their own country. Import quotas, or limits on the amount of goods imported, also protect home producers. Import quotas are applied to certain products for specific periods of time. For example, a government can put a limit on the amount of steel that can be imported. Once the limit has been reached, no more foreign steel can be ordered.

Countries use tariffs and import quotas to help them maintain a favorable *balance of payments*. A nation's balance of payments is the difference between its total payments to foreign countries and its total receipts from foreign countries. Payments include such things as the amounts spent for imports, foreign aid, and

business investments in foreign countries. Money from the sale of exports, aid received from other countries, and money spent by tourists from foreign countries are examples of receipts. Subtracting total annual payments from total annual receipts gives the balance of payments.

If a country receives more than it spends, it has a surplus in its balance of payments. If it spends more than it receives, it has a deficit. The United States had a deficit in its balance of payments for 1977 through 1979. The high price of foreign oil was an important factor in creating these deficits. Kuwait had a surplus in its balance of payments for those years. The surplus came from its oil exports.

Cooperation and Regulation

Many countries have formed organizations and signed agreements to eliminate or reduce tariffs and other trade barriers.

In 1947, the United Nations sponsored the General Agreement on Tariffs and Trade, or GATT. The more than 70 countries that signed this agreement work together to promote international trade. Import quotas are restricted and tariffs have been reduced between the nations who cooperate in GATT.

Smaller groups of nations have joined together to encourage trade. Some of these associations are called common markets. The countries that form a common market act as a unit in negotiating trade agreements with other nations. There are no tariffs or other trade restrictions between common market members.

FOREIGN CURRENCY EXCHANGE RATES			
COUNTRY		BANK SELLS	BANK BUYS
IRELAND	POUND	1.4443	1.3736
AUSTRALIA	$A	.9999	.9356
AUSTRIA	SCH	.0599	.0558
BELGIUM	FCS	.0219	.0185
CANADA	$CAN	.8232	.7970
DENMARK	KR	.1222	.1079
ENGLAND	POUND	1.7828	1.6830
FRANCE	FCS	.1520	.1386
GERMANY	DM	.4146	.3960
ITALY	LIR	.00080	.00069
JAPAN	YEN	.00400	.00371
MEXICO	PESO	.NQ	.NQ
NETHERLANDS	GLD	.3767	.3589
PHILIPPINES	PESO	.1237	.1015
SPAIN	PTA	.0096	.0085
SWEDEN	KR	.1697	.1505
SWITZERLAND	SFC	.4878	.4668
GREEK	DR	.0152	.0124
NORWAY	KR	.1571	.1421

NOT ACCEPTING COINS

Foreign currency exchange rates are often posted in large banks that buy and sell foreign money.

The Soviet Union formed a common market with some of its satellites and Mongolia, Vietnam, and Cuba in 1949. The group is called the Council for Mutual Economic Assistance, or COMECON. Six Western European nations formed the European Economic Community, or EEC, in 1957. There are ten members today. Eleven Latin American nations belong to the Latin American Free Trade Association, or LAFTA, which was formed in 1960.

The Organization of Petroleum Exporting Countries, or OPEC, is another kind of trade association. The 13 OPEC countries are major oil producers. Half of the world's oil supply comes from OPEC nations. OPEC establishes prices and policies for oil sales. In 1973, the cost of a barrel of crude oil from OPEC nations was $2.40. In 1980, the price was more than $30. This great increase in price affected the balance of payments for many nations that import oil.

Exchange Rates

Trade associations and agreements affect international trade. Another important influence on world trade is the exchange rate. The value of one nation's money is expressed in terms of another nation's money by an exchange rate. For example, a recent exchange rate table showed that one English pound had about the same value as $1.70 in United States currency. Exchange rates vary somewhat, depending on whether the currency is being bought or sold.

Exchange rates do not remain constant. A stable exchange rate is desirable, however. When a nation imports products from another country, the buying nation usually pays in the money of the selling country. With stable exchange rates, the price in foreign money is easily determined.

An agency of the United Nations was created in 1947 to work toward stabilizing exchange rates. This agency is the International Monetary Fund, or IMF. Another goal of the IMF is to help nations with their balance of payments by making loans available.

Do You Know?

1. What is money?
2. Name three inventions that have affected communication.
3. What are two ways countries protect their industries from outside competition?
4. What is an exchange rate?

Before You Go On

Using New Words

literacy   demography
profit   malnutrition
interest   investment
free trade   balance of payments
biosphere

Number a paper from 1 through 9. After each number write the word or term from the above list that matches the definition.

1. The study of populations
2. The part of the earth that supports life
3. The ability to read and write
4. Lack of enough food or the right kinds of food
5. Money gained after expenses have been paid
6. Money paid for the use or borrowing of money
7. An outlay of money for income
8. The difference between a nation's total payments to and total receipts from foreign countries
9. Buying and selling without restrictions

Finding the Facts

1. Where is the earth's biosphere?
2. How much of the earth's land is used for agriculture? What percent is covered by forests?
3. What are three ways of using forest lands to make a living?
4. What is the distribution of minerals related to?
5. What is the world's population expected to be by 2000? If it does reach this figure, how long will the doubling time have been?
6. How did the Industrial Revolution contribute to the increase in population after 1650?
7. What two factors must be considered when studying population growth?
8. What do population profiles show?
9. What do banks do with the money that people deposit?
10. Explain surplus and deficit in balance of payments.
11. What does GATT stand for?
12. What is the name of the common market the Soviet Union belongs to?

3
Sharing the World

Despite the advances of modern societies, the basic needs of people are the same as they have always been. People everywhere need food, clothing and shelter. Complex technology and industrialization have made it easier to secure these necessities. Today the world is so changed that few people are self-sufficient. Most nations of the world today depend on other nations for some of the things they need and want. Events in one part of the world can affect other parts of the world directly or indirectly. Growing populations, limited food supplies, dwindling resources, pollution, and the threat of war are problems shared by the entire world. Their solution will depend on the goodwill and cooperation of all nations.

Testing new ways to grow plants may help solve food shortages. Here plants are being grown without soil.

Living in a World of Limited Resources

Of all living things, only people are able to change the environment to any great degree. Until fairly recent times, however, the changes were few and took place slowly. Today the world is changing rapidly. The development of complex technologies and industrialization have made it possible for the world to support more and more people.

Industrialization has brought a high standard of living to many countries of the world. People in countries that are not industrialized have become aware of the differences between their standards of living and those in industrialized countries. They, too, want to share in a better life.

The demands of an increasing population on the world's resources have caused problems. The resources of the world are *finite* (fī′nīt), or fixed and limited. Even the amount of renewable resources is finite. Not only are the world's resources limited, they are also unevenly distributed. Some countries are rich in certain resources and poor in others. Many countries have few resources at all. Countries with goods and resources can trade with one another. Other countries have no goods or resources to exchange and therefore have no way to pay for the goods they need.

Industrialization has also caused unwanted changes in the environment. The effects of complex technologies on the habitat can be alarming. Erosion and floods sometimes result. Pollution affects the atmosphere and the water supply.

The problems facing the developing world include overpopulation, food shortages, poverty, low literacy rates, scarcity of resources, and pollution. People in many parts of the world are working together to find solutions to these and other problems.

Overpopulation and Food Shortages

Every day the world population increases by more than 200,000. Some scientists believe that the world will become overpopulated. Many parts of the developing world are already overpopulated. People in these regions do not get the food they need. They suffer from hunger and malnutrition. The increase in food production cannot keep up with the increase in population.

There are several ways to increase agricultural productivity. One way is to increase the amount of arable land. Marshes can be reclaimed by draining, and dry lands can be reclaimed by irrigation. Reclamation projects, however, may be successful only temporarily. The Aswan High Dam in Egypt, which was completed in 1970, allowed Egypt to double its agricultural output. By 1980, food shortages in Egypt were greater than before the dam was built. Egypt's food production could not keep up with its increase in population.

In many places, the cost of reclaiming land is too high. People are turning to methods of increasing the food supply by increasing the productivity of land already in use. Improved farming techniques, new varieties of grains, the use of fertilizer, and elimination of pests and diseases are some solutions.

In some developing nations, greater efforts have been made toward industrialization. Leaders of developing countries have seen the many benefits that industrialized nations have. They would like their own people to have more food, money, and goods, better health services, and longer lives. Unfortunately, industrialization is not always the answer.

Industrialization and Nonrenewable Resources

Included in the nonrenewable resources are the fossil fuels—coal, oil, and gas—and metals such as iron, copper, and aluminum. Until the Industrial Revolution, people used very little of these fuels and metals. Since the Industrial Revolution, the industrialized nations have used enormous quantities of these resources. The use of these resources grew as populations grew. More and more people demanded more and more manufactured goods. Today the industrialized countries of Western Europe, Canada, the United States, Japan, and the Soviet Union consume about 80 percent of the world's resources. Only about 25 percent of the world's population lives in these countries.

As developing countries turned to manufacturing and mechanization, they began to demand their share of the world's resources. Many of these countries were important producers of raw materials for industrialized nations. Until fairly recently, the production of minerals and fossil fuels was controlled by the industrialized nations. Many producing countries have claimed the right to control their own resources. These countries have nationalized many of their mineral industries. OPEC was formed by nations that took control of their own oil production.

Because of more people and more demands, many of the world's resources are becoming scarce. You have read in Unit 1 about the management of nonrenewable resources through conservation, the search for new supplies, and alternative materials. Population growth and industrialization, however, will continue to put greater and greater strain on scarce resources. Today many people realize the importance of nonrenewable resources. They are aware of the possibility that we may *deplete* (di plēt') them, or use them up. They realize the need to use them wisely.

Industrialization and the Environment

While industrialization has brought many benefits, it has also had many harmful effects. One result of industrialization is the depletion of resources. Another result is damage to the environment. In industrialized countries, pollution of air, water, and soil has become a serious problem.

Smoke from factories and exhaust from cars and trucks have blackened the skies and caused lung diseases. Dumping of chemical wastes underground and in rivers has affected the water supplies. Oil spills and industrial wastes in the ocean can be carried to all parts of the world.

The burning of fossil fuels increases the amount of carbon dioxide in the air. Some scientists believe that a buildup of this gas could cause a rise in the world's temperatures through a condition called the "greenhouse effect." Carbon dioxide, like the glass in a greenhouse, could trap heat within the earth's atmosphere. A rise of just a few degrees in the world's temperature might cause the polar icecaps to melt and raise the levels of the oceans. Areas along the shore would be flooded if the level of the oceans were raised.

The effects of pollution can be far reaching. Wastes in the atmosphere can combine with moisture in the air and fall as acid rain far from the source of pollution. Acid rain can pollute water, and damage buildings, soil, and plants.

Private industry and governments are working in many industrialized countries to protect the environment. Stricter regulations have been imposed in many places. Many large cities have reduced air pollution. Conservation efforts have also led to the renewal of many lakes and rivers. International agreements against dumping wastes into the ocean, however, have not always been effectively enforced. Pollution has also become a problem in developing countries that are becoming industrialized.

Conflict and Cooperation

No one knows the cost of all the wars that have been fought. There is no way to put a price on the deaths or the suffering caused by war. Numbers alone cannot describe the destruction of homes, farms, cities, and factories.

Despite their destructive effects, wars have been fought throughout history. Fighting still disrupts the lives of people in many parts of the world today. International conflicts have been caused by nations seeking more new land for their growing populations. Countries with limited resources have tried to acquire territory beyond their borders where needed resources exist. Growing industrialization has increased the demand for raw materials. Countries have been willing to risk war to insure a continued supply of resources such as oil and other minerals.

Economic considerations are not the only causes of war. Political and social beliefs have also led to conflict. Governments have been overthrown by revolutions and coups led by groups that believe their ideas should prevail.

The nature of warfare changed drastically when the first atomic bomb was dropped on Hiroshima in 1945. The death and destruction caused by the bomb led to increased concern about atomic, or nuclear, weapons.

In 1969, the United States and the Soviet Union met to discuss the development and limitation of nuclear weapons. These Strategic Arms Limitation Talks, or SALT, continued through 1972. Two treaties were signed as a result. One set limitations on the number of defensive missiles, and the other limited production of certain weapons.

Another series of meetings was held in Geneva, Switzerland. These meetings began in 1973 and resulted in an agreement to limit bombers and missiles. The treaty that would put this agreement into effect has not been signed.

The threat of nuclear war affects every nation on earth. The United States and the Soviet Union are not the only countries with nuclear weapons. Many nations believe that such weapons pose the greatest threat to life on earth today.

You have read about the alliances created by nations before and during World War I and World War II. These alliances were attempts to create a *balance of power*. A balance of power exists when there is equal economic or military power between nations or groups of nations. The trade organizations described earlier in this unit were established to promote a balance of economic power. Two major organizations were created after World War II to insure a balance of military power. The North Atlantic Treaty and the Warsaw Pact established these organizations.

Military Alliances

Many nations feared that the Soviet Union would try to gain control of Western Europe after World War II. The Soviet blockade of Berlin and the Communist takeover of Czechoslovakia in 1948 increased these fears.

To prevent Soviet expansion, the United States and eleven other countries formed the North Atlantic Treaty Organization, or NATO, in 1950. NATO is a military defense organization. If any member nation is attacked, the other members are pledged to aid that nation with military support. The United States has been the leader of NATO since it was founded. An American general has always been the chief commander of NATO forces.

To restore the balance of military power in Europe, the Soviet Union and six other European Communist nations signed the Warsaw Pact in 1955. This agreement established a unified defense system for the member nations. A Soviet army marshal is the commander of Warsaw Pact forces.

The United Nations

Preserving a balance of military power in the world is one way to maintain peace. Another way is to encourage understanding and cooperation among nations. Forming military alliances was not the only way nations tried to promote peace after World War II. Even before the war was over, meetings were held to organize an international peace-keeping organization. This organization, the United Nations, was established in 1945. Today more than 150 nations are members. The agencies of the United Nations, or UN, are involved in activities throughout the world.

Some agencies of the United Nations provide funds that help countries finance projects such as building or improving transportation or irrigation systems. Other agencies are involved in efforts to improve the use of resources and to develop better farming methods. Health care and education are other important concerns. Many of the UN's efforts are aimed at solving problems of growing populations, hunger, disease, and poverty. Another of the UN's important goals is to help keep peace. It has been involved in working out truces and cease-fire agreements. UN forces have patrolled buffer zones between hostile nations.

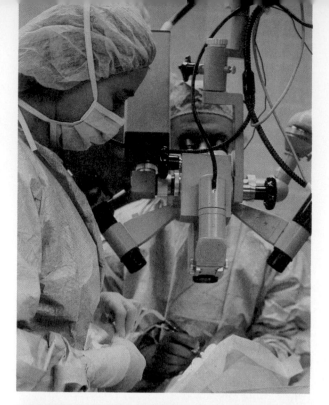

In highly developed countries, doctors in well-equipped hospitals use precision instruments. Doctors in developing countries often work with limited equipment on visits to small villages.

The United Nations has also tried to control the spread of nuclear weapons. In 1968, it proposed an agreement that limited the sale or trade of nuclear weapons. The United States, Great Britain, and the Soviet Union signed the treaty and agreed to withhold nuclear weapons from nations that did not already have them.

The success of the United Nations depends on the attitudes of its members. Serious differences and disputes among member nations have kept the UN from accomplishing as much as it might. As long as most countries are willing to stay in the UN and support it, the organization has a chance to work toward solving many of the problems facing the world today, including the preservation of peace.

Alliances for Peace and Progress

The United Nations represents nearly all of the world's nations. Smaller groups of nations have also established alliances to promote peace and cooperation.

Countries in North and South America formed the Organization of American States, or OAS, in 1948. This alliance was designed to strengthen the security of the Western Hemisphere. The member nations have agreed to give military aid to any threatened member nation. The organization is also committed to peaceful settlement of disputes among members. The OAS promotes improved communication, education, health, and welfare of its members by sharing information and resources.

In 1963, leaders of several African nations met in Ethiopia to establish the Organization of African Unity, or OAU. The members of this organization also work to resolve conflicts through peaceful settlements. The OAU also tries to assist newly independent African nations establish stable political and economic systems. Member nations work together to improve transportation and communication.

Other Ways Nations Cooperate

Nations cooperate through many organizations other than the United Nations and regional alliances. Different countries work together to make the world run more smoothly. Groups of people work together to promote the interests they share.

The Universal Postal Union

Because of the Universal Postal Union, letters can pass freely between many countries of the world. Letters from the United States, for example, if they bear the correct amount of United States stamps, will be sent to any foreign country in the world. Replies will be carried to the United States if they bear the correct postage of the country in which they are mailed.

The Universal Postal Union was founded in 1874 by 22 countries. Today 158 countries belong to the union, which is now an agency of the United Nations. Each member nation has agreed to accept and deliver letters mailed from the other member nations. These nations have a system of paying each other to handle the mail. The Universal Postal Union promotes understanding between people of different countries through the exchange of letters.

The International Bureau of Weights and Measures

The International Bureau of Weights and Measures establishes standards for metric measurements. Having standard units of measurement makes it easier for nations to work together and trade with one another. Before the metric system was developed, countries used many different systems of measurement. There was no way of knowing whether measurements of the same thing would be equal.

The standard system of weights and measures known as the metric system was created in France. After 1840, when the French officially adopted the system, other nations began to convert to it. Between 1870 and 1875, 17 nations held a metric convention. They established the International Bureau of Weights and Measures. From time to time, the bureau has made changes in the metric system.

Today almost every country in the world uses the metric system. Great Britain, Canada, and Australia began their changeover during the 1960s and 1970s. In 1975 Congress passed an act calling for voluntary conversion to the metric system in the United States.

The Olympic Games

Contests known as the Olympic games first took place in Greece in 776 B.C. The games were repeated every four years until 39 A.D., when the Romans, who then controlled Greece, ordered them stopped.

The discovery of the ruins of Olympia in 1878 interested the French educator Pierre de Coubertin (də kōō′bär tan). He suggested reorganizing the Olympic games as an international event. De Coubertin believed that sports competition would lead to better understanding among nations and promote world peace. The first modern Olympic Games took place in Athens in 1896. Since then, the games have been held every four years except in wartime. Each time the modern Olympics are opened, hundreds of doves are released into the air as a symbol of peace.

International Travel

Understanding among nations is broadened when people are permitted to move freely across borders. Each year, millions of people take international trips for a variety of reasons. Some people visit other nations on business. Others travel abroad for education or as tourists. Whatever the reason, travelers have an opportunity to meet people of other lands and learn how they live. These travelers return home with a better understanding of their world neighbors.

To travel in foreign countries, a person must have a *passport* (pas′pôrt′). An official document issued by the government of a country to a citizen giving permission to travel abroad is called a passport. Travel between some countries, for example, between the United States and Canada, does not require a passport.

The International Geophysical Year

A great scientific adventure began in the summer of 1957. Ten thousand scientists from about 70 nations launched a special study of the earth and sky. They set aside 18 months for the study and gave a name to this period of time. It became known as the International *Geophysical* (jē′ō fiz′i kəl) Year, or IGY. *Geophysical* means "related to the study of the earth and the forces that affect or change it."

As the great research project began, groups of scientists set out to measure tides, map the heavens, and probe beneath the earth's crust. They explored the Arctic and the Antarctic. They collected facts about earthquakes, hurricanes, droughts, floods, and currents. Geographers took new measurements of oceans and continents. Engineers observed the sun and tested its rays, hoping to learn how the rays might be used to furnish power for industry. Both the United States and the Soviet Union launched satellites and rockets with scientific recording devices.

For years to come, scientists will continue to study and share the facts collected during the IGY. By sharing, all nations will have a better understanding of the earth and its resources.

Geophysical studies in Antarctica have helped scientists learn more about the earth, its origin, and development.

Cooperation in Antarctica

During the IGY, several nations set up bases in Antarctica for collecting scientific data. After the IGY ended, most of these nations continued their research there. The question then arose as to who should control the continent. In 1959, the 12 nations that had worked there during the IGY signed a treaty. They agreed that Antarctica should remain free for scientific observation and used only for peaceful purposes. The treaty also included an agreement for delaying claims until 1989.

Continued exploration of Antarctica has revealed undersea oil pools and what may be the world's largest coalfield. Geologists also believe that the continent may have important uranium reserves.

Scarcity of resources, overpopulation, and pollution are problems that affect the whole world. The population explosion has put a strain on the world's resources. Uneven distribution of the world's riches has led to conflicts and disagreements. Only through understanding and working together can the nations of the world meet the challenge of trying to solve the world's problems.

Do You Know?

1. Name two ways to increase agricultural productivity.
2. What is the "greenhouse effect"?
3. What are two ways of maintaining peace in the world?
4. What were the terms of the 1959 treaty on Antarctica?

To Help You Learn

Using New Words

passport   finite

balance of payments deplete

balance of power   geophysical

Number a paper from 1 through 6. After each number write the word or term from the above list that matches the definition.

1. The difference between a nation's total payments to and its total receipts from foreign countries
2. Equal economic or military power
3. Related to the study of the earth and the forces that affect or change it
4. Fixed and limited
5. To use up
6. An official government document entitling the holder to travel abroad

Finding the Facts

1. What two main activities does agriculture include?
2. How is the growth of manufacturing and the growth of cities interrelated?
3. About how many people are there in the world?
4. How did colonies benefit colonial powers economically?
5. What is the cheapest way to move goods?
6. What does LAFTA stand for? EEC?
7. Name three problems shared by the entire world.
8. By how much does the population of the world increase each day?
9. What are the two main harmful effects of industrialization?
10. What considerations besides economic ones have led to wars and conflicts?
11. What did the SALT treaties accomplish?
12. What kind of alliances are NATO and the Warsaw Pact?
13. When was the Universal Postal Union founded? How many countries belong to it today?
14. Name four activities conducted by scientists during the International Geophysical Year.

Learning from Maps

1. Compare the maps on pages 521 and 14-15. What are the two most direct ways to ship goods by water from Karachi to London? From New York to San Francisco? What continent seems to have the greatest number of miles of railroads in proportion to its size? Where are most of the railroads in North America? In Australia? Compare the map on page 521 with the map on page 515. What relationship does there seem to be between railroads and population?

2. Compare the maps on pages 31 and 515. In what two climate regions are there un-inhabited areas? Now compare the maps on pages 511 and 515. What is the main land use in the parts of Europe that are the most densely populated? What are the major land uses in the parts of Australia where there are fewer than 25 people per square mile (10 people per sq. km)? Are areas where land is used for manufacturing generally areas of high population density or low population density?

Using Study Skills

1. **Graphs:** Look at the graphs on this page. What region shown has the largest percentage of the world's land area? What percent of the world's population does this region have? For what region shown are the percentages of the land area and population most nearly the same? What region shown on the land area graph is not represented on the population graph? What percent of the world's land area do the Soviet Union and southern and eastern Asia represent?

World Land Area and Population

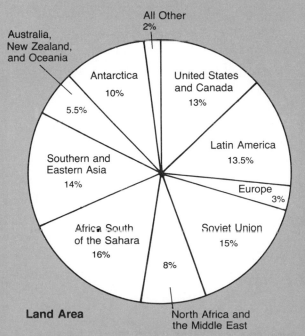

Land Area

All Other 2%
Australia, New Zealand, and Oceania
Antarctica 10%
5.5%
United States and Canada 13%
Southern and Eastern Asia 14%
Latin America 13.5%
Europe 3%
Africa South of the Sahara 16%
Soviet Union 15%
8%
North Africa and the Middle East

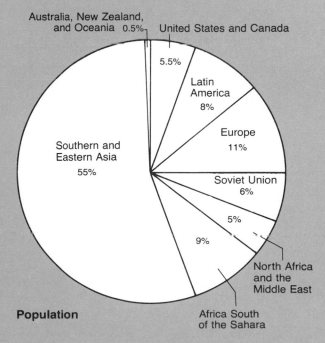

Population

Australia, New Zealand, and Oceania 0.5%
United States and Canada
5.5%
Latin America 8%
Southern and Eastern Asia 55%
Europe 11%
Soviet Union 6%
5%
9%
North Africa and the Middle East
Africa South of the Sahara

2. **Graphs:** Look at the graph on page 517. What does this graph show? What years does it cover? In 1800, was a greater percentage of the population urban or rural? In what twenty-year period were the percentages of urban and rural populations the same? During what twenty-year period did the proportion of urban population to rural population change the most? What percent of the population was urban in 1980?

Thinking It Through

1. Eminent domain is the right of the government to take private property that is needed for public use. In the United States, the federal, state, and local governments, and sometimes private corporations, have this right. Land can be taken for roads, railroads, schools, parks, libraries, housing projects, telephone lines, and gas pipelines. Land taken for these purposes must be paid for. Do you think governments and corporations should have the right of eminent domain? Explain your answer.

2. In 1975, Congress passed an act calling for voluntary conversion to the metric system in the United States. However, it took no steps requiring the use of metric measurements. What reasons are there for adopting the metric system in the United States? What reasons can you give for remaining with the conventional system of measurement?

Projects

Write a research report on a topic of your choice or on one of the following topics: land use in your state, emigration and population patterns in a specific country, cities and the growth of trade in the Middle Ages, the history of banking, energy consumption, the United Nations, the Olympic games, or the International Geophysical Year.

To find information on your topic, use the *Readers' Guide to Periodical Literature,* the card catalog, and an encyclopedia index. Be sure to check all cross-references. Consult almanacs, yearbooks, atlases, and biographical, geographical, or unabridged dictionaries.

After taking notes on what you have read, choose a title for your report and prepare an outline. Write the report by following the outline. You may wish to illustrate your report by including time lines, diagrams, charts, graphs, and maps.

Learning About Maps and Globes

Maps and globes are special tools. They help us to understand our earth and the people, places, and things on it. Maps and globes are useful tools only if we know how to use them. The lessons in this section will help you improve your skills in using maps and globes. These map and globe skills will help you to better understand the world around you.

Words to Learn

You will meet these words in this unit. As you read, you will learn what they mean and how to pronounce them. The Word List will help you.

annual temperature range
block diagram
cartography
coalition
exaggerated

in dispute
oceanography
potential
profile
terminal

1 Projections and Distortion

A globe, like the earth, is a sphere. Because a globe is really a scale model of the earth, it is the most accurate representation of the earth. On a globe, the position and proportion of land and water features are shown as they are on the earth's surface. Distance, size, shape, and direction are presented in their true relationship to one another.

Globes, however, are not always practical to use. They cannot be folded or easily carried. Only half the earth can be seen at one time on a globe. Geographers, however, have found ways to show the earth on a flat surface. A representation of the earth or part of the earth on a flat surface is called a map. The art or technique of making maps is called *cartography* (kär tog′rə fē).

To show the curved earth on a flat surface is difficult. It is like trying to flatten an orange peel or a rubber ball. Part of the surface must be stretched or torn. The resulting change in shape is called distortion. All maps have some kind of distortion, or error. Unlike a globe, no single map can show all distances, sizes, shapes, and directions accurately. At least one of these properties will be distorted. Distortion is not as great on maps of small areas as it is on maps of large areas.

Making maps requires some kind of projection. A map projection is a systematic way to transfer locations on the earth to locations on a map. The grid system can help us to understand projections.

The grid system is the network of lines of longitude and latitude used on a map or globe. Lines of longitude, or meridians, extend north and south. Longitude is measured in degrees east up to 180° and west up to 180° from the prime meridian. Lines of latitude, or parallels, extend east and west. Latitude is measured in degrees north and south of the equator. It increases from 0° at the equator to 90° at each pole.

Certain statements are true of the grid system on a globe. On a globe, all meridians are equal in length and meet at the poles. All parallels are the same distance from one another. Their length decreases from the equator to the poles. All meridians and parallels meet at right angles. Distances along meridians between any two parallels are equal.

The grid system of a map will never agree in all ways with that of a globe. By comparing the grid system of a particular map with that of a globe, we can discover in what ways the map is distorted. There are hundreds of different projections, but each is distorted in some way. No single map projection is best for all purposes.

Only a few projections are in common use. Most of them are worked out according to mathematical rules. Some can be explained, however, by imagining a transparent globe with a grid system and outlines of the coastlines. A light source casts shadows of the grid and coastlines onto a sheet of paper. Then the outlines are traced. The paper can be a cylinder, a cone, or a plane. Most map projections can be classified as cylindrical projections, conic projections, or plane projections.

A cylindrical projection is made as if a cylinder or tube of paper were placed around a globe. It may touch the globe along one line. If the cylinder touches along the equator, the equator has true length on the map. The grid and coastlines are projected by the light and traced on the cylinder. The cylinder is then unrolled and flattened.

The Mercator projection is an example of a cylindrical projection with true length along the equator. In this projection, the meridians and parallels are straight lines. The distance between parallels increases toward the poles. Is the distance between meridians equal everywhere on the map? The Mercator projection shows shapes, but not sizes, correctly. Compare the size of Greenland with that of South America on the Mercator projection. Which appears larger? Now compare the size of these areas on a globe. Which is truly larger?

The Mercator projection also shows direction correctly. Any straight line is a line of constant compass direction. For this reason, this projection is very useful to ship navigators. Where is east at any point on this map? North?

A conic projection is made as though a cone of paper were placed over the globe. The cone may intersect, or cut through, the globe. In the Lambert projection, the cone intersects the globe along two parallels. Along these parallels, distances are true. Between them, shape, distance, and direction are quite accurate. Conic projections are used for areas in the middle latitudes with greater east-west than north-south distances.

In a plane projection, the grid is transferred immediately to paper that is a flat surface or plane. The paper does not have to be unrolled, or flattened, as it does in cylindrical and conic projections. Plane projections are often used to show polar regions. In some plane projections, the plane is in contact with the globe at only one point. This point is the center of the map. The gnomonic projection is a projection of this kind. The central part of the map is good, but the outer parts are badly distorted. Pilots use gnomonic projections for plotting routes. On this projection, a straight line drawn between any two points is part of a great circle. A great-circle route is the shortest distance between two points. Where is north on the gnomonic projection? Where is 30° N. latitude?

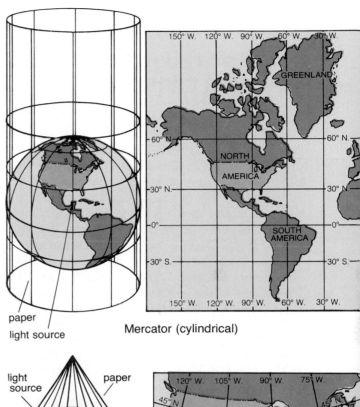

Mercator (cylindrical)

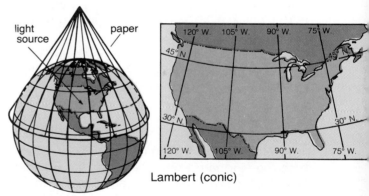

Lambert (conic)

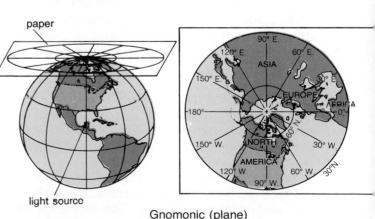

Gnomonic (plane)

2 Latitude, Altitude, and Climate

Latin America is a region that stretches through many degrees of latitude. Latitude is the distance in degrees north and south of the equator. Look at the map on the right to see how far north and south Latin America extends. How many degrees of latitude does this region cover? Latitude is one of the main factors affecting temperature and climate.

Because lines of latitude are always the same distance apart, we can convert degrees of latitude to miles or kilometers. All we need to know is that one degree of latitude covers about 70 miles (112 km). What is the greatest north-south extent of Latin America in miles? In kilometers?

Regions lying between 30° N. and 30° S. are in the low latitudes. These tropical regions receive the direct rays of the sun and are generally hot all year long. How much of Latin America is in the low latitudes?

Regions lying between latitudes 60° and 90° in both the Northern Hemisphere and the Southern Hemisphere are in the high latitudes. These polar regions receive no direct rays from the sun and are cold all year. Is any part of Latin America in the high latitudes?

Regions lying between latitudes 30° and 60° in both the Northern Hemisphere and the Southern Hemisphere are in the middle latitudes. The middle latitudes are also known as the temperate regions. These regions receive varying amounts of heat from the sun. Generally they are colder than the low latitudes and hotter than the high latitudes. What parts of Latin America are in the middle latitudes?

Regions that extend through many degrees of latitude usually have many different kinds of climate. Can you explain why Latin America, which extends through many degrees of latitude, lies mainly in one major climate zone?

We have seen that as latitude increases, temperature generally decreases. Latitude also affects temperature in another way. The difference be-

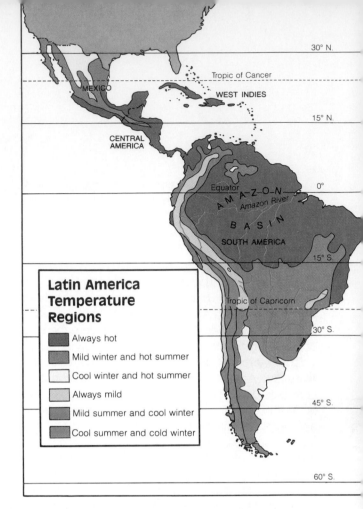

Latin America Temperature Regions

- Always hot
- Mild winter and hot summer
- Cool winter and hot summer
- Always mild
- Mild summer and cool winter
- Cool summer and cold winter

tween the highest temperature and the lowest temperature of a place during the year is called the *annual temperature range.* This figure is usually given as an average. Look at the map showing annual temperature range on page 541. In Latin America, does the range generally increase or decrease as latitude increases? Reread page 30 to explain the temperature range pattern in southern South America.

Even though much of Latin America is in the tropics, it has regions that are always cool or cold. The temperatures at sea level in the low latitudes are very hot. Mountainous areas or highlands in the same latitudes have much lower temperatures. Altitude, or elevation, affects temperatures in much the same way latitude does. In highland areas, altitude is more important in determining temperature than latitude is. Look at the altitude map on page 541. What parts of Latin America have elevations of more than 10,000 feet (3,000 m)?

Now look at the temperature regions map. What kinds of temperatures do these high altitude areas have?

We have seen that as altitude increases, temperature decreases. At a given latitude, temperatures drop about 3.6° F. (2° C) for each increase of 1,000 feet (300 m) in elevation. If the temperature at the seaport of Valparaiso is 90° F. (32° C), what would you expect the temperature to be at the top of Mount Aconcagua, which has an elevation of nearly 23,000 feet (7,000 m)?

Temperature is only a part of climate. Precipitation is another important part of climate. Tempera-ture, air pressure, winds, elevation, and ocean currents are factors that affect precipitation. On the temperature regions map you can see that the Amazon Basin in South America and much of Central America are always hot. If you look at the map on page 24, you will see that these areas also receive much precipitation. Now look at the map on page 31. What climate do these regions have?

Latitude and altitude are two important factors that affect climate. Climate in turn has a direct effect on vegetation. Compare the maps on pages 31 and 34. Notice the similarities between the distribution patterns of climate and vegetation.

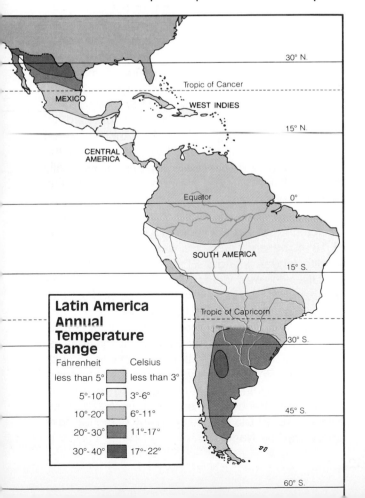

Latin America Annual Temperature Range

Fahrenheit	Celsius
less than 5°	less than 3°
5°-10°	3°-6°
10°-20°	6°-11°
20°-30°	11°-17°
30°-40°	17°-22°

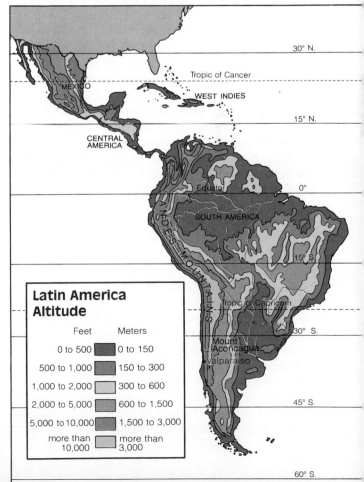

Latin America Altitude

Feet	Meters
0 to 500	0 to 150
500 to 1,000	150 to 300
1,000 to 2,000	300 to 600
2,000 to 5,000	600 to 1,500
5,000 to 10,000	1,500 to 3,000
more than 10,000	more than 3,000

Using Maps to Understand History: Europe from 1763 to 1815

Maps are often used to illustrate the events of history. Several maps of the same region at different times can show changes that took place over a period of years. Such maps are arranged in chronological order, as they are on page 543.

The first map of the series shows Europe in 1763. Six years later, Napoleon Bonaparte, a man who would change the map of Europe, was born in Corsica. The map of Europe in 1812 shows the empire that Napoleon created. In 1815, Napoleon was defeated and exiled. The peace treaty made following Napoleon's downfall established the boundaries shown on the map of Europe in 1815.

Napoleon was French by an accident of history. Corsica had been sold to France only 15 months before his birth. What country was Corsica a part of in 1763?

Napoleon was educated at military schools in France. He joined the French army and quickly rose through the ranks. When the French Revolution broke out in 1789, Napoleon joined the revolutionary forces and distinguished himself in battle. He was made a brigadier general in 1793.

The revolutionary government of France hoped to spread its ideas of "liberty, equality, and fraternity" throughout Europe. The monarchs of Europe feared that the spread of the revolutionary movement would lead to the loss of their thrones. By 1793, France was at war with almost all of Europe. Leading powers formed a *coalition* (kō′ə lish′ən) against the French. A coalition is a temporary alliance for some specific purpose.

Internal disorders led to the formation of a new government in France. The revolution ended and Napoleon became the ruler of France in 1799. Five years later he became Emperor of the French. By 1812, he controlled most of Europe. In size, his empire rivaled that of Charlemagne.

Look at the map of Europe in 1812. Compare the boundaries of France in 1799, when Napoleon came to power, with the boundaries of the French empire in 1812. What regions had been added? What countries were allies of Napoleon? Napoleon set up the Confederation of the Rhine, which was a group of German states under his control. What had been abolished in order to do this?

The map of Europe in 1812 shows when and where some of Napoleon's important battles were fought. Was the Battle of Austerlitz fought before or after the Battle of Marengo?

In 1812, Napoleon decided to invade Russia. The Russians had begun to trade with Britain after Napoleon had declared all of Europe closed to British goods. Napoleon wanted to teach the czar a lesson. He gathered an army of 600,000 men and moved it to the Russian border. The army marched eastward toward Moscow. What battle was fought before they reached that city? When Napoleon reached Moscow, he found it nearly deserted. The Russians who had stayed set fire to the city. The French army was surrounded by ruins with nothing to conquer. Napoleon decided to retreat. On the long march west, thousands of soldiers died of hunger and the terrible cold. Others deserted, and some were captured or killed. By the time it left Russia, the army had fewer than 30,000 men.

Napoleon did not recover from the Russian campaign. His enemies joined to defeat him, and in 1814, he abdicated. He was exiled to the tiny Mediterranean island of Elba. In 1815, he returned to rule. He was defeated a final time by the combined armies of several nations at the Battle of Waterloo. When was this battle fought?

After Waterloo, the leaders of Europe met to redraw the boundaries of Europe. Is the map of Europe in 1815 more like that of Europe in 1812 or Europe in 1763? What happened to the Confederation of the Rhine? What happened to Poland?

Compare the boundaries of France in 1815 with those of 1812. Did France keep any of the territory conquered by Napoleon?

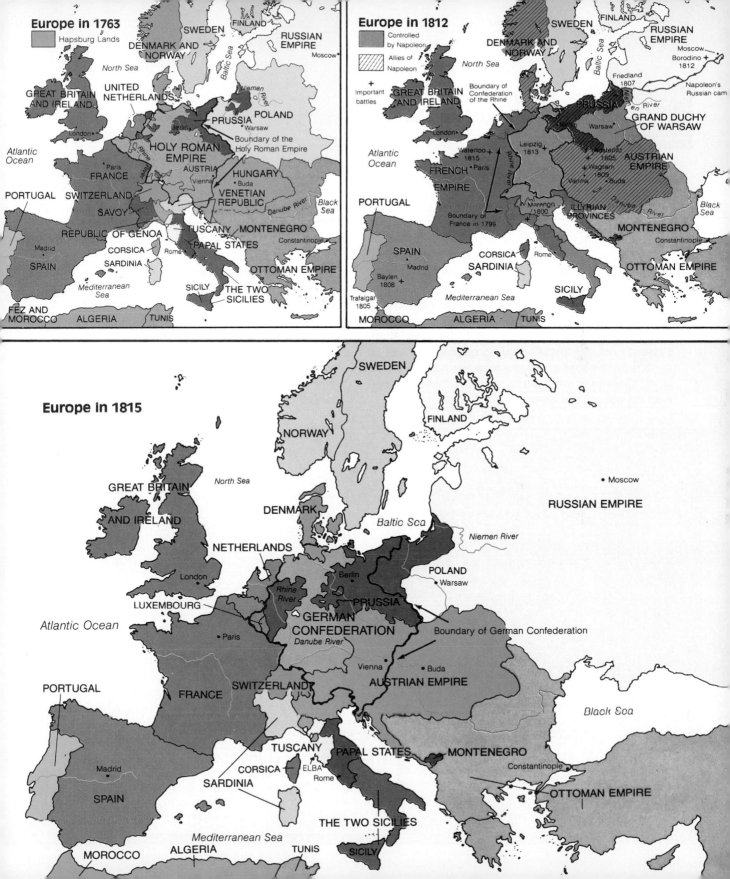

Europe in 1763

Hapsburg Lands

SWEDEN
FINLAND
DENMARK AND NORWAY
RUSSIAN EMPIRE
Moscow
North Sea
Niemen River
GREAT BRITAIN AND IRELAND
UNITED NETHERLANDS
POLAND
PRUSSIA
Berlin
Warsaw
London
HOLY ROMAN EMPIRE
Boundary of the Holy Roman Empire
Atlantic Ocean
Rhine River
FRANCE
Paris
AUSTRIA
Vienna
HUNGARY
Buda
SWITZERLAND
PORTUGAL
SAVOY
VENETIAN REPUBLIC
Danube River
Black Sea
REPUBLIC OF GENOA
TUSCANY
MONTENEGRO
Madrid
CORSICA
Rome
PAPAL STATES
Constantinople
SPAIN
SARDINIA
Mediterranean Sea
SICILY
THE TWO SICILIES
OTTOMAN EMPIRE
FEZ AND MOROCCO
ALGERIA
TUNIS

Europe in 1812

Controlled by Napoleon

Allies of Napoleon

+ Important battles

SWEDEN
FINLAND
RUSSIAN EMPIRE
DENMARK AND NORWAY
Moscow
Borodino 1812
North Sea
Boundary of Confederation of the Rhine
Napoleon's Russian cam
GREAT BRITAIN AND IRELAND
PRUSSIA
Berlin
Friedland 1807
Niemen River
London
Warsaw
GRAND DUCHY OF WARSAW
Atlantic Ocean
FRENCH EMPIRE
Waterloo 1815
Leipzig 1813
Austerlitz 1805
Paris
AUSTRIAN EMPIRE
Wagram 1809
Vienna
Buda
PORTUGAL
Boundary of France in 1799
Marengo 1800
ILLYRIAN PROVINCES
Black Sea
SPAIN
Madrid
CORSICA
Rome
MONTENEGRO
Baylen 1808
SARDINIA
Constantinople
Trafalgar 1805
Mediterranean Sea
SICILY
OTTOMAN EMPIRE
MOROCCO
ALGERIA
TUNIS

Europe in 1815

SWEDEN
FINLAND
NORWAY
North Sea
DENMARK
Baltic Sea
RUSSIAN EMPIRE
Moscow
Niemen River
GREAT BRITAIN AND IRELAND
NETHERLANDS
Berlin
POLAND
Warsaw
London
LUXEMBOURG
PRUSSIA
Rhine River
GERMAN CONFEDERATION
Atlantic Ocean
Boundary of German Confederation
Paris
Danube River
Vienna
Buda
FRANCE
SWITZERLAND
AUSTRIAN EMPIRE
PORTUGAL
Black Sea
TUSCANY
PAPAL STATES
MONTENEGRO
Madrid
CORSICA
ELBA
Rome
Constantinople
SARDINIA
SPAIN
OTTOMAN EMPIRE
Mediterranean Sea
THE TWO SICILIES
MOROCCO
ALGERIA
TUNIS
SICILY

4 Transportation and Geography

The Soviet Union is the world's largest country. It stretches about 6,000 miles (9,650 km) from east to west, and about 3,200 miles (5,150 km) north to south. Look at the climate map of the Soviet Union on page 545. What climate region covers the largest part of the country? Harsh climate and great distances have affected the Soviet Union's development. The geography of the country has always made transportation a problem.

Look at the transportation map of the Soviet Union on this page. What kinds of transportation systems does it show? Moving goods by water is generally cheaper and easier than moving them by land. Countries with good seaports have always had an advantage in carrying on trade.

The Soviet Union has the longest coastline in the world. In spite of its long coastline, the Soviet Union lacks good seaports. Most of the Arctic coast is frozen for much of the year. It is navigable only during the warm months. Look at the map to see which routes can be used in winter. What Arctic port is ice-free all year long? What southern ports do you think are important throughout the year for trade with other countries?

Inland waterways are also important to the Soviet Union. Look at the transportation map to find the navigable rivers. Most of the rivers that are navigable are navigable only during part of the year. They are frozen for many months. Into what bodies of water do the rivers of Siberia flow?

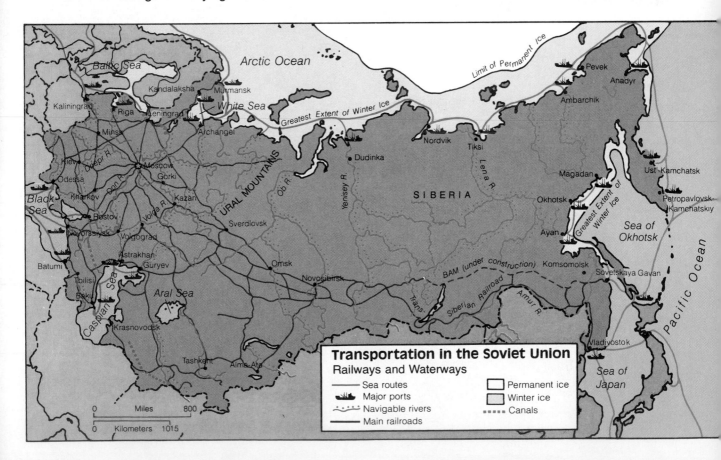

Transportation in the Soviet Union
Railways and Waterways

- Sea routes
- Major ports
- Navigable rivers
- Main railroads
- Permanent ice
- Winter ice
- Canals

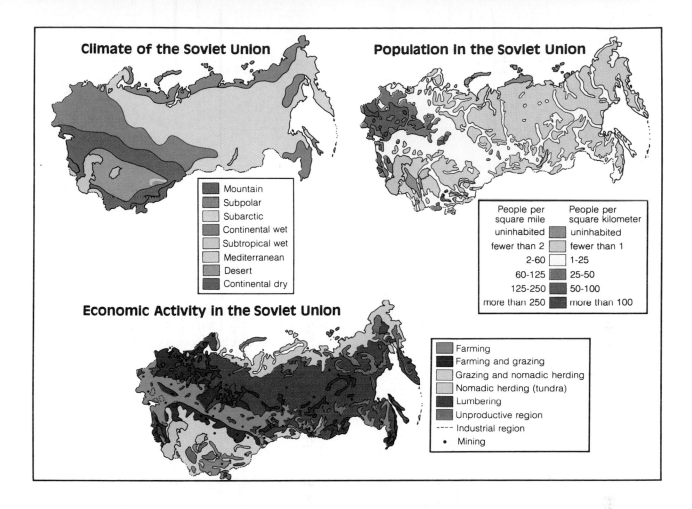

Climate of the Soviet Union

Mountain
Subpolar
Subarctic
Continental wet
Subtropical wet
Mediterranean
Desert
Continental dry

Population in the Soviet Union

People per square mile	People per square kilometer
uninhabited	uninhabited
fewer than 2	fewer than 1
2-60	1-25
60-125	25-50
125-250	50-100
more than 250	more than 100

Economic Activity in the Soviet Union

Farming
Farming and grazing
Grazing and nomadic herding
Nomadic herding (tundra)
Lumbering
Unproductive region
---- Industrial region
• Mining

You have read how the early rulers of Russia wanted ice-free ports and access to seas so that they could carry on trade with other countries. Today canals link rivers and seas to create a large transportation network east of the Urals. Moscow, near the center, is often called the "Port of Five Seas." With what seas is it connected?

Because many of its waterways cannot be used for much of the year, the Soviet Union has built many railroads. It has more miles of track than any other country in the world except the United States. Do you think more goods and passengers are carried by train or by boat in the Soviet Union?

Soviet railroads are concentrated in the region east of the Urals. Moscow is the hub of the railroad network. How many main rail lines radiate from Moscow? What railroad crosses southern Siberia? What major port is the eastern *terminal* (tur'mən əl), or end, of this transportation line?

Compare the climate, population and economic activity maps on this page with one another and with the transportation map. In what climate regions is the population densest? Economic activities in these areas support large numbers of people. Here also transportation systems are the most highly developed.

Sometimes the construction of transportation systems leads to the development of a region. This happened in Siberia. The Trans-Siberian Railroad was built after Russia acquired Vladivostok. The railroad was needed to link Siberia with the rest of Russia. Towns grew up along the railroad, and the government encouraged settlement. Siberia is a great storehouse of natural resources. BAM is being built to tap these resources and to develop Siberia's *potential* (pə ten'shəl). *Potential* means "the capacity for use or development." What resources give Siberia a great potential?

545

5 Maps That Show Trade

Most countries of the world do not produce all of the things their people need and want. Few countries are self-sufficient. One reason for this is the uneven distribution of natural resources. Another is differences in levels of technology. For these and other reasons, nations find it desirable to exchange, or trade, goods and raw materials.

Maps can help show what products are traded between different parts of the world. Each of the geographic units in this book has a world trade map. These maps show trade in a generalized way. Look at the world trade map for North Africa and the Middle East on page 324. This map shows the major imports, or goods brought in, and major exports, or goods sent out, for each of the two parts of this region. It also shows the parts of the world that are major trading partners of North Africa and the Middle East.

Now look at the maps on page 547. These maps are also trade maps for North Africa and the Middle East. These maps tell us about the goods imported and exported by each country in North Africa and the Middle East. The map at the top shows exports. The map at the bottom shows imports.

On the maps on page 547, information about the imports and exports of each country is given in a bar. In fact, these maps are really a kind of bar graph. The bases of the bars are not lined up neatly, however. Each bar is placed on or near the country for which it gives information.

The total height of each bar is related to volume of trade. Volume of trade tells us the value in United States dollars of the goods imported or exported. Volume of trade is usually given for a period of one year.

The bar in the map key shows the volume of trade represented by the different heights of the bars. We can measure the bar showing Saudi Arabia's exports, for example, and compare its height with the bar in the key. Saudi Arabia exports goods worth from $50 billion to $60 billion a year. What is the value of the goods Saudi Arabia imports in a year? Does any other country shown export goods with as high a value as those exported by Saudi Arabia? Does any other country shown import goods with as high a value as those imported by Saudi Arabia? What is the value of the goods exported by Turkey? Imported by Iran?

If you look at each bar carefully, you will see that it is divided into different colored parts. The key explains that each color stands for a different group of goods. What five groups of goods does the map show?

The proportions of the colored parts of each bar tell us how much of the total value of goods exported or imported is represented by a particular group of goods. For example, about 98 percent of the value of all Saudi Arabia's exports is represented by mineral fuels and other minerals. What group of goods is Saudi Arabia's largest single import in value? Do these goods make up more than half or less than half of the value of all of Saudi Arabia's imported goods? What accounts for more than half the value of Yemen's exports? Is the value of food imported by Tunisia greater than the value of the manufactured goods it imports?

The arrows on the map indicate the major regions with which the countries of North Africa and the Middle East trade. Each region is represented by a different color. The direction of the arrows shows where the exports go and where the imports come from. Does Morocco export many goods to North America? Does it import many goods from North America?

Now turn to the map on page 302 showing products of North Africa and the Middle East. What do you think is one of the important "mineral fuels and other minerals" exported by many countries of North Africa and the Middle East? What products might account for the raw materials exported by Egypt?

Trade in North Africa and the Middle East

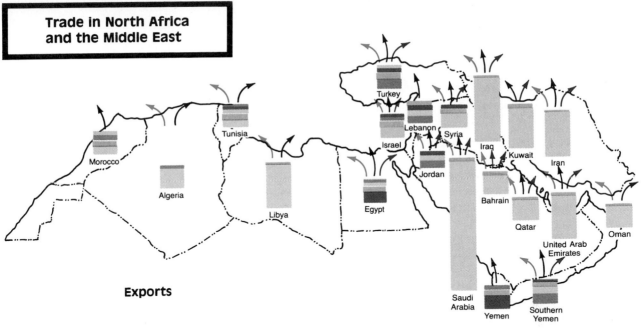

Exports

Volume of Trade
(in billions of U.S. dollars)

- $50-$60
- $40-$50
- $30-$40
- $20-$30
- $10-$20
- 0-$10

Goods Traded

- Mineral fuels and other minerals
- Manufactured goods
- Raw materials
- Food
- All other

Direction of Trade

- South America
- North America
- Europe
- Asia
- Australia and New Zealand

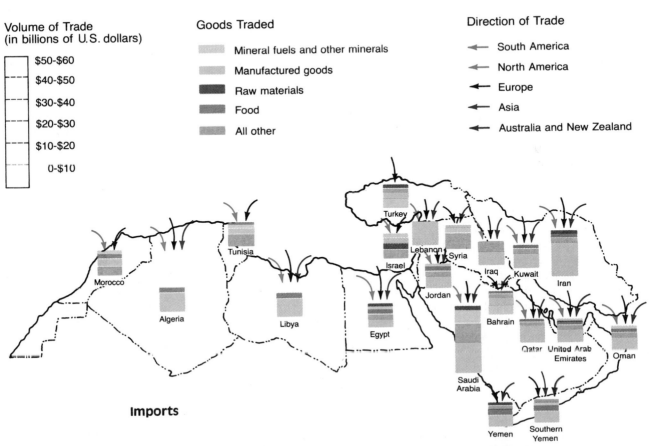

Imports

6 Map Scale, Geography, and Geology

Scale is relative size. The scale of a map tells how much of the earth's surface is represented by a given measurement on the map. In this book, a bar scale is used to show scale. It indicates how many miles or kilometers are represented by a line of a given length.

Maps can be grouped according to scale. Maps that show large areas of the earth in a general way are small-scale maps. Maps that show small areas of the earth in greater detail are large-scale maps. Compare the maps on these pages with the map on page 333. Which has the largest scale? The smallest?

The map on page 333 and the maps on these pages are relief maps. Relief, or variation in height, is shown by color or shading. One of the most spectacular relief features of Africa is the Great Rift Valley. This valley is a series of depressions, or low areas, that extends from Mozambique through East Africa into Syria. It was produced by giant faults in the earth's crust. Between the faults, parts of the African plateau dropped down. The steep cliffs that resulted rise nearly one mile (1.6 km) in some places.

The Great Rift Valley can be traced in a series of lakes that occupy its floor. Look at the map on page 333 to find these lakes: Lake Nyasa, Lake Tanganyika, Lake Edward, and Lake Rudolf. North of Lake Rudolf, the Great Rift Valley cuts across Ethiopia. It can then be traced northward as the Red Sea, the Dead Sea, and the Jordan River.

Between Ethiopia and Lake Nyasa, the Great Rift Valley forms two belts. Look at the map of Africa on this page to find the lakes that mark the western belt: Lake Tanganyika, Lake Kivu, Lake Edward, and Lake Albert. The eastern belt curves to the east of Lake Victoria. The small lakes of Eyasi, Natron, Magadi, and Lake Rudolf show the eastern belt of the Great Rift Valley.

Below the map on this page is a cross section. A cross section is a diagram, not a map. This cross section can be thought of as an imaginary cut through the earth. It is made along the line A–B on the map. Notice that the left side of the cross section is labeled A and that the right side is labeled B. The left side is also marked "West" and the right is marked "East." In what direction are you looking as you look at the diagram?

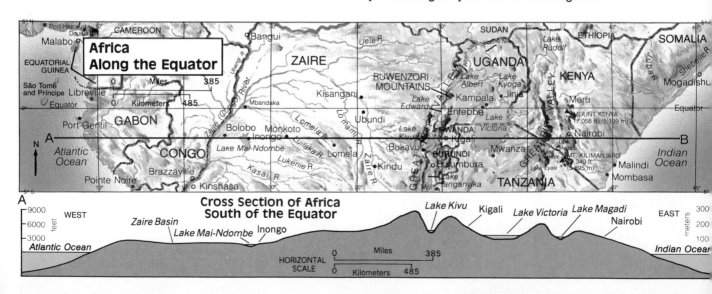

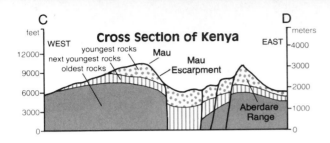

Cross Section of Kenya

C D
feet WEST EAST meters
12000
youngest rocks Mau 4000
next youngest rocks Mau
9000 oldest rocks Escarpment 3000
6000 2000
Aberdare
Range
3000 1000
0 0

Cross sections often give us a better idea of elevation than maps do. Notice that the horizontal scale of the cross section A–B on page 548 is the same as that of the map above it. Is the vertical scale the same? The vertical scale of cross sections of the earth is often *exaggerated* (igzaj′ərā′tid), that is, enlarged or increased, in relation to the horizontal scale. This is done to emphasize relief. Can you think why?

Study cross section A–B to see if the valley floors have dropped lower in the eastern rift belt or in the western rift belt. Now look at the map of Equatorial Africa. How do the lakes that occupy these belts differ?

Find Lake Victoria on the map and cross section on page 548. Does Lake Victoria lie in a rift valley? How does its shape differ from that of lakes Rudolf, Albert, and Tanganyika?

Now look at the map of Kenya to the right and the cross section above. Along what line on the map is this cross section made? Does this cross section show the eastern or the western rift belt? What distance does the line C–D represent?

Cross section C–D has more geological information than the cross section A–B. Cross section C–D shows several different kinds of rock. Are the oldest rocks at the top or at the bottom of the section?

Geologists sometimes use a *block diagram* to show landforms and geologic features. A block diagram is a drawing that shows a three-dimensional picture. It is often used to show relief of landforms. The front and sides of a block diagram are often cross sections. The diagram below is a block diagram of a rift valley. The top of the diagram shows how the surface of the earth looks. The front cross section shows faulted blocks of the earth's crust.

Block Diagram of a Rift Valley

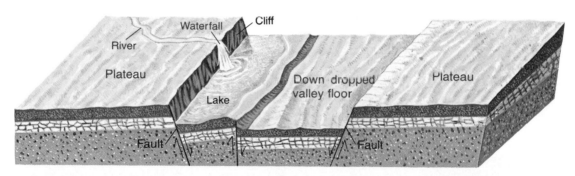

Comparing Maps: Religion, Language, and Political Boundaries

7

The countries labeled on the map below on the left became independent in 1947. Before that, most of this region was part of British India. Religious differences brought pressure to divide, or partition, the British-controlled area into two separate nations. As a result, India and Pakistan were created. Their boundaries were drawn according to religion. From the beginning, Pakistan was a nation in two parts, West Pakistan and East Pakistan. What was the main religion in Pakistan? In India? The two parts of Pakistan were united only by religion. What divided them?

The map below on the right shows the principal languages of South Asia. Language differences also influenced the boundaries established between India and Pakistan in 1947. In East Pakistan the language was Bengali. What languages were

spoken in West Pakistan? Language differences and other problems led to a civil war between West Pakistan and East Pakistan. After a bitter struggle, East Pakistan became independent in 1971. Look at the map on page 551 to see what name the new country adopted.

Political boundaries within India were also formed largely in accordance with language boundaries. After India became independent, some states were divided to please language groups in conflict with one another. Other states were renamed for the same reason. Compare the language map with the map on page 551. What state names are based on the name of the principal language spoken in the area?

You have seen how language and religion can influence the establishment of political boundaries.

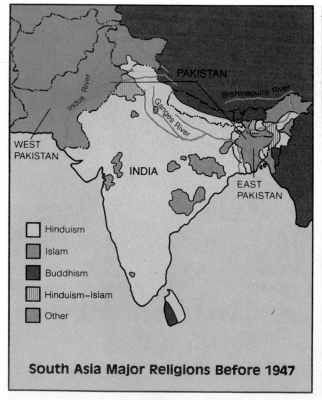

South Asia Major Religions Before 1947

Hinduism

Islam

Buddhism

Hinduism–Islam

Other

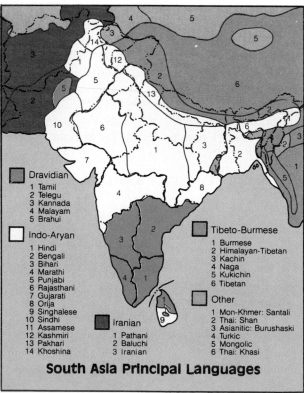

South Asia Principal Languages

Dravidian
1 Tamil
2 Telegu
3 Kannada
4 Malayam
5 Brahui

Indo-Aryan
1 Hindi
2 Bengali
3 Bihari
4 Marathi
5 Punjabi
6 Rajasthani
7 Gujarati
8 Orija
9 Singhalese
10 Sindhi
11 Assamese
12 Kashmiri
13 Pakhari
14 Khoshina

Iranian
1 Pathani
2 Baluchi
3 Iranian

Tibeto-Burmese
1 Burmese
2 Himalayan-Tibetan
3 Kachin
4 Naga
5 Kukichin
6 Tibetan

Other
1 Mon-Khmer: Santali
2 Thai: Shan
3 Asianitic: Burushaski
4 Turkic
5 Mongolic
6 Thai: Khasi

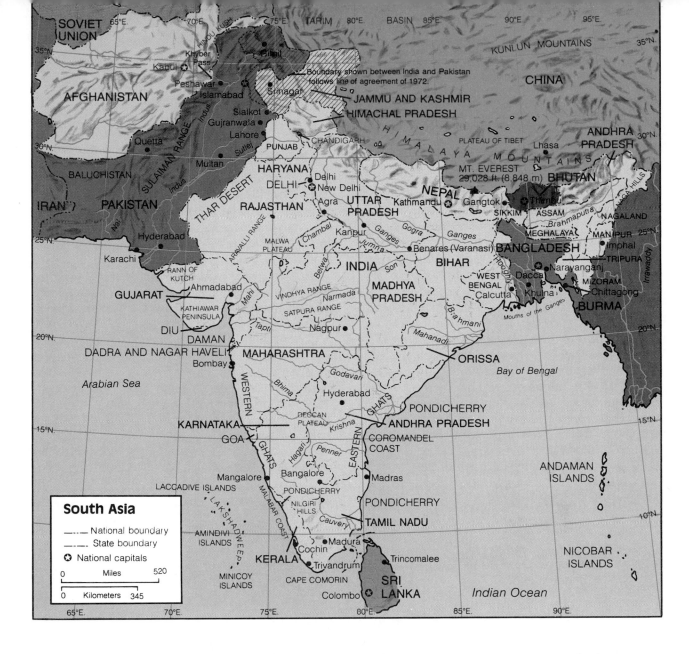

Physical features that act as barriers also help to determine political boundaries. What physical features shown on the map on this page have influenced the creation of political boundaries? Have these features acted as barriers for religion and language as well?

A large region known as Kashmir was not included in the division of the Indian subcontinent in 1947. This region is shown along the upper part of the Indus River on the religion map. Kashmir was ruled by a prince who did not want to join either India or Pakistan. When the Pakistanis invaded Kashmir, the ruler decided to make Kashmir a part of India. Fighting between India and Pakistan over this territory continued for many years. In 1972, an agreement established a cease-fire boundary line. However, the boundary between Pakistan and India is still *in dispute* (dis pyo͞ot′), or not settled, in this region. In religion, is Kashmir more like India or Pakistan? Can you determine whether it is more like India or Pakistan on the basis of language?

8 Maps of the Ocean Floor

Maps of the earth's land areas are the most familiar kinds of maps. Less familiar are maps of the part of the earth's crust that lies below sea level. Until about 50 years ago, it was thought that the ocean floor was a nearly flat plain. The scientific study of the ocean, or *oceanography* (ō'shənog'rəfē), has shown that the ocean floor is as irregular as the land's surface. Mountain ranges, ridges, canyons, and valleys are found there.

Elevation and relief of the ocean floor are shown on maps by color, shading, and contour lines. The map below shows features of the ocean floor by color and shading. What color are the deepest areas? How are areas above sea level shown?

Contour maps show differences in elevation by lines that connect all points having the same elevation. These lines are called contour lines. Elevation is indicated in feet or meters on the line. Look at the diagram showing contour lines on page 553. Contour lines on land measure distances above sea level. They indicate height. How is sea level indicated on a contour map? Contour lines are also used to measure distances below sea level. They indicate depth, and they are marked with a minus sign ($-$).

Contour lines that are drawn close together indicate steepness. Gentle slopes are indicated by contour lines drawn far apart. Compare the block diagram with the contour map.

Color can be added to contour maps to make it easier to visualize relief. Look at the map at the top of page 553. This map shows the same region shown by the map on page 552. How is depth indicated on this map? Are the lines separating colors contour lines? What depth does the darkest color indicate?

To visualize the topography, or features, of the ocean floor, it is helpful to look at a *profile* (prō'fīl).

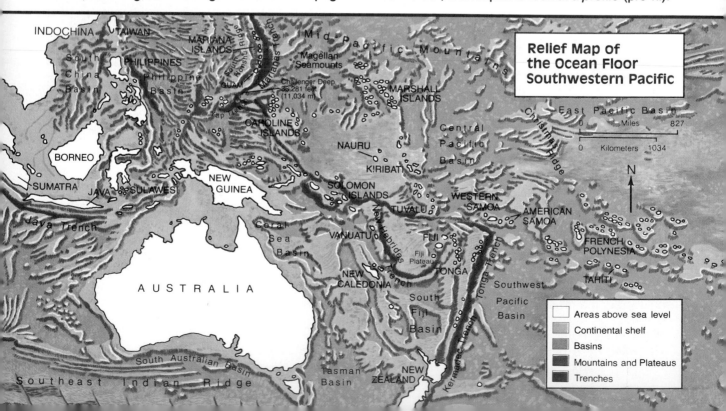

Relief Map of the Ocean Floor Southwestern Pacific

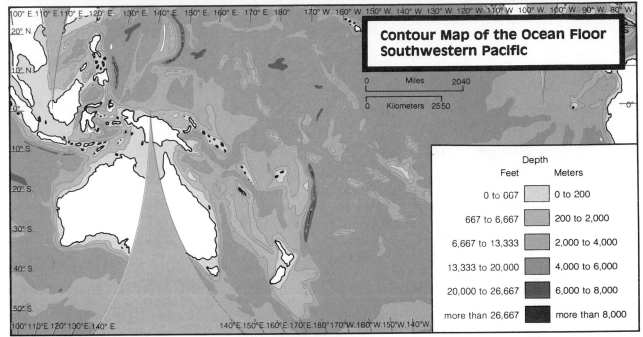

Contour Map of the Ocean Floor Southwestern Pacific

Depth	
Feet	Meters
0 to 667	0 to 200
667 to 6,667	200 to 2,000
6,667 to 13,333	2,000 to 4,000
13,333 to 20,000	4,000 to 6,000
20,000 to 26,667	6,000 to 8,000
more than 26,667	more than 8,000

Contour Lines

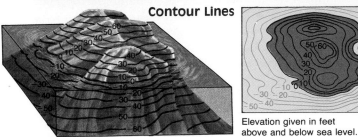

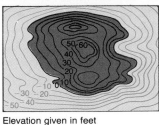

Elevation given in feet above and below sea level.

Profile of the Ocean Floor

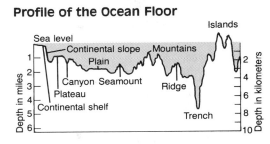

A profile is a representation of something in outline. It is like a cross section. The profile on this page shows some of the features on the ocean bottom. Extending out from the shoreline is the continental shelf. This shallow area slopes gently seaward. Its topography is generally like that of the nearby land. The continental shelf has an average width of 40 miles (65 km). It rarely exceeds depths of 666 feet (200 m). Find the continental shelf areas on the map above.

The seaward edge of the continental shelf is marked by the beginning of a steep slope called the continental slope. The boundary is very sharp. Look at the profile. The base of the slope is at depths of about 6,560 feet (2,000 m). Find the limits of the continental slope on the map on this page.

Even though the continental slope and the continental shelf are under water, they are considered part of the continents. Beyond the base of the continental slope are the ocean basins. Find the Pacific basins on the relief map.

Features of the ocean basins are shown on the relief map and on the profile. Long, narrow valleys called trenches are the deepest parts of the ocean floor. The deepest known spot in any ocean is the Challenger Deep. It is in the Mariana Trench, east of the Mariana Islands. Find the Challenger Deep on the map. How deep is it? You read in Unit 1 that the world's highest mountain, Mount Everest, is 29,028 feet (8,848 m) high. Is Mount Everest higher than the Challenger Deep is deep?

Other features of the ocean floor include ridges, mountains, plains, plateaus, and seamounts. Seamounts are isolated peaks rising from the ocean floor. Find examples of these features on the shaded relief map. Refer to the contour map to see how these features are represented there. Are ridges and trenches represented by widely spaced or closely spaced contour lines?

9 Using an Atlas

One of the special reference sections in your book is a collection of maps called an atlas. To find the atlas, turn to the table of contents. We use references to get information. Your atlas can be a valuable source of information if you use it efficiently.

There are five world maps in your atlas. World maps are valuable for comparing relationships between different parts of the world because all the continents and oceans are in view at the same time. On world maps, however, information usually is shown only in a general way. Maps showing only part of the world can give more details. There are 8 maps in your atlas that show only part of the world. Each shows one of the world's inhabited continents. Name these six continents.

Maps can be grouped according to the kind of information they show. Examples of three common groups of maps—political maps, physical maps, and special-purpose maps—are included in your atlas.

Political maps show places such as countries and cities. They sometimes show other political divisions such as states, provinces, and counties. You should know that political means "having to do with government." Political maps use symbols to show the location of capitals and other cities. Different kinds of lines are used to show boundaries between different political divisions. Sometimes colors are used to make it easier to see sizes and shapes.

Map A below is part of a political map in your atlas. What city on the map is a national capital? What is the capital of Victoria?

Physical maps help you understand how the earth looks. Landforms or altitude are shown by colors or shading. On physical maps, many natural features such as mountain ranges, mountain peaks, rivers, lakes, deserts, glaciers, and oases are indicated and named.

Maps are classified as political or physical according to the main kind of information they show. Political maps almost always show some physical features, and physical maps generally include some political features. Maps that show both kinds of information are often referred to as physical-political maps.

Map A

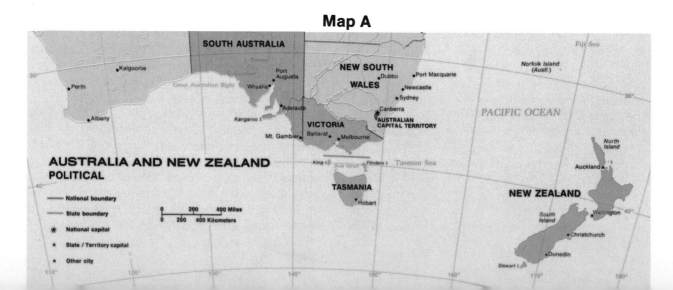

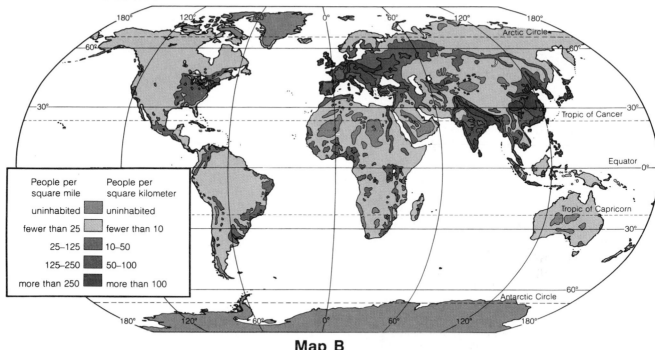

People per square mile | People per square kilometer
uninhabited | uninhabited
fewer than 25 | fewer than 10
25–125 | 10–50
125–250 | 50–100
more than 250 | more than 100

Map B

Special-purpose maps show such things as relief, rainfall, climate, vegetation, population, products, and weather. **Map B** above is one of the special-purpose maps in your atlas. What does it show?

When you study the maps in your atlas, you will need to use what you have learned about directions, latitude, longitude, and scale. You will need to know about symbols and how to interpret a key.

Some maps have a compass rose or a north arrow to help you find directions. It is useful to know that most maps are drawn so that north is toward the top of the page. Lines of latitude and longitude also can help you find directions. You know that lines of latitude run east and west and that lines of longitude run north and south. If a map is oriented, or fixed to be directed, with north toward the top, lines of latitude run from left to right, and lines of longitude run from top to bottom.

Latitude and longitude can help you find locations as well as directions. You can tell where any place on the earth is by giving its latitude and longitude in degrees. Use **Map B** to tell on what continent a point at 0° latitude and 60° W. longitude is located. Use **Map A** to give the approximate location of Canberra.

Scale is relative size. In your atlas, scale is shown by a scale bar. It shows what actual distance on the earth is represented by a given distance on the map. Use **Map A** to tell how many miles it is from Adelaide to Canberra. Is Adelaide closer to Canberra or Hobart?

Information on maps is shown by symbols. Symbols are often, but not always, explained in a key. Many commonly used map symbols are explained on page A–15 of your book.

Color is a special symbol. The same color on different maps may mean different things. It is particularly important to understand the color key on special-purpose maps. What color on **Map B** shows areas where there are fewer than 25 people per square mile? What does the red color show?

REFERENCE
SECTION

Reviewing the Text

Reread pages 12–23. Then number a paper from **1** through **10**. After each number, write the word or words in parentheses that correctly complete each sentence.

1. There are (six, seven, eight) large landmasses, or continents, on the earth.
2. A landmass smaller than a continent and completely surrounded by water is called (an island, a peninsula, an isthmus).
3. By definition, mountains must rise at least 2,000 feet above (sea level, the surrounding land, plains).
4. Another word for elevation, or height above sea level, is (relief, steepness, altitude).
5. The world's largest ocean is the (Atlantic, Pacific, Indian).
6. Glaciers are part of the (lithosphere, hydrosphere, atmosphere).
7. The outermost layer of the earth is called the (core, mantle, crust).
8. (Weathering, Glaciation, Mountain building) is a result of tectonic activity.
9. The breaking down of rocks into smaller pieces is called (weathering, erosion, deposition).
10. The single most important agent of erosion is (water, wind, glaciers).

Reading a Diagram

To follow page 26

The diagram below illustrates the section "The Earth and the Sun" on pages 24–26. Reread this section and study the diagram. Then number a paper from 1 through 5. After each number, write the answer to the question.

Seasons in the Northern Hemisphere

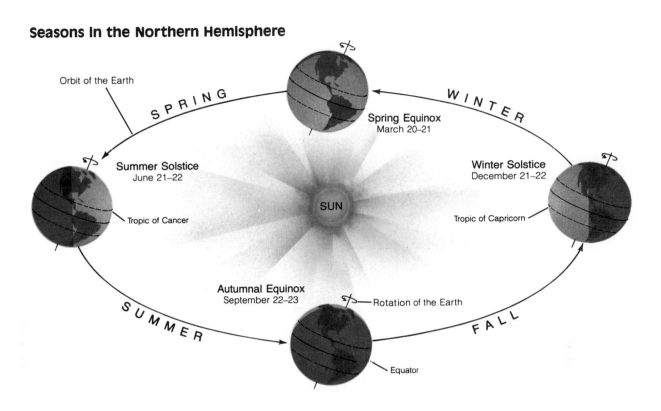

1. What does this diagram show?
2. How is the rotation of the earth indicated? Describe the direction of the earth's rotation.
3. During what two periods are day and night of equal length in all parts of the earth?
4. When are the direct rays of the sun over the Tropic of Cancer? The Tropic of Capricorn?
5. If the title of the diagram were changed to "Seasons in the Southern Hemisphere," several labels would also have to be changed to make the diagram correct. Tell which labels you would change and how you would change them.

A Time Zone Map of the United States

Reread the section "Time Zones" on pages 39–41 and study the map below. Then number a paper from 1 through 7. After each number, write the answer to the question.

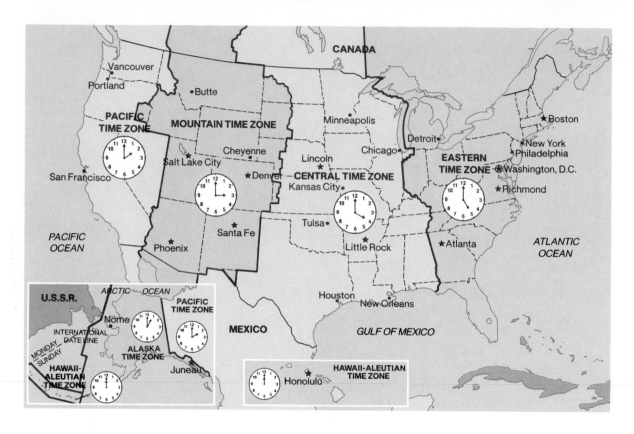

1. Compare the map on this page with the map on page 40. Which map is drawn to a larger scale?

2. How many time zones are there in the United States? What is the easternmost time zone in the United States? The westernmost?

3. How many hours' difference is there between the easternmost part of the United States and the westernmost part?

4. If it is 10:00 A.M. in Butte, Montana, what time is it in Atlanta, Georgia?

5. If it is 11:00 P.M. on Saturday in San Francisco, what day and time is it in New York?

6. Is the time difference between Denver and Washington, D.C., greater or smaller than the time difference between Denver and Honolulu?

7. A flight from Kansas City to Santa Fe takes two and one-half hours. If a plane leaves Kansas City at 3:00 P.M. local time what time will it arrive in Santa Fe?

To follow page 48

Study the graph below. Then number a paper from **1** through **8**. After each number, write the letter of the correct answer.

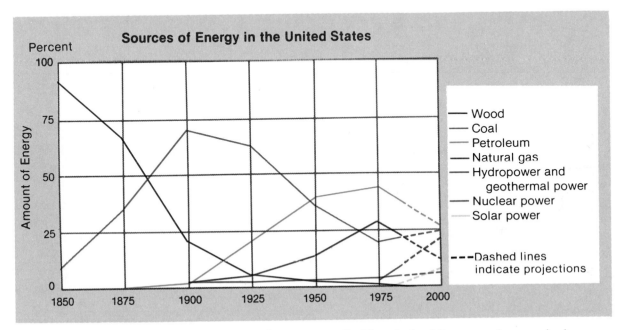

1. The graph above is a _____ graph.
   a. circle   b. line   c. bar

2. In 1850, _____ supplied most of the energy in the United States.
   a. wood   b. coal   c. petroleum

3. Coal and wood each accounted for about half the energy used in the United States in _____.
   a. 1885   b. 1915   c. 1950

4. Between 1900 and 1975, the percent of energy supplied by coal in the United States _____.
   a. increased   b. decreased
   c. remained the same

5. In 1975, petroleum supplied about _____ percent of the energy used in the United States.
   a. 35   b. 40   c. 45

6. The dashed lines on the graph show projections, or estimates for the future, made by scientists. The projected part of the graph shows what scientists _____ percentages of future energy sources will be.
   a. know   b. expect   c. hope

7. Solar energy began to grow as an important energy resource about the time _____ accounted for less than 1 percent of United States energy.
   a. nuclear power   b. hydropower and geothermal power   c. wood

8. In the year 2000, experts predict that Americans will use _____ different kinds of energy.
   a. five   b. six   c. eight

A geographical dictionary provides basic information about regions, countries, cities, and natural features of the world. Read the sample entries from a geographical dictionary below. Then number a paper from 1 through 4. After each number, write the answer to the question.

Eu·phra·tes \yủ-ˈfrāt-(ˌ)ēz\ *or Arab.* **Al-Fu·rāt** \ˌal-fə-ˈrät\. River, SW Asia; 2235 m. long; formed by confluence of the Murat Nehri (Eastern Euphrates) and the Kara Su (Western Euphrates, the main stream) in E Turkey; flows S and SE across NE Syria, through W and cen. Iraq to unite with the Tigris and continues, as Shatt-al-Arab, to Persian Gulf; has few important tributaries but in Syria on the N receives the Balikh and the Khabur; in middle course crosses Syrian Desert; in lower course in Iraq is used for irrigation, expands into swamps and side streams; navigable for small vessels below Hit. Has on its banks several modern cities of importance: Erzincan (on the Kara Su), Rakka, Deir-ez-Zor, An Najaf, An Nasiriya, and ruins of many ancient cities. Its valley was extensively irrigated in ancient times and gave growth to civilizations of Babylonia, Assyria, Chaldea (see MESOPOTAMIA).

Ti·gris / ˈtī-grəs\ *or Arab.* **Shatt Dij·la** \shät-ˈdij-lə\. River, SE Turkey and Iraq; 1180 m. long; rises in a lake in the mountains of Kurdistan, S of Elazig, Turkey; flows SSE past Diyarbakir in Turkey and Mosul and Baghdad in Iraq, and unites in SE Iraq at Al-Qurna with the Euphrates river to form the Shatt-al-Arab. Has many tributaries on left bank, esp. the Great Zab, Little Zab, and Diyala in Iraq. Navigable for small steamers bet. Baghdad and a point just above Al-Qurna. Since ancient times, tributaries connected with Euphrates in their lower courses by irrigation canals; probably in Sumerian times its lower course was much more to the W. Sites of ruins of many ancient cities are on its banks, as Nineveh, Calah, Ashur, Ctesiphon, and Seleucia.

1. What are the Tigris and the Euphrates?

2. In what modern country do both the Tigris and the Euphrates begin?

3. Which river—the Tigris or the Euphrates—is longer? At what city do they join, or unite? What river do they form where they join? Into what body of water does this river empty?

4. A cross reference tells you where to look for further information on a subject. Under what entry would you look to find further information about the Euphrates?

Read the introduction and passage below. Then number a paper from **1** through **5**. After each number, write the answer to the question.

Herodotus' Account of the Building of the Great Pyramid

Herodotus (5th century B.C.) was a Greek historian. He is known as "the father of history" because his classic *History* marks the beginning of Western history writing. Below is part of Herodotus' account of the building of the Great Pyramid.

Cheops succeeded to the throne, and plunged into all manner of wickedness. He closed the temples, and forbade the Egyptians to offer sacrifice, compelling them instead to labour, one and all, in his service. Some were required to drag blocks of stone down to the Nile from the quarries in the Arabian range of hills; others received the blocks after they had been conveyed in boats across the river, and drew them to the range of hills called the Libyan. A hundred thousand men laboured constantly, and were relieved every three months by a fresh lot. It took ten years' oppression of the people to make the causeway for the conveyance of the stones, a work not much inferior, in my judgment, to the pyramid itself. This causeway is five furlongs in length, ten fathoms wide, and in height, and the highest part, eight fathoms. It is built of polished stone, and is covered with carvings of animals. To make it took ten years, as I said—or rather to make the causeway, the works on the mound where the pyramid stands, and the underground chambers, which Cheops intended as vaults for his own use: these last were built on a sort of island, surrounded by water introduced from the Nile by a canal. The Pyramid itself was twenty years in building. It is a square, eight hundred feet each way, and the height the same, built entirely of polished stone, fitted together with the utmost care. The stones of which it is composed are none of them less than thirty feet in length.

HERODOTUS
The Histories, c. 455 B.C.

1. Who was Herodotus?
2. How long did Herodotus say it took to build both the causeway and the pyramid?
3. According to Herodotus, how high was the Great Pyramid? According to the diagram on page 64, what was the original height of the pyramid?

4. According to Herodotus, how many people were employed in building the Great Pyramid at any given time?
5. About how many years passed between the building of the Great Pyramid and Herodotus' description of it? (You may need to refer to the caption on page 64.)

ENRICHMENT

Below is a list of people who are connected with the early civilizations. Number a paper from 1 through 6. After each number, write the name of the civilization with which the person is associated. Then write two sentences about the person. You may need to refer to pages 61–71.

1. Nebuchadnezzar

2. Hammurabi

3. Hippocrates

4. Pericles

5. Caesar Augustus

6. Julius Caesar

Reading and Understanding a Graph

To follow page 78

Reread page 78 and study the graph below. Then number a paper from 1 through 7. After each number, write the letter of the correct answer.

1. The graph shows _____.
   a. gross national product in three countries and Greenland
   b. per capita gross national product in three countries and Greenland
   c. per capita income in three countries and Greenland

2. The graph is a _____ graph.
   a. circle
   b. line
   c. bar

3. Per capita gross national product is the _____ in a country (or region) in one year.
   a. value of all the goods produced and services performed
   b. value of all the goods produced and services performed divided by the population
   c. population divided by the value of all the goods produced and services performed

4. The country or region with the lowest per capita gross national product is _____.
   a. Canada
   b. Iceland
   c. Greenland

5. The per capita gross national product of the United States is about $2,000 more than the per capita gross national product of _____.
   a. Canada
   b. Greenland
   c. Iceland

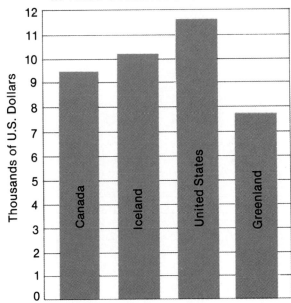

Per Capita Gross National Product in Three Countries and Greenland

6. Compare the graph above with the chart on page 126. The per capita gross national product of a country (or region) is always _____ its gross national product.
   a. the same as
   b. greater than
   c. smaller than

7. Refer to the chart on page 126. In order of decreasing gross national product, the countries and region are _____.
   a. the United States, Iceland, Canada, Greenland
   b. Greenland, Iceland, Canada, the United States
   c. the United States, Canada, Iceland, Greenland

565

ENRICHMENT

Landform Regions and Natural Features of the United States and Canada

To follow page 87

Number a paper from **1** through **22**. After each number, write the name of the landform region or natural feature indicated by the number on the map. Numbers **1** through **9** are next to the symbols in the key. Numbers **10** through **22** are on the map itself. You may need to refer to pages 84–87 and to the map on pages 100–101.

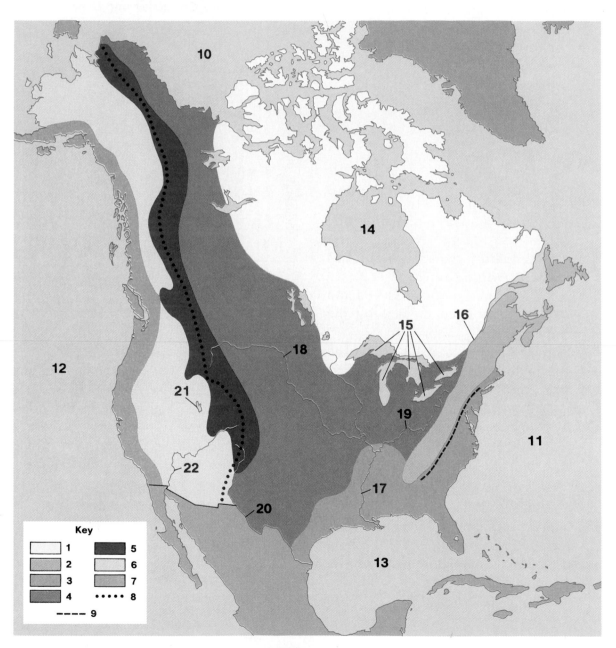

Reading Graphs

The graphs below compare the population and land area in six regions of the United States. Refer to the graphs to answer the questions that follow. Number a paper from 1 through 8. After each number, write the answer to the question.

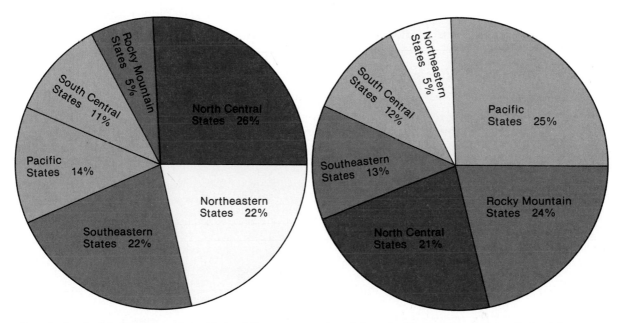

Population in Six Regions of the United States   **Land Area in Six Regions of the United States**

1. What kind of graphs—circle, line, or bar—are shown above?

2. What does the graph on the left show? The graph on the right?

3. Which region has the most land? The most people?

4. Which region has the least land? The fewest people?

5. Which two regions have the same number of people? Which two regions together include about half the land in the United States?

6. Which region ranks fifth in population? Which ranks fifth in land area?

7. Which two regions together have the same land area as the Pacific states?

8. Which single region has about as many people as the South Central states and the Pacific states together?

567

Making and Using a Time Line

List the events below in chronological order and add them to the time that has been started for you. Then number a paper from **1** through **6**. After each number, write the answer to the question.

St. Lawrence Seaway completed

First permanent European settlement in Canada

First Canadian transcontinental railroad completed

British gain control of New France

Alberta and Saskatchewan become provinces of Canada

Aluminum plant completed at Kitimat

British capture Quebec

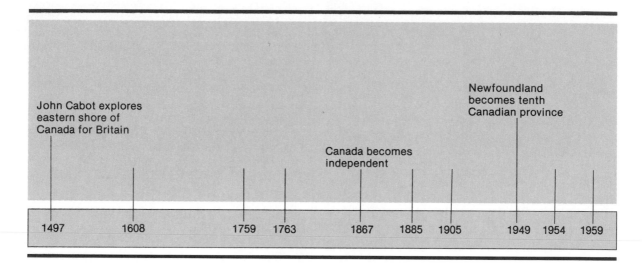

1. How long after the British captured Quebec did they gain control of New France?

2. How long after the settlement of Quebec did the French lose Quebec?

3. How long after the British gained control of New France did Canada become an independent country?

4. When was the first Canadian transcontinental railroad completed?

5. Did Newfoundland become a province before or after Saskatchewan and Alberta became provinces? How many years before or after?

6. Was the St. Lawrence Seaway completed before or after the Kitimat aluminum plant was completed? How many years before or after?

Using the Card Catalog

To follow page 136

A card catalog is a list on cards of all the books in a library. There are three cards for each book—a subject card, an author card, and a title card. The first line on each card gives the subject, the author, or the title of the book. The cards are all arranged in alphabetical order in drawers. The drawers are labeled with the letters of the first three and the last three cards they contain.

On a card in the card catalog, the author's last name is listed first, followed by a comma and the author's first name. The card also tells the name of the book's publisher and the place and date of publication. *Illus.* means that the book is illustrated. The number on the bottom is the call number. It tells you on what shelf to look for the book. The library shelves are labeled with the numbers of the first and last books they include.

Refer to the sample cards below to answer the questions that follow. Number a paper from 1 through 6. After each number, write the letter of the correct answer.

CARD I

Enterline, James Robert

Viking America
New York: Doubleday,
1972. 217 pp. *illus.*
973.13
E

CARD II

VIKINGS

Enterline, James Robert
Viking America
New York: Doubleday,
1972. 217 pp. *illus.*
973.13
E

CARD III

Viking America

Enterline, James Robert
New York: Doubleday,
1972. 217 pp. *illus.*
973.13
E

1. If you knew only the title of this book you would look for _____.
   a. Card I
   b. Card II
   c. Card III
2. Card I is _____ card.
   a. an author
   b. a subject
   c. a title
3. This book would be found on a shelf marked _____.
   a. 975–999
   b. 217–345
   c. 900–975

4. The subject of this book is _____.
   a. Vikings
   b. Viking America
   c. James Robert Enterline
5. Card II would be found in a drawer marked _____.
   a. VAC–WIL
   b. ELD–EXC
   c. VIM–WAD
6. The author of this book is _____.
   a. Enterline James Robert
   b. James Robert Enterline
   c. America Viking

ENRICHMENT

The written language of the Mayas used hieroglyphic signs. Among the hieroglyphics that have been deciphered are those expressing numbers. The Mayas used a system of counting based on 20s. The table below shows the Mayan numeral system for the numbers 0 through 19.

0	1	2	3	4
5	6	7	8	9
10	11	12	13	14
15	16	17	18	19

For numbers 20 and above, two rows were used, one above the other. The top row showed the number of 20s in the total. For example, the number 155 would be shown like this:

represents 7 groups of 20s, or 140

represents 15

$$140 + 15 = 155$$

Now number a paper from **1** through **6**. After each number, write the answer to the question.

1. The Mayas could express any number by the use of three symbols. What were these three symbols? What did each stand for singly?

2. What does •••• represent?

3. Show how the Mayas wrote 16.

4. Write your age in Mayan numerals.

5. What number does ≡ represent?

6. Show how the Mayas would have written 212.

The Conquest of the Inca Empire

Read the passage below and study the map. Then number a paper from 1 through 7. After each number, write the answer to the question.

Pizarro Conquers the Incas

Francisco Pizarro first heard stories of a rich land of gold to the south when he crossed the Isthmus of Panama with Balboa in 1513. Later, Pizarro led several expeditions in search of this rich Indian empire. His first voyage was unsuccessful because of bad weather. On his second voyage, Pizarro took refuge from unfriendly Indians on Gallo Island and waited for additional men. Here he received orders to turn back, which he ignored. He continued along the coast to 9°S. latitude and found the Inca Empire, which was centered in what is now Peru. Pizarro began his last voyage in 1531 after getting permission from the king of Spain to undertake the conquest of the Inca Empire. He arrived at Cajamarca in 1532, captured the Inca leader, Atahuallpa, and had him put to death the following year. Pizarro then continued to the royal capital of Cuzco and took control without a struggle. The capture of this city nearly completed the conquest of Peru.

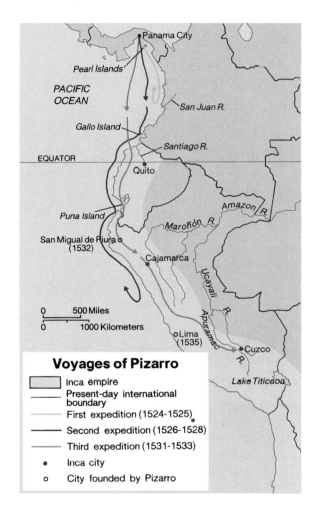

Voyages of Pizarro

- Inca empire
- Present-day international boundary
- First expedition (1524-1525)
- Second expedition (1526-1528)
- Third expedition (1531-1533)
- • Inca city
- ○ City founded by Pizarro

1. What was the name of the empire that Pizarro found and conquered?

2. How many expeditions did Pizarro undertake to find and conquer the Inca Empire? How many years did these expeditions take?

3. The northern limit of the Inca Empire reached as far as what present-day boundary?

4. On which expeditions did Pizarro cross the equator?

5. Near the mouth of what river did Pizarro begin his overland journey?

6. About how far did Pizarro travel between Cajamarca and Cuzco?

7. What cities were founded by Pizarro? Were they founded before or after the capture of Cuzco?

ENRICHMENT

Read the passage below and study the map. Then number a paper from 1 through 5. After each number, write the answer to the question.

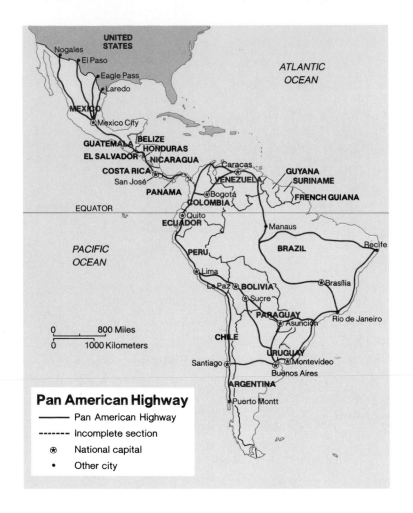

Pan American Highway
——— Pan American Highway
------- Incomplete section
⊛ National capital
• Other city

The Pan American Highway

The Pan American Highway is a network, or system, of highways connecting North and South America. It includes 29,525 miles (47,516 km) of roads. The idea of a road linking the two continents originated in the 1800s. Planning began in the late 1920s. By 1940, more than 60 percent of the highway between the United States and Panama was completed. In 1962, a highway bridge over the Panama Canal was completed. In the 1970s, construction was begun on a 250-mile (402-km) gap between Panama and Colombia. The Pan American Highway Congress meets every four years to talk about the progress of the highway and to plan its development.

1. The Pan American Highway begins at what four cities in the North? In what country are they?

2. Through what cities would you pass traveling from Caracas to Montevideo by the most direct route on the Pan American Highway?

3. What does the symbol -------- indicate?

4. What major division of Latin America that you have studied is *not* served by the Pan American Highway?

5. The section of the Pan American Highway that follows the western coast of South America reaches as far south as what city? In what country is this city?

Can You Match These?

To follow page 181

Match each person in Column I with the correct description in Column II. Number a paper from 1 through 14. After each number, write the letter of the correct answer.

Column I	Column II
1. Fidel Castro	a. Mexican president famous for the government reforms he began
2. Sebastian Cabot	b. liberated Chile from Spanish rule and became the country's first president
3. Pedro Cabral	c. became known as *El Libertador* for leading revolutions against the Spanish in Andean lands
4. Christopher Columbus	d. conquistador who conquered the Inca Empire
5. Hernando Cortés	e. landed in the West Indies in 1492 and claimed the islands for Spain
6. Porfirio Díaz	f. the first European to explore the Río de la Plata in 1516
7. Simón Bolívar	g. served as president of Mexico for 30 years after leading a revolt that overthrew the government
8. Juan de Solís	h. explored the coast of Argentina in the 1500s
9. Francisco Pizarro	i. led a successful coup in Cuba in 1959 and made himself prime minister
10. Miguel Hidalgo y Costilla	j. became emperor of Brazil in 1831
11. Pedro II	k. priest who led the Mexican revolution for independence
12. Bernardo O'Higgins	l. established the Portuguese claim to what is now Brazil in 1500
13. Benito Juárez	m. patriot of Argentina who led the country in its struggle for freedom from Spain
14. José de San Martín	n. conquistador who conquered the Aztec Empire

ENRICHMENT

573

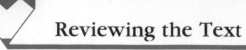

Reread pages 188–193 and study the map on page 189. Then number a paper from 1 through 14. After each number, write the letter of the correct answer.

1. Mountains that do *not* form part of the boundary between Europe and Asia are the _____.
   a. Urals
   b. Caucasus
   c. Alps

2. Europe is the _____ continent.
   a. smallest
   b. second-smallest
   c. largest

3. Europe includes _____ countries.
   a. fewer than 20
   b. 20 to 30
   c. more than 30

4. The Pyrenees are part of a cordillera that is known as the _____ mountain system.
   a. Alpine
   b. Apennine
   c. Carpathian

5. The _____ is an arm of the Mediterranean Sea.
   a. Gulf of Bothnia
   b. Bay of Biscay
   c. Adriatic Sea

6. A climate of dry summers and cool, wet winters is called _____ climate.
   a. an oceanic
   b. a Mediterranean
   c. a mountain

7. _____ is *not* an important natural resource of Europe.
   a. Coal
   b. Iron
   c. Oil

8. Europe's many waterfalls are important for _____.
   a. transportation
   b. irrigation
   c. hydroelectricity

9. The population density of Europe is _____ that of the United States.
   a. less than
   b. the same as
   c. greater than

10. An example of intensive farming is _____.
    a. increasing the amount of land under cultivation
    b. planting two or more crops in the same field at the same time
    c. selling crops for higher prices

11. The European Economic Community is an organization that _____.
    a. promotes trade through cooperation
    b. encourages competition among its members
    c. establishes taxes for its member countries

12. _____ extends farther north than any other country in Europe.
    a. Norway
    b. Sweden
    c. Finland

13. The Rhine River forms part of the border between France and _____.
    a. Luxembourg
    b. Switzerland
    c. the Federal Republic of Germany

Read the paragraph below and study the graph. Then number a paper from **1** through **4**. After each number, write the letter of the correct answer.

    The graph below shows the growth of the Roman Empire by comparing its size at different times. It shows in a different way much the same thing that the map on page 201 shows. Each square represents the same area as every other square. To compare the size of the empire for two given dates, you must consider the entire rectangle shown for each date. For example, to compare the size of the empire in 264 B.C. with its size in 201 B.C., you must compare the size of the dark red rectangle, marked 264 B.C., with the size of the larger light red rectangle (which includes the smaller rectangle of 264 B.C.) marked 201 B.C.

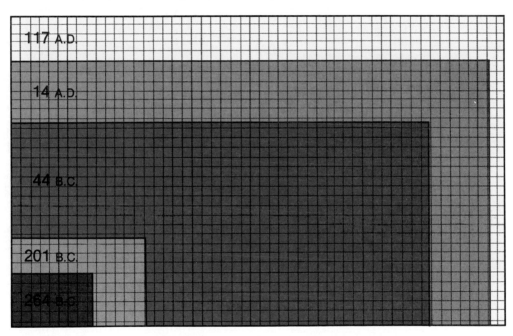

1. What is the best title for this graph?
   a. Divisions of the Roman Empire
   b. Important Dates in Roman History
   c. Growth of the Roman Empire

2. The comparative size of the Roman Empire is shown at how many different times?
   a. four
   b. five
   c. six

3. During what period did the empire grow the most?
   a. 201 B.C.–44 B.C.
   b. 44 B.C.–14 A.D.
   c. 14 A.D.–117 A.D.

4. During what period did the empire grow the least?
   a. 264 B.C.–201 B.C.
   b. 201 B.C.–44 B.C.
   c. 14 A.D.–117 A.D.

France, which has more miles of railroad track than any other country in Europe, operates a service of fast electric trains. The trains travel at speeds as great as 165 miles per hour (270 km per hour). The timetable below shows train service between Paris and Geneva. Note that the use of A.M. and P.M. is not necessary because the day is divided into 24 clock hours. For example, 18:30 is the same as 6:30 P.M.

Study the timetable below to answer the questions that follow. Number a paper from 1 through 8. After each number, write the answer to the question.

Paris to Geneva Read down				PARIS — GENEVA			Geneva to Paris Read up			
# 921	# 923	# 927	# 929				# 920	# 922	# 924	# 928
7:34	10:41	14:32	19:13	dep.	Paris	arr.	10:55	15:52	20:33	23:09
	12:24	16:15	20:56	dep.	Mâcon	dep.	9:10	14:07	18:46	
	12:44	16:35	21:16	dep.	Bourg	dep.	8:51	13:47	18:28	
10:11	13:29	17:20	22:01	dep.	Culoz	dep.	8:03		17:40	20:25
10:34	13:52	17:43	22:24	dep.	Bellegarde	dep.	7:37	12:35	17:13	19:58
11:04	14:23	18:14	22:55	arr.	Geneva	dep.	7:10	12:08	16:46	19:31

1. According to the schedule, how many trains are there from Paris to Geneva each day (24 hour period)? How many are there from Geneva to Paris?

2. Are the numbers of the trains going from Paris to Geneva odd or even? What kind of numbers, odd or even, do the trains from Geneva to Paris have?

3. Does train #921 stop at Mâcon? At Culoz?

4. Which train from Paris to Geneva is the fastest?

5. Which train from Geneva to Paris is the slowest?

6. If you wanted to be in Paris by noon of the day you leave Geneva, what train would you take?

7. How long does the trip from Bellegarde to Geneva take on train #921?

8. How long is the trip from Mâcon to Paris on train #920?

Reread the section titled "Using Study Skills" on page 183 and study the sample dictionary entries below. Number a paper from **1** through **7**. After each number, write the answer to the question.

Sample Entry A

mon•arch (mon' ərk) *n.* **1.** a ruler with the title of king, queen, emperor, or empress. **2.** a large orange and black butterfly.

Sample Entry B

mon•arch (mon' ərk) *n.* Latin *monarcha,* from Greek *monarchés,* a monarch, from *monarchos,* ruling alone; *monos,* alone and *archein,* to rule. **1.** the single or sole ruler of a state. **2.** the hereditary (often constitutional) head of a state; a king, queen, emperor, or empress. **3.** a person or thing that surpasses others of the same kind. **4.** a species of large, migrating butterfly (*Danaüs archippus*) of North America, having reddish-brown, black-edged wings, the larvae of which feed on milkweed.

1. Which entry is probably from an unabridged dictionary?
2. Which sample entry provides more information about the word monarch?
3. Which sample entry gives the etymology of monarch?
4. To what two languages is the word monarch traced in the etymology?
5. What does the word *monos* mean? The word *archein*? To what language do these words belong?
6. What meaning does the word monarch have in the following sentence:
The oak is the monarch of the forest.
7. How do you think the monarch butterfly got its name?

ENRICHMENT

Reading a Chart

The chart below also appears on page 252. Refer to the chart to answer the questions that follow. Number a paper from **1** through **6**. After each number, write the answer to the question.

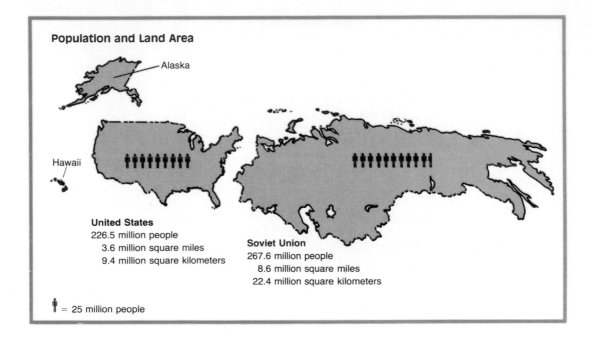

Population and Land Area

Alaska

Hawaii

United States
226.5 million people
3.6 million square miles
9.4 million square kilometers

Soviet Union
267.6 million people
8.6 million square miles
22.4 million square kilometers

♦ = 25 million people

1. What does this chart compare?
2. Which country, the United States or the Soviet Union, is larger? How much larger? Give the answer in both square miles and square kilometers.
3. About how many times larger is the Soviet Union than the United States?
4. Which country, the United States or the Soviet Union, has more people? How many more?
5. Reread the paragraph on population density on pages 191–192. Population density is found by dividing the number of people in a country or region by the number of square miles or square kilometers, in the country or region. What is the population density of the Soviet Union? Of the United States? Give the answers as both number of people per square mile and number of people per square kilometer.
6. How does the population density of the Soviet Union compare with that of the United States?

Read the following statements. Then number a paper from **1** through **14**. If the statement is true, write **T** after the number. If the statement is false, write **F** after the number. Then write the reasons for your answer in full sentences.

1. The Norse moved into the area that became Russia after the Slavic people were already established there.

2. The name *Russia* came from the term *Rus*, which was used to describe the Norse and Slavs who lived in the region.

3. During the 900s, Slav, Norse, and Tartar city-states arose throughout southern Russia.

4. The Tartar armies invaded Russia from the west.

5. The first czar of Russia was Ivan IV.

6. Peter the Great named the new capital he built Leningrad.

7. In World War I, Russia fought against Austria and Germany.

8. The reign of the czars came to an end in 1917 with the abdication of Nicholas II.

9. V.I. Lenin was the head of the republican government that was set up after the Russian Revolution.

10. The Soviet five-year plans were begun in 1928 under Stalin's regime.

11. In 1929, the Soviet government decided not to take control of any more privately-owned farms.

12. Since the revolution, the Soviet Union has expanded its borders.

13. Finland became a satellite of the Soviet Union after World War II.

14. The Soviet Union was the first country to establish a completely Communist state.

The Kremlin is where the leaders of the Soviet Union meet.

ENRICHMENT

A Climograph

Temperature and precipitation are two of the most important factors in climate. Sometimes information about temperature and precipitation is combined in a single graph called a climograph. The graph below is a climograph for Moscow. Number a paper from 1 through 9. After each number, write the answer to the question.

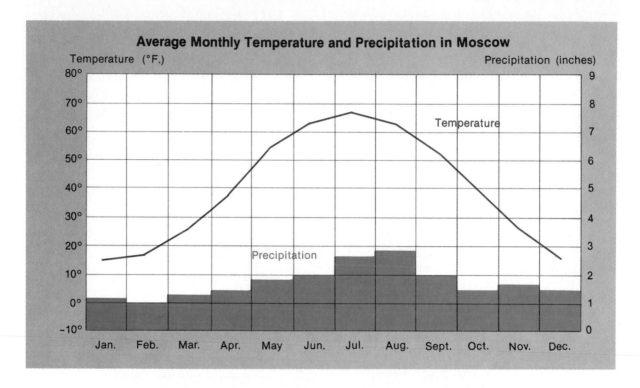

1. What kind of information is given in the graph? For what city is the information given? For what period of time?

2. On which side of the graph is the scale for temperature? Is temperature given in Fahrenheit or Celsius?

3. On which side of the graph is the scale for precipitation given? Is precipitation given in centimeters or inches?

4. This climograph is a combination of two kinds of graphs. What kind of graph is the temperature graph? What kind of graph is the precipitation graph?

5. In what month is the average temperature the highest for Moscow? The lowest?

6. What month has the highest average precipitation? The lowest?

7. Choose the words that describe summers in Moscow: short, long, mild, hot.

8. Choose the words that describe winters in Moscow: short, long, mild, cold.

9. Do you think the winter precipitation in Moscow is mainly rain or mainly snow? Explain your answer.

Learning from Graphs

Study the two graphs below, then number a paper from 1 through 9. After each number, write the answer to the question.

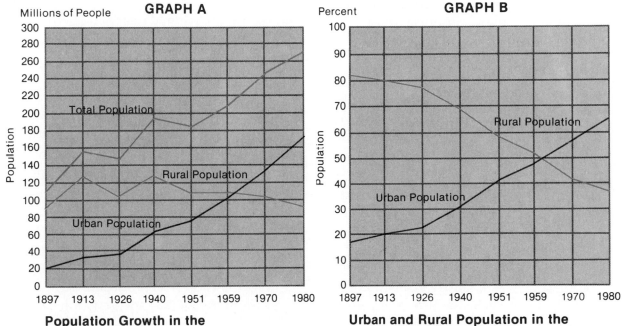

Population Growth in the Soviet Union—1897–1980

Urban and Rural Population in the Soviet Union—1897–1980

1. Both of the graphs above are line graphs. Which one—Graph A or Graph B—is a double line graph? Which is a triple line graph?

2. For what span of years do both graphs give information?

3. What do the lines on Graph A show? How are the populations given?

4. What do the lines on Graph B show? How are the populations given?

5. What was the total population of the Soviet Union in 1940? What percent was urban? What percent was rural?

6. Between what years did the urban population first become larger than the rural population?

7. The population of the Soviet Union decreased twice during the period shown on the graphs. Which graph shows this? Between what years did the declines in population take place? Can you think of any reasons for these declines? (<u>Hint</u>: Reread column 1 on page 259 and column 1 on page 261.)

8. What was the total population of the Soviet Union in 1980? How many people made up the urban population? The rural population? What percent of the population was urban? What percent was rural?

9. Which graph shows the changes in population more dramatically?

ENRICHMENT

John Bell (1691–1780) was a Scottish doctor who decided to become a traveler. He arrived in St. Petersburg, Russia, in 1714. During the next 25 years, he traveled throughout much of Asia. In 1722 he accompanied Peter the Great to Caucasia. Bell returned to Scotland in 1747 and published his *Travels* in 1763.

The following account is part of Bell's description of Siberia. Read the passage, then number a paper from **1** through **5**. After each number, write the answer to the question.

This vast extent of eastern continent is...not easy to ascertain [figure out]. Foreigners commonly are terrified at the very name of Siberia... [but] it is by no means so bad as is generally imagined. On the contrary, the country is really excellent, and abounds with all things necessary for the use of man and beast. There is no want of anything, but people to cultivate a fruitful soil, well watered by many of the noblest rivers in the world; and these stored with variety of such fine fish, as are seldom found in other countries. As to fine woods, furnished with all sorts of game and wild fowl, no country can exceed it....

Considering the extent of this country, and the many advantages it possesses, I cannot help being of opinion, that it is sufficient to contain all the nations in Europe; where they might enjoy a more comfortable life than many of them do at present. For my part, I think, that, had a person his liberty and a few friends, there are few places where he could spend life more agreeably than in some parts of Siberia.

Towards the north, indeed, the winter is long, and extremely cold. There are also many dreary wastes, and deep woods, terminated [bounded] only by great rivers, or the ocean; but these I would leave to the present inhabitants...where, free from ambition and avarice [greed], they spend their lives in peace and tranquility. I am even persuaded, that these poor people would not change their situation, and manner of life, for the finest climate, and all the riches of the east; for I have often heard them say, that God, who had placed them in this country, knew what was best for them and they were satisfied with their lot.

1. Who was John Bell? What region of Asia is he describing in the account above?

2. Was Bell favorably or unfavorably impressed with the region?

3. Name four natural resources that Bell found in the region.

4. What part of the region would Bell "leave to the present inhabitants"?

5. A *contemporary* (kən tem′ pə rer′ ē) is "a person who belongs to or lives at the same time as another or others." Bell was a contemporary of what czar?

Reading Diagrams

Read the paragraphs below and study the diagrams. Number a paper from **1** through **5**. After each number, write the answer to the question.

Dunes

Dunes are mounds or ridges of sand deposited by the wind. They develop where sand-carrying winds are slowed down by some obstacle. Once started, a dune itself becomes an obstacle and continues to grow.

Dunes not held in place by vegetation tend to move in the direction of the prevailing wind, as shown at right.

How Dunes Move

Dunes vary greatly in shape and size. Four types of dunes are shown below. They range from a few feet in height and length to more than 700 feet in height and several miles in length. Regardless of type, most dunes are similar in cross-section. The windward side has a more gentle slope than the leeward side (see page 28).

Barchan (bär kan′) Dune

Forms in open areas of little relief, little vegetation, and limited sand supply
Maximum height: 100 feet (30 meters)
Maximum width: 1,000 feet (300 meters)

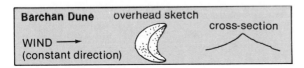

Longitudinal, or Seif (sīf) Dune

Forms in areas where small amounts of sand are available.
Maximum height: 600 feet (180 meters)
Maximum length: 60 miles (95 kilometers)

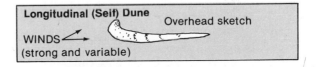

Transverse Dune

Forms in areas of little vegetation and abundant sand

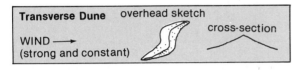

Parabolic (par′ ə bol′ ik) Dune

Forms in areas with some vegetation
Maximum height: 100 feet (30 meters)

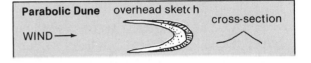

1. What agent is responsible for the creation of dunes?
2. Which side of a dune is steeper?
3. Which of the dune types shown has the greatest maximum height?
4. How are barchan and parabolic dunes alike? How are they different?
5. Which kind of dune forms in areas of strong winds, little vegetation, and abundant sand?

ENRICHMENT

About one-fifth of the world's population is Muslim. The map below shows the percentages of Muslims living in different countries. None of the countries you are studying in this unit is labeled on the map. Other countries where more than 10 percent of the population is Muslim are labeled.

Refer to the map below to answer the questions that follow. You may also need to refer to the maps on pages 76–77 and 289. Number a paper from 1 through 6. After each number, write the answer to the question.

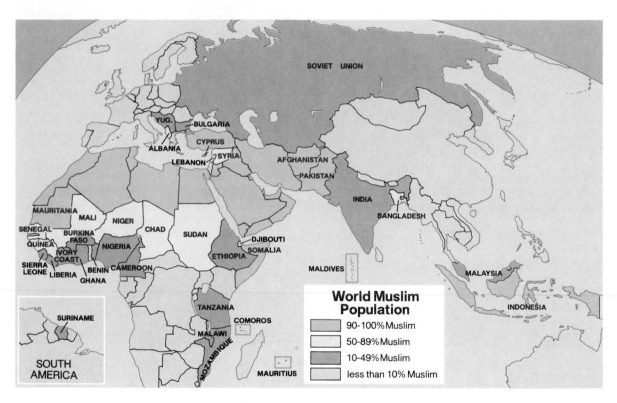

World Muslim Population

- 90-100% Muslim
- 50-89% Muslim
- 10-49% Muslim
- less than 10% Muslim

1. What does this color symbol ☐ represent on the map?

2. Only three countries you are studying in this unit have Muslim populations of less than 90 percent. What countries are they? What percent is the Muslim population of each?

3. In what hemisphere are all the countries where Islam is the dominant religion? In what continents are they?

4. How many countries in Europe have Muslim populations that are greater than 50 percent?

5. In what country in the Western Hemisphere is more than 10 percent of the population Muslim? In what continent is this country?

6. Compare the map on this page with the map on page 297. What similarity do you notice?

Read each group of words below. Then on a piece of paper, write a paragraph of four or five sentences using each group of words. Before you begin, think what the main idea of each paragraph will be. Remember that each sentence in the paragraph should be related to the main idea. Number each paragraph and underline each word from the list the first time you use it in the paragraph.

1.

Islam	Muslim	Mohammed
Koran	Moors	caliph

2.

Nasser	Aswan	benefits
irrigation	silt	electricity

3.

Dardanelles	Marmara	Straits
Constantinople	Black Sea	Mediterranean

4.

Saudi Arabia	oil	concession
royalty	government	income

ENRICHMENT

Using an Encyclopedia Index

Read the sample from an encyclopedia index as well as the explanation below. Refer to these to answer the questions that follow. Number a paper from 1 through 5. After each number, write the answer to the question.

Like other indexes, this encyclopedia index lists main topics and subtopics in alphabetical order. Because an encyclopedia includes many volumes, the index uses different kinds of type to help you find the information you want. Entries for a separate article in the encyclopedia appear in capital boldface letters (**ARABIA**). Entries for subjects having no separate article appear in boldface capitals and small letters (**Arabian Literature**). Subheadings refer to related material. They are set in lightface letters and are always indented (Arab). There are two kinds of cross references. *See* references refer to the alternative or synonymous heading under which the subject is treated. *See also* references refer to headings under which additional or related information can be found.

The volume is shown in boldface numerals and the page in regular numerals. The numerals 3-118, for example, refer to volume 3, page 118.

ARABIA 1–503
  Arab **1**–501
  Oman **13**–422
  petroleum **1**–504
  see also **Middle East;**
    and names of countries

ARABIAN DESERT, Egypt 1–506
Arabian Literature 12–406:
  see also **Islamic law; Koran**

ARABIAN NIGHTS, THE 1–508
  Aladdin **1**–222
  Burton, Sir R.F. **3**–419
  Sinbad **16**–498
Arabian Peninsula: *see* **Arabia**

ARABIAN SEA 1–508

ARABIC (lang.) 1–508, 145, 146;
  16–348
Arabic art & architecture: *see*
  Islamic art & architecture

ARABIC LITERATURE 1–509
Arabic numerals: *see* **Numeral**
Arab-Israeli War: *see* **Israel-Arab War**

1. How many entries shown in the sample have separate articles in the encyclopedia? What are the headings of the first two entries that have separate articles?

2. In what volume and on what page would you find information about Arabian literature? Under what other entries could you look to find additional or related information?

3. In what volume and on what page would you find an article on *The Arabian Nights*?

4. Under what entry would you look to find the volume and page where there is information on Arabic numerals?

5. Is there a separate encyclopedia article entitled "Arabian Literature"? How do you know?

Number a paper from **1** through **11**. After each number, write the letter of the correct answer. You may need to refer to pages 339-347 and to the map on page 333.

1. _____ is *not* a country of West Africa.
   a. Togo
   b. Mauritania
   c. Mali
   d. Malawi

2. _____ is a landlocked country.
   a. Guinea-Bissau
   b. Sierra Leone
   c. Burkina Faso
   d. Ivory Coast

3. The Niger River does *not* flow through _____.
   a. Guinea
   b. Burkina Faso
   c. Mali
   d. Niger

4. _____ important climate zones cross West Africa.
   a. Two
   b. Three
   c. Four
   d. Five

5. The climate of Cape Verde is much like that of _____.
   a. the desert
   b. the Sahel
   c. the rain forest
   d. the savana

6. _____ conquered the Kingdom of Ghana and became the first ruler of the Mali Empire.
   a. Askia
   b. Sonni Ali
   c. Mansa Musa
   d. Sundiata

7. Timbuktu was a famous and important city of the Kingdom of _____.
   a. Ghana
   b. Mali
   c. Songhai
   d. Morocco

8. Before the late 1800s, all of the following except _____ made much of Africa seem unfavorable for settlement by Europeans.
   a. malaria
   b. heat
   c. humidity
   d. lack of resources

9. The first independent country in West Africa was founded in _____.
   a. 1975
   b. 1967
   c. 1957
   d. 1847

10. An important city in the Sahel is _____.
    a. Dakar
    b. Lagos
    c. Abdijan
    d. Ibadan

11. One cause of the rapid growth rate of many West African coastal cities is _____.
    a. low birth rates
    b. high death rates
    c. migration from inland villages
    d. migration to inland villages

ENRICHMENT

587

Read the paragraphs and study the map below. Then number a paper from 1 through 6. After each number, write the answer to the question.

Alexandrine Tinné

Alexandrine Tinné (tēn nā′) (1839–1869) was a Dutch heiress who became one of the first women to explore Africa. Her first expedition led her up the Nile into the Sudd. Here she followed the shallow canal of the Bahr el Ghazal, a Nile tributary. Her party went by barge as far as possible, then traveled overland to the Jur and Kosango rivers. The area had been only partly explored up to this time. The expedition returned with much valuable information about the plants, animals, climate, and geology. A new species of plant collected on the trip was named in Tinné's honor. It was called *Cucumis tinneanus*.

Later, Alexandrine Tinné made her base in Cairo and traveled in Algeria and Tunisia. In Tripoli, she joined a caravan setting out for Lake Chad. South of Marzūg, she decided to make a side trip to the Oasis of Ghat. She was killed by her Tuareg guides at a camp in the Sahara.

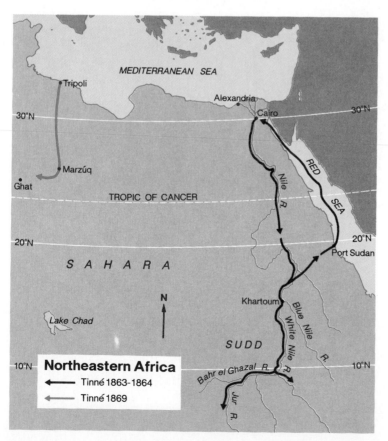

1. Who was Alexandrine Tinné? For what is she known?

2. During what year(s) did she make an expedition to the Bahr el Ghazal? Did the expedition reach the equator? Describe her return route on this expedition.

3. Through what modern-day countries did the Bahr el Ghazal expedition travel? (You may need to refer to the map on page 333.)

4. When did Tinné set out for Lake Chad? From what city did she start?

5. Why did Tinné turn west south of Marzūg? What happened to her before she reached Ghat?

6. How old was Tinné when she died?

Copy and complete the chart that has been started for you below. The chart tells about South Africa's production of certain resources. Information to complete the chart can be found in the tables on pages 604–606.

When you have completed your chart, number a paper from **1** through **6**. After each number, write the answer to the question.

Resource	World Rank	Amount	Standard Unit of Measure	Amount	Metric Unit of Measure
Corn	tenth	9,083,000	short tons	8,240,000	metric tons

1. What is a good title for this chart?
2. How many resources are included in the reference tables on pages 604–606? For how many of these resources does South Africa rank among the top ten producers?
3. For what resource listed in the chart does South Africa lead the world in production?
4. How does South Africa rank in the world production of uranium?

5. About how many times more tons of iron does South Africa produce than tons of uranium?
6. You have read that South Africa is rich in natural resources. It produces large quantities of minerals that are not included in your chart. List the mineral resources mentioned on page 367 that are *not* included in the chart.

ENRICHMENT

Fact and Opinion

A **fact** is something that is true or something that actually happened. An **opinion** is what someone believes to be true or how someone feels about something. A fact can be proven true; an opinion cannot.

Number a paper from **1** through **20**. After each number, write **F** if the statement is a fact. Write **O** if the statement is an opinion. You may want to refer to pages 364–373.

1. Madagascar, the Comoros, and Mauritius should not be considered part of Southern Africa.

2. South Africa is the southernmost country of Africa.

3. Afrikaans is more difficult to learn than English.

4. Most of South Africa lies south of the Tropic of Capricorn.

5. The king of Portugal was angry that Diaz named the tip of Africa the Cape of Storms.

6. The Boers chose not to live under British rule in Natal.

7. The war between the Boers and the British was more serious than the war between the Boers and the Zulus.

8. The Afrikaners took control of the government of South Africa in 1948.

9. Apartheid is a necessary policy in South Africa.

10. No one is happy about the policy of apartheid.

11. The government of South Africa set up homelands, or reserves, for the blacks.

12. The homelands should have self-government.

13. The people of Swaziland, Lesotho, and Botswana who work in South Africa's mines like their jobs.

14. South Africa is the world's largest producer of gold.

15. Lesotho is sometimes called the "Switzerland of Africa."

16. South Africa should give up its claims to Namibia and transfer power to the people of the territory.

17. Many nations support Namibia's independence movement.

18. The Zimbabwe kingdom was the greatest empire of Africa.

19. Southern Rhodesia changed its name to Zimbabwe to preserve the memory of a famous early African kingdom.

20. The island of Mayotte decided to retain its ties with France when the rest of the Comoro Islands became independent in 1975.

Finding the Main Idea

The three paragraphs below are from pages 390–391. Read each paragraph to find the main idea. After you have read the paragraphs, answer the questions. Number a paper from 1 through 4. After each number, write the letter of the correct answer.

When World War II broke out, Britain asked for India's help and promised independence after the war. Many Indian soldiers fought loyally in the British-Indian armies. After the war, Great Britain offered India independence as soon as a form of government could be agreed upon. This was difficult because of disagreements between the Muslims and the Hindus. The final decision was to partition, or divide, the country into the mainly Muslim nation of Pakistan and the mainly Hindu nation of India. In 1947, Britain granted independence to both countries.

As a result of the partition, millions of Muslims in India fled to Pakistan, and millions of Hindus fled from Pakistan to India.

Pakistan was divided into two parts at the time of the partition. West Pakistan was separated from East Pakistan by nearly 1,000 miles (1,600 km). The political power was in West Pakistan, but most of the people lived in East Pakistan. The people in the two countries differed in languages and traditions. In 1971, a civil war resulted in the establishment of two separate and independent countries. West Pakistan became Pakistan, and East Pakistan became Bangladesh.

1. The main idea of Paragraph 1 is:
   a. Britain asked for India's help in World War II.
   b. Many Indian soldiers fought loyally in World War II.
   c. Britain granted independence to Pakistan and India in 1947.

2. The main idea of Paragraph 2 is:
   a. Millions of Muslims fled from India to Pakistan.
   b. Millions of Hindus fled from Pakistan to India.
   c. The partition of India led to large-scale movements of Muslims and Hindus.

3. The main idea of Paragraph 3 is:
   a. Important differences between the two parts of Pakistan led to the establishment of two independent countries—Pakistan and Bangladesh.
   b. The political power of Pakistan was in West Pakistan.
   c. Nearly 1,000 miles separated East Pakistan from West Pakistan.

4. Which of the following phrases best expresses the main idea of all three paragraphs?
   a. How the British ruled India
   b. How the independent countries of India, Pakistan, and Bangladesh were established
   c. How the Hindus and Muslims settled their differences

ENRICHMENT

Two Maps of Singapore

To follow page 412

Reread the section ''Singapore'' on page 412 and study the maps below. Then answer the questions on page 593. Number a paper from **1** through **12**. After each number, write the letter of the best answer.

Map A

Map B

1. Singapore is _____.
   a. a city
   b. an island
   c. a country
   d. all three of the above

2. The _____ separates Singapore from Malaysia.
   a. Strait of Malacca
   b. Johore Strait
   c. Singapore Strait
   d. South China Sea

3. The symbol --- is used to show _____ boundary.
   a. an international
   b. a state
   c. a city
   d. a provincial

4. _____ airports or airfields are shown on Map B.
   a. Three
   b. Four
   c. Five
   d. Six

5. The Johore Strait is crossed by _____ between Johor Baharu and Woodlands.
   a. a railroad
   b. a bridge
   c. a railroad and a bridge
   d. an airport

6. Singapore Island is about _____ kilometers long from east to west.
   a. 25
   b. 30
   c. 35
   d. 40

7. An inch on Map A represents _____ an inch on Map B.
   a. the same distance as
   b. a greater distance than
   c. a smaller distance than

8. From Johor Baharu to the railroad station in the City of Singapore is about _____ miles by rail.
   a. 10
   b. 15
   c. 20
   d. 25

9. Singapore's oil refineries are in the _____.
   a. north
   b. east
   c. south
   d. west

10. The symbol ■ stands for _____.
    a. a shipyard
    b. an oil refinery
    c. a railroad station
    d. a point of interest

11. The City of Singapore occupies about _____ percent of Singapore Island.
    a. 25
    b. 50
    c. 75
    d. 100

12. Map B does *not* show a _____ within the city limits of Singapore.
    a. museum
    b. university
    c. war memorial
    d. stadium

ENRICHMENT

Reviewing the Text

To follow page 435

Number a paper from **1** through **12**. After each number, write the word or group of words that correctly completes each statement. You may wish to reread pages 430–435.

1. The population of Japan is about (one-fourth, one-half) that of the United States.

2. (Hokkaido, Honshu) is the largest island of Japan.

3. In the sixth and seventh centuries, Japan's culture was strongly influenced by the (Chinese, Portuguese).

4. The first Europeans to reach Japan were the (Dutch, Portuguese).

5. (Mutsuhito, Commodore Matthew Perry) was largely responsible for opening up trade between Japan and the United States.

6. The Japanese attack on (Korea, Pearl Harbor) brought the United States into World War II.

7. Most of Japan's population is (urban, rural).

8. (Silk, Tobacco) is one of Japan's important industries.

9. Farming in Japan is (extensive, intensive).

10. Japan has (few, many) mineral resources of its own.

11. Japan leads the world in the production of (rice, automobiles).

12. Most of the people in Japan live in (Tokyo, Honshu).

Read the paragraphs below, then number a paper from **1** through **5**. After each number, write the answer to the question.

James Cook (1728–1779) was an English explorer and navigator (pages 449 and 453). In his three great voyages to the Pacific (map, page 453), Cook contributed more to the geographical knowledge of the Southern Hemisphere than anyone before him. He traveled greater distances and discovered more new lands than any other explorer of his time. He has been called the first of the scientific navigators. The scientists and artists on board his ships made contributions to many fields of knowledge. Cook himself kept a journal in which he recorded his observations and adventures. Two passages from his journals appear below. The first was written in July 1770 on the Endeavour River in Australia. In the second passage, Cook describes how in August 1770 he and his crew narrowly missed being dashed to death on the Great Barrier Reef. They were saved by a slight breeze that moved their ship.

Passage 1:
One of the men saw an animal. It was of a Mouse Colour very slender and swift of foot. I saw this morning one of the Animals. It was the full size of a grey hound and shaped like one, with a long tail which it carried like a grey hound. I should have taken it for a wild dog, but for its walking or running in which it jumped like a Hare or a dear. Excepting the head and ears which was something like a Hare's, it bears no sort of resemblance to any European Animal I ever saw . . . we din'd of the animal & thought it excellent.

Passage 2:
Such are the vicissitudes [changes in situations or conditions] attending this kind of service and must always attend an unknown navigation. Was it not for the pleasure which naturally results to a man from being the first discoverer, this service [exploration] would be *insupportable.*

1. During which of Cook's three voyages to the Pacific were the above passages written? Where was Cook when he wrote the passages? Where is the Great Barrier Reef?

2. In what year did Cook write these passages? In what ways are they unlike modern writing?

3. What animal is Cook describing in the first passage?

4. *Insupportable* means:
   a. unbearable; b. desirable; c. wrong.

5. In the second passage, Cook expresses:
   a. his joy at being saved; b. disappointment in his discoveries; c. the satisfaction and pleasure of exploration.

ENRICHMENT

Match each person or place in Column I with the correct description in Column II. Number a paper from **1** through **21**. After each number, write the letter of the correct answer.

Column I

1. Tasman Sea

2. William Jansz

3. Aborigines

4. Cook Strait

5. Great Dividing Range

6. Botany Bay

7. Ferdinand Magellan

8. Tasmania

9. Abel Tasman

10. Canberra

11. Bass Strait

12. William Hobson

13. Southern Alps

14. Maoris

15. Northern Territory

16. Murray-Darling Plain

17. Wellington

18. Matthew Flinders

19. Sydney

20. Auckland

21. Captain James Cook

Column II

a. explorer who named New Holland, Van Dieman's Land, and New Zealand

b. mountain range in New Zealand

c. people living in New Zealand when the first Europeans arrived

d. separates Australia from New Zealand

e. first European to land in Australia

f. separates Tasmania from the rest of Australia

g. Australia's largest city

h. largest area of artesian wells in the world

i. claimed Australia for England

j. part of Australia that is not a state

k. signer of the Treaty of Waitangi for Great Britain

l. capital of Australia

m. people living in Australia when the first Europeans arrived

n. first European to cross the Pacific Ocean

o. separates South Island from North Island

p. proved that Australia was a single landmass

q. highlands in Australia

r. largest city in New Zealand

s. capital of New Zealand

t. where Cook first landed in Australia and where first English colony was founded

u. island state of Australia

Washington's Farewell Address

To follow page 485

Read the paragraphs below, then number a paper from **1** through **7**. After each number, write the answer to the question.

George Washington served as President of the United States for two terms, from 1789 to 1797. Although he was strongly urged to do so, he refused to run for a third term. In September 1796, Washington gave his *Farewell Address* to his country.

Dear Friends and Fellow Citizens:

As a new election year draws near, I wish to inform you that I will not run again . . . . This seems like a good time, therefore, to share with you some of my concerns for your safety as a nation . . . . The best role for us to follow in dealing with other nations is to develop good trade relations with them, but to have as few dealings with these governments as possible. The ties with those governments that we already have made should be carried out in good faith. But we should not do more than this. Europe has its own interests, and they have little or no relation to ours. As a result, Europe will often be involved in quarrels that have nothing to do with us. Therefore, it would be unwise for us to become involved in Europe's affairs by establishing artificial ties with the nations there . . . . The wisest policy for us is to steer clear of permanent alliances with any foreign country. Where we already have established certain ties, we should honor them. However, it would be unwise to extend such ties with other countries . . . .

George Washington
September 19, 1796

---

1. When did Washington deliver his *Farewell Address?*
2. How many terms did Washington serve as President? How long is a presidential term?
3. What is the first thing Washington announced in his address?
4. The main idea of Washington's advice is: a. the United States should develop good trade relations with other nations; b. the United States should remain neutral in foreign affairs; c. the United States should honor established ties with other nations.
5. What reasons did Washington give to support his advice?
6. What policy that you have read about in Unit 11 sums up Washington's views and advice?
7. Why do you think other American presidents have been unable to follow Washington's advice?

ENRICHMENT

Since its beginning, the United States has had many different flags. Some of them are shown below. Look at the flags and read the captions. Then number a paper from 1 through 7. After each number, write the answer to the question.

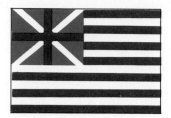

The first national flag, called the Continental Colors, was used from 1775 to 1777. The British Union Jack appeared in the upper left corner. The 13 stripes symbolized the 13 colonies in defense of their liberties.

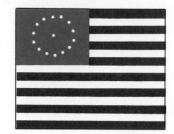

In 1795, Congress decided to add a star and a stripe for each new state. The design varied in arrangement of stars and the order of stripes.

Because of the growing number of states Congress voted in 1818 to add only a star for each new state. The number of stripes would remain at 13.

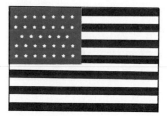

During the Civil War the flag had 34 stars for 34 states, including the southern states that had seceded.

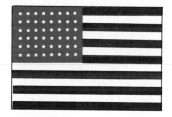

From 1912 until 1959, the flag had 48 stars.

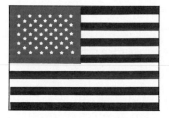

In 1959 and again in 1960, a star was added to the flag. This is the flag we use today.

1. What three colors are used in all the flags above?

2. What was the first national flag called?

3. What decision did Congress make about the flag in 1795? In 1818?

4. How do you think the flag would look today if Congress had not changed its decision of 1795?

5. What have the stripes of the flag stood for since 1818? The stars?

6. During the Civil War, the stars represented what two kinds of states?

7. The flag in the middle of the bottom row served as the nation's emblem longer than any other flag. How many years was this?

Number a paper from **1** through **16**. After each number, write the word or words in parentheses that correctly complete each sentence.

1. People inhabit (all, only part) of the biosphere.

2. Places where large areas of land support few people are called areas of (intensive, extensive) land use.

3. The use of land for commercial activities has been (increased, decreased) by modern technology.

4. More of the world's land is used for (manufacturing, agriculture) than for any other purpose.

5. Shifting cultivation and nomadic herding are part of (commercial, subsistence) agriculture.

6. Agriculture in the United States and western Europe is mainly (subsistence, commercial).

7. The distribution of minerals throughout the world is related to (climate, rock types).

8. (All, Only part of) the earth's crust is made up of minerals; (all, only some) minerals are natural resources.

9. Preservation of land for enjoyment has become (more, less) important with growing economic development.

10. Population density can be found by dividing (the amount of land in a given area by the number of people living there, the number of people in a given area by the amount of land).

11. The increase in the rate of population growth is due to improved health practices and (better weather conditions, industrialization).

12. Demographers estimate that the world population will be (two, three) times as great in 2000 as it was in 1970.

13. A country with a birth rate of 60 and a death rate of 10 has a rate of natural increase of (2, 5) percent.

14. The population growth rate for a country is not affected by (natural increase, internal migration).

15. A country with a pyramid-shaped population profile has a (high, low) birth rate and a (high, low) death rate; a pyramid-shaped profile indicates (an industrialized, a developing) country.

16. Developing countries usually have a (lower, higher) per capita GNP than industrialized countries.

ENRICHMENT

Global View

Refer to the global view and the distance chart to answer the questions below. Number a paper from 1 through 5. After each number, write the answer to the question.

The global view on the left helps you understand the true relationships of different places on the earth. The lines show Great Circle routes between some of the cities on the chart. Great Circle routes are the shortest and most direct routes along the curved surface of the earth.

Great Circle Distances Between Cities Shown on Global View

	Calcutta	Chicago	Dakar	Honolulu	Istanbul	London	Moscow	San Francisco	Tokyo	Washington, D.C.
Calcutta	•	7980	6799	7047	3638	4947	3321	7814	3194	8084
Chicago	7980	•	4530	4250	5477	3950	4974	1858	6299	597
Dakar	6799	4530	•	8777	3314	2719	4049	6388	8648	3957
Honolulu	7047	4250	8777	•	8109	7228	7037	2393	3853	4519
Istanbul	3638	5477	3314	8109	•	1552	1091	6703	5560	5215
London	4947	3950	2719	7228	1552	•	1555	5357	5940	3663
Moscow	3321	4974	4049	7037	1091	1555	•	5871	4647	4858
San Francisco	7814	1858	6388	2393	6703	5357	5871	•	5135	2442
Tokyo	3194	6299	8648	3853	5560	5940	4647	5135	•	6772
Washington, D.C.	8084	597	3957	4519	5215	3663	4858	2442	6772	•

Miles

1. What is the Great Circle route distance between Calcutta and Chicago? Between London and Dakar?

2. Which is greater, the Great Circle route distance between Washington, D.C., and London or the Great Circle route distance between Washington D.C., and Dakar? How much greater?

3. What city lies on the Great Circle route between Honolulu and Chicago?

4. Through what large island does the Great Circle route pass between Chicago and Moscow?

5. How much closer is London to Washington, D.C., than London is to Chicago by the Great Circle route?

Smallpox and the World Health Organization

To follow page 530

Read the paragraph below and study the maps. Then number a paper from 1 through 5. After each number, write the answer to the question.

Countries with Smallpox in 1967

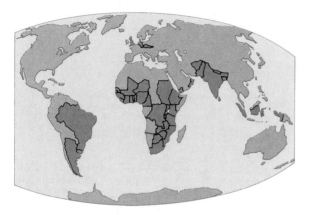

Countries with Smallpox in 1972

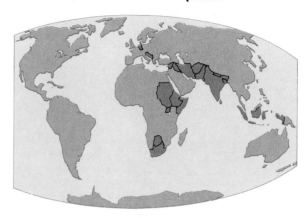

Countries with Smallpox in 1975

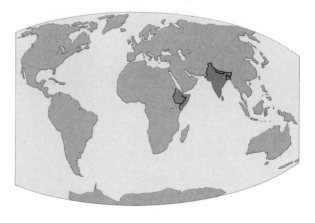

The World Health Organization (WHO) is an agency of the United Nations that works to improve health conditions throughout the world. In 1967 WHO began a program to eradicate (i rad′ ə kāt′), or wipe out, smallpox. Smallpox was a deadly disease that had been present in the world since ancient times. It was spread throughout Europe by returning Crusaders. Explorers and colonists introduced it to the Western Hemisphere. The maps show the success of WHO in eradicating smallpox. The last known naturally occurring case was reported in 1977.

1. What is WHO and what is its purpose?

2. In what continents were there cases of smallpox in 1967? What continents shown had no cases of smallpox?

3. From what continent was smallpox eradicated between 1967 and 1972?

4. In what countries did smallpox still exist in 1975? (You may need to refer to the map on page 77.)

5. How many years did it take WHO to stamp out smallpox? How successful do you think the WHO program was?

ENRICHMENT

Reference Tables

States of the United States

State	Capital	Largest city	Area		Population	Principal products
			Square miles	Square kilometers		
Alabama	Montgomery	Birmingham	50,708	131,334	3,890,100	Metals, paper products, coal, livestock
Alaska	Juneau	Anchorage	566,432	1,467,059	400,500	Oil, minerals, fish, wood products
Arizona	Phoenix	Phoenix	113,417	293,750	2,717,900	Machinery, electronics equipment, copper, livestock
Arkansas	Little Rock	Little Rock	51,945	134,538	2,285,500	Food products, soybeans, oil, bauxite, lumber
California	Sacramento	Los Angeles	156,361	404,975	23,668,600	Machinery, oil, food products
Colorado	Denver	Denver	103,766	268,754	2,888,800	Coal, oil, livestock, wheat, food products
Connecticut	Hartford	Bridgeport	4,862	12,593	3,107,600	Transportation equipment, machinery, metal products
Delaware	Dover	Wilmington	1,982	5,133	595,200	Chemicals, food products, livestock
Florida	Tallahassee	Jacksonville	54,090	140,093	9,740,000	Fruit, food products, cattle, phosphate, fish
Georgia	Atlanta	Atlanta	58,073	150,409	5,464,300	Textiles, transportation equipment, livestock, peanuts
Hawaii	Honolulu	Honolulu	6,425	16,641	965,000	Food products, sugarcane, pineapples, cattle
Idaho	Boise	Boise	82,677	214,133	943,900	Lumber, potatoes, minerals, chemicals
Illinois	Springfield	Chicago	56,400	146,076	11,418,500	Machinery, coal, corn, hogs, soybeans
Indiana	Indianapolis	Indianapolis	36,097	93,491	5,490,200	Electronics equipment, corn, coal, steel, soybeans
Iowa	Des Moines	Des Moines	55,491	144,887	2,913,400	Machinery, hogs, soybeans, corn, food products
Kansas	Topeka	Wichita	81,787	211,828	2,363,200	Wheat, cattle, transportation equipment, oil, coal
Kentucky	Frankfort	Louisville	39,650	102,694	3,661,400	Machinery, coal, tobacco, cattle
Louisiana	Baton Rouge	New Orleans	44,930	116,369	4,204,000	Chemicals, oil, gas, soybeans, sugarcane
Maine	Augusta	Portland	30,920	80,083	1,124,700	Paper products, wood, fish, potatoes
Maryland	Annapolis	Baltimore	9,891	25,618	4,216,400	Food products, electronics equipment, metals, dairy products, fish
Massachusetts	Boston	Boston	7,826	20,269	5,737,000	Machinery, electronics equipment, fish
Michigan	Lansing	Detroit	56,817	147,156	9,258,300	Transportation equipment, dairy products
Minnesota	St. Paul	Minneapolis	79,289	205,359	4,077,100	Machinery, food products, dairy products, oats, iron
Mississippi	Jackson	Jackson	47,296	122,497	2,520,600	Transportation equipment, soybeans, cotton, cattle, wood products, oil
Missouri	Jefferson City	St. Louis	68,995	178,697	4,917,400	Transportation equipment, food products, livestock, soybeans, corn, lead, coal
Montana	Helena	Billings	145,587	377,070	786,700	Wheat, cattle, lumber, coal, petroleum
Nebraska	Lincoln	Omaha	76,483	198,091	1,570,000	Livestock, corn, meat products, wheat
Nevada	Carson City	Las Vegas	109,889	284,613	799,200	Copper, gold, livestock
New Hampshire	Concord	Manchester	9,027	23,380	920,600	Electronics equipment, machinery, scientific instruments, dairy products
New Jersey	Trenton	Newark	7,521	19,479	7,364,200	Chemicals, food products, electronics equipment
New Mexico	Santa Fe	Albuquerque	121,412	314,457	1,300,000	Gas, oil, coal, uranium, livestock
New York	Albany	New York	47,831	123,882	17,557,288	Printed material, photo equipment, machinery, dairy products
North Carolina	Raleigh	Charlotte	48,798	126,387	5,874,400	Textiles, tobacco, chemicals, paper, corn
North Dakota	Bismarck	Fargo	69,273	179,417	652,700	Wheat, livestock, barley, coal, oil, flax
Ohio	Columbus	Cleveland	40,975	106,125	10,797,419	Transportation equipment, rubber products, machinery, metals, soybeans, coal
Oklahoma	Oklahoma City	Oklahoma City	68,782	178,145	3,025,300	Oil, gas, livestock, wheat, machinery
Oregon	Salem	Portland	96,184	249,117	2,632,700	Lumber, food products, wheat
Pennsylvania	Harrisburg	Philadelphia	44,966	116,462	11,866,700	Steel, machinery, food products, coal, stone
Rhode Island	Providence	Providence	1,049	2,717	947,200	Jewelry, metal products, chemicals
South Carolina	Columbia	Columbia	30,225	78,283	3,119,200	Textiles, tobacco, chemicals, machinery
South Dakota	Pierre	Sioux Falls	75,955	196,723	690,200	Wheat, corn, livestock, gold
Tennessee	Nashville	Memphis	41,328	107,040	4,590,800	Chemicals, food products, livestock, soybeans, coal
Texas	Austin	Houston	262,134	678,927	14,228,400	Chemicals, oil, gas, cattle, cotton, wheat
Utah	Salt Lake City	Salt Lake City	82,096	212,629	1,461,000	Metal products, livestock, oil, copper, coal
Vermont	Montpelier	Burlington	9,276	24,025	511,500	Electronics equipment, dairy products, machinery
Virginia	Richmond	Norfolk	39,780	103,030	5,346,300	Coal, chemicals, tobacco, cattle
Washington	Olympia	Seattle	66,570	172,416	4,130,200	Transportation equipment, food products, wood products, wheat

States of the United States (continued)

State	Capital	Largest city	Area — Square miles	Area — Square kilometers	Population	Principal products
West Virginia	Charleston	Charleston	24,070	62,341	1,949,600	Coal, chemicals, metals, cattle
Wisconsin	Madison	Milwaukee	54,464	141,062	4,705,300	Machinery, dairy products, paper products
Wyoming	Cheyenne	Casper	97,203	251,756	470,800	Oil, coal, livestock, uranium

Provinces and Territories of Canada

Province	Capital	Largest city	Area — Square miles	Area — Square kilometers	Population	Principal products
Alberta	Edmonton	Edmonton	255,200	660,968	2,135,900	Oil, gas, coal, cattle, food products
British Columbia	Victoria	Vancouver	366,255	948,600	2,687,000	Wood, paper products, minerals, fish
Manitoba	Winnipeg	Winnipeg	251,000	650,090	1,027,000	Minerals, food products, wheat, cattle
New Brunswick	Fredericton	St. John	27,633	71,569	709,100	Paper, wood products, minerals, potatoes, livestock
Newfoundland	St. John's	St. John's	156,185	404,519	583,600	Pulp and paper, iron, fish
Nova Scotia	Halifax	Halifax	20,743	53,724	858,100	Food products, paper, minerals, fish
Ontario	Toronto	Toronto	412,582	1,068,587	8,600,500	Automobiles, minerals, livestock, lumber
Prince Edward Island	Charlottetown	Charlottetown	2,184	5,656	124,100	Potatoes, livestock, fish
Quebec	Quebec	Montreal	6,301,200	16,320,108	6,325,200	Food products, paper products, clothing, dairy products, asbestos, iron
Saskatchewan	Regina	Regina	251,700	651,903	975,700	Wheat, potash, oil, cattle

Territory

Northwest Territories	Yellowknife	Yellowknife	1,304,903	3,379,699	42,800	Zinc, lead, gas, oil
Yukon Territory	Whitehorse	Whitehorse	207,000	536,130	21,500	Zinc, lead, silver

Republics of the Soviet Union

Republic	Capital and largest city	Area — Square miles	Area — Square kilometers	Population	Principal products
Armenia	Erevan	11,506	29,801	3,031,000	Chemicals, minerals, cotton, fruit
Azerbaijan	Baku	33,475	86,700	6,028,000	Oil, iron, cotton, potatoes, livestock
Byelorussia	Minsk	80,154	207,599	9,559,000	Livestock, machinery, potatoes, wood, peat
Estonia	Tallinn	17,413	45,100	1,466,000	Oil, farm products, wood products, fish
Georgia	Tbilisi	26,872	69,598	5,016,000	Fruit, tea, manganese, coal, steel
Kazakhstan	Alma-Ata	1,064,092	2,755,998	14,685,000	Wheat, coal, copper, livestock, cotton
Kirghizia	Frunze	76,641	198,500	3,529,000	Livestock, wheat, sugar, cotton
Latvia	Riga	24,595	63,701	2,521,000	Electronics equipment, machinery, steel, farm products
Lithuania	Vilnius	25,174	65,201	3,399,000	Electronics equipment, machinery, metals, farm products
Moldavia	Kishinev	13,012	33,701	3,948,000	Food products, textiles, shoes, wine, tobacco
Russia	Moscow	6,593,391	17,076,882	137,552,000	Transportation equipment, iron, coal, oil, metals
Tadzhikistan	Dushanbe	55,019	142,499	3,801,000	Livestock, fruit, cotton, coal, minerals
Turkmenistan	Ashkhabad	188,417	488,000	2,759,000	Cotton, wool, corn, minerals, fruit
Ukraine	Kiev	232,089	601,111	49,757,000	Coal, iron ore, steel, manganese, grains, sugar beets
Uzbekistan	Tashkent	158,069	409,399	15,391,000	Cotton, livestock, fruit, textiles, leather goods, minerals

World Production of Selected Resources

Wheat

	Short tons	Metric tons
Soviet Union	99,317,000	90,100,000
China	66,141,000	60,003,000
United States	64,252,000	58,289,000
India	38,561,000	34,982,000
France	21,377,000	19,393,000
Canada	19,561,000	17,746,000
Turkey	19,435,000	17,631,000
Australia	17,747,000	16,100,000
Pakistan	10,961,000	9,944,000
Italy	10,075,000	9,140,000
All other countries	101,577,000	92,150,000
World total	469,004,000	425,478,000

Corn

	Short tons	Metric tons
United States	217,382,000	197,208,000
China	44,775,000	40,620,000
Brazil	17,977,000	16,309,000
Romania	13,647,000	12,380,000
France	11,346,000	10,293,000
Yugoslavia	11,113,000	10,082,000
Mexico	10,202,000	9,255,000
Argentina	9,590,000	8,700,000
Soviet Union	9,259,000	8,400,000
South Africa	9,083,000	8,240,000
All other countries	80,186,000	72,744,000
World total	434,560,000	394,231,000

Rice

	Short tons	Metric tons
China	158,070,000	143,400,000
India	76,059,000	69,000,000
Indonesia	29,046,000	26,350,000
Bangladesh	21,335,000	19,355,000
Thailand	17,240,000	15,640,000
Japan	17,196,000	15,600,000
Vietnam	11,574,000	10,500,000
Burma	11,023,000	10,000,000
South Korea	8,875,000	8,051,000
Brazil	8,365,000	7,589,000
All other countries	59,886,000	54,329,000
World total	418,669,000	379,814,000

Sugar

	Short tons	Metric tons
Brazil	9,149,000	8,300,000
Soviet Union	8,377,000	7,600,000
Cuba	7,481,000	6,787,000
United States	5,740,000	5,207,000
India	4,740,000	4,300,000
France	4,685,000	4,250,000
China	4,049,000	3,673,000
Australia	3,654,000	3,315,000
Mexico	3,252,000	2,950,000
West Germany	3,235,000	2,935,000
All other countries	39,809,000	36,114,000
World total	94,171,000	85,431,000

Soybeans

	Short tons	Metric tons
United States	53,792,000	48,800,000
Brazil	16,755,000	15,200,000
China	8,708,000	7,900,000
Argentina	3,858,000	3,500,000
Canada	772,000	700,000
Indonesia	716,000	650,000
Paraguay	661,000	600,000
Soviet Union	551,000	500,000
India	441,000	400,000
Romania	441,000	400,000
All other countries	2,150,000	1,950,000
World total	88,845,000	80,600,000

Cotton

	Short tons	Metric tons
Soviet Union	3,527,000	3,200,000
China	2,984,000	2,707,000
United States	2,670,000	2,422,000
India	1,543,000	1,400,000
Pakistan	772,000	700,000
Brazil	637,000	578,000
Egypt	584,000	530,000
Turkey	507,000	460,000
Mexico	375,000	340,000
Argentina	161,000	146,000
All other countries	2,103,000	1,908,000
World total	15,863,000	14,391,000

World Production of Selected Resources (continued)

Cattle

	Number
India	181,651,000
United States	116,265,000
Soviet Union	112,690,000
Brazil	89,000,000
China	65,630,000
Argentina	61,280,000
Australia	29,379,000
Mexico	29,333,000
Ethiopia	27,500,000
Bangladesh	27,007,000
All other countries	473,357,000
World total	1,213,092,000

Sheep

	Number
Soviet Union	141,025,000
Australia	131,510,000
China	88,000,000
New Zealand	60,300,000
Turkey	42,708,000
India	40,432,000
Argentina	34,000,000
Iran	33,600,000
South Africa	31,400,000
United Kingdom	29,618,000
All other countries	423,104,000
World total	1,055,697,000

Coal

	Short tons	Metric tons
China	681,221,000	618,000,000
United States	584,219,000	530,000,000
Soviet Union	555,890,000	504,300,000
Poland	212,303,000	192,600,000
United Kingdom	135,803,000	123,200,000
India	111,112,000	100,800,000
West Germany	99,317,000	90,100,000
South Africa	97,994,000	88,900,000
Australia	80,468,000	73,000,000
North Korea	38,581,000	35,000,000
All other countries	200,729,000	182,100,000
World total	2,797,637,000	2,538,000,000

Petroleum

	Barrels (42 gallons or 159 liters)
Soviet Union	4,383,650,000
Saudi Arabia	3,514,950,000
United States	3,127,685,000
Iraq	962,870,000
Venezuela	790,955,000
China	773,435,000
Nigeria	750,805,000
Libya	652,525,000
Mexico	597,140,000
United Kingdom	590,935,000
All other countries	5,634,610,000
World total	21,779,560,000

Natural Gas

	Billions of cubic feet	Billions of cubic meters
United States	19,663	556
Soviet Union	14,359	406
Netherlands	3,407	96
Canada	2,660	75
United Kingdom	1,364	39
Romania	1,266	36
Norway	760	22
Mexico	753	21
West Germany	740	21
Venezuela	540	15
All other countries	6,848	195
World total	52,360	1,482

Uranium

	Short tons	Metric tons
United States	18,519	16,800
Canada	7,881	7,150
South Africa	6,775	6,146
Niger	4,519	4,100
Namibia	4,455	4,042
France	2,903	2,634
Australia	1,721	1,561
Gabon	1,139	1,033
Spain	209	190
Argentina	206	187
All other countries	135	122
World total	48,462	43,965

World Production of Selected Resources (continued)

Copper

	Short tons	Metric tons
United States	1,504,000	1,364,000
Soviet Union	1,212,500	1,100,000
Chile	1,161,500	1,053,700
Zambia	903,000	819,200
Canada	860,500	780,600
Zaire	470,900	427,200
Peru	378,800	343,600
Poland	318,500	289,000
Philippines	294,400	267,100
Australia	239,400	217,200
All other countries	1,474,900	1,338,000
World total	8,818,400	8,000,000

Tin

	Short tons	Metric tons
Malaysia	69,445	63,000
Thailand	37,478	34,000
Indonesia	32,408	29,400
Bolivia	30,423	27,600
Soviet Union	19,841	18,000
China	18,739	17,000
Australia	12,566	11,400
Brazil	7,716	7,000
Zaire	3,858	3,500
All other countries	28,881	26,200
World total	261,355	237,100

Iron

	Short tons	Metric tons
Soviet Union	144,841,000	131,400,000
Australia	66,358,000	60,200,000
Brazil	62,390,000	56,600,000
United States	38,580,000	35,000,000
China	35,825,000	32,500,000
Canada	35,053,000	31,800,000
India	29,211,000	26,500,000
South Africa	18,298,000	16,600,000
Sweden	17,747,000	16,100,000
Liberia	13,228,000	12,000,000
All other countries	70,656,000	64,100,000
World total	532,187,000	482,800,000

Bauxite

	Short tons	Metric tons
Australia	25,139,000	22,806,000
Jamaica	12,588,000	11,420,000
Guinea	11,950,000	10,841,000
Suriname	5,353,000	4,856,000
Soviet Union	5,070,000	4,600,000
Guyana	3,553,000	3,223,000
Hungary	3,251,000	2,949,000
Greece	3,168,000	2,874,000
France	2,270,000	2,059,000
Yugoslavia	2,253,000	2,044,000
All other countries	13,148,000	11,928,000
World total	87,743,000	79,600,000

Gold

	Troy ounces	Kilograms
South Africa	22,617,000	703,389
Soviet Union	9,740,000	302,914
Canada	1,644,000	51,128
China	1,625,000	50,538
United States	1,015,000	31,567
Papua New Guinea	639,000	19,873
Australia	632,000	19,655
Zimbabwe	600,000	18,660
Brazil	599,000	18,629
Philippines	547,000	17,012
All other countries	2,705,000	84,124
World total	42,363,000	1,317,489

Silver

	Troy ounces	Kilograms
Mexico	49,310,000	1,533,541
Soviet Union	46,000,000	1,430,600
Peru	43,415,000	1,350,207
Canada	38,068,000	1,183,915
United States	38,055,000	1,183,510
Australia	25,000,000	777,500
Poland	23,000,000	715,300
Japan	8,665,000	269,481
Chile	8,322,000	258,814
Bolivia	5,742,000	178,576
All other countries	58,880,000	1,831,168
World total	344,457,000	10,712,612

Countries That Have Become Independent Since World War II

Country	Year of independence	Controlling country at time of independence	Country	Year of independence	Controlling country at time of independence
Algeria	1962	France	Maldives	1965	Great Britain
Angola	1975	Portugal	Mali	1960	France
Bahamas	1973	Great Britain	Malta	1964	Great Britain
Bahrain	1971	Great Britain	Mauritania	1960	France
Bangladesh	1971[1]	Great Britain	Mauritius	1968	Great Britain
Barbados	1966	Great Britain	Morocco	1956	France and Spain
Belize	1981	Great Britain	Mozambique	1975	Portugal
Benin	1960	France	Nauru	1968	Great Britain/Australia
Botswana	1966	Great Britain	Niger	1960	France
Brunei	1984	Great Britain	Nigeria	1960	Great Britain
Burkina Faso	1960	France	Pakistan	1947	Great Britain
Burma	1948	Great Britain	Papua New Guinea	1975	Australia
Burundi	1962	Belgium	Philippines	1946	United States
Cameroon	1960	France/Great Britain	Qatar	1971	Great Britain
Cape Verde	1975	Portugal	Rwanda	1962	Belgium
Central African Republic	1960	France	St. Kitts-Nevis	1983	Great Britain
Chad	1960	France	St. Lucia	1979	Great Britain
Comoros	1975	France	St. Vincent and the Grenadines	1979	Great Britain
Congo	1960	France	São Tomé and Príncipe	1975	Portugal
Cyprus	1960	Turkey	Senegal	1960	France
Djibouti	1977	France	Seychelles	1976	Great Britain
Dominica	1978	Great Britain	Sierra Leone	1961	Great Britain
Equatorial Guinea	1968	Spain	Singapore	1965[5]	Great Britain
Fiji	1970	Great Britain	Solomon Islands	1978	Great Britain
Gabon	1960	France	Somalia	1960	Great Britain and Italy
Gambia	1965	Great Britain	Southern Yemen	1967	Great Britain
Ghana	1957	Great Britain	Sri Lanka	1948	Great Britain
Grenada	1974	Great Britain	Sudan	1956	Great Britain and Egypt
Guinea	1958	France	Suriname	1975	The Netherlands
Guinea-Bissau	1974	Portugal	Swaziland	1968	Great Britain
Guyana	1966	Great Britain	Syria	1961	Great Britain
India	1947	Great Britain	Tanzania	1964[6]	Great Britain
Indonesia	1949[2]	The Netherlands	Togo	1960	France
Israel	1948	Great Britain	Tonga	1970	Great Britain
Ivory Coast	1960	France	Trinidad and Tobago	1962	Great Britain
Jamaica	1962	Great Britain	Tunisia	1956	France
Jordan	1946	Great Britain	Tuvalu	1978	Great Britain
Kampuchea (Cambodia)	1953	France	Uganda	1962	Great Britain
Kenya	1963	Great Britain	United Arab Emirates	1971	Great Britain
Kiribati	1979	Great Britain	Vanuatu	1980	Great Britain and France
Korea	1945[3]	Japan	Vietnam	1954[7]	France
Kuwait	1961	Great Britain	Western Samoa	1962	New Zealand
Laos	1954	France	Zaire	1960	Belgium
Lesotho	1966	Great Britain	Zambia	1964	Great Britain
Libya	1951	Italy	Zimbabwe	1980	Great Britain
Madagascar	1960	France			
Malawi	1964	Great Britain			
Malaysia	1963[4]	Great Britain			

1. Until 1971, Bangladesh was part of Pakistan. Pakistan became independent in 1947.
2. In 1963, Netherlands New Guinea became part of Indonesia; Portuguese Timor became part of Indonesia in 1976.
3. Korea became independent when Japan was defeated in World War II. The countries of North Korea and South Korea were established in 1948.
4. The Federation of Malaya became independent in 1957. In 1963, Malaya, Sarawak, Sabah, and Singapore joined to form the Federation of Malaysia.

5. Singapore withdrew from the Federation of Malaysia and became an independent country in 1965.
6. Tanzania was formed in 1964 by the merger of the independent countries of Tanganyika and Zanzibar. Tanganyika became independent in 1961, and Zanzibar became independent in 1963.
7. Vietnam was divided into North Vietnam and South Vietnam after independence.

Continents

Name	Area		Population	Population density		Independent nations	Highest elevation	Lowest elevation
	Square miles	Square kilometers		per sq. mi.	per sq. km			
Asia (including southeastern archipelagoes, Soviet Asia, Asian Turkey)	17,120,000	44,339,000	2,800,000,000	164	63	40	Mount Everest, 29,028 feet (8,848 m)	Shore of Dead Sea, −1,299 feet (−396 m)
Africa (including Madagascar)	11,714,000	30,339,000	486,000,000	42	16	51	Mount Kilimanjaro, 19,340 feet (5,895 m)	Shore of Lake Assal, −509 feet (−155 m)
North America (including Arctic islands, Caribbean islands, Greenland)	9,421,000	24,495,000	380,000,000	40	15	21	Mount McKinley, 20,320 feet (6,194 m)	Death Valley, −282 feet (−86 m)
South America	6,883,000	17,896,000	250,000,000	36	14	12	Mount Aconcagua, 22,831 feet (6,959 m)	Península Valdés, −131 feet (−40 m)
Antarctica	5,100,000	13,209,000	—	—	—	0	Vinson Massif, 16,864 feet (5,140 m)	sea level
Europe (including Iceland, Soviet Europe, European Turkey)	4,063,000	10,524,000	670,000,000	165	64	34	Mount Elbrus, 18,481 feet (5,633 m)	Shore of Caspian Sea, −92 feet (−28 m)
Australia	2,968,000	7,687,000	15,000,000	5	2	1	Mount Kosciusko, 7,316 feet (2,230 m)	Shore of Lake Eyre, −52 feet (−16 m)

Oceans and Major Seas

Body of Water	Area		Greatest depth	
	Square miles	Square kilometers	Feet	Meters
Pacific Ocean	64,000,000	165,760,000	37,782	11,516
Atlantic Ocean	31,815,000	82,400,000	30,246	9,219
Indian Ocean	28,344,000	73,400,000	25,344	7,725
Arctic Ocean	5,427,000	14,056,000	17,850	5,441
Caribbean Sea	1,049,500	2,718,200	24,720	7,535
Mediterranean Sea	969,100	2,510,000	16,896	5,150
Tasman Sea	900,000	2,331,000	17,000	5,182
South China Sea	895,400	2,319,000	15,000	4,572
Bering Sea	884,900	2,291,900	15,659	4,773
Gulf of Mexico	615,000	1,592,800	12,425	3,787
Sea of Okhotsk	613,800	1,589,700	12,001	3,658
Barents Sea	542,300	1,405,000	2,000	610
East China Sea	482,300	1,249,200	9,126	2,782
Hudson Bay	480,000	1,245,000	2,846	867
Sea of Japan	389,100	1,007,800	12,276	3,742
Andaman Sea	308,100	797,700	12,392	3,777
North Sea	221,000	574,600	2,400	730
Black Sea	180,000	466,200	7,250	2,210
Red Sea	169,100	438,000	7,254	2,211
Baltic Sea	163,000	422,200	1,539	470

Major Lakes and Inland Seas

Lake	Location	Area		Greatest depth	
		Square miles	Square kilometers	Feet	Meters
Caspian Sea	Soviet Union-Iran	152,239	394,299	3,104	946
Superior	United States-Canada	31,820	82,414	1,333	406
Victoria	East Africa	26,828	69,485	270	82
Aral Sea	Soviet Central Asia	25,659	66,457	223	68
Huron	United States-Canada	23,010	59,596	750	229
Michigan	United States	22,400	58,016	923	281
Tanganyika	East Africa	12,700	32,893	4,708	1,435
Baikal	Southern Siberia	12,162	31,500	5,712	1,741
Great Bear	Northwest Territories, Canada	12,000	31,080	1,350	411
Nyasa	Southern Africa	11,600	30,044	2,316	706
Great Slave	Northwest Territories, Canada	11,170	28,930	2,015	614
Erie	United States Canada	9,930	25,719	210	64
Winnipeg	Manitoba, Canada	9,094	23,553	70	21
Ontario	United States-Canada	7,520	19,477	778	237
Ladoga	European Russia	7,000	18,130	738	225
Balkash	Soviet Central Asia	6,670	17,275	87	27
Chad	West Africa	6,650	16,835	23	7
Onega	European Russia	3,819	9,891	361	110
Eyre	Australia	3,700	9,583	4	1
Titicaca	Boliva-Peru	3,261	8,446	1,214	370
Athabasca	Alberta-Saskatchewan, Canada	3,120	8,081	407	124
Nicaragua	Nicaragua-Costa Rica	3,060	7,925	230	70

Major Rivers

Name	Length		Source	Mouth
	Miles	Kilometers		
Nile	4,187	6,738	East Africa	Mediterranean Sea
Amazon	3,915	6,300	Andes Mountains, Peru	Atlantic Ocean
Mississippi-Missouri	3,741	6,020	Montana and Minnesota	Gulf of Mexico
Ob-Irtysh	3,459	5,567	Altai Mountains, Soviet Union	Gulf of Ob, Arctic Ocean
Chang	3,434	5,526	Kunlun Mountains, Tibet	East China Sea
Huang	2,903	4,672	Kunlun Mountains, Tibet	Gulf of Chihili, Yellow Sea
Zaire	2,716	4,371	Zaire	Atlantic Ocean
Amur	2,704	4,352	Manchuria and southeastern Siberia	Tatar Strait, Sea of Okhotsk
Lena	2,652	4,268	Baikal Mountains, southern Siberia	Laptev Sea, Arctic Ocean
Mackenzie-Slave-Peace-Finlay	2,635	4,241	British Columbia, Canada	Beaufort Sea, Arctic Ocean
Mekong	2,600	4,184	Tibet	South China Sea
Niger	2,600	4,184	Guinea, West Africa	Gulf of Guinea
Yenisey	2,566	4,129	Southern Siberia	Kara Sea, Arctic Ocean
Paraná	2,450	3,943	Brazil	Río de la Plata
Murray-Darling	2,310	3,717	Australian Alps	Indian Ocean
Volga	2,291	3,687	Valdei Hills, European Russia	Caspian Sea
Madeira	2,012	3,238	Brazil-Bolivia border	Amazon River
Purus	1,993	3,207	Andes Mountains, Peru	Amazon River
São Francisco	1,987	3,198	Brazil	Atlantic Ocean
St. Lawrence	1,900	3,058	Lake Ontario, United States-Canada	Gulf of St. Lawrence
Rio Grande	1,885	3,034	Colorado	Gulf of Mexico
Yukon	1,875	3,017	Yukon Territory, Canada	Bering Sea

Major Islands

Island	Location	Area Square miles	Area Square kilometers	Status
Greenland	North Atlantic Ocean	839,999	2,175,597	Belongs to Denmark
New Guinea	Western Pacific Ocean	316,615	820,033	Part of Indonesia/part of Papua New Guinea
Borneo	Malay Archipelago	286,914	743,107	Part of Indonesia/part of Malaysia/Brunei (Great Britain)
Madagascar	Indian Ocean	226,657	587,042	Independent country
Baffin	Arctic Ocean	183,810	476,068	Part of Canada
Sumatra	Malay Archipelago	182,859	473,605	Part of Indonesia
Honshu	North Pacific Ocean	88,925	230,310	Part of Japan
Great Britain	North Atlantic Ocean	88,758	229,883	Part of the United Kingdom
Ellesmere	Arctic Ocean	82,119	212,688	Part of Canada
Victoria	Arctic Ocean	81,930	212,199	Part of Canada
Sulawesi	Malay Archipelago	72,986	189,034	Part of Indonesia
South Island	South Pacific Ocean	58,093	150,461	Part of New Zealand
Java	Malay Archipelago	48,990	126,884	Part of Indonesia
North Island	South Pacific Ocean	44,281	114,688	Part of New Zealand
Cuba	Caribbean Sea	44,218	114,525	Independent country
Newfoundland	North Atlantic Ocean	42,734	110,681	Part of Canada
Luzon	Malay Archipelago	40,420	104,688	Part of the Philippines
Iceland	North Atlantic Ocean	39,768	102,999	Independent country
Mindanao	Malay Archipelago	36,537	94,631	Part of the Philippines
Ireland	North Atlantic Ocean	32,597	84,426	Independent country of Ireland/part of the United Kingdom
Novaya Zemlya	Arctic Ocean	31,382	78,737	Part of the Soviet Union
Hispaniola	Caribbean Sea	29,355	76,029	Independent countries of Haiti and the Dominican Republic
Sakhalin	Sea of Okhotsk	28,215	73,077	Part of the Soviet Union
Tasmania	Indian Ocean	26,215	67,897	Part of Australia
Sri Lanka	Indian Ocean	25,332	65,610	Independent country

Major Deserts

Continent	Name	Location	Area Square miles	Area Square kilometers
Asia	Syrian	Syria, Jordan, Iraq, Saudi Arabia	100,000	260,000
	Great Arabian	Arabian Peninsula	500,000	1,300,000
	Nafud	Saudi Arabia	56,000	145,000
	Rub al-Khali	Saudi Arabia	250,000	650,000
	Dasht-i-Kavir	Iran	20,000	52,000
	Dasht-i-Lut	Iran	20,000	52,000
	Turkestan	Soviet Union, China	450,000	1,170,000
	Thar (Indian)	Pakistan, India	100,000	260,000
	Gobi	Mongolia, China	600,000	1,560,000
Africa	Sahara	North Africa	3,500,000	9,100,000
	Libyan (Western)	Libya, Egypt, Sudan	500,000	1,300,000
	Arabian (Eastern)	Egypt, Sudan	86,000	223,600
	Nubian	Sudan	120,000	312,000
	Namib	Namibia	50,000	130,000
	Kalahari	South Africa, Botswana, Namibia	120,000	312,000
North America	Great Basin	Western United States	180,000	468,000
	Colorado	California	2,000	5,200
	Black Rock	Nevada	1,000	2,600
	Great Salt Lake	Utah, Nevada	5,500	14,300
	Painted	Arizona	7,500	19,500
	Sonoran	United States, Mexico	120,000	312,000
	Mojave	California	15,000	39,000
South America	Atacama	Chile	60,000	156,000
	Patagonian (Argentine)	Argentina	10,000	26,000
Australia	Great Australian	Western part of Australia	1,250,000	3,250,000
	Great Sandy	Western Australia	200,000	520,000
	Gibson	Western Australia	130,000	338,000
	Great Victoria	Western Australia, South Australia	250,000	650,000
	Simpson	Northern Territory, South Australia, Queensland	120,000	312,000

Word List

A

abdicate (ab′də kāt′): to give up power and position

accessible (ak ses′ə bəl): easily reached

Afrikaans (af′ri käns′): a dialect of Dutch spoken in South Africa

aggression (ə gresh′ən): hostile actions

agribusiness (ag′rə biz′nəs): the industry related to the production, sale, and distribution of farm products

alliance (ə lī′əns): an agreement between two or more nations to cooperate closely

alluvial plain (ə lo͞o′vē əl plān′): an area built up of silt and other material left behind after a flood

Alpine (äl′pīn): of or relating to the Alps

altiplano (al′ti plän′ō′): the high plateau of the Andes

annex (ə neks′): to take possession of

annual temperature range: the difference between the highest temperature and the lowest temperature of a place during the year

anopheles (ə nof′ə lēz′): a mosquito that transmits malaria

antimony (an′ti mō′nē): a bluish-white brittle metal

aquifer (ak′wə fər): a rock layer that holds water and lets it pass through

arable (ar′ə bəl): suitable for cultivation

archaeologist (är′kē ol′ə jist): a scientist who studies ancient ruins and examines artifacts

archipelago (är′kə pel′ə gō′): a large group of islands

architecture (är′kə tek′chər): the art of designing and constructing buildings

aridity (ə rid′ə tē): dryness

armistice (är′mi stis): an agreement during a war or battle to stop fighting

artesian (är tē′zhən) **well:** a well in which water rises as a result of underground water pressure

artifact (är′tə fakt′): anything made or changed by humans

atoll (at′ôl): a ring-shaped coral island

B

balance of payments: the difference between a nation's total payments to and total receipts from foreign countries

balance of power: equal economic or military power

bayou (bī′o͞o): a marshy creek or sluggish backwater swamp

bight (bīt): a wide bay or gulf formed by a curve in a coast

bilingual (bī ling′gwəl): using or capable of using two languages

biosphere (bī′ə sfēr′): the part of the earth that supports life

block diagram: a drawing that shows a three-dimensional picture

Brahman (brä′mən): a member of the priest or scholar caste

buffer state (buf′ər stāt′): a small country lying between two larger countries that are rivals or enemies

butte (byo͞ot): a flat-topped hill with steep sides that is smaller than a mesa

C

caliph (kā'lif): the title given to the successors of Mohammed who were the leaders of Islam

capital (kap'itəl): anything that can be used to produce wealth

capitalist (kap'itəlist): a person who owns capital

cartography (kärtog'rəfē): the art or technique of making maps

cash crop (kash'krop'): a plant or plant product raised for income

cede (sēd): to give up rights to

channel (chan'əl): a wide stretch of water between two land areas

chernozem (cher'nəzem'): a fertile soil rich in humus

chromium (krō'mēəm): a silver-gray, hard metallic mineral

chronological (kron'əloj'ikəl): arranged according to the order in which events happened

civil servant (siv'əl sur'vənt): a person who works for a government department other than the armed forces

coalition (kō'əlish'ən): a temporary alliance for some specific purpose

cobalt (kō'bôlt): a heavy and strong metal that does not rust or tarnish

commerce (kom'ərs): the buying and selling of goods and services

concession (kənsesh'ən): the right to operate a business at a certain place

conquistador (konkēs'tədôr'): a Spanish conqueror in Latin America during the sixteenth century

constitutional monarchy (kon'stətoo'shənəl mon'ərkē): a form of government in which elected representatives have political power and the monarch has only symbolic authority

conterminous (kəntur'mənəs): contained within the same boundaries

cordillera (kôrdil'ərə): a long mountain chain

coup (koo): a sudden, unexpected action that overthrows a government

cryolite (krī'əlīt): a mineral used in refining aluminum

cultivate (kul'təvāt'): to improve the growth of plants by labor and care

D

demography (dimog'rəfē): the study of populations

deplete (diplēt'): to use up

depose (dipōz'): to remove from power

détente (dātänt'): the easing of strained relations between countries

developing (divel'əping) **country**: a country that is starting to develop industrially

diplomacy (diplō'məsē): a system for managing relations between nations and for carrying on negotiations between governments

doctrine (dok'trin): a principle or set of principles

domesticate (dəmes'təkāt'): to tame and keep animals for human use

dynasty (dī'nəstē): a line of rulers from the same family

E

economic (ek'ənom'ik): having to do with the production and use of goods and services

emigration (em'əgrā'shən): the act of leaving one place or country to live in another

emirate (əmēr'āt): in some Arab or Muslim areas, a nation ruled by a chief or prince

enclave (en'klāv): a country or an outlying portion of a country surrounded, or nearly surrounded, by the territory of another country

equinox (ē'kwənoks'): one of the two times of the year when the sun is directly over the equator at noon

escarpment (eskärp'mənt): a steep slope or cliff

estancia (estän'sēə): a large estate or cattle ranch in Argentina

ethnic (eth'nik) **group**: people who share similar customs, languages, and other characteristics

evacuate (ivak'yooāt'): to leave a country or place

exaggerated (igzaj'ərā'tid): enlarged or increased

exile (eg'zīl): to banish

F

famine (fa'min): a great and widespread scarcity or lack of food

fazenda (fəzen'də): a coffee plantation in Brazil

federalism (fed'ərəliz'əm): the division of powers between the national government and the state governments

federation (fed'ərā'shən): a political union of two or more states or countries, in which each keeps the right to manage its internal affairs

ferroalloy (fer'ōal'oi): a metal that is mixed with iron to make a special kind of steel

finite (fi'nīt): fixed and limited

fishing banks (fish'ing bangks'): fairly shallow parts of the ocean where fish are usually plentiful

foothills (foot'hilz'): a low line of hills lying between a mountain range and a plain

free port (frē pôrt): a port where goods may be moved in and out without payment of taxes, or duties

free trade: buying and selling without restrictions

G

geophysical (je'ōfiz'ikəl): related to the study of the earth and the forces that affect or change it

gorge (gôrj): a deep, steep-sided valley

gross (grōs) **national product**: the total value of a country's goods and services produced in one year

Gulf Stream (gulf' strēm'): a warm ocean current that flows north along the Atlantic coast of North America

H

heritage (her'ətij): values and traditions passed down from earlier generations

hieroglyphics (hī'ərəglif'iks): a form of picture writing used by the early Egyptians

homeland: the place where a people has its origins

humus (hyoo'məs): decaying plant and animal matter that in part makes up soil

hydrosphere (hī'drəsfēr'): all the water of the earth

I

in dispute (dispyoot'): not settled; still being argued about

industrial crop (indus'trēəl krop'): a plant or plant product that is used in manufacturing

industrialization (indus'trēəlizā'shən): the process of changing to an economy that is based on manufacturing

intensive farming (inten'siv fär'ming): working the land with special care to increase agricultural productivity

interest (in'trist): money paid for the use or borrowing of money

investment (invest'mənt): an outlay of money for income

isolationism (ī'səlā'shəniz'əm): a policy of avoiding involvements with foreign countries

J

junta (hoon'tə): a small group, such as a group of military leaders, that rules a country after a coup

K

kibbutz (kiboots'): a collective farm in Israel

Koran (kôran'): the holy book of the Muslims

L

lagoon (ləgoon'): the water lying between an island shore and a reef

literacy (lit'ərəsē): the ability to read and write

lithosphere (lith'əsfēr'): the crust, or outer rock layer, of the earth

loess (lō'əs): rich soil deposited by the wind

M

Maghrib (məg'rəb): the North African countries west of Egypt

mainland: the principal land of a continent

malnutrition (mal'nootrish'ən): lack of enough food or the right kinds of food

---

a bad, ā cake, ä father; e pet, ē me; i it, ī ice; o hot, ō open, ô off; oo wood; oo food, oi oil, ou out; u cup, ur turn, yoo music; ə ago, taken, pencil, lemon, helpful

---

613

mandate (man′dāt): a commission, or order, to administer some region

manifest destiny (man′ə fest′ des′tə nē): the idea that the United States was meant to expand and extend its boundaries to the Pacific

maritime (mar′ə tīm′): bordering on or close to the sea

marsupial (mär soo′pē əl): any mammal that rears its young in a pouch attached to the stomach of the mother

martial (mär′shəl) **law**: military rule of a country during a war or other emergency

mesa (mā′sə): a flat-topped hill or mountain with steep sides that is larger than a butte

moraine (mə rān′): a deposit of material carried by a glacier

mutton (mut′ən): the meat of a sheep more than one year old

N

nationalize (nash′ən əl īz′): to change from private to government ownership

negotiations (ni gō′shē ā′shənz): discussions for the purpose of bringing about an agreement

nitrogen (nī′trə jen): a colorless, odorless gas that makes up about four-fifths of the atmosphere

nonrenewable (non′ri noo′ə bəl) **resource**: a useful material that cannot be replaced

O

Oceania (ō′shē an′ē ə): the three island groups of the Pacific known as Melanesia, Micronesia, and Polynesia

oceanography (ō′shən og′rə fē): the scientific study of the ocean

Orient (ôr′ē ənt): a word meaning "east" that refers to the Far East

outback (out′bak′): the vast, isolated interior of Australia

P

pact (pakt): an agreement or treaty

passive resistance (pas′iv rə zis′təns): a method of resisting authority or protesting against some law or act by nonviolent means

passport (pas′pôrt′): an official government document entitling the holder to travel abroad

pastoral (pas′tər əl): relating to shepherds or their way of life

pilgrimage (pil′grə mij): a journey to a sacred place for religious reasons

policy (pol′ə sē): a general plan of action adopted by a government

political (pə lit′i kəl): having to do with government

population density (pop′yə lā′shən den′sə tē): the average number of people living on a square unit of land in a country or other region

potential (pə ten′shəl): the capacity for use or development

profile (prō′fīl): a representation of something in outline

profit (prof′it): money gained after expenses have been paid

proletariat (prō′lə ter′ē ət): the working class

propaganda (prop′ə gan′də): publicity to make known the ideas of a group

Q

quota (kwō′tə): a fixed amount or share of the total due

R

ratification (rat′ə fi kā′shən): official approval

reef (rēf): a ridge of coral rock that lies just above or just below water level

regime (rə zhēm′): a system of rule or government

renewable (ri noo′ə bəl) **resource**: a useful material that is capable of replacing or rebuilding itself

rift (rift) **valley**: a long, steep-sided valley lying between two parallel faults

royalties (roi′əl tēz): shares of the income from a product paid to the owner in return for permission to use the property

S

safari (sə fär′ē): an expedition to a game reserve to see wildlife

samurai (sam′oo rī′): formerly, a member of the warrior class in Japan satellite (sat'ə līt'): a country under the control of another more powerful nation

seismology (sīz mol'ə jē): the study of earthquakes

self-determination (self'di tur'mə nā'shən): the right of a nation to choose its own form of government

selva (sel'və): a vast tropical rain forest

shadoof (shä dōof'): an irrigation device consisting of a pole on a pivot with a bucket

shifting cultivation (shif'ting kul'tə vā'shən): the practice of moving farming to new land once the soil becomes infertile

shogun (shō'gun'): formerly, a military and political ruler in Japan

silt (silt): very fine particles of rock, smaller than sand

sirocco (si rok'ō): a hot wind that blows from Africa into southern Europe

sisal (sī'səl): a tropical plant with fibers used to make twine and bags

social (sō'shəl): having to do with human beings living together in groups

society (sə sī'ə tē): a group of people who form a community and have common interests and culture

solstice (sol'stis): either of two times during the year when the sun appears farthest from the equator

sovereignty (sov'rən tē): political authority or control

standard (stan'dərd) of living: the general level of goods and services available to a group or a country

station (stā'shən): in Australia, a farm or ranch

strait (strāt): a narrow channel that joins two larger bodies of water

subcontinent (sub'kon'tə nənt): a large landmass that is somewhat isolated from the rest of a continent

sub-Saharan (sub'sə har'ən): south of the Sahara

subsistence farming (səb sis'təns fär'ming): producing only enough food to supply the necessities of life

sultan (sult'an): the title given to the chief ruler in some Muslim countries

Swahili (swä hē'lē): a Bantu language used by many people in East Africa

T

taiga (tī'gə): needleleaf forests of far northern regions

terminal (tur'mən əl): either end of a transportation line

terra cotta (ter'ə kot'ə): a hard, brown-red earthenware

topography (tə pog'rə fē): the surface features of an area

tourism (toor'iz'əm): the business of providing accommodations and services for tourists

tsetse (tset'sē) fly: an insect that causes diseases in animals and humans

U

urbanization (ur'bən i zā'shən): the change from rural to urban living

V

vanadium (və nā'dē əm): a silver-white metallic mineral

W

wadi (wä'dē): a short, dry riverbed

wallaby (wäl'ə bē): a small or medium-sized kangaroo

Z

zebu (zē'byōo): a domesticated animal related to the ox

---

a bad, ā cake, ä father; e pet, ē me; i it, ī ice; o hot, ō open, ô off; oo wood; ōo food, oi oil, ou out; u cup, ur turn, yōo music; ə ago, taken, pencil, lemon, helpful

---

Index

For pronunciations see guide on page 611.

Boers (bôrz), 366–367
Bogotá (bō'gə tä'), Colombia, 164
Bohemia, 236
Bolívar, Simón, 161, 162, 166
Bolivia, 161, 170
Bolsheviks, 259, 261
Bonn, West Germany, 203, 207
Borneo, 402, 411, 412
Bosporus, Strait of, 315–316, 318
Botany Bay, 453–454
Botswana, 364–366, 368–369
Brahmaputra (bräm'ə poo'trə) River, 385, 391, 392, 393, 394–395
Brasília, Brazil, 174–175
Brazil, 142, 146, 161, 172–175, 177, 179
Brazilian Highlands, 142, 173, 174–175
Brezhnev, Leonid, 263
British East India Company, 389
British Empire, 124, 196. *See also* **Great Britain**
British Isles, 194
Britons, 194
Brunei (broo'nī), 411
Brussels, Belgium, 199
Budapest, Hungary, 236
Buddha, 387, 393, 420
Buddhism, 387–388, 393, 395, 396, 412–413, 431, 435
Buenos Aires (bwā'nəs er'ēz), Argentina, 176, 178, 181
Bulgaria, 233, 239, 261, 495
Burkina Faso, 339, 344
Burma, 402, 404, 405
Burundi (bə run'dē), 354, 363
Bushmen, 368, 369, 370
Byzantine (biz'ən tēn') Empire, 231, 316–317

C

Cabral, Pedro (kə bräl', pä'drō), 146, 173
Cairo (kī'rō), Egypt, 64, 296, 299–300
Cambodia. *See* **Kampuchea**
Cameroon, 334, 335, 347, 348, 349, 351
Canada, 84, 124, 527, 532; climate and vegetation, 87–88; farming, 127, 132, 133; geography, 84–87; government, 124; history, 84–89, 124–125; mining, 127, 130, 132; people, 88–89, 90–91; provinces, 124–135; transportation, 129
Canadian Shield, 84, 86, 130
Canberra, Australia, 460
Cape of Good Hope, 332, 366
Cape Town, South Africa, 366, 368
Cape Verde (kāp'vərd'), 339, 344, 345
capitalism, 261, 262
Caracas (kə rä'kəs), Venezuela, 162
Caribbean (kar'ə bē'ən) Sea, 15, 143
Caroline Islands, 472, 473, 474
Carpathian Mountains, 190, 236, 248
Carter, Jimmy, 504
Carthage (kär'thij), 300–301
Cascade Mountains, 84, 118, 119
Caspian (kas'pē ən) Sea, 246, 249, 250, 251, 266, 268, 274, 275, 288
caste system of India, 387, 391

Castro, Fidel (käs'trō, fē del'), 157, 502
Catherine the Great, 257
Caucasia, 273
Caucasus (kô'kə səs) Mountains, 188, 248, 258, 260–261, 273
Celts, 194
Central African Republic, 347, 349, 351, 352
Central America, 142, 153–154, 488. *See also* **Latin America**
Central Valley, 84, 119
Ceylon, 400. *See also* **Sri Lanka**
Chaco (chäk'ō'), 176–177
Chad, 334, 347, 348, 349, 352
Chad, Lake, 335, 347–348
Chaldeans, 66
Chang River, 418–419, 425
Charlemagne (shär'lə mān'), 200, 203, 207
Charles V, King of Spain, 198
chernozem (cher'nə zem'), 251, 281
Chiang Kai-shek (chäng'kī'shek'), 422
Chile, 161, 170–172, 178, 476
Ch'in Dynasty, 420
China, 383, 417, 418, 427–428; ancient, 57, 67–68, 419–420; cities, 425–426; climate and vegetation, 419; Communism in, 422; farming, 423–424; geography, 418–419; history 419–422; manufacturing and mining, 425; Republic of, 417, 426; and United States, 421, 422, 493, 503
Chongqing (choon'king'), *Chungking,* China, 418, 422
Chou (jō) Dynasty, 419–420
Christianity, 66, 228, 386, 391; in Africa, 296, 343, 349, 355, 356; in Middle East, 292–293, 307, 313, 317; in Russia, 255; in Scandinavia, 212
Churchill, Winston, 500, 501
cities, 61, 62, 196, 514, 517, 520
civilization, 61; classical, 68–71; Huang Valley, 61–62, 67; Indus Valley, 61–62, 66–68; Mesopotamia, 61–62, 65–66; Nile Valley, 61–62, 63–64
Cliff Dwellers, 58
climate, 23, 24; factors affecting, 24–30, 540–541; and vegetation, 32–35; zones, 30–32. *See also specific countries and regions*
clothing, 54, 56–57, 72
coal, 44, 46, 48, 513
Coast Mountains, 84, 121, 133
Cold War, 500–503
Colombia, 145, 161, 162–164, 166
Colorado Plateau, 84, 113
Colorado River, 87, 119
Columbia Plateau, 86, 113, 120
Columbus, Christopher, 144, 156, 157, 164
commerce. *See* **trade**
common market, 193, 523
Commonwealth of Nations, 124, 196–197, 366–367
Communism, in Afghanistan, 397; in

China, 422; in Cuba, 157, 502; in Europe, 229, 233, 234, 237, 239, 501; in Korea, 502; in Mongolia, 428; in Southeast Asia, 383, 405, 407, 408, 410, 502; in Soviet Union, 246, 259–263; and Truman Doctrine, 501
Comoros, 364, 371, 373
Confucianism, 420
Confucius (kən fyoo'shəs), *Kung Fu-tse,* 420
Congo, 347, 348, 349, 351–352
conquistadors, 145–146
Constantine, Emperor, 317
Constantinople, 231, 255, 294, 316, 317. *See also* **Istanbul, Turkey**
Constitution, United States, 94, 483
Continental Divide, 87
Cook, James, 121, 449, 452, 453, 463, 475
cooperation among nations, 503–504, 522–524, 528–533
Copenhagen, Denmark, 219
Cortés, Hernando, 145, 148
Costa Rica, 153, 155
Coubertin (də koo'bär tan), Pierre de, 532
Council for Mutual Economic Assistance (COMECON), 524
Crater Lake, 119
Creoles, 161
Crete, 68
Cuba, 153, 157, 491, 502, 524
cultivation, 55; shifting, 352, 362, 513
culture, 58, 61, 72, 511–512
Cyprus, 221, 229
czars, 246, 255–259, 269, 270, 271
Czechoslovakia (chek'ə slə vä'kē ə), 233, 236, 261, 498, 529

D

Dakar (də kär'), Senegal, 345
Damascus, Syria, 314
Danube River, 190, 207, 233, 236, 239
Dardanelles (därd ən elz'), Strait of the, 315–316
Dead Sea, 15, 291
Deccan Plateau, 384–385, 386, 392, 393
Declaration of Independence, 93, 102
deltas, 22
democracy, 68, 69, 390
Denmark, 135, 136, 157, 193, 204, 211–213, 214, 219, 342, 498
deposition, 21, 22
deserts, 31, 32, 35
developing countries, 355, 517, 518, 526–527
Diaz (dē'äs), Bartholomew, 366
Díaz, Porfirio, 150
District of Columbia, 105, 120
division of labor, 59, 72, 78
Djibouti (jə boot'ē), 354, 357
domestication of animals, 55–56, 61. *See also* **farming; herding**
Dominican Republic, 158

Mountains, 384, 386, 397
Hinduism, 386, 388, 390, 391, 395, 403, 412–413
Hippocrates (hipok'rətēz), 69
Hispaniola, 145, 146, 153, 157–158
Hitler, Adolf, 205–206, 497–498
Hittites, 66, 317
Hobson, William, 464
Hokkaido (häkīd'ō) Island, 430, 433
Holy Land, 307. *See also* **Palestine**
Holy Roman Empire, 203, 207, 208
Honduras, 153, 155
Hong Kong, 417–418, 426–427, 522–523
Hooghly (hōō'glē) River, 393
Horn of Africa, 332, 335, 354, 357
Hottentots, 364, 369
Huang (hwäng) River, 418, 419, 426; Valley, 61, 67–68, 71, 423–424
Hudson River, 95, 98, 99
Hugh Capet, 201
humidity, 23, 24
Hungary, 207, 233, 236–237, 261
hunting, 54–55

I

Ibadan (ēbäd'ən), 346–347
Iberian Peninsula, 221–222, 224
Ibn Saud, 322
Ibo (ē'bō), 343
Iceland, 135, 136
Ife (ē'fä), 341
Imperial Valley, 119
import duties, 522–523
Incas, 144, 145–146, 166
India, 383, 384, 391–393, 394, 396, 397, 403, 550–551; ancient, 56, 410; subcontinent of, 384, 386–391
Indian Ocean, 14, 364, 380, 400, 443
Indian Peninsula, 380, 384, 385–386
Indians, American, and farming, 55, 144; of Latin America, 144–146, 153, 161, 162, 170, 178; of North America, 88, 89, 90–91, 92, 115; shelter of, 57–58
Indochina, 402, 404, 407
Indonesia, 402, 412–414
Indus River, 385, 394; Valley, 61, 386, 394
Industrial Revolution, 73–74, 195–196, 513, 516, 520, 527
industrialization, effects of, 526–528, 529; in Great Britain, 195; and natural resources, 526, 527–528; and population, 515–516, 518–519; in Soviet Union, 260, 269
Inner Mongolia, 418, 419, 428
International Bureau of Weights and Measures, 531–532
International Court of Justice, 369, 497
International Date Line, 40, 41, 467
International Geophysical Year, 532–533
International Monetary Fund (IMF), 524

inventions, 72–73, 94–96, 195–196, 522. *See also* **technology**
Iran, 306, 319–321, 504
Iraq, 306, 307, 314–315, 321
Ireland, 57, 193, 194, 197–198
Irian Jaya (ir'ēän jī'yə), 412
Irrawaddy (ir'əwäd'ē) River, 403, 405, 406
Islam, 66, 292–294, 297, 386, 388, 400, 413
Islamabad, Pakistan, 394
islands, 12, 443, 446
Ismail, 320
Israel, 293, 297, 298, 306, 307, 308–309, 313, 504
Istanbul (is'tänbōōl'), Turkey, 316, 317, 318–319. *See also* **Constantinople**
Italy, 193, 221, 226–228, 317, 495–496, 497–498; and Africa, 294, 302, 338, 356–357
Ivan the Great, 255–256
Ivan the Terrible, 256
Ivory Coast, 339, 344, 345, 346, 347

J

Jackson, Andrew, 487
Jamaica, 153, 157
Jamestown, 92
Japan, 383, 417, 428, 430, 467, 492, 497–499, 527; and China, 421, 422, 431, 432; farming, 432–433; geography, 430–431; history, 431–432; manufacturing, 430, 433, 435; and Southeast Asia, 404, 406, 410; transportation, 435
Japan, Sea of, 249, 417, 428, 430
Japan Current, 29–30, 430
Java, 402, 412, 413
Jay, John, 93, 484–485
Jefferson, Thomas, 485–486, 488, 495
Jerusalem, 307, 309
Jews, 293, 306, 307–309. *See also* **Judaism**
John, King of England, 195
Jordan, 306, 309, 312
Jordan River, 291, 308, 312
Juan Carlos I, King of Spain, 224
Juárez, Benito (wär'ez, benē'tō), 148, 150
Judaism (jōō'dēizəm), 66, 292–293, 307, 386. *See also* **Jews**
Julius Caesar (sē'zər), 70–71, 200
Jutes, 194
Jutland Peninsula, 211, 212

K

Kalahari (kal'əhär'ē) Desert, 364–366, 368, 369
Kampuchea (kam'poochē'ə), 402, 403, 404, 405, 407–409
Kanem-Bornu, 348–349
Kano (kän'ō), Nigeria, 347
Kariba (kärē'bä) Dam, 371
Kashmir, 394, 551
Kemal Atatürk (Kemal Mustafa), 318

Kennedy, John, 502, 503
Kenya, 336, 337, 354, 360–362
Khmer (kəmer'), 403
Khmer Rouge (kəmer' roozh'), 408
Khoisan (koisän'), 337
Khomeini, Ayatollah (hōmān'ē, īyətō'lä), 321
Khrushchev, Nikita, 503
Khyber (kī'bər) Pass, 384
kibbutz (kiboots'), 309
Kilimanjaro, Mount, 27, 334, 360
Kiribati (kir'əbas), 472
Knights of St. John of Jerusalem, 228
Korea, 417, 428–430, 432
Korean War, 428, 502
Kremlin, 269
Kuala Lumpur (kwäl'ə loom'poor'), Malaysia, 410, 411
Kublai Khan (koo'blə kän'), 420, 427
Kush, 354–355, 356
Kuwait (kəwāt'), 321, 323, 523
Kuznetsk Basin (Kusbas), 282

L

Ladoga, Lake, 249
Lagos, Nigeria, 346
Lan Xang, 407
land, 12; use of, 510–514
landforms, 12–13
languages, in Africa, 295, 338–339, 351, 360, 363, 364; American Indian, 145; in Canada, 91, 129; in India, 390, 391, 550–551; in Latin America, 142, 147, 172; Romance, 71; in Soviet Union, 295; in United States, 89
Laos (lä'ōs), 392, 402, 404, 405, 407
Lapps, 218, 220
Latin America, 142, 488, 492, 503, 504; geography and climate, 142–144; people and history, 144–147. *See also* **Central America; Mexico; South America; West Indies**
Latin American Free Trade Association (LAFTA), 524
latitude, 27, 37–39, 538, 540–541
Latvia, 261, 271–272
Laurentian (lôren'shən) upland. *See* **Canadian Shield**
lava, 19–20
laws, 59; of Hammurabi, 65; Roman, 70, 71. *See also* **government**
League of Nations, 497
Lebanon, 293, 307, 312–313
Lenin, V.I., 259
Leopold, King of Belgium, 349
Lesotho (ləsō'tō'), 364, 368–369
Lesser Antilles, 153, 156, 158–159. *See also* **West Indies**
Liberia, 339, 342, 345, 346
Libreville (lē'brəvil'), Gabon, 352
Libya, 295, 300, 301–302
Libyan Desert, 295
Liechtenstein, 193, 194, 209
Lima, Peru, 161, 167
Lisbon, Portugal, 224–226

Acknowledgments

Cover:

Illustration by Robert LoGrippo

Maps:

Ligature Publishing Services, Inc.; Carter Clock; Eugene Derdeyn, General Cartography, Inc., Perspecto Map Company; Yvette M. Heyden; Susan Lovdjieff; Jeffrey M. Mellander, Precision Graphics, Inc.; Lowell Stumpf; George Suyeoka; John Walter & Associates: Joanne Adamska Koperska

Diagrams:

Leon Bishop; George Suyeoka; John Walter & Associates: Ed Huff, James Teason

Charts and Graphs:

Ligature Publishing Services, Inc., Hima Pamoedjo

Photographs:

Architect of the Capitol: 487

Art Resource/Scala: Vatican Museum, 564 bottom left and center

Art Resource/E.E.F.: Napoli, Museo Nazionale, 564 bottom right

Atoz Images: Doris DeWitt, 83

James L. Ballard, 538

The Bettmann Archive, Inc.: 89, 258, 259, 431, 484, 492, 496, 501, 520

Black Star Publishing Co., Inc.: Howarth and Bell, 348; Victor Englebert, 359 top; M. P. Kahl, 331; J. Launois, 128; Lawrence Manning, 337, 358 bottom; David Moore, 216 bottom; Fred Ward, 358 top

Cameramann, Int., Inc.: 106 bottom, 107 top, and center, 111, 112, 162, 202, 217 top left, 334, 393, 399 bottom left, 411, 412, 415, 427, 433, 434, 441, 443, 468 top and bottom, 469 top right and left, 470, 475, 523, 524

Bruce Coleman Incorporated: Bob and Clara Calhoun, 35; John Elk III, 69, 198; F. Erize, 73 left; J. S. Flannery, 245; Eugene Luttenberg, 169 bottom left; J. Messerschmidt, 237, 367; Norman Myers, 370; M. Timothy O'Keefe, 63, 159; Toby Richards, 169 bottom right; C. B. Schaller, 359 bottom right; Joy Spurr, 136; Rogers and Sullivan, 169 top; Jonathan T. Wright, 314

Leo deWys: F. Damm, 579

Drakewell Museum, 46

Fogg Art Museum, Harvard University, Theodore Roosevelt Collection: 491

Fort Ligonier Museum, 93

Robert Frerck, Odyssey Productions: 152, 158, 379, 392, 398 top left, 398 bottom, 455, 458, 460, 465, 469 bottom right

Gartman Agency: Michael Philip Manheim, 216 top

The Image Bank: Steve Dumwall, 73 right

Barbara Loudis: 522

Magnum: 499; Bruno Barbey, 175, 316, 359 bottom left, 398 top right

The Metropolitan Museum of Art: The Cultural Relics Bureau, Beijing, Department of Far Eastern Art, 68; The Michael C. Rockefeller Memorial Collection, Gift of Nelson A. Rockefeller, 1972, photograph by Jerry L. Thompson, 341

Miller Services: Edna Douthat, 129; Malak, 132; Michael Saunders, 106

NASA: 11, 43

New-York Historical Society: 96

Newberry Library: 349

The Oriental Institute, University of Chicago: 66

Nancy Palmer Photo Agency: 53

Photo Reseachers, Inc.: Brian Brake, 423; Nigel Cameron, 404; William Carter, 310 bottom; Ed Drews, 298 right; Jack Fields, 141, 471; Carl Frank, 147, 168 top left; Georg Gerster, 290, 469 bottom left, 476; Farrell Grehan, 74; Dan Guravich, 154; George Holton, 135, 399, 425; Paolo Koch, 276; Susan McCartney, 407; Frances Mortimer, 397; John Moss, 171; Carl Purcell, 399; Steve Proehl, Bradley Smith, 514

Photri: 489

Reynolds Aluminum: 48

James P. Rowan: 58, 116

Sovfoto: 248, 268, 270, 271, 272, 276 top right, 276 bottom right, 277 top, 277 bottom left, 277 bottom right, 278, 280, 281

Stock, Boston, Inc.: Eric Anderson, 75; Tom Bross, 70; Stuart Cohen, 385; Peter Dublin, 33; Terry E. Eiler, 107 bottom; Owen Franken, 190, 222; Tyrone Hall, 54; International Rice Research, 512; Diane M. Lowe, 518; Peter Menzel, 119, 230; John Running, 17, 105; Nich Sapieha, 311 top left; Harry Wilks, 530 top; Carl Wolinsky, 110; Cary Wolinsky, 200

Sygma: William Campbell, 513; Allen Green, 313

Taurus: 219; T. W. Bennett, 211; Vance Henry, 217 top right; M. L. Nolan, 192; L. L. T. Rhodes, 106 top; G. R. Richardson, 187; R. Thompson, 115

United Nations: 509, 530

United Press International: 500, 504

Woodfin Camp & Associates: Craig Aurness, 304; Robert Azzi, 287, 311 top right, 325; Marc and Evelyne Bernheim, 301, 344, 346, 503; Daily Telegraph Magazine, 533; Timothy Eagan, 481; Jeffrey Jay Foxx, 233, 298 left; Michael Friedel, 13; George Hall, 118; Hans Hoefer, 413; Anthony Howerth, 311 bottom; William Hubbell, 227; Sylvia Johnson, 526; Loren McIntyre, 168 bottom, 179, 217 bottom; John Marmaras, 220; Fred Mayer, 309, 310 top; Roland and Sabrina Michaud, 319, 389; Kal Muller, 405; Marvin Newman, 362; Roger Werth, 21; Baron Wolman, 168 top right; Adam Woolfit, 195, 196

Yale University Art Gallery: Joseph Szaszfai, 482

Photo research by Marilyn Gartman